Accountability for Mass Starvation

OXFORD MONOGRAPHS IN INTERNATIONAL HUMANITARIAN AND CRIMINAL LAW

This series emerged through the vision of the late Antonio Cassese. Since then the series has published original and innovative works on challenging issues in international humanitarian law and international criminal justice, primarily by emerging authors. Given the ever-growing intersection of these areas with other fields of international law such as the jus ad bellum, and disciplines such as criminology, sociology, and history, the scope of the series also incorporates these perspectives. Fresh approaches and new ideas for improving conceptual and practical challenges are welcomed. The series editors encourage submissions from around the world, and will consider edited collections, although the primary focus is on authored works.

General Editors

SUZANNAH LINTON
Member of the Expert Committee, International Academy of the Red Cross & Red Crescent at Suzhou University and Adjunct Professor at the School of International Law, China University of Political Science and Law (CUPL)

SALVATORE ZAPPALÀ
Professor of International Law at the University of Catania
Accountability for Mass Starvation

ALSO PUBLISHED IN THIS SERIES

The Use of Force against Individuals in War under International Law
A Social Ontological Approach
Ka Lok Yip

Non-Binding Norms in International Humanitarian Law
Efficacy, Legitimacy, and Legality
Emily Crawford

Doing Justice to History
Confronting the Past in International Criminal Courts
Barrie Sander

The Humanitarian Civilian
How the Idea of Distinction Circulates Within and Beyond International Humanitarian Law
Rebecca Sutton

Rules of Engagement and the International Law of Military Operations
J.F.R. Boddens Hosang

Accountability for Mass Starvation

Testing the Limits of the Law

Edited by

BRIDGET CONLEY,
ALEX DE WAAL,
CATRIONA MURDOCH,
and
WAYNE JORDASH QC

OXFORD
UNIVERSITY PRESS

OXFORD
UNIVERSITY PRESS

Great Clarendon Street, Oxford, OX2 6DP,
United Kingdom

Oxford University Press is a department of the University of Oxford.
It furthers the University's objective of excellence in research, scholarship,
and education by publishing worldwide. Oxford is a registered trade mark of
Oxford University Press in the UK and in certain other countries

First Edition published in 2022

Impression: 1

Published in the United States of America by Oxford University Press
198 Madison Avenue, New York, NY 10016, United States of America

British Library Cataloguing in Publication Data

Data available

Library of Congress Control Number: 2022938194

ISBN 978–0–19–286473–4

DOI: 10.1093/oso/9780192864734.001.0001

Printed and bound by
CPI Group (UK) Ltd, Croydon, CR0 4YY

This book is dedicated to the victims of mass starvation—all those who have suffered the pain, loss, and indignities of a crime that the world has yet to recognize.

Acknowledgements

Can the crime of starvation be prosecuted? This question sparked a collaboration between the international legal practice, Global Rights Compliance (The Hague), and the World Peace Foundation at The Fletcher School (Tufts University, Boston, Massachusetts). It resulted in a multi-year research and engagement project, *Accountability for Starvation: Testing the Limits of the Law (2018–20)*. This book is a product of the collaboration.

Over the course of the project, the project leaders—who are also the editors of this volume—gained valuable insights from expert colleagues in conversations, workshops, and seminars, including: Fiona Terry, Norah Niland, Antonio Donini, Mark Duffield, Sama'a al Hamdani, Andrew Clapham, Matthias Lanz, Eran Nagan, Marco Valentini, Martha Mundy, Tong Anei, Kristine Beckerle, Sarah Nouwen, Kirsten Young, Nathalie Weizmann, Tom Dannenbaum, Emanuela-Chiara Gillard, Dearbhla Minogue, Hilal Elver, UN Special Rapporteur for Food; Nathalie Weizmann of UN Office for the Coordination of Humanitarian Affairs; and Rebecca Richards and Brian Lander, both with World Food Programme.

We wish express our thanks to organizations we collaborated with over the course of the project, including Global Legal Action Network, The Yemen Data Project, The Oxford Institute for Ethics, Law and Armed Conflict, Mwatana for Human Rights (Yemen), Peace Track Initiative, Welt Hunger Hilfe, Save the Children, Action Against Hunger, Concern, and Damaan Humanitarian Organisation (Syria).

We reserve special thanks to our chapter authors, many of whom participated in conversations over multiple years: Senai Abraha, Ali Aljasem, Uzay Yasar Aysev, Randle C. DeFalco, Jane Ferguson, Joe Holmes, Simone Hutter, Susanne Jaspers, Mohammad Kanfash, Dan Maxwell, Dyan Mazurana, Chris Newton, Aditya Sarkar, Benjamin J. Spatz, Kinsey Spears, and Oliver Windridge.

At GRC, several additional colleagues made vital contributions to the project, including Margherita Stevoli, Rebecca Bakos Blumenthal, Kristine Fainveica, and Niriksha Sanghvi, who supported the drafts in a multitude of ways. WPF wishes to thank Lyndon Sam and Anna Cloud, and to extend special thanks to Lisa Avery, without whom nothing would get done.

This project was made possible through funds provided by the World Peace Foundation, and project donor, the Kingdom of the Netherlands Ministry of

Foreign Affairs (MoFA). In particular, we wish to thank the MoFA's UN Security Council and the Stabilisation and Humanitarian Aid department. With special thanks to Elianne Lambalk, Simon van der Staaij, Mariett Schuurman, and Jeroen Romeijn for their continued dedication to the work of addressing conflict and hunger.

Series Editors' Preface

It is unusual to publish edited volumes in a monograph series. However, when this Oxford University Press series was created over ten years ago, on the basis of an idea by Antonio (Nino) Cassese, he strongly argued for the possibility of including exceptional collections of important essays on urgent issues. The Press agreed, and we concurred with the advice to keep such occasions to a minimum.

Accountability for Mass Starvation, edited by Bridget Conley, Alex de Waal, Catriona Murdoch, and Wayne Jordash QC, and featuring contributions by themselves as well as from Susanne Jaspars, Randle Defalco, Senai Abraha, Joe Holmes, Simone Hutter, Chris Newton, Mohammad Kanfash, Ali Aljasem, Adyta Sarkar, Uzay Yasar Aysev, Dan Maxwell, Ben Spatz, Olivier Windridge, Dyan Mazurana, Kinsey Spears, and Jane Ferguson, represents a notable example of the exceptional circumstances which justify the publication of an edited volume. The collection tackles an extremely important and yet insufficiently researched topic, and it offers an innovative approach. The world, unfortunately, has for too long tended to react to the civilian population being deprived of food and of objects indispensable to their survival as inevitable effects of war; this being so even though resort to deprivation of food and other essential goods has, for centuries, served as a deliberate and pernicious tool of war. Nonetheless, as the authors illustrate, despite the existence of provisions prohibiting and criminalizing such conduct very little has happened on the side of actual prosecution of these crimes (described as 'starvation crimes').

We, and all those who reviewed the book for us, have been particularly impressed with the comprehensive, open-minded, and multi-disciplinary tackling of what has, shockingly, continued to plague humankind, and has been something of a 'blindspot' in international law. It is not just that the law has been lamentably weak but there has been a tendency to allow what little there is to become and remain 'dead letter' through lack of implementation. One can, of course, question whether law and the emphasis on legal responsibility are actually the right ways to tackle this complex phenomenon. Fortunately, *Accountability for Mass Starvation* is no mere challenge to impunity. It is a ground-breaking and well-rounded study that draws from the expertise of experts from a range of disciplines to engage with technical issues of law, present extensive empirical research particularly through case studies, engage with theoretical issues, grapple with political and social realities, and present practical and holistic ways of improving how the world handles mass starvation. In search of accountability for mass starvation, the editors and their fellow contributors take us on a journey that leads us to understand better the complexity of mass starvation situations. They demonstrate that the effort to prevent and respond to starvation requires the combined effort of scholars, practitioners, activists, by promoting measures to strengthen compliance with international rules.

The book is divided into four parts. In the first, the authors set the broader historical and conceptual framework. Over three chapters, the authors consider 'What is Starvation?' (Bridget Conley and Alex de Waal); 'Social Nutrition and Accountability for Mass Starvation' (Susanne Jaspars); and starvation as 'An Unprosecuted Crime' (Bridget Conley, Randle Defalco, Senai Abraha, and Alex de Waal). The second part focuses on the illustration of the law in theory (or in the books), with two chapters: 'A Comprehensive Review of Existing IHL and ICL As It Relates to Starvation' (Wayne Jordash QC, Catriona Murdoch, and Joe Holmes); and 'The Right to Food in Armed Conflict' (Simone Hutter). There are four chapters in the third part, demonstrating realistic options for law in action, discussing potential prosecution of 'starvation crimes' in various contexts: 'Not Never Again, but Next Time: Armed Conflict and Mass Starvation in South Sudan 2013–2019' (Chris Newton); 'Starvation as Strategy in the Syrian Armed Conflict: Siege, Deprivation and Detention' (Mohammad Kanfash and Ali Aljasem); 'Once We Control Them, We Will Feed Them': Mass Starvation in Yemen' (Aditya Sarkar); and 'Prosecution of Starvation in South Sudan' (Wayne Jordash QC and Uzay Yasar Aysev). Finally, the fourth part presents other options for a broader approach to countering starvation in conflict and the variety of tools that could be harnessed. The five chapters in this final part are 'Humanitarian Challenges and Implications for Famine Early Warning Systems' (Dan Maxwell); 'Sanctions as a Mechanism for Accountability for Starvation Crimes' (Ben Spatz, Catriona Murdoch, and Olivier Windridge); 'Sex, Gender, Age, and Mass Starvation' (Dyan Mazurana, Bridget Conley, and Kinsey Spears); 'Reporting Famine' (Jane Ferguson); and 'Truth, Memory, and Victims' (Alex de Waal).

Across these fifteen chapters, this edited collection makes a profound contribution that is deeper than a technical argument for accountability. As the editors of the present volume write in their introduction, '[d]emanding accountability for mass starvation—including prosecuting perpetrators of starvation crimes—is a crucial part of two linked broader agendas, namely eliminating famine and preventing all forms of mass atrocities, including those of deprivation'.

In keeping with the spirit of the founder of this series, who believed that each one of us can contribute to make the world a better place, we see this volume as a major contribution.

The Editors

Contents

Table of Cases

NATIONAL COURTS

Constitutional Court of Colombia

Demanda de inconstitucionalidad contra los artículos 135, 156 y 157 (parciales) de la Ley 599 de 2000, y 174, 175, 178 y 179 de la Ley 522 de 1999, Constitutional Case No.C- 291/ 07 (25 April 2007) 8–9n.25

District Court in Zadar, Croatia

Public Prosecutor v. Perišić et al. (Judgment, Trial Chamber) K. 74/96 (24 April 1997) 8–9n.25, 71n.1, 119n.49

Supreme Court of India

People's Union for Civil Liberties v. Union of India & Ors (Civil Original Jurisdiction, Writ Petition) No.196 of 2001 (9 July 2007) 8–9n.25

District Court of Jerusalem

Attorney General v. Eichmann, Case No. 40/ 61 (11 December 1961) 8n.25

Ethiopian Federal High Court

Special Prosecutor v. Hailamariam et al. (Judgment) File No. 1/ 87 (12 December 2006) 8–9nn.24–25, 71n.1, 119n.49

United Kingdom

Alcock and others v. Chief Constable of South Yorkshire Police, 1 AC 310 (1992) 120n.50
Bourhill v. Young, AC 92, UKHL 5, 110 (1943) 120n.50
Trial of Hans Renoth and Three Others, Case No. 68 (8–10 January 1946) 120n.50, 120n.53
Dulieu v. White & Son, EWHC KB 1 (1901) 120n.50
Page v. Smith, All ER 736, UKHL 7 (1995) 120n.50
R. v. Hyde, 1 QB 134 (1991) 121–22n.60
R. v. Anderson; R. v. Morris, 2 QB 110 (1966) 121–22n.60

INTERNATIONAL

African Commission of Human and Peoples' Rights

Centre on Housing Rights and Evictions v. Sudan, Communication No. 296/ 2005 (13–27 May 2009) 135n.18

European Court of Human Rights

Catan and Others v. Moldova and Russia, App no 43370/04, 8252/05, and 18454/06 (19 October 2012) 135n.19
Ilascu and others v. Moldova and Russia Judgment, App no 48787/998, 8 July 2004 . . . . . 135n.19

Extraordinary Chambers in the Court of Cambodia

International Court of Justice

International Criminal Court

International Criminal Tribunal for Rwanda

International Criminal Tribunal for the former Yugoslavia

International Military Tribunal at Nuremberg

Special Court for Sierra Leone

International Residual Mechanism for Criminal Tribunals

List of Figures and Tables

FIGURES

TABLES

List of Abbreviations

ACF	Action Contre la Faim
ACHPR	African Commission on Human and Peoples' Rights
AP I	Additional Protocol I
AP II	Additional Protocol II
ASP	Assembly of State Parties
AUCISS	African Union Commission of Inquiry on South Sudan
BMI	body mass index
BSA	Bosnian Serb Army
CAH	Crimes against Humanity
CBY	Central Bank of Yemen
CESCR	Committee on Economic, Social and Cultural Rights
CoI	Commission of Inquiry
CIA	Central Intelligence Agency
CMAM	community management of acute malnutrition
CPA	Comprehensive Peace Agreement
CPK	Communist Party of Kampuchea
DRC	Democratic Republic of Congo
DRK	Democratic People's Republic of Korea
ECCC	Extraordinary Chambers in the Courts of Cambodia
ECOWAS	Economic Community of West African States
EDF	Eritrean Defence Force
EHRC	Ethiopian Human Rights Commission
ENDF	Ethiopian National Defence Force
EPRDF	Ethiopian People Revolutionary Democratic Front
ESCR	Economic, Social and Cultural Rights
EU GHRS	European Union's Global Human Rights Sanctions Regime
EW	Early warning
EWS	Early Warning Systems
FAM	World Bank Famine Action Mechanism
FAO	Food and Agriculture Organization
FEWS NET	Famine Early Warning Systems Network
FMA	female mortality advantage
FSA	Free Syrian Army
FSNAU	Food Security and Analysis Unit
GAM	global acute malnutrition
GCC	Gulf Cooperation Council
GDP	Gross domestic product

GEE	Group of Eminent Experts on Yemen
GPC	General People's Congress
HDZ	*Hrvatska demokratska zajednica Bosne i Hercegovine*/Croatian Democratic Union
HRC	Human Rights Council
HRCte	Human Rights Committee
HRD	Human Rights Division
HRP	United Nations Humanitarian Response Plan
IAC	International Armed Conflict
ICC	International Criminal Court
ICCPR	International Covenant on Civil and Political Rights
ICESCR	International Covenant on Economic, Social and Cultural Rights
ICJ	International Court of Justice
ICL	International Criminal Law
ICRC	The International Committee of the Red Cross
ICTR	International Criminal Tribunal for Rwanda
ICTY	International Criminal Tribunal for the former Yugoslavia
IDPs	internally displaced persons
IHL	International Humanitarian Law
IHRL	International Human Rights Law
INGO	International non-governmental organization
IO-2	Sudan People's Liberation Army-in-Opposition led by Taban Deng Gai
IPC	Integrated food security Phase Classification
IPEP	International Panel of Eminent Personalities
IRG	Internationally Recognized Government of Yemen
ISIL	Islamic State of Iraq and the Levant
ISIS	Islamic State of Iraq and Syria
JCE	Joint Criminal Enterprise
JEM	Justice and Equality Movement
JIAT	Joint Incidents Assessment Team
JMP	Joint Meeting of Parties
KSA	Kingdom of Saudi Arabia
LSHTM	London School of Hygiene and Tropical Medicine
MERIAM	Modeling Early Risk Indicators to Anticipate Malnutrition
MSF	Médecins Sans Frontières
NDF	National Defense Forces
NGO	Non-governmental organization
NIAC	Non-international Armed Conflict
NSAs	non-state actors
OCHA	Office for the Coordination of Humanitarian Affairs
OECD	Organization for Economic Co-operation and Development
OHCHR	Office of the High Commissioner for Human Rights
OIAs	other inhumane acts
OIS	objects indispensable to survival
OLS	Operation Lifeline Sudan

OP	optional Protocol to the ICESR
PoC	Protection of Civilians
PoCAA	Protection of Civilians Site Adjacent Area
PDRY	People's Democratic Republic of Yemen
PITF	Political Instability Task Force
PTSD	post-traumatic stress disorder
PYD	Kurdish Democratic Union Party
RCT	Randomized Controlled Trials
RRC	Relief and Rehabilitation Commission
RUTF	ready to use therapeutic foods
SAF	Sudanese Armed Forces
SAMLA	Sanctions and Anti-Money Laundering Act 2018
SDA	*Stranka Demokratske Akcije*/Party of Democratic Action
SDGs	Sustainable Development Goals
SDF	Syrian Democratic Forces
SDS	*Srpska Demokratska Stranka*/Serb Democratic Party
SGBV	Sexual and Gender-Based Violence
SLC	Saudi/UAE-led coalition
SMART	Standardized Monitoring and Assessment of Relief and Transitions
SPLA	Sudan People's Liberation Army
SPLA-IO	Sudan People's Liberation Army-in-Opposition
SPLA-IO	(RM) Sudanese Liberation Movement in Opposition led by Riek Machar
SPLA-IO	(TD) Sudanese Liberation Movement in Opposition led by Taban Deng Gai
SPLM	Sudan People's Liberation Movement
SPO	Special Prosecutor's Office
SRK	Sarajevo Romanija Corps of the Army of *Republika Srpska* (VRS)
SSLM/A	South Sudan Liberation Movement/Army
STC	Southern Transitional Council
SUN	Scaling Up Nutrition
TGE	transitional Government of Ethiopia
TPLF	Tigray People's Liberation Front
TWG IPC	Technical Working Group
UK GHRS	United Kingdom's Global Human Rights Sanction Regime
UN	United Nations
UNICEF	United Nations Children's Fund
UNCHRSS	United Nations Commission on Human Rights in South Sudan
UNHAS	United Nations Humanitarian Air Service
UNMISS	United Nations Mission in South Sudan
UNPROFOR	United Nations Protection Force
UNSC	United Nations Security Council
USAID	United States Agency for International Development
VRS	*Vojska Republika Srpska*/Bosnian Serb army

WFP	The World Food Programme
WHO	World Health Organization
YAR	Yemen Arab Republic
YDP	Yemen Data Project
YPG	Kurdish People's Protection Units

List of Contributors

Senai Abraha is an officer at the US Department of Homeland Security. He specializes in human rights and refugee law, foreign policy decision-making, the role of force in politics, and China–Africa relations. He received his PhD in International Conflict Management in 2015 from Kennesaw State University and has served in the US Army, including NATO peacekeeping deployment to Kosovo.

Ali Aljasem is a PhD candidate at the Centre for Conflict Studies of Utrecht University. His research focuses on the rise of paramilitary groups (Shabbiha) and their repertoires of violence in the city of Aleppo after 2011. Previously, he worked as a researcher for the Institute for War, Holocaust and Genocide Studies (NIOD). Among his publications are: 'An Episode of the Revolution: Aleppo University Protest Movement 2011–2013', *British Journal of Middle Eastern Studies* (13 May 2021) 1–17, and 'In the Shadow of the State: The Rise of Kata'ib al-Baath at Aleppo University after 2011', Journal for Perpetrator Research 2, no. 3(2021), 87–113.

Uzay Yasar Aysev is a legal consultant for GRC, specializing in international criminal, humanitarian and human rights law and a PhD candidate at the University of Amsterdam. He holds an LL.M degree in Public International Law with a specialization in international criminal law from Leiden University. In the past, Uzay has worked for a number of organizations including the STL, the ICC, the International Bar Association, and the UNHCR.

Bridget Conley is Research Director of the World Peace Foundation (WPF) and Associate Research Professor at the Fletcher School, Tufts University. She leads the WPF's programs on protecting vulnerable civilians, including projects on tracking COVID-19 in detention and ending mass atrocities. She has published on issues related to the 1992–1995 war in Bosnia-Herzegovina, mass atrocities and genocide, memory and violence, and how museums can engage with human rights issues. She previously worked as Research Director for the US Holocaust Memorial Museum's Committee on Conscience, where she led the Museum's research and projects on contemporary threats of genocide, including curating the exhibition, *From Memory to Action: Meeting the Challenge of Genocide Today*. She is the author of *Memory from the Margins: Ethiopia's Red Terror Martyrs Memorial Museum* (London: Palgrave, 2019), and editor of *How Mass Atrocities End: Studies from Guatemala, Burundi, Indonesia, the Sudans, Bosnia-Herzegovina, and Iraq* (Cambridge: Cambridge University Press, 2016).

Randle C. DeFalco is an Assistant Professor of Law at the University of Hawai'i at Mānoa William S. Richardson School of Law. Professor DeFalco spent time researching the Khmer Rouge era famine in Cambodia as a Fulbright Fellow and Legal Advisor to the Documentation Center of Cambodia. He holds a JD from Rutgers Law School and LLM and SJD degrees from the University of Toronto Faculty of Law.

Alex de Waal is executive director of the World Peace Foundation, Research Professor at the Fletcher School, Tufts University. He has worked on the Horn of Africa and on humanitarian issues since the 1980s as a researcher and practitioner, with a special focus on famine and humanitarian crises. He served as a senior advisor to the African Union High Level Panel on Sudan and South Sudan. De Waal's recent books include: *The Real Politics of the Horn of Africa: Money, War and the Business of Power* (London: Polity, 2015), *Mass Starvation: The History and Future of Famine* (London: Polity, 2018), and *New Pandemics, Old Politics: 200 Years of the War on Disease and its Alternatives* (London: Polity, 2021).

Jane Ferguson is an award-winning broadcaster for PBS NewsHour and contributor to the *New Yorker*. Based in the Middle East for twelve years, she covered wars, humanitarian crises, and revolutions across Africa, South Asia, and the Middle East. Ferguson's reporting in Yemen exposed the humanitarian catastrophe caused by the war. Her reporting has covered war crimes committed by the US and its allies in Taliban-controlled areas of Afghanistan; the front lines of the battles against ISIS in Iraq and Syria for PBS, and the link between climate change and conflict across Somalia. Previously, she worked with Al Jazeera as its English correspondent and was the network's first journalist to be smuggled into Syria by rebels. She subsequently reported from Afghanistan, where she lived for a year. She has won a Peabody Award, Alfred I. duPont Columbia University Award, an Emmy, a Polk Award, and the Aurora Humanitarian Journalism Award.

Joe Holmes is a partner at Global Rights Compliance and an international criminal law specialist, having acted in trials and appeals at the ICTR, ICTY, SCSL, IRMCT, and the ICC. He practises as a barrister in the United Kingdom and is also licensed to practise in New York. He is recommended as a leading practitioner in international criminal law in the Legal 500 and Chambers and Partners UK.

Simone Hutter is an experienced business advisor specializing in business and human rights. She has a legal background with a PhD focused on international human rights and international humanitarian law. She works as Project Manager of International Cooperation and specialist on human rights and environmental due diligence at Fairtrade Max Havelaar Switzerland. She has published several works, including Leiden and Boston: *Starvation as a Weapon: Domestic Policies of Deliberate Starvation as a Means to an End under International Law* (Leiden: Brill- Nijhoff International Humanitarian Law Series, 2015).

Susanne Jaspars has researched the social and political dynamics of food security and nutrition in situations of conflict, famine, and humanitarian crises, for more than thirty-five years. Most of her work has been on the Horn of Africa, often in Sudan and Somalia. She published her PhD as a book entitled *Food Aid in Sudan. A History of Politics, Power and Profit* (London: Zed Books, 2018), adding to a range of other books, academic articles, and policy reports. She is an Independent Researcher and a Research Associate at the Food Studies Centre of the School for Oriental and African Studies.

Wayne Jordash QC is the Managing Partner of Global Rights Compliance. He has worked in all the international courts over the last two decades, representing governments, military and political leaders, and victims. Representation/advisory work has included for the Serbia Government at the International Court of Justice; the (post-revolution) Libyan Government, the Ukrainian Government, and Rohingya and Sri Lankan Tamils at the International Criminal Court; and the ex-head of the State Security of Serbia at the International Criminal Tribunal for the former Yugoslavia. Currently, focused on advising states and corporations on how to meet their responsibilities to protect and/or respect humanitarian and human rights law in conflict affected and high-risk areas.

Mohammad Kanfash is a researcher at the Law School of Utrecht University with a particular focus on state–society relations and post-conflict state-building in Syria. Mohammad previously worked for the UN refugee agency in the MENA region, including Syria, and Europe. On starvation, Mohammad has published 'Starvation in Syria: A Political Marketplace Analysis' for the Conflict Research Programme at London School of Economics and Political Science.

Daniel Maxwell is the Henry J. Leir Professor in Food Security at the Friedman School of Nutrition at Tufts University, and Research Director at the Feinstein International Center. His research focuses on food security emergencies and the re-emergence of famines in the twenty-first century. He teaches courses on humanitarian action, famine, and food insecurity. He co-authored *Understanding the Humanitarian World* (London: Routledge, 2019) with Kirsten Gelsdorf, and *Famine in Somalia: Competing Imperatives, Collective Failures* (Oxford: Oxford University Press, 2016) with Nisar Majid. He is a member of the Famine Review Committee for the Integrated Food Security Phase Classification system—the formal mechanism by which contemporary famines are analysed and declared. Previously, Dan worked for humanitarian agencies, including as Deputy Regional Director for Eastern and Central Africa for CARE International. He holds a B.Sc. from Wilmington College, a master's degree from Cornell University, and a Ph.D. from the University of Wisconsin.

Dyan Mazurana directs the Feinstein International Center's Research Program on Women, Children, and Armed Conflict, co-directs the Masters of Arts in Humanitarian Assistance (MAHA) Program, and is Professor of Practice at the Fletcher School at Tufts University. She focuses on gendered dimensions of humanitarian response to conflict and crises, documenting serious crimes committed during conflict, and accountability, remedy, and reparation. She has written and developed training materials regarding gender, human rights, armed conflict, and post-conflict periods for civilian, police, and military peacekeepers involved in UN and NATO operations. She has contributed to materials now widely used to assist in documenting serious violations and abuses against women and girls during conflict and post-conflict reconstruction periods; and has published more than 100 scholarly and policy books, articles, and international reports, and her work has been translated into more than thirty languages.

Catriona Murdoch is a Partner at Global Rights Compliance (GRC). Experienced in trial and appellate litigation across the international courts and tribunals, she was called to the Bar of England and Wales in 2009 and is ranked as a leading junior across the legal directories. Catriona is an expert on the crime of starvation and also advises on accountability for atrocity crimes more generally. Catriona manages GRC's strategy to advance accountability for the crime of starvation. In this role, she manages sizeable and complex grant programmes in support of the agenda, routinely engaging with donors, and providing legal advice to states, UN bodies, and CSOs to assess the legality, and accountability prospects of conflict-induced hunger. Separately, in support of GRC's broader conflict work, Catriona provides advice on accountability strategies and works with CSOs to investigate and prosecute international crimes.

Chris Newton previously worked in South Sudan for five years with several humanitarian organizations, including most recently the United Nations World Food Programme. He is currently enrolled in the Food and Nutrition Policy and Programmes MS at the Friedman School of Nutrition Science and Policy at Tufts University.

Aditya Sarkar is an independent researcher and a visiting fellow at the World Peace Foundation, the Fletcher School of Law and Diplomacy, Tufts University. His research focuses on the political economy of transactional political systems, labour, and migration/displacement. He is currently advising the Government of Sudan on developing a National Employment Policy, and has advised the Federal Government of Somalia, as well as the Job Creation Commission in Ethiopia on similar issues. He has worked with the World Bank, the International Labour Organization, and the Open Society Foundations, and is qualified as a lawyer in India and in England and Wales. He is a graduate of the Fletcher School of Law and Diplomacy, and the National Law School of India University in Bangalore, India.

Benjamin J. Spatz is a Fellow at the World Peace Foundation at Tufts University's Fletcher School of Law and Diplomacy. He is a scholar-practitioner focused on conflict, sanctions, corruption, and African politics, and is the recipient of awards from the United States Institute of Peace, United States Department of Defense, Harry Frank Guggenheim Foundation, and Eisenhower Institute. He has held research fellowships at the University of Notre Dame's Kroc Institute for International Peace Studies and Harvard Law School. As an internationally recognized expert in sanctions, Dr Spatz was appointed by the UN Secretary-General to serve as a member of the United Nations Panel of Experts on Liberia. He holds a Ph.D. from the Fletcher School of Law and Diplomacy, an M.S. in Foreign Service from Georgetown University and undergraduate degrees from the University of Washington. He is a Term Member of the Council on Foreign Relations.

Kinsey Spears is a doctoral candidate at the Fletcher School of Law and Diplomacy at Tufts University, where her work focuses on gender, security studies, and Women, Peace, and Security. While completing her doctoral work, Kinsey has worked as a research assistant at the Feinstein International Center; a Teaching Fellow at the Fletcher School and a Research Fellow at the United States Army War College. Prior to pursuing her doctoral work Kinsey worked as a Director of Scheduling in the US Senate, served in the Peace Corps in Cambodia. She is a graduate of the University of Georgia.

Oliver Windridge is a British lawyer specializing in international criminal law and international human rights law. Oliver has worked on human rights and anti-corruption submissions to sanctions regimes in the United States, the United Kingdom, the European Union, and Australia. Oliver's international criminal law practice includes cases at the International Criminal Tribunal for Rwanda, International Criminal Tribunal for the former Yugoslavia, the Extraordinary Chambers in the Courts of Cambodia, International Residual Mechanism for Criminal Tribunals, and the International Criminal Court. Oliver has a prominent expertise in the African human rights system and acts as counsel in cases pending before the African Court on Human and Peoples' Rights and African Commission on Human and Peoples' Rights. Oliver's international human rights law practice spans six continents, advising individuals and NGOs on litigation, policy, and advocacy. He regularly writes and lectures on international criminal law and international human rights law.

1

Introduction

Rendering Starvation Unthinkable-Preventing and Punishing Starvation Crimes

Bridget Conley, Alex de Waal, Catriona Murdoch, and Wayne Jordash QC

1. Introduction

'Carthage must be destroyed!' pronounced Roman senator Marcus Porcius Cato, before a brutal and thorough attack on the ancient city in 149 BC. Not only did Roman soldiers destroy the city, kill many of its residents, and enslave the survivors but, according to myth, they sowed salt into the earth to render its farmlands permanently uninhabitable. No nourishment would ever be produced from the soil—starvation was tactic, goal, and punishment.

Salt became the signature detail in modern narratives of the effort to erase Carthage from the map and from history. However, it is an apocryphal story of relatively recent vintage.[1] What historians and chroniclers of Carthage noted at the time was the use of starvation as a means to destroy an entire people. A siege was intended to deprive soldiers and civilians alike of the means to survive, and thereby the means to resist. In 149 BC, Roman forces surrounded the city and blocked all supplies with a rigour that intensified over nearly three years, as a means to force capitulation. As historian Richard Miles writes, in the last desperate months, many of the city's inhabitants began to starve:

> During the last difficult years of the city, the only waste that seems to have been regularly removed was the corpses of the many who died as starvation and disease took hold. Now in the last terrible months of the city's existence, in contrast to the care that had traditionally been taken of the dead, the corpses of both rich and poor were unceremoniously dumped in a number of mass graves just a short distance away from where they had lived.[2]

Finally, when the walls were breached, Romans stormed into the city-state, murdering those who had survived the siege by sword or flame. Of the population of

[1] R. T. Ridley, 'To be Taken with a Pinch of Salt: The Destruction of Carthage', 81 *Classical Philology* (1986), 140–146.

[2] R. Miles, *Carthage Must Be Destroyed: The Rise and Fall of an Ancient Civilization* (New York: Viking, 2010), at 3.

Bridget Conley, Alex de Waal, Catriona Murdoch, and Wayne Jordash QC, *Introduction* In: *Accountability for Mass Starvation*. Edited by: Bridget Conley, Alex de Waal, Catriona Murdoch, and Wayne Jordash QC, Oxford University Press.
 DOI: 10.1093/oso/9780192864734.003.0001

an estimated 200,000 to 400,000, perhaps 145,000 perished, the survivors were sold into slavery.[3] Salt was hardly necessary.

Acts such as these have occurred throughout history. If committed today, and facets of such crimes are, they would undoubtedly fall within the definition of the crime of starvation in the Rome Statute of the International Criminal Court (ICC), the central element of which is 'intentionally using starvation of civilians as a method of warfare by depriving them of objects indispensable to their survival'. Contemporary actions of this kind would be subject to criminal prosecution under laws prohibiting genocide, crimes against humanity (CAH) (such as extermination), and war crimes, as well as being prohibited under human rights law. However, starvation has been side-lined in legal debates and prosecutions. In the past few years, important developments—considered later in this chapter—have occurred, but starvation remains under-addressed and too readily overlooked or even dismissed by investigators and prosecutors.

Application of international law is subject to international norms, which evolve alongside political and public pressure. These factors, combined with prosecutorial innovation, determine which cases are reviewed and what crimes are given attention. This volume addresses starvation today at the nexus of policy, public interest, and prosecution.

To this end, we deploy the term 'starvation crimes' as a useful way of encapsulating all actions that deliberately cause starvation or famine, irrespective of which body of law is most appropriate, providing a chapeau that allows us to focus our attention.[4] It aims to provide a vocabulary that can be used by a range of international actors who seek to advance both policy and prosecution towards the goal of ending starvation. Starvation crimes are common and intense across conflicts from antiquity to the current day. In recent years, water facilities in Yemen have been routinely targeted by air strikes. Besieged Syrians have been reduced to eating cattle fodder to survive. South Sudanese have been driven from their homes, all their means of sustenance destroyed or stolen. Tigrayans have seen their entire food system deliberately smashed and their region subjected to a hunger siege. The examples are numerous, the methods similar, and the outcomes shoehorned into metrics of food balance sheets rather than forensically explored. In all these cases, starvation is carried out in tandem with other crimes, including murder, rape, persecution, and forced displacement. Yet for purposes of attributing responsibility and pursuing accountability, starvation remains out of focus: widely inflicted but rarely considered sufficiently important to warrant special attention.

[3] B. Kiernan, *Blood and Soil: A World History of Genocide and Extermination from Sparta to Darfur* (New Haven: Yale University Press, 2007), at 51.

[4] Chapter 2 in this volume; B. Conley and A. de Waal, 'The Purposes of Starvation: Historical and Contemporary Uses', 17 *Journal of International Criminal Justice* (2019) 699–722.

One reason has been that the legal consensus appeared to allow for certain forms of starvation, including siege, blockade, and state discretion over whether aid should be allowed to reach vulnerable civilian groups. There are lacunae in the law itself, which have been interpreted conservatively, allowing states and belligerents considerable latitude to starve entire populations.[5] This is changing.

Another reason for lack of focus has been misunderstanding of why starvation occurs. The common understanding of 'famine' has been as mass hunger as the product of a food crisis caused by natural disaster. The word 'famine' is sometimes used in a metaphorical sense to refer to a shortage of a commodity (e.g., a 'book famine'). Those who have experienced famines and scholars who have studied the topic see mass starvation as the product of power relations: the weak starve while the powerful are immune or may benefit.[6] It is increasingly commonplace to describe famines as 'man-made', a depiction that begs the question of who are the men (and it is generally men) who made them, and how and why they did so. In many cases, episodes of mass hunger are deliberately perpetrated: the verb 'to starve' can be transitive as well as intransitive. Paradigmatic famines of the modern era, from Ireland in the 1840s, to Ukraine in the 1930s, China's 'Great Leap Forward' catastrophe of 1958–1961, the Nigerian breakaway province of Biafra in the late 1960s, Cambodia in 1975–1979, and Ethiopia in 1984–1985, all had causes that included direct political and military policies.

Lack of definitional clarity is a further complication. Famine and starvation each are subject to important issues of definition and measurement. In the case of famine, while historians tend to measure famines on the basis of total excess deaths, current famine early-warning and prevention systems focus on the severity of key indicators (malnutrition, excess deaths, loss of access to food) according to location. Each approach has its strengths and weaknesses depending on the use to which it is put. Decades ago, there was a controversy over whether famines should be diagnosed as food deficits or whether the collapse in some people's ability to obtain food was more crucial.[7] The consensus was that while decreases in food availability were commonly a contributory factor in famine, they were neither necessary nor sufficient, and that famines were better seen as episodes in which substantial numbers of people were starving, regardless of the cause.

[5] C. A. Allen, 'Civilian Starvation and Relief During Armed Conflict: The Modern Humanitarian Law', 19 *Georgia Journal of International & Comparative Law* 31 (1989) 1–85. N. Mulder and B. van Dijk, 'Why Did Starvation Not Become the Paradigmatic War Crime in International Law?', in K. J. Heller and I. Venzke (eds), *Contingency and the Course of International Law* (Oxford: Oxford University Press, 2021) 370–388.

[6] D. Keen, *The Benefits of Famine: Political Economy of Famine and Relief in Southwestern Sudan, 1983–1989* (Princeton: Princeton University Press, 1994).

[7] A. Sen, *Poverty and Famines: An Essay on Entitlement and Deprivation* (Oxford: Clarendon Press, 1981); P. Bowbrick, 'The Causes of Famine: A Refutation of Professor Sen's theory', 11 *Food Policy* (1986) 105–124; S. Devereux, 'Sen's Entitlement Approach: Critiques and Counter-critiques', 29 *Oxford Development Studies* (2001) 245–263.

Starvation itself also has several definitional dimensions. While famine is always a collective phenomenon, starvation can be individual. The everyday concept of starvation refers to extreme hunger to the point of endangering life. For a nutritionist, the closest referent is acute protein-energy malnutrition with heightened risk of death. In a collective, population-centric sense, 'mass starvation' corresponds to the deterioration in the ecology of health and nutrition that causes an increase in death rates. Used in this latter manner, starvation would include not just the reduced intake of food, but also many other deprivations—lack of healthcare, poor-quality housing and shelter, contaminated or lack of water supplies and inadequate sanitation, the stresses of displacement, and reduced maternal care for young children—which separately and in combination contribute to higher risks of death. In law, starvation is the act of intentional deprivation or destruction of that which sustains life, which could include each one of these elements. For lawyers, 'to starve' is a verb that it refers primarily to something that one person does to another, as well as the experience of that harm.

Another reason why starvation has been neglected in law is that during the years in which international criminal law (ICL) was making its most notable advances, the worst outcomes of starvation crimes—widespread death—was rare.[8] At the same time, famines almost disappeared. After the mid-1980s, famines declined in frequency and severity and between 2000 and 2011 there were no famines according to either the severity criteria used by the Integrated food security Phase Classification (IPC) system, which combines measurements of mortality, malnutrition and food availability or the magnitude criterion of 100,000 excess deaths used by historians.[9] This progress was partly due to greater expertise in predicting, preventing, mitigating, and responding to crises before they reached the level of famine. International Humanitarian Law (IHL) was stronger and humanitarian lesson-learning was more robust. Over a generation, the humanitarian agenda was ascendant.

Then famines returned. In 2017, the United Nations identified four situations of acute food insecurity that threatened famine or breached the IPC threshold—in north-eastern Nigeria, Somalia, South Sudan, and Yemen. The gravest disaster was Yemen but these 'four famines' do stand alone. Deliberate mass starvation also

[8] Starvation was considered during the establishment of the UN International Criminal Tribunal for the former Yugoslavia in light of the sieges, obstruction of humanitarian aid, and the systematic deprivation of food and water in the camps. However it did not make it onto the statute of the ad hoc tribunal. The justification is aptly summarized in the words of the final report of the UN Commission of Experts (Frenrik Report) of 27 May 1994: 'The tendency of both sides to control food, water and electricity for publicity purposes, the intermingling of military forces and the civilian population and the fact that no one appears to have died during the siege from starvation, dehydration or freezing, combine to make difficult the establishment of a solid case that starvation is being used as a method of warfare. The conduct of this matter has been deplorable, but its criminality is debatable' (S/1994/674, § 204).

[9] On the two different criteria and the measurements that underpin them, see: P. Howe and S. Devereux, 'Famine Intensity and Magnitude Scales: A Proposal for an Instrumental Definition of Famine', 28 *Disasters* (2004) 353–372.

occurred in Syria. Warring parties recurrently inflicted humanitarian crises in pockets across the Democratic Republic of Congo. Economic collapse and state policies transformed Venezuela into a land of want and desperation. And carefully calculated restrictions kept Palestinians in Gaza deprived but not subject to mass starvation.[10] In all of these and similar cases in this century, political decisions have driven the re-emergent threat and reality of famine. Some famines derive from intentional political and military decisions while others are allowed to develop because the most powerful actors have other priorities that overrule an effective response.[11] The hunger crises that follow in the wake of the COVID-19 pandemic is also likely to create a new configuration of political and economic contributors to food insecurity. While the global integration of food production and supply chains was crucial in the sustained reduction in international food prices, when that system was disrupted by the pandemic, the repercussions disproportionately affected the poor and food insecure, especially those in urban areas or dependent on daily wage labour.

During the final stages of preparing this volume, starvation was inflicted upon the people of the Tigray region of Ethiopia. Formerly a poster child for overcoming poverty and hunger, Ethiopia was once again the land of famine. In scenes redolent of Carthage, Ethiopian and Eritrean soldiers cut down fruit orchards, prevented farmers from ploughing their lands, and laid siege to areas not under their control. This crisis is unfolding, and these crimes are being perpetrated at the time of writing. It is too early to provide a definitive account of the scale and nature of the acts and their consequences. In section 3 of this introduction, we provide a succinct account of the genesis and trajectory of this famine.

Every famine today is occurring in the context of armed conflict. Indeed, all result from military actions and exclusionary, authoritarian politics conducted with—at minimum—reckless disregard for the well-being or even the survival of people, which cascades into intent. These famines, and other contemporary near-famine conditions, arise because a political or military actor is actively pursuing policies that starve a community or entire population. Many of these are already specifically criminalized under international law. Yet across conflicts today, violations of IHL, including blockading ports, attacks on health facilities, violence against humanitarian workers, and obstruction of relief aid are all carried out with a sense of renewed impunity. As stated by Sigrid Kaag, Minister for Foreign Trade and Development Cooperation of the Kingdom of the Netherlands, during a discussion of famine and extreme hunger in the United Nations Security Council on

[10] Dov Weisglass, an adviser to Ehud Olmert, the Israeli Prime Minister, is reputed to have said, 'The idea is to put the Palestinians on a diet, but not to make them die of hunger'. C. Urquhart, 'Gaza on brink of implosion as aid cut-off starts to bite', *The Guardian*, 15 April 2006, available online at <https://www.theguardian.com/world/2006/apr/16/israel> (visited 5 August 2021).

[11] P. Howe, 'Priority Regimes and Famine', in S. Devereux (ed.), *The New Famines: Why Famines Persist in an Era of Globalization* (London: Routledge, 1994).

23 March 2018: 'Flouting the law of war not only turns these norms into hollow phrases; it erodes the rules-based international order itself.'[12] Famines strike when accountability fails.

Addressing this demands a new infusion of resources and energy to ensure that there is sufficient political will to end the political and military acts that cause famine. At a time when more authoritarian, militaristic, xenophobic, and cynically self-interested politics are on the rise, we must defend the humanitarian imperative and the right of life and dignity. Our ultimate goal is to render mass starvation so morally toxic that it is universally publicly vilified. Because mass starvation demonstratively can be ended, it cannot be tolerated. Man-made famine—that is, all contemporary famine—can become unthinkable such that leaders in a position to inflict it or fail to prevent it will unhesitatingly ensure that it does not occur, and the public will demand this of them.

A portmanteau term that draws on David Scheffer's coinage of the term 'atrocity crimes',[13] 'starvation crimes' does not refer to a legal category as such but rather brings together a range of crimes under different provisions of law in a manner that gives them political salience.[14] Specifically, by starvation crimes we mean the unlawful processes of deprivation that occur when actors impede the capacity of targeted persons to access the means of sustaining life, as prohibited under IHL,[15] the corollary provisions of the Rome Statute,[16] acts constitutive of genocide under the Genocide Convention, and other relevant provisions of International Human Rights Law (IHRL) and ICL. It is important to stress that the means to sustain life and the term 'objects indispensable to survival' (OIS)[17] include objects broader than just food, encompassing water (including water installations, supplies, and irrigation works,[18] medicine, clothing,[19]

[12] United Nations Security Council 8213th meeting, UN Doc. S/PV.8213, 23 March 2018, at 6.

[13] D. J. Scheffer, 'Genocide and Atrocity Crimes', 1 *Genocide Studies and Prevention* (2006) 229–250.

[14] Conley and de Waal, see note 4, at 702.

[15] Art. 54 of Additional Protocol I to the Geneva Conventions (applicable in IACs) and Art. 14 of Additional Protocol II to the Geneva Conventions (applicable in NIACs).

[16] Art. 8(2)(b)(xxv) of the Rome Statute, applicable to IACs. In 2019, the Rome Statute was amended to include the war crime of starvation in NIACs. Art. 8(2)(e)(xix) will only come into force for each State that ratifies it a year after. At the national level, acts of starvation are criminalized in at least six national jurisdictions as a crime in both a NIAC and an IAC. See e.g. the Netherlands, International Crimes Act (2003), Section 5(5)(l). The deprivation of access to food, medicine, and other essential foodstuffs could fall within a number of other Rome Statute crimes. For example, attacks on civilian objects as a war crime; inhuman acts and/or persecution as crimes against humanity; and/or serious bodily and mental harm and/or conditions of life calculated to destroy as underlying acts of genocide. See Global Rights Compliance, The Starvation Training Manual (2019), available at <https://starvationaccountability.org/wp-content/uploads/2019/12/Manual-Primer-Jan-2020-.pdf> (visited 31 March 2022).

[17] As defined under Additional Protocol I, Art. 54, and Additional Protocol II, Art. 14 and featured in the war crime definition under the Rome Statute.

[18] Additional Protocol I, Art. 54; Additional Protocol II, Art. 14.

[19] Geneva Convention IV, Art. 59, which is considered to be part of customary international law applicable also in NIACs (ICRC, IHL Database, Customary IHL (ICRC Customary IHL) Rule 55). See also Geneva Convention IV, Art. 23, which includes 'clothing and tonics intended for children under fifteen, expectant mothers and maternity cases'.

shelter,[20] fuel and electricity,[21] and—we would argue—maternal care for young children.[22] Under ICL, attacking, destroying, damaging, or otherwise rendering useless OIS and wilfully impeding relief supplies for the purpose of starving civilians is prohibited, and may constitute a war crime. It is not necessary for the outcome to be that civilians starve to death, provided the required purposive requirement is met.[23]

In 2018, the UN Security Council (UNSC) responded to the 'four famines' by unanimously passing UNSC Resolution 2417. This marked the first time that the Council explicitly addressed the link between conflict and hunger, and carved a new opening for public and legal consideration of the prohibition of starvation under IHL. The resolution underscored that the use of starvation as a method of warfare may constitute a war crime.

Accountability for starvation crimes covers a span of actions from labelling the crime and acknowledging the dignity and humanity of victims and survivors, naming and shaming those responsible, sanctioning the perpetrators, enacting transitional justice provisions such as restitution and reparation, and—the legal gold standard—prosecution of those culpable. The aim of this volume is to catalyse discussion of the available legal instruments that might support pursuit of the ultimate goal: rendering mass starvation so morally reprehensible that it is universally and reflexively reviled, and is halted where it is threatened.

A fundamental contribution to achieving this goal is sharpening the conceptual and practical applications of international law. The power of the law in shaping public opinion can be witnessed throughout history, and within its judgments and proclamations the red lines of permissible and impermissible conduct are drawn and often clearly stated to both perpetrator and survivor. If the law doesn't reflect political will, it can engender it. The pursuit of our ultimate goal, and the means in which we aim to achieve it, raises several questions. Is the law as it exists sufficient

[20] See e.g. Additional Protocol I, Art. 69.

[21] O. Triffterer and K. Ambos (eds), *The Rome Statute of the International Criminal Court: A Commentary* (3rd edn, Munich: C.H. Beck, 2016), at 513. See also M. Bothe, K. J. Partsch, and W. A. Solf, *New Rules for Victims of Armed Conflicts: Commentary on the Two 1977 Protocols Additional to the Geneva Conventions of 1949* (2nd edn, Leiden: Martinus Nijhoff Publishers, 2013), at 382; K. Dörmann, L. E. Doswald-Beck, and R. Kolb, *Elements of War Crimes under the Rome Statute of the International Criminal Court: Sources and Commentary* (Cambridge: Cambridge University Press, 2003) 363–364; SC Res. 2451, 28 December 2018 (which links respect for medical facilities to the protection of civilians from starvation, linking them contextually to objects indispensable to survival (OIS), and noting paragraph 10 that the definition of OIS appears to have been slightly enlarged to include 'all those objects which are necessary for food distribution, processing and storage').

[22] See Chapter 13 in this volume; H. Clark and R. Kyte, 'In Tigray, Sexual Violence Has Become a Weapon of War', *Foreign Policy*, 27 April 2021, available online at <https://foreignpolicy.com/2021/04/27/in-tigray-sexual-violence-has-become-a-weapon-of-*war*/> (visited 5 August 2021).

[23] See Chapter 5 in this volume; D. Akande and E.-C. Gillard, 'Conflict Induced Food Insecurity and the War Crime of Starvation of Civilians as a Method of War', 17 *Journal of International Criminal Justice* (2019) 753–779; T. Dannenbaum, 'Encirclement, Deprivation, and Humanity: Revising the *San Remo Manual* Provisions on Blockade', 97 *International Legal Studies* (2021) 307–394; T. Dannenbaum, 'Siege Starvation: A War Crime of Societal Torture', 22 *Chicago Journal of International Law* (2022) 1–73.

to ensure accountability for starvation crimes? Specifically with regard to the prospect of prosecuting perpetrators, are there gaps in the law as it stands today, or major constraints on a successful prosecution (such as obtaining the necessary evidence)?

The question concerning whether the current law is sufficient to prosecute individuals for crimes of starvation cannot be considered without understanding the way in which law is developed; unless and until there is a culture of focused prosecutions for starvation, this question and its answer will remain in the abstract and the law will be found wanting. While ICL has become increasingly sophisticated and robust over the past decades, it almost entirely failed to address crimes related to starvation. This was partially due to lacunae in the relevant law, but more due to prosecutorial and political will, or rather the lack thereof, to apply the existing law. As the last thirty years of law-making at the international criminal tribunals have shown, once the relevant conduct for a serious international violation moves beyond the textbooks and into the courtroom, the relevant law can be identified, clarified, and developed. As with the recognition and prosecution of sexual violence and gender-based crimes, this process is what brings clarity to the law and ensures it is a useful instrument for accountability.

Although deprivation of food, water, and medicine has appeared in a few prosecutions in ICL over the modern era, there has been a dearth of prosecutions resting squarely on the crime of starvation. Of the approximate twenty cases in which starvation has featured, only two have pleaded it as a distinct crime.[24] Generally, it has been included as context in other CAH often as part of misconduct in detention situations.[25]

[24] Our research indicates that only two prosecutions of the modern era have pleaded starvation as a distinct crime, all on the domestic level (Croatia and Ethiopia): *Public Prosecutor v. M.P. et al.*, in the District Court in Zadar, Croatia, K. 74/96, Verdict, 24 April 1997; and *Special Prosecutor v. Col. Mengistu Hailamariam et al.*, Ethiopian Federal High Court, File No. 1/87, (2006).

[25] Our research indicates that approximately twenty-one cases have featured starvation as context in other distinct CAH, often in detention situations. *The International Military Tribunal* at Nuremberg, at 34, 43, 54, 230, 297, 251, 298, 214; Judgment, *United States of America v. Wilhelm von Leeb et al.*, (Case No. 12), The High Command Case, US Military Tribunal, Nuremberg, Trial Chamber, 27 October 1948, at 562, 573; Judgment, *Attorney General v. Adolf Eichmann*, (Case No. 40/61) District Court of Jerusalem, 11 December 1961, §§ 244(5); Judgment, *Prosecutor v. Kayishema & Ruzindana*, (ICTR-95-1-T), Trial Chamber, 21 May 1999, §§ 146, 548, at 560; Closing Order, *Prosecutor v. Chea Noun and Samphan Khieu*, (Case No.002), Extraordinary Chambers in the Court of Cambodia, Trial Chamber, 7 August 2016, §§ 1435–1438; Judgment, *Prosecutor v. Chea Noun and Samphan Khieu*, (Case No.002), Extraordinary Chambers in the Court of Cambodia, Trial Chamber, 7 August 2004, §§ 457, 648; Judgment, *Prosecutor v. Kaing Guek Eav*, (Case No. 001), Extraordinary Chambers in the Court of Cambodia, Trial Chamber, §§ 335, 372; 26 July 2010; Judgment, *Prosecutor v. Zejnil Delalić, Zdravko Mucić, and Esad Landzo*, (IT-96-21-T) Trial Chamber, 16 November 1998, §§ 1113, 1119; Judgment, *Prosecutor v. Radislav Krstić*, (IT-98-33-T), Trial Chamber, 2 August 2001, §§ 15, 26, 28, 566; Judgment, *Prosecutor v. Milorad Knrojelac*, (IT-97-25-T), Trial Chamber, 15 March 2002, § 9; Judgment, *Prosecutor v. Dragan Nikolic*, (IT-94-2-S), Trial Chamber, 18 December 2003, § 69; Judgment, *Prosecutor v. Zdravko Tolimir*, (IT-05-88/2-T), Trial Chamber, 12 December 2012, §§ 830; Judgment, *Prosecutor v. Jadranko Prlić et al.*, (IT-04-74-T), Trial Chamber, 29 May 2013, §§ 1176–1177, 1181–1184, 1192–1199, 1201–1205; Judgment, *Prosecutor v. Radovan Karadžić*, (IT-95-5/18-AR98*bis*.1), Appeals Chamber, 11 July 2013, § 49; Judgment, *Prosecutor v. Stanislav Galić*, (IT-98-29-T), Trial Chamber, 5 December 2003, §§ 609, 765; Judgment, *Prosecutor v. Dragomir Milošević*, (IT-98-29/1-T), Trial Chamber, 12 December

Despite the lack of prosecutions, there is no reason to believe that the crime of starvation cannot follow a trajectory similar to other international offences, such as sexual violence and gender-based crimes. Before the 2001 judgment in the case of *The Prosecutor v. Jean-Paul Akayesu*[26] at the International Criminal Tribunal for Rwanda, rape was not recognized as a form of genocide or a CAH. The Court's finding served as the departure point for several international prosecutions of sexual and gender-based crimes and a further elucidation of the law. What was historically observed as a natural consequence of war, an unhealthy belief that 'boys will be boys', became universally viewed as abhorrent behaviour demanding prosecution and lengthy prison sentences. What is now required are prosecutions for starvation offences leading to understanding of the law, robust legal findings of individual criminal responsibility, the recognition and removal of accountability gaps, and the comprehensive labelling of the crime as repugnant to all.

To advance this agenda, the international community requires a taxonomy for the acts that constitute starvation and a will to respond to these acts as prosecutable crimes. Several recent developments indicate that both issues are gaining momentum.

2. Indications of Change?

Given the global trend towards focusing on national prerogatives, this may be an inauspicious time to promote innovations in international law. Nevertheless, the question of whether starvation could be prosecuted sparked a collaboration between the international legal practice, Global Rights Compliance (The Hague), and the World Peace Foundation at the Fletcher School (Tufts University, Boston, Massachusetts) in support of the project, Accountability for Starvation: Testing the Limits of the Law (2018–20). This book is one product of the collaboration and includes contributions by leading legal scholars, humanitarian aid professionals, activists, journalists, and country experts. Over the course of the project, the project

2007 (hereafter '*Milošević* Trial Judgment'), §§ 208, 910–911, 937; Judgment, *Prosecutor v. Athanase Seromba*, (ICTR-2001-66-I), Trial Chamber, 13 December 2006, § 327; Second Decision on the Arrest Warrant, *Prosecutor v. Omar Hassan Ahmad Al-Bashir*, (ICC-02/05-01/09), Pre-Trial Chamber, 12 July 2010, §§ 34, 39; *Public Prosecutor v. Momčilo Perišić et al.*, in the District Court in Zadar, Croatia, K. 74/96, Judgment, Trial Chamber, 24 April 1997; Civil Original Jurisdiction, Writ Petition, *People's Union for Civil Liberties v. Union of India & Ors*, (No.196 of 2001), Supreme Court of India, 9 July 2007; Judgment, *Special Prosecutor v. Col. Mengistu Hailamariam et al.*, (File No. 1/87), Ethiopian Federal High Court, 12 December 2006; Decision, *Demanda de inconstitucionalidad contra los artículos 135, 156 y 157 (parciales) de la Ley 599 de 2000, y 174, 175, 178 y 179 de la Ley 522 de 1999*, (Constitutional Case No. C-291/07), Constitutional Court of Colombia, 25 April 2007. For additional starvation jurisprudence see, Global Rights Compliance, *Starvation Digests* 12 July 2021, available online at <https://starvationaccountability.org/news-and-events/starvation-jurisprudence-digest-december-2020> (visited 29 September 2021).

[26] Judgment, *Prosecutor v. Jean-Paul Akayesu*, (ICTR-96-4-T), Trial Chamber, 2 September 1998.

leaders (also the editors of this volume) benefitted from extended conversation with colleagues at the World Food Programme, the Oxford Institute for Ethics, Law and Armed Conflict, colleagues working within non-governmental organizations (NGOs) on the ground in impacted countries—like Mwatana for Human Rights (Yemen) and Damaan Humanitarian Organisation (Syria)—colleagues in the foreign ministries of the Netherlands and Switzerland, and many others from the legal, policy, and humanitarian sectors. Our work suggested that the time was indeed ripe to transform concern for mass starvation into a new movement to end it—or, at minimum, to set into motion the wheels of change that might eventually bring about this goal.

During those years, states and other international actors reached a faltering consensus that international law prohibits starvation as a weapon of war. This was demonstrated in two key advances. First, as discussed earlier in this chapter, was the adoption of UNSC Resolution 2417, and second was an amendment to the Rome Statute articulating that the prohibition of starvation applies in both International Armed Conflicts (IAC) and in Non-international Armed Conflicts (NIAC). In addition, the award of the Nobel Peace Prize of 2020 to the World Food Programme, explicitly recognizing the links between hunger and war, is an affirmation of this wider consensus. Legal scholarship has also begun to probe the law, finding more room for accountability than previously governed consensus.[27] This volume is situated at the nexus of policy, international relations, and law, seeking to illuminate how action might be taken in the arenas of international policy and prosecution.

A. United Nations Security Council Resolution 2417

On 23 March 2018, the Netherlands, during its term as president of the UNSC, introduced a discussion of the connections between food insecurity, hunger, and conflict. The discussion revealed a wide range of understandings among various country representatives of how these issues intersect with the UNSC's mandate.[28]

Various national representatives expressed concern about structural issues, like root causes of conflict, development, agricultural policies, cycles of poverty,

[27] Akande and Gillard, Dannenbaum (2021), and Dannenbaum (2022), see note 23; P. Drew, 'Can We Starve the Civilians?: Exploring the Dichotomy between the Traditional Law of Maritime Blockade and Humanitarian Initiatives', 95 *International Law Studies* (2019) 302–321; M. Nijs, 'Humanizing Siege: Applying the Principle of Proportionately to Sieges', 102 *International Review of the Red Cross* (2020) 683–704. See also essays in A. Coco, J. Hemptinne, and B. Lander (eds), 'Special Issue on Starvation in International Law', 17 *Journal of International Criminal Justice* (2019).

[28] The session began with presentations by Mark Lowcock, Under-Secretary General for Humanitarian Affairs, and David Beasley, Executive Director of the United Nations World Food Programme, was highly influenced by the Secretary General's presentation in 2017 regarding the four threatened famines in Somalia, South Sudan, Yemen, and northern Nigeria; and by a Food and Agriculture Organization report, 'Global Report on Food Crises 2018', published 22 March 2018.

and unemployment. Others focused more narrowly on the nexus with conflict, drawing attention to violations of international law, including through obstruction of humanitarian aid and attacks against humanitarian aid workers. Concern that the issues of hunger and food insecurity went beyond the UNSC's mandate were expressed by Russia, Ethiopia, China, and Kazakhstan, which argued that the Security Council should restrict its definition of international peace and security to actual and imminent cases of conflict between and within states.

Emerging out of this discussion and responding to stated concerns, on 24 May 2018, the UNSC unanimously passed Resolution 2417, which ensured a focus upon the context of hunger in armed conflict. It explicitly placed for the first time the issue of starvation in the peace and security arena, signalling a move away from its associations with food systems or climatic impacts.[29] UNSC Resolution 2417 drew on existing IHL and ICL to address three criminalized acts: starvation, depriving civilians of OIS (notably mentioned, those required for food production and distribution), and impeding humanitarian access (including protection for humanitarian aid workers), underscoring that such conduct could amount to a war crime. In so doing, the resolution echoes language found in Article 8(2)(b)(xxv) of the Rome Statute, which prohibits '[i]ntentionally using starvation of civilians as a method of warfare by depriving them of objects indispensable to their survival, including wilfully impeding relief supplies as provided for under the Geneva Conventions'.

While the resolution recalled that the UNSC can impose sanctions for obstructing the delivery of aid, it did not make explicit a mechanism to attend to such a process. Rather, the resolution tasked the Secretary General with providing information on risks of famine and food insecurity in conflict-affected countries as part of already-existing monitoring requirements on specific countries and in the annual report on civilian protection. A third, more ambiguous reporting requirement was also included: 'to swiftly bring to the Council's attention when there is a risk of conflict-induced famine or food insecurity in countries with armed conflict'. While risk of famine is circumscribed, the inclusion of broader language regarding risk of 'food insecurity' in conflict-affected countries suggests latitude for interpretation.

Following passage of the resolution, it was swiftly and separately referenced by the governments of the Netherlands (23 October 2018)[30] and Sweden (31 December 2018),[31] in reference to Yemen. Likewise, Adama Dieng, the UN Special

[29] Country-specific resolutions had done this on occasions beforehand, notably resolution 794 (1992) on Somalia. See M. Ventura, 'Prosecuting Starvation under International Criminal Law: Exploring the Legal Possibilities', 17 *Journal of International Criminal Justice* (2019) 881–906, at 902.

[30] United Nations Press Release, 'International Community Must Act to Stop Catastrophic Famine in Yemen, Top Humanitarian Affairs Official Tells Security Council', (SC/13550) 23 October 2018, available online at <https://www.un.org/press/en/2018/sc13550.doc.htm> (visited 5 August 2021).

[31] O. Skoog, 'Swedish Statement at the UN Security Council Briefing on Yemen', Swedish Ministry of Foreign Affairs, 23 October 2018, available online at <https://www.government.se/statements/2018/10/swedish-statement-at-the-un-security-council-briefing-on-yemen/> (visited 5 August 2021).

Advisor on Genocide Prevention, referenced 2417 in his condemnation of the coalition offensive on the crucial port city of Hudaydah in Yemen (14 June 2018):

> Starvation of civilians as a method of war is a war crime and was condemned by the Security Council in resolution 2417 of 24 May 2018. It seems that the first test of this resolution is Yemen: the Yemeni port of Hudaydah is a lifeline for the delivery of aid and the Coalition's air strikes can kill many more people over time through famine and hunger when damaging such civilian infrastructure.[32]

A subsequent UN resolution related to Somalia (UNSC 2431, 30 July 2018), referenced Resolution 2417 as it related to the 'ongoing humanitarian crisis', in relation to the obstruction of humanitarian aid, including through attacks on humanitarian aid workers.

Developments concerning South Sudan, as expressed in a closed-door meeting of the UNSC of August 2018 demonstrate how UNSC 2417 might be further harnessed to galvanize action in response to critical situations of starvation,[33] even when it is not directly referenced. The Netherlands and co-penholders of UNSC 2417, requested a briefing on the food security risks in South Sudan, followed by the circulation to the Council in July of a white paper by the UN Office for the Coordination of Humanitarian Affairs (OCHA), drawing attention to the extreme malnutrition in the country. As a result, UNSC S/RES/2428 (2018) was swiftly passed on 13 July 2018, imposing an arms embargo and additional targeted sanctions, expressing grave alarm and concern at the conflict, which had led to 'great human suffering', including 'conflict-induced food insecurity and threat of famine' in the country.

The UNSC has also been briefed on an ad hoc basis, through the submission of confidential White Papers by OCHA. These briefings have focused on country-specific situations, apprising the Council of food security challenges stemming from armed violence in South Sudan in July 2018 as noted earlier,[34] Yemen in October 2018,[35] the Democratic Republic of Congo (DRC), north-east Nigeria,

[32] 'Note to Correspondents: Statement by Adama Dieng, United Nations Special Adviser on the Prevention of Genocide, on the situation in Hudaydah, Yemen', UN Secretary General, 14 June 2018, available online at <https://www.un.org/sg/en/content/sg/note-correspondents/2018-06-14/note-correspondents-statement-adama-dieng-united-nations> (visited 5 August 2021).

[33] 'UN gravely concerned at South Sudan's "food security crisis"', Associated Press, 10 August 2018, available online at <https://apnews.com/article/c3091aa26df24f9f85eae8d7e375c7e3> (visited 5 August 2021).

[34] Security Council Report, 'What's in Blue: South Sudan Consultations', 9 August 2018, available online at <https://www.securitycouncilreport.org/whatsinblue/2018/08/south-sudan-consultations-10.php> (visited 5 August 2021).

[35] Security Council Report, 'What's in Blue: Yemen: Briefing on the Humanitarian Crisis', 22 October 2018, available online at <https://www.securitycouncilreport.org/whatsinblue/2018/10/yemen-briefing-on-the-humanitarian-crisis.php> (visited 5 August 2021).

South Sudan, and Yemen in September 2020,[36] and Ethiopia in May[37] and July[38] 2021, prompting the UNSC to convene conference sessions to address the issues facing these countries. In addition to convening high-level briefings to spotlight critical issues, the UNSC has also taken further action. Following the White Paper on South Sudan in 2018, the UNSC swiftly passed resolution 2428, imposing an arms embargo, targeted sanctions and recognizing the 'conflict-induced food insecurity and threat of famine' prevalent in the country.[39] The Yemen White Paper ultimately led to the adoption of resolution 2451 in December 2018, which explicitly called on the warring parties to protect objects indispensable to civilians.[40]

In addition to the mechanisms for reporting, as noted earlier, there are several other aspects of UNSC 2417 that are open to interpretation.

Resolution 2417 includes discussion of 'the destruction of OIS to civilians' which is broad enough to include both acts of intentionally starving people, and acts that may not have the express goal of starvation, but nonetheless produce starvation conditions. Such acts would particularly be subject to sanction if and when they were committed repeatedly and over a long duration. This is reflected UNSC Resolution 2451 (2018) relating to Yemen, which includes within the definition of OIS 'all those objects which are necessary for food distribution, processing and storage'.

Of concern is whether the resolution will be referenced primarily in relation to obstruction of humanitarian aid and targeting of humanitarian actors. While the language of UNSC 2417 does not suggest this limitation, if reporting is primarily compiled by humanitarian organizations, a risk arises that this important focus might become the primary issue, leaving aside criminal acts that create conditions under which people become reliant on aid in the first place.

A different concern arises in relation to whether UNSC 2417 will be applied broadly, in regard to generalized food insecurity or hunger, and indeed whether it is applicable in situations that do not rise to the definition of armed conflict but rumble along as civil disturbances or intercommunal violence, as can be seen in South Sudan after the end of major hostilities.[41] While the Resolution focuses on

[36] Security Council Report, 'What's in Blue: Videoconference on Conflict-induced Hunger', 16 September 2020, available online at <https://www.securitycouncilreport.org/whatsinblue/2020/09/videoconference-on-conflict-induced-hunger.php> (visited 5 August 2021).

[37] Security Council Report, 'What's in Blue: Ethiopia (Tigray): Informal Interactive Dialogue on the Humanitarian Situation', 14 June 2021, available online at <https://www.securitycouncilreport.org/whatsinblue/2021/06/ethiopia-tigray-informal-interactive-dialogue-on-the-humanitarian-situation.php> (visited 5 August 2021).

[38] 'Statement by Acting Under-Secretary-General for Humanitarian Affairs and Emergency Relief Coordinator, Ramesh Rajasingham—Briefing to the Security Council on the humanitarian situation in Ethiopia', Reliefweb, 2 July 2021, available online at <https://reliefweb.int/report/ethiopia/statement-acting-under-secretary-general-humanitarian-affairs-and-emergency-relief-1> (visited 5 August 2021).

[39] SC Res. 2428, 13 July 2018.

[40] SC Res. 2451, 21 December 2018.

[41] C. Newton, 'Pandemic of Hunger Symposium: Famine in a NIAC's Shadow—Other Situations of Violence and a Challenge for UNSCR 2417', Opinio Juris, 20 May 2021, available online at <http://opin

conflict contexts, it introduces some imprecision through reference to increases in undernourished and food insecure populations, root causes of conflict, and 'a vicious cycle between armed conflict and food insecurity'. While all of these points are valid, they stray from the narrower set of acts that might be criminalized. There are two specific issues. The consensus supporting Resolution 2417 at the UNSC could be jeopardized if situations in which there is not clear criminality are brought to the attention of the UNSC through this mechanism. Further, the specific prohibition on starvation could be diluted by reference to other factors creating hardship, such as crop failure related to drought or locusts, thus depoliticizing the actions that create famine. Additionally, they may introduce areas of enormous complexity that require response through many different sets of policy tools. Blurring the lines and weakening the implications of criminal behaviour by actors who should be sanctioned for creating and perpetrating starvation conditions remains an ever-present concern.

B. Amending the Rome Statute

A quieter and subtler, but significant development also occurred in relation to how the Rome Statute addresses starvation. Until 2019, the Rome Statute only criminalized starvation in an IAC—an odd omission, the (non) reasons for which will be noted later in this chapter. Switzerland proposed in April 2018 an amendment to Article 8 of the Rome Statute to include within the list of war crimes capable of being committed in an NIAC, precisely the same prohibition found in Article 8(2)(b)(xxv) regarding IACs.

In 2018, there was general support for the substance of the proposal from state delegates.[42] However, in October 2018, Switzerland deferred the decision to the 18th session of the Assembly of States Parties to the Rome Statute (December 2019), abiding by states' general reluctance to amend the Rome Statute until it was clear that there was an overwhelming consensus to proceed. There was significant precedent in favour of the Swiss Amendment. Starvation has long been prohibited under IHL in both an NIAC and an IAC[43] and has been included as a rule

iojuris.org/2021/05/20/pandemic-of-hunger-symposium-famine-in-a-niacs-shadow-other-situations-of-violence-and-a-challenge-for-unscr-2417/> (visited 5 August 2021).

[42] *Report of the Working Group on Amendments, Annex IV Non-paper submitted by Switzerland: proposed amendments to article 8 of the Rome Statute on the inclusion of starvation as a war crime in non-international armed conflicts*, ICC-ASP/17/3520, 29 November 2018, § 11.

[43] Protocol Additional to the Geneva Conventions of 12 August 1949, and relating to the Protection of Victims of International Armed Conflicts 8 June 1977, Art. 54(1); and Protocol Additional to the Geneva Conventions of 12 August 1949, and relating to the Protection of Victims of Non-International Armed Conflict, 8 June 1977, Art. 14. See also Arts 23, 55, 59 of the Geneva Conventions IV which introduced relevant obligations relating to the free passage of humanitarian relief.

from which no derogation can be made.[44] The International Committee of the Red Cross (ICRC) considers the prohibition to be part of customary international law, regardless of conflict classification.[45] The ICRC also includes starvation of civilians within its list of serious violations of IHL applicable in an NIAC.[46] There is increasing evidence of state acceptance of the customary status of starvation with eight national jurisdictions criminalizing starvation in both an NIAC and an IAC.[47] It is also a crime in both conflict designations under the Protocol on Amendments to the Protocol on the Statute of the African Court of Justice and Human Rights (the Malabo Protocol).[48] It is further recognized as a crime in an NIAC in a range of authoritative military manuals.[49]

[44] Commentary on the Additional Protocols, at 1456, § 4795.

[45] J. Henckaerts and L. Doswald-Beck (eds), *Customary International Humanitarian Law* (Cambridge: Cambridge University Press, 2005), Commentary on Rule 53.

[46] ICRC, *War Crimes: Working Paper Prepared by the ICRC for the United Nations Preparatory Committee for the Establishment of an International Criminal Court* (1997), available online at <https://www.icrc.org/en/doc/resources/documents/misc/57jngx.htm> (visited 29 September 2021), at 1.

[47] Croatia, Criminal Code (2011), Art. 91, available online at <https://narodne-novine.nn.hr/clanci/sluzbeni/2011_11_125_2498.html>; the Netherlands, International Crimes Act, 2003, Art. 5(5)(I), (amended 2018), available online at <https://iccdb.hrlc.net/documents/implementations/pdf/Netherlands_ICC_Implementation_Act_2002.pdf>; Republic of Korea, Act on the Punishment of Crimes within the Jurisdiction of the International Criminal Court (2007), art. 13, available online at <https://cjad.nottingham.ac.uk/en/legislation/206/>; Germany Law Introducing the International Crimes Code (2002), Section 11(1)(5), available online at <https://www.iuscomp.org/gla/statutes/VoeStGB.pdf>; France, Criminal Code, Art. 461-1, 461–25, (consolidated version up to November 2017), available online at <https://www.legifrance.gouv.fr/> (visited 29 September 2021). Nicaragua, Draft Penal Code [1999] Art. 463 relating to the impediment of humanitarian aid; and El Salvador, Draft Amendments to the Penal Code [1998], Article entitled 'Omission y obstaculización de medidas de socorro y asistencia humanitaria' relating to the impediment of humanitarian aid, Nicaragua and El Salvador taken from J.-M. Henckaerts and L. Doswald-Beck, *Customary International Humanitarian Law, Volume I: Practice* (Cambridge: Cambridge University Press, 2005). There are approximately twenty-two countries which reference starvation or wilfully impeding humanitarian access in their criminal legislation but do not specify whether the conduct is criminalized in an NIAC or IAC. Approximately eight countries follow the ICC and feature the crime only in an IAC (Australia, Georgia, Iraq, Mali, New Zealand, Slovenia, Trinidad and Tobago, and the United Kingdom).

[48] Art, 28 D War Crimes (e) (xvi).

[49] Argentina Law of War Manual (1989) Leyes de Guerra, PC-08-01, Público, Edición 1989, Estado Mayor Conjunto de las Fuerzas Armadas, aprobado por Resolución No. 489/89 del Ministerio de Defensa, 23 April 1990, § 9; Australia LOAC Manual (2006) The Manual of the Law of Armed Conflict, Australian Defence Doctrine Publication 06.4, Australian Defence Headquarters, 11 May 2006, 10–11; Benin, Le Droit de la Guerre, III fascicules, Forces Armées du Bénin, Ministère de la Défense nationale, (Military Manual, 1995), § 13; Canada, The Law of Armed Conflict at the Operational and Tactical Levels, Office of the Judge Advocate General, 13 August 2001, § 14; Colombia (Directive on IHL) Normas de Derecho Internacional Humanitario, Directiva Permanente No. 017, Ministerio de Defensa Nacional, 17 August 1993, § 15; Croatia, 'Basic Rules of International Humanitarian Law Applicable in Armed Conflicts', Republic of Croatia, Ministry of Defence, 1993, §16; France (OAC Manual) Manuel de droit des conflits armés, Ministère de la Défense, Direction des Affaires Juridiques, Sous-Direction du droit international humanitaire et du droit européen, Bureau du droit des conflits armés (2001), § 18; Germany (IHL Manual), ZDv 15/1, Humanitäres Völkerrecht in bewaffneten Konflikten—Grundsätze, DSK VV230120023, Bundesministerium der Verteidigung, June 1996, § 19; Hungary (Military Manual) A Hadijog, Jegyzet a Katonai, Föiskolák Hallgatói Részére, Magyar Honvédség Szolnoki Repülötiszti Föiskola, (1992), § 20; Kenya (LOAC Manual) Law of Armed Conflict, Military Basic Course (ORS), 4 Précis, The School of Military Police, § 23; Republic of Korea, Military Law Manual (1996), § 24; Madagascar (Military Manual) Le Droit des Conflits Armés, Ministère des Forces Armées, August 1994, § 25; the Netherlands, see note 47, § 26; New Zealand (Military Manual, 2005); Humanitair Oorlogsrecht: Handleiding, Voorschrift No. 27-412, Koninklijke Landmacht, Militair

UNSC 2417 also appears to reflect this apparent customary international law position, drawing no distinction between the use of starvation of civilians as a method of warfare in an NIAC or an IAC. As the resolution clearly underlines (without any apparent limitation on its applicability), 'using starvation of civilians as a method of warfare may constitute a war crime'.[50]

The above enumeration of the customary international law position thus begs the question of why the Rome Statute failed to criminalize starvation in an NIAC in the first place. There appeared to be no principled or practical reason for this omission. The Preparatory Committee of the Rome Statute first considered the offence of starvation in 1996 and it originally included 'starving of the civilian population and prevention of humanitarian assistance from reaching them',[51] this then evolved into the present wording under Article 8(2)(b)(xxv). The delegations agreed that the deprivation of OIS was not limited to food and drink but should include a broader approach of something necessary to live.[52] Notwithstanding that this was the first time the war crime of starving civilians was criminalized under ICL, its passage was not controversial and the delegation quickly reached agreement on the draft text.[53]

There is no indication from the drafting history regarding why starvation was only criminalized in an international armed conflict. Indeed in 1998 there was a provision penalizing starvation in an NIAC, yet the final 'package' of the Rome Statute did not include it, leading to the conclusion that its omission was unintentional.[54] If it was indeed a mere slip of the drafting pen, the omission may be further evidence of the low level of interest in starvation crimes at that time. There were no states or NGOs championing the issue who would have been vigilant to it being overlooked. Fortunately, the reassessment of the status of the war

Juridische Dienst (2005), § 27; Nigeria (Military Manual) International Humanitarian Law (IHL), Directorate of Legal Services, Nigerian Army (1994), § 28; Russian Federation (Military Manual), Instructions on the Application of the Rules of International Humanitarian Law by the Armed Forces of the USSR, Appendix to Order of the USSR Defence Minister No. 75 (1990), § 29; Spain (LOAC Manual) Orientaciones, El Derecho de los Conflictos Armados, Tomo 1, Publicación OR7-004 (Edición Segunda), Mando de Adiestramiento y Doctrina, Dirección de Doctrina, Orgánica y Materiales, 2 November 2007, § 30; Togo (Military Manual) Le Droit de la Guerre, III fascicules, État-major Général des Forces Armées Togolaises, Ministère de la Défense nationale (1996), § 33; and the Former Yugoslavia (Military Manual) Propisi o Primeri Pravila Medjunarodnog Ratnog Prava u Oruzanim Snagama SFRJ, PrU-2, Savezni Sekretarijat za Narodnu Odbranu (Pravna Uprava) (1988), § 36.

[50] SC Res. 2417, 24 May 2018, at 2.

[51] M. Cottier, 'War Crimes—Para. 2(b)(xxv) Starvation of Civilians as a Method of Warfare' in O. Triffterer (ed.), *Commentary on the Rome Statute of the International Criminal Court* (Baden-Baden: Nomos, 1999), at 510, citing to the 1996 Preparatory Committee II 61.

[52] K. Dörmann, L. E. Doswald-Beck, and R. Kolb, *Elements of War Crimes under the Rome Statute of the International Criminal Court: Sources and Commentary* (Cambridge: Cambridge University Press, 2003), online publication 2009.

[53] Cottier, see note 51, at 510. See also W. Schabas, *The International Criminal Court: A Commentary to the Rome Statute*, (2nd edn, Oxford: Oxford University Press, 2010), at 285.

[54] *Report of the Working Group on Amendments*, see note 42, §7.

crime of starvation in NIACs reached critical international consensus by 2019 when the Swiss successfully renewed their efforts to advance the amendment. At the Assembly of States Parties meeting on 6 December 2019, the Parties unanimously passed resolution ICC-ASP/18/5, adopting Article 8(2)(e)(xix) which amended the Rome Statute.[55] On 10 October 2020 New Zealand became the first country to ratify it. However, at the time of writing, only five further states had ratified.[56]

C. Investigative and Accountability Mechanisms

Another indication of change can be seen in the clear trends of including starvation in investigative mandates. For instance, the mandate of the Human Rights Council (UNCHRSS) has explicitly recognized the use of starvation during war, most recently in a March 2021 resolution.[57] In 2020, the UNCHRSS released a landmark report concluding that both government and opposition armed forces in South Sudan had deliberately used the starvation of civilians as a method of warfare, often as an instrument of collective punishment to punish non-aligning communities.[58] This report expanded on the UNCHRSS' examination of conflict-induced hunger and the right to food as part of their regular reporting on the wider human rights situation in South Sudan.[59]

Moreover, in renewing the mandate of the Group of Eminent Experts on Yemen (GEE) for 2021, the HRC called for an end to the use of starvation as method of warfare and for the full implementation of UNSC 2417.[60] In its most recent report, the GEE also relied on UNSC 2417 as part of their legal analysis of the factual situation on the ground towards determining the violation of the right to adequate food.[61]

In addition to HRC investigative bodies, UN Special Rapporteurs have examined the link between armed violence and food security. In his planned vision for his tenure, the new Special Rapporteur on the Right to Food referenced UNSC

[55] Assembly of States Parties to the Rome State, Resolution ICC-ASP/18/Res. 5, 6 December 2019.

[56] At time of writing, Andorra, Croatia, the Netherlands, Norway, and Portugal have ratified, see UN, *Treaty Collection*, available online at <https://treaties.un.org/Pages/ViewDetails.aspx?src=TREATY&mtdsg_no=XVIII-10-g&chapter=18&clang=_en> (visited 29 September 2021).

[57] HRC Res. 46/23, 30 March 2021, § 3.

[58] Commission on Human Rights in South Sudan, *'There is nothing left for us': starvation as a method of warfare in South Sudan*, UN Doc. A/HRC/45/CRP.3, 5 October 2020.

[59] See, for example, *Report of the Commission on Human Rights in South Sudan*, UN Doc. A/HRC/46/53, 4 February 2021, §§ 48–63; *Detailed findings of the Commission on Human Rights in South Sudan*, UN Doc. A/HRC/46/CRP.2, 18 February 2021.

[60] HRC Res. 45/15, 12 October 2020, § 6.

[61] *Situation of human rights in Yemen, including violations and abuses since September 2014: Detailed findings of the Group of Eminent International and Regional Experts on Yemen*, UN Doc. A/HRC/45/CRP.7, 29 September 2020, §112.

2417, among other instruments, while outlining his plan to investigate 'the power of international humanitarian law and international criminal law to prevent hunger, famine and malnutrition'.[62] Most recently, the Special Rapporteur for Myanmar called for action to address humanitarian access blockades and mass deaths from starvation, particularly in Kayah state.[63]

Conflict-driven food insecurity has also featured more prominently in accountability processes, with the ICC Prosecutor making explicit reference to the destruction of food sources prompting mass displacement in the request to investigate crimes committed against the Rohingya people,[64] and submissions being made before the International Court of Justice on the forced starvation and food supply deprivations suffered by Rohingya in Myanmar.[65]

D. Hunger and Peace

On 9 October 2020, the Norwegian Nobel Committee announced the award of the Nobel Peace Prize to the World Food Programme. As the Committee stated:

> The link between hunger and armed conflict is a vicious circle: war and conflict can cause food insecurity and hunger, just as hunger and food insecurity can cause latent conflicts to flare up and trigger the use of violence. We will never achieve the goal of zero hunger unless we also put an end to war and armed conflict.
>
> The World Food Programme plays a key role in multilateral cooperation on making food security an instrument of peace, and has made a strong contribution towards mobilizing UN Member States to combat the use of hunger as a weapon of war and conflict. The organisation contributes daily to advancing the fraternity of nations referred to in Alfred Nobel's will. As the UN's largest specialised agency, the World Food Programme is a modern version of the peace congresses that the Nobel Peace Prize is intended to promote.[66]

[62] *Right to Food, Report of the Special Rapporteur on the right to food, Michael Fakhri*, UN Doc. A/HRC/46/33, 24 December 2020, § 95–97.

[63] T. Andrews, *Statement by Thomas Andrews, UN Special Rapporteur on the Situation of Human Rights in Myanmar*, Human Rights Council, 7 July 2021, available online at <https://www.ohchr.org/en/NewsEvents/Pages/DisplayNews.aspx?NewsID=27283&LangID=E> (visited 29 September 2021).

[64] Request for authorization of an investigation pursuant to Art. 15, *Situation in the People's Republic of Bangladesh/Republic of the Union of Myanmar* (ICC-01/19), Pre-Trial Chamber III, 4 July 2019, § 111.

[65] *Case concerning Application of the Convention on the Prevention and Punishment of the Crime of Genocide (The Gambia v. Myanmar)*, Public Sitting: Verbatim Record, of 10 December 2019, available online at <https://www.icj-cij.org/public/files/case-related/178/178-20191210-ORA-01-00-BI.pdf> (visited 29 September 2021), § 19.

[66] 'The Nobel Peace Prize for 2020', Nobel Peace Prize Committee, 9 October 2020, available online <https://www.nobelprize.org/prizes/peace/2020/press-release/> (visited 25 August 2021).

The Prize sends a signal that mass starvation is antithetical to international peace. It suggests that in global opinion, there remains a strongly held view that regards those who perpetrate starvation crimes as beyond the pale.

3. Starvation in Tigray, Ethiopia

In the weeks between the announcement of the 2020 Nobel Peace Prize and its award, Ethiopia returned to war: a war of starvation. It was a test of the progress made in overcoming famine and ostracizing starvation crimes, and especially of the efficacy of resolution 2417. On all counts, the assessment at the time of writing (July 2021) is that the principles and institutions failed.[67]

Hostilities erupted in November 2020, pitting the regional government of Tigray and its ruling party, the Tigray People's Liberation Front (TPLF) against the Federal Government of Ethiopia, militias and special forces from the neighbouring Amhara region, and their coalition partner the state of Eritrea. The first weeks of the war were a conventional military offensive in which the Ethiopian National Defence Force (ENDF), the Eritrean Defence Force (EDF), and Amhara militia, rapidly defeated the TPLF and occupied all the major towns. All parties bore a share of responsibility for the outbreak of the war, but overwhelming evidence available at the time of writing indicates it was the coalition of Ethiopian Federal forces, Amhara regional forces, and Eritrean troops who committed starvation crimes on a large scale, thereby creating a famine of a scale and depth that is likely to surpass that of Somalia (2011) and Yemen (2015 to the present).

Tigray was historically a food deficit region and was the epicentre (with neighbouring Wollo Province) of the famine of 1984–1985. That famine, and other severe food crises, also struck many other parts of the country. After a rebel coalition led by the TPLF overthrew the military government in 1991, food security became a national priority. Ethiopia's national economy was developed and restructured by active government intervention in partnership with international donors. The national security strategy identified poverty and hunger as the most significant threat to the country's stability.[68] Along with the rest of Ethiopia, Tigray became more food secure through the promotion of diversified and sustainable

[67] World Peace Foundation, 'Starving Tigray: How Armed Conflict and Mass Atrocities Have Destroyed an Ethiopian Region's Economy and Food System and Are Threatening Famine', April 2021, available online at <https://sites.tufts.edu/wpf/starving-tigray/> (visited 5 August 2021); T. Dannenbaum, 'Famine in Tigray, Humanitarian Access, and the War Crime of Starvation', Just Security, 26 July 2021, available online at h<ttps://www.justsecurity.org/77590/famine-in-tigray-humanitarian-access-and-the-war-crime-of-starvation/> (visited 6 August 2021); S. Annys et al., 'Tigray: Atlas of the humanitarian situation', Research Gate, July 2021, available online at <https://www.arcgis.com/apps/webappviewer/index.html?id=e7538a480f004487927852d75a90bb69>(visited 15 July 2021).

[68] Government of Ethiopia, Ministry of Information, 'The Federal Democratic Republic of Ethiopia Foreign Affairs and National Security Policy and Strategy', Addis Ababa (2002).

smallholder agriculture, commercial sesame production, artisanal mining, industries, and various components of a Productive Safety Net Programme that moved beyond traditional humanitarian response to a package of comprehensive livelihood support. This was a major achievement that took three decades to build. When drought caused a major nationwide food deficit in 2015, the government responded expeditiously and effectively, providing assistance to more than 20 million people. Ethiopia, it seemed, was no longer the land of famine.[69]

As such, Tigray benefited from the national politics and economics of famine prevention and economic development. Ironically, those successes exposed the population to new vulnerabilities when, in 2020, the Ethiopian government dismantled those new structures and the different armed forces in the coalition arrayed against Tigray attacked the recently developed infrastructure. The economy and food system were hard hit by the hostilities and consequent closure of banks and microfinance institutions and the interruption of government resource transfers. The Ethiopian army, the Eritrean army, and the militia and special forces of the neighbouring Amhara region took control of the region and committed a wide range of atrocities including pillage, the war crime of starvation, and rape.

Numerous reports indicate that the Ethiopian, Eritrean, and allied militias systematic looted and destroyed factories, shops, banks, schools, and universities. They ransacked, burned, and pillaged farms, grain stores, and livestock, with satellite imagery appearing to show large swathes of land burnt in what many are calling 'scorched earth tactics'. Crops and food stores were stolen or destroyed. Livestock from herds of cattle to chickens were seized or slaughtered. Fruit trees were cut down. Farming was disrupted with peasants reportedly being told, 'you will not plough, you will not harvest, and if you try we will punish you'. Water pipes, wells, and even basic household utensils were smashed. The majority of the region's health infrastructure was stripped of everything and vandalized, and some hospitals and clinics were turned into army camps. The destruction of these OIS, in particular, will have long-term implications for food security and resilience. Refugee camps appear also to have been targeted, with a UNHCR spokesman stating that Eritrean refugees in Tigray have resorted to drinking from muddy puddles and eating plants, tree bark, and leaves.[70] On 22 June an airstrike struck a crowded market, and according to reports, ambulances were prevented from attending the wounded.[71] Forty-two civilians died.

Before the conflict, the food economy of Tigray depended on food crops and export crops grown in the fertile lands of western Tigray. These districts were claimed

[69] A. de Waal, *Mass Starvation: The History and Future of Famine* (Cambridge: Polity, 2017).

[70] 'Tigray crisis: Ethiopia region at risk of huge "humanitarian disaster"', *BBC*, 2 February 2021, available online at <https://www.bbc.com/news/world-africa-55905108> (visited 5 August 2021).

[71] K. Houreld, 'Medical official: air strike kills at least 43 in Ethiopia's Tigray', *Reuters*, 23 June 2021, available online at <https://www.reuters.com/world/africa/witness-airstrike-kills-dozens-ethiopias-tigray-region-2021-06-23/> (visited 5 August 2021).

by Amhara region in a territorial dispute dating back many decades. Amhara regional forces invaded and (in the terminology of the US State Department)[72] ethnically cleansed western Tigray, foreclosing migrant labour and forcibly truncating the region's food economy.

Reports from medical workers indicate that rape and sexual violence was organized and widespread.[73] They provide testimony that Ethiopian and Eritrean troops perpetrated gang rape, mutilation, and torture. Some reports have also indicated that women have been held in captivity as sexual slaves. In addition to the profound physical, emotional, and psychological trauma inflicted on the women and girls, rape may also be considered in the context of starvation crimes for its impact on a mother's ability to care for her children. Some women were so grievously injured that they could no longer perform basic tasks such as preparing food or washing their children.[74] Thousands of mothers were separated from their children, often by abduction by soldiers for sexual violation.[75] There will be many children born of rape. In Tigray, fear of rape meant that women and girls were confined to hiding and unable to undertake essential activities. Additionally, the longer-term impacts of rape complicate a woman's status within her own community, harming the long-term economic, social, and emotional prospect for both her and her children, often resulting in deep poverty and hunger.[76] For all these reasons, rape may qualify as a starvation crime.[77]

The government imposed an information blackout starting with shutting off phone and Internet connectivity, including preventing journalists from travelling to the worst hit areas and intimidating, jailing, and even murdering local reporters. Human rights organizations and media were compelled to rely on innovative methods such as of geolocating video footage that had been smuggled

[72] D. Walsh, 'Ethiopia's war leads to ethnic cleansing in Tigray region, U.S. report says', *New York Times*, 26 February 2021, available online at <https://www.nytimes.com/2021/02/26/world/middleeast/ethiopia-tigray-ethnic-cleansing.html> (visited 5 August 2021).

[73] United Nations Press Release, 'United Nations Special Representative of the Secretary-General on Sexual Violence in Conflict, Ms. Pramila Patten, urges all parties to prohibit the use of sexual violence and cease hostilities in the Tigray region of Ethiopia', 21 January 2021, available online at <http://bit.ly/2NiLx55> (visited 5 August 2021); International Rescue Committee, 'Gender Analysis key findings: women's exploitation & gender-based violence across Ethiopia's Tigray crisis', 4 May 2021, available online at <https://www.rescue.org/sites/default/files/document/5868/irctigraygenderanalysiskeyfindingsmay.pdf> (visited 5 August 2021).

[74] L. Kassa, '"A Tigrayan womb should never give birth": Rape in Tigray', *Al Jazeera*, 21 April 2021, available online at <https://www.aljazeera.com/news/2021/4/21/a-tigrayan-womb-should-never-give-birth-rape-in-ethiopia-tigray> (visited 5 August 2021).

[75] Save the Children, 'Six months on: Almost 5,000 children separated from parents by conflict in Tigray', 4 May 2021, available online at <https://reliefweb.int/report/ethiopia/six-months-almost-5000-children-separated-parents-conflict-tigray> (visited 5 August 2021).

[76] D. Mazurana and K. Proctor, 'Gender and Humanitarian Action', in R. Mac Ginty and J. H. Peterson (eds), *Handbook on Humanitarian Action* (London: Routledge, 2014) 49–61; E. von Joeden-Forgey, 'Gender and the Future of Genocide Studies and Prevention', 7 *Genocide Studies and Prevention* (2012) 89–107; H. Slim, *Killing Civilians: Method, Madness and Morality in War* (New York: Columbia University Press, 2008), at 37–119.

[77] See Chapter 13 in this volume

out and laboriously confirmed by phone interviews.[78] This also applied to humanitarian reporting. One of the ironies of the development of sophisticated institutional mechanisms for measuring food crisis and determining the levels of food insecurity including famine, meant that when such information was deliberately withheld, international agencies were reluctant to declare famine, even when it was clearly happening.

According to numerous reports from the UN and humanitarian agencies, Ethiopian and Eritrean forces limited humanitarian access, stole essential aid, and attacked humanitarian workers, killing at least ten. In a region that was ranked as broadly food secure in October 2020, within seven months, at least 350,000 people were estimated to be in famine conditions and a further 2 million in a situation fast approaching famine. Of Tigray's 6 million people, 5 million were in need of food assistance. The IPC analysis of early June 2021 concluded: 'Notwithstanding some incremental improvements in access, this cannot meaningfully offset the scale of conflict-induced hunger. Even on a best-case scenario, with a cessation of hostilities and aid able to reach the population, it is still predicted that 400,000 people will face Catastrophe (IPC Phase 5) famine-like conditions by September.'[79] At the time of writing, that 'best-case scenario' seemed hopelessly optimistic.

In June 2021, the war took a dramatic turn with the military victory of the Tigray Defence Forces over the Ethiopian army, which lead to the latter fleeing from Tigray, and the prompt withdrawal of the Eritrean army. The starvation crimes of pillage and destruction of OIS, along with rape and massacre of civilians, appear promptly to have ceased. However, the Ethiopian government placed Tigray under siege, encircling it and cutting off essential services, commercial traffic, and humanitarian access. Given the scale of escalating deprivation, this was tantamount to a starvation siege.

The overall picture, from numerous reports, indicates that the Ethiopian–Eritrean onslaught on Tigray was a campaign of scorched earth and starvation.[80] It was a shocking reminder that the progress made in overcoming famine over the previous half century was fragile, and that the commission of widespread and systematic starvation crimes could unleash human suffering on an atrocious scale. Meanwhile, the international norms, principles, and institutions for the prevention of such crimes proved woefully inadequate. Ignoring its own commitments and the

[78] B. Feleke et al., '"Two bullets is enough": Analysis of Tigray massacre video raises questions for Ethiopian Army', *CNN*, 2 April 2021, available online at <https://www.cnn.com/2021/04/01/africa/tigray-mahibere-dego-massacre-video-cmd-intl/index.html> (visited 5 August 2021); 'Ethiopia: video of Tigray massacre lifts lid on "war without photos"', *France24*, 10 March 2021, available online at <https://observers.france24.com/en/africa/20210312-ethiopia-tigray-video-massacre-war-mai-harmaz-investigation> (visited 5 August 2021).

[79] IPC, 'Ethiopia: Acute Food Insecurity Situation May–June 2021 and Projection for July–September 2021', June 2021, available online at <http://www.ipcinfo.org/fileadmin/user_upload/ipcinfo/docs/IPC_Ethiopia_Acute_Food_Insecurity_2021MaySept_national.pdf> (visited 6 August 2021).

[80] World Peace Foundation and Annys et al., see note 67.

authoritative reporting, the African Union tamely fell into line with the Ethiopian government's account. The United Nations Security Council met in public session on the crisis only on 2 July 2021, eight months after the war began and six months after the first warnings that armed conflict could lead to widespread food insecurity—a delay that shockingly showed the weakness of UNSC 2417, in both its preventative and punitive functions.

Two investigative bodies were launched in the early months of the conflict. The first is a joint investigation under the auspices of the United Nations High Commissioner for Human Rights (OHCHR) and the Ethiopian Human Rights Commission (EHRC). This initiative faces the obstacle that the EHRC is a government body that is not trusted by most Tigrayans and therefore it is unlikely to have access to the crime scene. The second is a Commission of Inquiry (CoI) set up by the African Commission on Human and Peoples' Rights (ACHPR) to investigate violations of international humanitarian and human rights law and identify perpetrators. The resolution establishing the CoI noted 'with concern the humanitarian crisis in Tigray, the challenges to the population's access to humanitarian assistance, and reports of the use of starvation as a weapon of war'.[81] The formation of the CoI was strongly rejected by the government of Ethiopia. Whether out of the UNSC's ashes an investigative phoenix may rise with a robust and dedicated investigative focus on the starvation crimes in Tigray is at the time of writing unknown. The short mandate cycles of both investigations coupled with the inevitable access restrictions is likely to curtail, at least initially, the scope of their findings.

The war in Ethiopia and crimes of starvation are unfolding at the time of writing. The very fact of this calamity and the half-hearted international response shows that progress in adopting principles and policies does not translate into real change. The men who made famine in Tigray in 2021 appear to have done so confident that they would enjoy impunity for their crimes. This is testament to the need to make acts of starvation not only unlawful but so morally reprehensible that they cannot be contemplated.

4. Overview of Chapters

This volume offers the first of its kind: a comprehensive introduction to how international humanitarian and criminal law, in addition to other international monitoring and response mechanisms, might be deployed to confront processes of mass starvation. It does so by addressing the conceptual, historical, legal, and social

[81] African Commission on Human and Peoples Rights, *Resolution on the Fact-Finding Mission to the Tigray Region of the Federal Democratic Republic of Ethiopia*, 12 May 2021, ACHPR/Res. 482, available online at <https://www.achpr.org/sessions/resolutions?id=513> (visited 6 August 2021).

frameworks and tools that have defined the past and that are likely to be most relevant to on the future of accountability for starvation.

Chapters 2 through 4 introduce the conceptual and historical background for the discussion of starvation and international law. In Chapter 2, Bridget Conley and Alex de Waal explore the question 'What is Starvation?', presenting the historical and conceptual framework for 'starvation' that informs this volume. They contextualize mass starvation within discussions concerned with defining famine, arguing that the term 'starvation' captures a key element often missed in 'famine'. 'Starvation' is a *process* of deprivation that occurs when actors impede the capacity of targeted persons to access the means of sustaining life, during which preexisting vulnerabilities interact with policies that create starvation conditions. The term 'starvation crimes' is presented as a means to capture the way various legal regimes already criminalize an array of acts and omissions that move populations from conditions of need to life-threatening catastrophe. Conley and de Waal detail how starvation has been used to by various military and political actors to achieve strategic and tactical goals, illustrating them with historical examples from the nineteenth century until today, ranging across every continent.

Susanne Jaspars' contribution (Chapter 3), 'Social Nutrition and Accountability for Mass Starvation', examines social nutrition as a framework for understanding the social and political factors that expose populations to risk of mass starvation. Jaspars provides a multi-factorial and synergistic framework for understanding patterns of vulnerability and trajectories of deprivation leading to increased mortality from malnutrition, disease, and other harms. The framework, she argues, can contribute to strengthening accountability for mass starvation. The chapter discusses obstacles that may arise and ends with a focus on issues that require further discussion in order to develop a socially and politically oriented framework for food and nutrition at the level of populations that is relevant to today's crises.

Chapter 4, 'An Unprosecuted Crime' by Bridget Conley, Randle DeFalco, Senai Abraha, and Alex de Waal, presents four cases where starvation crimes featured in a conflict and were investigated in the course of subsequent transitional justice efforts, but were not prosecuted as such: Cambodia under the Khmer Rouge (1975–1979), Ethiopia under Mengistu Haile Mariam (1974–1991), the war in Bosnia-Herzegovina (1992–1995), and the conflict and atrocities in Darfur, Sudan (2003–2008). In both Cambodia and Ethiopia, famine conditions resulted from policies directed against entire civilian populations. In Bosnia, through concerted international humanitarian intervention, only discrete pockets of extreme deprivation occurred, despite the fact that throughout the conflict access to food, water, and other life-supporting supplies was manipulated to serve war aims. Only prosecutions related to Cambodia addressed starvation, and even there, only partially. In Darfur, the humanitarian crisis claimed at least 200,000 lives and the ICC Prosecutor framed charges against President Omar al-Bashir that included the destruction of objects indispensable to the survival of the civilian population and obstructing humanitarian assistance, with genocidal intent. Although al-Bashir was overthrown and at the time of writing is in custody in Sudan, no prosecutions on this basis have yet been commenced. Together, the case studies reveal the prosecutorial caution and evidential complexities of prosecuting starvation.

Chapters 5 and 6 offer comprehensive discussions of how international humanitarian, criminal ,and human rights law apply to starvation and the most salient questions posed for a prosecutor who might decide to pursue charges.

Chapter 5, 'A Comprehensive Review of Existing IHL and ICL as it Relates to Starvation' by Wayne Jordash QC, Catriona Murdoch, and Joe Holmes begins by drawing attention to the fact that deliberate starvation is a crime under international law. Notwithstanding, there has yet to be a prosecution of an individual suspected of committing the crime or engaging in any of the underlying conduct upon which such a charge might be based. The reasons for this neglect may be many, including a lack of clarity around the elements of the crime and particularly the element of intent that must be established. This chapter explores the challenges that might exist in investigating and prosecuting the crime of starvation and seeks to clarify its elements with a particular focus on the *mens rea* requirement under Article 8(2)(b)(xxv) of the Rome Statute. This chapter provides a roadmap for practitioners to ensure better international recognition of deliberate starvation as an international crime, and in order that attribution of fault and accountability become less elusive.

Human rights law, argues Simone Hutter in Chapter 6, 'The Right to Food in Armed Conflict', presents clear guidance on the right to food as pertains to states' obligations, as opposed to individual criminal responsibility articulated in ICL and IHL. As Hutter points out, the right to food and the right to be free from hunger are not only indivisibly linked to the survival of populations but also to the inherent dignity of individuals. Access to food, water, and other indispensable objects is a precondition for the fulfilment of other human rights. Hutter considers what is meant by the 'progressive realisation' of the right to food and water and associated IHRL law linked to starvation, and the obligations to respect, protect, and fulfil IHRL related to starvation and how economic accessibility and economic, social, and cultural rights are important. She also reviews the applicability of IHRL in times of armed conflict and what avenues for accountability flow specifically from IHRL violations.

Having presented an extended discussion of the law, the chapters now turn to three of the most prominent cases of starvation crimes of the new century: South Sudan, Syria, and Yemen. These are far from the only cases that might have been examined. Other important contemporary cases that are not developed in separate chapters include both those in which political decision is paramount (such as Venezuela and Nigeria) and those in which chronic poverty and climate crisis also play a role (such as Somalia). The famine in the Tigray region of Ethiopia was too recent for a detailed or definitive examination. The three cases developed were chosen both for their prominence and because they highlight themes that help illuminate the patterns of starvation as a method of war.

Chapter 7 by Chris Newton presents a case study of South Sudan. It provides background on the history of mass starvation in South Sudan and pre-conflict vulnerabilities. Its primary focus, however, is to document the starvation crimes that occurred during the civil war (2013–2019), with emphasis on two regions of particular concern: Unity State and Wau/Baggari (western Bahr el Ghazal), with comparisons from elsewhere. This chapter provides a detailed examination of how conflict actors' strategic and tactical choices have produced the conditions of famine in three locations across South Sudan.

Syria is the focus of Chapter 8, and is authored by Mohammad Kanfash and Ali Aljasem who draw on their professional experience as humanitarian relief workers during the armed conflict in Syria, as well as a broader analysis of the dynamics of starvation. They address the issue of starvation crimes committed during the war in Syria (2012–2018), including the goals and methods of the perpetrators, the outcomes for the victims, and the possibilities for legal redress. It includes a case study of the use of starvation during the war and case studies of Eastern Ghouta (in the Damascus suburbs), Aleppo, and Deir Alzor.

Chapter 9 is the study of Yemen by Aditya Sarkar that addresses the causes of the protracted food security crisis in that country and the specific factors that have led to acute starvation in several localities. Pre-war Yemen was the poorest and most food-insecure country in the Arab world, a condition well known to those who chose to pursue a war of starvation. Conditions of extreme deprivation and even famine arose from the combination of economic policies by the internationally recognized government and its regional backers (the Saudi-led coalition), conditions that appear to have been designed to strangle the capability of the areas controlled by the Houthis and military actions that were either aimed to destroy livelihoods, agriculture, water infrastructure, and medical facilities (or had that as a reasonably foreseeable outcome), or to restrict humanitarian access. At the outset of the conflict, the warring parties—especially the Saudi-led coalition—might have pleaded ignorance as to the devastating consequences of their chosen means of pursuing their military and political goals, but as the conflict wore on and those calamitous humanitarian outcomes became clear, no such pleas are credible. Yemen is the largest and most protracted case of man-made famine of our times.

Chapter 10, 'Prosecution of Starvation in South Sudan' by Wayne Jordash QC and Uzay Yasar Aysev, fuses the legal analysis carried out in Chapter 5 and the factual circumstances described in Chapter 8 to provide a roadmap for the prosecution of the war crime of using starvation as a method of warfare in South Sudan in the course of the civil war which started in December 2013. To this end, the authors analyse the factual patterns that emerge from the conduct of the governmental armed forces during the civil war and discuss the potential issues that future prosecutors may face in prosecuting the war crime of starvation in South Sudan. The authors provide an assessment of the evidence currently available as derived from publicly available sources and discuss if/how the legal elements of the war crime of starvation as well as certain applicable modes of liability (such as co-perpetration, joint criminal enterprise, and command responsibility) could be established in order to affect the potential prosecution of senior South Sudanese perpetrators. Parallels are drawn with other cases developed in this volume, including Syria and Yemen, where applicable.

The final chapters of the book highlight broader humanitarian, policy, and social issues that define—or should define—how the global public understands and responds to incidents of mass starvation today.

Dan Maxwell's contribution, 'Humanitarian Challenges and Implications for Famine Early Warning Systems' (Chapter 11) provides an overview of famine early warning systems (EWS) that have developed since the 1970s. With advances in the measurement and monitoring of malnutrition, augmented by new information and communication technologies, these systems have become increasingly sophisticated in the past decade but they still tend to be based on the assumption that extreme food insecurity is an amplified version of regular seasonal stresses in agrarian societies, and driven primarily by environmental and economic factors. The systems are also distinct from and rarely speak to those designed to provide early conflict warning, which have the counterpart shortcoming of not addressing the likely consequences of conflict for food insecurity. Despite internationally agreed priorities about the links between armed conflict and extreme hunger, neither type of EWS directly deals with question of deliberately inflicted hunger. For the case of famine early warning, this is partly because they are either government-owned systems (and governments are, without contemporary exception, parties to the conflicts that cause contemporary famines) or they are managed by UN agencies that have to negotiate their presence within and access to affected populations, and they therefore are reluctant to anger parties to the conflict (be they government or non-state actors). Even attempting to track and analyse conflict can be difficult; tracking or analysing the use of hunger as a weapon of war is universally out of the question for these formal, government, or UN-led systems. Maxwell exemplifies his points in discussion of Somalia, South Sudan, Syria, and Yemen. He investigates reasons why—despite international consensus statements like UNSCR 2417—it remains so difficult to incorporate violent conflict into humanitarian information systems, and the ways in which the very technology that seems to be a distraction could, in fact, be helpful.

Chapter 12, 'Sanctions as a Mechanism for Accountability for Starvation Crimes' by Benjamin J. Spatz, Oliver Windridge, and Catriona Murdoch, addresses accountability mechanisms at the UN, including mandated investigative and reporting functions and sanctions. The sole mechanism referenced in Resolution 2417 is sanctions, specifically targeted against individuals and entities that obstruct humanitarian assistance. This reflects the contemporary preference for targeted sanctions, which differ markedly in their design and outcomes from national-level sanctions and are designed to avoid negative humanitarian consequences. The chapter examines the evolution of sanctions regimes at the UN and by the European Union, United States, United Kingdom, and Canada, and their potential use in the case of starvation crimes, with goals that may include exposing and punishing perpetrators, bringing pressure to bear to end such violations, and as a step towards other forms of accountability such as prosecutions.

Chapter 13, 'Sex, Gender, Age, and Mass Starvation' by Dyan Mazurana, Bridget Conley, and Kinsey Spears, applies an analysis of sex, gender, and age to issues related to mass starvation, including risks, protection, and accountability. Discussing the evidence from cases of famine and mass starvation, the chapter proposes that in contexts where sexual and gender-based violence (SGBV) inhibits maternal care, SGBV might be considered as a specific starvation crime. It further argues that mass starvation and SGBV are mutually reinforcing atrocity crimes. Widespread conditions of deprivation and starvation can increase the risk of SGBV. At the same time, SGBV, and in some cases even the threat of SGBV, can increase the risk of starvation, in ways that differ by sex, gender, age, and context. The authors document and analyse the long-term, intergenerational gender and age-influenced health and socio-cultural risks associated with exposure to mass starvation. They conclude with recommendations for how to improve the investigation, analysis, research, and prosecution of SGBV in the context of mass starvation.

Independent journalist Jane Ferguson provides insight into how stories about famine enter the public realm through news media in Chapter 14, 'Reporting Famine'. Drawing on her experience covering famine and conflicts in Yemen and South Sudan, Ferguson details the immense challenges and need for investigative journalism. The causes of hunger must be investigated by a wide variety of leading news organizations so the public can be made aware when famine victims are in fact the victims of war. Otherwise, there is a very real risk of successful attempts by combatants and governments to manipulate the news by making it unclear to both journalists reporting from afar and their viewers and readers why certain famines are happening. In South Sudan, for example, few news organizations sent their own reporters to the country to report on the famine in 2017, instead taking updates on the famine from aid agencies that avoided discussion of its causes (attacks on ethnic communities by government troops) for fear of being thrown out of the country by the government. When she arrived in South Sudan to report, senior NGO officials told her they could not call this famine man-made because it would risk their entire operation, but that it was indeed caused by the government's brutal counter-insurgency tactics. In Yemen, there has been a more concerted effort by the Saudi-led coalition to prevent journalists from reporting on the famine, aware that its cause is a direct result of the tactics being used in the war.

Chapter 15, 'Truth, Memory, and Starvation' by Alex de Waal, opens up the neglected agenda of transitional justice mechanisms for the victims and survivors of mass starvation. He focuses on the commemoration of famine, opening with the observation that silence commonly shrouds memory of mass starvation. One reason for this, he argues, is the sense of shame, loss of dignity, and self-blame felt by the survivors. During times of the utmost deprivation, death, life, and dignity depend on the tiniest increments of resources and standing among the dispossessed and destitute. Victims are often forced into terrible decisions: who will eat today? With perpetrators often distant from the scene, many victims blame themselves for the hardships they suffered and the micro-deprivations they end up perpetrating against others. For these reasons, famine is particularly demoralizing and memories are suppressed. This has too often allowed the deliberate perpetration of starvation crimes to remain unrecognized or fade away in time. This chapter discusses efforts to memorialize past instances of mass starvation, with notable examples of the Great Irish Famine and Ukraine, and the role that memorialization might play in honouring victims and changing the narrative for today's famines. It concludes with the insight that criminalizing starvation serves the vital purpose of emancipating victims, survivors, and their descendants from a sense of shame and failure, dignifying them as victims of a crime.

5. Conclusion

Demanding accountability for mass starvation—including prosecuting perpetrators of starvation crimes—is a crucial part of two linked broader agendas, namely eliminating famine and preventing all forms of mass atrocities, including those of deprivation. We have long known that mass starvation is not primarily the product of poverty or forces of nature but is a man-made condition associated with armed conflict and political repression. Although starvation crimes are central to contemporary famines, this discomforting reality has yet to be recognized in policy and legal responses. This volume seeks to remedy this shortcoming. We begin with framing the issue, turn to the law, and then to policy. We insist that the people who suffer from acts of starvation are not victims of a lesser crime, and those whose actions produce deprivation and death should be held to account.

Despite having international laws on the book that were drafted to address such acts, there has to date been little effort to expose and prosecute the crimes. However, as this volume demonstrates, the law can and should be applied to starvation crimes. Recent experience indicates both the widespread recognition that the law needs to be strengthened and applied more firmly, and also that the political obstacles to doing so are formidable. Those who perpetrate starvation crimes are getting away with mass murder.

In order to capitalize on the momentum and confront the continuing resistance, we suggest six main areas in which policy and politics should be developed.

The first is continued pressure for, and clarity about how, UNSC resolution 2417 will be turned from aspiration into reality. There are a host of specific actions within the UN system, including how to improve existing country-specific and thematic reporting, and when special briefings should be undertaken. Specifically, greater clarity is needed to specify when the 'risk of conflict-induced famine and wide-spread food insecurity in armed conflict contexts occurs' that would enable a coordinated and coherent response from states and humanitarian organizations.

A second area is the development of standards for understanding how to investigate, document, and pursue accountability effectively with regard to acts of starvation.

Third is addressing other mechanisms involving the full range of transitional justice tools. This might include truth telling, reparations, reform, memorialization, and guarantees of non-recurrence.

Fourth is incorporating the element of intentionality, including criminality, into famine early warning and measurement metrics and measures. Part of this is factoring intent into the functioning of predictive mechanisms such as the IPC. Another element is attending to the particular vulnerabilities of targeted groups, whether targeted by ethnic or religious identity, political views, location, or gender, among other differences. Once we analyse and measure the degree of intention that drives episodes of mass starvation, we also need to develop policy and response mechanisms that are alert to variations in exposure to and experiences of deprivation of the objects and activities indispensable to life.

Fifth is engaging with the broader humanitarian community on how their work intersects with the law, including in the sphere of negotiating with conflict actors. The tension between practical humanitarian action and human rights advocacy has long been a contentious issue among humanitarian agencies in the field. The ethical problem was succinctly formulated by an aid worker in Sudan in 1988 who said, 'I would sup with the devil to get food to [the starving in] Abyei'.[82] Many humanitarians have found themselves compromised by practices they see as regrettable necessities. The sharpening of accountability mechanisms may provide guidance for humanitarian negotiations, helping to clarify the limits beyond which there can be no compromise with perpetrators of starvation crimes.

Finally, developing public awareness is essential to all of the above: our envisaged developments in law and humanitarian practice will be far more effective if they are backed by public opinion. Journalists and engaged professionals—lawyers, scholars, relief practitioners—are all crucial in shaping and sustaining wider understanding and public pressure. It is our hope that this volume contributes to advancing the discussions of how international and domestic actors can support accountability for starvation, as part of the project of building and sustaining sufficient political will to end the political and military acts that cause famine.

[82] Personal correspondence with Alex de Waal, 1989.

PART I

THE HISTORICAL AND CONCEPTUAL CONTEXT

While the suffering caused by lack of access to sufficient food, water, shelter, medicine, and other items and activities required to sustain life is perhaps as old as human history itself, the occurrence of such deprivations at scale has proven challenging to define. This gap impedes the work of crafting policies and other interventions that can end deliberate starvation. The chapters in this section review conceptual frameworks at play in contemporary contexts, with emphases on where, when and how different approaches have offered advantages and introduced complications. Across the chapters, authors provide critical examination of discursive practices that naturalize starvation and thereby obscure the work of prevention and response. Offering alternative analysis embedded in interdisciplinary historical, conceptual, nutritional, and legal discourses, the chapters reveal how contemporary mass starvation is the product of socio-political policies. This revised starting conceptual point opens the door for new potential response mechanisms, including legal accountability.

2
What is Starvation?

Bridget Conley and Alex de Waal

1. Introduction

From October to April, the Polish sun fades behind grey clouds and a deep cold extends its reach under the skin. In 1944, Primo Levi, who had already survived one winter in Auschwitz, painfully anticipated the coming season's unforgiving tolls: cold would combine with constant hunger to torment the survivors and thin their numbers. The camp, he wrote '*is* hunger: we ourselves are hunger, living hunger'.[1] The predicament defied language: hunger, tiredness, pain, fear, winter—these words were created for everyday experiences. To capture what concentration camp prisoners experienced, Levi wrote: 'a new, harsh language would have to been born'.[2]

Mass starvation is rarely implemented alongside systematic murder to the degree found in the Holocaust. Nonetheless, the task Levi set for himself, to couple description of the rigour of cruelty with making sense of it, accompanies all efforts to capture human suffering. Lacking a newly invented language to describe and detail severe hunger and its companion diseases and deprivations, efforts to explain 'famine' and 'mass starvation' include a range of metrics and conceptual parameters. Embedded within the various definitions is an articulation of how to spur a response: a capable humanitarian operation, a demographic diagnosis, a political contract, or—the purpose of this chapter—recognition that starvation, like atrocity, is the result of intentional actions and should be deemed unacceptable.

This chapter addresses efforts to define 'famine' and 'starvation', noting several critical challenges. 'Mass starvation', we argue, is most fitting to contemporary conditions as it draws attention to the core observation that Levi made more than half a century ago and the implications of which remain under-appreciated today:[3] it is

[1] P. Levi, *If This Is A Man and The Truce* (London: Abacus, 1987), at 80.

[2] Levi, see note 1, at 129.

[3] As counter-examples, see: S. Devereux, *Theories of Famine* (London: Harvester Wheatsheaf, 1993); A. de Waal, *Famine Crimes: Politics and the Disaster Relief Industry in Africa* (London: African Rights & the International African Institute in association with James Currey, Oxford & Indiana University Press, Bloomington, 1997); J. Edkins, *Whose Hunger? Concepts of Famine, Practices of Aid* (Minneapolis: University of Minnesota Press, 2008); and D. Marcus, 'Famine Crimes in International Law', 97 *The American Journal of International Law* (2003) 245–281; and D. Keen,

Bridget Conley and Alex de Waal, *What is Starvation?* In: *Accountability for Mass Starvation*. Edited by: Bridget Conley, Alex de Waal, Catriona Murdoch, and Wayne Jordash QC, Oxford University Press.
DOI: 10.1093/oso/9780192864734.003.0002

perpetrated by one group of people against another group. Starvation is a powerful tool for perpetrators—we detail nine specific uses—that can be calibrated to achieve war or oppressive aims. Many of the acts that create mass starvation are already criminalized under various forms of international law, and together they can be described as 'starvation crimes', a designation designed not just to sharpen the legal consequences for such acts but also to mobilize political accountability.

2. What is Famine?

The endeavour to define famine is entangled with theories of its causation and descriptions of its impacts on populations. Writing in 1993, Stephen Devereux, categorized major definitions into five dominant types: (1) simple dictionary presentations focused on lack of food that causes widespread hunger and death; (2) theories of decline in food availability; (3) theories of food consumption deficits; (4) behavioural descriptions of responses to widespread hunger; and (5) 'insider' definitions based on how the people who suffer famine describe it.[4] None, he concluded, manages the feat of balancing brevity and comprehensive scope that characterizes an authoritative definition.

A key challenge is that no single definition is sufficiently robust to capture the variety and combinations of contributing factors and outcomes across examples, and famine's shape-shifting as societies and economies change. We can, however, begin by dismissing theories of famine that treat it as an 'act of God', or a natural (if regrettable) consequence of food supply failures, like crops failing from vermin or adverse weather, population surges beyond the means of production, or inadvertent displacements and disruptions of armed conflict. These are, at best, weak explanations of historic famines and none explains contemporary examples.[5]

Amartya Sen's seminal *Poverty and Famines* (1981) showed, both deductively and inductively, that famines were the result of collapses in peoples' ability exchange labour or goods for food, due to poverty, adverse shocks, or market failures. Access, not availability, determined when famine would occur and who would starve. However, he hesitated to introduce a new definition. Indeed, he added in a footnote that definitions often serve better 'in providing a pithy description of what happens in a situation clearly diagnosed as one of famine rather than in helping one to do the diagnosis'.[6] Famines, he argued, could be identified, 'like a flood or a

The Benefits of Famine: A Political Economy of Famine and Relief in Southwestern Sudan, 1983–1989 (Princeton: Princeton University Press, 1994).

4 Devereux, see note 3, at 10.

5 A. de Waal, *Mass Starvation: the History and Future of Famine* (Cambridge: Polity Press, 2018) at 15-29.

6 A. Sen, *Poverty and Famines: An Essay on Entitlement and Deprivation* (Oxford: Clarendon Press, 1981), at 40, footnote 3.

fire—even without being armed with a precise definition'.[7] Offering only a limited corrective, he observed that 'famines imply starvation'[8] and are distinguished from chronic hunger in that they are 'a particularly virulent manifestation' that causes 'widespread death'.[9]

This approach left two major concerns unaddressed. First, it did not clarify what counts as 'particularly virulent' starvation or serves as a threshold for 'widespread' death. Second is the extent to which famine, as distinct from 'normal conditions' and food insecurity, is the product of deliberate action.

A partial response to these concerns can be found in the work of the operational humanitarian mainstream, which endeavoured to bridge entitlement gaps during crises by improving delivery systems, and to develop metrics to quantify and specify famine. They, too, largely ignore the second concern about responsibility, focusing instead on response. One consequence of this focus was real improvement in humanitarian relief systems—to the point that the culpability is pointedly heightened in today's examples. Humanitarian operations can effectively mitigate the impacts of famine except where deliberately impeded.

The essence of famine is scale: it is a matter for public action because it is a severe hardship, veering into fatally absolute dispossession, that affects a large number of people, and it can be prevented or at least ameliorated by government policy and (to a lesser degree) by private advocacy and charity.

In the last twenty years, a small but influential group of humanitarian practitioners has been preoccupied with the challenge of developing an operational definition for famine and a metric for diagnosing it,[10] with the implication that this would serve for initiating and calibrating aid responses. Their starting point was the same intuition as Sen's: famine is constituted by widespread starvation causing excess death. The key diagnostic tool, with a working definition of famine attached, is the Integrated food security Phase Classification (IPC) scale.[11] This has become an invaluable assessment method and classificatory metric. The IPC relies on measurements of nutritional status among a population: indicators for food security (actually existing and anticipated), data for mortality levels, and the basis of an aggregate score on these elements. It determines whether the people in a locality

[7] Sen, see note 6, at 39–40.

[8] Sen, see note 6, at 39.

[9] Sen, see note 6, at 40. Also note: Sen's writings have generated much misunderstanding, some of them originating from his use of the term 'entitlement' to mean 'real economic demand' and not 'legal right or claim'. His early writing on famine is strictly economistic. He later shifted course and addressed famine as an outcome of political systems and decisions, drawing attention to the links between democracy, civil and political rights, freedom of the press, and protection against famine (see, for example, A. Sen, *Development as Freedom* (New York: Random House, 1999). However, he did not delve into the issue of famine as the outcome of deliberate policies or acts by policy-makers.

[10] For further discussion on this topic, see Chapter 11 in this volume.

[11] Integrated Food Security Phase Classification, 'Technical Manual Version 2.0: Evidence and Standards for Better Food Security Decisions', (2012) available online at <http://www.fews.net/sites/default/files/uploads/IPC-Manual-2-Interactive.pdf> (visited 10 November 2020), at 439.

may be said to be suffering 'food insecurity', 'emergency', or 'famine'. The IPC does not use the term 'starvation', though it may be said to have an implicit definition of starvation as the amalgam of its measures.

The famine scale exercise served three purposes. First, it categorized historical famines, distinguishing among famines based on the numbers of dead. Thus, 100,000 or more deaths was a 'great famine' and a million or more counted as a 'calamitous famine'. Given the variations in measurement methods over time and place, compiling this record is an imprecise exercise, but it demonstrates trends.[12] It is, however, of limited use to those trying to prevent or relieve a famine, who do not want to wait until a certain death toll is verified before declaring 'famine'.

Second, it served as a diagnostic tool for humanitarian practitioners, to put their decision-making on a more objective basis. The IPC scale was developed in the Horn of Africa at the turn of the Millennium. Following a food crisis in southeast Ethiopia in 1999, there was controversy over whether this should constitute 'famine' or not. Given the Ethiopian government's political sensitivities over the label 'famine', it was clearly important to agree an objective metric. Shortly afterwards the challenge arose of humanitarian aid allocation across different locations in Somalia, where local militia commanders and clan leaders asked why certain localities received more aid, while others received less. There were perils of political or ethnic bias in aid distribution. The outcome was a standardized method for assessing need.

The IPC has become the standard method and metric for diagnosing and defining 'famine'. It is an operational tool, which reflects the purposes for which it was designed. Its main strength is that it introduces the possibility of an objective and widely respected assessment of need into the diagnosis of famine. This was an essential step forward for international humanitarian policy, minimizing the extreme subjectivity in assessments and declarations of 'famine' that previously persisted—the IPC's third purpose.

The IPC scale suffers from some internal weaknesses. It was developed in agrarian societies in the Horn of Africa where community food security is closely tied into local production and livelihoods. It is therefore less well-suited to the kinds of famines in which a class of people (such as wage labourers) starves because of a class-specific collapse in income. The IPC focuses on the severity of suffering in particular locations, putting the overall magnitude and persistence of that suffering into the background. This has the odd and unanticipated consequence that famine can be declared for a small geographically bounded population, which suffers a highly elevated mortality rate but which has a small aggregate mortality.

12 S. Devereux, *Famine in the Twentieth Century*, University of Sussex, The Institute of Development Studies (IDS), Working Paper 105 (2000), available online at <https://www.ids.ac.uk/files/dmfile/wp105.pdf> (visited 9 October 2019); de Waal, see note 5, at 55–67.

In South Sudan in 2017, for example, famine (IPC level 5) was declared for two counties, Leer and Mayendit, in which many hundreds, possibly 1,500 people, perished. However, this pocket of extreme deprivation took place against a background of a much wider humanitarian crisis, affecting several million people over a four-year period. Using a 'survey of surveys' method, Francesco Checci and colleagues estimated that there was a total excess mortality of 383,000, half of which was attributable to hunger and disease.[13] It follows that, even without the famine declaration for the two counties, South Sudan would have suffered excess mortality which would have qualified it for 'great famine' status (deaths exceeding 100,000).

In other protracted and widespread food crises, such as Yemen, it is possible that hundreds of thousands of people could die, without any one locality breaching the IPC level 5 threshold. This shortcoming can be remedied by attending to the demographic consequences of lower IPC levels. Indeed, a calculation of the estimated excess deaths in South Sudan based on the (relatively modestly) elevated mortality rates in IPC levels 3 and 4 results in an aggregate death toll very close to that calculated by the 'survey of surveys' method.[14]

Another weakness arrives as a backhanded compliment to the efficacy and legitimacy of the IPC scale. Host governments, belligerents, and donors have politicized it. Keen to avoid a 'famine' determination, political actors try to influence the IPC process to get the outcome they want. This is attempted by limiting access—IPC findings are only as strong as the capacity of researchers to access areas. Political sensitivities are most acute where starvation has been perpetrated for political or military purposes. As a result, the IPC's biggest weakness is addressing deliberate starvation.

3. What is Mass Starvation?

The English word 'starvation', in the contemporary context of famine and humanitarian emergency, contains three ambiguities.

In the first instance, 'starvation' can mean either act or outcome; the verb 'to starve' can be either transitive or intransitive. In the transitive sense, person A can starve person B, deliberately depriving them of food. In the intransitive sense, person C can be in the condition of lacking food, leading to hunger and malnutrition, without attributing cause or blame. To the limited extent that they

[13] F. Checci et al., *Estimates of Crisis-attributable Mortality in South Sudan, December 2013–April 2018: A Statistical Analysis* London School of Hygiene and Tropical Medicine, September 2018, available online at <https://www.lshtm.ac.uk/south-sudan-full-report> (visited 9 October 2019).

[14] D. Maxwell et al., *Constraints and Complexities of Information and Analysis in Humanitarian Emergencies: Evidence from South Sudan* (Medford: Feinstein International Center, Tufts University, 2018), available online at <https://fic.tufts.edu/assets/SouthSudan-Case-Study-Report.pdf> (visited 22 October 2021).

use the word 'starvation', humanitarian assessments use the word in its intransitive sense: their concern is with the objective, medical, and nutritional status of people, not who might have done this to them. A prosecutor seeking to establish culpability for a starvation crime would primarily be concerned with the transitive sense, but would also make use of evidence for starvation as a state of affairs in establishing the gravity of the act.

Another area of ambiguity is individual malnutrition versus collective excess mortality. 'Starvation' sits uneasily within the terminology and frameworks of nutritional science and epidemiology. Nutritionists tend not to use the word. Instead they prefer a raft of more precise terms such as protein-energy malnutrition, kwashiorkor, or (with when speaking about the condition of a population) the malnutrition rates and excess mortality. One reason for this is the imprecision of the everyday term. Another is the rarity of starvation as a distinct medical condition. It takes approximately sixty days for an individual, consuming no food at all, to starve to death. Such outright or frank starvation is extraordinarily rare and tends to occur in prisons. The highest profile case of this in recent times was the hunger strike in 1981 by Republican prisoners in Northern Ireland, ten of whom starved to death after refusing food.

More common is semi-starvation, namely reduced intake of nutrients over a long period of time. The Minnesota Starvation Experiment of 1944–1945,[15] in which the leading physiologist Ancel Keys observed thirty-six men (conscientious objectors who volunteered for the study) during a twenty-four-week period during which these individuals were put on a severely reduced diet and lost approximately 25 per cent of their body weight. The reason for the experiment was to study the effects of famine, in the correct anticipation that this would be a major challenge at the close of the Second World War. The experiment is more correctly described as semi-starvation under quasi-laboratory conditions. The individuals studied were adult men, previously healthy, in a controlled environment free from infectious disease.

A specialist in emergency nutrition today would point out that the Minnesota experiment did not take into account the social ecology of food, nutrition, and health.[16] In almost all famines, the immediate cause of death is infectious disease and is concentrated among young children. Death rates increase because malnourished children are either more susceptible to disease (their weakened immune systems mean that they are more likely to become infected, or to die of an infection) or more exposed (because infectious diseases are more prevalent in a distressed population, especially one that is displaced to overcrowded and unsanitary camps).

[15] A. Keys et al., *The Biology of Human Starvation* (2 vols, Minneapolis: University of Minnesota Press, 1950).

[16] See Chapter 3 in this volume.

Hence the nutritionists' professional discomfort with 'starvation': it implies a physical condition that is rare and is not their principal concern.

Finally, there is a difference between the lay and legal senses of 'starvation'. In lay terms, starvation means deprivation of food, and is extended to items other than food only in a metaphorical sense.[17] The legal sense of 'starvation' is not confined to food and includes other essentials. The most definitive statement of this is Article 8(2)(b)(xxv) of the Rome Statute, specifies the following as a war crime: 'Intentionally using starvation of civilians as a method of warfare by depriving them of objects indispensable to their survival, including wilfully impeding relief supplies as provided for under the Geneva Conventions.'

Following the word 'by' is the substantive definition of acts of starvation under the law, which include any acts that deprive people of objects indispensable to survival (OIS), including not only food but clean water, medicine, shelter, blankets, and maternal care.

4. 'Starvation Crime': Uses and Complications

Our focus in this volume is on the transitive meaning of 'starvation' and what this entails for law and policy. The term 'starvation crimes' is a chapeau for starvation-related acts that are prohibited under one or more legal regimes. The term is influenced by the coinage of 'atrocity crimes' by David Scheffer, which was intended to circumvent the problems that arose with controversies over whether a particular atrocity qualified as genocide, crimes against humanity, war crimes, and so forth. Similarly, 'starvation crime' refers to prohibited acts under four different but related legal regimes: crimes against humanity; international humanitarian law; the Genocide Convention; and human rights law.

The concept further develops Alex de Waal's articulation of 'famine crimes',[18] which foregrounded the concern that most famines, as large-scale societal events, are caused by human actions, and usually and specifically by government policies. De Waal defined famine crimes by identifying these crises as (at least) failures of political accountability and (at most) deliberate actions. This was an exercise in political sociology rather than law.

Reframing this discussion within legal terms complicates definitional approaches centred on outcomes. The perpetrator of famine is often remote and operates through a bureaucracy; the tools are often those of regular economic and social policy turned to more malign ends. Famine is a white-collar crime against humanity. A criticism of the concept is that it implicitly criminalizes a range of

[17] Interestingly, there is a rarer Scottish and north English vernacular use that refers to deprivation of shelter or warmth, leading to risk of death.

[18] de Waal, see note 3.

economic and social policies that fall outside the perimeter of what is considered a crime, including, for example, interventions in grain markets, public spending policies, or changes to land tenure systems.[19] David Marcus brought a legal lens to the concept of 'famine crime' and refined it through specifying what he called 'faminogenic' actions and policies, and identifying whether they contribute to famine through direct commission and deliberate intent, through recklessness, or through acts of omission.[20] Using the closely related concept of 'state food crimes', Rhoda Howard-Hassmann brought human rights law into the frame, and advocated for a convention outlawing mass starvation as such.[21]

Each of these approaches starts with the outcome—famine—and work backwards to identify its causes. These arguments threaten to get caught in the definitional morass of what constitutes 'famine'. Actions constitute famine crimes only if they contribute to a sufficiently bad outcome that it qualifies as famine, and not so if the outcome falls short. Thus posed, severe instances of starvation are marginalized: episodes of forcible mass starvation, such as in populations of prisoners of war, are difficult to categorize as famines.

By contrast, the concept of 'starvation crime' begins with the action of the perpetrator, his purposes and intentions, and considers as secondary whether the result is famine or some other form of deprivation.

A. Purposes of Starvation

What do perpetrators accomplish through starvation crimes? The question of objectives points our attention to the linkage between political-military strategic goals and the use of starvation as a weapon of war or repression. We introduce a preliminary categorization of nine uses of mass starvation.[22]

The first and simplest aim is mass killing; it is a corollary of the crimes of extermination and genocide, but inflicted through deprivation. Just as with killing as an act of genocide, such policies need not culminate in the actual death by starvation of an entire population. Key is that a perpetrator demonstrates the *intent to destroy* a significant part of the population.

Second is deprivation as part of a policy to reduce the capacity of a group to mount resistance. A common context is counterinsurgency, with resettlement camps providing a stark, emblematic context for examining starvation crimes. In

[19] See Chapter 9 in this volume.

[20] Marcus, see note 3.

[21] R. Howard-Hassmann, *State Food Crimes* (Cambridge: Cambridge University Press, 2016).

[22] de Waal, see note 5; B. Conley, *Mass Atrocity Endings* (Somerville, MA, USA: World Peace Foundation, 2017), available online at <https://sites.tufts.edu/atrocityendings/> (visited 8 July 2019). The authors first introduced this typology and provide historical examples in B. Conley and A. De Waal, 'The Purposes of Starvation: Historical and Contemporary Uses', 17 *Journal of International Criminal Justice* (2019) 699–722.

camps, responsibility is clear; perpetrators exercise direct control over the targeted group. A common feature of colonial, post-colonial, and Cold War counterinsurgency, camps established through forcible displacement, with little or no measures to provide for a population's basic needs, and where they are bereft of their livelihoods creates a dependent and despondent population. In this manner, perpetrators exert control over and punish a civilian population perceived as an enemy. Policies ostensibly designed to control and separate a civilian population from armed groups, when pursued over time and without concern for civilians' well-being, become indistinguishable from an intended policy of starvation.[23]

Third, is starvation as a means to seize territorial control. Siege is the signature context for starvation crimes as part of a military effort to seize territorial control. While in theory, siege can be lawfully conducted, when perpetrators fail to differentiate between civilian and military populations under siege, such policies may cross the line into intentional attacks against civilians.[24] A complication of siege is that it requires one side to control access to a location, while the other refuses to leave (sometimes with good reason, fearing that a fate worse than starvation may follow should they surrender or evacuate). Siege endures as long as one or both sides are willing to prioritize political-military goals over humanitarian concern. For besieged soldiers, a civilian population can serve as a shield, a source of conscripts and labour, or a source of revenue or aid that is utilized by armed forces. While in some cases civilians support the armed forces that are associated with them, rarely is such support consistent across a group or unwavering over time, especially over a long duration, as resources dwindle and if soldiers prioritize their needs at the expense of civilians.

Fourth is flushing a population out of a remote area into perpetrator control. There are some similarities to both siege and counterinsurgency starvation, but this follows a variant pattern. Here, the primary goal is to control people rather than territory, forcing them to move into an area controlled by perpetrators.

Fifth is using deprivation as a means to alter a targeted group's political calculus, without obliging the perpetrator to take control over either territory or civilian population, and thereby assuming responsibility for governing. This may occur in the form of widespread sanctions, blockade, siege, and persecution as forms of collective punishment.

Sixth, starvation can be a tool for material extraction.[25] Conflicts offer many opportunities for enrichment; profiteering can be accelerated through sustaining deprivation. In a besieged town, the price of basic goods will soar and people will

[23] A. Pitzer, *One Long Night: A Global History of Concentration Camps* (Boston: Little, Brown and Company, 2017); I. R. Smith and A. Stucki, 'The Colonial Development of Concentration Camps (1868–1902)', 39 *The Journal of Imperial and Commonwealth History* (2011) 417–437.

[24] J. Kraska and S. Power, 'Siege Warfare in Syria: Prosecuting the Starvation of Civilians', 8 *Amsterdam Law Forum* (2016) 1–22.

[25] Keen, see note 3.

pay for passage out. Where the goal is taking land, as in colonial settler contexts, starvation is an efficient means to this end. Proxy groups such as tribal militia can be licensed to pay themselves through looting, creating starvation as a by-product.

Seventh, and related to the above, is starvation as a means to provision combatants. In all non-industrial countries, armies have typically lived off the land, feeding themselves from the local communities. Famines followed in the wake of campaigns in Europe, Asia, and Africa—including in those armies' own countries. In these cases, hunger is inflicted not just on 'enemy' populations but also on those who are the supporters or the subjects of the perpetrators. A contemporary variant is when an aid operation provides a perverse rationale for maintaining a population in starvation conditions, used as a magnet to attract humanitarian aid that soldiers then steal for their own use.

Eighth, creating or sustaining starvation conditions can be a means of coercing labour. Where there are large captive populations but meagre food resources, the outcome is usually severe hunger. In labour camps, such as the Soviet Gulag, the authorities use rationing to incentivize labour.

Ninth, starvation has played an enormous role in engineering massive societal transformation. These economic and social policies are not themselves crimes. The question of culpability is raised, however, when policies clearly demonstrate harmful outcomes and yet are adhered to over a longer duration even as people die *en masse*. The question of culpability comes into play chiefly as a side effect of the inhuman consequences of flawed policies, and increases in parallel as three further factors come into play. First, societal transformations of this scale can be affected only with coercion and repression. Second, these policies are often implemented selectively and punitively, in pursuit of other goals, such as ethnic repression. Third, as the calamitous consequences of these policies become evident, no efforts are made to change course or mitigate the suffering.

B. Complications and Cross-Purposes

Several issues arise that are relevant for identifying starvation crimes, how and by whom it might be perpetrated, and what might be done to prevent, prosecute, or otherwise remedy it.

Many different acts qualify. The clearest instances are acts of destroying, removing or rendering useless OIS of a civilian population, such as food stores, water supplies, or farms. Other OIS include water supplies, sanitation, shelter, and health facilities. Although not specified in this manner in the relevant law, preventing or impeding *activities* indispensable to survival can have the same impact. Examples would be impeding maternal care for young children, halting labour migration, or preventing people from foraging for wild foods in forests.

Starvation crimes are usually perpetrated in the context of other prohibited acts, ranging from killing, enslavement, and torture through sexual and gender-based violence, to denial of freedom of the press and suppression of democratic liberties and cultural rights. This has practical implications for trials, insofar as a prosecutor who is pressed for time and resources will find it more straightforward to obtain a conviction for an atrocity such as a massacre rather than for starvation. This appears to have been the case in the Extraordinary Chambers in the Courts of Cambodia and under Ethiopia's Office of the Special Prosecutor, as examples.[26] It also means that explorations of motives and intentions may be complicated.

Starvation crimes almost invariably intersect with other causes of deprivation, such as generalized food insecurity, poverty, inequality, poor health infrastructure, or environmental degradation. There may be other intersecting triggers of disaster, such as climatic calamities including drought, economic crisis, or international factors such as an increase in the price of foods on the global market. Political leaders prefer to blame famine on these factors—especially the weather—and the staff of relief agencies also like to depoliticize famine, for reasons of fundraising from a donating public that finds the victims of 'natural' disasters more deserving of their charity, and because averting their gaze from the politics of starvation makes it easier to work in the affected country. A full investigation of the causes of mass starvation requires that these different elements are all weighed. Nonetheless, if a country is already highly vulnerable to food crisis and famine, this makes the perpetration of starvation more blameworthy, not less. For example, an army commander who destroys food crops in a poor, food-insecure country does so in the knowledge that this is more likely to create intense hunger than one who does so in a more prosperous country with plentiful food.

More complicated are situations in which clearly identified acts of starvation, such as aerial bombardment of food supplies, are perpetrated alongside economic policy decisions that, while a clear cause of distress, would not normally be considered criminal. An example is Yemen, where the military campaigns by the Saudi-led coalition (including, for example, bombing of medical facilities) combined with harsh economic decisions (including, for example, the non-payment of civil service salaries in Houthi-controlled areas) combined to cause famine.[27] In a case such as this, Marcus' framework of types of faminogenic action becomes relevant for specifying the actions that contributed to starvation.

Another complicating scenario involves micro-dynamics within the affected society. There are winners and losers in all famines, and while some of the winners may well be those who designed and implemented policies of starvation, others who gain may not be perpetrators, or at least not the principal ones. Small-town grain traders may profit from the high price of food; village landlords may benefit

[26] Chapter 4, in this volume.
[27] Chapter 9, in this volume.

from being able to buy up smallholdings from destitute farmers at fire-sale prices; smugglers may get rich from trading scarce commodities across the front lines.

Finally, starvation crimes typically take a long time to unfold. While a massacre may be perpetrated within a single day, the infliction of starvation takes at least several weeks and often a whole year or longer. This has several implications. It complicates tracing cause and effect, as many intervening factors intrude, and different contributory causes can wax and wane over time. It reinforces the problems associated with perpetrator remoteness and complex causes. The long process of deprivation prior to mass starvation means that actions that caused starvation may not initially have been taken with that purpose, or even with an awareness of that outcome.

The duration also means that as events unfolded and the reality or imminence of starvation became clear, the perpetrator had opportunities to halt or remedy the process of starvation. Failing to take such remedial actions would render a perpetrator culpable. In assessing the responsibility of a political or military authority who presided over starvation, it would therefore be necessary to ascertain what information was—or should have been—available about the impact of policies, and what actions could have been taken to halt or remedy those impacts.

5. Conclusion

Efforts to articulate a comprehensive definition of famine have not yet achieved success. To proffer a definition of famine is to reveal one's hand: to point attention simultaneously to a theory of causation and a plan of action. This is the case for influential treatments of the subject, including endeavours to quantify and depoliticize famine so as to improve humanitarian relief operations.

Our contribution does not depart from this pattern. It aims to serve as a corrective to past approaches that have illuminated important components of famine, but too often by minimizing the degree to which today, populations starve when those more powerful than they create and sustain conditions of extreme deprivation. We have argued for the term 'mass starvation' to describe the processes through which a perpetrating regime deprives a population of the basic means of sustenance, with severe medical and nutritional outcomes as indicative evidence. While food is a central concern, the legal definition, which informs our work, offers helpful expansion to 'objects'—to which we add 'activities'—'indispensable to survival', including destroying, removing, or rendering useless such objects and activities. In parallel, assessing outcomes should be expanded beyond starvation unto death; most people exposed to these conditions suffer or die from disease, lack of medical care, and displacement stresses long before they perish from lack of food.

However, mass starvation cannot be defined based solely on outcomes for affected populations. Perpetrators' actions and purposes require analysis as well.

Starvation and policies of deprivation serve war or oppressive aims, many of which are already criminalized under various bodies of international law, and together can be labelled as 'starvation crimes'. Assessing policies as starvation crimes is not without complication. But given that such acts often occur in the context of violent assaults against a population, and frequently endure over a period during which well-intentioned actors would have sufficient time and knowledge to alter policies, responsibility can—and in our view, must—be ascertained. Defining such actions as mass starvation and starvation crimes is one step towards this goal.

3
Social Nutrition and Accountability for Mass Starvation

Susanne Jaspars

1. Introduction

Starvation crimes comprise a range of actions prohibited under different international legal regimes that deprive populations of items indispensable to their survival—commonly the result of deliberate political or military acts. Wider political and economic decisions may also lead to famine.[1] The key question that this chapter attempts to answer is what do we need from nutrition science to strengthen accountability for mass starvation, and can it actually achieve this? First, nutrition science would be required to provide evidence about the nature of the starvation crime and the way in which it is perpetrated. In a legal sense, prosecution requires showing intent, action, and outcome. Second, criminal acts include specific actions such as policy decisions or military strikes and their effects on access to food or other items indispensable to survival. To strengthen accountability for starvation crimes, we therefore need nutrition to help us determine how mass starvation has come about through a series of policies and actions, structural causes, and the interactions between them. It needs to assist with an examination of the process by which people were deprived of items indispensable for survival and how the combined effects of different causes can lead to elevated levels of acute malnutrition and mortality.

This chapter first examines social nutrition as a possible means of examining causes of mass starvation, its concepts, and evolution over time, and then discusses social nutrition in the context of promoting accountability. The second half of the chapter examines evidence from situations of calamitous famine and war, and addresses the challenges to using a social or politically oriented approach to nutrition to advance accountability for starvation crimes.

[1] A. de Waal and B. Conley, 'What Justice for Starvation Crimes?', in J. Bhabha and M. Matache (eds), *Time for Reparation? Addressing State Responsibility for Collective Injustice* (Philadelphia: University of Pennsylvania Press, 2021) 272–290.

Susanne Jaspars, *Social Nutrition and Accountability for Mass Starvation* In: *Accountability for Mass Starvation*.
Edited by: Bridget Conley, Alex de Waal, Catriona Murdoch, and Wayne Jordash QC, Oxford University Press.
 DOI: 10.1093/oso/9780192864734.003.0003

2. Concepts of Social and Medicalized Nutrition

There are a number of different approaches to nutrition, each of which results in very different interventions. According to Lang, nutrition is currently fragmented intellectually, with different nutritions including social nutrition, nutrition epidemiology, sports nutrition, animal nutrition, etc.[2] He identifies two broad directions, however: nutrition as a social science and nutrition as a life, or medical, science;[3] his later work adds nutrition as an ecological science.[4] A key feature of social nutrition is an analysis of nutrition within its social, political and economic context, at the level of populations or society. The approach commonly includes an acceptance of multi-causality at population as well as household level, in particular socio-economic and political causes, the interactions between different causes, and the development of flexible and context-specific interventions.[5] Such interventions may focus specifically on food systems or livelihoods.

Social nutrition has been variously defined as follows:

> Social nutrition examines how society determines who eats, what, when, how, and with what effects.[6]

> A subject which examines those social, environmental, economic and political factors that determine the degree to which people have access to food … Malnutrition, they argued, has 'multiple causes which are closely linked to the conditions of inequality of resources, or poverty, and of social discrimination' … [new ideas] include food systems, the epidemiology of malnutrition, and livelihoods' [and] 'understanding *how* people became malnourished … and *who* such people are …[7] What is needed is a systematic procedure for identifying the various contributory causes of malnutrition and the nature of their interactions,[8] including *simultaneity* (factors which reinforce each other, which could also be termed *synergy*) and *feedback*.'[9]

> … a broad-based problem-solving approach to addressing nutrition problems of communities. A Public Nutrition approach is based on the assessment and analysis of the underlying and basic causes of malnutrition, available resources (human, financial and infrastructural) and constraints that influence action

[2] T. Lang, 'Food Control or Food Democracy? Re-Engaging Nutrition with Society and the Environment', 8(6A) *Public Health Nutrition* (2005) 730–737.

[3] Lang, see note 2.

[4] T. Lang, D. Barling, and M. Caraher, 'Nutrition', in T. Lang, D. Barling, and M. Caraher (eds), *Food Policy: Integrating Health, Environment and Society* (Oxford: Oxford University Press, 2009) 101–142.

[5] A. Pacey and P. Payne, *Agricultural Development and Nutrition* (London: Hutchinson & Co., 1985).

[6] Lang, see note 2, at 731.

[7] Pacey and Payne, see note 5, at 18–20.

[8] Pacey and Payne, see note 5, at 107.

[9] Pacey and Payne, see note 5, at 111.

within a specific context. Components include: a focus on populations, cross-disciplinary analysis of causes, broad-based problem solving (including constraints that influence action), development of relevant actions in a socially and politically aware manner and local capacity building.[10]

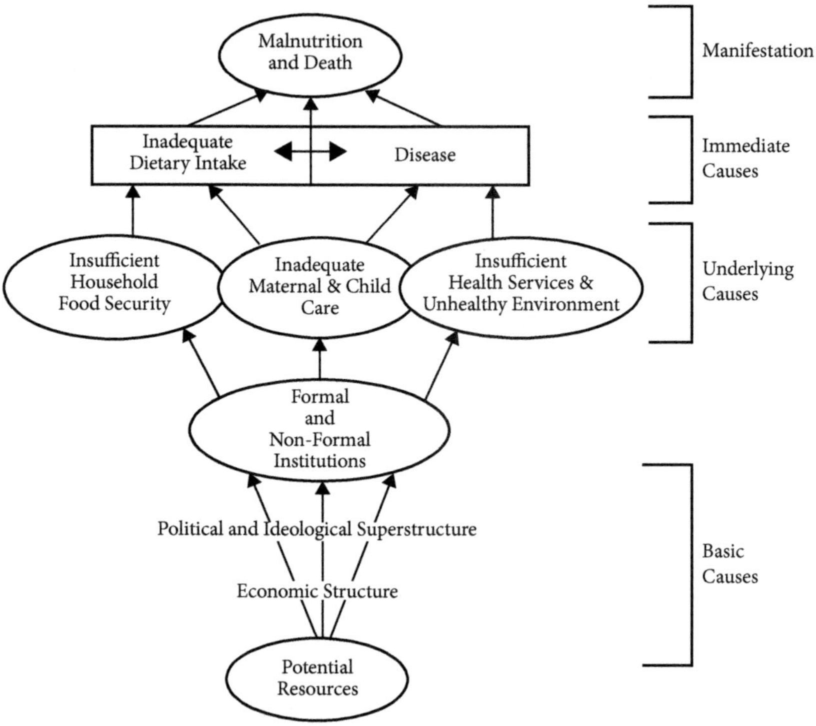

Figure 3.1 Causes of malnutrition and death

Source: UNICEF, *Strategy for Improved Nutrition of Children and Women in Developing Countries* (New York: UNICEF, 1990). Available online at <https://digitallibrary.un.org/record/132779?ln=en>.

The adoption of the UNICEF conceptual framework on causes of malnutrition in the 1990s facilitated this broader social approach[11] (see Figure 3.1). It formed the basis of a social approach to nutrition in emergencies for much of the 1990s, and was included in the Sphere Project's Humanitarian Charter and the Minimum Standards for humanitarian response, in 1998, 2004, and 2011.

The UNICEF framework was pioneered in 1990 in Iringa, Tanzania, to develop a nutrition strategy that reflected the biological and social causes of malnutrition,

[10] H. Young, 'Public Nutrition in Emergencies: An Overview of Debates, Dilemmas and Decision-making', 23(4) *Disasters* (1999) 277–291, at 283.

[11] UNICEF, *Strategy for Improved Nutrition of Children and Women in Developing Countries* (New York: UNICEF, 1990).

as well as causes at micro and macro levels.[12] This strategy was based on an analysis of the particular context, rather than the application of pre-packaged technical interventions.[13] The framework shows inadequate food intake and disease as immediate causes of malnutrition at the individual level. The framework shows three clusters of underlying causes: insufficient household food security,[14] insufficient health services and an unhealthy environment, and inadequate care for women and children. Each cluster may contribute to inadequate food intake or disease, alone or in combination. It is important to note that the framework shows an overlap (interaction) between the three clusters of underlying causes. For example, food insecurity may hinder childcare if the mother has to spend long hours working away from home. Of critical importance in relation to starvation crimes is that the framework also shows basic or structural causes, which relate to the unequal distribution of resources within society.[15] In other words, what is produced or consumed depends on economic, social, political, and ecological factors. Social conditions include property relations, labour relations, and power structures. Political and ideological superstructure reflects the structure and functions of the state, including income and tax policies, subsidies, the legal system, and the role and power of national institutions. Ideology includes religion, culture, tradition, and beliefs. Historical conditions, external (relating to aid policies) or internal (discrimination of certain groups), all contribute. Formal and informal institutions can be seen as the interface between underlying and basic causes, and may, for example, include extended family, social networks, community institutions (churches, local organizations), or schools as well as customary law, for example concerning land. In other words, what is produced or consumed depends on economic, social, political, and ecological factors.

The originators of the framework[16] saw it as an entry point, and when a problem is identified, it is necessary to carry out a deeper analysis of specific causes which are highly varied and context specific.

Medicalized nutrition in contrast, focuses on nutrition at the level of the individual or household, tries to identify the single most important cause, and promotes predetermined packages of interventions. Methods are largely quantitative (see the *Lancet* articles, 2008, discussed later in this chapter). For our purposes, therefore, social nutrition is the most relevant approach to provide evidence on the nature and causes of malnutrition, the different causes and levels of causation,

[12] UNICEF, see note 11, at 13.

[13] UNICEF, see note 11, at 14.

[14] Note that the definition of food security has changed over time but since this framework was produced in 1990 we can assume that they are referring to the 1986 World Bank definition: 'access by all people at all times to enough food for an active, healthy life'. World Bank, *Poverty and Hunger: Issues and Options for Food Security in Developing Countries* (Washington, DC: World Bank, 1986), at 1.

[15] World Bank, see note 14, at 21.

[16] D. Pelletier and U. Jonnson, 'The Use of Information in the Iringa Nutrition Programme: Some Global Lessons for Nutrition Surveillance', 19 *Food Policy* (1994) 301–313, at 303.

and the process by which people were deprived of items indispensable to survival. Although medicalized nutrition has always been the dominant approach, calls for a more socially or politically oriented approach to nutrition have occurred at particular points in time. This evolution of social nutrition is explored further in the next section.

3. Evolution of Social Nutrition and Calls for its Revival

Notions of social nutrition have often followed times of crisis or famine. It has been applied to Western populations and to those in the Global South, in emergency and in more stable contexts to address malnutrition within its wider social, political, and economic context. Each time, the role of social practices and their disruption, food systems, the health environment, politics, and inequality have been a key feature.

Social nutrition first emerged during the depression of the 1930s. According to Scott-Smith,[17] the establishment of the League of Nations in 1920s was a highpoint of social nutrition. Audrey Richards, an anthropologist who briefly worked for the League, 'introduced the idea that nutrition was a matter of cultural practices, agricultural systems, and political organization, and John Boyd Orr (later the first director of the Food and Agriculture Organization (FAO), connected nutrition with public health, productivity, economic growth, trade, and peaceful global relations'.[18] He considered that malnutrition was the result of social inequality and could best be addressed with equitable access and affordable food as part of a welfare system.[19] The approach came about because the League of Nations Health Organization set out to determine the effect of the economic crisis of the 1930s on health. However, while ill-health (including low weight and avitaminosis) was highest amongst the poorest, the stable mortality rate was taken as indicating that the crisis had no effect on public health.[20]

In the late 1970s and 1980s, the Nutrition Department at the London School of Hygiene and Tropical Medicine (LSHTM) provided another brief period when social nutrition appeared. It followed the experience of the global food crisis and the Sub-Saharan famines of the 1970s. Two examples are given here. First, Rivers et al.[21]

[17] T. Scott-Smith, *On an Empty Stomach: Two Hundred Years of Hunger Relief* (Ithaca: Cornell University Press, 2020), at 75–89.

[18] S. Jaspars, T. Scott-Smith, and E. Hull, *Contested Evolution of Nutrition for Humanitarian and Development Ends. Report of an International Workshop*, Refugee Studies Centre Working Paper Series No. 125 (2018), available online at <https://www.rsc.ox.ac.uk/publications/contested-evolution-of-nutrition-for-humanitarian-and-development-ends> (visited 25 August 2021), at 3.

[19] Lang, Barling, and Caraher, *Food Policy*, see note 4, at 119.

[20] C. Sathyamala, *Nutrition: contested meanings. A theoretical and empirical enquiry* (PhD thesis on file at Erasmus University, Rotterdam, 2016), at 68.

[21] J. Rivers, et al., 'Lessons for Epidemiology from the Ethiopian Famines', 56(4–5) *Annales Societe Beige de Medecine Tropicale* (1976), 345–360, at 56.

drew attention to famine in Ethiopia as a social phenomenon, not one simply defined as high levels of acute malnutrition. Famines, they argued, were qualitatively different from periods of extreme poverty. They are sudden and distinct events, as different from extreme poverty as ice is from freezing water. Famines are different because they are characterized by social disruption, including distress migration and the need to carry out precarious or degrading work as servants, labourers, or prostitutes.[22] By waiting for signs of starvation before responding, international response was late. They suggested examining early social and economic signs of famine more carefully. Second, Pacey and Payne[23] found that by the mid-1980s agricultural production and supplementary feeding interventions developed in response to the 1974 food crisis had little impact on nutrition.[24] As a result, they recommended a new more socially oriented approach to nutrition (see earlier).

A social nutrition approach was also adopted briefly in emergencies in the late 1980s and 1990s. When working in the refugee crises and famines of the 1980s and 1990s, nutritionists soon realized that 'in famine ... what matters is access to food, which relates to political, economic, social and environmental factors. In this context, nutrition is a social and human science'.[25] International nutrition conferences in 1988 and 1991 concluded that the political priorities of donor countries and international aid practices contributed enormously to the nutritional crises.[26] Nutritionists developed a large number of new practices, ranging from famine early warning, to food security assessments, and agricultural, market- and employment-based interventions as well as approaches to food distribution that took into account the social and political constraints in reaching the most vulnerable.[27]

In the past decade, however, social nutrition has rarely, if at all, been used in emergencies. Nutrition continued and intensified on a path of medicalization in the 2000s, including in emergencies. The period of social or public nutrition in emergencies has in fact largely been excluded from mainstream histories of nutrition[28] which presents emergency nutrition as focusing on treatment. In development contexts, the UNICEF framework has been criticized for facilitating a focus on the biomedical, by placing an emphasis on disease and lack of care as underlying

[22] Rivers et al., see note 21, at 346.

[23] Pacey and Payne, see note 5.

[24] Note that John Rivers, the lead author of the article on the Ethiopian famine, worked at the Nutrition Department of LSHTM and Philip Payne was its head in the 1980s.

[25] *Report of a workshop on the improvement of the nutrition of refugees and displaced people in Africa, University of Nairobi, Machakos, Kenya* (United Nations Administrative Committee on Coordination/ Standing Committee on Nutrition (UN SCN), 1994), at 134.

[26] *Nutrition in Times of Disaster. Report of an international conference held at the World Health Organization Headquarters* (UNSCN, 1988).

[27] S. Jaspars, *Food Aid in Sudan. A History of Power, Politics and Profit, Politics and Development in Contemporary Africa* (London: Zed Books, 2018).

[28] See, e.g. S. Gillespie and J. Harris, 'How Nutrition Improves: Half a Century of Understanding and Responding to the Problem of Malnutrition', in S. Gillespie et al. (eds), *Nourishing Millions: Stories of Change in Nutrition* (Washington DC: International Food Policy Research Institute, 2016), 1–13.

causes and therefore providing an means of moving attention away from its political and economic causes.[29] Sathyamala[30] also points out that while the framework identifies the structural causes of malnutrition, it does not mean that UNICEF will want to address them—as their policy on '[structural] adjustment with a human face' shows. The application of the framework has received criticism because of it its focus on technical issues at the individual and household level—also leading to a depoliticization of nutrition.[31] The political and economic reasons for the marginalization of social nutrition are further discussed in section 6 of this chapter.

The only approach that currently comes close to social or public nutrition analysis is Action Contre la Faim's (ACF) nutrition causal analysis. However, its analysis is largely limited to the underlying causes at the community rather than population level and known risk factors at individual level. Qualitative methods focus on local perceptions of malnutrition and its causes, the practices of caregivers, and to understand historical change.[32] As it is estimated to take about four to five months to complete, it has largely been applied to protracted rather than acute crisis contexts or famine. The wider political and economic processes that determine why some people have plenty of food whereas others do not have enough are generally not analysed. When social factors are considered at all, it tends to be at the level of the household or individual and limited to 'caring behaviours' or the interaction between caregiver and child. A few exceptions exist, however, in the literature. Engle et al.[33] for example, consider the social systems in a child's environment (e.g. schools, community organizations, extended families) and the larger forces which influence social systems, such as government policies, culture, and legal systems. Studies in Yemen and Jamaica showed the importance of social inclusion for good nutrition,[34] and in Niger showed the importance of women's income and access to social networks to secure nutritional resources.[35] By extension, the social disruption associated with famine would have a serious impact on nutrition whether due to the splitting of families, contraction of social networks, or displacement.

[29] Sathyamala, *Nutrition: contested meanings*, see note 20, at 111; C. Sathyamala, 'Assessment: Global Nutrition Report: Towards a Global Governance in Nutrition', 48(5) *Development and Change* (2017) 1227–1242.

[30] Sathyamala, *Nutrition: contested meanings*, see note 20.

[31] H. Young and A. Marshak, *Persistent Global Acute Malnutrition: A Discussion Paper on the Scope of the Problem, Its Drivers, and Strategies for Moving Forward for Policy, Practice, and Research*, Feinstein International Center, January 2018, available at <https://fic.tufts.edu/publication-item/persistent-global-acute-malnutrition-discussion-paper/> (visited 22 October 2021); N. Nisbett, 'Understanding the Nourishment of Bodies at the Centre of Food and Health Systems—Systemic, Bodily and New Materialist Perspectives on Nutritional Inequity', 228 *Social Science and Medicine* (2019) 9–16.

[32] Action Contre la Faim (ACF), *Link-NCA. Nutrition Causal Analysis* (2017).

[33] P. Engle, S. Castle, and P. Menon, 'Child Development: Vulnerability and Resilience', 43(5) *Social Science and Medicine* (1996) 621–635.

[34] Engle, Castle, and Menon, see note 33, at 628.

[35] K. Hampshire et al., 'The Social Context of Childcare Practices and Child Malnutrition in Niger's Recent Food Crisis', 33(1) *Disasters* (2009) 132–151.

Recently, there have been calls by some nutritionists but mainly by anthropologists, food policy analysts, and social movements for the need to re-examine nutrition within its social and political context. In non-emergency contexts, a recent article in *Public Health Nutrition* argues that the social needs to be seen as central to nutrition science,[36] calling in particular for more attention to agency. It also highlights that socially engaged nutrition studies tend to be done by sociologists, anthropologists, and geographers, and that they tend to be qualitative or ethnographic rather than quantitative. Nisbett[37] too argues the need for nutritionists to engage more with insights from the critical social sciences to move beyond the biomedical; learning, for example, from food systems models, ecological and adaptive systems models, biopolitics, or new materialist approaches. Anthropology, development studies, and politics researchers have criticized medicalized approaches because the focus on behaviour and biotechnology takes attention away from government policy and the food industry itself in causing malnutrition. They particularly raise issues of conflict of interest arising from business involvement in solving malnutrition.[38] Social and human rights movements are advocating re-engaging nutrition with society and argue for the necessity of seeing nutrition as a profoundly political issue which touches on rights, livelihoods, and health.[39] For emergency contexts, a recent study on persistent global acute malnutrition found that several respondents raised issues of society and politics as causes. The study report is clear about the importance of analysing basic social, political, and economic causes to improve understanding of persistently high levels of acute malnutrition, and about the need to look beyond simplistic interpretations of the UNICEF framework.[40] De Waal[41] has called for social nutrition to be part of an agenda for prohibiting famine.

To conclude, the concept of social nutrition is largely a historical one and has been defined in different ways. Its role needs to be redefined in light of today's famines and humanitarian crises (including protracted crises), taking into account the considerable obstacles in bringing about a shift away from medicalized approaches.

[36] L. Schubert et al., 'Re-imagining the "Social" in the Nutrition Sciences', 15(2) *Public Health Nutrition* (2011) 352–359.

[37] Nisbett, see note 31.

[38] A. Street, 'Food as Pharma: Marketing Nutraceuticals to India's Rural Poor', 25(3) *Critical Public Health* (2015) 361–372; R. Patel et al., 'Cook, Eat, Man, Woman: Understanding the New Alliance for Food Security and Nutrition, Nutritionism and its Alternatives from Malawi', 42(1) *The Journal of Peasant Studies* (2015) 21–44; C. Sathyamala, 'Nutritionalizing Food: A Framework for Capital Accumulation', 47(4) *Development and Change* (2016) 818–839; Sathyamala, 'Assessment', see note 29; Jaspars, *Food Aid in Sudan*, see note 27.

[39] S. Prato and N. Bullard, 'Editorial: Re-embedding Nutrition in Society, Nature and Politics', 57(2) *Development* (2014) 129–134; Civil Society Forum, 'Social Movements Statement on Nutrition', 57(2) *Development* (2014) 305–309.

[40] Young and Marshak, see note 31.

[41] A. de Waal, 'Social Nutrition and Prohibiting Famine', 9(1) *World Nutrition* (2018).

4. How Can Social Nutrition Strengthen Accountability for Mass Starvation?

Accountability for mass starvation entails making it unthinkable for political and military leaders in a position to inflict starvation to unambiguously act to avoid it. This will happen when the public demands it and the law is fit for purpose.[42] One element of a strategy to bring this about is to sharpen the practical application of the relevant international law, and how criminal and humanitarian law might be used to prosecute individuals for crimes of starvation. Another is to find a means of gathering and analysing evidence of actions which can lead to mass starvation, such as the way in which wars are being fought, and the process by which these actions and the combined effects of different underlying causes lead to extremely heightened levels of acute malnutrition and mortality. A socially or politically oriented approach to nutrition may have a role in this.

The law already recognizes the multi-dimensionality of starvation, as illustrated by the Rome Statute of the International Criminal Court. Article 8(2)(b)(xxv) of the Rome Statute, provides that '*intentionally* using starvation of civilians as a method of warfare by depriving them of objects indispensable to their survival, including wilfully impeding relief supplies as provided for under the Geneva Conventions' is a war crime. International Humanitarian Law (IHL) also prohibits the starvation of civilian populations and, like International Criminal Law (ICL), states that the parties to the conflict have an obligation to allow and protect speedy and unhindered access to humanitarian workers and the distribution of supplies for civilians.[43] Sieges and blockades are considered unlawful if the intent is to starve the population.

The law recognizes that starvation is not limited to the deprivation of food directly but also of other objects indispensable to survival. This has the potential to link it to the underlying causes of malnutrition and mortality. In other words, food insecurity (e.g. food, markets, land, livestock), social networks and caring behaviours (e.g. relations between groups, distress migration, family separation), healthcare and the environment (e.g. medicine, shelter, blankets), and the things that link or influence all three such as access to water, displacement, and restriction of movement, depending on the severity of crisis. The following section examines malnutrition in situations of calamitous famine. In particular, the process by which populations are deprived of items indispensable to survival and the how the combined effects of different causes can lead to elevated levels of acute malnutrition and mortality.

[42] A. de Waal, *Mass Starvation. The History and Future of Famine* (Cambridge: Polity, 2018).

[43] Three main principles of IHL: (1) *Distinction* between civilian populations and combatants. (2) *Proportionality*. Parties to the conflict may not launch an attack on military objectives if it will result in excessive civilian deaths. (3) *Precaution*. Take all measures to protect the civilian population.

5. Calamitous Famine and Malnutrition

A. Famine, Malnutrition, and Mortality

Some of the highest rates of malnutrition have been associated with calamitous famines, usually as a result of conflict and displacement. In these cases, malnutrition is often the result of deliberate war strategies to undermine livelihoods and to restrict food supplies. Examples of great or calamitous famines in recent history include Ethiopia and Sudan in 1984, Sudan (South: Bahr el-Ghazal) in 1988, Somalia in 1992–1993, Sudan (South) in 1998, Democratic Republic of Congo in 1998–2002, Darfur (Sudan) in 2003–2005, and Somalia in 2011.[44] Such famines have been defined as those resulting in more than 100,000 or 1 million or more excess deaths.[45] With the exception of Sudan in 1984, all famines mentioned in this paragraph were linked to war. One recent example is war-ravaged South Sudan, prevalences of acute malnutrition were between 23 per cent and 39 per cent when famine was declared in 2017.[46] Acute malnutrition rates in these famines are shown in Table 3.1 and have also been some of the highest levels recorded; many times the generally accepted World Health Organization (WHO) threshold for emergencies of 15 per cent.[47]

In calamitous famines, crude mortality rates are also well above the emergency threshold of 1/10,000/day, for example 16/10,000/day amongst Ethiopian refugees in Sudan in 1985, 90/10,000/day amongst displaced populations in Sudan in 1988 and 26/10,000/day in South Sudan in 1998.[48] As for acute malnutrition, refugee and displaced contexts often present situations of the greatest severity.[49] These highly elevated acute malnutrition and mortality rates illustrate well the qualitatively different nature of great or calamitous famines and an exponential increase in malnutrition and mortality when a crisis affects all underlying causes simultaneously. A recent example is the sudden (and apparently exponential) increase in the most recent famine in Somalia[50] (see Figure 3.2).

Together with Helen Young, I examined this exponential relationship between malnutrition and mortality in situations of different categories of severe food

[44] D. Maxwell and N. Majid, *Famine in Somalia. Competing Imperatives, Collective Failures, 2011–12* (Oxford: Oxford University Press, 2016); de Waal, *Mass Starvation*, see note 42.

[45] S. Devereux, *Famine in the Twentieth Century, IDS Working Paper 105* (Brighton: University of Sussex, 2000); de Waal, *Mass Starvation*, see note 42.

[46] D. Maxwell et al., 'Viewpoint: Determining Famine: Multi-dimensional Analysis for the Twenty-First Century', 92 *Food Policy* (2020) 1–13.

[47] WHO World Health Organization, *The Management of Nutrition in Major Emergencies* (Geneva: World Health Organization, 2000).

[48] CDC, 'Famine-affected', see note 47; P. Howe and S. Devereux, 'Famine Intensity and Magnitude Scales: A Proposal for an Instrumental Definition of Famine', 28 *Disasters* (2004) 353–372.

[49] See on Somalia more recently: G. Moloney et al., 'Malnutrition and Mortality—Southern Somalia, July 2011', 60(30) *Morbidity and Mortality Weekly Report* (2011).

[50] Salama et al., see note 55.

Table 3.1 Examples of prevalences of acute malnutrition in situations of mass starvation

Date	Country	Prevalence acute malnutrition	Specific location
1985	Ethiopia	70%[a]	Korem
1988	Sudan	36%[b]	internally displaced persons (IDP) South Darfur
1992-1993	Somalia	70%[c]	Baidoa, Bardera, Huddur
	Ethiopia	44%[d]	Ogaden Region, Gode town, IDPs and refugees
1998	Sudan (South)	48-80%[e]	Ajiep, Gogrial County
		71.6%[f]	Wau IDPs
2004	Sudan	21.8%[g]	Darfur
2011	Somalia	19.6-55%[h]	Crisis-affected areas
2017	South Sudan	20-39%[i]	Leer, Mayendit, Koch

Source: Susanne Jaspars 2022; Data: as noted.

[a] CDC, 'Famine-affected, Refugee and Displaced Populations: Recommendations for Public Health Issues', 41(13) *Morbidity and Mortality Weekly Report* (1992).

[b] CDC, see note 48.

[c] C. Cambrezy, *Nutrition Surveys in Somalia. 1980–1996* (Rome: World Food Programme, 1997).

[d] H. Young et al., 'Public Nutrition in Complex Emergencies', 364 *The Lancet* (2004) 1899–1909.

[e] Young et al., see note 51.

[f] Young et al., see note 51.

[g] World Food Programme and UNICEF, *Emergency Food Security and Nutrition Assessment* (Rome: World Food Programme, 2005).

[h] P. Salama et al., 'Famine in Somalia: Evidence for a Declaration', 1 *Global Food Security* (2012) 13–19.

[i] Maxwell et al., 'Viewpoint: Determining Famine', see note 46.

insecurity or famine.[51] In reviewing the malnutrition–mortality relationship, we found that:

- Mortality risk in individuals increases as anthropometric status declines. Malnourished children who are exposed to higher baseline mortality and morbidity have a higher risk of dying: malnutrition and infection have a synergistic effect on mortality.[52]

[51] H. Young and S. Jaspars, 'The Meaning and Measurement of Acute Malnutrition in Emergencies. A Primer for Decision-makers', 56 *Humanitarian Practice Network Paper* (2006); H. Young and S. Jaspars, *Review of Nutrition and Mortality Indicators for the Integrated Food Security Phase Classification (IPC): Reference Levels and Decision-making*, SCN Task Force on Assessment, Monitoring and Evaluation, and The Integrated Food Security Phase Classification (IPC) Global Partners (2009).

[52] Note that the relationship is different for different nutritional indices.

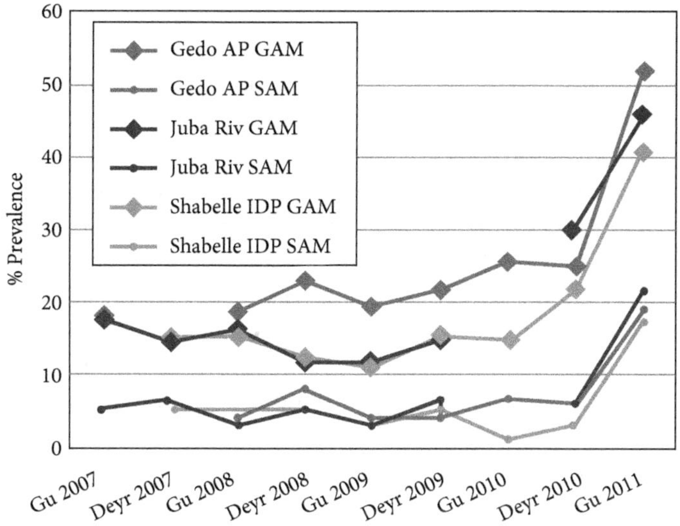

Figure 3.2 Trends in prevalence of global and severe acute malnutrition in selected areas of southern Somalia, 2007–2011

Source: This chart was published P. Salama et al., 'Famine in Somalia: Evidence for a Declaration', 1(1) Global Food Security (2012), at 3. Copyright Elsevier (2012).

- The few studies that exist on the relationship between food security, nutritional status, and mortality suggest that for a given level of nutritional status, mortality is higher during a period of food insecurity. Furthermore, as food insecurity worsens, and the prevalence of wasting[53] increases, the risk of dying for *all* children increases.
- Studies of prevalences of wasting and mortality rates in situations of humanitarian crises (in particular, camp situations) in the 1980s and 1990s strongly suggest a synergism between underlying causes—leading to an exponential relationship. This explains the sometimes rapid deterioration in situations of increasingly severe crisis.

These findings led us to develop a theory of how the relationship between underlying causes changes as food security deepens and famine develops. We suggested that in a non-emergency phase the three underlying causes are on a par: each necessary, but insufficient on their own to ensure good nutrition. When food insecurity worsens, it affects the social and care environment and the health

[53] Another term for acute malnutrition.

environment as, for example, people migrate for work and reduced income lowers access to healthcare. It also constrains caring behaviours. In the next stage of severity, a humanitarian emergency or social disruption influences both food security and the health environment. This may include increased migration, displacement, and social unrest, all of which affect the integrity of the household. In the most severe famines or humanitarian catastrophes all underlying causes are extremely elevated and produce the extremely elevated malnutrition and mortality rates found in the most severe famines. This is also shown in Figure 3.3.[54] The changing relationship between the underlying causes of malnutrition and mortality could be a crucial element in social nutrition's role in determining the outcomes of famine acts. Further analysis is needed of recent studies of the malnutrition and mortality relationship, and to test the proposed theory about the interaction between different underlying causes with increasing severity of food insecurity and famine.

B. Famine as a Political Act

The interaction between food insecurity, social factors, and the health environment in situations of famine may explain the highly elevated rates of malnutrition and mortality, but the high malnutrition rates are not linked to their structural or basic causes (see Figure 3.2). In the most severe famines, the destruction of livelihoods is a deliberate political and military act, or the result of a failure to act, in particular when it is known that war strategies are leading to the starvation of civilians. Macrae and Zwi[55] divided these into acts of commission, omission, and provision. Acts of commission are attacks on production (agriculture and livestock, and items needed to maintain them), markets, and the restriction of movement; that is blocking of people's attempts to access food or preserve their livelihoods. Acts of omission include failures to act, such as the obstruction of relief or failure to use local reserves to feed civilians affected by conflict. Acts of provision entails the selective provision of food for one side of the conflict, or its supporters. Importantly, as Keen[56] has shown in Sudan, famine has beneficiaries as well as victims. The restriction of food and other items essential to survival may benefit the government, for example when used in siege tactics, but also merchants benefit

[54] Young and Jaspars, *Review of Nutrition*, see note 60.

[55] J. Macrae and A. Zwi (eds), *War and Hunger. Rethinking International Responses to Complex Emergencies* (London: Zed Books, 1994).

[56] D. Keen, *The Benefits of Famine: A Political Economy of Famine and Relief in Southwestern Sudan 1983–89* (Oxford: James Currey, 1994).

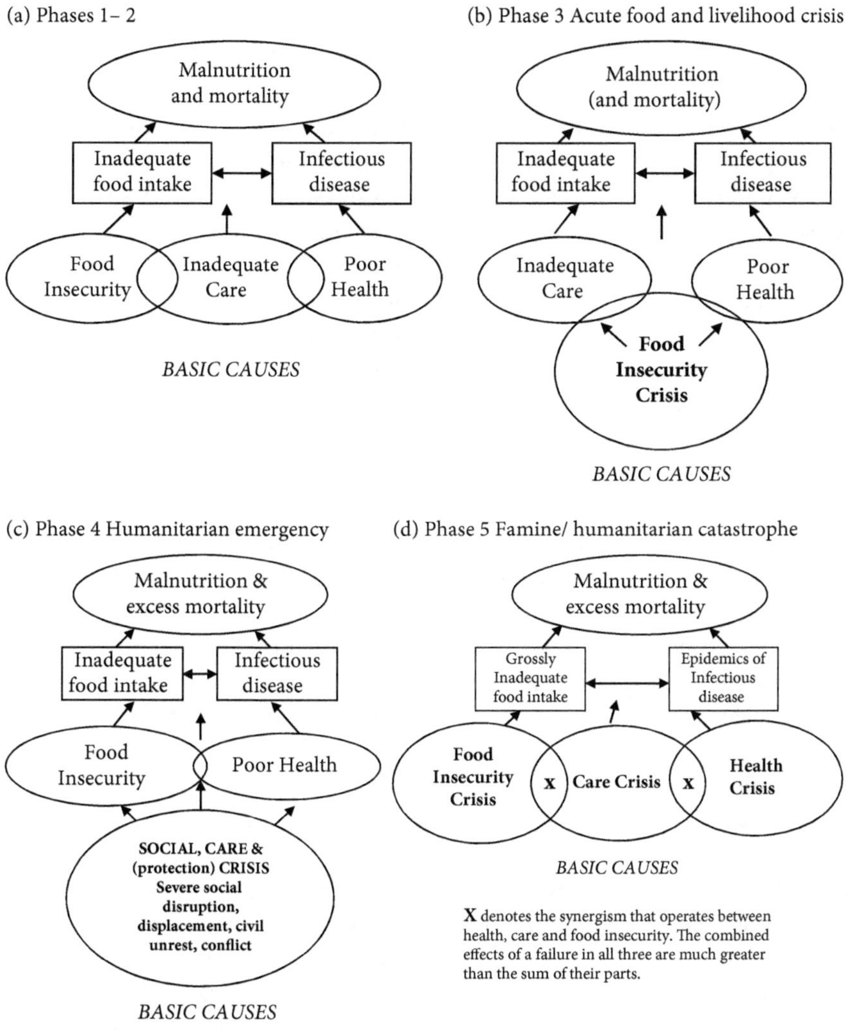

Figure 3.3 The changing relationship between food, health, and care as food security deteriorates

Source: adapted from H. Young, and S. Jaspars (2009) Review of Nutrition and Mortality Indicators for the Integrated Food Security Phase Classification (IPC). Reference Levels and Decision-making, Rome: UN Standing Committee on Nutrition.

from increased food prices and farmers may benefit from cheap labour from the forcibly displaced.[57] These benefits include those gained from the manipulation of food aid, which continues to the present day.[58]

A number of populations are at risk of mass starvation at the time of writing including in Yemen, South Sudan, and Syria, all of which are in the midst of war.[59] As de Waal[60] suggests, the resurgence of mass starvation is not only a result of an increase in conflict globally but also a global trend of counter-humanitarianism. This is linked both to the War on Terror and a return to geopolitical objectives of aid and national security, a rise in authoritarian governments, and—in some cases—a reluctance in declaring famine or humanitarian crisis on the part of the international community for fear of losing access. In Somalia, for example, US anti-terrorism legislation delayed the 2011 famine response and continues to limit humanitarian operations today. In Yemen, the war between the US- and UK-supported Saudi coalition and Iran-backed Houthi rebels has led to a severe humanitarian crisis. Saudi bombing of markets, sieges, and destruction of roads and bridges, combined with coalition closure of airspace and a naval and land blockade led to a total collapse of food supplies. In South Sudan, the Integrated Phase Classification (IPC) team hesitated in declaring a famine in 2016 because it feared government reprisals.[61] Similarly, in Sri Lanka, Sudan, and Syria, government denial of aid and access to crisis-affected populations in rebel-held areas was not challenged, thus inadvertently strengthening the government's hand.[62]

If famine is a result of political decisions and of power relations, the key question is not what causes famine but how were acts of starvation committed and by whom?[63] If mass starvation is the result of a political process or of a series of political acts, it needs to be seen as a crime. Once considered a crime, the language changes from causes and solutions to responsibility, perpetrators, bystanders, victims, and survivors.[64] It can also lead to prosecution, using the legal instruments described earlier in this chapter. Using social nutrition to demonstrate connections between highly elevated levels of malnutrition and political acts or decisions,

[57] Keen, see note 65.

[58] Keen, see note 65; Jaspars, *Food Aid in Sudan*, see note 27.

[59] de Waal, *Mass Starvation*, see note 42.

[60] de Waal, *Mass Starvation*, see note 42.

[61] de Waal, *Mass Starvation*, see note 42.

[62] Keen, see note 65; J. C. Martinez and B. Eng, 'The Unintended Consequences of Emergency Food Aid: Neutrality, Sovereignty and Politics in the Syrian Civil War, 2012–15', 92(1) *International Affairs* (2016) 153–173; Jaspars, *Food Aid in Sudan*, see note 27.

[63] J. Edkins, 'The Criminalisation of Mass Starvations; From Natural Disaster to Crime Against Humanity', in S. Devereux (ed.), *The New Famines: Why Famines Persist in an Era of Globalisation* (Abingdon: Routledge, 2007); de Waal, *Mass Starvation*, see note 42.

[64] Edkins, see note 72.

however, faces many challenges. These challenges are discussed in the following section.

6. Challenges in Using Social Nutrition to Strengthen Accountability for Mass Starvation

For the discipline of social nutrition to function as a tool to strengthen accountability for mass starvation it must overcome several hurdles. The first set of challenges has to do with the marginalization of social nutrition and the domination of a medicalized approach to nutrition, along with powerful motivations for maintaining the status quo. The second relates to the difficulties of applying a social nutrition approach to promote accountability in practice. Analysis would need to link famine acts and underlying causes explicitly, and by understanding the process leading to malnutrition and mortality promote political accountability. The analysis would also have to determine what constitutes plausible evidence from which to infer causation. Finally, analysts would need to overcome the considerable political, economic, and scientific incentives that are currently promoting a medicalized approach to nutrition. In effect, a paradigm shift in nutrition is required. This section discusses each of these challenges in turn.

A. Why the Domination of Medicalized Nutrition?

There are a number of reasons why medicalized nutrition currently dominates both academia and practice, briefly mentioned here.[65] First, the development of community management of acute malnutrition (CMAM) and commercially prepared ready to use therapeutic foods (RUTF) improved dramatically methods for treating malnutrition. This led many emergency nutritionists to focus on treatment.[66] Second, two influential series of papers in the *Lancet* in 2008 and 2013 reported on meta-analyses of the causes of malnutrition and 'what works' in terms of interventions. However, they explicitly excluded deprivation and inequity from their analysis, and focused on identifying risk factors at the individual level, and 'what works' based on impact evaluations using Randomized Controlled Trials (RCT) of medical and behavioural interventions.[67] They concluded that

[65] For a more detailed analysis see Jaspars, *Food Aid in Sudan*, see note 27.

[66] Jaspars, *Food Aid in Sudan*, see note 27, at 51.

[67] R. Black et al., 'Maternal and Child Undernutrition: Global and Regional Exposures and Health Consequences', 371 *Lancet* (2008) 243–246; Z. Bhutta et al., 'What Works? Interventions for Maternal and Child Undernutrition and Survival', 371 *Lancet* (2008) 417–440.

interventions such as fortification, supplements, and nutrition education were effective in addressing malnutrition (later called 'nutrition-specific' interventions). The later series introduced nutrition-sensitive interventions such as agriculture, safety nets, and education.[68] These articles form the basis of most nutrition strategies today—whether donors or aid organizations—including in emergencies. These articles coincided with the 2008 global food crisis, following which a resilience ideology dominated development and in which nutrition became key to resilience.[69] Since 2010, donors, aid organizations, and researchers all work together with private sector institutions to promote a standard package of interventions as part of the Scaling Up Nutrition (SUN) movement.

The move away from a socially oriented approach is highlighted by the adaptations of the UNICEF framework in the *Lancet* articles. The social and political have been almost entirely removed. In 2008, the underlying causes no longer overlap and a different level of entirely economic causes—income, employment, medicalized, etc.—replaces the formal and informal institutions. Basic causes are indicated as capital (financial, physical, social, natural), and the 'social, political and economic context'.[70] By 2013, the framework is medical on actions to achieve optimal foetal and child nutrition, rather than analysing the causes of malnutrition.[71] The framework lists nutrition-specific and nutrition-sensitive interventions, thus promoting standardized packages of interventions rather than interventions based on a context-specific analysis. Furthermore, Ruel and Alderman[72] argue that there is little evidence of impact for nutrition-sensitive interventions, further justifying a purely medical approach. The fact that only RCT studies are considered valid evidence of impact highlights the dominance of methodologically individualistic quantitative studies that generate statistically significant results over ethnographic and qualitative information on context-specific causal linkages and interactions.

The third reason that a medicalized approach is dominant is that it is economically and politically convenient. As Sathymala[73] highlights, medicalized nutrition includes a number of biotechnical products such as micro-nutrient supplementation and nutraceuticals, all of which further business interests. It is politically convenient for governments because malnutrition is not linked to their war strategies or development policies; they know they will not be held to account. For

[68] M. Ruel and H. Alderman, 'Nutrition-sensitive Interventions and Programmes: How Can They Help to Accelerate Progress in Improving Maternal and Child Nutrition?', 382 *Lancet* (2013) 536–551.

[69] Jaspars, *Food Aid in Sudan*, see note 27.

[70] Black et al., 'Maternal and Child Undernutrition', see note 67.

[71] R. Black et al., 'Maternal and Child Undernutrition and Overweight in Low-Income and Middle-Income Countries', 382 *Lancet* (2013) 427–451.

[72] Ruel and Alderman, see note 68.

[73] Sathyamala, 'Assessment', see note 29.

international organizations, the benefit arises because they are able to maintain a presence by not highlighting the political causes of malnutrition.[74] For aid agencies, it is also easier logistically to implement a standard package of interventions for populations which are hard to access (as is frequently the case in situations of conflict).[75]

B. The Challenges of Applying a Social Nutrition Approach

Social nutrition could potentially provide the analytical link between structural causes or famine acts, and the process and outcome of heightened malnutrition and mortality. However, in practice, determining accountability is difficult, so is proving causality, and such an approach by its very nature will have political repercussions.

Few attempts to classify famine link it with accountability. The IPC and its predecessor, Howe and Devereux's famine intensity and magnitude scale,[76] attempt to classify severity of food insecurity and famine using indicators of food security, malnutrition, and mortality. While the Howe and Devereux scale went some way in trying to promote accountability, it is telling that the IPC manual[77] states that the aim is to produce 'technical consensus' and that the host government is one of its stakeholders, which is likely to be problematic in situations of civil war and repression.[78] The 2019 manual produced a combined food security and nutrition conceptual framework, which also incorporates elements from a livelihoods framework, and which includes structural causes. However, the interaction between structural and underlying causes is not well explained and the main classification relies almost entirely on quantitative data. It also assumes an almost linear progression in severity. Howe and Devereux[79] in contrast, distinguish between famine and severe famine, place much greater emphasis on the social and political dimensions of famine, and examine the implications for accountability. Acts of commission, or where famine is used as a weapon of war, they write, could in theory lead to referrals to the International Criminal Court (ICC) for crimes against humanity. They also argue that accountability needs a clear definition of famine and clear

[74] Jaspars, *Food Aid in Sudan*, see note 27.
[75] Jaspars, Scott-Smith, and Hull, see note 18.
[76] Howe and Devereux, see note 57.
[77] 'Technical Manual Version 3.0. Evidence and Standards for Better Food Security and Nutrition Decisions', The Integrated Food Security Phase Classification (IPC) Global Partners (2019), available online at <http://www.ipcinfo.org/fileadmin/user_upload/ipcinfo/manual/IPC_Technical_Manual_3_Final.pdf> (visited 25 August 2021).
[78] Note that the IPC was originally used when in Somalia when there was no government.
[79] Howe and Devereux, see note 57.

responsibilities for famine prevention, but the latter is made difficult by the diffusion of responsibilities between national and international actors.

Proving causality is difficult, whether in a legal or in a statistical sense. In the 2000s, nutrition studies largely analyse statistical associations of malnutrition with, and the prevalence of, immediate risk factors. This cannot prove causality and does not involve an examination of structural causes or the effects of political acts. The latter are more likely to be examined by anthropologists, political analysts, and other social scientists through qualitative enquiry or ethnography, but such evidence is unlikely to be accepted as proving causality by epidemiologists or medical nutritionists. In presenting the case for prosecuting starvation crimes, however, the ability to demonstrate causal links between political acts such as sieges or blockades and the consequential deprivation of items that leads to starvation is necessary. ICL permits a conclusion on causality from circumstantial evidence as long it is the only reasonable inference available from the evidence taken as a whole. In theory, this sounds similar to ACF's nutrition causal analysis. The aim of ACF's nutrition causal analysis is to determine causal pathways and to develop evidence-based consensus around plausible causes of under-nutrition. However, it currently considers basic causes as background information and in practice does not link it with underlying or immediate causes of malnutrition. A key question arising from current approaches to nutrition is therefore whether evidence permissible for prosecution may in fact be accepted as proving causal links by medical nutritionists. Alternatively, linking nutrition with legal instruments to prevent starvation may lead to new ways of gathering plausible evidence on the process that ultimately leads to heightened malnutrition and mortality. An examination of the structural causes of malnutrition needs to be a starting point. This includes an examination of how famine acts lead to hugely elevated levels of malnutrition.

Nutritionists rarely consider the structural causes of malnutrition partly because they feel it is beyond their control, and partly because it can become a highly political exercise. The importance of being aware of structural causes has been stressed only occasionally. Young and Jaspars,[80] for example, urge the importance of examining structural factors because they reflect the overarching processes that are shaping and influencing the nutrition of communities, and possibly the preconditions for recovery from emergencies. Young and Marshak[81] have more recently called for a more systematic exploration of basic causes to understand persistently high levels of acute malnutrition, and Jaspars[82] for a reconsideration of nutrition within its social and political context to examine contemporary nutrition

[80] Young and Jaspars, 'The Meaning and Measurement of Acute Malnutrition', see note 60.
[81] Young and Marshak, see note 31.
[82] Jaspars, *Food Aid in Sudan*, see note 27.

approaches critically. Well before this, Pacey and Payne[83] write that nutritionists need to be aware of the political and social dimensions of the food system because, with a degree of independence, they might take up an advocacy role on behalf of the poor.

An analysis of the structural causes of malnutrition can be seen as a political exercise and may have political repercussions, particularly when used to strengthen accountability for mass starvation. Such an analysis requires explicitly linking war strategies or obstruction of aid with malnutrition and mortality as an outcome by analysing the link between basic, underlying, and immediate causes and the interactions between them. Assigning responsibility and intent will take this even further. Pacey and Payne[84] discuss some of the dilemmas that analysing the social and political dimension of nutrition creates in relation to advocating for 'problem-solving education' rather than traditional nutrition education. According to Freire (the originator of this approach) a problem-solving approach involves people in a reflection on their situation and it should lead to revolutionary action for change. A resulting interest in social change is therefore inevitable, as are its political repercussions. At the same time, the fact that social approaches may lead to political repercussions can also be taken as an indication of the relevance of the programme, whereas the more conventional forms of nutrition intervention—for example nutrition education—are so ineffective that no-one could object. However, if a relevant programme is withdrawn or prevented because it is so controversial, it does not have an effect. Unless local organizations are strong enough to take on the political repercussions, a balance needs to be reached. Howe and Devereux[85] also state it is important to ensure that strengthening accountability for famine does not create perverse incentives, for example just trying to prevent populations from crossing the malnutrition or mortality threshold for famine rather than addressing the underlying causes.

In Darfur, Sudan, the use of a medicalized approach to nutrition can also in part be explained by its apolitical nature and therefore enabling aid organizations to maintain a presence in Sudan.[86] Darfur in fact warrants further investigation as to why the referral by the UN Security Council to the ICC for a situation described as a situation of mass atrocities including possibly genocide has not, at the time of writing, led to justice. It was the first time that anyone responsible for a situation described as famine faced the prospect of being brought to justice by the ICC.[87] Almost immediately after the ICC issued an arrest warrant for President al-Bashir

[83] Pacey and Payne, see note 5, at 203.
[84] Pacey and Payne, see note 5, at 198.
[85] Howe and Devereux, see note 57.
[86] Jaspars, *Food Aid in Sudan*, see note 27.
[87] Edkins, see note 72.

in March 2009 (on counts of war crimes and crimes against humanity), however, the Sudan government expelled thirteen international non-governmental organizations (INGOs) and revoked the licenses of three local NGOs. It accused them of violating their humanitarian mandates by, for example, false reporting and co-operating with the ICC.[88] For international organizations that remained, access to conflict affected populations got worse, while President al-Bashir continued to be able to travel freely within the region.

Humanitarian agencies were concerned that the ICC actions jeopardized their activities, and hence the well-being of the victims, and argued that prosecution would not therefore be in the victims' interests. They also criticized the factual claims of the ICC prosecutor for exaggerating ongoing mortality levels.[89] Prosecutorial overreach discredited a potentially valuable exercise in seeking accountability for starvation crimes. In December 2014, the ICC prosecutor shelved the investigation into war crimes in Darfur due to lack of action by the UN Security Council in pushing for arrests.[90] Gathering and using evidence to strengthen accountability for mass starvation clearly needs an approach that has been thought through more thoroughly. Sudan's new transitional government pledged in August 2021 to hand Omar al-Bashir to the ICC.[91] Before the military coup in October 2021, this seemed to provide an opportunity for accountability for starvation crimes.

Finally, the interests in maintaining the status quo are very powerful. As indicated earlier, an approach that identifies the multiple causes of malnutrition, including political, will be controversial. In contrast, a medicalized approach to nutrition is more acceptable as it focuses on disease or individual behaviour rather than the government's unequal development or war strategies (and their international sponsors). In addition, most aid organizations have signed up to the SUN movement and the standardized package of nutrition interventions it promotes. A standardized package of biotechnical interventions also promotes the interests of business, and business involvement is actively promoted by nutritionists, aid organizations, and their donors, despite the conflict of interest this entails. Sathymala[92] has additionally noted the conflict of interest of many of the authors of

[88] Humanitarian Aid Commission, *Humanitarian Situation in Sudan*, Ministry of Humanitarian Affairs (2009), at 4.

[89] R. Brauman, 'Darfur: The International Criminal Court is Wrong', MSF Crash (2010), available online at <https://www.msf-crash.org/en/publications/rights-and-justice/darfur-international-criminal-court-wrong> (visited 20 November 2020).

[90] African Globe, 'ICC shelves Darfur case for lack of UN support', 13 December 2014, available online at <https://www.africanglobe.net/africa/icc-shelves-darfur-case-lack-support/> (visited 8 January 2015).

[91] L. Chutel, 'Will Sudan Send Bashir to the Hague?', *Foreign Policy*, 18 August 2021, available online at <https://foreignpolicy.com/2021/08/18/sudan-bashir-icc-hague-justice-darfur-hemeti/> (visited 6 March 2021).

[92] Sathyamala, 'Assessment', see note 29.

the *Lancet* papers. A change in approach, in particular establishing responsibility, will also highlight that current medicalized approaches implicitly assign responsibility to mothers or households themselves for causing malnutrition, rather than those who obstruct access to items essential to survival. Furthermore, in changing to a more socially or politically oriented approach it may also become apparent that medicalized and quantitative aid practices can be seen as making aid agencies complicit in hiding the political acts that cause food insecurity or famine.[93] To strengthen accountability for mass starvation, a key issue is therefore not only that it requires a paradigm shift in nutrition (or at least recognition of social nutrition as a discipline) but also that it needs to find a way to overcome the political and economic benefits of a medicalized approach to nutrition or find political and economic incentives to promote a social nutrition approach.

7. Social Nutrition and Famine in Context: Somalia

This section provides a brief case study to illustrate how different approaches to nutrition can lead to very different conclusions, and the importance of taking a social approach to nutrition. Without an analysis of structural causes, a nutrition causal analysis can feed into the processes of marginalization and discrimination of particular social or political groups. This is the case for Somalia, which provides a good illustration of how famines occur in populations which already suffer protracted crises.

It is often the same politically marginalized populations which suffer repeated famines, particularly in wars fought along ethnic lines, such as in Somalia and Sudan. In Somalia, the riverine and inter-riverine populations in Somalia (Bay and Bakool regions) suffer persistently high rates of acute malnutrition and experienced the most severe famines in 1992 and in 2011.[94] These populations (including the Rahanweyn, Gabaweyn, and Bantu) have historically been powerless. During the 1980s, they were the victims of land grabs by more powerful groups, reducing their land holdings and—in some cases—turning them into labourers. They were particularly vulnerable to looting and destruction of assets during the conflict in the early 1990s, because they were unarmed. Many were displaced or forced off their lands. Land grabs accelerated, increasing the number of small-holders and

[93] Jaspars, *Food Aid in Sudan*, see note 27.

[94] S. Jaspars, *Solidarity and Soup Kitchens: A Review of Principles and Practice for Food Distribution in Conflict*, Humanitarian Policy Group, Report 17, Overseas Development Institute (2000), available online at <https://cdn.odi.org/media/documents/301.pdf> (visited 25 August 2021); S. Jaspars and D. Maxwell, *Targeting in Complex Emergencies: Somalia Country Case Study*, Feinstein International Center (2008), available online at <https://fic.tufts.edu/publication-item/targeting-in-complex-emergencies-2/> (visited 25 August 2021); Maxwell and Majid, see note 44.

day labourers, which made them more vulnerable to food insecurity.[95] These power dynamics were replicated in food distribution: many politically vulnerable populations were excluded or had their aid heavily taxed by local more powerful clans.[96] The same clans continued to be exploited and displaced in the 2000s, and suffered disproportionately during the humanitarian crises and famines of 2008, 2011, and 2017. They received little assistance as by 2006, many rural areas in southern Somalia were held by al-Shabaab (an Islamist movement and designated terrorist group). This is where many of the most marginalized populations live. Conflict between government and African and Western allies, combined with restriction of aid to al-Shabaab held areas, has increased displacement to urban areas. Within these urban areas, many of the most vulnerable clans continue to be excluded from assistance or exploited by 'gatekeepers' and a small elite continues to benefit from aid and from cheap labour.[97] Even with the shift from food aid to cash transfers, al-Shabaab-held rural areas are hard for international organizations to reach, and diversion and taxation continues.

In contrast to these dynamics of food and power, a recent nutrition causal analysis highlights issues of weak infant and child feeding, poor hygiene, lack of health facilities, and women's workload (in addition to 'insecurity' and 'seasonal factors').[98] A focus on behaviour change makes people themselves responsible for their malnutrition and implies that people have a choice in what they do. The politics, or structural factors that put people at risk, is made invisible. By focusing on individual actions and choice (in both cash transfer and nutrition strategies), the political and economic processes that lead to inequalities in the distribution of land, production, and aid, and the exploitation and exclusion this involves, is edited out. Furthermore, positing that some people are malnourished because of their own actions itself feeds into the ongoing discrimination of these groups.[99] Rather than asking how conflict and Somali politics causes malnutrition in particular groups, such an approach asks what certain groups (like the Gabaweyn) are doing to cause malnutrition.

Issues of protracted crisis are relevant well beyond Somalia. Populations in South Sudan, Yemen, and Syria who are at risk of mass starvation are also already suffering protracted crises associated with persistently high levels of malnutrition.

[95] African Rights, *Land Tenure, the Creation of Famine, and Prospects for Peace in Somalia* (New York: African Rights, 1993); A. de Waal, *Class and Power in a Stateless Somalia*, Social Science Research Center (2007), available online at <https://items.ssrc.org/crisis-in-the-horn-of-africa/class-and-power-in-a-stateless-somalia/> (visited 25 August 2021).

[96] Jaspars, see note 103.

[97] S. Jaspars, G. Adan, and N. Majid, *Food and Power in Somalia: Business as Usual? A Scoping Study on the Political Economy of Food Following Shifts in Food Assistance and in Governance*, London School of Economics and Political Science (2020), available online at <https://eprints.lse.ac.uk/103138/7/Food_and_Power_in_Somalia_business_as_usual_v5.pdf> (visited 25 August 2021).

[98] '*Nutrition Causal Analysis Study. South and Central Somalia*', SNS Consortium (2015), available online at <https://www.wfp.org/publications/nutrition-causal-analysis-study> (visited 25 August 2021).

[99] Jaspars, Adan, and Majid, see note 106.

Young and Marshak[100] found that acute malnutrition in populations in South Sudan, Chad, Niger, and Bangladesh rarely went below the 15 per cent mark. One question is therefore how to distinguish situations of protracted crisis with persistently high levels of acute malnutrition from situations of famine and mass starvation, or rather how to identify the point when protracted crisis turns into mass starvation. At the same time, a focus on mass starvation or the threshold between protracted crisis and mass starvation, should not lead to a normalization of protracted crises. In the end, more people may die during a protracted crisis or a lesser famine than in pockets of calamitous famine. Each situation needs to be considered for response.

8. Conclusions and Way Forward

This chapter has shown that a social nutrition approach as such does not really exist at present, but that a number of nutritionists, human rights activists and anthropologists are calling for a more socially or politically engaged approach to nutrition. The reasons for this vary from the return of severe famines, persistently high levels of acute malnutrition in some populations, and because of the crises in food systems due both to climate change, ecological crisis, and the industrialization of food products. In situations of famine, the task for the nutritionist is both social and forensic. It is social in that it must examine the community or population as a whole, not just individuals. It is forensic in that it requires an examination of not only the outcomes (extent of deprivation) but also how that state was arrived at: the processes whereby people were deprived of sufficient (and sufficiently good) food, water, healthcare, and caregiving.

What a future social nutrition looks like depends on its purpose and, in the case of mass starvation, whether and how it can be linked to the legal instruments that prohibit starvation, and who should be doing this. This chapter can provide a starting point for such discussions. It has shown that in the past, a social nutrition approach consisted of a population-level analysis, an examination of the socio-economic and political factors or acts that cause famine and humanitarian crises and that obstruct response. It includes an analysis of the process leading to deprivation (for some but not for others), and the interaction between multiple causes in leading to highly elevated levels of malnutrition and mortality. Other aspects have included a focus on livelihoods, food systems, and participatory or qualitative methods of enquiry. Another feature is an analysis of the actual political and economic effects of existing interventions, in particular the role of business. It also raises the possibility that at least some nutritionists need to become social or political activists.

[100] Young and Marshak, see note 31.

On the issue of purpose, it will be necessary to determine whether the UNICEF framework is still valuable, or do its various adaptations and depoliticizations mean it has been too debased for a genuinely social or political approach? A return to the document accompanying the original UNICEF framework may prove instructive. The originators were clear that it is a deliberate abstraction of a complex reality, and that it functions as an entry point. At the same time, the model clearly incorporates basic causes such as the unequal distribution of resources in society, power structures, access to legal systems, and issues of historical marginalization, which covers many of the basic causes in today's crises. In addition, a closer look at how social scientists examine the causes of hunger and malnutrition may prove valuable and this needs a more in-depth review of anthropological, sociological, and political approaches to hunger. In the case of mass starvation, an additional element is to examine how linking nutrition with legal instruments may lead to new ways of gathering plausible evidence on causation and the process that ultimately leads to heightened malnutrition and mortality. These issues need to be discussed between nutritionists, development and humanitarian specialists, anthropologists, political scientists, and legal experts. A new approach is necessary to strengthen accountability for mass starvation, and because current approaches are not actually reducing acute malnutrition levels.

In addition, there is need for further analysis of malnutrition and mortality relationships, in particular in situations of crisis and famine, and further testing of the proposed theory on the interaction between different underlying causes for a number of famine situations. Key will be to examine the link between different famine acts and decisions, underlying causes, and heightened malnutrition and mortality, and what constitutes plausible qualitative evidence from both a legal and nutritional perspective. Another key issue will be to examine the temporal dimension that distinguishes situations of protracted crisis with persistently high levels of acute malnutrition from situations of famine and mass starvation, or rather how to identify the point when protracted crisis turns into mass starvation. Again, this should not be done by nutritionists alone.

Finally, each famine and crisis context will need careful examination of the political, economic, and logistical interests in maintaining the status quo (i.e. a medicalized nutrition), and the obstacles towards a more politically oriented approach. Part of this will need to be an examination of any political and economic incentives for promoting a social nutrition approach as well as the limits of a social nutrition approach in facilitating prosecutions for famine crimes.

4

'An Unprosecuted Crime'

Bridget Conley, Randle DeFalco, Senai Abraha, and Alex de Waal

1. An Unprosecuted Crime

Mass starvation is a largely unacknowledged and almost entirely unprosecuted crime. There has yet to be a stand-alone prosecution of starvation on the international level.[1] Even in situations wherein a state or non-state belligerent intentionally deprived civilian populations of the basic requirements for sustaining life—food, water, medicine, shelter, and maternal care for small children—and for which criminal proceedings were held, these actions received little if any attention from prosecutors. Even among legal scholars and analysts, and despite significant harm to civilian populations, starvation crimes[2] were too often treated as secondary to direct killing.

There are several probable reasons for the lack of a stand-alone prosecution of starvation. Most importantly, there was no distinct crime of starvation in the International Criminal Tribunal for the former Yugoslavia (ICTY), International Criminal Tribunal for Rwanda (ICTR), or Extraordinary Chambers in the Courts of Cambodia (ECCC) statutes, thus procedurally barring a direct prosecution of the crime. Its low profile in the Rome Statute, which came into force in 2002, is linked to the crime's application initially being limited to International Armed Conflict (IAC), until amended in 2019. Further, the conduct simply did not arise in some of the conflicts, such as during the Rwandan genocide where the *modus operandi* of mass killing was too rapid for starvation crimes to play a major role.[3]

[1] Noting that while the Extraordinary Chambers in the Courts of Cambodia (ECCC) and ICTY did adjudicate upon starvation, they did so in the context of alternative crimes. This is principally because there was no distinct crime of starvation in the ICTY, ICTR, or ECCC statutes, thus procedurally barring a direct prosecution of the crime. Our research indicates that only two prosecutions of the modern era have pleaded starvation as a distinct crime, all on the domestic level (Croatia and Ethiopia, at District Court in Zadar, *Public Prosecutor v. M.P. et al.*, K. 74/96, Verdict 24 April 1997; and Ethiopian Federal High Court, *Special Prosecutor v. Col. Mengistu Hailamariam et al.*, File No. 1/87, 2006).

[2] Introduction in the current volume.

[3] Note, that Judgment in *Kayishema and Ruzindana*, (ICTR-95-1-I, 146), Trial Chamber II, 21 May 1999, §§ 548, 560 analysed the deprivation of food and water in the context of extermination, but held the conduct was insufficient in length and scale to bring about the destruction of the group. Similarly, in Judgment, *Seromba*, (ICTR-2001-66-I), Trial Chamber, 13 December 2006, § 327, considered the prohibition of access to food was considered in the context of the crime of genocide. Here it was held that the refusal to allow the refugees to get food from the banana plantation substantially contributed

Bridget Conley, Randle DeFalco, Senai Abraha, and Alex de Waal, *'An Unprosecuted Crime'* In: *Accountability for Mass Starvation.* Edited by: Bridget Conley, Alex de Waal, Catriona Murdoch, and Wayne Jordash QC, Oxford University Press.
 DOI: 10.1093/oso/9780192864734.003.0004

While currently undergoing a period of re-evaluation, scholarly legal consensus has tended to side with a limited application of the law to starvation conditions. As examples, international law has been understood broadly to allow sieges and blockades, which function through systematic deprivation of an entire population (regardless if composed of civilians and combatants).[4] In terms of states' legal responsibilities to allow humanitarian relief to vulnerable civilian groups, the law has been interpreted as ceding considerable discretion to state authorities,[5] and the oft-times spatial and temporal distance between a perpetrators' acts and the consequential civilian suffering of deprivation has been treated as an insurmountable gulf in terms of proving criminal intent.[6]

Contemporary international criminal law (ICL) prosecutions have primarily focused on violent deaths. Even though prosecutors have sought to convict the most senior political and military leaders, who may not have personally committed homicide, the crimes that have preoccupied the courts are those most frequently associated with policies to perpetrate violent killing on a large scale. Determined to obtain convictions and to do so rapidly, prosecutors have focused their energies on the best-documented and highest-profile crimes, which also allow them to pursue more conservative and less controversial legal strategies.

Nonetheless, prosecutors always had the option of including other crimes that do not have such well-worn paths to conviction. Among these are prosecutions for rape and for the recruitment of children into armed groups. There is no doubt that the reason for these innovative charges was clamour from advocacy groups which had made these offences internationally salient. International tribunals are creations of the political moment and they require public support and funding, and for these reasons it is understandable that their senior prosecutors are attentive to issues that are in the public eye. This can contribute to legal creativity, though it can also overreach, if a prosecutor is seen as a follower of fashion at the expense of legal rigour. Starvation crimes did not have such a level of attention. Political

to their physical weakening, as they were deprived of food. The Chamber was satisfied that this contributed towards the commission of acts causing serious bodily harm to the Tutsi refugees.

[4] C. A. Allen, 'Civilian Starvation and Relief During Armed Conflict: The Modern Humanitarian Law', 19 *Georgia Journal of International & Comparative Law* 31 (1989) 1–85; N. Mulder and B. van Dijk, 'Why Did Starvation Not Become the Paradigmatic War Crime in International Law?', in K. J. Heller and I. Venzke (eds), *Contingency and the Course of International Law* (Oxford: Oxford University Press, 2021) 370–388. More recent work that suggests stronger legal limits on siege, see T. Dannenbaum, 'Encirclement, Deprivation, and Humanity: Revising the *San Remo Manual* Provisions on Blockade', 97 *International Legal Studies* (2021) 307–394; D. Akande and E.-C. Gillard, 'Conflict Induced Food Insecurity and the War Crime of Starvation of Civilians as a Method of War, 17 *Journal of International Criminal Justice* (2019) 753–779; and M. Nijs, 'Humanizing Siege: Applying the Principle of Proportionately to Sieges', 102 *International Review of the Red Cross* (2020) 683–704. See also Chapter 5 in the current volume.

[5] Akande and Gillard, see note 4.

[6] Akande and Gillard, see note 4.

and popular attention to the sufferance of starvation crimes has largely been channelled into humanitarian aid, rather than political and criminal responsibility for creating and perpetrating conditions of starvation.[7] Thus, even when prosecutors could have tested the limits of the existing laws prohibiting starvation-related acts, there was an absence of demand from international political and public opinion.

In this chapter, we engage in an exercise of thinking 'how the law might have been otherwise', as Ingo Venzke refers to it.[8] We present four short cases in which deprivation was a central component of the harms perpetrated against civilian populations, and to which courts have thus far paid relatively little attention. In three cases, criminal prosecutions were carried out by national, hybrid, or international courts: Cambodia under the Khmer Rouge, Ethiopia under President Mengistu Haile Mariam, and the war in Bosnia-Herzegovina. In the fourth, the conflict and atrocities in Darfur, Sudan, there remains a real possibility of prosecutions at the time of writing.

Among the most striking examples of state policies that caused mass starvation in the twentieth century were attempts at rapid radical agricultural, social, and economic transformations by Communist regimes. In this chapter, Cambodia under the Khmer Rouge provides an example of such an event. Earlier instances of such short-term radical transformations include Stalin's (USSR) and Mao's (China) forced collectivization policies and nineteenth-century incorporations of entire economies into imperial systems of production, which caused some of the worst-recorded famines on record.

Socio-economic transformation is not the only relevant context to examine. The 1983–1985 famine in Ethiopia, which became a humanitarian *cause célèbre*, demonstrates how a regime may use food deprivation as a central component of counter-insurgency. In Ethiopia, food shortages and a resettlement programme that intensified already dire living conditions, were deployed to punish and control a civilian population, while separating it from insurgents in an effort to 'drain the sea'.

A third example, Bosnia-Herzegovina, presents a more complicated picture. Access to food and other objects necessary for life were weaponized, while the impacts were calibrated to remain below the threshold where mass starvation might result, greatly supported through the international priority on maintaining the delivery of humanitarian aid. In this instance, except for a few limited examples, people did not experience severe acute malnutrition or heightened mortality as a direct result of deprivations; nonetheless, the manipulation of aid served battlefield and political objectives.

[7] A. de Waal, *Famine Crimes: Politics and the Disaster Relief Industry in Africa* (London: African Rights & the International African Institute in association with James Currey, Oxford & Indiana University Press, Bloomington, 1997) and A. de Waal, *Mass Starvation: The History and Future of Famine* (Cambridge: Polity Press, 2018).

[8] I. Venzke, 'Situating Contingency in the Path of International Law', in K. J. Heller and I. Venzke (eds), *Contingency and the Course of International Law* (Oxford: Oxford University Press, 2021) 3–19.

The final case, the war and atrocities in Darfur, Sudan, during 2003–2008, achieved a very high international profile. There was a vigorous debate as to whether it constituted genocide, and the UN Security Council referred the case to the ICC, resulting in an arrest warrant against President Omar al-Bashir on ten counts of war crimes, crimes against humanity, and genocide. The Sudanese government's war strategy in Darfur utilized militia tactics familiar from earlier campaigns in the country and had the foreseeable outcome of mass killing, displacement, and hunger. The ICC prosecutor's framing of the charges includes elements of starvation, but they are subsumed within a genocide charge that is unlikely to stand up to scrutiny. After al-Bashir was overthrown and arrested by the Sudanese authorities in 2019, the prospect of prosecution became real, although the 2021 military coup raises new questions.

Together, these examples demonstrate a failure to investigate fully and sanction those who use deprivation as a weapon of war. This failure, we argue, directly contributes to ongoing impunity and lack of understanding concerning why and how entire civilian populations are intentionally harmed through acts that render their lives unliveable.

2. Cambodia under the Khmer Rouge (1975–1979)

A. Background

To discuss food security in Cambodia is essentially to focus on rice production and distribution. Rice accounts for up to 80 per cent of the total caloric intake and up to 70 per cent of the protein intake of the average Cambodian.[9] In 1970, a coup against the Prince Sihanouk regime by General Lon Nol helped trigger a civil war. The planting, harvesting, and processing of rice—which previously produced relatively plentiful supplies—were all negatively affected by the fighting between the Lon Nol government and insurgent forces of the Communist Party of Kampuchea (CPK), popularly known as the Khmer Rouge. Further reducing Cambodia's agricultural production was the massive US bombing campaign in support of the Lon Nol regime, which devastated vast areas throughout the country, often indiscriminately,[10] killing farmers and draft animals and rendering huge areas of croplands unusable.[11]

[9] J. L. Maclean et al. (eds), *Rice Almanac: Source Book for the Most Important Economic Activity on Earth* (3rd edn., Wallingford: CABI Publishing, 2002), at 141; K. A. S. Murshid, *Food Security in an Asian Transitional Economy: The Cambodian Experience*, UNRISD, Working Paper 6 (1998), available online at <https://www.unrisd.org/unrisd/website/document.nsf/(httpPublications)/06D24C68979175DF80256B67005B708D?OpenDocument> (visited 20 November 2020).

[10] T. Owen and B. Kiernan, 'Bombs over Cambodia', *The Walrus* (2006), at 63.

[11] J. A. Tyner, *The Politics of Lists: Bureaucracy and Genocide under the Khmer Rouge* (Morgantown: West Virginia University Press, 2018), at 11–15, and 48 (internal citations omitted).

As the civil war raged on and the bombing campaign intensified, Cambodians flooded into cities, especially its capital, Phnom Penh. Meanwhile, Khmer Rouge insurgents progressively controlled more and more of Cambodia's food-producing agricultural areas. By 1975, residents in the capital suffered from serious food insecurity and were rendered almost completely reliant on food aid delivered by the US military and humanitarian organizations. By 1975, Cambodia's rice production had dropped by 84 per cent compared to the 1970 crop.[12]

B. Famine

The Khmer Rouge won the civil war, taking control of the capital city on 17 April 1975. They established the most ambitious totalitarian regime ever envisaged: referred to in-country as the ominous *Angkar Padevat* (the 'Revolutionary Organization'), it sought to control every aspect of life. Rather than taking steps to reduce food insecurity, the regime enacted a series of policies that deepened the crisis, and produced, and thereafter sustained, nationwide famine. The regime espoused two main policy priorities: national self-reliance and the pursuit of a rapid transformation into a model socialist state.[13] The leadership planned to achieve both by relying on agricultural production, primarily rice, to feed the population and military, and to export in order to fund state projects.[14] Indeed, rice and other raw goods were the only commodities available to the regime that could facilitate engagement in international trade of any sort, as the regime banned markets and money shortly after taking power, and thus lacked any currency of its own.[15]

To achieve its goals, the Khmer Rouge leadership estimated that the nation would need to triple its rice yield, from roughly one tonne of rice produced per hectare, to three tonnes per hectare.[16] It was an impossible feat, especially on the extremely accelerated timetable envisioned by the Khmer Rouge leaders, as outlined in their draft 1976 'Four-Year Plan'.[17] A small, impoverished nation, just emerging

[12] H. J. Nesbitt (ed.), *Rice Production in Cambodia* (Manila: International Rice Research Institute, 1997), at 5; Tyner, see note 11, at 15.

[13] R. C. DeFalco, 'Justice and Starvation in Cambodia: International Criminal Law and the Khmer Rouge Famine', LLM Thesis, *University of Toronto TSpace* (2013) 32–34; P. Chandler, B. Kiernan, and C. Boua (eds and trans), *Pol Pot Plans the Future: Confidential Leadership Documents from Democratic Kampuchea* (New Haven: Yale University Press, 1988); Judgment, *Case 002/01 Trial Judgment* (Doc. E313), Trial Chamber, Extraordinary Chambers in the Court of Cambodia (ECCC), 7 August 2014, (hereafter 'Case 002/01 Trial Judgment') §§ 325, 538, 726 note 2260, 737 note 2310, 755.

[14] On 'standing' on agriculture, see DeFalco, see note 13; Tyner, see note 11, at 48–59.

[15] Tyner, see note 11, at 49 and generally at 48–59; Case 002/01 Trial Judgment, see note 13, at §§ 736–777.

[16] DeFalco, see note 13, at 32–75; Chandler, Kiernan, and Boua, see note 13, at 1–176; see also Case 002/01 Trial Judgment, see note 13, at §§ 604, 736–776.

[17] Chandler, Kiernan, and Boua, see note 13, at 37; D. Chandler, *Voices from S-21: Terror and History in Pol Pot's Secret Prison* (Berkeley: University of California Press, 1999), at 60.

from a brutal five-year civil war, preceded by various other conflicts and roughly a century of colonization, was barely positioned to feed its own population, let alone produce massive rice surpluses sufficient to fund a rapid process of modernization and industrialization.

Regime policies, however, brooked no dissent and were predicated on forced labour under the harshest of conditions. Upon taking power, the new regime forcibly evacuated Phnom Penh and expelled all foreigners, including humanitarian aid organizations, from the country.[18] Beginning in 1976, the leadership exacted large quotas of rice for party use and provided virtually nothing in return to average civilians. The civilian population was systematically overworked in rice fields and on the overhaul of irrigation systems. Children and adults worked long hours with insufficient rest and food rations. Although the precise amount of food provided to the civilian labour force varied throughout the country, generally communal rations consisted of twice daily rations of rice soup. In areas especially hard hit by famine, survivors recall this soup being extremely watery and lacking in salt and proteins. In relatively good areas, salt and small amounts of proteins, such as fish, were provided.[19]

All vestiges of private ownership were abolished, including private cultivation of food in subsistence gardens and ownership of cooking implements. By mid-1977 communal eating was enforced nationwide.[20] Cooking or eating privately was banned. As regime policy dictated that everything in the country, including wild game and other food sources, belonged to *Angkar*, foraging for food was treated as theft.[21] Punishments for such relatively minor offences varied considerably, ranging from relatively light punishments, such as a beatings or brief periods of imprisonment, to torture and execution.[22]

Additionally, sanitation and medical care were woefully lacking. Civilians suffering from starvation and related diseases were viewed as lazy and punished.[23] Civilians had to obtain special permission to go virtually anywhere

[18] Case 002/01 Trial Judgment, see note 13, at § 737.

[19] DeFalco, see note 13, at 64–65; Closing Order, *Case 002* (Doc. No. D427) Office of the Co-Investigating Judges, Extraordinary Chambers in the Court of Cambodia (ECCC), 15 September 2010, (hereafter 'Case 002 Closing Order'), at §§ 338, 341–342, 378–379, 392, 408.

[20] B. Kiernan, *The Pol Pot Regime: Race, Power and Genocide in Cambodia under the Khmer Rouge, 1975–19* (New Haven: Yale University Press, 2008), at 58 ('Communal eating was probably foreshadowed in May 1975, but it was not ordered until 1976.'); Chandler, Kiernan, and Boua, see note 13, at 107; Case 002/01 Trial Judgment, see note 13, at §§ 106, 217.

[21] H. Locard, *Pol Pot's Little Red Book: The Sayings of Angkar* (Chiang Mai: Silkworm Books, 2005), at 277, 83, 183.

[22] Tyner, see note 11; C. Chanda Pheakdey, 'Five Sons in the Khmer Rouge Butchery', 2nd Quarter *Searching for the Truth: Magazine of the Documentation Center of Cambodia* (2007), at 56; K. Cheam aka Kosal, 'My Life During the Pol Pot Regime', 2nd Quarter *Searching for the Truth: Magazine of the Documentation Center of Cambodia* (2005), at 53; Case 002 Closing Order, see note 19, at §§ 365, 379, 479, 524, 542, 560, 578, 602, 653.

[23] Locard, see note 21, at 188–190; S. Em, 'Female Patients', 33 *Searching for the Truth: Magazine of the Documentation Center of Cambodia* (September 2002), at 25 (Interview with Khmer Rouge period survivor named Vanna).

and leaving the country was strictly forbidden.[24] Those who tried to forage or flee and were caught doing so were viewed as potential traitors and hence risked imprisonment, torture, and/or execution.

The existence of famine appears to have become obvious to local actors in various locations by mid-1976 and spread to a nationwide phenomenon by late 1977, at which point evidence suggests that regime leaders were aware of conditions. The Khmer Rouge's top leaders obsessively monitored rice production and demanded regular reports from the countryside.[25] Local leaders directly oversaw worksites and cooperatives where large swathes of the population were obviously in the process of starving. National leaders, including Pol Pot, Nuon Chea, and others also regularly visited worksites in the countryside, including areas where large-scale starvation was occurring.[26] The regime also allocated ration provisions according to the perceived importance of the work being undertaken. For example, child labour units, assigned to hard labour at important irrigation project worksites, were often given much more substantial rations than other segments of the civilian population.

There are a limited number of documents in which members of the Khmer Rouge top leadership obliquely acknowledge or reference the existence of famine and mass starvation. For example, at a December 1976 CPK Party meeting, a senior party official, believed to be Pol Pot himself, discussed the successes and failures of the preceding year. In his speech, the speaker even acknowledges that 'three-quarters of the country has failed [to feed] the civilian population [adequately] and that this affects the health of the people'. These shortfalls, the speaker concludes, would be avoided in the future by adhering more strictly to the political line of the Party, rather than altering the party 'line' in any way, as the CPK leadership still believed in itself 'completely'.[27] Such documents generally demonstrate that the leadership was aware that people were starving, and yet Khmer Rouge leaders continued to collect and export Cambodia's primary foodstuff—rice—while starvation was widespread in the countryside. Additionally, the regime purged individuals, including those at or near the highest echelons of authority, who resisted or critiqued the Party's various famine-inducing policies.[28]

Witness testimony further demonstrates that it was manifestly obvious that civilians were dying by the thousands of starvation. The effects of famine could hardly have gone unnoticed: the Khmer Rouge regime oversaw what is estimated to have been the most severe famine, in terms of the increase in excess death rates

[24] Case 002 Closing Order, see note 19, at § 1393.

[25] Case 002/01 Trial Judgment, see note 13, at § 278 (internal citations omitted); DeFalco, see note 13, at 43–46.

[26] DeFalco, see note 13, at 55–56; Chandler, *Voices from S-21*, see note 17, at 68–70.

[27] Quotations from translated version of document, available in Chandler, Kiernan, and Boua, see note 13, at 182–195.

[28] DeFalco, see note 13, at 53–62.

attributable to famine, since the Irish famine of the nineteenth century, claiming the lives of approximately 10 per cent of the population.[29]

C. Prosecutions

The ECCC were established in 2001; additional agreements with the UN governing international support for it were signed in 2003. The Court has jurisdiction over various domestic and international crimes committed within the territory of Cambodia between 17 April 1975 and 6 January 1979,[30] and is tasked with prosecuting 'senior leaders' and those 'most responsible' for Khmer Rouge-era crimes.[31] As a hybrid court, the ECCC statute blends national and international law, and it applies the Cambodian Penal Code of 2009 for certain procedural and substantive provisions. Starvation as a distinct crime does not feature, instead a prosecution for starvation would need to be channelled through either genocide or crimes against humanity (CAH). Despite the ubiquity of starvation as a harm experienced by the population during the Khmer Rouge period, the ECCC has addressed issues related to famine and starvation in only a limited fashion.

In total, ten suspects were investigated by the ECCC: Kaing Guek Eav alias Duch, Nuon Chea, Khieu Samphan, Ieng Sary, Ieng Thirith, Sou Met, Ao An, Meas Muth, Im Chaem, and Ta Tith. Duch was convicted of various crimes for his role in overseeing S-21 *Tuol Sleng* prison in Phnom Penh in Case 001. In Case 002, which was bifurcated into a series of trials, Nuon Chea and Khieu Samphan were convicted with various crimes in two trials. Ieng Sary, Ieng Thirith, and Sou Met died prior to being tried. It is highly unlikely that the Court will try the remaining suspects as it appears poised to shut down after completing its second Case 002 trial.

Both Cases 001 and 002 referenced instances of starvation under specific conditions, such as at prisons and worksites, in conjunction with forced population transfers, or other narrowly targeted policies against Cham Muslims and Vietnamese-Cambodians.[32] This focus fails to address broader issues of famine

[29] C. Ó Gráda, *Famine: A Short History* (Princeton: Princeton University Press, 2009), at 24 (Table I.I) (comparing the excess death rates of various famines).

[30] Agreement between the United Nations and the Royal Government of Cambodia Concerning the Prosecution Under Cambodian Law of Crimes Committed During the Democratic Kampuchea Period, 6 June 2003, Art. 1 (hereafter 'Agreement'); Law on the Establishment of the Extraordinary Chambers in the Courts of Cambodia for the Prosecution of Crimes Committed during the Period of Democratic Kampuchea (with amendments), doc. no. NS/RKM/1004/006, 27 October 2004, at Arts 1–2 (hereafter 'ECCC Law').

[31] Agreement, see note 30, at preamble, Arts 1, 2(1), 5(3); ECCC Law, see note 30, at Arts 1–2. For an overview of how this requirement has been interpreted in ECCC jurisprudence, see R. C. DeFalco, 'The Uncertain Relationship between International Criminal Law Accountability and the Rule of Law in Post-Atrocity States: Lessons from Cambodia', 42(1) *Fordham International Law Journal* (2018), at 43–44.

[32] See note 30, at §§ 1381–1390.

and starvation nationwide.[33] An opportunity to address these broader issues arose in Case 002. In the Closing Order (indictment equivalent), the Co-Investigating Judges found that

> the policy implemented by the Democratic Kampuchea authorities between 17 April 1975 and 7 January 1979 consisted of a widespread and systematic attack against the entire civilian population of Cambodia.[34]

Given the breadth of this alleged attack, and the specific reference to Khmer Rouge 'policy', starvation-related CAH would appear to be major components of the attack. The Co-Investigating Judges issued indictments for the CAH of enslavement, other inhumane acts (OIAs), and persecution on political grounds, based at least partially on the enforcement of living conditions marked by the denial of adequate food.[35] Most notably, the Order states that

> [r]egarding the *actus reus* [for OIAs], by depriving the civilian population of adequate food, shelter, medical assistance, and minimum sanitary conditions, the CPK authorities inflicted on victims serious mental and physical suffering and injury, as well as a serious attack on human dignity of similar gravity to other CAH.[36]

In its first Case 002 Judgment, the ECCC Trial Chamber focused on the forced evacuation of Phnom Penh in 1975 and other major population transfers from 1975–1977. The Chamber found that in regards to the forced evacuation of Phnom Penh, Khmer Rouge soldiers had committed the CAH of murder, extermination, OIAs, and persecution on political grounds, and that Nuon Chea and Khieu Samphan are responsible for such crimes as members of a joint criminal enterprise (JCE).[37] These findings were based on both the violence committed during the evacuation of the cities and also on the conditions suffered by the evacuees and lack of assistance provided by the regime. Denial of access to food was a major aspect of such enforced conditions:

> The evacuees' journeys were marked by the almost complete absence of food, water, medical care, shelter and hygiene facilities for periods ranging from several days to several weeks. Coupled with the peak of the hot season and duped into believing they would only be gone for several days, many left unprepared and were forced to improvise food and accommodation in the face of a grim situation. In particular, the sick, the injured, the elderly, the pregnant and the young suffered,

[33] See generally, Case 002/01 Trial Judgment, see note 13.
[34] Case 002 Closing Order, see note 19, at § 1350.
[35] Case 002 Closing Order, see note 19., at §§ 1391–1396, 1414–1418, 1434–1440.
[36] Case 002 Closing Order, see note 19, at § 1435.
[37] Case 002/01 Trial Judgment, see note 13, at §§ 553–574.

and countless victims succumbed to the unforgiving conditions throughout the journey. People were also forced to bury their dead children in forests or to abandon their elderly or sick family members by the roadside to a fate of certain death.[38]

Similar conditions were enforced on civilians forcibly relocated throughout Cambodia during the second major population transfer. Again, the Trial Chamber found that Khmer Rouge soldiers committed CAH through both the commission of violence and the enforcement of extremely harsh conditions marked by deprivation and starvation during the second population transfer.[39]

However, on appeal, the Supreme Court Chamber overturned Nuon Chea and Khieu Samphan's extermination convictions, finding that the Trial Chamber had erred in its characterization of the requisite *mens rea* by finding *dolus eventualis* sufficient, and in its assessment of the evidence in terms of the death toll associated with both the evacuation of Cambodia's cities in 1975 and the second population transfer from 1975 to 1977.[40]

The Trial Chamber pronounced its second, and final, Case 002 judgment in November 2018. While the Chamber's written judgment was not released at the time of writing, the Chamber had released a summary of its main findings. This second judgment is notable vis-à-vis famine and starvation in Khmer Rouge-era Cambodia because the charges against Nuon Chea and Khieu Samphan were predicated on their alleged participation in a JCE, the goal of which was 'to implement rapid socialist revolution in Cambodia through a "great leap forward" and to defend the Party against enemies by whatever means necessary'.[41] Moreover, 'in order to achieve this common purpose', Nuon Chea and Khieu Samphan were accused with having 'designed, together with other JCE participants, five policies, the implementation of which resulted in and/or involved the crimes charged in Case 002/02' including, *inter alia*, 'the establishment and operation of cooperatives and worksites'.[42]

While a complete analysis of the Case 002/02 Judgment is beyond the scope of this overview, the Trial Chamber's summary of its findings sheds light on the degree to which famine and starvation are addressed in it. Reference is solely made to periods of 'acute food shortages' rather than any explicit mention of endemic nationwide famine or starvation, although the Chamber notes that people died as a result of food shortages as well as malnutrition.[43] In focusing exclusively on four

38 Case 002/01 Trial Judgment, see note 13, at § 564.

39 Case 002/01 Trial Judgment, see note 13, at §§ 627–657.

40 Appeal Judgment, *Case 002/01* (Doc. No. F36), Supreme Court Chamber, Extraordinary Chambers in the Courts of Cambodia (ECCC), 23 November 2016, (hereafter 'Case 002/01 Appeal Judgment'), §§ 580, 529–562.

41 Summary of Judgment, *Case 002/02*, Trial Chamber, Extraordinary Chambers in the Court of Cambodia (ECCC), 16 November 2018, at § 6.

42 Summary of Judgment, *Case 002/02*, see note 41, at § 6.

43 Summary of Judgment, *Case 002/02*, see note 41, at §§ 14–18.

disparate sites, the Chamber also appears to have found that killings, including presumably those attributable to food shortages and malnutrition, did not reach the scale necessary to establish the elements of extermination as a CAH, opting instead to focus on individual murders.

At the time of writing, the ECCC is in the process of completing its operations. It appears poised to address famine and starvation in Khmer Rouge-era Cambodia in the same way other mass starvation events have been treated within international criminal law practice. That is, through oblique referencing and limited direct engagement rather than any kind of thorough analysis of the full scale and scope of either the famine itself, or the crimes that may have been involved. In the process, what appears to have been a nationwide set of socio-economic policies, enforced through the commission of extreme acts of violence, which directly caused the deaths of at the very minimum, several hundred thousand victims, and brutalized over 6 million more victims, is at risk of being juridically interpreted as the creation of inhumane conditions at specific sites and a selection of individual murders.

3. Ethiopia (1983–1985)

A. Background

Ethiopia provides another case where a government came into power promising to redress injustices and address rural poverty and hunger and ended up committing atrocities and driving its people into famine. The revolution of 1974 overthrew the feudal regime of Emperor Haile Selassie, discredited in part because of failure to prevent and relieve a famine in Wollo province in 1973. The revolutionary government swiftly turned into a military dictatorship, headed by Colonel Mengistu Haile Mariam turning against the idealistic young revolutionaries who had brought it to power. During the 'Red Terror' of 1977–1978, government agents mercilessly repressed political opposition in the cities, killing tens of thousands of young people in a murderous spree. In the rural areas, the military government unleashed its army to suppress provincial rebellions. In some parts of the country the regime's offensives succeeded, reducing liberation fronts in the south to scattered resistance. In the north—Eritrea and Tigray—it failed, and the war intensified over the seventeen years of dictatorship. In the midst of the war, a great famine killed between 500,000 and 1 million Ethiopians.[44]

Rebels defeated the military regime in 1991 and put its senior officials on trial three years later. The trials lasted sixteen years. Despite initial promises to engage with the full range of crimes committed across the country, they focused on the

[44] A. de Waal, *Evil Days: Thirty Years of War and Famine in Ethiopia*, (New York, NY, USA: Africa Watch, 1991).

egregious human rights violations committed during the Red Terror.[45] The prosecutors did not hold officials of the military regime responsible for starvation crimes or for their role in causing the Ethiopian famine. This section explains how the military regime caused the famine and why the post-1994 trials overlooked this fact.

B. Famine and Starvation

The most common explanations for the Ethiopian famine of 1983–1985 attributed it to natural factors such as drought and pest infestations.[46] Some even criticized political explanations as Cold War ploys to discredit communist regimes.[47] However, scholarship on the links between respect for civil and political rights and the occurrence of famine points to the importance of free flow of information and mechanisms for calling governments to account for policy failings and human sufferings.[48] By contrast, authoritarian regimes have limited incentives to prevent natural adversities or economic shocks translating into famine, and may even see famine as a powerful instrument for suppressing resistance. These phenomena were evident in Ethiopia during the 1980s.[49]

It would not be correct to attribute the 1984–1985 famine to an overall food shortage. There was a severe drought, which would have led to hardship in the stricken areas, but famine was not inevitable and the pattern of who starved, when, and where was the result of political decisions. National food production was increasing in the years immediately prior, and the Food and Agriculture Organization (FAO) and the Ethiopian Relief and Rehabilitation Commission (RRC) reported surplus food production in several provinces such as Illubabor, Arssi, and Gojjam.[50] Even in the drought-stricken northern provinces, there were areas of surplus production alongside areas of shortage. Cultural Survival interviewed 227 Ethiopian farmers from the northern provinces who fled to Sudan,

[45] K. Tronvoll, C. Schaefer, and G. Alemu Aneme (eds), 'The "Red Terror" Trials: The Context of Transitional Justice in Ethiopia,' in *The Ethiopian Red Terror Trials* (New York: Boydell & Brewer Inc., 2009), 1–16; G. Alemu Aneme, 'Apology and Trials: The Case of the Red Terror trials in Ethiopia,' *African Human Rights Law* (2006) 64–84.

[46] R. Pankhurst, 'The Ethiopian Famine: Cultural Survival's New Report,' 2(3) *Anthropology Today* (1986) 4–5; R. Kaplan, *Surrender or Starve: The Wars Behind the Famine* (London: Routledge, 1988); G. Kumar, *Ethiopian Famines 1973–985: A Case Study*, Working Paper 26, United Nations University World Institute for Development Economics Research (1987).

[47] Pankhurst, see note 46, 4–5.

[48] A. Sen, *Development as Freedom* (Oxford: Oxford University Press, 1999).

[49] Kaplan, see note 40. De Waal, *Evil Days*, see note 44.

[50] Food and Agriculture Organization of the United Nations (FAO), *The State of Food and Agriculture 1983* (1984), available online at <http://www.fao.org/3/a-ap663e.pdf> (visited 28 September 2018); Kumar, see note 46.

who attested to food surplus.[51] Rainfall data and satellite imagery from the Gondar province in 1983 and from Tembien district in Tigray also indicated a surplus, but restrictions on trade prevented that food from moving to nearby deficit areas.[52]

One set of political causes of famine was that the communist regime implemented misguided economic policies throughout the country. The government levied fixed quotas of grain from farmers and controlled grain prices, rendering farmers destitute.[53] It compelled farmers to abandon their traditional cultivation methods in favour of planned villages.

Another and more substantial set of causes was military. The government pursued a war strategy that drove already fragile rural communities into famine.[54] Between 1978 and 1984, the military regime launched twenty-three armed offensives in northern Ethiopia.[55] Its counterinsurgency strategy had several elements relevant to generating starvation. These included military offensives that destroyed food crops, burned food stores, destroyed farm production capacity (e.g. by killing plough oxen or breaking ploughs), and forcibly displaced villagers; military checkpoints that strangled local trade; aerial bombardment of markets and commercial vehicles in rebel-held areas; restrictions on humanitarian aid including an attempt at a total blockade of relief food to the people living in rebel-held areas; using relief distributions as a magnet to draw hungry people away from their villages to government-controlled camps, and the forced resettlement of over 600,000 rural people from the insurgent area, of whom at least 100,000 died.[56]

The famine as a whole can be considered a crime. Within it there were numerous acts of deliberately depriving civilians of objects indispensable for their survival, with the intent of causing them to move away, surrender, become dependent on government for their sustenance, or die.

The resettlement programme was the best-documented instrumentalization of hunger for military purposes. Officially, the regime portrayed resettlement as a key part of relief efforts, but its primary purpose was to implement the classic counterinsurgency mantra, 'drain the sea to catch the fish'. Occurring in three phases, between 1984 and 1988,[57] the resettlement programme was presented as an ambitious plan to move 1.2 million people residing in the northern highlands in areas

[51] J. Clay, and B. H. Holcomb, *Politics and the Ethiopian Famine 1984–1985* (Cambridge: Cultural Survival Inc., 1986).

[52] De Waal, *Evil Days, see* note 44, at 146–147.

[53] Clay and Holcomb, see note 51; E. Chole, *Underdevelopment in Ethiopia*, Organization for Social Science Research in Eastern and Southern Africa (2004); A. A. Balema, *Economic Development and Democracy in Ethiopia* (Rotterdam: Erasmus University, 2003).

[54] De Waal, *Evil Days*, see note 44; Kaplan, see note 40; D. Korn, *Ethiopia, the United States, and the Soviet Union* (Illinois: Southern Illinois University Press, 1986); D. Woldegiorgis, *Red Tears: War, Famine, and Revolution in Ethiopia* (New Jersey: The Red Sea Press, 1988).

[55] De Waal, *Evil Days*, see note 44.

[56] Kaplan, see note 46.

[57] Kaplan, see note 46, at 211.

stricken by drought to fertile areas in the south and west of the country. It was also an attempt to deplete the able-bodied population of the rebellious northern provinces, separating the people from the rebel groups. Although the regime lacked the resources to achieve this goal, the cadres disseminated false propaganda by telling people they were moving to a better place. Nonetheless, most farmers did not want to abandon their lands and had to be coerced to do so. The cadres rounded up people randomly to fulfil their quota, in the process separating many families. The forced settlers arrived in malaria-infested areas that lacked proper housing. The resettlement camps were not equipped to meet the basic needs of the relocated. Many died of illness, lack of food, shelter, and water; and the absence of the tools and seeds needed to plant and survive on their livelihoods.[58] The military regime fulfilled only half of its resettlement quota and one-fifth of the people resettled died in the process. The US Chargé d'Affairs to Ethiopia, David Korn, reported his exchanges with Ethiopia's leaders that elucidate the military-political motives. According to Korn, Mengistu told a group of diplomats: 'only the able-bodied would be resettled; the old and young would be left in the drought-stricken areas'.[59]

The weaponization of food became apparent to the international community in the context of efforts to provide international aid to the hungry, which transformed into a high-profile issue in the wake of the 1984 Band Aid/Live Aid fundraising concerts. Aware that many—perhaps most—of the hungry people lived in areas controlled by rebel forces, several international donors including the United States provided clandestine cross-border relief aid from Sudan. The Ethiopian government objected strenuously. Korn also relates a conversation with Tibebu Bekele, Ethiopia's acting Foreign Minister, concerning US support for the cross-border relief operation:

> In the course of our exchange, Tibebu blurted out with more candor than he probably intended that 'food is a major element in our strategy against the secessionists.' The Ethiopian army, Tibebu added, tries to cut the rebels off from food supplied. He threatened that it would destroy any food it found being brought into Ethiopia from Sudan . . . .[60]

Despite evidence of manipulation and violent obstruction, international aid became embroiled in the regime's counterinsurgency. The regime's RRC began appealing for international aid in 1980.[61] Foreign donors were initially ready to adopt the story that the famine was caused solely by drought and turn a blind eye to government responsibility for starvation. In retrospect, the willingness of international

[58] J. Young, *Peasant Revolution in Ethiopia: The Tigray People's Liberation Front, 1975–1991* (New York: Cambridge University Press, 2006), at 146.
[59] Korn, see note 54.
[60] Korn, see note 54, at 137.
[61] Woldegiorgis, see note 54.

donors, including the UN, to provide assistance with only modest monitoring and accountability, is remarkable. There is no doubt that international funds were used to support forced resettlement.[62] The government also misused relief aid to supply garrisons that it established during its military offensives and divert aid to feed its soldiers and militiamen, to the extent that some militia were colloquially known as 'wheat militia' on account of how their wages were paid.[63] There was, however, international pressure against the resettlement, and Médecins Sans Frontières (MSF) was expelled after its public exposure of the coercive element of the programme in December 1985.[64]

It was only several years after the famine that detailed investigation into the impact of the government's counter-insurgency policies on food production and transport, marketing, and rural incomes, became possible. Those revealed the extent to which the sustained and comprehensive counter-insurgency suppressed the livelihoods and food security of the areas in which the war was fought. There is no doubt that the military regime turned hardship and stress into mass starvation. The entire famine can be categorized as a crime, committed by a regime determined to stay in power with reckless indifference to the human cost.[65] The lowest credible estimates suggest that 275,000 to 367,000 people died in the 1983–1985 famine.[66] A further 100,000 died during the forced resettlement. The most commonly cited figures for excess deaths are higher, at 1 million, but there are too little good data to come to definitive conclusions about the human toll.

C. Prosecutions

The military regime was defeated in May 1991 by the fighters of the Ethiopian People's Revolutionary Democratic Front (EPRDF). The EPRDF invited political parties in Ethiopia that ratified a national charter to form the transitional Government of Ethiopia (TGE). One of the steps taken by the TGE the following year was to establish the Special Prosecutor's Office (SPO) through Proclamation 22/1992. In parallel, the Eritrean People's Liberation Front took power in Eritrea, which became an independent state following a referendum two years later. There was no process of accountability for past violations in Eritrea.

Proclamation 22/1992 granted the SPO with authority to bring the military regime's officials to justice using the Ethiopian Penal Code, and to preserve an account of atrocities as a means to educate the next generation.[67] The TGE detained

[62] De Waal, *Evil Days*, see note 44.
[63] De Waal, *Evil Days*, see note 44.
[64] De Waal, *Evil Days*, see note 44, at 211–217; de Waal, see note 8.
[65] De Waal, *Evil Days*, see note 44, at 120.
[66] de Waal, *Evil Days*, see note 44, at 173–176, 224–227.
[67] Tronvoll, Schaefer, and Alemu Aneme (eds), see note 45.

around 2,000 officials of the military regime in 1991–1992. Some officials were released on bail—reducing the number of the detainees to 1,300.[68] Trials began in 1994 and lasted for twelve years (1994–2006).

The SPO proceeded by dividing offences into four sets of major crimes: the Red Terror, war crimes, forced relocation, and manipulating food aid.[69] It then divided the defendants into three categories: high-level policy- and decision-makers, mid-level civilian administrators and military commanders, and low-level officials who executed orders on the ground.[70] The charges drew on the 1957 Ethiopian Penal Code (see Table 4.1).[71]

The SPO's plans, reports, and statements from early in the prosecution process indicate that the SPO intended to include charges related to forced resettlement and creating the conditions of famine. For example, a 1994 SPO report, intended to solicit external funding stated:

> The forced resettlement programme consisted of moving hundreds of thousands of peasants from the north of the country to the south. Originally dubbed a famine relief programme, we have evidence of the political nature of the relocation. According to non-government relief organizations, between 15–20 per cent of those resettled died either in transport upon arrival in the resettlement camps. Given that 600,000 people were resettled between 1984–86, about 100,000 people lost their lives due to this governmental policy.[72]

[68] Human Rights Watch Africa, *Ethiopia: Reckoning Under the Law*, 1 December 1994, available online at <https://www.hrw.org/sites/default/files/reports/ethiopia94d.pdf> (visited 30 October 2018).

[69] S. Vaughan, 'The Role of the Special Prosecutor's Office' in Tronvoll, Schaefer, and Alemu Aneme (eds), see note 45, 51–67; HRW/Africa, see note 68.

[70] Alemu Aneme, see note 45.

[71] Perhaps surprisingly the Ethiopian Penal Code 2004 is very progressive for its time, and whereas the Rome Statute was only amended in 2019 to reflect the customary international law that starvation is a war crime in both a non-international armed conflict and international armed conflict. Ethiopia's Criminal Code of 2004, had the following provisions: Art. 270—War Crimes against the Civilian Population. 'Whoever, in time of war, armed conflict or occupation organizes, orders or engages in, against the civilian population and in violation of the rules of public international law and of international humanitarian conventions: (b) Wilful reduction to starvation, destitution or general ruination through the depreciation counterfeiting or systematic debasement of currency; (i) the confiscation, destruction, removal, rendering useless or appropriation of property such as foodstuffs, agricultural areas for the production of foodstuffs, crops, livestock, drinking water installations and supplies and irrigation works, health centres, schools.' Art. 523—Creation of Distress or Famine: '(1) Whoever intentionally, directly or indirectly, creates within the country a grave state of misery, want or famine, epidemic or epizootic disease or distress, especially by improperly hiding or hoarding, destroying or preventing the transport or distribution of grain, foodstuffs or provisions, or remedies or products necessary to the life or health of man or domestic animals, is punishable with rigorous imprisonment not exceeding fifteen years. (2) Whoever, in time of such distress, fails to fulfil, or to fulfil properly, without justification of force majeure, the obligations or liabilities incumbent upon him, whether as a purveyor, middleman, subcontractor, carrier or agent, or in any other capacity, in respect to the delivery or handing over of provisions, remedies or any other products to be used to prevent, limit or arrest the distress, is punishable under sub-art. (1); (3) Where the crime is committed for gain, the punishment shall be rigorous imprisonment not exceeding twenty years, and fine not exceeding one hundred thousand Birr.'

[72] United States Institute of Peace, *Ethiopia: Report of the Office of the Special Prosecutor*, February 1994, available online at <https://www.usip.org/sites/default/files/Ethiopia-SPODossier-2.pdf> (visited 23 October 2018), at 3.

Table 4.1 The charges against the military regime per the 1957 Ethiopian Penal Code

Charges	Penal Code Violated
Public provocation and preparation to commit genocide from 1975 to 1983 against members of political groups dubbed: 'anti-people' and 'reactionaries'	Art. 32 (1)(a) Art. 286(a)
The Commission of Genocide: Murder, Injury (physical/mental), detaining to kill or disappear	Art. 32 (1)(b) Art. 281(a) and (c)
Unlawful Detention: imprisonment under squalid conditions	Art. 32(1)(b) Art. 486
Abuse of Power: illegal confiscation of property and money	Art. 32(1)(b) Art. 414

Source: Aneme (2009, pp. 3–5)

However, it soon became apparent that the prosecutions would focus overwhelmingly on killings conducted during the Red Terror, with only a few prosecutions addressing the conduct of the war, and none focused on starvation as such. The trials were criticized by both parties within and outside the country, but primarily on procedural grounds, concerns about the politicization of the process, or the slow pace. Specific concerns included questions about the rights of the accused, the sometimes haphazard prosecutorial strategy, and the use of trials *in absentia.* The failure to pursue charges related to the famine and resettlement programme received very little attention.

The most significant SPO decision was to frame the charges as acts of genocide. Ethiopia was one of the first states to ratify the 1948 Genocide Convention and the same provisions were incorporated into the Ethiopian Penal Code. The domestic law contains the controversial provision that the protected groups under the definition of the crime of genocide include political groups.[73] This meant that it was possible to prosecute senior officials of the former regime for crimes committed during the Red Terror, which was directed against political groups—initially the members and sympathizers of the Ethiopian People's Revolutionary Party, and subsequently other radical groups opposed to the government. The SPO quoted Article 281 of the 1957 Ethiopian Penal Code in accusing the defendants:

> Art. 281: Whosoever, with the intent to destroy, in whole or in part, a national, ethnic, racial, religious or political group, organizes, orders or engages in, be it in time of war or in time of peace:

[73] M. T. Tessema, *Prosecution of Politicide in Ethiopia: The Red Terror Trials* (Berlin: Springer, 2018), at 191.

(a) Killings, bodily harm or serious injury to the physical or mental health of members of the group, in any way whatsoever; or
(b) Measures to prevent the propagation or continued survival of its members or their progeny; or
(c) The compulsory movement or dispersion of peoples or children, or their placing under living conditions calculated to result in their death or disappearance, is punishable with rigorous imprisonment from five years to life, or in cases exceptional gravity, with death.

Additionally, the SPO quoted Article 32(1)(b) which allows for indirect perpetration, which would have been highly relevant to prosecutions for starvation crimes:

> A person shall be regarded as having committed an offence and punished as such: if (a) he actually commits the offence either directly or indirectly, for example by means of an animal or natural force.

These articles in combination could have been used for prosecuting those responsible for creating famine. However, they were not used in this manner. Rather the SPO came to focus almost exclusively on acts of violence committed during the Red Terror.[74] Those decisions on whom to prosecute and for what crimes were taken on the basis of the ready availability of evidence. Such evidence was ample in the Red Terror cases because the violence was heavily documented by the perpetrators themselves and because survivors and relatives of victims were assiduous in collecting evidence and clamouring for justice. Overwhelmed by documentation, the SPO made some decisions on an *ad hoc* basis. For example, a 1993 SPO report confessed that it made most of the charges 'simply because a particular file cabinet was searched first, as opposed to a policy decision based upon a full understanding of the environment in which the prosecutions would be held'.[75]

Pressure for speedy trials was also a significant factor that reduced the scope of the proceedings, and the possibilities of innovative prosecutorial strategies. From a pragmatic vantage point, the SPO was confident that the thousands of pages of evidence collected on the Red Terror sufficed to obtain convictions for the senior officials and other well-known violators, in a manner that satisfied the demands of victims' families for justice. In fact, since the SPO focused its energy on the Red Terror, some observers called the entire process 'the Red Terror trials'. The court reached a verdict on fifty-five high-level officials of the military regime, whom it charged with genocide.

[74] F. Elgesem and G. A. Aneme 'The Rights of the Accused', in Tronvoll, Schaefer, and Alemu Aneme (eds), see note 45, at 37–41.
[75] Vaughan, see note 69, at 59.

The judges barred all of them from participating in elections or holding public offices. They sentenced forty-eight of the high-level defendants to life imprisonment, two defendants to twenty-five years' imprisonment, and five defendants to twenty-three years of imprisonment.[76] On 4 October 2011, the Ethiopian President pardoned and released sixteen of the senior officials sentenced to life in prison.[77]

A footnote to Ethiopia's limited pursuit of criminal accountability is that the EPRDF government initiated an important step towards international norms of non-indifference to atrocities. After taking power in 1991, the EPRDF leadership considered whether to initiate an inquiry into political responsibilities for famine, including international failures, but decided against because it was a new and fragile government that could not afford to court international controversy. However, following the genocide in Rwanda in 1994, Prime Minister Meles Zenawi took the initiative to propose an International Panel of Eminent Personalities (IPEP) to investigate the genocide and surrounding events, with a view to informing African and international norms and principles for preventing such atrocities happening again. The IPEP report[78] was the foundation for the principle of 'non-indifference', which is the African counterpart of the 'responsibility to protect'. It is enshrined in Article 4(h) of the Constitutive Act of the African Union: 'The right of the Union to intervene in a Member State pursuant to a decision of the Assembly in respect of grave circumstances, namely war crimes, genocide and crimes against humanity.'

4. Bosnia-Herzegovina (1992–1995)

A. Background

Events in Bosnia-Herzegovina from 1992 to 1995 complicate discussion of starvation crimes because in this particular context, no widespread elevation of mortality due to malnutrition (i.e. famine) occurred. Strictly speaking, the law that addresses starvation does not require the outcome of increased mortality, rather it hinges on the interpretation of the 'purpose' of deprivations.[79] The political, legal, and humanitarian responses to the Bosnian conflict largely dismissed the matter of starvation crimes as irrelevant, since almost no-one starved to death. However, there were geographically isolated and context-specific instances of extreme need—including deaths by starvation in detention settings—in the context

[76] G. A. Aneme, 'The Anatomy of Special Prosecutor v. Colonel Mengistu Hailemarriam et al. (1994–2008)', 4(1–2) *International Journal of Ethiopian Studies* (2009) 1–53.

[77] M. Mezgebu, *In Search of Truth*, World Peace Foundation, 8 May 2012, available online at <https://sites.tufts.edu/reinventingpeace/2012/05/08/in-search-of-truth/> (visited 15 July 2019).

[78] African Union, International Panel of Eminent Personalities, 'Rwanda: The preventable genocide', July 2000.

[79] Dannenbaum, see note 4, at 6.

of systematic manipulation of humanitarian aid as an instrument of warfare. The ICTY, mandated to prosecute crimes committed during the 1992–1995 war, prioritized prosecution for incidents involving the commission of relatively large-scale acts of direct, physical violence. Given the scale of torture, rape, and murder that occurred during this conflict, this was a logical approach. Nonetheless, the Tribunal did address multiple instances in which people were deprived of food, water, medicine, and other objects necessary for life, notably in detention settings. It also cracked open the door for considering conditions in the so-called safe havens areas besieged by the Bosnian Serb Army (BSA), while largely leaving unaddressed the matter of whether criminal sanctions should apply to the broader context of using access to food, water, and medicine as a point of tactical leverage in a conflict.

Before the 1990s, the main nutrition issue in the former Yugoslavia was obesity.[80] The war in Bosnia-Herzegovina occurred in the context of the dissolution of the former Yugoslavia. As tensions escalated regarding the political and economic structure of the former Yugoslavia, politicians in the constituent republics and the autonomous region of Kosovo, began asserting claims to independence. The war in Bosnia was the longest and most deadly of the Yugoslav conflicts. It was fought between all three of the major ethnic groups within the country: Bosnian Muslims (43 per cent of the population) (today often referred to as 'Bosniaks'), Bosnian Serbs (31 per cent), and Bosnian Croats (17 per cent).[81] Throughout the conflict in Bosnia, the neighbouring, newly independent countries of Serbia (aka: former Yugoslavia; Serbia and Montenegro) and Croatia provided significant political, military, and economic support to Bosnian Serb and Bosnian Croat political and military leadership (respectively). The Bosnian government forces, which became increasingly dominated by Bosniaks over time, and Bosnian Croats formed a shaky alliance that violently splintered in 1993–1994, resulting in widespread violence against civilians. However, both fighting and targeting civilians overwhelmingly occurred in relation to fighting between the Bosnian Serbs and the Bosnian government, the focus of examples in this case study.

The first multi-party elections occurred in Bosnia in 1990, and the results were dominated by three nationalist political parties: the Serb Democratic Party (SDS: *Srpska Demokratska Stranka*) which aimed to represent the Bosnian Serbs under Radovan Karadžić; the Party of Democratic Action (SDA *Stranka Demokratske Akcije*) which was largely Muslim, and led by Alija Izetbegović; and the Croatian Democratic Union (HDZ: *Hrvatska demokratska zajednica Bosne i Hercegovine*) representing Bosnian Croats under Stjepan Kljuić.

Throughout 1991, the SDS worked to unify and connect areas where it had won elections, created parallel state institutions, like the Assembly of the Serbian

[80] S. Zeć et al., 'Nutrition in Pre-war Sarajevo', 49 *European Journal of Clinical Nutrition* (1995) 6–10.
[81] The remainder of the population self-selected as Yugoslav or other in the 1991 Census.

People of Bosnia-Herzegovina (Bosnian-Serb Assembly), and issued secret orders instructing SDS municipal leaders to take over the municipality and establish a crisis staff either overtly where Serbs formed a majority or covertly where they formed a minority.[82] A referendum on independence was held from 19 February to 1 March 1992. While boycotted by Serbs, the majority of respondents endorsed independence, which was declared by the Bosnian Parliament on 6 March and recognized by the international community. Shortly thereafter, the conflict between armed units loyal to the Bosnian Serb political leadership and those loyal to the Bosnian government began.

On 12 May 1992, as violence escalated, Bosnian Serb leader Radovan Karadžić presented six 'strategic goals' that emphasized separation of Serbs from other nationalities and outlined the geographic claims of their 'Serb Republic', including the division of Sarajevo; the Serbian Parliament then adopted the goals. By the end of August 1992, the Bosnian Serb army (VRS: *Vojska Republika Srpska*), which managed to take control over many resources of the Yugoslav National Army that were positioned in Bosnia, controlled over 70 per cent of Bosnian territory, from which the non-Serb populations were violently displaced, accompanied by killing, rape, torture, and detention.

According to the Research and Documentation Center of Sarajevo, a minimum total of 39,684 civilians and 57,523 soldiers were killed during the 1992–1995 war.[83] These numbers represent people directly killed during the war, not excess mortality, and do not capture the wider range of suffering inflicted on civilian populations: displacement, torture, wounding, and sexual violence, for instance, or the widespread confiscation of property which impoverished large portions of the population.[84] Bosnian Muslims represent the overwhelming number of civilian victims.

B. Starvation Crimes without Famine?

Throughout the conflict, starvation crimes occurred in prisons and in areas under siege. Responsibility ultimately resides with those directly engaged in obstruction.

[82] On 19 or 20 December 1991, the SDS leadership circulated a memo to municipal leaders instructing them to undertake actions to 'enhance the preparedness of the Serbian people and its readiness to defend its interests.' (Judgment, *Krajišnik*, (IT-00-39-T) Trial Chamber, 27 September 2006, §§ 86–99).

[83] Research and Documentation Center Sarajevo, 'Human Losses in Bosnia and Herzegovina 1991–1995', (2008). The data are derived from individual documented deaths and arrived at by cross-checking multiple sources, including family and eyewitness testimony, and diverse other databases, international and national. It is the best-documented minimal number of murders from the war. Demographers from the International Criminal Tribunal for the former Yugoslavia have suggested a slight increase of the number of civilians killed, up to around 40,000.

[84] This background section draws from B. Conley (ed.), *How Mass Atrocities End: Studies from Guatemala, Burundi, Indonesia, the Sudans, Bosnia-Herzegovina, and Iraq* (New York: Cambridge University Press, 2016).

However, international interventions into the conflict, which largely consisted of humanitarian aid, helped shape and produce the context in which aid became a powerful weapon of war. Lacking political consensus on how to respond to the conflict, world leaders found the only policy they could agree on was delivering humanitarian relief to civilians. To this end, the UN authorized the UN High Commissioner for Refugees (UNHCR) as the lead organization, and in June 1992 deployed a UN peacekeeping force (UNPROFOR: United Nations Protection Force), with a mission to *protect the delivery of humanitarian supplies*, not to protect civilians. The mission was altered in 1993, with the creation of the safe haven policy, which expanded UNPROFOR's role to *protect areas at risk* (again, not civilians) of falling to Bosnian Serb military: Sarajevo, Srebrenica, Gorazde, Žepa, Bihać, and Tuzla.

The international prioritization of aid had several impacts. In the first instance, it prevented mass starvation,[85] leaving some critics of the policy to prioritize humanitarian deliveries to refer to Bosnians as the 'well-fed dead'.[86] Secondarily, it produced fundamental dilemmas for humanitarians, whose continued activities were cited by international policy-makers as reason for making concessions with belligerents, despite the fact that aid could not be distributed based on need. As the greatest humanitarian needs were located in areas besieged by Bosnian Serbs, the emphasis on humanitarian access gave advantage to the Bosnian Serbs who could manipulate access in exchange for concessions elsewhere.[87] For the Bosnian government, which began the conflict with a severe military equipment disadvantage, the international emphasis on humanitarian access incentivized maintaining a civilian population in hostile areas as a way to keep control of areas that they otherwise could not defend militarily. Many civilians supported the government aims but not all, and support waivered as conditions worsened. The above points are

[85] J. Vespa and F. Watson, 'Who is Nutritionally Vulnerable in Bosnia-Hercegovina?', 311 *British Medical Journal* (1995) 652–654, at 218. See also F. Watson, 'Why Are There No Longer "War Famines" in Contemporary Europe?', in S. Devereux (ed.), *The New Famines: Why Famines Persist in an Era of Globalization* (London: Routledge, 2007), 269–289. Watson points to pre-war factors that increased the populations resilience: general good health and nutritional status of the population, low rates of infectious disease, an age distribution that favoured 'able-bodied adults' over children and the elderly. She also highlights coping strategies that included cultivating gardens, selling assets, and the black market, among others, as crucial for avoiding mass starvation (at 279).

[86] *New York Times*, 'The Well-Fed Dead in Bosnia', 15 July 1992, available online at <https://www.nytimes.com/1992/07/15/opinion/the-well-fed-dead-in-bosnia.html> (visited 25 August 2021).

[87] M. Cutts, *The Humanitarian Operation in Bosnia, 1992–1995: Dilemmas of Negotiating Humanitarian Access*, UNHCR Working Paper No. 8, Policy Research Unit, 21 May 1999, 14. UNHCR was the lead organization throughout the war. Mark Cutts of the organization's Policy Research Unit, authored a review of the UNHCR's wartime programmes in Bosnia. He notes that the primary difficulty was obstruction by the Bosnian Serbs, and to a lesser degree the Bosnian Croats. UNHCR began the war with a policy of notifications to the armed forces, so that their convoys would not be fired upon. However, over the course of the conflict, the Bosnian Serbs and later Croats (the government had little opportunity for such action, even should it have wanted to do so) treated this as a clearance policy, claiming authority over access.

crucial for understanding how humanitarian aid was politicized and obstructed throughout the conflict.

In detention centres, populations were deprived of objects necessary for life while under the direct and total control of perpetrators. For populations held in detentions camps run by the armed parties in the Bosnian War, severe deprivation of food, water, proper shelter, and medical care was common. Across the country, there were 600 detention sites and camps where around 160,000 people, almost entirely Bosnian nationals, were imprisoned during the war, including 88,000 Bosniak, 12,000 Serb, and 4,500 Croat detainees.[88] The duration of time that civilians were detained and the conditions in which they were kept varied considerably, but almost nowhere were conditions adequate. Detention frequently served as a prelude to forcibly displacing civilians based on religious/ethnic identities. Particularly severe treatment was often reserved for men of fighting age, as a form of punishment and humiliation. For the wider population, deprivation regularly functioned as a mode of persecution, serving the aims of ethnic cleansing by separating out a targeted population and making their lives unbearable so that deportation appeared as their only option. During the process of detaining people and once they were held in camps, deprivation was regularly accompanied by torture, rape, forcible impregnation, and murder.

Areas under siege demonstrated variant patterns of starvation crimes. Here we examine two: Sarajevo and Srebrenica.

C. Sarajevo

Sarajevo, the country's capital, was divided by early 1992 into areas control by the Bosnian government and those controlled by Bosnian Serb forces. Bosnian Serbs held the high ground, surrounded the city, and controlled access into and out of the city. Over the course of the conflict, the city's population shrank from 500,000 to 300,000.[89] For those who remained, the siege was an exhausting experience that exposed them to hardship and terror.

According to the Bosnia-Herzegovina Department of Public Health, over 10,000 people were killed in Sarajevo, with over 75 per cent of these victims dying in 1992 alone.[90] The Bosnian Serbs did not appear to want to destroy the city, but it remains unclear how much of its area they sought to control. More evident was the Serb strategy of terrorizing the city's population as both

[88] E. Skrgic Mikulic, '600 Wartime Detention Sites Identified in Bosnia', *Balkan Investigative Reporting Network*, 13 December 2016, available online at <https://balkaninsight.com/2016/12/13/600-wartime-detention-sites-identified-in-ex-yugoslavia-12-13-2016/> (visited 25 August 2021).

[89] S. Ramet, *The Three Yugoslavias: State-Building and Legitimation, 1918–2005* (Bloomington: Indiana University Press, 2006), at 431.

[90] R. Donia, *Sarajevo: A Biography* (Ann Arbor: University of Michigan Press, 2006), at 334.

a demonstration of power and negotiating tactic.[91] Tactics included bombardment of the city following military or negotiating setbacks, as a way to punish the population in front of the international media, who swarmed to the city,[92] and depriving the population of basic necessities. The BSA targeted the supply of electricity and water. The population was largely reliant on aid, the flow of which the BSA controlled, by dictating the terms of using the key international access point: the airport. In a post-crisis assessment for UNHCR, Mark Cutts writes:

> UNHCR, UNPROFOR and the international community had decided that it was better to have the airlift operating on terms laid down by the Bosnian Serb authorities, than not at all. The problem was that this further empowered the Bosnian Serbs, who turned the tap on and off as they pleased. It gave them enormous leverage over the international community.[93]

Various studies deploying a range of methodologies examined malnutrition (including body mass and micronutrients) in Sarajevo over the course of the war.[94] They found gaps in needs, but no crisis-level deprivation. This raises a question of whether starvation crimes can be said to have occurred based on perpetrators' actions alone, not outcomes for the civilian population. Complicating any response to this question is recognition that the reason there was no mass starvation was international aid that mitigated the negative impacts of Serb military policies.[95]

D. Srebrenica

The siege of Srebrenica presents a different pattern. There, the Serb military sought to displace the entire non-Serb civilian population. Following an initial wave of ethnic cleansing in 1992, Srebrenica was completely surrounded, and its population swelled to an estimated 40,000 Bosnian Muslims, many of whom were displaced people having fled there from towns across eastern Bosnia. The isolated Bosnian Muslim fighters mounted a limited defence, carving out a small zone of Bosnian government-affiliated territory deep within areas claimed by the Bosnian Serb leadership for the Serb Republic.

[91] Donia, see note 91, at 288–289.
[92] Donia, see note 91, at 289–290.
[93] Cutts, see note 87.
[94] N. Andersson et al., 'Childhood Malnutrition during the Bosnian Conflict: Four Linked Cross-sectional Studies', 5(3) *Vulnerable Children and Youth Studies* (2019) 197–207, at 198–199.
[95] Until 1993, when the Bosnian government was able to dig a tunnel under the airport and supply the city.

Through early 1993, the Bosnian Muslim armed forces based in Srebrenica raided neighbouring Bosnian Serb-held towns to supply themselves and the civilian population of Srebrenica with food. By February 1993, the Bosnian Serbs made military advances, further concentrating the Muslim population into the town of Srebrenica and cutting off access to outside supplies and farmlands. At the time, the World Health Organization warned that 'malnutrition and related infections could be responsible for 20–30 additional deaths per day in Srebrenica'.[96] The desperate conditions were only relieved with the April establishment of the 'UN safe haven policy' that was supposed to guarantee that the town's defenders would disarm in exchange for protection from UNPROFR forces stationed there.

The situation again escalated in Spring 1995. On 8 March 1995, Bosnian Serb President Radovan Karadžić issued Operational Directive 7, which commanded VRS forces to tighten access to the enclave, directing:

> the physical separation of the Srebrenica and Žepa enclaves as soon as possible, preventing even communication between individuals between the two enclaves. By planned and well-thought out combat operations, create an unbearable situation of total insecurity, with no hope of further survival or life for the inhabitants of Srebrenica or Žepa.[97]

Blocking aid convoys, the Court continued, 'was also part of the plan'.[98] Coupled with a military offensive in July 1995 and mass killing, this policy successfully led to the deportation of the entire non-Serb populations of Srebrenica and Žepa. In Srebrenica, where tensions between the besieged population (civilian and armed forces) and local Serb forces was already very high, deportation was accompanied by mass executions amounting to genocide. In Žepa, the civilian population and men of fighting age managed to flee without suffering large-scale massacres. This was arguably because, international aid workers accompanied civilians on buses and that men fled on foot in multiple directions rather than as a group, as they had done in Srebrenica.[99]

E. Prosecution

The ICTY was mandated through the United Nations in 1993 to bring to justice those responsible for serious crimes in the former Yugoslavia since 1991. The ICTY addressed conditions of deprivation in several contexts, but always in conjunction

[96] Andersson, see note 95, at 198.
[97] Judgment, *Krstić*, (IT-98-33-T), Trial Chamber, 2 August 2001, §199.
[98] Conley, see note 84.
[99] Conley, see note 84.

with acts of direct violence, killing, raping, and torture; and with caveats pointing to the need for deaths caused by deprivation in order to substantiate charges.

The Tribunal issued a significant number of judgments concerning detention centres, most of which addressed inhumane conditions in the camps, including lack of food, water, sanitation, proper sleeping quarters, and medicine.[100]

Defendants Stanislav Galić and Dragomir Milošević were convicted for crimes that occurred as part of the siege of Sarajevo. These cases demonstrated that the siege disproportionately targeted civilian sites that had no military purpose, and emphasized crimes related to the killing of civilians as part of a campaign of terror. Neither was charged with counts related to the destruction of civilian infrastructure, nor with the obstruction of food aid or other objects indispensable for life. Instead, charges focused on acts of violence: sniping, bombing and otherwise targeting the civilian population of the city. Later trials of Ratko Mladić, the military head of the VRS and Radovan Karadžić, the Bosnian Serb political leader, with being part of a joint criminal enterprise, included similar charges related to Sarajevo.

The conditions of severe deprivation in Srebrenica in 1993, including lack of food, 'appalling' hygienic conditions, absence of running water and medical supplies, were documented by the Tribunal in the Naser Orić case. Orić, who led the Bosnian Muslim forces inside Srebrenica, was charged with war crimes relate to the wanton destruction of cities, towns, or villages not justified by military necessity and with command responsibility for acts of violence against Serb detainees. The conditions of extreme deprivation in Srebrenica were admitted as mitigating evidence on Orić's behalf[101] in relation to charges of plunder as a war crime. However, this understanding of the severity of conditions in Srebrenica in 1993 did not factor into any charges against VRS officials responsible for creating and maintaining those conditions.

The Tribunal addressed the deterioration of conditions in Srebrenica following the issuance of Operational Directive 7 in March 1995 in several judgments, notably confirmed the evidence in the Appeals judgment against Karadžić, which found that:

> following the issuance of Directive 7, humanitarian aid deliveries fell considerably, the conditions in Srebrenica deteriorated to 'disastrous levels', and by the end of June 1995, some residents had died of starvation. According to the Trial Chamber, the restriction of access to Srebrenica, which was implemented by Mladić, allowed Karadžić to maintain control over goods and personnel entering

[100] Including in the ICTY cases against Aleksovski, Banović, Blaškić, Delalić, Delić, Hadžihasanović, Krnojelac, Krajisnik, Kubura, Kvočka et al., Mucić, Nikolic, Prlić et al., Karadžić, Mladić, Sikirica et al, Simić et al., among others.

[101] Judgment, *Orić*, (IT-03-68-T), Trial Chamber, 30 June 2006, §§108 – 115.

> Srebrenica during the period leading to its take-over. The Trial Chamber concluded, partly based on the considerations, that, by the time Directive 7 was issued, Karadžić and Mladić had devised a long-term strategy aimed at the eventual forcible removal of the Bosnian Muslims from Srebrenica through, inter alia, the deliberate restriction of humanitarian aid, and that Karadžić shared the common purpose of and significantly contributed to the Srebrenica JCE.[102]

The starvation conditions in Srebrenica were also recognized as persecution and murder in the Trial Judgment against Radislav Krstić, when the Court noted that 'several persons died from starvation on 7 and 8 July 1995 and a report from the command of the 28th Division, dated 8 July 1995, warned that the civilian population would very soon be forced to flee the enclave if it wished to survive'.[103] Conditions in another safe haven, Žepa, were also considered under the charge of forcible deportation, in terms of how starving and weakening the population created a situation in which they had no choice but to leave.[104]

Despite several important contributions to reviewing evidence of use of starvation as a weapon of war, addressing the intentional deprivation of objects indispensable for life was not a priority issue for the Tribunal. The conflict in Bosnia-Herzegovina could have been a significant context for addressing starvation, notably, whether the crime requires a particular outcome of death within the civilian population, but the Tribunal left this matter for future consideration.

5. Darfur, Sudan, 2003–2008

Darfur is an important case for several reasons. First, it is a case in which starvation crimes were perpetrated on a large scale. Second, the case of Darfur was referred to the ICC by the UN Security Council (resolution 1593, 31 March 2005), and the Prosecutor requested arrest warrants for several senior government officials on charges of war crimes, crimes against humanity, and genocide.[105] Of particular interest in this case is the case made against President Omar al-Bashir, on ten counts of these crimes. For our purposes, the significance of these charges is that crimes explicitly included acts of depriving civilians of items indispensable for their survival, driving them into inhospitable places where they could not survive, and obstructing relief, all of which fall within the compass of starvation crimes. There were significant shortcomings in how the evidence was compiled and the

[102] Judgment, *Karadžić*, (MICT-13-55-A), Appeals Chamber, 20 March 2019, § 565.
[103] *Krstić*, see note 98, at §566.
[104] Judgment, *Tolimir*, (IT-05-88/2-T), Trial Chamber, 12 December 2012, §830.
[105] The OTP also laid charges against three rebel commanders for crimes committed when attacking an African Union peacekeepers base. Those will not be considered here.

analysis constructed, especially with respect to the counts of genocide, but these should not detract from the possibility of a future prosecution reformulating the charges in a more credible manner.

A third reason why Darfur is important is that President Omar al-Bashir was overthrown in April 2019 by Sudanese citizens who, among other things, demanded accountability for the crimes committed during his twenty-nine years in power. Al-Bashir was arrested and detained, and the Transitional Government decided to cooperate with the ICC, as well as bringing charges in national courts. One militia leader, Ali Abd al-Rahman 'Kushayb' handed himself over to the ICC and has been brought to trial in The Hague on charges of war crimes and crimes against humanity. It appears unlikely that the ICC will depart substantially from the pattern of tribunals not addressing starvation as a standalone crime, but a full review of how the ICC treats starvation crimes in Darfur will have to await further developments as the trial proceeds.

A. The Use of Starvation

In response to a rebellion in Darfur that escalated in 2003, the Sudanese government conducted a military campaign according to a well-established template utilized over the previous twenty years, namely using irregular militia recruited from provincial communities to destroy the social and economic base of the insurgents, supported by the army and air force. These militia were supported by military intelligence officers and sometimes by regular army units, motivated by opportunities to loot cattle and other livestock and take over land, and promises of other future rewards from the government. It has been termed 'counter-insurgency on the cheap'.[106] In earlier campaigns mobilized on this basis in southern Sudan and elsewhere in the Sudanese peripheries, this had led to severe famine,[107] and the government's leaders had every reason to expect that in the normal course of events, it would do so again. This had been well-documented and was well-understood by all involved.

The Darfur variant of this counterinsurgency primarily made use of a militia popularly known as *Janjaweed*, drawn from Darfur's nomadic Arab tribes to target entire communities suspected of sympathizing with the rebels. Hundreds

[106] A. de Waal, 'Counter-insurgency on the Cheap', 26 *London Review of Books*, 5 August 2004, 716–725.

[107] D. Keen, *The Benefits of Famine: A Political Economy of Famine and Relief in Southwestern Sudan* (Princeton: Princeton University Press, 1994); A. de Waal, 'Starving out the South', in M. Daly and A. Alsikainga (eds), *Civil War in Sudan* (London: IB Taurus, 1994); A. de Waal, 'Patterns of Violence and Imperfect Endings', in B. Conley-Zilkic (ed.), *How Mass Atrocities End: Studies from Guatemala, Indonesia, the Sudans, Bosnia-Hercegovina and Iraq* (Cambridge: Cambridge University Press, 2016).

of villages were destroyed. Crops and food stores were burned, animals were slaughtered or stolen, fruit trees were cut down or burned, irrigation ditches were broken, presses for cooking oil and flour mills were destroyed. More than 1 million people were driven from their homes, becoming refugees in Chad or seeking relative safety and assistance in camps for internally displaced persons (IDPs) around Darfur's major towns. The principal goal of the Sudanese government was to defeat the rebellion by dispersing the communities that supported the rebels, destroying their material resources, and terrorizing them into submission. That goal intersected with punishing the rebels and their supporters, deterring further insurgency through conspicuous violence and the nomadic groups' agenda of driving villagers off land that they could then take over. Starvation was ancillary to those goals and was inflicted alongside killing, torture, rape, and ransacking. In one village (Keilak, in early 2004), the militia mounted a starvation siege, causing exceptionally high death rates,[108] but were persuaded to relent after intervention by the UN and government officials.

B. The Outcome of Starvation Crimes

The best estimates are that 30,000 people died in direct violence and approximately 200,000 died from the effects of hunger, disease, and displacement.[109] Violent killing dramatically reduced in April 2004 following a 'Humanitarian Ceasefire Agreement' facilitated by the African Union, while the famine-related deaths peaked in June that year and fell away more slowly. A prompt and very large international humanitarian relief operation meant that nutrition and mortality rates among the affected population, especially in IDP camps, had returned to normal levels by mid-2005 and fluctuated thereafter, with some places relatively well provided and others undergoing much more serious deprivation. The government imposed many restrictions on humanitarian aid, and interfered with agencies that it suspected of supporting the rebel cause or were involved in documenting violations of human rights. Smaller and more remote communities were often cut off from aid for long periods and people suffered life-threatening shortages of food and medicine. Sometimes, government actions to restrict relief were aimed as much at punishing international agencies as harming the recipients of their assistance. Following the issuing of the ICC arrest warrant against President al-Bashir

[108] J. Flint and A. de Waal, *Darfur: A New History of a Long War* (London: Zed Books, 2008), at 146.

[109] D. Guha-Sapir and O. Degomme, *Darfur: Counting the Deaths: Mortality Estimates From Multiple Surveys*, Brussels: Centre for Research on the Epidemiology of Disasters (2005), available online at <http://hdl.handle.net/2078.1/179719> (visited 25 August 2021); US General Accountability Office, 'Darfur Crisis: Death estimates demonstrate severity of crisis, but their accuracy and credibility could be enhanced' (2006), available online at <https://www.gao.gov/products/GAO-07-24> (visited 25 August 2021).

in March 2009, the government expelled thirteen international non-governmental organizations (NGOs) and revoked the licenses of three local NGOs, accusing them of violating their humanitarian mandates by, for example, false reporting and cooperating with the ICC.[110] Sufficient warning had been given of this action that most of those NGOs had made plans to hand over their operations to other agencies, reducing the negative impact.

The main specific allegation made against the international NGOs was that they were said to have gathered (allegedly, fabricated) evidence on sexual violence. The recriminations levelled against the humanitarians focused on this and not on the starvation crimes listed in the application for an arrest warrant. We may speculate that one reason for the government's focus on rape rather than starvation was that it was a higher-profile and more sensitive issue in the public realm. A second reason was perhaps because the humanitarians publicly took the side of the government of Sudan against the prosecutor on the issue of hunger, refuting his claims that the population of the IDP camps was being eradicated by starvation. Overall, while there were numerous cases of obstruction of relief to the affected population in Darfur, there was no wholesale blockade. The humanitarian operation was remarkably effective, especially in light of logistical and security problems and continuous harassment by officialdom.

C. The ICC Approach to Prosecution, 2008

The ICC Office of the Prosecutor compiled evidence for mass atrocities including killings, sexual violence, torture, forced displacement, and starvation. It considered the whole of Darfur to be a crime scene. The first two arrest warrants were issued for a militia leader, Ali Kushayb, and a government minister who had coordinated the government's 'Darfur desk', Ahmed Haroun. The charges focused on direct responsibility for specific incidents of large-scale killing of civilians. The prosecutor's public application for an arrest warrant against President al-Bashir, announced and dated July 2008 and published two months later, was much more significant in every respect, and ignited huge controversy.[111] Most of the debate swirled around the wisdom of seeking to arrest a sitting head of state at a time of unresolved conflict (the peace versus justice argument) and ongoing humanitarian operations (the life-saving aid versus accountability argument). The application expanded the scope of the crimes from individual incidents to Darfur in its entirety during the whole period of the conflict and the preparation for it. A less-noticed discussion

[110] Humanitarian Aid Commission, 'Humanitarian Situation in Sudan' (2009), Khartoum: Ministry of Humanitarian Affairs, at 4.

[111] Public Redacted Version of the Prosecutor's Application under Article 58, *Situation in Darfur, the Sudan* (ICC-02/05), Pre-Trial Chamber I, 14 July 2008 (hereafter 'Prosecutor's Application').

focused on the nature of the evidence and analysis put forward by the prosecutor, Luis Moreno Ocampo.

The prosecutor alleged that al-Bashir had implemented the genocide of the African tribes of Darfur through a two-stage plan. The first stage was the active war of 2003–2005, during which there were numerous well-substantiated incidents of large-scale killing, torture, rape, and destruction of objects indispensable for the survival of the population. The prosecution claimed that President al-Bashir directly perpetrated these crimes with genocidal intent.

Had the prosecutor limited his ambition to charges of war crimes and crimes against humanity, including acts that qualify as starvation crimes under the definition used in this volume, he would have had a strong case. However, by developing a socio-political theory of genocide, the prosecutor undermined his credibility. He imputed a grand genocidal plan to al-Bashir, claimed that the accused had absolute control over a totalitarian state apparatus and had, over more than a decade, engaged in systematic planning for eradicating Darfur's African tribes.[112] No scholar of Sudan could take this seriously:[113] the patterns of violence and deprivation are properly understood against the long history of government conduct of counter-insurgency in different parts of the country, resorting to indiscriminate violence more out of weakness than strength.

Equally problematically, the prosecutor argued that the second stage of President al-Bashir's genocidal plan unfolded in the IDP camps during 2005–2008, and was indeed ongoing at the time of the application for an arrest warrant. Moreno Ocampo alleged that the confinement of the African tribes to these camps was the concluding part of a plan to exterminate them. He included the charge of 'hindering of humanitarian aid to persons displaced—subjecting members of each target group to protracted malnutrition and lack of medical care'.[114] Having cited (in an unsystematic manner) some cases of relief obstruction and some statistics for malnutrition and mortality, he noted also that 'the humanitarian operation in Darfur was the world's largest'.[115]

The demographic and health data for the displaced population indicate that nutrition and death rates had fallen to pre-conflict levels by 2006, such that the population size was in fact increasing.[116] The prosecutor's claims about ongoing levels of attacks against displaced people, systematic obstruction of humanitarian aid, and

[112] Prosecutor's Application, see note 113, at §40, §§250–346, and §373.

[113] A. de Waal, 'A Critique of the ICC Prosecutor's Case against President Bashir', *Making Sense of Darfur/African Arguments*, 27 January 2009, available online at <https://sites.tufts.edu/wpf/files/2020/12/Bashir-public-application-critique-d6-250109.pdf> (visited 25 August 2021).

[114] Prosecutor's Application, see note 113, at §§185–198.

[115] Prosecutor's Application, see note 113, at §192.

[116] Darfur would therefore be an unusual instance of genocide in which the size of the targeted population was larger at the end of the genocide than at the beginning, and growing normally. This would not, in itself, disprove genocidal intent, though it would at minimum indicate the lack of capacity to carry it out.

consequently highly elevated death rates in the camps were not supported by evidence and were contradicted by the UN, African Union, and relief agencies.[117] One prominent humanitarian leader dismissed the argument as 'insane'[118] and many feared that a prosecution mounted on this basis would most probably result in the acquittal of al-Bashir—an end result that his critics did not desire.[119] A potentially seminal legal case of identifying and prosecuting atrocity crimes including starvation was undermined by the prosecutor's casual approach to facts and analysis, which probably stemmed from his evident enjoyment of the publicity that came from consorting with the celebrities who supported the Save Darfur campaign. The possibilities and pitfalls of the prosecution remained moot, however, while al-Bashir remained in power, defying the arrest warrant.

D. Opportunities for Prosecuting Starvation Crimes in Darfur

The scope and ambition of the charges against al-Bashir require that a prosecutor consider starvation within the elements of war crimes and crimes against humanity, and there is plentiful evidence for such crimes having been perpetrated. Moreover, such a prosecution would be an opportunity to set precedents that clarify crucial elements in the law.

The case of the siege of Keilak, which appeared intended to inflict death by starvation on the inhabitants of the town, is a documented extreme case. The starvation tactics used in this case included the denial of activities indispensable for the survival of the population, such as the ability to move freely to get access to markets, to gather wild foods from the bush, and to seek charitable assistance from other communities and from aid agencies. Some of these activities and objects (e.g. wild roots, berries, and grasses) were not indispensable in normal times but became so during times of hardship and distress.[120] More widely, the counter-insurgency included destruction of the means of survival of members of the target groups[121] and their forcible displacement into inhospitable terrain.[122] There were

[117] US General Accountability Office, see note 111; R. Brauman, 'Darfur: The International Criminal Court is Wrong', MSF Crash, 10 September 2010, available online at <https://www.msf-crash.org/en/publications/rights-and-justice/darfur-international-criminal-court-wrong> (visited 25 August 2021).

[118] R. Brauman, 'The ICC's Bashir Indictment: Law Against Peace', World Politics Review, 23 July 2008, available online at <https://www.worldpoliticsreview.com/articles/2471/the-iccs-bashir-indictment-law-against-peace> (visited 25 August 2021).

[119] A. de Waal, 'A Critique of the ICC Prosecutor's Case Against President Bashir', African Arguments, 27 January 2009, available online at <https://africanarguments.org/2009/01/a-critique-of-the-icc-prosecutors-case-against-president-bashir/> (visited 25 August 2021).

[120] Chapter 7 in the current volume.

[121] Prosecutor's Application, see note 113, at §§ 172–173 and §§199–208.

[122] Prosecutor's Application, see note 113, at §§177–178.

numerous incidents of obstruction of relief assistance in violation of the Geneva Conventions, though these did not add up to the wholesale denial of assistance to the entire population.

In April 2019, the overthrow of al-Bashir by citizens' actions, and his subsequent arrest and imprisonment, revived the possibility of a path-breaking prosecution. The Transitional Government in Sudan convicted al-Bashir on charges of corruption under domestic law. It also indicated its willingness to cooperate with the ICC, though this option vanished with a military coup in October 2021. In framing charges against the militia leader Ali Kushayb the prosecutor followed well-trodden paths. Of the 31 counts of war crimes, two were pillage and destruction of the property of an adversary as war crimes.[123] The trial opened in April 2022. It would be eminently feasible for the court to include reference to destruction of OIS, and in doing so it would set an important precedent in ICL, clarifying some of the outstanding questions over criminal responsibility for starvation.

6. Conclusion

The situations discussed in this chapter are far from the only ones that have been, to some extent, addressed in international fora. Important formal international investigations have revealed strong evidence of intentional creation of mass starvation in Somalia, Nigeria, North Korea, Venezuela, and, as discussed in later chapters, Yemen, South Sudan, and Syria, and significant use of deprivation of basic needs in other contexts, notably the Gaza blockade and sanctions against Iraq.

Prosecutions are a limited tool. The degree to which they deter new acts of violence, foster reconciliation, or provide solace to victims remains unclear. However, criminal proceedings provide extensive reviews of the evidence and convict individuals. In so doing, they contribute to social and political narratives about the past. Further, and perhaps most importantly, they sanction acts, and thereby alter public conversation about what can and cannot be justified.

Each the above situations involved the weaponization of objects indispensable for life as a crucial part of perpetrators' strategic and tactical aims. While circumstances differed in each of these scenarios, each case makes clear that over time leaders became aware of the impact of their policies and decided not only to continue them but to reinforce them. All four also provide examples of how prosecutors have missed opportunities to apply existing laws to real-world famine

[123] ICC, Pre-Trial Chamber II, Corrected version of 'Decision on the confirmation of charges against Ali Muhammad Ali Abd-Al-Rahman ('Ali Kushayb')', 9 July 2021, ICC-02/05-01/20-433, 23 November 2021, §91 and §94.

and starvation events. Without question, prosecuting starvation crimes presents distinct challenges: the relationship between acts that create starvation and pre-existing conditions, distinctions between poor policy and criminal acts, and establishing intent, are examples of such challenges. However, as is demonstrated in subsequent chapters, these challenges are far from insurmountable. Failing even to try leaves acts of enormous harm unsanctioned.

PART II
THE LAW

This section provides a comprehensive overview of international law as it applies to deliberate starvation. It begins with a survey of International Criminal Law and International Humanitarian Law as each addresses starvation. The analysis aims to provide a roadmap for practitioners to ensure better international recognition of deliberate starvation as an international crime or violation, in order that attribution of fault and accountability become less elusive. Human Rights law offers another avenue, addressed through a focus on the right to food and human rights-based obligations, which impose clear duties on states with respect to the rights to food and be free from hunger. Both chapters argue that, despite important caveats and lacunae, there is ample room within existing legal regimes to address the individual and state responsibility for creating and sustaining conditions in which people are starved.

5

A Comprehensive Review of Existing IHL and ICL as it Relates to Starvation

Wayne Jordash QC, Catriona Murdoch, and Joe Holmes

1. Introduction

The pathway to a successful international criminal prosecution for the crime of starvation is entirely untrodden. The intersection of this crime with a wide range of other, more familiar violations also remains broadly unexplored.[1] Yet the recurrent use of starvation in conflict and the associated scale of suffering and death as a result is unprecedented in modern history. It leaves wounds well beyond the rising death tolls, significant intergenerational physical and cognitive harm,[2] economic repercussions,[3] instability and mass displacement[4]—to mention just a few.

In light of the re-emergence of famine and rise in the deliberate use of starvation, the United Nations Security Council (UNSC) responded by unanimously passing S/RES/2417 (UNSC 2417), which underscored that the deliberate use of starvation as a method of warfare is a war crime, and implored member states to investigate robustly and, where appropriate, seek accountability. Two years on from this landmark consensus much has changed: the legal landscape, with the historic amendment to the Rome Statute ensuring that the crime of starvation is a crime in

[1] Global Rights Compliance jointly with the World Peace Foundation lead a project entitled Mass Starvation: Testing the Limits of the Law, supported by the Netherlands Ministry of Foreign Affairs, see <http://www.starvationaccountability.org>. Launched in June 2019 were a compendium of expert policy papers entitled 'Accountability for Mass Starvation: Testing the Limits of the Law' (GRC-WPF Starvation Compendium) these will foreshadow the publication of the forthcoming starvation textbook, the first authoritative assessment of starvation for practitioners in international law, policy-makers and related humanitarian actors.

[2] N. M. Zagre and G. Quince, 'Child hunger and its long-term effects', UNICEF connect, 24 September 2014, available online at <https://blogs.unicef.org/blog/child-hunger-and-its-long-term-effects/> (visited 20 March 2019); P. E. Kamper, 'Independent and Additive Association of Prenatal Famine Exposure and Intermediary Life Conditions with Adult Mortality between Age 18–63 Years', 119 *Social Science & Medicine* (2014) 232–239.

[3] Kamper, see note 2, at 1; 'The social and economic consequences of malnutrition in ACP countries', Background document, (European Parliament) available online at <http://www.europarl.europa.eu/meetdocs/2009_2014/documents/acp/dv/background_/background_en.pdf> (visited 20 March 2019); see also 'Famine Action Mechanism (FAM)', (The World Bank) available online at <http://www.worldbank.org/en/programs/famine-early-action-mechanism> (visited 18 July 2019).

[4] See this chapter, section 4.

Wayne Jordash QC, Catriona Murdoch, and Joe Holmes, *A Comprehensive Review of Existing IHL and ICL as it Relates to Starvation* In: *Accountability for Mass Starvation*. Edited by: Bridget Conley, Alex de Waal, Catriona Murdoch, and Wayne Jordash QC, Oxford University Press.
DOI: 10.1093/oso/9780192864734.003.0005

both a non-international and an international armed conflict (IAC);[5] international courts and accountability mechanisms have begun to consider the crime of starvation;[6] international scholars debate starvation more frequently,[7] an increased international momentum surrounding the sustainable development goals (SDGs), with just ten years to go to achieve zero hunger; and, more profoundly, globally we are grappling with a 'new normal' as we confront COVID-19. Famines of 'biblical proportions' have been forecast and a 'hunger pandemic' which will catastrophically compound the effect of COVID-19.[8] Amidst these changes, there remains a consensus that conflict remains the driving force behind food insecurity and accountability is essential to its prevention.[9]

[5] Art. 8(2)(e)(xix) of the Rome Statute was unanimously adopted in December 2019 following a two-year campaign by the Government of Switzerland to amend the law and close the accountability gap.

[6] GRC have engaged closely with the UN Office of the High Commission of Human Rights (OHCHR) Group of Eminent Experts on Yemen since the inception of its mandate in 2018, including providing training, advice, and legal submissions on starvation. Over the last two years there has been a measurable increase in their reports on the investigation and reporting on starvation; The UN OHCHR Commission in Human Rights in South Sudan have also increased their investigation and reporting on starvation, with a standalone starvation report due to be released in 2020; the prospects of accountability before the ICC following ICC ruling on jurisdiction in Bangladesh and the decision to constitute a Pre-Trial Chamber to consider an investigation into the situation in the People's Republic of Bangladesh/Republic of the Union of Myanmar offers an opportunity for the ICC to investigate the reports of deliberate starvation deployed against the Rohingya. Decision on the constitution of Pre-Trial Chamber III and on the assignment of the situation in the People's Republic of Bangladesh/Republic of the Union of Myanmar, (ICC-01/19-1), Presidency, 25 June 2019. Decision on the Prosecution's Request for a Ruling on Jurisdiction Under Article 19(3) of the Statute, (ICC-RoC46(3)-01/18-37), Pre-Trial Chamber I, 6 September 2018, § 53. This links to the Republic of the Gambia which filed its submissions in November 2019 at the International Court of Justice (ICJ) against Myanmar for alleged violations of the Genocide Convention. Citing reports of the UN Special Rapporteur, Committee on the Elimination of Discrimination against Women and the UN Fact-Finding Missions, Gambia argued that 'to implement its policy of forced starvation of the Rohingya group, Myanmar has engaged in widespread confiscation of agricultural lands on which the Rohingya grow subsistence crops essential to their survival' and that the Rohingya population still present in Myanmar is in grave danger of further genocidal acts and continue to 'face daily threats of death, torture, rape, starvation and other deliberate actions aimed at their collective destruction, in whole or in part'. (§§ 104, 131), see <https://www.icj-cij.org/files/case-related/178/178-20191111-APP-01-00-EN.pdf> ; See also Chapter 7 and Chapter 10 in this volume, for more detail on the increase in international investigations and accountability for starvation.

[7] D. Akande and E.-C. Gillard, 'Conflict Induced Food Insecurity and the War Crime of Starvation of Civilians as a Method of War', 17 *Journal of International Criminal Justice* (2019) 753–779; T. Dannenbaum, 'Encirclement, Deprivation, and Humanity: Revising the *San Remo Manual* Provisions on Blockade', 97 *International Legal Studies* (2021) 307–394; T. Dannenbaum, 'Siege Starvation: A War Crime of Societal Torture', 22 *Chicago Journal of International Law* (2022) 1–73; T. Dannenbaum, 'Criminalizing Starvation in an Age of Mass Deprivation in War: Intent, Method, Form, and Consequence', *Vanderbilt Journal of Transnational Law*(forthcoming), available at https://papers.ssrn.com/sol3/papers.cfm?abstract_id=3953922>. M. Nijs, 'Humanizing Siege: Applying the Principle of Proportionately to Sieges', 102 *International Review of the Red Cross* (2020) 683–704. See also essays in A. Coco, J. Hemptinne, and Brian Lander (eds), 'Special Issue on Starvation in International', 17 *Journal of International Criminal Justice* (2019).

[8] United Nations World Food Programme, 'WFP Chief warns of hunger pandemic as COVID-19 spreads (Statement to UN Security Council)', 20 April 2021, available online at <https://www.wfp.org/news/wfp-chief-warns-hunger-pandemic-covid-19-spreads-statement-un-security-council> (visited 1 October 2021).

[9] United Nations, 'As famines of "biblical proportion" loom, Security Council urged to "act fast"', 21 April 2020, available online at <https://news.un.org/en/story/2020/04/1062272> (visited 1 October 2021); Norwegian Refugee Council, 'Briefing on Protecting Civilians affected by Conflict-induced

The existing momentum therefore suggests that the problem is not that states fail to recognize that using starvation as a method of warfare is an international crime, or that international law obliges them to investigate and take appropriate penal action when violations occur. The problem seems to suggest, perhaps, a lack of understanding of the contours of the crime and how it may be successfully prosecuted.

This chapter comprises two principal sections:

(i) Law: including an analysis of the elements of the war crime of starvation and its IHL underpinning.
(ii) Practice: entailing a discussion on the potential strategies for prosecuting the crime, including an overview of some of the modes of liability, the chain of causation, and how intent may be inferred in particular scenarios.

It then concludes by arguing that prosecutions and international accountability play a significant role in rendering deliberate starvation morally toxic, an essential aim if we are to begin the journey towards starvation being deemed a medieval practice with no justifiable or lawful use in modern warfare.

2. The Law

A. The Development of the Legal Prohibition

The Hague Regulations concerning the Laws and Customs of War on Land (18 October 1907), began a slow process of restraint and moderation, limiting the destruction of the enemy's property to cases of imperative military necessity.[10] Some twelve years later, in 1919, we find one of the earliest references to starvation as a prosecutable crime.[11]

Despite these early flashes of recognition, starvation of civilians was not criminalized during the Nuremberg Trials.[12] However, shortly after the Second World

Hunger', 21 April 2020, available online at <https://www.nrc.no/resources/briefing-notes/briefing-on-protecting-civilians-affected-by-conflict-induced-hunger/> (visited 1 October 2021).

[10] Convention (IV) respecting the Laws and Customs of War on Land and its annex: Regulations concerning the Laws and Customs of War on Land, (The Hague, 18 October 1907), available online at <https://ihl-databases.icrc.org/ihl/INTRO/195> (visited 4 October 2019).

[11] 'Commission on the Responsibility of the Authors of the War and on Enforcement of Penalties—Report Presented to the Preliminary Peace Conference, 29 March 1919', 14 *American Journal of International Law* (1920) 95–154, at 144.

[12] Including analysis that starvation should be considered as a form of genocide by R. Lemkin, *Axis Rule in Occupied Europe* (Washington, DC: Carnegie Endowment for International Peace, 1944); *United States v. Wilhelm von Leeb ('High Command Case')* in *Trials of War Criminals Before the Nuremberg Military Tribunals Under Control Council Law No. 10, October 1946–April 1949*, Volume X (1950), 563 (hereafter the '*United States v. W. von Leeb*') Despite expressing significant unease with the state of the

War, the legitimacy and legality of starvation as a method of warfare began to be challenged with the enactment of the Geneva Conventions.[13] The prohibition of deliberate starvation of the civilian population as a method of warfare was introduced in the Additional Protocols to the Geneva Conventions of 1977,[14] in Article 54(1) of Additional Protocol I (AP I) and Article 14 of Additional Protocol II (AP II), rendering it unlawful for parties to starve civilians both in IACs and non-international armed conflicts (NIACs),[15] a development considered by some as 'one of the great achievements' of the Additional Protocols.[16]

Under AP I and AP II, it is prohibited to attack, destroy, remove, or render useless objects indispensable to survival (OIS). AP I and AP II provide non-exhaustive examples of OIS including 'foodstuffs, agricultural areas for the production of foodstuffs, crops, livestock, drinking water installations and supplies and irrigation works'.[17]

In order to qualify as starvation, the attack, destruction, removal, or rendering useless of the OIS has to be carried out with 'the specific purpose of denying them for their sustenance value to the civilian population or to the adverse Party, whatever the motive, whether in order to starve out civilians, to cause them to move away, or for any other motive'.[18]

law, the judges stated: 'The propriety of attempting to reduce it by starvation is not questioned. Hence the cutting off every source of sustenance from without is deemed legitimate ... We might wish the law were otherwise, but we must administer it as we find it.'

[13] Geneva Convention for the Amelioration of the Condition of the Wounded and Sick in Armed Forces in the Field, 12 August 1949 (hereafter the 'First Geneva Convention' or 'GC I'); Geneva Convention for the Amelioration of the Condition of Wounded, Sick and Shipwrecked Members of Armed Forces at Sea, 12 August 1949 (hereafter the 'Second Geneva Convention' or 'GC II'); Geneva Convention relative to the Treatment of Prisoners of War, 12 August 1949 (hereafter the 'Third Geneva Convention' or 'GC III'); Geneva Convention Relative to the Protection of Civilian Persons in Time of War, 12 August 1949, (hereafter the 'Fourth Geneva Convention' or 'GC IV'). See also obligations under Art. 23 GC IV and Art. 17 GC IV.

[14] Protocol Additional to the Geneva Conventions of 12 August 1949, and relating to the Protection of Victims of International Armed Conflicts 8 June 1977 (hereafter the 'Additional Protocol I' or 'AP I'); Protocol Additional to the Geneva Conventions of 12 August 1949, and relating to the Protection of Victims of Non-International Armed Conflict, 8 June 1977 (hereafter 'Additional Protocol II' or 'AP II').

[15] With regard to NIACs which do not fall into the definition of Art. 1(1) AP II, and are therefore only regulated by Common Art. 3, the prohibition of starvation is included in the obligation to treat humanely all persons taking no active participation in the hostilities, included in para. 1 of said article.

[16] Y. Sandoz, C. Swinarski, and B. Zimmermann (eds), *Commentary on the Additional Protocols of 8 June 1977 to the Geneva Conventions of 12 August 1949* (Leiden: Martinus Nijhoff Publishers, 1987) 653, at 2087.

[17] Commentary to Rule 54, ICRC Customary IHL Database (2005), at 186, available online at <https://www.icrc.org/en/doc/assets/files/other/customary-international-humanitarian-law-i-icrc-eng.pdf> (visited 20 March 2022).

[18] Art. 54(2) API and Art. 14 APII. Two exceptions to this prohibition are listed under Art. 54(3) API when the OIS are used by an adverse Party: (1) as sustenance solely for the members of its armed forces; or (2) if not as sustenance, then in direct support of military action, provided, however, that in no event shall actions against these objects be taken which may be expected to leave the civilian population with such inadequate food or water as to cause its starvation or force its movement.

Rules 54 to 56 of customary IHL are a corollary to the prohibition of starvation of civilians as a method of warfare in both IACs and NIACs. This includes attacking OIS of the civilian population (Rule 54) and denying access of humanitarian aid intended for civilians in need, including deliberately impeding humanitarian aid (Rule 55) or restricting the freedom of movement of humanitarian relief personnel (Rule 56).

From the point of the Additional Protocols, the status of the IHL prohibition was accepted and considered firmly to be part of customary law,[19] leading to the recognition that its violation amounted not only to a gross affront to the protection of civilians in armed conflict but also an international crime.[20] Notwithstanding this significant development, debate remained about the practical protection these laws would offer civilians.[21]

1. Article 8(2)(b)(xxv) and Article 8(2)(e)(xix) of the Rome Statute

The Rome Statute entered into force in 2002, featuring for the first time on the international level the war crime of starvation (noting the crime did not feature in either the UN *ad hoc* tribunals created to prosecute crimes committed during the Rwandan genocide and the Yugoslavia war). Article 8(2)(b)(xxv) of the Rome Statute criminalizes '[i]ntentionally using starvation of civilians as a method of warfare by depriving them of objects indispensable to their survival, including wilfully impeding relief supplies as provided for under the Geneva Conventions'.

Following the government of Switzerland's proposal to amend the Rome Statute to close the illogical accountability gap, removing the distinction between the two conflict designations and enabling the deliberate use of starvation as a method of

[19] Rule 53, ICRC Customary IHL Database, available online at <https://ihl-databases.icrc.org/customary-ihl/eng/docs/v2_rul_rule53> (visited 20 March 2022). See also Rule 54 available online at <https://ihl-databases.icrc.org/customary-ihl/eng/docs/v2_rul_rule54> (visited 20 March 2022) on attacks against objects indispensable to survival; EECC, Partial Award: Western Front, Aerial Bombardment and Related Claims, 19 December 2005, §§ 104–105, available online at <http://legal.un.org/riaa/cases/vol_XXVI/291-349.pdf> (visited 20 March 2022).

[20] For a general overview on IHL and starvation see J. Pejic, 'The Right to Food in Situations of Armed Conflict: the Legal Framework', 83 (844) *International Review of the Red Cross* (2001) 1097–1109; D. Akande and E. Gillard, 'Conflict-induced Food Insecurity and the War Crime of Starvation—The Underlying Rules of International Humanitarian Law', 17(4) *Journal of International Criminal Justice* (2019) 753–779; ICRC, War Crimes: *Working Paper Prepared by the ICRC for the United Nations Preparatory Committee for the Establishment of an International Criminal Court* (1997) 1 May 2004; *Reports of International Arbitral Awards, 'Eritrea Ethiopia Claims Commission—Partial Award: Western Front, Aerial Bombardment and Related Claims*, UN Doc, Vol. XXVI, 291–349, at 104–105; see also J.-M. Henckaerts and L. Doswald-Beck (eds), *Customary International Humanitarian Law ('ICRC Customary IHL Database')*, Vol. I (Geneva: ICRC, 2005), Rule 54, at 186. Noting that the prohibition does not feature as a grave breach in Art. 85 AP I.

[21] C. A. Allen, 'Civilian Starvation and Relief During Armed Conflict: The Modern Humanitarian Law', 19 *Georgia Journal of International & Comparative Law* 31 (1989) 1–85;N. Mulder and B. van Dijk, '*Why Did Starvation Not Become the Paradigmatic War Crime in International Law?*', in K. J. Heller and I. Venzke (eds), *Contingency and the Course of International Law* (Oxford: Oxford University Press, 2021) 370–388; P. Drew, 'Can we Starve the Civilians?: Exploring the Dichotomy between the Traditional Law of Maritime Blockade and Humanitarian Initiatives', 95 *International Law Studies* (2019) 302–321.

warfare to be investigated and prosecuted in a NIAC, the Assembly of State Parties (ASP) to the International Criminal Court (ICC) historically and unanimously voted to adopt the Swiss proposal in December 2019.[22] The importance of this amendment cannot be overstated, its adoption (1) enhances the protection of civilians in conflicts; (2) aligns the Rome Statute with the position in IHL and customary law which prohibits starvation in both types of conflict designation; and (3) significantly pushes the accountability envelope, encouraging states to mirror these legal provisions in their domestic laws. Article 8(2)(e)(xix) mirrors almost identically the crime in an IAC, save for there is no reference to 'as provided for under the Geneva Conventions'.

For both crimes the Elements of the Crimes are the same, there are four elements required to establish the offence: (1) the perpetrator deprived civilians of OIS; (2) the perpetrator intended to starve civilians as a method of warfare; (3) the conduct took place in the context of and was associated with an international armed conflict; and (4) the perpetrator was aware of factual circumstances that established the existence of an armed conflict.

Elements (3) and (4) are the well-established chapeau elements applicable to any war crime, therefore we consider here only the physical and mental elements contained in elements (1) and (2).

(a) The actus reus

Element (1) describes the only *actus reus* of the offence, namely depriving civilians of OIS. It appears clear from a plain reading of Article 8(2)(b)(xxv) and Article 8(2)(e)(xix) (Article 8 Starvation) that one of the ways in which this element may be achieved is through 'wilfully impeding relief supplies'. The absence of any reference to this in the Elements of Crimes seems to confirm that it is a non-essential and merely illustrative means of fulfilling the *actus reus* of the offence. Generally, any conduct that restricts civilians' use of an object would be considered as causing 'deprivation'.[23] This includes acts such as attacking, destroying, removing objects or rendering them useless,[24] as well as omissions such as refusing to take measures to ensure civilians' access to them.[25]

It is also important to note that the *actus reus* requires the deprivation of OIS to be aimed at civilians. Civilians are all persons who are not members of the

[22] GRC are privileged to have worked alongside Switzerland and the Netherlands on the amendment. GRC and the World Peace Foundation's project 'Accountability to Mass Starvation: Testing the limits of the law', has actively supported the amendment. In particular, GRC have collaborated with the Swiss throughout 2019, and the Amendment has underpinned all of GRC's starvation outputs, such as high-level panel events, including co-sponsoring with the Swiss the only side event during ASP 18 which focused on the starvation amendment; policy papers, advocacy interviews, and analysis.

[23] ICRC Commentary to the APs, § 2101.

[24] See Art. 54 AP I and Art. 14 AP II. See also ICRC Commentary to the APs, § 2795.

[25] O. Triffterer and K. Ambos (eds), *The Rome Statute of the International Criminal Court: A Commentary* (3rd edn., Munich: C.H. Beck, 2016), at 516.

armed forces,[26] and they are always protected from being targeted under IHL. If in doubt, a person shall always be considered a civilian.[27] There are exceptions to this, depriving enemy combatants of OIS is not prohibited under IHL, unless they are wounded, sick, shipwrecked, or captured/detained.[28] Furthermore, if the object in question is entirely and exclusively used by the armed forces of the enemy (such as food supplies in an enemy military base), deprivation would not be prohibited.[29] Similarly, objects that are being used in direct support of military action, even if also used by civilians, may be lawfully attacked (e.g. a military vehicle sometimes used to transport civilians).[30] Finally, a party to a conflict may deprive civilians on their own territory (as opposed to enemy territory) of OIS if required by military necessity, for instance, as defence against invasion.[31] How these exceptions would be interpreted in a prospective prosecution has yet to be clarified.

(b) The mens rea

Element (2), the *mens rea* requirement of Article 8 Starvation has two components: (1) the perpetrator must have *intentionally* deprived civilians of OIS; and (2) the perpetrator must have *intended* to starve civilians as a method of warfare.

The first of these requirements follows from the application of Article 30 of the Rome Statute that mandates that 'unless otherwise provided', all material elements of crimes within the jurisdiction of the Rome Statute are committed 'with intent and knowledge'. Thus, 'depriving civilians of OIS' is a distinct and severable 'material element' for the purpose of Article 30 with its own distinct mental element standard.[32] By virtue of Article 30(2)(a), the perpetrator must 'mean' (i.e. desire) to engage in conduct which deprives civilians of OIS. In addition, the requirement that a material element be committed 'with knowledge ... means [that such conduct will amount to the relevant crime if performed with an] awareness that a circumstance exists' (Article 30(3) ICC Statute). Thus, it is an essential feature of the commission of starvation that the perpetrator is aware that the objects of which he or she is depriving the civilian population are essential to their survival.

[26] GC III, Art. 4 and AP I, Art. 50; AP II does not contain a definition of civilians or the civilian population even though these terms are used in several provisions, see AP II, Arts 13–15 and 17–18; ICRC Customary IHL Study, Rule 5: Definition of Civilians, available online at: <https://ihl-databases.icrc.org/customary-ihl/eng/docs/v1_rul_rule5> (visited 20 March 2022).

[27] AP I, Art. 50(1).

[28] AP I, Art. 54(3). See ICRC Commentary to the APs, at 657.

[29] AP I, Art, 54(3). See ICRC Commentary to the APs, at 657.

[30] For guidance see ICRC Commentary to the APs, at 655.

[31] AP I, Art. 54(5).

[32] § 2 of the General Introduction to the Elements of Crimes, containing guidance for the application of Art. 30 to the Elements of Crimes, provides that '[w]here no reference is made in the Elements of Crimes to a mental element for any particular conduct, consequence or circumstance listed, it is understood that the relevant mental element, i.e., intent, knowledge or both, set out in Art. 30 applies. Given that the essential element of depriving civilians of objects indispensable to their survival is conduct (and a consequence) without an express associated mental standard, Art. 30 operates to require that that element be committed intentionally.'

The interpretation of the second of these *mens rea* requirements is likely to pose the most significant challenges to prosecutorial practice, the principal amongst which are considered in the sections to follow.

2. Clarifying 'Intention to Starve as a Method of Warfare'

(a) 'Intention to starve' does not require proof of consequence

Whilst the crime requires the deprivation of OIS as both a conduct *and* a consequence, the crime does not appear to require proof that civilians did in fact starve in terms of the intention to starve requirement. This is apparent from a plain reading of Article 8 Starvation, as well as the Elements of Crimes. The phraseology employed in both is familiar to ICL and to national systems of criminal law in that it refers to an intention to bring about a consequence but is silent as to whether proof is required that the consequence is actualized. Conventionally, in those circumstances, proof of consequence is not required.

The Statute's drafters during the Rome Conference considered proposals during the drafting of Article 8(2)(b)(xxv) that would have included the phrase 'as a result of the accused's acts, one or more persons died of starvation' within the definition of the crime. However, these proposals were not adopted.[33] In addition, it is now generally accepted that IHL prohibits starvation as a method of warfare, independently of whether its effects become visible on the population.[34]

This is not to argue that the consequences of any deprivation will be irrelevant to an assessment of individual criminal responsibility. On the contrary, *mens rea* is very often inferred from the consequences of the defendant's conduct. Any consequences that flow will also be important at the sentencing stage and during any reparations to be awarded.[35]

[33] The United States had proposed to include the element '[t]hat as a result of the accused's acts, one or more persons died from starvation', see United States of America, *Proposal regarding an Annex on Definitional Element for Part 2 Crimes*, UN Doc. A/CONF.183/C.1/L.10, 19 June 1998; *Proposal Submitted by the United States of America: Draft Elements of Crime*, UN Doc. PCNICC/1999/DP.4/Add.2, 4 February 1999, at 18.

[34] Triffterer and Ambos (eds), see note 26, at 517, § 790: '[t]he only material element required by the elements of crimes is that there is a deprivation of certain objects. This suggests that it is ... sufficient that civilians are deprived of objects indispensable to their survival, that is, a deprivation that would cause them in the future to starve, without requiring that the deprivation takes its effect over time'; see also, S. Hutter, *Starvation as a Weapon: Domestic Policies of Deliberate Starvation as a Means to an End under International Law* (Leiden: Brill-Nijhoff International Humanitarian Law Series, 2015), at 32; R. Provost, 'Starvation as a Weapon: Legal Implications of the United Nations Food Blockade Against Iraq and Kuwait', 30 *Columbia Journal of Transnational Law* (1992) 577–639. Other authoritative commentators have also likened starvation with incitement to genocide, denying quarter, displacing civilians, and intentionally directing attacks against civilians not taking direct part in hostilities. These are all offences that do not require proof of the consequences intended; R. S. Lee, *The International Criminal Court: The Making of the Rome Statute: Issues, Negotiations, Results* (Amsterdam: Kluwer Law International, 1999), at 141–142; Triffterer and Ambos (eds), see note 26, at 448, § 531, citing to *Report of the Preparatory Committee on the Establishment of an International Criminal Court*, GA Supplement No. 22 (A/51/22), 1996, at 635, fn. 74; T. Dannenbaum, 'Siege Starvation: A War Crime of Societal Torture', 22 Chicago Journal of International Law (2022) 1–73.

[35] Judgment, *Karadžić*, (IT-95-5/18-T), Trial Chamber, 24 March 2016 (hereafter the '*Karadžić* Trial Judgment'), § 5669; Judgment, *Popović et al.*, (IT-05-88-T), Trial Chamber II, 10 June 2010 (hereafter

As the only essential act or consequence within the offence of starvation is depriving civilians of OIS, the crime requires an intent that goes beyond this act and *toward* starvation and is, therefore, as defined, a specific intent crime.[36]

(b) Oblique intent: a knowledge-based approach to the intention to starve

The starting point for addressing this issue is Article 30 of the Rome Statute. As described earlier, this sets out the 'default' mental standard that needs to be established in relation to each material (physical) element. It does this in two ways. First, Article 30(1) attaches a mental standard of intent and/or knowledge to each material element—conduct, consequence, or circumstance[37] of an offence, 'unless

the '*Popović* Trial Judgment'), § 820; A. Cassese and P. Gaeta (eds), *Cassese's International Criminal Law* (3rd edn., Oxford: Oxford University Press, 2013), at 57–58; K. Ambos, 'Karadzic's Genocidal Intent as the "Only Reasonable Inference"?', EJIL: Talk! Blog of the European Journal of International Law, 1 April 2016, available online at <https://www.ejiltalk.org/karadzics-genocidal-intent-as-the-only-reasonable-inference/ (visited 2 May 2019).

[36] We note that 'specific intent' has also been used in international criminal law in the context of genocidal intent to describe direct intent (a concrete desire that genocide occur (i.e. that the group is destroyed in whole or in part)), rather than oblique intent (a mere awareness that the genocide is a consequence of pursuing certain qualifying acts (e.g. murder or physical harm)). This definition was first adopted in ICL in the International Criminal Tribunal for Rwanda (CTR') case of *Akayesu* that described genocidal intent as 'the specific intention, required as a constitutive element of the crime, which demands that the perpetrator clearly seeks to produce the act charged', Judgment, *Akayesu*, (ICTR-96-4-T), Trial Chamber I, 2 September 1998 (hereafter the '*Akayesu* Trial Judgment'), §§ 498, 518 and has been adopted in ICTR and ICTY cases since Judgment, *Rutaganda*, (ICTR-96-3-T), Trial Chamber I, 6 December 1999, §§ 47–49; Judgment, *Seromba*, (ICTR-2001-66-I), Trial Chamber, 13 December 2006, §§ 319–320; Judgment, *Kambanda*, (ICTR 97-23-S), Trial Chamber, 4 September 1998, § 16; Judgment, *Krstić*, (IT-98-33-T), Trial Chamber, 2 August 2001 (hereafter the '*Krstić* Trial Judgment'), § 571; Judgment, *Blagojević and Jokić*, (IT-02-60-T), Trial Chamber I, 17 January 2005 (hereafter the '*Blagojević and Jokić* Appeal Judgment'), § 656; Judgment, *Jelisić*, (IT-95-10-A), Appeals Chamber, 5 July 2001 (hereafter the '*Jelisić* Appeal Judgment'), §§ 51–52. However, as discussed later in this chapter, this type of intent is more accurately described as direct intent. We consider whether or not the specific intent to starve requires proof of direct intent or whether oblique intent will suffice. See, W. Schabas, *Genocide in International Law: The Crime of Crimes* (2nd edn., Cambridge: Cambridge University Press, 2009), at 214.

[37] The *conduct* of a crime includes a prohibited action (see e.g. Art. 6, Elements of Crimes ('killing', 'causing serious bodily or mental harm', 'inflicting . . . conditions of life', 'imposing measures', and 'forcibly transferring')) or prohibited omission (see e.g. Art. 28(a)(ii) and (b)(ii), Rome Statute ('failed to take all necessary and reasonable measures') that is described in the definition of a crime). The *consequences* of a crime can refer either to a completed result, such as the causing of death (see e.g. Art. 8 (2)(b)(vii) Elements of Crimes (improper use of a flag of truce 'resulting in death or serious personal injury')); Art. 8 (2)(b)(x), Elements of Crimes (subjecting persons to physical mutilation or to medical or scientific, or the creation of a state of harm or risk of harm, such as endangerment (see e.g. Art. 8 (2)(b)(x) Elements of Crimes (subjecting persons to physical mutilation or to medical or scientific)). 'Material element of a crime' can also include some kind of harmful result. Needless to say, that for harm to be a constituent element of a crime, it must be provided for by a definition thereof (Art. 22 (Elements of an International Crime) of the Draft Convention on the Establishment of an International Penal Tribunal for the Suppression and Punishment of the Crime of Apartheid and other International Crimes provided that '[t]he element of harm shall depend upon the definition of the crime'. See GA res. 3068 (XXVIII), 28 UN GAOR Supp. (No. 30) at 75; UN Doc. A/9030 (1974), 1015 UNTS 243, entered into force July 18, 1976, E/CN.4/1426, 1981, 37). The *circumstances* of a crime qualify the conduct and consequences. They may, for example, describe the requisite features of the persons (e.g., that the victims who are killed must be 'members of the group' (Art. 6(a), Elements of Crimes or be 'combatants' (Elements of Crimes, Art. 8 (2)(b)(vi)) or that the persons who are forcibly transferred must be 'children

otherwise provided' within the specific definition of the offence. Second, Article 30(2) and (3), respectively, define and interpret the scope of the intent and knowledge standards created by Article 30(1) and their relationship to the conduct, consequence, or circumstance (as the case may be) to which they attach.

Where the intent is 'in relation to a consequence', Article 30(2)(b) provides that such intent may be shown where the perpetrator:

(i) 'means to cause that consequence' (i.e. with direct intent); or
(ii) 'is aware that it will occur in the ordinary course of events' (i.e. with oblique intent).

In relation to the depriving conduct and consequence discussed earlier, there can be little doubt that Article 30(2)(a) will engage to attach a specific mental standard to the first of the essential elements of starvation, meaning that the perpetrator must intend, that is 'mean' to deprive civilians of OIS.[38] We further conclude that the intention should be interpreted in line with the same mental standards as those contained within Article 30(2)(b), namely that the 'intention to starve' element of the crime might be satisfied by either direct or oblique intent.[39] This conclusion is based upon two rationale: first, Article 30 only applies to define the mental element requirement, 'unless [one is] otherwise provided'. Since starvation does expressly provide for its own mental element requirement, namely 'intentionally using starvation', no other mental element requirement is required and that Article 30 does not operate; second, the 'intention to starve' is not comprised of any 'material element' (i.e. consequence, conduct, or circumstance) immediately capable of engaging Article 30(1). Where an element is defined as an intent *not* requiring

of the group' (Art. 6(e), Elements of Crimes or things (e.g. that the attacks or bombardment must be directed against 'towns, villages, dwellings or buildings which are undefended and which are not military objectives' (Art. 8 (2)(b)(v), Elements of Crimes) or 'buildings dedicated to religion, education, art, science' (Art. 8(2)(b)(ix), Elements of Crimes) mentioned in the conduct and consequence elements). (Triffterer and Ambos (eds), see note 26, at 1115–1116 and 20 cc).

38 Art. 8(2)(b)(xxv)(1), ICC Elements of Crimes.

39 For a longer debate on this analysis see W. Jordash QC, C. Murdoch, and J. Holmes, 'Strategies for Prosecuting Mass Starvation' 17 *Journal of International Criminal Justice* (2019) 849–879. Public Redacted Judgment on the appeal of Mr Thomas Lubanga Dyilo against his conviction, Judgment, *Lubanga* (ICC-01/04-01/06 A 5), Appeals Chamber, 1 December 2014 (hereafter the '*Lubanga* Appeal Judgment'), § 447: 'absolute certainty about a future occurrence can never exist; therefore the Appeals Chamber considers that the standard for the foreseeability of events is virtual certainty'; Decision Pursuant to Article 61(7)(a) and (b) of the Rome Statute on the Charges of the Prosecutor Against Jean-Pierre Bemba Gombo, *Bemba et al.*, (ICC-01/05-01/08), Pre-Trial Chamber II, 15 June 2009 (hereafter the '*Bemba* Pre-Trial Decision'), § 362: 'Nevertheless, the words "will occur" read together with the phrase "in the ordinary course of events", clearly indicate that the required standard of occurrence is close to certainty. In this regard, the Chamber defines this standard as "virtual certainty" or "practical certainty", namely that the consequence will follow, barring an unforeseen or unexpected intervention that prevent its occurrence.' See the discussion on the legal basis for the application of this mental element standard to the war crime of starvation, in section 2 of this chapter.

the establishment of a conduct, consequence or circumstance, then Article 30(1) does not apply.

Read in the context of the Elements of Crimes, it seems clear that 'depriv[ing] civilians of OIS' (the first element) will be analysed and treated as a distinct element to the requirement that the 'perpetrator intends to starve civilians as a method of warfare' (the second element). On that analysis, whilst the Elements of Crimes refer to an intention to bring about the consequence of starvation, neither the consequence of starvation per se nor any other material conduct, consequence, or circumstances is intrinsic within the 'intention to starve' element. In these circumstances, whilst the first element described in the Elements of Crimes does appear to require the deprivation of OIS as both a conduct *and* a consequence, in terms of the *additional* intent requirement under the second element, that is the intent to starve, the crime does not appear to require either any additional proof that civilians did in fact starve or any proof of any conduct distinct from the latter prohibited deprivation. In sum, the intent to starve sits alone without any (direct) reference to a consequence or any conduct that might constitute a 'material element' for the purpose of Article 30. As such, in our view, Article 30 does not technically apply to it.

Furthermore, there is nothing within the Rome Statute, or the general principles of criminal law, to suggest that, absent the application of Article 30(1), the applicable intent must be automatically interpreted and restricted to direct intent.

Notwithstanding this analysis, as referred to earlier, it is essential that although individual responsibility for the war crime of starvation does not require the establishment of any 'starvation consequence', many, if not most, prosecutions will still require a focus upon *some* 'starvation consequences'. This evidence will be highly probative of any intent to starve. Thus, the practical distinction between a crime of starvation requiring proof of 'starvation consequences' as matter of law and Article 8 Starvation may in practice be less significant. In relation to future prosecutions, a direct intent to starve may well look very similar to, if not indistinguishable from, oblique (knowledge-based) intent. As with genocide,[40] a desire to commit the offence may form extemporaneously and temporarily amidst a course of otherwise lawful (or unlawful) purposes.

(c) The meaning of 'as a method of warfare'

Article 8 Starvation appends a qualification to the intent to starve by requiring the establishment of an intent to starve civilians *as a method of warfare*. There are a variety of views concerning the meaning of methods of warfare,[41] we endorse Gaggioli

[40] Judgment, *Niyitegeka* (ICTR-96-14-A), Appeals Chamber, 9 July 2004 (hereafter the '*Niyitegeka* Appeal Judgment'), § 53; *Jelisić* Appeal Judgment, see note 37, § 49.

[41] See Jordash, Murdoch, and Holmes, see note 39 and N. Melzer and G. Gaggioli, 'Methods of Warfare', in D. Akande and B. Saul (eds), *Oxford Guide to International Humanitarian Law* (Oxford: Oxford University Press, 2019), citing the ICRC Commentary to the Additional Protocols, § 4799. Sandoz et al., see note 16, §§ 1402 and 1957; Art. 54(1) AP I, Art. 14 AP II; Art. 38 AP I, Art. 37 AP I.; Art. 40 AP I; D. Akande and E.-C. Gillard, 'Conflict Induced Food Insecurity and the War

and Melzer's proposition that 'methods of warfare' may be defined as: '(i) the way and manner in which the weapons are used; and (ii) any specific, tactical or strategic, ways of conducting hostilities that are not particularly related to weapons and that are intended to overwhelm and weaken the adversary'.[42] This definition has the merit of highlighting that methods of warfare are more than just the manner in which weapons are used[43] and may be more accurately understood as 'referring to any particular manner of using weapons *or otherwise* conducting hostilities irrespective of permissibility or appropriateness, and ranging from the use of emblems, flags, uniforms and weapons or other equipment to the choice of targets for attack'.[44] This broader definition of 'method of warfare' also has the practical benefit of encompassing a subcategory of military operations,[45] which includes aerial and naval blockades, sieges, or the establishment of a no-fly zone.[46] The intended starvation must have been intended to be a 'specific, tactical or strategic, way of conducting hostilities'[47] but nothing more (such as a purposive requirement to 'overwhelm and weaken the adversary') demanding than this is required.[48]

Crime of Starvation of Civilians as a Method of War, 17 *Journal of International Criminal Justice* (2019) 753–779; Dannenbaum, see note 7, available at <https://papers.ssrn.com/sol3/papers.cfm?abstract_id=3953922>.

[42] Melzer and Gaggioli, see note 42, at 4.

[43] Melzer and Gaggioli, see note 42, at 4.

[44] Melzer and Gaggioli, see note 42, at 4.

[45] Military operations such as re-supply, transportation of troops, and communications 'do not constitute methods of warfare unless they adversely affect the enemy's military operations or military capacity'. See Humanitarian Policy and Conflict Research (eds), *Commentary on the Humanitarian Policy and Conflict Research Manual on International Law Applicable to Air and Missile Warfare* (Cambridge: Harvard University, 2010), at 44.

[46] Humanitarian Policy and Conflict Research (eds), see note 45, at xlviii; According to the ICRC Commentary to the APs (Sandoz et al., see note 16), §§ 1402 and 1957, the term 'methods of warfare' generally refers to the way in which weapons are used. This definition includes aerial and naval blockades and sieges. On the legality of sieges under IHL, see § 4796: 'the use of blockade and siege as methods of warfare remain legitimate, provided they are directed exclusively against combatants'. For the use of sieges as methods of warfare, see § 2096, which recognizes that the prohibition of the use of starvation as a method of warfare, applies in case of besiegement. See also E. Rosenblad, 'Starvation as a Method of Warfare, Conditions for Regulation by Convention', 7 *International Lawyer* (1973) 252–270. For blockades as methods of warfare, see Sandoz et al., see note 16, §§ 2092–2095; L. Doswald-Beck (ed.), *San Remo Manual on International Law Applicable to Armed Conflicts at Sea* (Cambridge: Cambridge University Press, 1995), Arts 93–104.

[47] See also P. J. Cameron, 'The Limitations on Methods and Means of Warfare', 9 *Australian Yearbook of International Law* (1980) 247–261, at 247, which similarly defines them as 'all strategies and tactics and every other measure which, by the use of manpower and weapons systems, an armed force may employ'; Another interpretation is given in Humanitarian Policy and Conflict Research (eds), see note 44, at 43, which defines them as 'attacks and other activities designed to adversely affect the enemy's military operations or military capacity'. This interpretation has been criticized since it does not include attacks against enemy civilians, see S. Casey-Maslen and S. Haines, *Hague Law Interpreted: The Conduct of Hostilities Under the Law of Armed Conflict* (Oxford: Hart Publishing, 2018), at 54–55.

[48] The Commentaries to the Additional Protocols state that the term 'methods of warfare' refers to the way in which weapons are used. However, as Gaggioli and Melzer argue, this definition appears to be too restrictive 'given that even methods not necessarily involving the use of a weapon, such as starvation, improper use of emblems, perfidy, or denial of quarter are either expressly described as 'methods of warfare' or as a 'method of combat' or are systematically included in Part III, Section I of Additional

In sum, despite the vagueness in the construction of Article 8 Starvation, a literal or teleological interpretation of 'methods of warfare', and an examination of it in context, does not appear to demand the establishment of a purposive or direct intent to starve. On the contrary, there appears to be little to exclude oblique intent, rendering a perpetrator, not desiring the starvation of civilians as a method of warfare, but who nevertheless became aware that act(s) of deprivation would inevitably lead to the starvation of civilians *and* that this would become a part of the overall military endeavour, individually criminally responsible.

3. The Practice

A. Strategies for Prosecuting Starvation

There has yet to be a prosecution of starvation on the international level.[49] Thus, the process of identifying the contours of the material elements of starvation will rest in large part upon judges of an actual case discerning the intention of the drafters of Article 8 Starvation. As the earlier analysis suggests, establishing the intent to starve is likely to be the most pressing challenge for any trial.

There may be 'starvation cases' that are straightforward or lend themselves to easier analysis, the deprivation of OIS in military detention centres for example. However, many starvation prosecutions will be called upon to assess crowded causal environments where lawful military activity and violations of IHL are inextricably linked. In these cases, identifying the relevant misconduct and drawing inferences concerning criminal intent will be challenging.

This analysis will invariably raise specific issues that include: (1) challenges arising from the need to map causation (i.e. the connection between the alleged perpetrator's acts and omissions and deprivation of OIS and any consequential impacts upon civilian populations); (2) the role of direct and indirect (circumstantial) evidence in establishing the elements of the offence, particularly the intent requirement; and (3) the possible approaches to identifying intent in a multi-causal environment, particularly where the deprivation of OIS occurs during the pursuit of a lawful purpose (including sieges and blockades). These will be discussed now.

Protocol I on Methods and Means of Warfare' (Arts 35–42 AP I). Melzer and Gaggioli, see note 40, at 4; Sandoz et al., *Commentary to the APs*, see note 16, §§ 1402 and 1957.

[49] Our research indicates that only two prosecutions of the modern era have pleaded starvation as a distinct crime, all on the domestic level (Croatia and Ethiopia): *Public Prosecutor v. M.P. et al.*, in the District Court in Zadar, Croatia, K. 74/96, Verdict, 24 April 1997; and *Special Prosecutor v. Col. Mengistu Hailamariam et al.*, Ethiopian Federal High Court, File No. 1/87 (2006).

1. Mapping the Chain of Causation

Establishing causation is important as a matter of evidence, not law. Whilst intention to starve does not require proof of result, linking the actions of individuals to the deprivation of OIS and these in turn to the result of the population suffering from such deprivation will provide the clearest illustration of the required intention to starve.

A range of evidence will need to be carefully examined to assess causation, especially any alleged perpetrators' awareness of, and proximity to, relevant deprivations. Starvation and famines rarely occur in a vacuum; countries often face pre-existing or concurrent food insecurity, malnutrition, and disease, resources may be limited, and climate and other natural factors may impact upon the availability of OIS, as well as the ability of communities to absorb, or at least survive, fluctuations in the availability of food, shelter, or medicine. Despite the 'eggshell skull rule',[50] by which pre-existing conditions or circumstances will not automatically break the chain of causation,[51] these challenges will be many and varied. Teasing out the factors that led to the deprivation and ascertaining their foreseeability (that they would lead to the starvation of a civilian population) will undoubtedly tax judicial minds.

However, these challenges ought not to be considered unique or insurmountable in the context of ICL prosecutions before international or national courts more generally. Assessing an accused's acts and conduct in the midst of complex, fluctuating circumstances and contributory factors as part of regional or even countrywide enterprises are the bread and butter of ICL. Usually, these issues can be disentangled through a common-sense analysis of context, cause, effect, and an accused's awareness of risk.[52] It is worthwhile recalling that, generally, it is no defence to claim that circumstances were already dire, that others were engaged in prohibited conduct, or that other causes may have contributed to the prohibited harm.[53]

[50] Also known as the 'thin skull' rule; *Dulieu v. White & Son* [1901] EWHC KB 1, § 12; *Page v. Smith* [1995] All ER 736, UKHL 7; British Military Court, Elten, Germany, *Trial of Hans Renoth and Three Others*, Case No. 68, 8–10 January 1946, at 76; *Alcock and others v. Chief Constable of South Yorkshire Police* [1992] 1 AC 310; *Bourhill v. Young* [1943] AC 92, [1942] UKHL 5, 110; Judgment, *Samphan and Chea* (002/19-09-2007- ECCC/SC), Supreme Court Chamber, 23 November 2016 (hereafter the '*Samphan and Chea* ECCC Judgment'), § 534.

[51] Judgment, *Čelebići*, (IT-96-21-T), Trial Chamber, 16 November 1998 (hereafter the '*Čelebići* Trial Judgment'), § 909: 'To establish criminal liability in situations where there are pre-existing physical conditions which would cause the victim's death, therefore, it is only necessary to establish that the accused's conduct contributed to the death of the victim.'

[52] *Samphan and Chea* ECCC Judgment, see note 49, §§ 529–535. The defence raised on appeal that the multiplicity of plausible causes of death broke the chain of causation, excluding the accused from criminal responsibility for those who starved to death. This argument was rejected as 'inapt' in breaking the lack of a causal link between the conditions of the evacuation and the death of the victims. The Appeals Chamber held that it was irrelevant whether the victims might have died for other reasons, or that the conditions generally in the area were dire. The civilians had died because of the conditions to which they were exposed during the evacuation.

[53] *Samphan and Chea* ECCC Judgment, see note 51, §§ 529–535, *Čelebići* Trial Judgment, see note 52, § 823; British Military Court, Elten, Germany, *Trial of Hans Renoth and Three Others*, Case No. 68, 8–10 January 1946, at 76.

2. Modes of Liability

The intent analysis outlined earlier will need to factor in the 'mode of liability' that the individual is being charged with to understand how this will affect what a prosecutor will have to prove. Broadly, an individual may be criminally responsible for international crimes if he/she:[54]

- (i) Committed the crime either (1) as an individual (i.e. direct perpetration); (2) jointly with another (co-perpetration); (3) through another person, regardless of whether that other person is criminally responsible (indirect perpetration); or (4) through other persons, together with co-perpetrators (indirect co-perpetration);[55]
- (ii) Ordered, solicited, or induced the crime;[56]
- (iii) Aided, abetted, or otherwise assisted the crime;[57]
- (iv) Contributed to the commission (or attempted commission) of a crime by a group of persons acting with a common purpose (complicity);[58] and
- (v) Failed to prevent, repress, or punish the commission of the crime (command or superior responsibility);[59]

Generally speaking, ICL aims to prosecute senior leaders or those who are the most responsible for the criminal conduct who often operate far removed from the scene of the crimes. Accordingly, in order to establish their liability, it must be proven that such persons have contributed to the crimes committed by others without being physically involved in their commission to a degree that attracts individual criminal responsibility. Therefore, in charging such individuals, prosecutors often favour modes of liability that allow those at the top of a criminal organization/group who exercise control over or contribute to criminal plans or objectives to be held criminally accountable.[60] These include co-perpetration, indirect perpetration,

[54] A detailed exploration of the specific legal elements of various modes of liability are outside the scope this article. For an overview of the various modes of liability see, GRC's Basic Investigative Standards App, (BIS App). BIS is available in mobile app (Android and Apple), desktop, or hard copy format. It is a live tool that distils international documentation for accountability standards into user-friendly guidance and empowers users with a succinct and practical knowledge of the relevant legal standards for documenting IHL, IHRL, and ICL violations.

[55] Art. 25(3)(a) Rome Statute.

[56] Art. 25(3)(b) Rome Statute.

[57] Art. 25(3)(c) Rome Statute.

[58] Art. 25(3)(d) Rome Statute.

[59] Art. 28(a) and (b) Rome Statute.

[60] These modes of liability are often also reflected in domestic criminal codes. For a description of common purpose liability in domestic law, see Judgment, *Tadić*, (IT-94-1-A), Appeals Chamber, 15 July 1999.(hereafter the '*Tadić* Appeals Chamber Judgment'), §§ 224–225. See e.g. Germany: Strafgesetzbuch, § 25(2); France: Code Pénal, Art. 121-7; England and Wales: *R. v. Hyde* [1991] 1 QB 134; *R. v. Anderson*; *R. v. Morris* [1966] 2 QB 110; Canada: Criminal Code, Section 21(2); Australia: McAuliffe v. R. (1995) 183 CLR 108 at 114; Zambia: Penal Code, Art. 22. See N. Piacente, 'Importance of the Joint Criminal Enterprise Doctrine for the ICTY Prosecutorial Policy', 2 *Journal of International Criminal Justice* (2004) 446–454, at 446; L. Yanev, 'Joint Criminal Enterprise', in J. De Hemptinne, R. Roth, and E. van Sliedregt (eds), *An Introduction to International Criminal Law and Procedure*, (Cambridge: Cambridge

indirect co-perpetration, superior/command responsibility, complicity, ordering, soliciting, or inducing. These modes may be relevant in situations where:

(i) **There is a common criminal plan among multiple perpetrators** which led to the commission of the crime (required for co-perpetration and indirect co-perpetration). To establish liability under the modes that require this element, it must be proven that the accused made an essential contribution to that plan in awareness of its criminal consequences;[61]

(ii) **The accused exercises control over the acts of direct perpetrators** who automatically comply with the orders of the accused due to his/her leadership position in an organized and hierarchical organization (required for indirect perpetration and indirect co-perpetration);[62]

(iii) **The accused's contributed to a crime committed by a group acting with a common purpose** with the knowledge of the fact that the group will commit crimes *but* without necessarily belonging to such group or sharing such purpose (required for complicity);[63] or

(iv) **The accused (who may either be a military commander or a civilian superior) failed to prevent or repress crimes committed by persons who are under his/her effective command, authority, and control.** For military commanders, establishing this mode requires a demonstration that the

University Press, 2019) 121–170; the predecessor being joint criminal enterprise, also heavily utilized and expanded upon by the *ad hoc* tribunals for the former Yugoslavia and Rwanda, since its first articulation in the ICTY's *Tadić* Appeals Chamber Judgment, § 227 (noting that this mode of liability was not expressly included in the ICTY and ICTR Statutes, attracting criticism that it is a judge-made artificiality, see Judgment, *Martić*, (IT-95-11-A), Appeals Chamber, 8 October 2008, Separate Opinion of Judge Schomburg on the Individual Criminal Responsibility of Milan Martić, § 9). See e.g. Judgment, *Kvočka et al.*, (IT-98-30/1-A), Appeals Chamber, 28 February 2005, §§ 79–119; Judgment, *Stakić*, (IT-97-24-A), Appeals Chamber, 22 March 2006, §§ 58–65; Judgment, *Brđanin*, (IT-99-36-A), Appeals Chamber, 3 April 2007, §§ 357–432; Judgment, *Popović et al.*, (IT-05-88-A), Appeals Chamber, 30 January 2015, § 806 et seq.; Judgment, *Stanišić & Simatović*, (IT-03-69-A), Appeals Chamber, 9 December 2015, §§ 77–90; Judgment, *Simba*, (ICTR-01-76-A), Appeals Chamber, 27 November 2007, §§ 243–255; Judgment, *Munyakazi*, (ICTR-97-36A-A), Appeals Chamber, 28 September 2011, §§ 156–164; Judgment, *Karemera and Ngirumpatse*, (ICTR-98-44-A), Appeals Chamber, 29 September 2014, §§ 623–634; Judgment, *Ngirabatware*, (MICT-12-29-A), Appeals Chamber, 18 December 2014, §§ 242–252; SCSL: Judgment, *Brima, Kamara and Kanu*, (SCSL-2004-16-A), Appeals Chamber, 22 February 2008, §§ 72–75; Judgment, *Sesay, Kallon and Gbao*, (SCSL-04-15-A), Appeals Chamber, 26 October 2009, §§ 474–475; ECCC: Judgment, *Kaing Guek Eav alias Duch*, Trial Chamber, (001/18-07-2007/ECCC/TC), 26 July 2010, §§ 504–517; Judgment, *Nuon Chea and Khieu Samphan*, Trial Chamber, (002/19-09-2007/ECCC/TC), 7 August 2014, §§ 690–691.

[61] Judgment, *Lubanga Dyilo*, (ICC-01/04-01/06-2842), Trial Chamber I, 05 April 2012, §§ 980-1006.

[62] Decision on the Confirmation of Charges, *Ntaganda*, (ICC-01/04-02/06-309), Pre-Trial Chamber II, 14 June 2014, §§ 104–135. See also Decision on the Confirmation of Charges, *Bemba Gombo*, (ICC-01/05-01/08-424), Pre-Trial Chamber I, 15 June 2009, §§ 350–351; Decision on the Confirmation of Charges, *Katanga and Ngudjolo Chui*, (ICC-01/04-01/07-716-Conf), Pre-Trial Chamber I, 26 September 2008, §§ 500–514, 527–539; Warrant of Arrest for Omar Hassan Ahmad Al Bashir, *Al Bashir*, (ICC-02/05-01/09-1), Pe-Trial Chamber I, 04 March 2009, §§ 209–213.

[63] Requisite elements of mode of complicity.

> accused had either actual knowledge of the crimes committed by his/her subordinates or, alternatively, he/she should have known the commission of the crimes.[64] For civilian superiors, on the other hand, it must either be shown that the accused knew the commission of the crime or consciously disregarded information indicating their commission (required for command/superior responsibility).[65]

As the various factual scenarios in places such as Yemen, Syria, South Sudan, or Myanmar suggest, these types of modes of responsibility are germane for the prosecution of starvation crimes since they capture the collective/joint responsibility of a number of perpetrators who commit crimes through their control over and use of (military or civilian) organizations.

In such circumstances, prosecutors must take into account the indicators listed above and seek evidence establishing their existence in relation to the crime of starvation by the perpetrators. For instance, they may seek to find out whether a common plan or agreement to commit the crime of starvation was in place and whether the accused made an essential contribution to it (whether through laying a siege or a blockade, repeatedly targeting of civilian objects which are indispensable to survival such as food production facilities, medical facilities, and food markets, etc.). Similarly, the accused's control over the chains of command and military organization(s) contributing to the deprivation of OIS of a civilian population and his/her material ability to ensure automatic compliance with his/her orders would also be highly relevant. The establishment of these facts or circumstances will be vital in establishing the *mens rea* of starvation.

3. Direct and Circumstantial (Indirect) Evidence

By its nature, intent is not usually susceptible to direct proof because '[o]nly the accused himself has first-hand knowledge of his own mental state, and he is unlikely to testify to his own ... intent'.[66] Accordingly, prosecutions at the international level often piece together intent through an examination of the underlying and surrounding circumstances that show beyond reasonable doubt either that a perpetrator must have harboured a concrete desire to commit the prohibited conduct or a continuation of conduct that left it practically impossible for the individual

64 Art. 28(a) Rome Statute; The higher standard of 'actual knowledge' has usually been reserved as a basis for convicting commanders who ordered or participated in the crime, or were present during their commission. Čelebići TJ, § 769. 567 Krnojelac TJ, §§ 309, 311–312. 568 Naletilić & Martinović TJ, § 435. 569 Aleksovski TJ, § 114. 570 Bagosora TJ, §§ 2038–2041, 2065–2067, 2082–2083. 571 AFRC TJ, §§ 1729–1734. The more physically distant a commander is to the commission of the acts 'the more difficult it will be, in the absence of other indicia, to establish [actual knowledge]' Hadžihasanović TJ, § 94, citing Aleksovski TJ, § 80.

65 Art. 28(b) Rome Statute.

66 Judgment, *Gacumbitsi* (ICTR-2001-64-A), Appeals Chamber, 7 July 2006 (hereafter the '*Gacumbitsi* Appeal Judgment'), § 40.

to envisage that the consequence would not occur—the virtual certainty (intent) requirement.[67]

In other words, most ICL prosecutions (be they before national or international courts or tribunals) rest in large part upon circumstantial evidence. The various factual scenarios that are amenable to prosecution for the crime of starvation are no exception. These range from attacks against humanitarian workers in South Sudan, to the imposition of sieges and the cutting off of relief supplies in Syria, or the blocking of access to Rohingya markets and access to rice fields at harvest in tandem with the restriction of humanitarian access by Myanmar security forces,[68] or the adoption of a combination of different acts such as the imposition of blockades coupled with impediments of humanitarian relief and the targeting of agricultural areas, agricultural equipment, and livestock in Yemen.[69] It is inevitable in the context of an international case involving any of these starvation scenarios that circumstantial evidence will play a critical role in establishing the elements of the crime.

Distinct from direct evidence, calculations based upon circumstantial evidence require that the various strands of evidence when considered together lead to an irresistible inference that a particular result was intended or would result in the ordinary course of events.[70]

4. Identifying Intent in a Multi-Causal Environment

As outlined earlier, the question of the existence of an intention to starve will ultimately rest upon a thorough analysis of the chain of causation. Defined instances

[67] *Lubanga* Appeal Judgment, see note 40.

[68] Amnesty International, *'We Will Destroy Everything': Military Responsibility for Crimes Against Humanity in Rakhine State, Myanmar*, 26 June 2018, available online at <https://www.amnesty.org/en/documents/asa16/8630/2018/en/> (visited 4 October 2021)

[69] See Chapter 7 for more detail and see further detailed analysis in conjunction with country experts on South Sudan, Syria, and Yemen in the GRC-WPF Starvation Compendium on <http://www.starvationaccountability.org> (visited 20 March 2022). Human Rights Watch, *'They Burned It All,' Destruction of Villages, Killings, and Sexual Violence in Unity State South Sudan* (2015), available online at <https://www.hrw.org/report/2015/07/22/they-burned-it-all/destruction-villages-killings-and-sexual-violence-unity-state> (visited 19 September 2019). The Yemen data project database recorded between March 2015 and May 2020, 21,147 airstrikes, with the majority targeting Sa'ada and Sana'a: available online at <http://yemendataproject.org> (visited 19 September 2019). See also M. Mundy, 'The Strategies of the Coalition in the Yemen War: Aerial Bombardment and Food War', World Peace Foundation, available online at <https://reliefweb.int/sites/reliefweb.int/files/resources/Strategies%20of%20Coalition%20in%20Yemen%20War.pdf> (visited 19 September 2019); *Report of the Group of Eminent International and Regional Experts as submitted to the UN High Commissioner for Human Rights*, UN Doc. A/HRC/42/17, 9 August 2019, §§ 51–56; Amnesty International, *Syria: Surrender or Starve Strategy Displacing Thousands of Amounts to Crimes Against Humanity* (2017), available online at <https://www.amnesty.org/en/latest/news/2017/11/syria-surrender-or-starve-strategy-displacing-thousands-amounts-to-crimes-against-humanity/> (visited 23 September 2019); the UN Human Rights Council's 2014 damning report detailing violations of international law, entitled OHCHR, '*Living Under Siege: The Syrian Arab Republic*', February 2014.

[70] Judgment on the appeals of Mr Jean-Pierre Bemba Gombo, Mr Aimé Kilolo Musamba, Mr Jean-Jacques Mangenda Kabongo, Mr Fidèle Babala Wandu, and Mr Narcisse Arido against the decision of Trial Chamber VII entitled 'Judgment pursuant to Article 74 of the Statute', *Bemba et al.*, (ICC-01/

of deprivation of OIS that are accompanied by a clear causative link to human starvation, such as deprivation in a detention environment or repeat destruction of clearly identified food stores or hospitals, may allow relatively straightforward assessments of a perpetrator's criminal intent. However, intention to starve may develop extemporaneously in the course of otherwise lawful or unlawful conduct, in which case the task of the tribunal will be to disentangle intention to starve from multiple coexisting purposes (whether lawful or unlawful). This presents obvious analytical challenges. Given the dearth of starvation prosecutions at the international level, no jurisprudence exists that directly guides how an array of circumstantial evidence might be approached to arrive at a fair and irresistible conclusion concerning the existence of criminal intent to starve.

In assessing whether an individual intended to use the starvation of civilians as a method of warfare by depriving them of OIS, relevant evidential considerations (or indicators) will include a vast array of assessments including: the nature, manner, timing, and duration of any deprivations of OIS or attacks on civilians,[71] including whether such attacks were long-term, persistent, and/or indiscriminate;[72] whether the attacks were widespread and perpetrated in an organized manner;[73] and whether they took place as part of a campaign that systematically targeted civilians

05-01/13 A A2 A3 A4 A5), Appeals Chamber, 8 March 2018, § 868: '[w]here a factual finding is based on an inference drawn from circumstantial evidence, the finding is only established beyond reasonable doubt if it was the only reasonable conclusion that could be drawn from the evidence. It is indeed well established that it is not sufficient that a conclusion reached by a trial chamber is merely a reasonable conclusion available from that evidence; the conclusion pointing to the guilt of the accused must be the only reasonable conclusion available. If there is another conclusion reasonably open from the evidence, and which is consistent with the innocence of the accused, he or she must be acquitted'; *Lubanga* Appeal Judgment, see note 40, § 447; *Bemba* Pre-Trial Decision, see note 40, § 362; Judgment pursuant to Article 74 of the Statute, *Bemba et al.*, (ICC-01/05-01/08-3343), Trial Chamber, 21 March 2016, § 192; Judgment, *Brđanin*, (IT-99-36-T), Trial Chamber, 1 September 2004 (hereafter the '*Brđanin* Trial Judgment'), § 970.

[71] See e.g. the prohibition against acts or threats of violence, the primary purpose of which is to spread terror among the civilian population (Art. 51(2) AP I; Art. 13(2) AP II). The *mens rea* of this crime is composed of the specific intent to spread terror among the civilian population, however, the purpose of the unlawful acts or threats to commit such unlawful acts needs not be the only purpose of the acts or threats of violence. The fact that other purposes may have coexisted simultaneously with the purpose of spreading terror among the civilian population would not disprove this charge, provided that the intent to spread terror among the civilian population was principal among the aims. Such intent can be inferred from the circumstances of the acts or threats, that is from their nature, manner, timing, and duration. Judgment, *Galić*, (IT-89-29-A), Appeals Chamber, 30 November 2006 (hereafter the '*Galić* Appeal Judgment'), § 104; Judgment, *Prlić et al.*, (IT-04-74-A), Appeals Chamber, 29 November 2017, §§ 424, 1774.

[72] Attacks during ceasefires and truces or long-term and persistent attacks against civilians, as well as indiscriminate attacks, may be taken as indicia of the intent to spread terror. The specific intent may also be inferred from the site of the attack; Judgment, *Milošević*, (IT-98-29/1-T), Trial Chamber, 12 December 2007 (hereafter the '*Milošević* Trial Judgment'), § 881.

[73] See Judgment, *Mladić*, (IT-09-92-T), Trial Chamber, 22 November 2017, §§ 3514, 3515, 3519, 3524, where the intent to destroy by the physical perpetrators was inferred from the intensity of the prohibited acts, their widespread and discriminatory nature, and the fact that many were perpetrated by the same individuals or units.

including on account of their membership of a particular group.[74] The analysis will encompass all relevant issues, including the general context in which the crime was committed,[75] the repetition of destruction and discriminatory acts,[76] attacks against civilians more generally,[77] involvement of a range of modes of perpetration,[78] the scale of those attacks,[79] and relevant policies or speeches encouraging the targeting of those civilians.[80]

The overall challenge will involve assessing the evidence, especially with regard to the central question of whether and how civilians and civilian objects were attacked or otherwise subject to interference. How to approach the array of indicators will be key to a successful prosecution.

In many 'military' campaigns where the lawful and unlawful action is temporally and geographically wide in scope and intermingled, these issues will test the analytical skills of all concerned. In circumstances where the deprivation occurs in circumstances where no lawful purpose can reasonably be discerned, such as the attacks upon humanitarian workers in South Sudan, or the 'kneel or starve' tactics adopted against civilians in Syria,[81] a court will have a wide discretion concerning how to approach the evidence, providing that the burden of proof remains on the prosecution and any finding of intent is made beyond a reasonable doubt. In cases where the alleged deprivation(s) occurred during ostensibly lawful action, a more systematic examination of those indicators will be required.

At a minimum, triers of fact will be required to consider the following four factors:

[74] *Karadžić* Trial Judgment, see note 36, § 5825. Indications of genocidal intent are rarely overt, and thus intent must often be inferred on the basis of the totality of the evidence, taking into account such factors as the scale of atrocities and the systematic targeting of victims on account of their membership in a particular group; See also the ICC Elements of Crimes, which add a 'contextual element' to the *actus reus*, requiring that the conduct for which the defendant is on trial takes place in the context of 'a manifest pattern of similar conduct'; and Decision on the Prosecution's Application for a Warrant of Arrest against Omar Hassan Ahmad Al Bashir, *Al Bashir*, (ICC-02/05-01/09-3), Pre-Trial Chamber, 4 March 2009, § 119. Contrast this with the Separate and Partly Dissenting Opinion of Judge Anita Ušacka, Decision on the Prosecution's Application for a Warrant of Arrest against Omar Hassan Ahmad Al Bashir, *Al Bashir*, (ICC-02/05-01/09-3), Pre-Trial Chamber, 4 March 2009, § 19, fn. 26.

[75] *Jelisić* Appeal Judgment, see note 37, § 47; Judgment, *Nyiramasuhoko et al.*, (ICTR-98-42-T), Trial Chamber, 24 June 2011(hereafter the '*Nyiramasuhoko et al.* Trial Judgment'), § 5732.

[76] *Jelisić* Appeal Judgment, see note 37, § 47.

[77] *Popović* Trial Judgment, see note 36, §§ 1314–1318, 1399; *Jelisić* Appeal Judgment, see note 37, §§ 47, 494; Judgment, *Karadžić*, (IT-95-5/18-AR98*bis*.1), Appeals Chamber, 11 July 2013, § 80; Judgment, *Tolimir*, (IT-05-88/2-A), Appeals Chamber, 8 April 2015, § 246.

[78] *Brđanin* Trial Judgment, see note 61, § 983; Judgment, *Ndindabahizi*, (ICTR- 2001-71-I), Trial Chamber, 15 July 2004, § 460.

[79] *Akayesu* Trial Judgment, see note 37, §§ 523, 730; *Krstić* Trial Judgment, see note 37, § 549.

[80] *Nyiramasuhoko et al.*, Trial Judgment, see note 77, § 6012.

[81] GRC-WPF Compendium on Syria. The strategy of 'kneel/surrender or starve' was initially used in Homs and shortly thereafter was deployed across Syria, where the warning to 'kneel/surrender or starve' appeared on the walls in the areas where the Assad regime established check-points around the areas outside his control. See Amnesty International, see note 71.

(i) Awareness of the risk that interference with OIS would lead to starvation (including where the deprivation occurs in pursuit of an ostensibly lawful purpose);
(ii) Respect for the full range of relevant IHL prohibitions (e.g. the prohibition against terrorizing the civilian population,[82] the prohibition against collective punishment,[83] the prohibition on the use of human shields,[84] and the prohibition against displacement);[85]
(iii) Implementation of positive obligations flowing from IHL principles applicable in the context of the conduct of hostilities;[86] and
(iv) The concrete steps taken (or not taken) to alleviate civilian suffering, especially those that are capable of facilitating delivery of OIS to affected civilian populations.

In assessing these essential factors in cases where the deprivation is connected to a lawful purpose, the trier of fact will need to wrestle with IHL that permits, in limited circumstances, the interference with OIS. Warring parties are permitted to attack OIS in a range of circumstances or for different purposes, including:

[82] Art. 51(2) AP I, Art. 13(2) AP II, and Rule 2, ICRC Customary IHL Database for the prohibition against acts or threats of violence with the primary purpose of terrorizing the civilian population, prohibit acts such as indiscriminate and widespread shelling, and the regular bombardment of cities.

[83] Art. 75 AP I, Art. 4 AP II, and Rule 103, ICRC Customary IHL Database for the prohibition against collective punishment, prohibit the imposition of collective penalties such as sanctions and harassment of any sort, administrative, by police action or otherwise, except on the basis of individual criminal responsibility.

[84] See Art. 51(7) AP I, Rule 97, ICRC Customary IHL Database, and Art. 8(2)(b)(xxiii) Rome Statute for the prohibition on the use of human shields, prohibit utilizing the presence of a civilian or other protected persons to render certain points, areas or military forces immune from military operations.

[85] Art. 49 GC IV, Art. 17 AP II, and Rule 129, ICRC Customary IHL Database for the prohibition against displacement, prohibit the deportation or transfer of civilians unless the security of the civilians involved is endangered or imperative military reasons so demand.

[86] The principle of precaution places a duty on warring parties to avoid or, in any event, minimize the infliction of collateral damage occurring from military attacks, (Arts 57(1) and 58 AP I, Rules 15 and 22, ICRC Customary IHL Database) including the desirability of warnings to enable civilians to evade the worst effects of any military operation (Art. 57(2)(c) AP I and Rule 20, ICRC Customary IHL Database). There is also an obligation to protect the natural environment (Art. 55 AP I) which may be relevant when considering destruction to agricultural areas. The obligation to allow humanitarian aid is paramount (Art. 70(2) AP I and Arts 59 and 61 (for occupied territories) GC IV, Art. 18(2) AP II, and Rule 55, ICRC Customary IHL Database). For blockades, *San Remo Manual*, see note 47, §§ 103–104. Art. 70(1) AP I states that such operations must take place when the civilian population is 'not adequately provided with the supplies mentioned in Article 69'. The ICRC Commentary to Art 70 AP I (Sandoz *et al.*, see note 17), § 2794 states that '[t]he expression 'not adequately provided', similar to the wording of Art. 55 of the fourth Convention, is not very precise, but this is justified. The need for a relief action and the extent of its urgency must be assessed in every case individually, depending on the real requirements. It is the 'essential' character of such requirements that must be the determining factor. This is a matter of common sense which cannot be formulated in precise terms.' Moreover, if it is established that civilian population is threatened with starvation and a humanitarian organization which provides relief on an impartial and non-discriminatory basis is able to remedy the situation, a party is obliged to give consent. See Rule 55, ICRC Customary IHL Database.

(i) If OIS are used solely by the armed forces of the opposing Party;[87]

(ii) If such targeting or other forms of interference with OIS are used 'in direct support of military action' and such attacks will not be expected to leave the civilian population with such inadequate food or water as to cause its starvation or force its movement;[88]

(iii) If such attacks are pursuant to an imperative military necessity (employed in order to prevent or slow down the enemy from invading a territory).[89] AP I allows Parties to adopt these necessary actions only in defence of their own national territory that is under their effective control;[90] and

(iv) Pursuant to the use of sieges and blockades, provided they are imposed with a view to gain a military advantage, even if they incidentally cause starvation[91] (provided that such starvation is not a virtually certain consequence of the siege, as explained in section 2).

As a preliminary and defining issue, for each of the aforementioned scenarios to remain lawful, such methods of warfare must not be imposed with the aim of causing starvation of the civilian population (which remains unlawful in all cases).[92] Additionally, there is an unconditional and absolute prohibition on the targeting of civilians in customary international law,[93] which aligns with the fundamental IHL protection against starving civilians.[94] It follows that the pursuit of any of the said objectives *sub* (i)–(iv) cannot insulate any individual from a finding that they intended to starve civilians as a method of warfare and therefore from individual responsibility for starvation pursuant to Article 8 Starvation (or the equivalent crime before tribunals other than the ICC).

In sum, in the circumstances where an alleged perpetrator pursues a lawful purpose but, in that pursuit, adopts the requisite starvation intent, Article 8 Starvation may, with all the other elements being fulfilled, be established. It will not be a

[87] Art. 54(3)(a) AP I.

[88] Art. 54(3)(a) AP I.

[89] Art. 54 (5) AP I.

[90] Art. 54(5) AP I, which speaks to territory under the own control of the Party. The ICRC Customary IHL Database states that '[i]t is doubtful, however, whether the exception of scorched earth policy applies to non-international armed conflicts because Article 14 of Additional Protocol II does not contain it'.

[91] For sieges: on the purpose requirement see Rule 53, ICRC Customary IHL Database: 'the prohibition of starvation as a method of warfare does not prohibit siege warfare as long as the purpose is to achieve a military objective and not to starve a civilian population'. See also, Independent International Commission of Inquiry on the Syrian Arab Republic, *Sieges as a Weapon of War: Encircle, Starve, Surrender, Evacuate*, 29 May 2018, available online at <https://www.ohchr.org/Documents/HRBodies/HRCouncil/CoISyria/PolicyPaperSieges_29May2018.pdf> (visited 18 July 2019). For blockades: see *San Remo Manual*, see note 7, § 102(a): '[t]he declaration or establishment of a blockade is prohibited if: it has the sole purpose of starving the civilian population or denying it other objects essential for its survival'.

[92] Art. 54 AP I, Art. 14 AP II, and Rule 53, ICRC Customary IHL Database.

[93] Rule 1, ICRC Customary IHL Database.

[94] See note 88.

defence for any alleged perpetrator to assert that they intended to achieve another lawful purpose, even if that was the primary intent.

The challenge for any ICC Chamber or national court adjudicating upon an Article 8 Starvation or associated starvation case will be to discern whether the alleged perpetrator, whilst pursuing other lawful or unlawful purposes—such as for example attacking OIS used in supporting military action or in besieging areas primarily to starve out combatants to hasten their surrender—nonetheless *also* intended to starve the civilian population as a method of warfare. When attempting to ascertain whether a particular individual possessed the relevant criminal intent, a tribunal will be obliged to consider whether any lawful purpose was superseded by a subsequent intention to starve. An examination of these factors will provide useful indications that allow conclusions to be drawn concerning the ongoing lawfulness or otherwise of any military attack and whether, in the circumstances, an intent to starve developed.

Thus, attacks that begin lawfully but cause excessive damage to the civilian population, when viewed in relation to the military advantage anticipated, will violate the principle of proportionality.[95] When this damage concerns the 'collateral' starvation of civilians,[96] it will be highly relevant to any assessment of the warring party's Article 8(2)(b)(xxv) intent.

This is especially true of the principle of precaution that places a duty on warring parties to avoid or, in any event, minimize the infliction of collateral damage occurring from military attacks.[97] This fundamental IHL precept will be viewed in a concrete way, including alongside a range of other IHL rules that lay out with some specificity what is expected of warring parties in relation to ensuring the passage of humanitarian relief.

As is well known, warring parties have a clear obligation to allow humanitarian access.[98] Warring parties must allow the rapid and unimpeded passage of relief when the population is inadequately supplied.[99] Aside from these obligations, it is logical to presume that those who do not intend starvation would show good faith attempts to abide by these strictures to ensure that civilians obtained OIS. It must

[95] Arts 51(5)(b) and 57(2)(a)(iii) AP I, Rule 14, ICRC Customary IHL Database.

[96] See Henckaerts and Doswald-Beck (eds), see note 21, Rule 53 'Practice', referring to several Military Manuals which adopt the principle of proportionality in the context of sieges. See also S. Watts, 'Under Siege: International Humanitarian Law and Security Council Practice concerning Urban Siege Operations', Harvard Law School: Counterterrorism and Humanitarian Engagement Project, May 2014, available online at <http://blogs.harvard.edu/cheproject/files/ 2013/10/CHE-Project-IHL-and-SC-Practice-concerning-Urban-Siege-Operations.pdf> (visited 18 July 2019), at 3–4: '[o]nly civilian starvation on a scale that is clearly excessive in relation to the anticipated military advantage of enemy defeat through encirclement and isolation from support or relief is prohibited', mentioning US Manual, § 5.20.1.

[97] Arts 57(1) and 58 AP I, Rules 15 and 22, ICRC Customary IHL Database.

[98] Art. 70(2) AP I and Arts. 59 and 61 (for occupied territories) GC IV, Art. 18(2) AP II, Rule 55, ICRC Customary IHL Database. For blockades, see *San Remo Manual*, see note 47, §§ 103–104.

[99] Art. 70 AP I. See also Henckaerts and Doswald-Beck (eds), see note 21, Rule 54.

be noted that there are only limited circumstances where it is lawful to impede aid before it becomes arbitrary and unlawful under IHL.

They broadly fit into three categories:

(i) Where the relief supplies are not humanitarian in nature[100] or do not emanate from an organization being impartial and humanitarian in character;[101]
(ii) Where supplies are impeded on the basis of reasonable military necessity (i.e. where the relief personnel may hamper military operations or is suspected of engaging in a behaviour in favour of the other Party[102] or if the consignments may be diverted from their destination);[103] and
(iii) Where technical arrangements are imposed for the passage of humanitarian relief,[104] including searches of the relief consignments of convoys transporting them,[105] the imposition of the condition to provide delivery under the local supervision of the Protecting Power,[106] or the temporary limitation of movements of relief personnel.[107] The diversion of relief consignments from the purpose for which they are intended or the delay of their forwarding is only allowed in cases of urgent necessity in the interests of the civilian population concerned.[108]

Of course, each course of impeding will have to be assessed on its own merits, taking into consideration the various justifications advanced by the warring parties and the entirety of the evidence concerning the range of IHL rules and the overall treatment of civilians. However, any failure to abide by these narrow exceptions may be probative of the required intent.

As is obvious from the foregoing, blanket assertions of the lawfulness of sieges,[109] ignoring the adverse impact to the besieged civilians, will not shield a commander

[100] For example, Israel blocked some relief supplies intended to reach Gaza because they were transporting cement which was then used by Hamas to build bunkers, see C. Levinson, 'UN Aid Group: Israel Deliberately Hampering West Bank, Gaza Relief Efforts', *Haaretz*, 30 May 2010, available online at <https://www.haaretz.com/1.5126675> (visited 18 July 2019).

[101] Arts 59 and 61 GC IV require the humanitarian organization to be impartial, and Art. 70 AP I requires relief actions to be humanitarian and impartial in character. See also Art. 71(4) AP I.

[102] Art. 71(4) AP I allows parties to terminate the mission of relief personnel if they exceed their mandate. See also Art. 23(2)(c) GC IV.

[103] Art. 23(2)(a) GC IV.

[104] Art. 70(3) AP I, Arts 23(a), 59, and 61 (for occupied territories) GC IV.

[105] Art. 70(3)(a) AP I, Art. 59(3) GC IV.

[106] Art. 70(3)(b) AP I, Arts 23(3) and 61 GC IV. These safeguards must in no case be misused 'in order to make the rule itself inoperative or unduly delay the forwarding of relief'. See ICRC, Commentary of 1858 to Art. 59 GC IV, at 322, available online at <https://ihl-databases.icrc.org/applic/ihl/ihl.nsf/Comment.xsp?action=openDocument&documentId=15B5740DF2203BE4C12563CD0042C966> (visited 18 July 2019).

[107] Art. 71(3) AP I allows temporary restriction only for imperative military necessity.

[108] Art. 70(3)(c) AP I, Art. 23(4) GC IV, Art. 60 GC IV.

[109] As explained earlier, sieges imposed in areas where only combatants are present or those imposed without the intent to cause the starvation of the population and not causing disproportionate effects among civilians are considered to be lawful.

from criminal responsibility. On the contrary and as mentioned earlier, whilst a siege may begin as lawful, conduct associated with it may move it along the spectrum and into violations of IHL, including intentional starvation of the civilian population, fulfilling the requirements of Article 8 Starvation.

4. Conclusion

An international criminal prosecution criminal prosecution for the crime of starvation, whilst long overdue, is not the panacea. We must aim to increase the likelihood that global leaders act to avoid mass starvation when they are in a position to inflict it, facilitate it, or prevent it. One of the vital steps must be to encourage the use of prosecutions for the crime of starvation with a proper criminal label, to ensure effective penal sanction and proportionate stigma for the underlying misconduct. However, this will only be a step along the road, albeit a significant one. We cannot rest on this aim alone, but we must be more ambitious and seek to render mass starvation morally toxic. As Alex de Waal quotes in his work, the Governor General of Poland, Hans Frank, prophetically wrote in his diary, 'that we sentence 1.2 million Jews to die of hunger should be noted only marginally'[110] and that remains true today eighty years on, with a crime noted only marginally. We are on the precipice of a critical turning point in the history of the crime of starvation, let us seize the current momentum and confront unquestionably both the recurrence of, and responsibility for, the crime of starvation.

[110] A. de Waal, *Mass Starvation: The History and Future of Famine* (Cambridge: Polity, 2017).

6

'The Right to Food in Armed Conflict'

Simone Hutter

1. Introduction

While much of this book is focused on situations of armed conflict, it is important to understand that human rights apply earlier and are essential for the prevention of conflicts. With food insecurity and social inequality as key drivers of conflict, and *vice versa* conflict as one of the leading causes of hunger, addressing the root causes of conflict and tackling food insecurity as a sign of future instability is vital.[1]

Human rights obligations to respect, protect, and fulfil impose clear duties on states to prevent starvation in armed conflict.[2] Human rights law also raises a fundamental question: is a state unwilling or unable to prevent starvation? Starvation during conflict today is not only caused by human decisions; it can also be prevented and alleviated by policy choices.

The focus of this chapter is on the right to food[3] and is centred around the special features and benefits of Economic, Social, and Cultural Rights (ESCR); this approach dissociates it from the distinct concepts of international humanitarian law

[1] Humanitarian Policy Group at the Overseas Development Institute (ODI), *Conflict and Hunger: Breaking A Vicious Cycle*, December 2017, available online at <https://www.permanentrepresentations.nl/latest/news/2017/12/14/release-report-conflict-and-hunger> (visited 11 February 2020) (hereafter the 'ODI report'), at 1, 5. On socio-economic inequalities as a root cause of conflict, see *Prevention of Armed Conflict: Report of the Secretary General*, UN Doc. A/55/985-S/2001/574, 1 June 2001, § 7; CESCR, Concluding Observations: Colombia, E/C.12/1/Add.74, 6 December 2001, § 8; Guatemala, UN Doc. E/C.12/1/Add.3, 28 May 1996, §§ 10–11. For a detailed examination of this interrelation in C. Breen, *Economic and Social Rights and the Maintenance of International Peace and Security* (London: Routledge, 2017).

[2] The controversial question whether non-state actors (NSAs) might also have human rights obligations is discussed in M. Ssenyonjo, *Economic, Social and Cultural Rights in International Law* (Oxford: Hart Publishing, 2016), at 177–187; and in particular on armed NSAs see A. Bellal, *Human Rights Obligations of Armed Non-State Actors: An Exploration of the Practice of the UN Human Rights Council*, Geneva Academy of International Humanitarian Law and Human Rights, Academy Briefing No. 7, December 2016, available online at <https://www.geneva-academy.ch/joomlatools-files/docman-files/InBrief7_web.pdf> (visited 11 February 2020); S. Hutter, 'Starvation in Armed Conflicts—An Analysis Based on the Right to Food', 17 *Journal of International Criminal Justice (JICJ)* (2019) 723–752, at 747–751.

[3] Other human rights are affected by starvation in armed conflict, such as the right to life, which has already been comprehensively analysed. See, most recently, I. Park, *The Right to Life in Armed Conflict* (Oxford: Oxford University Press, 2018).

Simone Hutter, *'The Right to Food in Armed Conflict'* In: *Accountability for Mass Starvation.* Edited by: Bridget Conley, Alex de Waal, Catriona Murdoch, and Wayne Jordash QC, Oxford University Press. © Simone Hutter 2022.
DOI: 10.1093/oso/9780192864734.003.0006

(IHL) (section 3.A), the 2030 Agenda for Sustainable Development with its seventeen Sustainable Development Goals (SDGs) (section 3.B.1), and international criminal law (ICL) (section 3.B.2).

2. The Right to Food

The right to food is enshrined in Article 11 of the International Covenant on ESCR (ICESCR),[4] which is ratified by almost all states, and consists of two different approaches: the right to adequate food (Paragraph 1), and the right to be free from hunger (Paragraph 2).[5]

The *right to adequate food*, as defined by the UN Committee on ESCR (CESCR),[6] is 'realized when every man, woman and child, alone or in community with others, has physical and economic access at all times to adequate food or means for its procurement'.[7] The adequacy requirement implies a certain standard of food and is closely linked to human dignity.[8] In the same vein, Article 25(1) of the Universal Declaration of Human Rights (UDHR)[9] entitles everyone to 'the right to a standard of living adequate for the health and well-being of himself and of his family, including food'.

The *right to be free from hunger* does not go as far. It grants only the minimum nutritional intake necessary for survival, regardless of the adequacy standard, and is directly linked to the right to life.[10] As Kälin and Künzli rightly point out, the right to freedom from hunger constitutes the indispensable basis for the exercise of all other human rights and is the only human right of the two UN Covenants

[4] 16 December 1966, 993 UNTS 3.

[5] The right to food is also affirmed by a range of international and regional human rights treaties, as for instance, Art. 15 of the Protocol to the African Charter on Human and Peoples' Rights on the Rights of Women in Africa, Assembly of the African Union, 11 July 2003, (hereafter the 'Maputo Protocol'). For an overview see Ssenyonjo, earlier at note 2, at 473–481; S. Hutter, *Starvation as a Weapon: Domestic Policies of Deliberate Starvation as a Means to an End under International Law* (Leiden: Brill/Nijhoff, 2015), at 32–41.

[6] The CESCR was established under ECOSOC Res. 1985/17, 28 May 1985, to carry out the monitoring functions. Neither the committee's concluding observations on the submitted state reports nor its general comments are binding, but its interpretations of the right to food, particularly its *General Comment No. 12: The right to adequate food* (UN Doc. E/C.12/1999/5, 12 May 1999, (hereafter the 'General Comment No. 12')) play a crucial role in promoting this right.

[7] General Comment No. 12, see note 6, at § 6.

[8] General Comment No. 12, see note 6, at § 4. For details see Hutter, see note 5, at 36–38.

[9] Adopted by the GA on 10 December 1948, Res. 217 (III). The UDHR is not a legally binding treaty, but it is considered part of an authoritative interpretation of Arts 55 and 56 of the UN Charter, which obligates the members of the UN to promote higher standards of living and solutions for international economic, social, health and related problems (L. Cotula and M. Vidar, *The Right to Adequate Food in Emergencies*, FAO-Legislative Study No. 77, FAO, (2002), available online at <http://www.fao.org/3/a-y4430e.pdf> (visited 3 February 2020)).

[10] *Interim Report of the Special Rapporteur on the Right to Food*, UN Doc. A/72/188, 21 July 2017 (hereafter the 'Interim Report 2017'), § 52.

on human rights referred to as 'fundamental'.[11] While *prima facie* the right to be free from hunger seems to be most relevant to counter mass starvation, the right to adequate food should not be overlooked and is key to prevent armed conflicts from erupting and to make population resilient to mass starvation when conflicts do occur.[12]

A. State Obligations

Like any other human right, both the right to adequate food and the right to be free from hunger impose three different obligations on state parties, namely, (1) the obligation to respect, (2) to protect, and (3) to fulfil.[13]

(i) The *obligation to respect* existing access to adequate food requires state parties not to take any measures that prevent access, such as by destroying foodstuff or infrastructure required for food production (e.g. poisoning water, burning crops). The CESCR emphasized that precisely because rights holders must primarily realize the right to adequate food themselves through their economic and other activities, member states have the duty not to hinder the exercise of those activities.[14]

(ii) The right to food can also be violated through a state's failure to regulate the activities of third or private parties sufficiently in cases where such activities prevent a state's population from gaining access to sufficient food.[15] The *obligation to protect* requires states to prevent human rights violations committed by third or private parties (e.g. individuals, companies, or armed groups), and to investigate, punish, and ensure redress where preventive measures have failed.[16] According to the Maastricht Guidelines, states are

[11] W. Kälin and J. Künzli, 'Das Recht auf Nahrung', *Jusletter* 6 January/13 January 2003, Part 1, § 3, referring to Art. 11(2) ICESCR.

[12] See the details in section 3.A.

[13] See, first and foremost, A. Eide, the former UN Special Rapporteur on the Right to Food, UN Doc. E/CN.4/Sub.2/1987/23, 7 July 1987; or the Maastricht Guidelines on Violations of ESCR, UN Doc. E/C.12/2000/13, 22–26 January 1997 (hereafter the 'Maastricht Guidelines'). For a critical voice, e.g. A. Müller, *The Relationship between Economic, Social and Cultural Rights and International Humanitarian Law, An Analysis of Health-Related Issues in Non-International Armed Conflicts* (Leiden: Martinus Nijhoff Publishers, 2013), at 71–74.

[14] General Comment No. 12, see note 6, § 15. See also OHCHR, *Protection of economic, social and cultural rights in conflict*, UN Doc. E/2015/59 (hereafter the 'OHCHR Report'), § 70.

[15] General Comment No. 12, see note 6, § 19.

[16] OHCHR, *International Legal Protection of Human Rights in Armed Conflict* (2011), available online at <https://www.ohchr.org/Documents/Publications/HR_in_armed_conflict.pdf> (visited 12 February 2020), (hereafter the 'OHCHR 2011 Report'), at 17–18; T. Eatwell, *State Responsibility for Human Rights Violations Committed in the State's Territory by Armed Non-state Actors*, Geneva Academy of International Humanitarian Law and Human Rights, Academy Briefing No. 13, December 2018, available online at visited 7 February 2020), at 21–25; Ssenyonjo, see note 2, at 162–177.

responsible for violations of ESCR that result from their failure to exercise due diligence in controlling the behaviour of non-state actors (NSAs).[17] An example of a violation of the obligation to protect during an armed conflict is the Sudanese government's inaction in the face of the large-scale destruction by the *Janjaweed* rebels in Darfur since 2003, which led to serious food insecurity among the Darfurian population.[18]

In an armed conflict, states often lack control over parts of their territory. Control might then be exercised by either a foreign state (during military occupation) or armed non-state actors. However, the lack of control over a territory does not discharge a state from its human rights obligations within the whole national territory, as long as its government exercises a certain degree of effectiveness.[19] This is challenging since measures taken by a state that has no control or authority over an area are unlikely to be effective.

(iii) The right to food is not a right to be fed. It is about being guaranteed the right to feed oneself, which requires that food is available and accessible (i.e. that each household either has the means to produce or buy its own food).[20] The *obligation to fulfil* the right to food thus primarily requires states to *facilitate* people's access to food by strengthening the ability of individuals to feed themselves. States must therefore proactively strengthen people's access to resources and means to ensure their livelihood, including social protection mechanisms.[21] This obligation clearly requires long-term measures established long before the outbreak of a crisis.[22]

Only when people are not able to feed themselves for reasons beyond their control, do states have the obligation to *provide* access to food directly.[23] In the event of an armed conflict, mere facilitation is usually not possible. War

[17] Maastricht Guidelines, see note 13, Guideline 18. See also the discussion of duties of NSAs see note 2.

[18] *Report of the International Commission of Inquiry on Darfur to the UN Secretary-General*, 25 January 2005, § 99. Similar, *Centre on Housing Rights and Evictions v. Sudan*, African Commission of Human and Peoples' Rights, Communication No. 296/2005, 13–27 May 2009, §§ 209–212.

[19] See, *Ilascu and others v. Moldova and Russia*, ECtHR (2004), Judgment, 8 July 2004, §§ 331–334; confirmed in *Catan and Others v. Moldova and Russia*, ECtHR (2004), Judgment, 19 October 2012, § 109.

[20] Information page on the right to food by former Special Rapporteur on the Right to Food, Jean Ziegler, available online at <http://www.righttofood.org/work-of-jean-ziegler-at-the-un/what-is-the-right-to-food> (visited 11 November 2020).

[21] See also *Interim Report of the Special Rapporteur on the Right to Food*, UN Doc. A/74/164, 15 July 2019 (hereafter the 'Interim Report 2019'), §§ 16–19.

[22] See the details on the long-term approach of IHRL at section 3.A.2.

[23] OHCHR/FAO, 'Fact Sheet No. 34', *The Right to Adequate Food* (2010), available online at <https://www.ohchr.org/sites/default/files/Documents/Publications/FactSheet34en.pdf> (visited 27 October 2021), at 3–4; General Comment No. 12, see note 6, § 15.

often interrupts access to food, thereby leaving malnutrition and starvation in its wake. In these situations, the state needs to provide humanitarian assistance directly.[24]

The right to adequate food requires both the availability of food in a quantity and quality sufficient to meet the dietary needs of individuals, and the economic and physical accessibility of such food.[25] During armed conflict, often the problem is not lack of food itself but that those who are starving are unable to acquire food. In a strictly economic sense, it is useful to frame starvation as an 'entitlement failure': Sen describes three basic forms of food entitlement: (1) access to resources to collect or to produce food; (2) the exchange of resources for food; and (3) the receipt of grants of food or the resources to procure food.[26]

B. Progressive Realization

The tripartite obligation to respect, protect, and fulfil is severely weakened by the requirement that ESCR be achieved only 'progressively' and 'to the maximum of its available resources': Article 2(1) ICESCR requires the state parties 'to take steps' to achieve the full realization of the rights recognized in the ICESCR 'progressively' and 'by all appropriate means'.[27] This obligation is weak in comparison to Article 2(1) of the second of the two UN Covenants on human rights, the International Covenant on Civil and Political Rights (ICCPR),[28] which contains an immediate obligation 'to respect and to ensure'. ESCR are therefore often declared as merely 'programmatic' rights, while CPR are directly enforceable 'legal' rights.[29]

But states still have an immediate obligation to ensure a minimum essential level of subsistence, that is the core content of the right to food, which is directly linked to the right to life.[30] In addition, prohibition against discrimination pursuant to

[24] General Comment No. 12, see note 6, § 6.

[25] General Comment No. 12, see note 6, §§ 3, 8.

[26] For details, A. Sen, *Poverty and Famines, An Essay on Entitlement and Deprivation* (Oxford: Oxford University Press, 1982), at 1–7.

[27] See note 4.

[28] 16 December 1966, 99 UNTS 171.

[29] On the effect of this limitation on the justiciability of ESCR, see CESCR, *General Comment No. 9: The Domestic Application of the Covenant*, 3 December 1998, UN Doc. E/C.12/1998/24, § 10; CESCR, *General Comment No. 3: The Nature of States Parties' Obligations*, UN Doc. E/1991/23, 14 December 1990 (hereafter the 'General Comment No. 3'), §§ 5–6, 9. For a critical assessment of the historical development of ESCR and the primacy of CPR, see I. Cismas, The Intersection of Economic, Social, and Cultural Rights and Civil and Political Rights, in E. Riedel, G. Giacca, and C. Golay (eds), *Economic, Social, and Cultural Rights in International Law: Contemporary Issues and Challenges* (Oxford: Oxford University Press, 2014) 448–472; Hutter, see note 5, at 21–26.

[30] General Comment No. 12, see note 6, at § 14; General Comment No. 3, see note 29, § 10. See also the Voluntary Guidelines to Support the Progressive Realization of the Right to Adequate Food in the Context of National Food Security, adopted by the 127th Session of the FAO Council, November 2004 (hereafter the 'FAO Voluntary Guidelines'), Guideline 16.

Article 2(2) ICESCR is immediately effective, which means that discrimination with regard to access to food cannot be justified under any circumstances, including low levels of resources.[31] This also pertains to an armed conflict.[32] But what does the 'progressive realization' concept of ESCR mean for the state obligations set out earlier under section 2.A.?

States have an immediate negative duty to abstain from any action that could create starvation (*obligation to respect*).[33] By virtue of its purely negative character, justification on the basis of a realization over time shall not satisfy the requirements of this specific obligation. The Special Rapporteur on the Right to Food equates 'the prevention of access to humanitarian food aid in internal conflicts or other emergency situations' through the direct action of states or other entities insufficiently regulated by states with unwillingness of the state and a violation of the right to adequate food.[34]

The progressive realization of the *obligation to protect* people's resource base for food, pursuant to Article 2(1) ICESCR, also requires immediate steps to be taken, including the adoption of legislative measures. But 'positive budgetary measures' only need to be achieved progressively.[35]

The *obligation of states to fulfil* the right to food corresponds with the obligation 'to take steps' up to the maximum of their available resources. Article 2(1), in conjunction with Article 11 ICESCR, requires a state progressively to ensure the full realization of the right to food through all appropriate means.[36] Similar to the obligation to protect, the obligation to fulfil often requires positive budgetary measures. But the CESCR held that resource constraints alone cannot justify inaction and that the availability of resources does not alter the immediacy of the obligation to take steps.[37] It can be expected that the basic resources required to allow individuals to be free from threats to their survival are available in every state, if necessary, through international cooperation.[38] In the same vein, retrogressive measures (i.e. measures which directly or indirectly lead to a backward movement in the enjoyment of the rights)[39] in the enjoyment of the core content of ESCR 'cannot be justified exclusively on the basis of the existence of a conflict: States have

[31] General Comment No. 12, see note 6, § 18; OHCHR Report, see note 14, §§ 31–32.

[32] See the details in section 3.

[33] For example, CESCR, *Statement on 'An evaluation of the obligation to take steps to the maximum of available resources' under an optional Protocol to the Covenant'*, UN Doc. E/C.12/2007/1, 21 September 2007 (hereafter the 'CESCR Statement'), § 7.

[34] Interim Report 2017, see note 10, § 56 (referring to General Comment No. 12, see note 6, § 19).

[35] CESCR Statement, see note 33, §§ 4 and 7.

[36] General Comment No. 12, see note 6, §§ 16–17.

[37] CESCR Statement, see note 33, § 4.

[38] Müller, see note 13, at 83–84; and the details on the minimum-core approach in general, at 74–99. He questions the actual feasibility of determining an internationally defined minimum core content (at 83 and 91–93); see also G. Giacca, *Economic, Social, and Cultural Rights in Armed Conflicts* (Oxford: Oxford University Press, 2014), at 35.

[39] OHCHR Report, see note 14, § 24. An example would be the reduction or removal of subsidies, without adequate alternative support measures.

to demonstrate that any retrogression was unavoidable and that all the possible measures have been taken, including seeking international cooperation and assistance, to overcome the resource constraints.'[40] Otherwise, they risk being held accountable. While the monitoring system of ESCR will be dealt with later,[41] it is already helpful to understand the difficulties of human rights bodies to assess a state's capacity as there is a presumption of a state's discretion in determining what resources are available.[42] Therefore it is essential that a state has to demonstrate that every effort has been made to use all resources that are at its disposal to satisfy the minimum core obligation.[43]

Monitoring bodies should not easily accept a lower adequacy level due to resource constraints. It is important to keep in mind that war is human-made and it would be wrong to excuse its adverse consequences as an impediment to the progressive realization of ESCR. The CESCR has on several occasions affirmed its expectations that governments must make serious attempts to solve existing conflicts through political negotiations taking into account the negative effect that armed conflicts have on the implementation of ESCR.[44] In addition, the availability of resources is often a question of prioritization, especially in emergency situations. Military spending and arms acquisitions can have adverse consequences on the protection and fulfilment of ESCR.[45] While states generally see it as their sovereign prerogative to decide on military expenditure,[46] it is still important to assess a state's alternatives from a human rights perspective. Human rights bodies have expressed their concern in different cases in which the military expenditure contrasted with allocations for social services.[47] They further clearly expressed that '[e]ven when conflicts result in resource constraints, states are required to prioritize the availability, accessibility and acceptability of goods and services to groups

[40] OHCHR Report, see note 14, § 70. CESCR Statement, see note 33, § 10, provides a list of objective criteria for states to justify retrogressive measures based on resource constraints. See also General Comment No. 3, see note 29, § 9. Stricter, the Maastricht Guidelines, see note 13, Guideline 14(e), declaring that any deliberate retrogressive measure that reduces the extent to which the right to food is guaranteed is a violation of the covenant. For a detailed discussion with many examples of the CESCR assessing state's retrogressive measures in its concluding observations, Ssenyonjo, see note 2, at 93–95.

[41] See the details on the accountability in section 3.B.

[42] Detailed on budget analysis, see A. Nolan, Budget Analysis and Economic and Social Rights, in Riedel, Giacca, and Golay (eds), see note 29, 369–390; see also Müller, see note 13, at 99–102. See, in contrast, the many available indicators to measure people's access to food (details in section 3.B.1).

[43] General Comment No. 12, see note 6, § 17; General Comment No. 3, see note 29, § 10.

[44] CESCR, Concluding Observations: Colombia, E/C.12/1/Add.74, 6 December 2001, §§ 4 and 30; Guatemala, UN Doc. E/C.12/1/Add.3 28 May 1996, §§ 4, 23, and 33; Nepal: UN Doc. E/C.12/NPL/CO/2, 16 January 2008, §§ 4 and 33; Sri Lanka, UN Doc. E/C.12/1/Add.24, 16 June 1998, §§ 5 and 21; Sudan, UN Doc. E/C.12/1/Add.48, 1 September 2000, § 9. Note that the Maputo Protocol includes a right to peace with an obligation of states to reduce military expenditure significantly in favour of spending on social development (see note 5, Art. 10(3)).

[45] See details in Müller, see note 13, at 200; Hutter, see note 2, at 729–730.

[46] Giacca, see note 38, at 46–50; see also 40–41 (on priorities in resource allocation).

[47] See, for instance, Committee on the Rights of the Child, Concluding Observations: Sudan, UN Doc. CRC/C/SDN/CO/3-4, 22 October 2010, § 17; CESCR, Concluding Observations: Democratic Republic of the Congo, UN Doc. E/C.12/COD/CO/4, 16 December 2009, § 16.

rendered vulnerable by conflict'.[48] In reality, this is often not the case in emergency situations. For example, in the ongoing humanitarian crisis in Venezuela which was triggered by an economic collapse and a political crisis, it was reported that the difference between those who have access to the goods supplied by the state at subsidized rates and those who do not is determined by party affiliation. Those not in favour are forced into the black market, where food and supplies are sold at prices that are unaffordable for the vast majority.[49]

C. Other Restrictions during Armed Conflict

It is now widely accepted that international human rights law (IHRL) continues to apply during armed conflicts and in situations of occupation.[50] Further, in contrast to many human rights treaties,[51] the ICESCR does not contain an explicit derogation clause (i.e. the temporary suspension of a right as a whole in public emergency situations).[52]

But this does not mean that the right to food cannot be restricted. Limitation clauses in IHRL instruments permit states lawfully to limit the scope of the

[48] OHCHR Report, see note 14, § 71. See also CESCR, Concluding Observations: Sudan, UN Doc. E/C.12/1/Add.48, 1 September 2000, § 40.

[49] *Report of the General Secretariat of the Organization of American States (OAS) and the Panel of Independent International Exerts on the Possible Commission of Crimes against Humanity in Venezuela*, 29 May 2018 (hereafter the 'OAS Report'), at 238. Another example of Democratic People's Republic of Korea (DRK) is described in Hutter, see note 5, at 79–81 (during a humanitarian catastrophe military personnel, Communist Party members, and those thought to be most loyal to the regime, purportedly received the largest allotments). See also *Report of the detailed findings of the Commission of Inquiry on human rights in the DRK*, UN Doc. A/HRC/25/CRP.1, 7 February 2014 (hereafter 'DRK Report'), § 1125.

[50] See in depth, OHCHR 2011 Report, see note 16. The International Court of Justice (ICJ) confirmed this for the ICESCR in its Advisory Opinion of 9 July 2004 on the *Legal Consequences of the Construction of a Wall in the Occupied Palestinian Territory*, available online at <https://www.icj-cij.org/files/case-related/131/131-20040709-ADV-01-00-EN.pdf> (visited 11 February 2020), §§ 112, 130. Reaffirmed in *Armed Activities on the Territory of the Congo (Democratic Republic of the Congo v. Uganda)*, Judgment of 19 December 2005, available online at <https://www.icj-cij.org/files/case-related/116/116-20051219-JUD-01-00-EN.pdf> (visited 11 February 2020), § 216. This was also repeatedly emphasized by the UN General Assembly (e.g. GA Res. 2444 (XXII), 9 December 1968). See also Human Rights Committee (HRCte), *General Comment No. 31: The nature of the general legal obligation imposed on States Parties to the Covenant*, UN Doc. CCPR/C/21/Rev.1/Add. 13, 26 May 2004 (hereafter the 'HRCte General Comment No. 31'), § 11.

[51] For example, Art. 4 ICCPR, but also instruments aiming at the protection of ESCR, such as the European Social Charter (1 July 1999, 2151 UNTS 277, Art. 30).

[52] The applicability of ESCR during armed conflicts has been confirmed by the practice of international human rights bodies, such as in the Concluding Observations of the CESCR on Israel, UN Doc. E/C.12/1/Add.69, 31 August 2001, §§ 12 and 15. With regard to the right to food: Interim Report 2017, see note 10, § 48. An in-depth analysis on ESCR in armed conflicts is provided in OHCHR Report, see note 14, at 6–15; Giacca, see note 38; E. Mottershawa, 'Economic, Social and Cultural Rights in Armed Conflict: International Human Rights Law and International Humanitarian Law', 12 *The International Journal of Human Rights* (2008) 449–470. For a more extensive approach on derogation, Y. Arai-Takahashi, *The Law of Occupation: Continuity and Change of International Humanitarian Law, and its Interaction with International Human Rights Law* (Leiden: Brill/Nijhoff, 2009), at 371–373.

protected human rights in order to protect public health, public safety, and morals, to restore order, and to protect fundamental rights and freedoms of others. In contrast to derogation, limitations are not restricted to exceptional situations and are considered general elements of the human rights treaty machinery. Article 4 ICESCR allows member states to restrict the free exercise of its rights as 'determined by law only in so far as this may be compatible with the nature of these rights and solely for the purpose of promoting the general welfare in a democratic society'.

But the ICESCR's limitation clause 'was not meant to introduce limitations on rights affecting the subsistence or survival of the individual'.[53] Starvation is likely to touch upon the core content, namely the right to be free from hunger. The minimum core content of the right to food—the right to be free from hunger—must not be subject to restrictions as this would deprive the ICESCR of its *raison d'être*.[54] Accordingly, the CESCR points out that states have a 'core obligation to take the necessary action to mitigate and alleviate hunger as provided for in Paragraph 2 of Article 11, even in times of natural or other disasters'.[55]

The right to adequate food can be limited, provided that the state concerned meets the burden of justifying the restriction (i.e. the conditions pursuant to Article 4 ICESCR).[56] When justifying the restriction, the state needs to adhere to the principles of legality, legitimacy, and proportionality.[57]

In addition, a state's action or omission due to *force majeure* does not amount to a violation of the ICESCR.[58] *Force majeure* is defined by the International Law Commission (ILC) as 'the occurrence of an irresistible force or of an unforeseen event, beyond the control of the state, making it materially impossible in the circumstances to perform the obligation'.[59] Armed conflicts do not qualify, in themselves, as creating an impossibility to respect human rights. A defence of *force majeure* will only be accepted if the eruption of violence, such as attacks by rebels,

[53] The Limburg Principles on the Implementation of the ICESCR, UN Doc. E/CN.4/1987/17, 8 January 1987 (hereafter the 'Limburg Principles'), § 47.

[54] General Comment No. 3, see note 29, § 10; in general, M. Sepulveda, *The Nature of the Obligations under the International Covenant on Economic, Social and Cultural Rights* (Cambridge: Intersentia, 2003), at 281. See also Interim Report 2017, see note 10, § 50.

[55] General Comment No. 12, see note 6, § 6. See also the *Report on the Situation of Human Rights in Kuwait under Iraqi Occupation*, prepared by W. Kälin, Special Rapporteur of the Commission on Human Rights, UN Doc. E/CN.4/1992/26, 16 January 1992, § 52.

[56] See, inter alia, CESCR, *General Comment No. 14: The Right to the Highest Attainable Standard of Health*, UN Doc. E/C.12/2000/4, 11 August 2000, §§ 28–29 (regarding the right to health).

[57] See the Limburg Principles, see note 53, § 60. For details about these principles shall be referred to Müller, see note 13, at 120–129.

[58] Art. 61 Vienna Convention on the Law of Treaties (VCLT), 23 May 1969, 1155 UNTS 331; Maastricht Guidelines, see note 13, Guideline 14(f).

[59] Art. 23(1) of the ILC Draft Articles on State Responsibility, 9 August 2001, submitted to the GA (A/56/10), (hereafter the 'ILC-Articles').

was totally unforeseeable and the state was unable to use any means to try to ensure the respect of human rights.[60]

In summary, Article 2(1) ICESCR, the limitation clause of Article 4 ICESCR, and the defence of *force majeure* are sufficiently flexible tools to counter emergency situations, including armed conflicts. But while the core content of the right to food—the right to be free from hunger—must not be restricted even during armed conflict, the allowed adequacy standard of the right to adequate food may be lowered legitimately if resources are scarce or if military forces operate under time constraints during an armed conflict.

3. Importance of Right to Food in Conflict

IHRL, IHL, and ICL interact in complex ways. The same factual background can be a violation of both ESCR and IHL as well as constitute an international crime.[61] The prevention of access to humanitarian food aid in an internal conflict, for example, constitutes a violation of the right to food under Article 11 ICESCR, as well as a grave violation of IHL.[62] In addition, a state's failure to take measures to improve the nutritional security of its population also contravenes states' commitments towards the implementation of the SDGs at the national level.[63]

While the various fields of law remain distinct, they are generally characterized as complementary and mutually reinforcing.[64] A correct interpretation of ICL frequently depends upon precise understanding of the legal terms employed in IHRL or IHL.[65] While the complex relationship between IHRL and IHL obligations and

[60] ILC-Articles, see note 59, Commentary on Art. 23, § 7. Doswald-Beck is rightly calling for a strict interpretation (L. Doswald-Beck, *Human Rights in Times of Conflict and Terrorism* (Oxford: Oxford University Press, 2011), at 41).

[61] A profound examination of the protection of ESCR in general through international criminal law is provided in E. Schmid, *Taking Economic, Social and Cultural Rights Seriously in International Criminal Law* (Cambridge: Cambridge University Press, 2015), see in particular at 69, and details at 41–45. And focusing on starvation, M. Ventura, 'Prosecuting Starvation under International Criminal Law: Exploring the Legal Possibilities', 17 *Journal of International Criminal Justice* (2019) 781–814; W. Jordash, C. Murdoch, and J. Holmes, 'Strategies for Prosecuting Mass Starvation', 17 *Journal of International Criminal Justice* (2019) 849–879. See the details in section 3.B.2.

[62] See, for instance, in CESCR, Concluding Observations: Sri Lanka, UN Doc. E/C.12/LKA/CO/2-4, 9 December 2010, § 28.

[63] See, for example, CESCR, Concluding observations on the fifth periodic report of Sri Lanka, 4 August 2017, E/C.12/LKA/CO/5, §§ 55–56, 74.

[64] HRCte, General Comment No. 29: Derogations during a State of Emergency, UN Doc. CCPR/C/21/Rev.1/Add.11, 31 August 2001, § 3; confirmed in HRCte General Comment No. 31, see note 50, § 11. Repeated in Interim Report 2017, see note 10, § 48; OHCHR Report, see note 14, § 69. See also the Conclusions of the work of the ILC Study Group on the Fragmentation of International Law: Difficulties arising from the Diversification and Expansion of International Law, 2006, submitted to the GA (A/61/10, § 251).

[65] Schmid, see note 61, at 69.

the influence of IHL on the assessment of IHRL is examined elsewhere,[66] the purpose of this section is to highlight the particular importance of the right to food during conflict situations (section 3.1) and its importance for the accountability for starvation (section 3.2).

A. Right to Food vs. IHL

In times of armed conflict, IHRL and IHL may apply simultaneously and both aim to ensure that civilians are not denied food.[67] This protection is essential, as in many conflicts more civilians die due to deprivations of food, medicine, and other non-violent causes than as a direct result of hostilities.[68]

The right to food adds a long-term perspective to the IHL provisions which primarily regulate what means and methods are permitted in war and generally do not foresee positive obligations of states to provide humanitarian relief.[69] Additionally, there are procedural advantages to the complementary application of ESCR and IHL. Unlike the IHL treaty regime, IHRL is endowed with a wide range of accountability and enforcement mechanisms. Not only ICESCR proper but also many IHL rules—if framed in human rights terms—are enforceable through human rights mechanisms.[70] ESCR have also been evaluated by commissions of inquiry and fact-finding missions. In comparison to human rights treaty bodies, the mandates of these mechanisms are generally not limited to IHRL.[71]

1. Broad Scope

IHL applies only if the threshold of an armed conflict is reached. Internal confrontations only rise to the level of armed conflict when the threshold of violence

[66] See the detailed analysis in Giacca, see note 38; G. Giacca, 'The Relationship between Economic, Social, and Cultural Rights and International Humanitarian Law', in Riedel, Giacca, and Golay (eds), see note 29, 308–342; Hutter, see note 2.

[67] An overlap primarily exists when IHL regulates domestic situations of a state and thus concurs with the provisions of IHRL. A state has human rights obligations primarily within its national territory. But the ICESCR applies also extraterritorially to individuals abroad when they are under effective control of a state party (CESCR, *General Comment No. 1: Reporting by States Parties*, UN Doc. E/1989/22/, 27 July 1981, § 3; Giacca, see note 38, at 108–127; Doswald-Beck, see note 59, at 40, and in detail, at 9–21. For details shall be referred to the Maastricht Principles on Extraterritorial Obligations of States in the Area of ESCR, 28 September 2011, available online at <https://www.etoconsortium.org/nc/en/main-navigation/library/maastricht-principles/?tx_drblob_pi1%5BdownloadUid%5D=23> (visited 4 February 2020); Giacca, see note 38, at 130–149; M. Langford et al., *Global Justice, State Duties: The Extra-Territorial Scope of Economic, Social and Cultural Rights in International Law* (Cambridge: Cambridge University Press, 2013).

[68] See, for instance with regard to children, the *Report of the UN Secretary-General on the Protection of Civilians in Armed Conflict*, UN Doc. S/1999/957, 8 September 1999, at 16.

[69] Hutter, see note 2, at 738–739 and 745.

[70] Giacca, see note 38, at 166–167; Arai-Takahashi, see note 52, at 413–414.

[71] Giacca, see note 38, at 204–210 (with many concrete illustrations).

requires the use of military means and methods employed.[72] However, many internal confrontations fall short of this measure, such as the recurring large-scale protests in Venezuela.[73] According to the United Nations Office for the Coordination of Humanitarian Affairs (OCHA), 7 million Venezuelans (or 24 per cent of the population) were estimated to be in need of humanitarian assistance in February 2020.[74] Doctors reported that hunger was killing children at an alarming rate with nearly 2,800 cases of child malnutrition, which resulted in approximately 400 deaths in 2017 alone.[75]

Globally, internal violence related to non-conflict economic collapse, and civil and political demonstrations are also the root cause for hunger and malnutrition. Crucially, starvation that occurs in non-conflict situations (and are thus not governed by IHL) are covered by IHRL.[76] It is also important to keep in mind that in states with totalitarian political systems, the regime is often so repressive that opponents are unable to confront the government (such as in the Democratic People's Republic of Korea (DRK) where officials implemented actions, decisions, and policies known to have led to mass starvation and death by starvation).[77]

From an ESCR perspective, the question of whether a situation has reached the threshold of an armed conflict within the meaning of IHL generally only matters to the extent that the concurrent application of IHL can impact the assessment of state duties. IHRL allows a broader, continuous approach that is not limited to the time of the armed conflict. This is important in light of the complexity of contemporary armed conflicts which cannot always easily be compartmentalized into distinct categories of pre-, during, and post-conflict situations.[78] The emergency character of an armed conflict might influence the adequacy level of the right to food or justify other restrictions (Articles 2(1) and 4 ICESCR).[79]

[72] Cf. Art. 1 (2) APII. See also Decision on the Defence Motion for Interlocutory Appeal on Jurisdiction, *Dusko Tadić*, (IT-94-1-AR72), Appeals Chamber, 2 October 1995, § 70. See the details in Giacca, see note 38, at 8–9, and 168–172.

[73] The details of the political crisis are described in the OAS Report, see note 49.

[74] OCHA, *Venezuela: Situation Report*, 18 February 2020.

[75] M. Kohut and I. Herrera, 'As Venezuela Collapses, Children Are Dying of Hunger', *The New York Times*, 17 December 2017, available online at <https://www.nytimes.com/interactive/2017/12/17/world/americas/venezuela-children-starving.html> (visited 5 February 2020).

[76] The Martens Clause supports this logical conclusion (see, *inter alia*, the preamble to AP II).

[77] DRK Report, see note 49, § 1115, 512–518 and on the crimes against humanity in political prison camps §§ 1033–1067. See also the database by the Committee for Human Rights in North Korea available at <https://www.hrnk.org> (visited 9 December 2019); S. Haggard, M. Noland, and E. Weeks, *North Korea on the Precipice of Famine* (New York: Peterson Institute for International Economics, 2008), at 746–747.

[78] Giacca, see note 38, at 10.

[79] See in sections 2.B and 2.C. See the details in Giacca, see note 38, at 10; and Hutter, see note 2, at 734 and 746.

2. Long-term Approach and Nutritious Food

Both natural and human-made disasters (such as armed conflicts) have a devastating effect on the environment and human populations, but not all classes of society are equally affected. Disasters often exacerbate existing inequalities and increase the vulnerability of at-risk populations.[80] In countries where inequality is greater, economic slowdowns and downturns have a disproportionately harmful effect on low-income populations' food and nutrition security because they use large portions of their income to buy food.[81]

The world's poor are mostly rural and depend on agriculture for their employment and income.[82] This makes them particularly vulnerable to emergency situations and price fluctuations. Even in cases when food is not scarce in the country, peasants may suffer entitlement losses when their farming land, water facilities, or harvest is destroyed (Yemen provides an example).[83] As explained under section 2.A., starvation during war is often caused by a lack of economic accessibility rather than the lack of food in the country.[84]

Therefore, food aid measures should expand their focus beyond the delivery of goods.[85] First aid facilities, such as the provision of commodities and materials during an emergency, may help to meet the urgent and immediate needs. But longer-term rehabilitation and development is necessary to encourage recovery and build capacity to satisfy future needs.[86] It is important to recreate the

[80] ILC Report 2012, UN Doc. A/67/10, at 89, § 69; FAO and others, *The State of Food Security and Nutrition in the World 2019: Safeguarding against Economic Slowdowns and Downturns* (2019), available online at <http://www.fao.org/3/ca5162en/ca5162en.pdf> (visited 6 February 2020) (hereafter the 'Food Security 2019'), at 97; B. Conley and A. de Waal, 'The Purposes of Starvation: Historical and Contemporary Uses', 17 *Journal of International Criminal Justice* (2019) 699–722, at 701. Devereux demonstrates that mortality rates among vulnerable socio-economic groups can be considerably higher than the average (S. Devereux, *Famine in the Twentieth Century* (Institute for Development Studies, 2000), at 9–10).

[81] Food Security 2019, see note 80, at 68.

[82] A 2016 World Bank report found that 80% of the extreme poor live in rural areas and 65 per cent of poor working adults make a living through agriculture (World Bank Group, *Who Are the Poor in the Developing World?* (2016), available online at <http://documents.worldbank.org/curated/en/187011475416542282/pdf/WPS7844.pdf> (visited 6 February 2020), at 1, 13).

[83] *Report of the detailed findings of the Group of Eminent International and Regional Experts on Yemen* UN Doc. A/HRC/42/CRP.1, 3 September 2019, §§ 128, 429, 440, and § 752 citing a report published by the World Peace Foundation (WPF), describing that agricultural zones were impacted by Coalition strikes, following an apparent 'strategy of hitting the resources of rural life.' (M. Mundy, *The Strategies of the Coalition in the Yemen War: Aerial Bombardment and Food War*, World Peace Foundation, October 2018, at 9).

[84] See the details in Chapter 2 in this volume. See also A. Sen, *Development as Freedom* (Oxford: Oxford University Press, 1999), at 167; Sen, *Poverty and Famines*, see note 26, at 7; World Food Programme, *Global Report on Food Crisis*, 2 April 2019, at 25. See also, OHCHR-FAO Fact Sheet No. 34, see note 23, at 4.

[85] See the 2011 ECOWAS Charter for Food Crisis Prevention and Management in the Sahel and West Africa, § 6 ('choose alternatives to food aid wherever possible'); and also Art. 2(a)(i) of Food Assistance Convention 2012.

[86] See, for instance, Art. 2(a)(ii)/(v) of the Food Assistance Convention 2012; or §§ 2 and 4 of the 2011 ECOWAS Charter, see note 85. For details see Cotula and Vidar, see note 9, at 63–64.

lost entitlements for those who are hit the hardest by the emergency (e.g. through public employment programmes or insurance).[87]

Inclusive development policies, which address the vulnerability of the poor and increase resilience, are vital and need to be in place long before the outbreak of a possible war or other emergency situations.[88] While IHL aims at alleviating the direct and immediate effects of armed conflicts, the positive obligations flowing from the right to food go beyond this first aid approach and can add a long-term perspective.[89]

IHRL is the appropriate framework to assess the standard of food required for the civilian population in armed conflict.[90] The right to adequate food is focused on the long term. The CESCR interprets the notion of sustainability as intrinsically linked to the notion of adequate food or food security, implying food being accessible for both present and future generations. While the meaning of 'adequacy' is to a large extent determined by prevailing social, economic, cultural, climatic, ecological, and other conditions, 'sustainability' incorporates the notion of long-term availability and accessibility.[91]

The importance of the need to provide an adequate standard of nutrition as opposed to providing the minimum calories necessary to survival is increasingly recognized.[92] This is also evident in SDG Indicator 2.1.2 which provides a perspective on global food insecurity that looks beyond hunger towards the goal of ensuring access to nutritious and sufficient food for all.[93] Vitamin and mineral deficiencies play a substantive role in shaping crisis-related morbidity and mortality. Malnourished people are at higher risk of mortality in the case of an emergency.[94] But it is hard to translate the right to adequate food into a specific list of entitlements, since good nutrition depends in complex ways on a wide range of factors (such as clean water, basic healthcare, and good hygiene).[95]

[87] Food Security 2019, see note 80, at 102–119. See also FAO Voluntary Guidelines, see note 30, Guidelines 16.7 and 16.8.

[88] Food Security 2019, see note 80, at 97. See also the ILC Draft Articles on the Protection of Persons in the Event of Disasters, 2016, submitted to the GA (UN Doc. A/71/10, chapter IV), dealing with aspects of prevention, including disaster risk reduction.

[89] See Hutter, see note 2, at 746–747.

[90] See the discussion on the context-sensitive effective complementary application of the right to food and IHL in Hutter, see note 2, at 746–747.

[91] General Comment No. 12, see note 6, § 7.

[92] See, for instance, Food Security 2019, see note 80, at 27–42; Global Strategic Framework for Food Security and Nutrition (GSF) (2017), available online at <http://www.fao.org/cfs/home/activities/gsf/en/> (visited 7 February 2020).

[93] See note 109.

[94] P. Webb and A. Thorne-Lyman, *Entitlement Failure from a Food Quality Perspective: The Life and Death Role of Vitamins and Minerals in Humanitarian Crises*, UNU-WIDER, Research Paper No. 2006/140 (2006), at 5–9. See the discussion in Hutter, see note 5, at 121–122.

[95] J. Drèze, 'Democracy and the Right to Food', in P. Alston and M. Robinson (eds), *Human Rights and Development: Towards Mutual Reinforcement* (Oxford: Oxford University Press, 2005) 45–64, at 55.

B. Accountability

The compliance of all contracting states with the obligations of the ICESCR is monitored within the framework of a reporting system: States must give an account of measures designed, improvements achieved, and difficulties encountered in the domestic implementation (Articles 16 and 17 ICESCR). The CESCR examines states' reports and monitors 'the measures which they have adopted' and 'the progress made'.[96] Based on reporting and following direct dialogue between the expert delegation of a state and the CESCR, the CESCR adopts its Concluding Observations.[97] Although the CESCR's observations are not legally binding, the CESCR can find a violation of the ICESCR and request detailed information on the steps a 'condemned' state has taken to implement the recommendations. But a report-based system alone has proven to be insufficient to result in any real changes, particularly in states which are not subject to internal scrutiny by its population.[98]

Since the 2008 Optional Protocol to the ICESCR (OP) entered into force in 2013, the CESCR has examined individual complaints (so-called communications).[99] These communications can be submitted by individuals (Article 2 OP) or by state parties (Article 10 OP). In addition, an inquiry procedure can be invoked by the CESCR on its own initiative (Article 11 OP).[100] Even though many states remain sceptical,[101] this new complaint procedure can potentially enhance the effective protection of ESCR at the international level and has already been used.[102] This section aims to put this monitoring system in comparison to the concepts underlying the SDGs (section 3.B.1) and ICL (section 3.B.2).

1. Development Goals vs. Progressive Realization Standard

In 2015, the 2030 Agenda for Sustainable Development was adopted by the General Assembly and signed by 193 countries.[103] The SDGs represent an important

[96] See the details in Ssenyonjo, see note 2, at 39–40. See note 6 on the CESCR.

[97] For details see CESCR: *Overview of the present working methods of the Committee*, available online at <https://www.ohchr.org/EN/HRBodies/CESCR/Pages/WorkingMethods.aspx> (visited 28 November 2019).

[98] Ssenyonjo, see note 2, at 41–43.

[99] Optional Protocol to the ICESCR, adopted by the HRC (Res. 8/2, 18 June 2008) and by the UN GA (UN Doc. A/RES/63/117, 10 December 2008).

[100] For an overview of these mechanisms and the history of the Optional Protocol, see Ssenyonjo, see note 2, at 43–51; M. Langford, 'Closing the Gap? An Introduction to the Optional Protocol to the International Covenant on Economic, Social and Cultural Rights', 27 *Nordic Journal of Human Rights* (2009) 1–28; B. A. Simmons, 'Should States Ratify? Process and Consequences of the Optional Protocol to the ICESCR', 27 *Nordic Journal of Human Rights* (2009) 64–81, both available online at <https://www.jus.uio.no/ior/english/people/aca/malcolml/NTMR109-1.pdf> (visited 28 November 2019); Giacca, see note 38, at 22 (note 92).

[101] As of 9 March 2022, 26 states have ratified the OP and 24 states have signed it (see <https://indicators.ohchr.org/> (visited 31 May 2022)).

[102] See the first communications brought against Spain (e.g. *IDG v. Spain*, Communication No. 2/2014, UN Doc. E/C.12/55/D/2/2014, 13 October 2015 in which the CESCR found that Spain violated Arts 2(1) and 11(1) ICESCR). See the details in Ssenyonjo, see note 2, at 49–50.

[103] Replacing the Millennium Development Goals which from 2000 sought to tackle poverty.

universal call to action and are guiding global development efforts from 2016 to 2030. Among the seventeen SDGs is SDG 2 'Zero Hunger' which aims to end hunger, achieve food security and improved nutrition, and promote sustainable agriculture by 2030.[104] Achieving zero-hunger within the next ten years will prove a challenge: hunger has risen globally since 2015, affecting more than 820 million people in 2019.[105]

The greatest weakness of development goals resides in monitoring states' advancement.[106] The UN developed indicators to measure progress towards the SDGs.[107] The main indicator for eradicating global hunger is the prevalence of undernourishment (SDG Indicator 2.1.1)[108] and prevalence of moderate or severe food insecurity based on the Food Insecurity Experience Scale (SDG Indicator 2.1.2).[109] While the progress can be measured by these indicators, it is difficult to monitor the corresponding state efforts, identify negligent states, and address offences. Persistent disagreement on optimal strategies for eradicating poverty and hunger and providing social protection exacerbate the problem.[110] This section aims to shed light on the advantages of using the legal mechanisms to monitor ESCR.

While the SDGs have clearly given fresh impetus to the realization of ESCR and among them the right to food, they also harbour the risk that the political debate moves away from granting concrete entitlements to legal state obligations. The use of the term 'goals' underlines that these are not legally binding obligations or human rights.[111] The SDGs cannot grant people concrete entitlements to legal obligations or substitute for the correlative legal duties of states. Abstract ideas about development must be translated into human rights and formulated in concrete detail.[112] A rights-based approach is required to effectively tackle hunger and poverty

[104] UN Department of Economic and Social Affairs, Statistics Division, SDG Goal 2, available online at <https://unstats.un.org/sdgs/report/2016/goal-02/> (visited 18 November 2019).

[105] Food Security 2019, see note 80, at 3.

[106] Detailed in Hutter, see note 5, at 142–145.

[107] See the SDG indicators website presenting the relevant official data, definitions, and methodologies available online at <http://www.fao.org/sustainable-development-goals/goals/goal-2/en/> (visited 2 February 2020).

[108] 'Indicator 2.1.1—Prevalence of Undernourishment', Sustainable Development Goals, FAO, available online at <http://www.fao.org/sustainable-development-goals/indicators/211/en/> (visited 6 February 2020).

[109] 'Indicator 2.1.2—Prevalence of moderate or severe food insecurity in the population, based on the Food Insecurity Experience Scale', Sustainable Development Goals, FAO, available online at <http://www.fao.org/sustainable-development-goals/indicators/212/en/> (visited 6 February 2020).

[110] An overview of the debates on social protection is provided by S. Devereux and R. Sabates-Wheeler, 'Editorial Introduction: Debating Social Protection', 38 *IDS Bulletin* (2007), at 1–7.

[111] C. Kaufmann and M. Grosz, 'Poverty, Hunger and International Trade: What's Law Got to Do with It?', 51 *German Yearbook of International Law* (2008) 75–110, at 97; Interim Report 2019, see note 21, § 2.

[112] See, for example, CESCR, Concluding observations on the fifth periodic report of Sri Lanka, 4 August 2017, E/C.12/LKA/CO/5, § 74 (recommending for the achievement of the SDGs that the state party establish independent mechanisms to monitor progress and treating beneficiaries of public programmes as rights holders who can claim entitlements). See already the former UN High Commissioner

and to implement the 2030 Agenda holistically.[113] States should therefore implement the SDGs in a manner which is consistent with their obligation to respect, protect, and fulfil ESCR, that is their commitments in their fight against hunger should be implemented in light of the obligations stemming from the right to food. One way to do this would be to systematically integrate human rights processes (such as the universal periodic review process) into national SDGs strategies.[114]

Owing to state resistance during the drafting process, the 2030 Agenda provides only for follow-up and review consisting of voluntary national reviews and peer-reviewed soft guidance, rather than accountability.[115] Under IHRL, more stringent monitoring mechanisms are in place. But as with the SDGs, there is a certain vagueness inherent in ESCR which makes it challenging to define the exact content of corresponding obligations. It is difficult to establish when a breach of ESCR obligations arises, given the progressive realization concept of ESCR, and to determine what resources are available to a state and to assess if the state has used such resources to the 'maximum' as required under Article 2(1) ICESCR.[116]

Still, the mandatory obligation of states to demonstrate which steps were taken (as explained under section 2.B) makes the difference. Even though the CESCR clearly respects the varying capacities of states to take steps and adopt measures most suited to their specific circumstances, it suggests a standard of review.[117]

The CESCR asks states to report the efforts they have taken to continuously improve the living conditions of the local population.[118] As a benchmark for the right to adequate food, the CESCR applies a standard elaborated in the FAO Voluntary Guidelines and asks states to indicate if the state party has adopted or envisages the adoption of these guidelines; if not, they are asked to explain why.[119] In addition, it should be reiterated that there are immediate obligations which are not subject to progressive realization: (1) to ensure a minimum essential level of subsistence,

for Human Rights, Mary Robinson, in the preface to the Draft Guidelines: A Human Rights Approach to Poverty Reduction Strategies, OHCHR, 10 September 2002.

[113] Interim Report 2019, see note 21, § 50. See already OHCHR, *Principles and Guidelines for a Human Rights Approach to Poverty Reduction Strategies* (2006), UN Doc. HR/PUB/06/12.

[114] Human Rights Council, Summary of the intersessional meeting for dialogue and cooperation on human rights and the 2030 Agenda for Sustainable Development, A/HRC/40/34, 5 March 2019, § 23; Interim Report 2019, see note 21, §§ 52 and 75; CESCR, Concluding observations on the fifth periodic report of Sri Lanka, 4 August 2017, E/C.12/LKA/CO/5, § 74.

[115] Interim Report 2019, see note 21, § 53.

[116] See the deliberations in section 2.B. For details, Ssenyonjo, see note 2, at 95–96; Hutter, see note 5, at 131–132; A. Chapman, A 'Violations Approach' for Monitoring the International Covenant on Economic, Social and Cultural Rights, 18 *Human Rights Quarterly* (1996) 23–66, at 31.

[117] See the details in B. Porter, 'The Reasonableness of Article 8(4) – Adjudicating Claims from the Margins', 27 *Nordic Journal of Human Rights* (2009) 39–53, at 44–45.

[118] The CESCR adopted detailed reporting guidelines on 24 March 2009 (E/C.12/2008/2, §§ 42–47).

[119] E/C.12/2008/2, §§ 42, 47. Relevant is in this context particularly Guideline 14.1 of the FAO Voluntary Guideline (see note 30), since it asks states 'to consider, to the extent that resources permit, establishing and maintaining social safety and food safety nets to protect those who are unable to provide for themselves'. See also Guideline 17 on monitoring, indicators, and benchmarks.

(2) not to actively hinder existing access to food (obligation to respect), and (3) not to discriminate with regard to access to food.

With regard to the communications under the 2008 Optional Protocol to the ICESCR, the CESCR provides a list of objective criteria to examine whether the steps taken by states are adequate.[120] The CESCR notes that in case of failure to take any steps or of the adoption of retrogressive steps, the burden of proof rests with the state party to show that such a course of action was based on the most careful consideration and can be justified by reference to the totality of the rights provided for in the Covenant and by the fact that full use was made of available resources.[121]

This means that also for poorer countries immediate steps are necessary to overcome resource constraints, including seeking international cooperation and assistance.[122] A state's failure to prove that it was unable to carry out its obligation and it has unsuccessfully sought to obtain international support is interpreted by the CESCR as unwillingness to fulfil its obligations.[123]

2. ICL vs. IHRL

ICL acts to enforce the common denominator of IHL and IHRL in a uniform and overarching fashion.[124] Grave violations of both IHL and IHRL incur criminal responsibility if committed deliberately. As explained earlier in this chapter, the same factual background can be an ESCR violation and give rise to state responsibility for internationally wrongful acts, and can also be an international crime leading to criminal responsibility.[125] If the perpetrator of the crime is a state actor (i.e. the conduct of the criminal perpetrator, such as a state official, is attributable to a state)[126] the same conduct might be identified as violation of a treaty protecting ESCR and might constitute an international crime. Or, in cases of a state's failure to protect ESCR, the perpetrator of the crime might be a non-state actor whose conduct must be prevented and criminalized by the state at the national level.[127]

Hence, the focus of ICL lies on the individual, as ICL primarily serves to decide on the guilt or innocence of individuals accused of criminal conduct.[128] The *mens rea* elements of the individual person are therefore at the centre of focus. IHRL, on the other hand, focuses on state duties. As human rights treaties are concluded by states, it is necessary to impute conduct onto a state to identify a violation of an

[120] CESCR Statement, see note 33, § 8.
[121] CESCR Statement, see note 33, §§ 9–10. See more sources at note 39.
[122] OHCHR Report, see note 14, § 70. See also General Comment No. 3, see note 29, § 9.
[123] General Comment No. 12, see note 6, § 17.
[124] Similarly, ICTY Judgment, *Zejnil* (IT-96-21-T), Trial Chamber, 16 November 1998, § 200.
[125] See note 61.
[126] ILC-Articles, see note 59, Art. 2(a); see also the discussion in Hutter, see note 5, at 12–14; Schmid, see note 61, at 46.
[127] Schmid, see note 61, at 45.
[128] Schmid, see note 61, at 68. See also Giacca, see note 38, at 21.

ESCR treaty.[129] It is important to note that only the internationally wrongful act can be attributed to a state, not the *mens rea* elements.

Distinct from ICL, under IHRL there is no need to demonstrate purpose or to analyse what motivates a potential violation.[130] However, in order to assess whether a IHRL violation has occurred and to find ways to address the problem, it is important to determine if a state is unable or unwilling to prevent starvation.[131] In the light of the obligation to take steps by all appropriate means to achieve progressively the full realization of ESCR (Article 2(1) ICESCR), it must be determined if starvation was caused by the state's inability to feed its own population or rather a lack of political will to respect the right to food. Furthermore, the intention behind an encroachment is relevant: the state may limit the enjoyment of the right to adequate food 'solely for the purpose of promoting the general welfare in a democratic society' if it can limit it at all.[132]

It is thus crucially important to differentiate unwillingness from inability in terms of addressing the problem, albeit not as pronounced as in ICL in which everything revolves around the question of intention and guilt. One of the main advantages of IHRL is, as explained in the previous section, that the burden of proof lies on the state to prove its inability, including that every effort has been made to seek international support: '[f]ailure to prove would indicate unwillingness', and constitutes a violation of the ICESCR.[133] In contrast, in ICL, the prosecution has the burden to prove that the accused is guilty. The standard of proof used by most existing international tribunals is 'proof beyond a reasonable doubt.'[134]

Similar to IHRL, ICL also has an 'indirect protective purpose by deterring future crimes and by affirming the importance of the normative values protected'.[135] But international criminal justice reflects a failure of the protective mechanisms of IHL and IHRL: ICL only steps in when the provisions of IHL and IHRL have already failed to prevent the population from deliberate starvation.[136] Then, ICL can be

[129] Schmid, see note 61, at 46. See also Hutter, see note 5, at 12–16. But cf. the obligations of non-state actors, see note 2.

[130] Hutter, see note 5, at 64. See explicitly, Inter-American Court of Human Rights, *Velazquez Rodriguez*, Judgment, 29 July 1988, available online at <http://www.corteidh.or.cr/docs/casos/articulos/seriec_04_ing.pdf> (visited 9 February 2020), § 173.

[131] General Comment No. 12, see note 6, § 17. See the details in Hutter, see note 5, at 131–132.

[132] Art. 4 ICESCR. See Limburg Principles, see note 53, §§ 46–56; Cotula and Vidar, see note 9, at 6; and the details see in Section 2.C.

[133] Interim Report 2017, see note 10, § 56.

[134] S. Wilkinson, *Standards of Proof in International Humanitarian and Human Rights Fact-Finding and Inquiry Missions* (Geneva Academy of International Humanitarian Law and Human Rights), available online at <https://www.geneva-academy.ch/joomlatools-files/docman-files/Standards%20of%20Proof%20in%20Fact-Finding.pdf> (visited 27 November 2019), at 20–24 (with an overview at 24).

[135] Schmid, see note 61, at 46.

[136] Similarly, Lattimer describes the significant advances in international criminal justice in the context of a crisis in the system of IHRL protection (M. Lattimer, 'Enforcing Human Rights through International Criminal Law', in M. Lattimer and P. Sands (eds), *Justice for Crimes against Humanity* (Oxford: Hart Publishing, 2003) 387–415, at 387).

used to account for violations of ESCR.[137] The international protection of human rights and the international criminalization of its most serious breaches (such as the crime against humanity or genocide) are both rooted in the movement to identify and promote the individual as a new participant in international law and entrench the concept of individual rights.[138]

4. Conclusion

Within this article the benefits and special features of the right to adequate food to prevent starvation have been elaborated. The following key principles can be summarized:

(i) The long-term perspective of the right to food aiming at an adequate standard including nutritious food. Sufficient measures must already be in place before a possible conflict scenario. The broad approach of IHRL is also essential in cases of internal disturbances in which IHL is not (yet) applicable (i.e. Venezuela) and for the post-conflict phase.

(ii) The preventive function of ESCR. While they continue to apply during conflict, ESCR are particularly important to reduce the risk of conflict.[139] And *vice versa*, armed conflicts and internal violence are a major cause for hunger and malnutrition worldwide. In the same spirit, SDG 16, the so-called peace goal recognizes that '[t]here is no peace without development, and there is no development without peace, and none of the above without respect for human rights and the rule of law'.[140] Studies demonstrate that 'chronic impunity and lack of accountability for violations of IHRL and IHL not only contribute to further violence during conflict, ... but also significantly reduce the prospects for peace-building'.[141]

[137] E. Schmid, 'War Crimes Related to Violations of Economic, Social and Cultural Rights', 71 *Heidelberg Journal of International Law* (2011) 523–540, at 523; L. van den Herik, 'Economic, Social, and Cultural Rights International Criminal Law's Blind Spot?', in Riedel, Giacca, and Golay (eds), see note 29, 343–366, at 352–356.

[138] However, Van den Herik points out that ICL is primarily concerned with violations of CPR (den Herik, see note 136, at 343).

[139] ODI report, see note 1, at 8; J. Moore, *Humanitarian Law in Action within Africa* (Oxford: Oxford University Press, 2012), at 80 (explaining how social development may alleviate or prevent the pressures that contribute to the outbreak of armed conflict, and contribute to the peace process).

[140] See the statement by Jan Eliasson when he was still UN Deputy Secretary-General (Fred Dews, 'No Peace without Development, No Development without Peace', Brookings, 17 October 2013, available online at <https://www.brookings.edu/blog/brookings-now/2013/10/17/un-deputy-secretary-general-jan-eliasson-no-peace-without-development-no-development-without-peace/> (visited 7 February 2020)). Similarly, SC Res. 2417, 24 May 2018, § 4 (indicating that the denial of humanitarian relief 'may constitute a threat to international peace and security'); Res. GA/11425, 25 September 2013, Sixty-eighth Plenary Meeting of the GA, 'World Leaders Highlight Link between Peace, Development as General Assembly's Sixty-eighth Session Holds Second Day of Annual Debate'; Report of the Secretary-General, UN Doc. S/2004/616, 23 August 2004, § 4.

[141] ODI report, see note 1, at 7. See also Giacca, see note 38, at 5 (criticizing that ESCR abuses have only rarely been included within transitional justice processes and mechanisms). Detailed in A. Nolan

The SDGs and the promotion of human rights standards are two mutually reinforcing agendas.[142] The right to food extends beyond SDG 2 and requires considering all the goals, which collectively seek to empower those who have been left behind.[143] Ignoring the nexus between economic growth, poverty, food security, and nutrition, and the role inequalities play within this nexus, could push policies and programmes designed to end hunger and malnutrition to miss their mark and fail. Rooting out hunger and malnutrition in all its forms will require an integrated understanding to inform solutions that are not exclusively relevant for SDG 2 (ending hunger and malnutrition in all its forms), but also other SDGs, particularly SDG 1 (ending poverty), SDG 8 (promoting inclusive and sustainable economic growth), and SDG 10 (reducing inequalities).[144]

and E. Schmid, '"Do No Harm"?: Exploring the Scope of Economic and Social Rights in Transitional Justice', 8 *International Journal of Transitional Justice* (2014) 362–382; F. Haldemann and R. Kouassi, Transitional Justice Without Economic, Social, and Cultural Rights?, in Riedel, Giacca, and Golay (eds), see note 29, 498–516.

[142] Interim Report 2019, see note 21, §§ 51, 76.

[143] Interim Report 2019, see note 21, in particular §§ 3, 10.

[144] Food Security 2019, see note 80, at 80. On the interrelation of all human rights, Cotula and Vidar, see note 9, at 5; Hutter, see note 5, at 36, see also 25–26.

PART III
THE CASE FOR PROSECUTIONS TODAY

Prosecutions go beyond legal theory into the application of law to real situations with all their evolving complexity. This section offers insight into how the law related to starvation intersects with three major contemporary cases of severe deprivation of objects indispensable to survival in conflict zones: South Sudan, Syria, and Yemen. The case studies focus on the distinct social, historical, political, and economic logics at play as belligerents deploy starvation tactics in pursuit of their military and political objectives. Fusing legal analysis to evolving conditions, this section also offers an example of how questions of evidence, the legal elements of the war crime of starvation under the International Criminal Court's Rome Statute, and various modes of liability might be addressed in relation to potential prosecution of senior South Sudanese perpetrators, with parallels to other cases discussed in this volume.

7

'Not Never Again, but Next Time'

Armed Conflict and Mass Starvation in South Sudan 2013–2019

Chris Newton

1. Introduction

Dak—a general situation of forced displacement, violent asset seizure, and death lasting from several months to many years

—Definition given 13 August 2018 by all-female Focus Group Discussion in Thaker Centre Boma, Thaker Payam, Mayendit County, Unity State

'The county has been flattened'

—Male Focus Group Discussion respondent speaking about Leer County, conducted in Nyal town, Panyijiar County, Unity State in December 2017

Dak is experienced by the targeted population in five main ways:

1. Burning of houses and community infrastructure
2. *Buoth* (hunger) of the highest severity
3. Widespread sexual violence
4. Death
5. Canings and beatings of civilians, especially of women who resist sexual violence

—Given in that order 7 August 2018 by all-female Focus Group Discussion in Kak Boma, Dablual Payam, Mayendit County, Unity State

Humanitarians and others in South Sudan debated whether or not famine was occurring, or was likely to occur in the short-term, almost annually for five years as the same small area of the country was subjected to repeated government military offensives. Before employing the word 'famine', humanitarians look for a limited set of quantified outcomes at or above universal thresholds. Those considering possible legal accountability for starvation may look for the deprivation of objects considered indispensable for survival while emphasizing perpetrator intent. The general public and media might expect images of skeletal victims in

Chris Newton, *'Not Never Again, but Next Time'* In: *Accountability for Mass Starvation.* Edited by: Bridget Conley, Alex de Waal, Catriona Murdoch, and Wayne Jordash QC, Oxford University Press. © Chris Newton 2022.
DOI: 10.1093/oso/9780192864734.003.0007

arid environments headed towards famine camps in search of assistance. These perspectives all truncate the lived reality of famine and mass starvation, especially within armed conflict. Such narrow views can be difficult to match to reality and definitional confusion can delay humanitarian response and other life-saving action, or what Maxwell and Lautze called 'death by definition' as a cause of famine mortality.[1]

The people at risk of or experiencing famine are rarely consulted beyond the documentation of their hunger, soft tissue loss, diseases, and death, if they are reached at all. The narrative of their experience, including how they describe the situation, explain how it developed, and forecast where it may be headed, is overlooked. In the case of central and southern Unity State from 2014–2018, the populations hit hardest by organized violence, including the Nyuong Nuer of Panyijiar County, Hak Nuer of Mayendit County, and Dok Nuer of Leer County, did not appear to commonly use the word famine to describe their experience of the civil war.[2] Instead, they often invoked the term *dak̲*. Among these and other Nuer communities, the term *dak̲* is used to refer to exceptional periods of organized violence, forced displacement, extreme hunger, and high levels of death. The entirety of an extended crisis may also be taken as a single period of *dak̲* collectively.[3]

This word is used to refer to situations in which a substantial number of deaths occur and where the causes of death are linked to violence, hunger, and disease—rather than famine alone. In several humanitarian assessments in central and southern Unity State in 2017 and 2018, the Nuer phrase for famine—*buoth mi diit e lang*—was not generally used to describe any period within the current crisis.[4] Respondents explained that *buoth mi diit e lang* captures only a subset of their experience, primarily hunger, disease, and distress migration in search of food. *Dak̲* captures a wider range of experiences and causes of death primarily due to intense organized violence.

Dak̲ is generally meant as a superlative—it is the worst situation or experience possible, though may still occur to varying degrees over space and time. It is a time of indiscriminate destruction, where a geographic area is subject to a general flattening—literally of structures, and more figuratively regarding the violent, wholesale dislocation of livelihood systems, social networks, and a way of life.

[1] D. Maxwell and S. Lautze, 'Why Do Famines Persist in the Horn of Africa? Ethiopia 1999–2003', in S. Devereux (ed.), *The New Famines: Why Famines Persist in an Age of Globalization* (New York City: Routledge, 2007) 222–244.

[2] Although the Nuer generally refer to themselves as *naath*, this chapter will maintain the common English usage of the exonym Nuer.

[3] 'The county has been flattened' is borrowed from REACH Initiative, *Now the Forest Is Blocked: Shocks and Access to Food—South Sudan*, April 2018, available online at <http://www.reliefweb.int/report/south-sudan/now-forest-blocked-shocks-and-access-food>. The remaining two quotations are from humanitarian assessments on file with the author, authorship confidential.

[4] Humanitarian assessment on file with the author, authorship confidential.

In the pursuit of accountability for starvation crimes in South Sudan, *da̱k* can serve as a starting point for considering four elements of these crimes that are not fully captured by legal framings. First and most importantly, considering *da̱k* helps to keep the perspective and lived experience of the communities targeted by weaponized starvation—in this instance, a subset of Nuer—at the centre of accountability efforts. The term can help to broaden other standard conceptions of mass starvation and support a more comprehensive description of the scope and depth of starvation as a weapon of war. Second, *da̱k* suggests an expansion of the legal view of starvation as primarily the deprivation of objects. It points to the need for greater focus on the entire process of bringing about mass starvation, including causal pathways to and risk factors for mass starvation in conflict.

Third, *da̱k* is an inherently politicized term. While *da̱k* does not necessarily make moral claims on its own, its emphasis on violence leaves little room for doubt about causation and preventability as applied in this period in Unity State: *da̱k* was the result of deliberate actions, with each occurrence prompting questions of why, how, who, and to whom. It may also assist in understanding how the use of starvation as a weapon of war can serve a variety of functions for different actors. Fourth, this inherent politicization of the starvation encompassed by *da̱k* also forces a reconsideration of analytical efforts intended to be apolitical, such as humanitarian famine early warning. If *da̱k* is political, so too are any efforts to analyse and report on characteristics of it.

While *da̱k* is a Nuer term and refers to extreme circumstances, similar cases of mass starvation are common and widespread in South Sudan. From January 2015 to January 2020, thirty-two cases of localized famine conditions and one famine were documented across the country, as classified through the government-led Integrated Food Security Phase Classification (IPC). This sets a minimum for the extent of mass starvation that has most likely occurred across the country through the entire crisis period under consideration here (December 2013 through January 2020), given that the count is known to be incomplete.[5] Where any single occurrence of mass starvation is a catastrophe, South Sudan averaged approximately one such event every two months for five consecutive years, at a minimum—a majority of the country's nine years of independence. Perhaps nowhere else in the world has

[5] This observation is based on technical consensus within the government-led national IPC Technical Working Group vetting team. It covers the IPC Key Messages of all full IPCs—not IPC updates—beginning May 2014 and ending January 2020. For all public IPC reports, see the data portal at <http://www.ipcinfo.org/>. The tally does not include localized famine conditions identified through IPC-compatible analyses, such as provided by the Famine Early Warning Systems Network (FEWS NET) for Ayod County in 2015 in their Food Security Outlook July-December 2015, or other publicly available data indicating likely famine conditions that did not lead to technical consensus within the South Sudan IPC Technical Working Group, such as a household survey done by REACH Initiative in lowland areas of Pibor County in March–April 2018.

publicly reported mass starvation with such frequency for so long in the twenty-first century.[6]

2. Armed Conflict, Famine, and Early Warning in South Sudan

Respondent 'XY' to the African Union Commission of Inquiry on South Sudan (AUCISS) paraphrased a conversation that occurred between himself, a senior military officer, and President Salva Kiir less than six months before the outbreak of civil war. With tensions rising between different political factions, President Kiir reportedly claimed that 'this one is not going to be like 1991, if Riek [Machar] does anything he is going to face it'. XY recalled the devastating and politically inconclusive violence of that period, saying 'I told him, then the people will also suffer, what will be the end game?'[7] In the view of the AUCISS, the unaddressed 'ghosts of 1991'—when the rebel Sudan People's Liberation Army (SPLA) fragmented and fought internally—helped to bring about a new civil war in late 2013.[8] Fought by many of the leaders from the 1991 split, this new war rapidly led to mass starvation and one officially declared famine.

Fifteen years after the last great famine in South Sudan—the 1997–1998 Bahr el Ghazal famine, the second famine in that region in ten years—political and military leaders drawn from the worst-affected communities, particularly Northern Bahr el Ghazal State and central Warrap State, entered into a new war at the head of national government.[9] This time, however, they found themselves directing a counter-insurgency campaign rather than trying to survive one. They had seen first-hand the effectiveness of weaponized starvation in counterinsurgency in the 1983–2005 Second Sudanese Civil War that ultimately led to South Sudan's independence. The Sudanese Armed Forces (SAF) and their allies, including a series of southern Sudanese armed actors, brought about several famines among civilian populations in areas under SPLA control over the course of that war.

[6] This would appear to be true at least since the advent of a standardized humanitarian framework for acute food insecurity analysis in the form of the IPC in 2004.

[7] Separate Opinion of Professor Mahmood Mamdani, AUCISS, Respondent XY to the African Union Commission of Inquiry on South Sudan (AUCISS), 29 July 2014.

[8] O. Obasanjo et al., *Final Report of the African Union Commission of Inquiry on South Sudan*, African Union, 15 October 2014, available online at <https://www.peaceau.org/en/article/final-report-of-the-african-union-commission-of-inquiry-on-south-sudan> (visited 23 March 2022).

[9] Luka Biong Deng observes that the two famines in Greater Bahr el Ghazal in 1987–1988 and 1997–1998 reportedly caused more than 300,000 excess deaths, likely the worst on record for southern Sudan. See L. Deng, *Famine in the Sudan: Causes, Preparedness and Response—A Political, Social and Economic Analysis of the 1998 Bahr el Ghazal Famine*, Institute for Development Studies (1999), available online at https://www.ids.ac.uk/publications/famine-in-the-sudan-causes-preparedness-and-response-a-political-social-and-economic-analysis-of-the-1998-bahr-el-ghazal-famine/> (visited 23 March 2022).

The SPLA had also attempted to starve out SAF garrisons. John Garang, the first leader of the SPLA, openly acknowledged his intentional use of starvation as a weapon of war. In 1987, he stated that '[SAF] garrison towns in the South are famine-stricken and are real disaster areas, and this is good; it means our military strategy is working'.[10] Rather than avoid repeating the atrocities of past wars, those in power today inflicted them once again with devastating efficacy to defeat their rivals. While the ghosts of 1991 may have contributed to the outbreak of South Sudan's civil war, the ghosts of 1998 helped guide how it would be fought.[11]

Mass starvation is inflicted because it is functional and able to further a variety of political, economic, and social objectives. In examining how weaponized starvation was used in the 1987–1988 Bahr el Ghazal famine, David Keen invoked Michel Foucault in asking: 'what use is famine, what functions does it assure, in what strategies is it integrated?'[12] In answer, Keen described how the counter-insurgency tactics of Sudan produced an extensive set of winners and losers in that famine. He argues that mass starvation produced not only a massive number of victims, but also brought sizeable benefits to politically and economically empowered individuals and communities. Mark Duffield extended this analysis further for both Sudan as a whole and regionally within the Greater Horn of Africa. He argued that industrial-scale asset transfer was central to strategies of political survival within what he termed permanent emergency in a context of macro-economic deterioration or collapse.[13]

Nearly thirty years later, de Waal deepened this political economy view of the region in describing its transactional, dollarized, and male-dominated 'real politics'. He observed that political systems functioned more as a marketplace in which loyalties were traded, often for cash and opportunities to collect cash rent. In the case of South Sudan, actors in such a political marketplace used weaponized starvation to wage war and to feed the transactions needed for their own political survival in an extreme revival of the political economy Duffield described.[14] In Sudan and South Sudan, the political marketplace and weaponized starvation appear inseparable.

South Sudan's civil war began in December 2013, less than three years after independence. Political rivalries could no longer be contained by the new country's nascent institutions, including the former rebel political wing-turned-political-party,

[10] African Rights, *Food and Power in Sudan: A Critique of Humanitarianism* (1997), available online at <https://www.sudanarchive.net/> (visited 23 March 2022), at 86.

[11] Elite legacies as a major contributing factor in the use of mass violence would seem to have at least some empirical backing. See S. Straus, *Making and Unmaking Nations: War, Leadership, and Genocide in Modern Africa*, (Ithaca: Cornell University Press, 2015).

[12] D. Keen, *The Benefits of Famine: A Political Economy of Famine & Relief in Southwestern Sudan 1983–1989* (Princeton: Princeton University Press, 1994), at 12.

[13] M. Duffield, 'The Political Economy of Internal War: Asset Transfer, Complex Emergencies and International Aid', in J. Macrae and A. Zwi (eds), *War and Hunger: Rethinking International Responses to Complex Emergencies* (London: Zed Books, 1995) 50–69.

[14] A. de Waal, *The Real Politics of the Horn of Africa: Money, War and the Business of Power* (Cambridge: Polity, 2015).

the Sudan People's Liberation Movement (SPLM), and the national military, the SPLA. South Sudan was a one-party state holding together a diverse collection of political, military, and economic elites—many maintaining or capable of raising independent, often identity-based militias—through free-flowing patronage resources. The causes of the civil war extend far back into the previous war—a conflict marked by political, economic, and social rivalries, shifting allegiances, and mass atrocity.

Only one of many armed actors in southern Sudan, the SPLA, was permitted to sign the Comprehensive Peace Agreement (CPA) with the Sudanese government in 2005 that brought that war to a close. From this position, the SPLA leadership negotiated the incorporation of other southern armed actors into the southern regional government—including those that broke away from the SPLA in 1991. This coalition largely held together until late 2013. To achieve this political incorporation required the integration of numerous, often ethnically based militias into a national military unified only on paper. These constituent militias had until recently inflicted grievous harm on the diverse communities of the south on a regular basis. Despite a series of peripheral rebellions, including multiple after the 2010 southern elections, major national actors remained in government through independence, when South Sudan's security concerns were largely focused on Sudan.

Economic collapse following a voluntary 2012 shutdown of oil production and export deepened cracks in the national governing coalition never previously mended. Patronage networks were hit with severe challenges in cash flow. When the question of national leadership of the SPLM arose in 2013, the fiction of a unified SPLM government and of the SPLA as a national, unified army began to unravel. President Salva Kiir eventually sacked much of his government, including then-Vice President Riek Machar, a leader of the 1991 breakaway faction. The SPLM leadership contest—linked to eventual control of the Office of the President and other national institutions—turned violent within Juba in December 2013. This rapidly led to civil war through the fragmentation of the SPLA and widespread mobilization of paramilitaries and militias of varied affiliation. Political and social networks activated all the support they could draw on, with opposition groups initially coalescing around the SPLA-in-Opposition, or IO, led by Machar.

While the early years of the war saw most organized violence, including major military offensives and territorial exchanges, occur within the Greater Upper Nile region, a failed peace process in 2015–2016 led to the expansion of conflict into most areas of the country. Throughout the war, armed actors sought to mobilize any network they could to avoid military defeat, including through transactional politics. Such transactions could involve cash, licencing or at least acceptance of rent collection, looting, and other forms of formal and informal resource accumulation, the provision of ammunition and other material support for organized violence, and other political services like redrawing administrative boundaries to favour some social groups over others.

Even as the SPLA, IO, and their affiliates clashed throughout the country, the means used by the main actors in pursuit of their war aims exacerbated and often exploited many sub-national and local issues. Organized violence increased across the country beyond the war for control of the national government, sometimes with far deadlier effect. It is within and through these overlapping national, sub-national, and local conflicts that mass starvation regularly occurred, including through the use of starvation as a weapon of war.

A. Famine Early Warning in South Sudan: The Invisibility of *Dak*

Contemporary humanitarianism declares famine only when key quantitative thresholds for food consumption, acute malnutrition, and mortality are met or exceeded within a defined period of time—perhaps only a few months—and for a specific geographic area. There are also some caveats for special situations like limited humanitarian access. Humanitarians rely on IPC to engage in this analysis. As a framework and set of tools, IPC allows for agreement that famine under a standard humanitarian definition is occurring or is most likely to occur within a certain number of months, which is a landmark technical achievement. However, analysis through IPC as practised within humanitarian crises tends to lose sight of the process of famine in favour of famine as an event. Within a conflict setting, this analysis also faces challenges in maintaining humanitarian neutrality and independence. In addition to the glaring and enduring capacity gap for incorporating analysis of conflict into famine early warning, IPC analysis does not escape the politics of numbers inherent to any armed conflict.[15] Together, this renders *dak* invisible, even as famine occurs within it.

Successive IPC analyses produce a series of discrete snapshots of acute food insecurity by design, rather than considering a famine process as a unit of temporal analysis. Regarding IPC in South Sudan, 'IPC is useful for declaring an ongoing famine and identifying the start and end points of mortality peaks'.[16] It is not an appropriate means of identifying and monitoring a growing risk of famine due to successive shocks and their cumulative impact, which is how most famines tend to develop. Cormac Ó Gráda observed that historically 'even the poorest societies could muster the resources to guard against occasional failures' like a lost harvest. He uses the term 'bang-bang famines' to describe how successive shocks, such as those leading to back-to-back harvest failures, were needed to cause famine.[17] This

[15] Chapter 11 in this volume.

[16] C. Newton and K. Rickard, *Living Memory of Famine in South Sudan: Using Local Knowledge to Inform Famine Early Warning*, Humanitarian Practice Network of Overseas Development Institute, 10 October 2018, available online at <http://www.odihpn.org/blog/living-memory-famine-south-sudan-using-local-knowledge-inform-famine-early-warning/> (visited 23 March 2022).

[17] C. Ó Gráda, 'The Third Horseman', in *Famine: A Short History*, (Princeton University Press, 2010) 1–44, at 31–32.

term is perhaps unintentionally though aptly onomatopoeic for describing how a succession of military offensives can inflict mass starvation in South Sudan.

The development of *da̱k*, and the use of weaponized starvation generally, fits well within Paul Howe's five-part model of famine as both a process and event. For Howe, an archetypal famine process begins with a form of pressure that inhibits access to food, such as drought or organized violence. When this pressure or its impact on food access is maintained over time, a hold develops. In a hold, strategies for sustainably coping with inadequate access to food may give way to unsustainable and irreversible options in a self-reinforcing downward spiral. Once this spiral begins, the likelihood of famine starts to grow absent intervention.

Eventually, coping cannot continue or provides negligible food access and the capacity to do so collapses. This collapse is when famine as an event, or Howe's famine system, is expected—a period of elevated mortality due to the interaction of starvation, acute malnutrition, and disease, often in relation to distress migration, across a geographic area. A famine system ends, or collapses, through rebalancing, including due to the ending of the conditions that brought on the famine system and the high death toll among the affected population.[18] While *da̱k* can encompass elements of Howe's famine systems model involving pressure, hold, self-reinforcing downward spiral, and famine system, IPC analysis in practice tends to focus on the onset of the famine system only.

IPC in South Sudan also lacks humanitarian neutrality and independence, initially by design and now as grandfathered in despite revised global IPC protocols. At the time of writing, the IPC Technical Working Group (TWG) in South Sudan has been and remains chaired by the national Ministry of Agriculture and Food Security, with representation by the National Bureau of Statistics and national Ministries of Health and of Humanitarian Affairs and Disaster Management, along with a range of state ministries. There has never been representation or direct analytical engagement with any armed opposition group or civilian representatives from territory under their control, despite famine and numerous cases of localized famine conditions occurring in territory under prolonged opposition civil administration. This is to say that those inflicting *da̱k* officially manage famine early warning, while those controlling and living in areas experiencing *da̱k* are categorically excluded from formal IPC analysis. This often leads to sanitized causal analysis, sometimes manifesting as a sort of *deus ex machina* explanation of how starvation somehow occurred within a chaotic mix of vaguely defined shocks, including a passive description of insecurity.

Beyond the impact on causal analysis, IPC in South Sudan is also subject to a brutal politics of numbers, in addition to diverse logistical and technical challenges. The result is often a form of the front-stage and back-stage humanitarianism described by Isabelle Desportes in Ethiopia, where IPC and its supporting

[18] P. Howe, 'Famine Systems: A New Model for Understanding the Development of Famines', 105 *World Development* (2018) 144–155.

data systems are presented outwardly as well-functioning, accurate, and apolitical while in private the severe toll taken by the political and technical realities of civil war is readily acknowledged by practitioners.[19] Public knowledge of mass starvation in South Sudan results from a long and complex process of data collection, analysis, and publication that must navigate layers of political battles, including accessing the worst-affected areas, collecting certain kinds of problematic information like deaths and their causes, and publishing technical confirmation of outcomes in politically salient areas of the country.

It can be difficult, for example, to indicate widespread starvation in an area recently subjected to a high-profile government military offensive or, more delicately, in the President's home area. The numbers of severely and extremely food insecure individuals published are a direct commentary on the winners and losers of organized violence. Where mass starvation is overwhelmingly man-made, to count the starving at all is to acknowledge culpability—an often overlooked reality in humanitarian efforts within armed conflict.[20]

In a country that has been no stranger to famine over the last thirty years, the primary famine early warning system—IPC and supporting data collection—is too important to fail. Yet through the many obstacles to tracking mass starvation, it is possible if not most likely that as many as three false negatives (where famine occurs and yet no declaration is made) and one false positive (where famine does not occur and is still declared) occurred in the first four years of civil war in South Sudan. While a false positive may facilitate a no-regrets approach to humanitarian response and most likely save lives regardless, a false negative is most likely to result in a preventable mass loss of life. That even the possibility of one false negative or false positive per year of armed conflict on average existed in South Sudan through the first half of its civil war is concerning. This is to say nothing of the incomplete reporting on the even larger number of individuals who experienced some form of famine conditions in geographically diffuse pockets spread across the country.[21]

[19] I. Desportes, 'The Humanitarian Theatre: Drought Response during Ethiopia's Low-Intensity Conflict of 2016', 57 *Journal of Modern African Studies* (2019) 31–59.

[20] It should not be surprising that such numbers are hard to come by, as the difficulties faced in the production of knowledge on mass starvation are only a subset of a larger problem. Until the London School of Hygiene & Tropical Medicine (LSHTM) published an estimate of crisis-attributable excess mortality in late 2018, only a single analyst, Casie Copeland, at the International Crisis Group (ICG) had previously attempted to collate and publicize tallies of violent deaths, let alone those due to less direct causes. This lonely effort was halted by the end of 2014. For the LSHTM estimate of crisis-attributable mortality, see F. Checchi et al., *Estimates of Crisis-attributable Mortality in South Sudan, December 2013–April 2018: A Statistical Analysis*, London School of Hygiene & Tropical Medicine, September 2018, available online at <https://www.lshtm.ac.uk/south-sudan-full-report> (visited 9 October 2019). For the initial ICG estimates and commentary on the overall lack of mortality data, see N. Kulish, 'New estimate sharply raises death toll in South Sudan', *The New York Times*, 9 January 2014, available online at <https://www.nytimes.com/2014/01/10/world/africa/new-estimate-sharply-raises-death-toll-in-south-sudan.html> (visited 27 October 2021); P. Martell, 'South Sudan is dying, and nobody is counting', *Agence-France Presse*, 10 March 2016, available online at <https:/sg.news.yahoo.com/south-sudan-dying-nobody-counting-045835128.html> (visited 5 October 2021).

[21] Although no definitive retrospective analyses have been undertaken, some have questioned the 2017 famine declaration and suggested it may not have been famine under the IPC definition or other common understandings of famine. This is not to say that the situation was not extreme, but mortality

3. The Interaction of Organized Violence and Food Security in Rural South Sudan

A. Vulnerability to Weaponized Starvation: Ecology, Mobility, and Seasonality

Most of South Sudan's population is exposed to organized violence as a shock in unique ways, particularly through how flood plain and wetland ecology structure settlement patterns and livelihood systems. In South Sudan, an agro-pastoralist centre politically and economically dominates at the expense of an agriculturalist periphery. The transhumant agro-pastoralism that characterizes politically salient and densely settled communities residing on flood plains and within wetlands across the geographic core of the country gives rise to a paradox of resilience in South Sudan. Households utilize both agriculture and pastoralism, along with supplementary activities like fishing and casual labour, to meet food needs throughout a given year. Transhumant pastoralism involves seasonal patterns of livestock migration, though with permanent settlements maintained and returned to annually, unlike nomadic pastoralism.

As Deng argues, the asset base of an agro-pastoralist household that makes it resilient to natural shocks like drought may also render it vulnerable to man-made shocks like conflict. To maintain a large livestock herd in areas of southern Sudan deemed in rebellion and open to asset stripping in the Second Sudanese Civil War was to attract the predatory attention of Khartoum-aligned armed actors.[22] The same remains true in South Sudan today, though more so regarding militarized asset stripping than ideas of "traditional" raiding.[23]

Looking at a regional topographical map, South Sudan appears at first glance as a major depression nearly surrounded by highlands and plateaus. The White Nile—one of the two branches of the Nile River that meet at Khartoum, Sudan—and a series of other large rivers all descend thousands of metres as they flow into and across South Sudan from the west, south, and east, many emptying into the Sudd wetlands that nearly bisect the country. On the clay flood plains to the east

consistent with famine may not yet have developed by the time of the declaration. The possible false negatives include, but may not be limited to, Unity State in 2015, as discussed in the first case, Greater Baggari in mid-2017, as described in the second case, and Ayod County in mid-2017. In Ayod County, where FEWS NET independently assessed localized famine conditions in 2015, famine may have occurred in mid-2017. A mix of published and unpublished humanitarian assessments show that indicators appear to have converged at or near famine outcomes during a period of extreme food insecurity, a cholera outbreak, and the severing of a final trade link to Sudan during a government offensive in Upper Nile State, most likely in the period April–July 2017.

[22] L. Deng, 'Are Non-Poor Households Always Less Vulnerable? The Case of Households Exposed to Protracted Civil War in Southern Sudan', 32 *Disasters* (2008) 377–398.

[23] D. Felix da Costa, N. Pendle, and J. Tubiana, ''What is happening now is not raiding, its war: The growing politicisation and militarisation of cattle-raiding among the Western Nuer and Murle during South Sudan's civil wars', in J. Bach, J. Abbink, S. Ancel, A. A. Abdel Aziz, E. Fantini, P. Ferras, H. Mwakimako, C. Nallet, A. Ylönen, and J. Záhořík (eds), *Routledge Handbook of the Horn of Africa* (New York: Routledge, 2022) 224–238; H. Wild, J. Madut Jok, and R. Patel, 'The Militarization of Cattle Raiding in South Sudan: How a Traditional Practice Became a Tool for Political Violence' 3 *Journal of International Humanitarian Action* (2018).

and west of the Sudd as well as within the wetlands, rural livelihoods track marginal shifts in elevation. Access to relative high ground and relative low ground, the availability of which changes with rainfall and river level, determines the ability of households and communities to access food and meet other basic needs.

Strategies for livelihoods and coping with insufficient access to food are operationalized through mobility, particularly on flood plains and in wetlands. Relative high ground, even marginally elevated above a flood plain or wetland, is essential for settlement, agriculture, and pastoralism in the rainy season. Relative low ground, where water, more nutritious grass for grazing, and fish may be concentrated in the dry season, is likewise essential for pastoralism and other activities. These features can only be taken advantage of when local communities have sufficient mobility.

This means that freedom of movement is central to livelihoods and coping, establishing a critical intersection of organized violence and food security. This includes the freedom to move as basic needs and natural shocks require and freedom from forced mobility, such as to occupy relative high ground freely and safely through the rainy season. Mobility can be viewed as a key resource that can expand and contract in relation to hazards. Natural and man-made restrictions on movement, from floodwaters to armed actor activity, always interfere with mobility to some degree, with hunger often close behind.

In a 2006 synthesis of over 3,000 food security and livelihoods reports produced under Operation Lifeline Sudan (1989–2005), Muchomba and Sharp, in collaboration with Deng, explained that '[t]he success or failure of all livelihood systems in southern Sudan rests on the ability of people to move and to trade ... it is only when insecurity keeps people or cattle from moving that periods of unusually acute hunger occur'.[24]

The idea of mobility as a key resource supports analysis of famine as a process. Howe describes how a famine system may be either open or closed, depending on the mobility of those experiencing famine and of those trying to assist them. To improve consideration of the effect of organized violence on mobility, this can be extended to cover mobility in pressures, holds, and self-reinforcing downward spirals, as well as movement within a famine system. As Stephen Lubkemann argues in relation to the Mozambican civil war (1977–1992), the impact of conflict on mobility should consider forced mobility and forced immobility. Mobility must be compared to a baseline in terms of what atypical movement is occurring as well as what normal movement is reduced or absent, such as when distress migration expected in famine is inhibited through organized violence.[25]

Vulnerability and mobility are also informed by seasonality. Absent interruption, livelihood systems tend to follow a consistent seasonal calendar. Each year, agriculture proceeds through periods of land preparation and planting, growing, and harvesting just as transhumant pastoralism is characterized by regular

[24] E. Muchomba and B. Sharp, *Southern Sudan Livelihood Profiles*, Southern Sudan Commission for Census, Statistics and Evaluation/Livelihoods Analysis Forum (2006), available online at <http://www.sudanarchive.net> (visited 27 October 2021).

[25] S. C. Lubkemann, 'Involuntary Immobility: On a Theoretical Invisibility in Forced Migration Studies', 21 *Journal of Refugee Studies* (2008) 454–475.

livestock migration. Most of South Sudan has one annual rainy season. Peak rainy season in these areas tends to be the period of greatest hunger, as the remainder of the previous harvest is exhausted and the next harvest has not yet arrived. For agro-pastoralists, this hunger period, or lean season, is normally mitigated through livestock, trade, and other strategies.

The timing of this lean season is contingent on livelihood outcomes, like a successful harvest at the expected time of year. While normally guided by seasonality, this changes when livelihoods outcomes are impacted by conflict. Short periods of organized violence have the potential to produce long periods of food insecurity. If agriculture is affected at a critical juncture, such as through the looting and destruction of recently harvested crops, the next harvest is twelve months away. If a planting season is lost, the next potential harvest may be almost eighteen months away at the earliest, assuming no other shocks. Pastoralism may see the highest impact when vital dry season water and grazing access are denied, leaving cattle to die, be sold off, or be slaughtered.

Once a harvest or most livestock are lost, alternative means of accessing food are required. Many strategies for coping, however, follow their own seasonal calendars. For example, the availability of wild foods tends to decline in the dry season, when harvested crops would normally be available. Absent that harvest, what is normally the most food secure period of the year may become the most food insecure for those reliant on wild foods. In this way, seasonality can be exploited by an armed actor seeking to starve a population.

From this perspective, objects and their indispensability to survival are contingent on vulnerability and likely to change as a conflict progresses. Conventionally, objects indispensable to survival are understood as the basic means of engaging in activities like agriculture and obtaining potable water. In South Sudan, this must broaden to include the range of objects needed for livelihood systems on the flood plains and in wetlands, the activities required for utilizing these objects, and activities for coping with the loss of these initial objects.

Objects must cover those needed for the immediate production of food like livestock, agricultural tools and seeds, fishing equipment, and fruit trees, as well as a wide range of household assets. Household assets range from those needed for the utilization of food, like cooking utensils, as well as milk and water containers, to assets needed for other basic needs, like shelter and blankets. Depending on the livelihood system, they may also include basic means of transport such as dugout canoes and bicycles. These objects may also be rendered useless if the activities that utilize them are inhibited, such as farming, movement to and from agricultural land, markets, and pastoral camps, livestock migrations, and movement for collecting natural resources like cooking fuel and wild foods.

Once the deprivation of these initial objects occurs, other objects and the activities that utilize them take on greater importance for survival. A waterlily root may not be indispensable in normal times. Under extreme duress after the loss of livestock, agricultural production, and markets, it may be the only means of survival.

As vulnerability to starvation increases, what was previously supplemental or marginal becomes indispensable. To deprive a population of access to something like wild foods in a time of severe food insecurity is to starve that population. As coping collapses, it becomes increasingly difficult to define the remaining objects as mobility itself is likely to function as the last means of survival. Faced with starvation, individuals and households may move within an affected area in search of food, such as from any remaining social connections, or seek to exit the area. Blocking these final coping strategies and distress migration could be considered an additional deprivation, though not involving physical objects. Table 7.1 summarizes key impacts that can cause famine, or faminogenic impacts, their coverage in international humanitarian law, a concrete example of an object or activity or concern in rural South Sudan, and how the impact can occur through a natural shock and the use of starvation as a weapon of war.

Table 7.1 South Sudan: Faminogenic impacts, international humanitarian law, natural shocks, and the use of starvation as a weapon of war

Faminogenic Impact	International Humanitarian Law	South Sudan Example	Natural Shock	Weaponized Starvation
Loss of Objects/ Physical Assets	Deprivation of objects indispensable to survival—'attack, destruction, and removal'	Cattle	Livestock disease outbreak	Asset stripping; pillage
Inhibition of Activities Utilizing Objects	'Rendering useless' aspect of deprivation	Cattle migration	Drought	Use and threat of organized violence; pillage
Inhibition of Activities Not Utilizing Conventional Objects (Coping Strategies)	Contextualized and contingent deprivation	Collecting wild foods	Drought	Use and threat of organized violence
Inhibition of Civilian Mobility: Within and to Exit from a Given Geographic Area	Humanitarian access and mobility, but civilian mobility within targeted area and ability to exit the area unclear	Within area—transit among humanitarian distribution points, villages seeking food and other support; Exit from area—distress migration	Severe flood	Use and threat of organized violence; siege

Source: Chris Newton, 2022

B. The Political Economic Logic of Weaponized Starvation

A primary goal of armed actors in civil war is often to weaken their adversary rather than to defeat them outright. This can be cost-effective, saving the efforts of total military victory while allowing the achievement of other political, economic, and social objectives. A weakened adversary can be negotiated with and potentially rehabilitated as an ally or affiliate. One effective means of weakening another armed actor is to attack the civilian population within the territory under its control. This may be especially true in asymmetric or symmetrically unconventional conflicts.[26] While the nature and severity of civilian targeting in civil war varies, environments with a small number of dense population clusters spread across large rural areas may encourage the use of mass dispossession, as in South Sudan.[27]

Forcing civilians to move can accomplish a variety of objectives, including emptying high-value territory, such as around an oilfield, and concentrating population in low-value territory, like deep wetlands where civilian mortality is likely to rise, or within one's own territory. One effective means of forcing civilian movement is to deprive them of objects and activities indispensable to survival, rendering them destitute. A destitute population facing starvation will move if allowed to do so, as seen in famines historically. When not allowed to do so, as in Howe's closed famine system, the population is likely to face rising mortality absent external transfers like humanitarian assistance.

However, the creation of mass starvation over a large geographic area or among a large population can be resource-intensive and time-consuming. Absent a recent famine or major shock, an armed actor will likely have to invest substantially in the effort over two or more cycles of a livelihoods system, such as multiple progressions of agriculture from planting through harvest. However, this approach can also be pursued in a way that generates distributable resources, delegates direct implementation, and becomes self-reinforcing.

If civilian dispossession is desired, and an effective and efficient method of achieving dispossession is to deprive civilians of indispensable objects and activities, then questions arise not only of who is best to enact this deprivation but also what will happen to the objects deprived. Weaponized starvation, especially in a rural livelihoods system characterized by lootable assets like livestock and grain, often functions as a massive redistribution of wealth away from a target population. Beneficiaries of this transfer are likely to include direct perpetrators, the political, economic, and social elites of the communities from which the perpetrators mobilized, and a mix of national elites that set the process in motion or at

[26] L. Balcells and S. N. Kalyvas, 'Does Warfare Matter? Severity, Duration, and Outcomes of Civil Wars', 58 *Journal of Conflict Resolution* (2014) 1390–1418.

[27] Geographically concentrated populations with inflexible loyalties have also been associated with greater efficacy in the use of indiscriminate violence against civilians in counterinsurgency. See A. Downes, 'Draining the Sea by Filling the Graves: Investigating the Effectiveness of Indiscriminate Violence as a Counterinsurgency Strategy', 9 *Civil Wars* (2007) 420–444.

least supported it. National elites pursuing civil war objectives may transact for the cooperation of sub-national and local actors in attacking a bloc of civilians, potentially without much overlap in national political interests between them. Sub-national and local actors may not be heavily invested in the national war effort, but they may desire the material gains and what these gains enable for the pursuit of their own objectives. Where sub-national and local grievances predate a civil war, the costs to national elites of delegating the implementation of weaponized starvation may be relatively low.

This resource transfer can help trigger two self-reinforcing dynamics that increase the likelihood of a famine system beginning, even after the active use of organized violence ends. As Howe theorizes, self-reinforcing dynamics are a crucial component of a famine process. To stave off starvation and death, coping strategies are likely to become increasingly unsustainable, irreversible, and even zero-sum in relation to a variety of basic needs. A population pushed into this sort of downward spiral may be forced to deliver their own assets to those using organized violence against them and other actors benefitting from the results, such as through distress sales of livestock that perpetrators were unable to locate during the use of organized violence. This may intensify if an armed actor effectively suppresses other means of coping, like denying a targeted population access to areas for wild foods collection.

Along a similar logic, the self-payment of perpetrators within a process of violently depriving a population of objects indispensable to their survival may give way to a self-reinforcing dynamic of asset seizure and destruction. Different groups of fighters and a range of national and sub-national elites may end up in a competition of self-aggrandizement while an environment of impunity lasts and the balance of power remains in their favour. Where cash is scarce, impunity itself can become a resource for transactions. This can sometimes lead to an otherwise greater intensification of asset stripping than was originally intended and in some circumstances it may be difficult—though not impossible—to gauge the original objectives of the elites involved. As the assets of a given target population are depleted, there may be a rush to capture what remains as perpetrators face diminishing returns on the use of organized violence.

C. Social and Physical Distance Between Perpetrator and Targeted Population

In an echo of research on ethnic defection in civil wars,[28] Deng has shown how narrowing the social and physical distance between an armed actor and targeted civilian populations increases the negative impacts of organized violence in South

[28] See, for example, S. N. Kalyvas, 'Ethnic Defection in Civil War', 41 *Comparative Political Studies* (2008) 1043–1068; J. Lyall, 'Are Coethnics More Effective Counterinsurgents? Evidence from the

Sudan. The smaller the social and physical distance between the low-ranking perpetrators of organized violence and a target population, the greater the efficacy of asset stripping and the damage to livelihoods and social capital. Deng demonstrated the differential impact for counter-insurgency perpetrated by armed actors drawn from communities different from that of the target communities and from communities the same as or similar to that of the target communities. In the case of Greater Bahr el Ghazal in the Second Sudanese Civil War, he traced the effects of organized and systematic raiding by predominantly Arab militias on Dinka communities in Abyei and primarily Dinka militias on closely related Dinka communities in Greater Gogrial.[29]

Where perpetrators are recruited from outside the targeted communities, Deng uses the term 'exogenous counter-insurgency'. Where the armed actor is drawn from the same, or a similar, community as the target community, he uses 'endogenous counter-insurgency'. Using data covering the period and locations of the two Bahr el Ghazal famines, Deng found that endogenous counter-insurgency had a detrimental effect on the likelihood of mortality, social capital, and asset base of households in targeted communities, especially non-poor households, and that exogenous counter-insurgency had a lower, though still negative, impact.[30] The degree of endogeneity can often be at least partially determined by considering the segmentary lineage system that socially organizes most of South Sudan's population. It offers a guiding, though not deterministic, logic for considering how different social units, including sub-ethnic groups, are likely to view their social identity in relation to others.[31]

D. Gendered Livelihoods, Gendered Attacks: Sexual and Gender-Based Violence (SGBV) and the Use of Starvation as a Weapon of War

> *'You must live through the barrels of your guns. Food, wife, and property wherever you find them are to be acquired through your might.'*
>
> SPLA message to graduating trainees, 1987[32]

Second Chechen War', 104 *American Political Science Review* (2010) 1–20; P. Staniland, 'Between a Rock and a Hard Place: Insurgent Fratricide, Ethnic Defection, and the Rise of Pro-State Paramilitaries', 56 *Journal of Conflict Resolution* (2012) 16–40.

[29] Although the Dinka generally refer to themselves as *jieng*, this chapter will maintain the common English usage of the exonym Dinka.

[30] L. Deng, 'Increased Rural Vulnerability in the Era of Globalization: Conflict and Famine in Sudan in the 1990s', in S. Devereux (ed.), *The New Famines: Why Famines Persist in an Era of Globalization* (Routledge, 2007) 245–268; Deng see note 22; L. Deng, 'Social Capital and Civil War: The Dinka Communities in Sudan's Civil War', 109 *African Affairs* (2010) 231–250.

[31] J. Ryle and M. Amuom, *Peace Is the Name of Our Cattle-Camp*, Rift Valley Institute (2018), available online at <http://riftvalley.net/publication/peace-name-our-cattle-camp#:%7E:text=Following%20the%202005%20Comprehensive%20Peace,and%20cycles%20of%20revenge%20killing> (visited 27 October 2021).

[32] African Rights, see note 10.

> *'Go get what you can. Food, a chicken, a goat, a cow, a woman, whatever you find is for you.'*
> *'For those of you who are yet to get married, it is your chance now to find a nice woman.'*
>
> Two different government-aligned commanders speaking to proxy forces before 2018 military operations in central Unity State, Annex 1 of Letter dated 9 April 2019 from the Panel of Experts on South Sudan addressed to the President of the Security Council

SGBV is not incidental to the use of starvation as a weapon of war in South Sudan—it is integral to creating starvation and inhibiting recovery. Any attempted analysis of weaponized starvation in conflict unable to account for SGBV will fail to explain fully how starvation was inflicted. As explained by two different government-aligned commanders operating in central Unity State in 2018, armed conflict can take the logic of the commodification of women and girls to the extreme of objects to be seized and used in the same way as food items or livestock.

In South Sudan's civil war, the use of SGBV has been systematic and widespread. In a 2015 survey of four Protection of Civilians (PoC) sites across the country, the United Nations Population Fund found that 72 per cent of women had been raped, largely by soldiers or police officers, since the outbreak of the war.[33] While SGBV is detrimental to those targeted serves a variety of purposes for the perpetrators, it also has severe consequences for food security. Analysing the use of what she considers to have been genocidal gang rape in Unity State and Central Equatoria State, Clemence Pinaud argues that '[t]hese gang-rapes physically, morally, and economically destroyed the target groups and prevented their moral, material, and demographic regeneration'.[34]

To attack women and girls in rural South Sudan is to attack rural food and nutrition security. Livelihoods and coping strategies are highly gendered, with women and girls handling a wide variety of tasks in food production and utilization in agro-pastoralist communities. They contribute significantly to agricultural and pastoral production in normal times, with the scope of their work increasing during periods of organized violence.

Women and girls are also typically tasked with all food preparation, gathering firewood or other cooking fuel, childcare, and ensuring adequate water for a given household. Even in normal times, these tasks may consume most of the available daylight in a given day. In times of hunger, women and girls will also take the lead in coping strategies like gathering wild foods and undertaking different forms of

[33] Amnesty International, '*Do Not Remain Silent': Survivors of Sexual Violence in South Sudan Call for Reparations and Justice* (2017), available online at <https://www.amnesty.org/en/latest/news/2017/07/south-sudan-sexual-violence-on-a-massive-scale-leaves-thousands-in-mental-distress-amid-raging-conflict/> (visited 27 October 2021).

[34] C. Pinaud, 'Genocidal Rape in South Sudan: Organization, Function, and Effects', 42 *Human Rights Quarterly* (2020) 667–694.

petty income generation. They are also most likely to be the household members dispatched to other households or communities to seek out kinship and social support or to beg outright as well as sent to humanitarian distribution sites to pick up food and other assistance. Women and girls are expected to undertake travel even in the most intense periods of organized violence, as they may face a lower risk of death compared to men and boys, even if they face a higher likelihood of SGBV.

When men are unavailable, women and girls may also fulfil roles in fishing, land clearance, and other tasks generally the purview of men and boys. Together, the food security status of a household and the nutritional status of children under five years old—those most likely to die during a time of extreme food insecurity—are most often in the hands of women and girls. These tasks involve high demands on time, with time becoming a key resource in a similar way to mobility as household food security declines. Trade-offs must be made among an impossible list of tasks to be accomplished with the same finite amount of time, even if limited to those critical for the survival of all household members.

The constant use of SGBV against women and girls does severe physical and mental damage, with long-lasting impacts, and often leads to loss of life. Strategies used to cope with this constant threat impose additional costs, especially in time and mobility or in not utilizing other coping strategies for mitigating hunger. Changing how essential tasks are done in response to the activities of armed actors—such as using alternative locations for fetching water or gathering firewood—can have severe knock-on effects due to the increased time required for each task, such as reducing time spent on childcare. Abandoning tasks like gathering wild foods or going to a functional market to reduce exposure to SGBV in turn further reduces access to food.

In livelihood systems where resource transfers are necessary for marriage, SGBV may also have a severe impact on the asset base of a household, community, or set of communities. In much of rural South Sudan and particularly in agro-pastoralist and pastoralist areas of the country, a would-be husband's extended family typically has an obligation to transfer livestock, primarily cattle, and other resources to the bride's extended family. Referred to commonly as bride-wealth or bride-price, this transfer is generally the result of considerable negotiation and reflective of the perceived value of the bride, her extended family and kinship network, and the prevailing socio-economic conditions in which the marriage occurs. The goal is not only to cement a single marriage but also to establish wider and more durable linkages to build social capital that may be drawn upon during crises.

Household recovery periods after shocks can be shortened if a household with marriageable female members drops its expected bride-price and negotiates for marriage with social networks not affected by the same shock and that still have their herds. In this way, marriages can be a mechanism for shifting productive assets from unaffected to shock-affected areas, including across ethnicities.[35] The shame

[35] D. H. Johnson, 'Political Ecology in the Upper Nile: The Twentieth Century Expansion of the Pastoral "Common Economy"', 30 *The Journal of African History* (1989) 463–486.

and social stigma surrounding victims of SGBV may lower that victim's potential bride-wealth and inhibit or eliminate a historical means of recovery after shocks.

4. Mass Starvation in South Sudan's Civil War

This section provides a brief overview of two cases of mass starvation within South Sudan's civil war: central Unity 2014–2018 and Greater Baggari 2016–2018. While both cases feature the occurrence of publicly released localized famine conditions or famine under the national IPC, they vary in geographic scope, the scale and forms of organized violence used, the involvement of government security forces and other armed actors, and other key factors in the onset of famine conditions or famine. These are not intended as comprehensive or legal analyses of each case but rather brief descriptions of some of the ways in which organized violence brought about mass starvation in service of varied objectives.

A. Counterinsurgency and *Da̠k*: Leer and Mayendit Counties, Unity State 2014–2018

This case is a brief exploration of *da̠k* in Unity State. The use of starvation as a weapon of war has been best documented in Leer and Mayendit counties of Unity State, or central Unity. If anywhere in the country was to see famine in this conflict, it was most likely going to be Unity State. Lying west of the White Nile and occupying much of the land where the Sudd wetlands give way to the western flood plain, its livelihood systems are agro-pastoralist. Livestock are essential to survival and agricultural production alone is typically insufficient for household food needs in a given year.

It is the only state with a Nuer majority, the country's second largest ethnic group, and it contains several oilfields. The prospect of formal and informal state-level sharing of oil revenue fosters tumultuous intra-ethnic political competition among the seven Nuer sub-groups that each predominate in their own county, in addition to a small Dinka population in the north of the state.

In February 2017, famine was declared for Leer County by humanitarian agencies and a host government for the first time since the 2011 declaration in Somalia.[36] Following the declaration, the United Nations (UN) Panel of Experts on South Sudan concluded:

> The bulk of the evidence suggests that the famine, which had been predicted for two years, has resulted from protracted conflict and, in particular, the cumulative toll of military operations undertaken by the leadership in Juba, the denial

[36] Concurrently, it was determined that famine had been prevented at the time of the declaration but was likely to imminently begin in a second county, Mayendit, there was an insufficiency of data

of humanitarian access, primarily by SPLM/A in Government, and population displacement resulting from the war.[37]

The 2017 famine declaration followed after a late 2015 non-declaration of famine, despite some indications of famine at the time. The official reason[38] for the non-declaration was an insufficiency of data, including a still routine lack of mortality data. This was partially due to how the IPC TWG described all deaths due to disease as unrelated to food security, despite IPC globally considering the interaction of starvation, acute malnutrition, and disease to be the primary cause of mortality in famine under its own definitions.[39] Deaths due to causes like drowning during displacement or wild foods collection in wetlands were also considered unrelated to famine, despite these activities being inherent to any contemporary understanding of famine, again including a customary IPC understanding.

Additionally, the Food Security and Nutrition Monitoring System in South Sudan—the primary source of data for IPC analysis in South Sudan—was unable to collect sufficient data in Unity State. Efforts to fill this data gap at the time contributed to the departure of the UN Deputy Humanitarian Coordinator and Country Representative of the UN's Food and Agriculture Organization (FAO). This official coordinated the rapid collection of mortality data in the worst-affected areas of Unity State—where the IPC TWG claimed such data collection was not feasible—and engaged in assertive advocacy that famine had occurred by the end of the year, contrary to the published IPC findings of the time.[40] The UN Humanitarian Coordinator, Toby Lanzer, was also expelled that year.[41]

for confirming or disproving the occurrence of famine in a third county, Koch, and that the onset of famine in a fourth county. Panyijiar, would be prevented only through the provision of the planned humanitarian food assistance. Contrary to popular understanding, only one county was declared as experiencing famine in real-time. See the South Sudan IPC Full Report for January 2017, available online at <http://www.ipcinfo.org/ipcinfo-website/resources/resources-details/en/c/1151919/> (visited 27 October 2021).

[37] K. Ryan et al., *Letter dated 13 April 2017 from the Panel of Experts on South Sudan established pursuant to Security Council resolution 2206 (2015) addressed to the President of the Security Council*, United Nations Security Council, 13 April 2017, available online at <https://reliefweb.int/report/south-sudan/letter-dated-13-april-2017-panel-experts-south-sudan-established-pursuant> (visited 27 October 2021).

[38] Some question whether the entire story is one of data. For example, de Waal has argued that the 2017 declaration represented a shift in the government's political and economic calculus from a non-declaration of famine in 2015 when actual conditions were quite likely worse. See A. de Waal, *Mass Starvation: The History and Future of Famine* (Cambridge: Polity, 2018).

[39] For example, the South Sudan IPC Key Messages for December 2015 refer to fever, diarrhoea, and respiratory illness as 'non-food security' causes of death and not indicative of near or actual famine.

[40] For the report detailing the more than 10,000 civilian deaths attributable to the year from the 2014 rainy season up through the 2015 rainy season, including nearly 900 drownings with a heavy concentration among female children, see United Nations Office of the Deputy Humanitarian Coordinator in South Sudan, *Crisis Impacts on Households in Unity State, South Sudan, 2014–2015* (2016) available online at <https://reliefweb.int/report/south-sudan/crisis-impacts-households-unity-state-south-sudan-2014-2015-initial-results> (visited 27 October 2021).

[41] 'Ban condemns South Sudan's decision to expel UN humanitarian coordinator', UN News: United Nations, 1 June 2015, available at https://news.un.org/en/story/2015/06/500352 (last visited 19 May 2022).

Prior to the current civil war, the most recent famine in the state was likely in the period 1988–1992, locally called *Ruon Nyakajuok*, or the time of eating a local wild food. In a pattern that would come to repeat itself, this earlier famine was brought about through years of violent attacks on livelihoods as local, regional, and national armed actors vied for supremacy of strategic and rent-producing locations, in addition to proximate natural shocks.[42] Many of these political and economic rivalries continued after the CPA or only became latent with the end of the Second Sudanese Civil War, later structuring the evolution of the war in Unity State.

State-level political and military leaders and their followers entered the current war with personal experience of this period and similar episodes. They knew how certain tactics would bring about mass starvation. The relatively younger fighters, though potentially lacking direct experience with mass starvation, grew up with passed-down knowledge of these events and, coming from within the same livelihoods system, were intimately familiar with what the simultaneous loss of livestock herds, agricultural production, market access, and various coping strategies would mean for a community.

Additionally, Machar, chairman of the IO and at the time of writing First Vice President of the Transitional Government of National Unity, is a Dok Nuer from Leer County. Prior to the most recent civil war, Machar was the commander of a series of Khartoum-aligned armed groups during the 1983–2005 war, having first led a breakaway faction of the SPLA in 1991. Machar's home county and the Dok Nuer that reside there have probably experienced the most concerted campaign to bring about mass starvation of any geographic area or social group within the current civil war.

Numerous other elites and armed actors from Unity State have also played and continue to play pivotal roles in national politics and the civil war, highlighting the political salience of the area beyond the oil underneath it. Illustrative of their importance and capacity for organized violence, had some of these key figures and groups decided to align with the IO and not the government when the civil war began, it is possible that the story of the civil war would instead be about the successful IO offensives into Warrap and Lakes states, including the home area of President Salva Kiir.

This case features repeated and large-scale military offensives by government security forces and their allies, including in 2014, 2015, and 2018, as well as additional fighting in the second half of 2016 after the collapse of a peace agreement and in late 2017. These led to the conventional military defeat of the armed opposition and the recurrent devastation of rural livelihoods with extreme levels of civilian targeting. It is unique in that it also shows the dynamic Deng highlighted regarding social and physical distance between perpetrator and target. With each successful

[42] REACH Initiative 2018, see note 3.

offensive, IO military capacity and political influence among competing Nuer subgroups in the state decreased. Concurrently, the government was increasingly able to narrow the physical and social distance between its attacking forces and the targeted communities by mobilizing members of communities further south in the state. As the sub-national politics of Unity State shifted through the use of these military tactics, so too did the social networks that the government could call upon at scale, increasing the efficacy of its strategy year by year even as less remained to be looted in the main areas targeted.

1. Ruon Tora Bora: Sudanese Rebels and Movement by Road in the 2014 Offensive

The first major offensive of the war in Unity State occurred in a period of time often referred to as *Ruon Tora Bora* in Nuer by central and southern communities. It is a reference to the collaboration between government forces and the Justice and Equality Movement (JEM), a Darfuri armed group. JEM operated alongside remaining SPLA forces after the dissolution of the resident SPLA Division 4 as well as local paramilitaries and other Sudanese armed groups. A major government paramilitary also took form among the Bul Nuer of Mayom County. Built around a pre-existing armed group, the South Sudan Liberation Movement/Army (SSLM/A), it did not yet deploy far beyond the county's borders.

Fighting occurred largely from April to June and was concentrated in northern Unity, though several areas of central and southern Unity were attacked for the first time. The state capital of Bentiu and several oilfields in northern Unity State changed hands multiple times. By the end of 2014, the IO—composed overwhelmingly of Nuer forces that defected or mobilized with the onset of the war—was confined to a key border location north of Bentiu and south of a tentative frontline south of Bentiu running east to west across the entire north of the state.

JEM provided much of the force that hit central Unity in 2014, including Leer County. Infamous for their use of retrofitted Land Cruisers and Toyota 4 × 4s, JEM preferred mobile lightning raids and vehicle swarms rather than the infantry and artillery formations preferred by the SPLA as well as the IO while it retained conventional military capability. In the 2014 offensive, these tactics were not suited to flood plains and wetlands, while in time the IO reportedly obtained additional rocket-propelled grenades and grew more adept at ambushing JEM convoys. JEM and similar Sudanese forces appeared to have stayed close to main roads where their vehicles could operate effectively, preferring to loot high-value assets that could be transported quickly, such as generators.[43]

[43] J. Craze and J. Tubiana with C. Gramizzi, *A State of Disunity: Conflict Dynamics in Unity State, South Sudan, 2013–15*, Small Arms Survey (2016), available online at <http://www.small arms surv eysudan.org/fileadmin/docs/working-papers/HSBA-WP42-Unity-Dec-2016.pdf> (visited 27 October 2021).

This JEM incursion was the first major disruption to livelihoods in central Unity, occurring within the main planting season and severing trade routes into IO territory in central and southern Unity. Agriculture, particularly the production of cereals like sorghum and maize, collapsed in 2014 and did not show even marginal recovery until 2019.[44] In particular, Leer County was targeted for the first time as senior IO figures arrived via the White Nile and Adok port. However, JEM members did not seize large numbers of livestock as this would likely have required a substantial number of lorries or travel by foot to transport the animals. In the words of one IO commander at the time, 'JEM don't walk and they're very dangerous'.[45] Prior to the start of the offensive, there were fewer than 5,000 individuals residing in the PoC site in Bentiu established by the peacekeeping forces of the United Nations Mission in South Sudan (UNMISS) as an *ad hoc* safe area for civilians within its base. At the end of the offensive, there were over 40,000.[46]

2. Counter-insurgency Moves Closer: Co-ethnic Militias and Mass Cattle Seizure in the 2015 Offensive

The 2015 offensive was a multi-pronged operation against the IO throughout Unity State, lasting approximately from February to August, with additional operations through the end of the year. This was the second consecutive planting and harvest season lost for many targeted communities and substantially increased the likelihood of famine, especially in Leer County. While the main thrust of the attack came from northern Unity, additional government forces and allied militia attacked from the south via Lakes State and the White Nile river. This included the destruction of Tayer, a riverside trade hub in Panyijiar County and a commercial lifeline for southern Unity communities.

The government pursued the seizure of territory only so far as it was required to regain control of most oil infrastructure, including the Tharjath area of Koch County. Beyond this, a buffer zone was sought to ensure adequate protection of oil facilities and at least nominally loyal Nuer communities. South of the Chotjiok River dividing Koch and Mayendit counties and what by December 2015 would become the short-lived Northern Liech State–Southern Liech State border—the government enacted a scorched-earth policy. Everything in central Unity outside

44 See the annual reports for 2014, 2015, 2016, 2017, 2018, and 2019 from the Food and Agriculture Organization, World Food Programme, and Government of the Republic of South Sudan Crop and Food Security Assessment Missions to South Sudan (CFSAM). While some have cautioned that the assumptions built into the calculations of the annual CFSAM to South Sudan conducted by the UN and South Sudanese government have regularly biased cereals production estimates downwards for much of Unity State, basic production data may still be taken at least indicatively in terms of a massive decrease in the first year of the war, followed by a general lack of recovery until 2019. It is noted that assessment of cereals production in central Unity has remained remote for the leading UN and government bodies involved for the duration of the civil war. All CFSAM annual reports are available online at <http://www.fao.org/publications/en/> (visited 27 October 2021).

45 Craze (2016), see note 39, at 163.

46 International Organization for Migration Displacement Tracking Matrix, *Conflict and Displacement Timeline: Bentiu/Unity 2014–2016* (2016).

of government garrison towns like Mayendit Headquarters and Leer town was considered open for looting, property destruction, abduction, killings, and rampant SGBV.

A joint report by UNMISS and the UN's Office of the High Commissioner for Human Rights (OHCHR) noted:

> From the middle of 2015, a new pattern emerged, particularly in the central and southern counties of Unity, with entire villages being burned down, food crops destroyed and livestock looted. There are indications that this may have been a deliberate strategy by the government or the SPLA aimed at depriving civilians of any source of livelihood with a view to forcing their displacement.[47]

Other authors described the initial stage of this offensive as 'the beginning of a sustained demographic war on the Nuer south, intended to disrupt the population's ability to sustain itself, notably by displacing thousands of people, abducting women, and garnering resources such as aid, vehicles, and cattle, which were to be brought to the north and west of the state'.[48]

The UN Panel of Experts on South Sudan agreed, writing that:

> The ferocity with which people were deliberately pursued —sometimes for days— into the swamps to kill them is particularly indicative of further escalation of the level of brutality and intensity of violence. These methods employed for fighting were aimed at annihilating SPLM/A in Opposition's support base, and led to a systematic destruction of villages and towns, forcing people into the PoC sites and creating an 'empty area' across the main transport axes in Central and Southern Unity....[49]

Within the main thrust of the offensive in April to August, the composition of counterinsurgency forces shifted sharply closer to the composition of target communities. Sudanese rebels played a minimal role, while a large body of co-ethnic fighters were instead drawn from the Bul Nuer and the network of the SSLM/A—relatively closer to the Hak and Dok of central Unity physically and socially as compared to JEM and other Sudanese fighters, but still distant relative to most other Nuer sub-groups of Unity State.

The centrality of Bul Nuer fighters to the 2015 offensive was noted by the UN Panel of Experts, who also directly observed approximately 8,000 Bul Nuer fighters marching past the Bentiu PoC site in June 2015:

[47] UNMISS Human Rights Division, *The State of Human Rights in the Protracted Conflict in South Sudan*,4 December 2015, available online at <https://unmiss.unmissions.org/sites/default/files/human_rights_update_report_of_4_december_2015_final.pdf> (visited 27 October 2021), at 1.

[48] Craze (2016), see note 40, at 55.

[49] P. Knopf et al., *Letter dated 21 August 2015 from the Panel of Experts on South Sudan established pursuant to Security Council resolution 2206 (2015) addressed to the President of the Security Council*, United Nations Security Council, 21 August 2015, available online at <https://reliefweb.int/report/

> In the SPLA offensive in Unity State from April to June, cattle were the main trophies for the thousands of Bul Nuer young people who aided SPLA. The offensive gave the Bul Nuer the opportunity to extensively loot the cattle of Nuer communities in southern Unity State (see annex V). Cattle-raiding has become the basis for a symbiotic relationship between SPLA and many of its allied militias. Within that relationship, SPLA aims to destroy SPLM/A in Opposition, whereas its allied forces aim to loot as many cattle as possible while contributing to the attainment of the SPLA military objectives.[50]

These Bul Nuer paramilitaries, tallied at almost an additional SPLA division, targeted livestock in Rubkona, Guit, and Koch counties of northern Unity State, with estimated losses in these counties of around 100,000 heads of cattle. In many cases, entire herds were taken, leading to immediate destitution and increasing migration to the Bentiu PoC site and other potentially safe areas.[51]

This asset stripping also extended into northern Mayendit County and deep into Leer County with much greater and more widespread violence.[52] Bul paramilitaries and the SPLA moved on foot throughout rural central Unity and targeted a large number of villages and cattle camps outside the immediate vicinity of roads, in contrast to the movements of JEM and other Sudanese rebels during the 2014 offensive. The primary goals of the Bul Nuer participants appear to have been the acquisition of cattle and the commission of mass sexual violence.

In the aftermath of this offensive, a combination of regular SPLA forces, Bul Nuer militia, and a form of Jegai Nuer militia from Koch County remained in central Unity garrisons and continued to target civilian populations almost to the end of the year. Amnesty International summarized the operations in Leer County at the time, using a description characteristic of government tactics for the entire war in central Unity: 'Witnesses described a regular pattern of attacks where government

south-sudan/letter-dated-21-august-2015-panel-experts-south-sudan-established-pursuant> (visited 27 October 2021), at 37.

[50] Knopf et al., see note 44, at 18.

[51] D. F. da Costa, S. Hutchinson, and N. Pendle, *Pastoralism in Greater Upper Nile: Socio-political Report*, VISTAS and Vétérinaires Sans Frontières-Suisse (2015).

[52] See, for example, South Sudan Protection Cluster, *Protection Situation Update: Southern and Central Unity (April–September 2015)* (2015) available online at <https://reliefweb.int/report/south-sudan/protection-situation-update-southern-and-central-unity-april-september-2015> (visited 27 October 2021); South Sudan Protection Cluster, *Protection Situation Update: Leer County, Southern Unity (October–December 2015)* (2015), available online at <https://reliefweb.int/report/south-sudan/protection-situation-update-leer-county-southern-unity-october-december-2015> (visited 27 October 2021); South Sudan Protection Cluster, *Protection Situation Update: Leer County, Southern Unity State (May 2016)* (2016), available online at <https://reliefweb.int/report/south-sudan/protection-situation-update-leer-county-southern-unity-state-may-2016> (visited 27 October 2021); Human Rights Watch, *'They Burned It All': Destruction of Villages, Killings, and Sexual Violence in Unity State, South Sudan* (2015), available online at <https://www.hrw.org/report/2015/07/22/they-burned-it-all/destruction-villages-killings-and-sexual-violence-unity-state> (visited 27 October 2021).

forces targeted men and boys for killing, women and girls for abduction and rape, and property, including cattle and homes, for looting or destruction.'[53]

The sustainment of a campaign of comprehensive livelihoods targeting by a series of government and affiliated forces for almost an entire year, particularly in Leer County, was instrumental in bringing about destitution and starvation. The introduction of large numbers of Jegai fighters is most likely to have improved the efficacy of civilian targeting—the Jegai Nuer being physically and socially closer than JEM and the Bul Nuer to the Hak and Dok, including through extensive pre-war intermarriage and trade. The duration of operations also kept communities displaced and bereft of their main livelihoods through an entire agricultural cycle and into the dry season, when wild food availability declines, in an example of a combined man-made and natural hold in Howe's famine systems model.

The highest risk period of the calendar year for extreme food insecurity in central Unity appears to be the mid-dry season from approximately January through March. The lack of rain and consequent decline in vegetation lowers milk production from livestock as well as access to alternative food sources, such as most wild foods and fish. As the availability of alternative food sources declines, accessing what remains often requires time-consuming travel deep into wetlands resulting in zero-sum trade-offs with other essential activities. In this way, reduced access to food may constrict further due to seasonality, even without additional organized violence. Without humanitarian assistance or other breaks in this hold, the risk of famine is likely to rise. It is not coincidental that the most extreme situations published under IPC for Mayendit and Leer counties were almost all within the period December–March, including the December 2015 declaration of insufficient evidence for famine classification, the January–February 2017 famine declaration, and the September 2018 projection of famine prevention only through humanitarian food assistance for January–March 2019.

While a degree of functionality began returning to key northern Unity markets through 2015, including in the capital Bentiu, central Unity markets remained dysfunctional and would not become fully operational until 2020 with limited exceptions for low-volume, high-value goods. As monitored by the Famine Early Warning Systems Network (FEWS NET), markets in central Unity would experience the longest period of minimal to no market activity of any markets that they consistently monitored in this time period.[54] In an area of the country heavily

[53] Amnesty International, *'We Are Still Running': War Crimes in Leer, South Sudan* (2016), available online at <https://reliefweb.int/report/south-sudan/we-are-still-running-war-crimes-leer-south-sudan#:~:text=%E2%80%9CWe%20are%20still%20running%E2%80%9D%3A,between%20August%20and%20December%202015> (visited 27 October 2021), at 40.

[54] The Food Security Outlook October 2015 to March 2016 maps the initial loss of functionality for key markets in central Unity. Each subsequent Food Security Outlook market functionality mapping shows non-functioning central Unity markets until the Food Security Outlook June 2020 to January 2021 shows improvement to 'significant disruption and/or limited activity'. All Food Security Outlooks are available online at <https://fews.net/east-africa/south-sudan> (visited 27 October 2021).

reliant on trade flows of outgoing cattle and incoming grain in normal times, the removal of this pillar of the livelihood system was detrimental to civilian food access.[55]

Sustained organized violence also led to the mass suspension of humanitarian programming in central Unity for much of the year, including food assistance provision. Even the International Committee of the Red Cross (ICRC), typically capable of maintaining humanitarian access under duress, was forced to withdraw from Leer County in May, where it was conducting food distributions. The ICRC did not return to Leer County permanently until September, though was forced to evacuate as soon as October.[56] The World Food Programme (WFP) was not active in Leer County in 2015 and did not begin handling most food distribution there until the famine declaration in 2017. For most of 2015, the provision of humanitarian assistance was prevented for months at a time, often due to active conflict and direct threats to humanitarian staff and assets. One of the last means of ensuring access to food was lost for much of the rainy season and typical lean season.

As livelihoods collapsed and coping strategies began to fail, civilians in central Unity faced a rising need to engage in distress migration. Movement options were severely constrained, however. In discussions with humanitarians in April–May 2017 regarding the entire period of conflict, respondents in Leer described the trade-offs between food security and physical security they faced with any movement decision they made, even when humanitarian assistance was available (see Table 7.2).

Movement to increase access to food may involve increased risks of violence, while moving to the safest locations might further constrict access to food. While movement out of the county presented the greatest potential benefits in security and food access if achieved, it also posed the greatest risks during migration.[57]

Changing or unexpected counter-insurgency tactics further contributed to the near impossibility of making movement decisions with the best chance of survival. The deployment of amphibious vehicles by the SPLA allowed their forces to penetrate deeper into wetlands, including seasonal islands on the mainland and permanent islands deeper within the Sudd, for what appeared to be the first time. Pursuit into hiding places was generally considered by central Unity residents to be unprecedented, a high risk to the pursuers, and evidence that civilians were the real targets of the campaign, not only cattle or other assets. While some civilians were

[55] Mercy Corps, *Emergency Market Mapping and Analysis (EMMA): Livestock Off-take and Sorghum Market Systems in Leer County, Unity, South Sudan*, January 2015, available online at <https://www.emma-toolkit.org/report/emma-livestock-take-and-sorghum-market-systems> (visited 27 October 2021).

[56] International Committee of the Red Cross, *South Sudan: ICRC Forced to Withdraw from Leer County Following Threats and Looting*, 5 October 2015, available online at <http://www.icrc.org/en/document/south-sudan-conflict-leer-looting-icrc-forced-withdrawal#:~:text=In%20May%202015%2C%20the%20ICRC,from%20carrying%20out%20its%20activities> (visited 27 October 2021).

[57] Humanitarian assessment on file with the author, authorship confidential.

Table 7.2 South Sudan: Trade-offs between physical security and food security

Household Priority		*Food Security*	
Physical Security	*Degree Achieved*	**Low**	**Improved**
	Low	Static in Active Conflict Zone	Close Proximity to Leer County Humanitarian Food Distribution Site
	Improved	Migration to Deep Wetland Island	Migration Out of Leer County (Bentiu PoC, Panyijiar County, etc.)

Source: Chris Newton, 2022

able to flee further east into core IO territory in the remote Nuer areas of northern Jonglei, such as Ayod and Fangak counties, this was a prohibitively difficult and expensive displacement route for most.

Dugout canoe prices rose exponentially due to the mass loss of canoes and the exceptional demand for water transport to take displaced people to safer areas. Additionally, the main channel of the White Nile, and the navigation of floating reed pathways, free-floating and static islands, and dangerous wildlife like crocodiles and hippopotami proved an insurmountable barrier for most. The assessment coordinated by the UN's Office of the Deputy Humanitarian Coordinator found 829 deaths due to drowning in the period November 2014–November 2015 in areas affected by the 2015 offensive, with girls under age five most likely to have drowned.[58]

Efforts to reach the PoC in Bentiu—approximately 110 kilometres from Leer town—involved navigating the territory of a series of militias, sometimes of shifting affiliation, as well as the SPLA itself. It was nearly impossible for men and boys to make this journey safely, while women and girls faced an almost certain likelihood of SGBV. This risk during movement endured alongside repeated government calls, including through the use of the main radio station in Bentiu, for civilians to come to government garrisons with their livestock.[59]

The only potentially safe area to which central Unity civilians could displace to was Panyijiar County, even then only after the main thrust of the offensive had concluded. Residents of both Mayendit and Leer counties took various land and water routes to reach the towns, villages, and Sudd islands throughout Panyijiar County.[60] The government offensive only managed to reach Nyal town in Panyijiar County and occupy it for about one day before being forced to withdraw.[61] Had

[58] Office of the Deputy Humanitarian Coordinator in South Sudan (2016), see note 37.
[59] Human Rights Watch (2015), see note 47.
[60] REACH Initiative, *Situation Overview: Greater Nyal West, South Sudan*, December 2015.
[61] Craze (2016), see note 40.

Nyal town become another government garrison for the staging and resupply of counterinsurgency forces, it is likely that Panyijiar County would not have served as the safe area that it did for the remainder of the war. Without this function, it is probable that much more of the central Unity population would have died through violence and the subsequent starvation, acute malnutrition, and disease that followed.

This offensive and its aftermath shattered the tenuous frontline running west to east across northern Unity State. The IO would not demonstrate any meaningful conventional military capacity after this offensive, nor would any stable frontlines come to exist again in Unity State. The offensive violently transferred tens of thousands of cattle from target communities to perpetrators and their home areas and scattered the targeted civilian populations, including deep into wetlands along the White Nile and south into Panyijiar County. By October 2015, the Bentiu PoC population had tripled in size to approximately 120,000 individuals, many as partial households as families separated through dislocation and to spread risk.[62]

3. A Militia of Neighbours: Looting a Destitute Population in the 2018 Offensive

Almost one year after famine was formally declared to have ended in Leer County in mid-2017, with no meaningful livelihoods recovery having occurred, another government offensive was directed against Leer and Mayendit counties. If there was ever any doubt as to the virtual certainty that government security forces operated with regarding the likely food security outcomes of their campaigns, a public declaration of famine by the government itself put that to rest. To undertake another offensive in the same area as the famine declaration, utilizing the exact same tactics, suggests the continuation of a policy to deliberately use starvation to completely dispossess and/or eliminate civilians.

Lasting from mid-April through June, the 2018 offensive was the shortest of the three main offensives, though no less impactful. This was due to the extreme vulnerability of the target population by this point in the war as well as the choice of government proxy forces. These included the IO-2, a government-aligned breakaway faction of the IO led by Taban Deng Gai, a western Jikany Nuer from Guit County, and a predominantly Jegai Nuer militia, supported by the SPLA.

With the SPLA's Division 4 leadership in Bentiu reluctant to launch another major operation into central Unity, 'the Government decided to effectively hand control of Unity's military campaign to Taban Deng Gai, which also offered an opportunity to test the loyalty of their new ally'.[63] Gai remained with much to prove,

[62] Office of the Deputy Humanitarian Coordinator in South Sudan (2016), see note 37.

[63] M. Gibb et al., *Letter dated 9 April 2019 from the Panel of Experts on South Sudan addressed to the President of the Security Council*, United Nations Security Council, 9 April 2019, available online at <https://digitallibrary.un.org/record/3801695?ln=en> (visited 27 October 2021), at 48.

as his relationship with the Bul Nuer remained fraught after a predominantly Bul Nuer rebellion during his gubernatorial tenure in Unity State before the civil war.[64] It was increasingly likely at the time that control of Unity State and its oil revenue were likely headed to Bul Nuer elites.

The offensive used the same scorched-earth tactics as earlier operations, including complete village destruction, stripping whatever assets remained to be found in Mayendit and Leer counties, killing large numbers of civilians and displacing others back into wetlands and Panyijiar County, and committing mass SGBV.[65] The opening shots of this offensive also appeared to be directed at humanitarian staff in order to trigger their evacuation before major operations began. Multiple humanitarian staff were killed or wounded in Leer County in early April. The offensive itself prevented humanitarian assistance provision for several months. It also occurred in the planting season, severely disrupting another agricultural season and pushing the next possible harvest back around eighteen months.

In one humanitarian assessment in July to August of that year, a detailed examination of shelter destruction in a single village in Mayendit County was undertaken as an example of patterns of attacks on villages. Just before the offensive began, the full village contained 106 residential structures. By the conclusion of the attack on the village during the offensive, only three residential structures remained standing, including at least one thought by attackers to be spiritually protected.[66]

Destroyed structures were confirmed through examination of charred wood, clay, and other building materials in the shape and location of reported pre-attack structures. At the time of the visit on 5 August, forty-nine structures were in various states of being rebuilt, with many household plots abandoned. This pattern of village destruction was reportedly comparable across many attacked villages, with at least forty villages documented as attacked in what the UNMISS Human Rights Division (HRD) and OHCHR termed a 'scorched-earth strategy: the deliberate destruction of villages not justified by military necessity, accompanied by pillage.'[67]

64 Small Arms Survey, *Legitimacy, exclusion, and power: Taban Deng Gai and the South Sudan peace process*, December 2016, available at https://www.smallarmssurvey.org/resource/legitimacy-exclusion-and-power-taban-deng-gai-and-south-sudan-peace-process-hsba-issue (visited 19 May 2022).

65 See, e.g. Ceasefire and Transitional Security Arrangements Monitoring and Verification Mechanism, *CTSAMM Report 2018/22—Violations against Civilians, including SGBV, in Southern Unity State April–May 2018*, 7 July 2018, available online at <https://www.jmecsouthsudan.com/index.php/reports/ctsamm-violation-reports> (visited 27 October 2021); Amnesty International, *War Crimes in Unity State, South Sudan*, September 2018, available online at <http://www.amnesty.org/en/latest/news/2018/09/war-crimes-in-unity-state-south-sudan/> (visited 27 October 2021); UNMISS HRD and OCHCR, *Indiscriminate Attacks Against Civilians in Southern Unity April–May 2018*, July 2018, available online at <https://reliefweb.int/report/south-sudan/indiscriminate-attacks-against-civilians-southern-unity-april-may-2018> (visited 27 October 2021).

66 Humanitarian assessment on file with the author, authorship confidential.

67 UNMISS HRD and OHCHR, *Report on Indiscriminate Attacks Against Civilians in Southern Unity, South Sudan* (2018), available online at <https://www.ohchr.org/EN/Countries/AfricaRegion/Pages/SouthSudanReports.aspx> (visited 27 October 2021).

It is likely that once again the participating Jegai Nuer found it much easier to navigate the rural areas of Mayendit and Leer counties due to a greater familiarity with local topography and settlement locations as compared to Bul Nuer, JEM, and other regular SPLA forces. Due to longstanding connections through intermarriage and trade, they may also have had intimate knowledge of non-poor households, livestock holdings and locations, and typical grazing and cattle camp locations at the time of the initial attacks in the late dry season. Given the former control of Koch County by the IO, participating individuals may have also previously fought under the IO and remained familiar with the disposition and tactics of remaining opposition forces and aligned militias in central Unity State.

Armed actors seeking cattle and other lootable assets may have been disappointed by the now meagre livestock holdings of communities in Mayendit and Leer counties, however. In an area where livestock, especially cattle, are equated with survival, 33 per cent of households in Mayendit County and 15 per cent of households in Leer County reported owning any livestock, with fewer than 5 per cent of households actually owning household cattle, by mid-2017. Nearly all reported livestock ownership was of goats, sheep, and poultry. Following the 2018 offensive, Mayendit County registered a 14-point drop in livestock ownership. In comparison, Koch County, where the Jegai Nuer predominate, 41 per cent of households reported owning livestock, with average cattle ownership at 5.2. This average cattle ownership was approximately triple that of Mayendit County and double that of Leer County, where only a few households accounted for nearly all remaining cattle ownership.[68]

The first IPC analysis published after the 2018 offensive issued a conditional famine warning, the last such warning of the civil war up to the time of writing. Indirectly, it warned of famine in the event that a period like mid-2018 was repeated in central Unity State. Only under the conditions of a subsequent military offensive was famine likely to recur in the area.[69]

4. Discussion

Through the deliberate use of starvation as a weapon of war, government and affiliated forces sought to retake geographic areas considered critical to the survival of the incumbent regime, including the state capital and oil installations. Concurrently, they aimed to contain and degrade, if not eliminate, the armed opposition in remaining areas in order to protect what was retaken and to insulate the government's core ethnic heartland in Warrap and Lakes states to the west. Elites

[68] World Food Programme, Food and Agriculture Organization, United Nations Children's Fund, Government of the Republic of South Sudan, FEWS NET, and REACH Initiative, Food Security and Nutrition Monitoring System rounds 20 and 22, June–August 2017 and June–August 2018, available online at <https://fscluster.org/sites/default/files/documents/fsnms_round_20_bulletin.pdf> (visited 27 October 2021) and <https://fscluster.org/south-sudan-rep/document/food-security-and-nutrition-monitoring-1> (visited 27 October 2021).

[69] See the IPC Key Messages from September 2018, available online at <http://www.ipcinfo.org/ipcinfo-website/ipc-alerts/issue-10/en/> (visited 27 October 2021).

and communities from the Nuer sub-groups of Unity State were effectively offered a choice between joining the government effort or having their home county declared an 'ethics-free zone' where total impunity reigned.[70] No middle ground was allowed.

The threat of having a livelihood system completely destroyed and the offer of becoming the perpetrator and beneficiary of destroying another population's livelihood system were essential to political transactions between the national government and state and local elites. That the Bul Nuer joined the government rather than the IO likely determined the course of the war in Unity State and potentially nationally. Thousands of Bul Nuer were then given the exceptional licence—and requisite ammunition—to loot the cattle of nearly all of their co-ethnic communities in the state. As politics shifted, key actors within devastated northern Unity Nuer sub-groups began shifting allegiances. By 2018, it was the turn of actors and networks from among the western Jikany and Jegai to plunder what could still be found in central Unity.

The use of starvation as a weapon of war functioned as an element of transactional politics sub-nationally—among layers of elites and their networks—and as a strategy for the conduct of the civil war. The objective of eliminating an entire social group, such as Machar's own Dok Nuer of Leer County, cannot be ruled out. Given the concerted effort to bring about starvation over three large offensives and extensive use of organized violence between and after these operations, including the pursuit of civilians deep into hiding locations and the killing of civilians as they attempted to exit the targeted area, it is difficult to conclude that the only intended functions were political transactions and the degradation or destruction of the IO in central and southern Unity.

As argued earlier, had the government taken Nyal town or other key locations in Panyijiar County as they sought to do in 2014 and 2015, Mayendit and Leer counties would have been caught with Warrap and Lakes states to the west and southwest, government security forces and affiliated militias to the south and north, and the main channel of the White Nile to the east. As seen in the Greater Baggari case, this may have resulted in a state of rural besiegement, with much higher civilian mortality.

B. Reconsidering Rural Besiegement: Greater Baggari, Wau County, Western Bahr el Ghazal State 2016–2018

In response to questions regarding forced displacement in the Greater Baggari area[71] of Wau County, Western Bahr el Ghazal State, several respondents compared their experiences to that of different animals. The phrase '*Ka nako ti nangele*

[70] A. de Waal, 'Counter-Insurgency on the Cheap', London Review of Books, 5 August 2004, available at https://www.lrb.co.uk/the-paper/v26/n15/alex-de-waal/counter-insurgency-on-the-cheap (visited 19 May 2022).

[71] Greater Baggari is a name in common usage at least among humanitarians, though is not an official administrative name. The term refers to portions of Bessilia and Baggari payams within Wau County.

kala ka nvatara dji wii ([People] running like bush rats from fire)' compared the displacement of the Greater Baggari civilian population from their areas of permanent residence into the surrounding forest to the flight of bush rats during the annual dry season burning of grass.[72] '*Ka nako ti wala la ka nanuu muru nguu* ([People] living like birds on trees)' referred to scratching out survival in the dirt, including living on limited wild foods in the forest, while remaining ready to flee at any moment. Elaborating on the comparison, the respondent that described living like a bird on a tree added that she only thought about two questions: 'Where am I running next? What am I eating next?'[73]

Greater Baggari contains a series of settlements along a triangle of roads southwest of Wau town, the state capital. The largest towns of the area are within a forty-kilometre radius of Wau town. It is predominantly home to various sub-groups of the Balanda, an ethnicity that falls under the umbrella term Fertit, which encompasses a range of minority groups.

The area relies on rain-fed agriculture, including a single harvest of cereals like maize and sorghum, groundnuts, and sesame, as well as ongoing production of eighteen to thirty-six month cassava and various garden vegetables. Livestock help to supplement agricultural production, though typically this is limited to goats, sheep, and poultry and not cattle. The area is often considered the breadbasket of Western Bahr el Ghazal State and especially Wau town, even serving as an area of local procurement for WFP prior to the onset of civil war.

No famine declaration was ever made for Greater Baggari, though famine conditions were observed multiple times and famine may have occurred in mid-2017. A famine warning was almost issued for early 2018 largely based on the likelihood of a government offensive. There was no analytical consensus on this famine warning within the IPC TWG and it was never issued.

1. Tightening the Noose: Government Counter-insurgency against the Fertit Lions 2015–2018

May 2015 saw the first full clashes between the IO-affiliated Fertit Lions, a grassroots armed actor built on pre-existing militia networks from the previous war, and the SPLA. Conflict escalated in December 2015 with the arrival of a new SPLA Division 5 commander in Wau town—Tayeb Gatluak, otherwise known as Tai Tai. This Bul Nuer officer played a central role in the 2015 offensive in Unity State as the commander of Division 4 in Bentiu and would utilize the same scorched-earth tactics of the Unity State offensives against the Fertit.[74] Few humanitarians

[72] Elderly female respondent at an IDP site in the forest south of Faranjallah, Baggari payam, Wau County, 7 December 2018, taken from humanitarian assessment on file with the author, authorship confidential.

[73] All-female FGD at an IDP site in the forest south of Faranjallah, Baggari payam, Wau County, 5 December 2018, taken from anonymous humanitarian assessment on file with the author.

[74] S. Vuylsteke, *Identity and Self Determination: The Fertit Opposition in South Sudan*, Small Arms Survey, December 2018, available online at <http://www.smallarmssurveysudan.org/fileadmin/docs/briefing-papers/HSBA-BP-Fertit.pdf> (visited 27 October 2021).

appeared to recognize what the change in divisional command meant for the area, though this was a clear early warning indicator of a coming scorched-earth campaign. Tai Tai remained in command until August 2017, when Greater Baggari was at the edge of—or even already experiencing—famine and a long period of denied humanitarian access. With his departure, humanitarian access was intermittently restored until the late 2018 offensive.[75]

In June 2016, following further rural clashes, an ethnic pogrom directed primarily at Fertit residents took place within Wau town. This led to the establishment of the Wau Protection of Civilians Site Adjacent Area (PoCAA), which came to house approximately 16,000 overwhelmingly Fertit residents of Wau town. By September, SPLA reinforcements—including helicopter gunships—arrived in Wau town. As rural military operations intensified, the population of the PoCAA rose to nearly 25,000 individuals.[76]

Major government offensives in Greater Baggari occurred in 2017 and 2018, each utilizing scorched-earth tactics comparable to the offensives in Unity State. Humanitarian access was largely denied from April to August 2017, with intermittent access through the end of the year, and from mid-June to early September 2018. In November 2017, the UN Panel of Experts on South Sudan characterized the denial of access and its effect on the civilian population in the following terms:

> It is the view of the Panel that the Government has, during much of 2017, deliberately prevented lifesaving food assistance from reaching some citizens. Such actions amount to using food as a weapon of war, with the intent to inflict suffering on civilians whom the Government views as opponents to its agenda. The denial of aid has caused extreme food insecurity among large sections of the population, the documented outcome being malnutrition and death by starvation, in particular in the greater Baggari area in Wau County.[77]

The Commission on Human Rights in South Sudan (UNCHRSS) also reviewed both the 2017 and 2018 offensives in Greater Baggari, noting the use of scorched-earth tactics, including widespread and systematic looting and destruction of property within a 'concerted campaign against the civilian population'.[78]

[75] 'Tayeb Gatluak "Tai Tai"', MAAPSS–Mapping Actors and Alliances Project–South Sudan: Small Arms Survey, available at https://maapss.org/person?id=5cc812f47ea6140461fdbc70 (visited 19 May 2022).

[76] International Organization for Migration Displacement Tracking Matrix, *Conflict and Displacement Timeline: Wau/Western Bahr el Ghazal 2014–2016* (2016).

[77] K. Ryan et al., *Letter dated 20 November 2017 from the Panel of Experts on South Sudan addressed to the President of the Security Council*, United Nations Security Council, 20 November 2017, available online at <https://reliefweb.int/report/south-sudan/letter-dated-20-november-2017-panel-experts-south-sudan-addressed-president> (visited 27 October 2021), at 13.

[78] Commission on Human Rights in South Sudan, *'There is nothing left for us': starvation as a method of warfare in South Sudan* Conference room paper of the Commission on Human Rights in South Sudan*, OHCHR, 5 October 2020, available online at <https://www.ohchr.org/en/hrbodies/hrc/cohsouthsudan/pages/index.aspx> (visited 27 October 2021); Commission on Human Rights in South Sudan, *Report of the Commission on Human Rights in South Sudan*, OHCHR, 12 March 2019, available online at <https://www.ohchr.org/en/hrbodies/hrc/cohsouthsudan/pages/index.aspx> (visited 27 October 2021).

In each period of denied humanitarian access, government military operations forced civilians to either displace into the previously uninhabited forest further west and south of the triangle of roads or risk the up to forty-kilometre journey by foot to Wau town. Travelling to Wau town required facing similar, gendered risks of loss of life, looting, and SGBV faced by Nuer civilians seeking to reach Bentiu. While PoC sites may have been generally protected, accessing them rarely was.

In contrast to the offensives in Unity State, which featured the use of co-ethnic militias of decreasing physical and social distance from the targeted communities, attacks on Greater Baggari featured almost mono-ethnic forces drawn from communities physically and socially distant to the targeted population. The SPLA's Division 5 was largely comprised of Dinka sub-groups from across Greater Bahr el Ghazal. They were at times accompanied by other Dinka forces like the Mathiang Anyoor paramilitary, its ranks heavily drawn from among the Malual Dinka of Northern Bahr el Ghazal State. Government forces appeared to lack the insider information available to them in Unity State, most likely reducing the efficacy of their livelihoods targeting.

The Fertit Lions frontline was also never broken in the same manner as the IO frontlines in Unity State. When the Fertit Lions were defeated, it typically involved a loss of territory that shifted the frontline rather than collapsed it. No government offensive ever reached the Fertit Lions' rear areas within the forests. Government forces seemed to accept that the Fertit Lions would keep control of the forests, so long as they remained outside a buffer zone around Wau town and all main roads.

Rather than pursue the civilian population into the forest, which would have likely led to prohibitively high losses for the SPLA and its paramilitaries, the government sought to maintain an effective state of besiegement on Greater Baggari. In addition to mass displacement, this was achieved through the disruption of four consecutive agricultural seasons, the severing of rural-urban trade links, the denial of humanitarian access through two consecutive lean seasons, the patrolling in force of the roads through Greater Baggari, and the killing and sexual assault of many civilians caught near roads or who sought to reach Wau town or the PoCAA.

The imposition of extreme movement restrictions on the population of Greater Baggari, especially where it inhibited distress migration, was instrumental in bringing about starvation. As explained by a displaced local chief within the forest south of Greater Baggari: 'We are not here because we do not want to be in the town. We are here because the government does not want us in the town.'[79] Referring to the behaviour of government patrols along the main road, he added: 'When they see you, *bullets*.'[80]

[79] Humanitarian assessment on file with the author, authorship confidential.
[80] Humanitarian assessment on file with the author, authorship confidential.

2. Surviving in the Forest but Nowhere Else: Fertit Civilian Coping and Starvation Behind the Frontline

The displaced civilian population unable or unwilling to attempt to reach Wau town found themselves pushed into the forests to the south-west. Those that arrived first, such as in 2015 and 2016, found land never previously cleared for cultivation and faced shortages of the labour, tools, and seeds needed to restart agricultural production, a severe lack of access to potable water, especially during the dry season, and labour productivity limited by already severe hunger.

The first populations to attempt to resettle in the forests, and later new arrivals unable to be supported by either other displaced civilians or humanitarian agencies, had to find sufficient wild foods, hunt, and seek out social and kinship support before the first opportunity came to clear new land in the forest and restart agriculture. They survived heavily on *ambeshe*, a local yam that is poisonous if cooked improperly and is only available from December through June—not the typical lean season linked to agriculture.[81]

Typically, two-year 'cassava is the major safety net and the preferred staple crop' in this area.[82] In normal times, growing cassava can provide a steady supply of cassava roots and leaves, particularly when other crops like cereals fail. During periods of conflict and displacement, the multi-year growth period of new cassava is a serious disadvantage. On several occasions, including in front of humanitarian teams, government security forces burned, uprooted, or stole locally produced cassava throughout Greater Baggari. Displaced civilians continually attempted to plant new cassava in the forest, but the main roots would not become available for harvesting for one to two lean seasons.

Respondents to the same assessment described how the first lean season after displacement—June–July 2017 for many—was the closest they came to, or was, famine under their own definition of the term. Not only would most *ambeshe* have become unavailable by the end of June but minimal agricultural production was available, most livestock had been lost, market access was negligible, and humanitarian assistance was highly limited for most of the area through that lean season.

The arrival of displaced civilians from other rural areas of Wau and Raga counties into Greater Baggari—themselves undertaking distress migration due to a loss of access of food and organized violence—worsened food security as extremely limited resources had to be shared further. The first humanitarian assessment of

[81] As an example of how eating wild tubers in South Sudan requires specialized knowledge and brings high risks to health, many elite Nuer soldiers that travelled with Machar through the forests of Central Equatoria State during their July 2016 escape from Juba to the Democratic Republic of the Congo reportedly died after mistaking a toxic root for the tuber their Equatorian comrades instructed them to consume. See Small Arms Survey, *Spreading fallout: The collapse of the ARCSS and new conflict along the Equatorias–DRC border*, May 2017, available online at <http://www.smallarmssurveysudan.org/fileadmin/docs/issue-briefs/HSBA-IB28-Spreading-Fallout.pdf> (visited 27 October 2021).

[82] WFP, FAO, and GRSS (2020), see note 39.

Greater Baggari in August 2017 after access denials were lifted found one of, if the not the greatest, concentrations of bilateral pitting oedema among children under five years old recorded in the course of the civil war, especially relative to the small estimated population of Greater Baggari at the time. A life-threatening condition manifesting as a result of Severe Acute Malnutrition, this finding alone indicated extreme deterioration in food security, nutritional status, potable water access, and the overall childcare and health environment for the embattled population.[83]

Echoing previous humanitarian findings, respondents to the December 2018 humanitarian assessment also indicated that further penetration of the forest was not a viable option for additional displacement. Even if food sources were completely exhausted in their current locations or if the government finally broke through the Fertit Lions frontline, there was nowhere left to go in the view of the affected population. Distress migration would be limited by poor water availability and low food access, including due to the difficulty of finding *ambeshe* sufficient to feed a family. While some respondents indicated that they might attempt travel to Wau town and the PoCAA, most indicated that they would wait in their current location for either humanitarian assistance or starvation, whichever arrived first.[84]

3. Discussion

The government objectives of maintaining this state of besiegement for months at a time in two consecutive lean seasons, alongside the use of scorched-earth tactics, indicates that mass starvation was most likely a desired outcome in this time period. Ultimately, the government did end denials of humanitarian access and by December 2018 reopened the roads between Wau town and Greater Baggari. Had these actions not been taken, it is highly likely that famine would have led to a massive loss of life in the area, potentially decimating the remaining civilian population. There was no safe zone similar to Panyijiar County in Unity State for the entrapped civilian population of Greater Baggari.

It appears most likely that the government sought one set of war aims comparable to Unity State—the containment and degradation if not elimination of armed opposition forces and the civilian population around them—which it viewed as practically the same. The Fertit Lions and the wider Fertit population perceived as disloyal was to be confined within low-value land where they posed as small a threat as possible to core government interests, such as ensuring domination of Wau town as well as the Western Corridor trade route that passes through it, serving as the main commercial and military logistics artery of the Greater Bahr el Ghazal region.

83 Humanitarian assessment on file with the author, authorship confidential.
84 Humanitarian assessment on file with the author, authorship confidential.

5. Conclusion

Across the two cases of central Unity and Greater Baggari, localized famine conditions and at least one famine occurred through the widespread and systematic use of organized violence directed against objects and activities indispensable for survival. In the view of the UNCHRSS the cases of central Unity and Greater Baggari are unambiguous:

> The Commission notes with grave concern that, beyond climate-induced factors, both government forces and armed groups have pursued policies responsible for the starvation of the population in Wau and Unity States. Such policies were envisaged and implemented as part of a wider strategy to deprive enemy communities of resources and thus force their capitulation, allow soldiers and militias to reward themselves, forcibly displace communities from ancestral lands that could then be expropriated or simply to compel individuals to join different factions engaged in the conflict.[85]

In both case studies, mass starvation appeared to serve the functions of dispossession and negotiating the price of loyalty with a range of elites and networks. Dispossession was achieved in both cases, if at different scale between central Unity and Greater Baggari. Where co-ethnics perpetrated the worst of the organized violence leading to starvation—central Unity—there appear to be the strongest political calculations regarding the transaction of loyalty and political services. Elites from different intra-ethnic sub-groups saw their networks and wider constituencies targeted in different ways, with the option of either joining armed actors involved in the use of starvation as a weapon of war or being the target of those actors. While intra-ethnic rivalry plagued the Fertit Lions throughout the period of analysis, no similar success was seen in government efforts to transact for a co-ethnic counterinsurgency force. Despite the high civilian casualties observed in each case, and the potential for eliminating an entire social group at some level of a segmentary lineage system, elimination does not appear to have been a primary objective in either case. If this were thought to be an objective of the use of mass starvation, it would only be in relation to specific sub-ethnic groups within limited geographic areas.[86] Table 7.3 summarizes the inferred objectives for the use of starvation as a weapon of war in each case.

[85] Commission on Human Rights in South Sudan (2020), see note 70.

[86] In the most extreme, in addition to well-documented, case of central Unity, elimination of one or both Nuer sub-groups, and particularly Machar's own Dok Nuer of Leer County, remains a distinct possibility. A counterfactual scenario for the 2015 offensive in Unity State in which government security forces and their affiliates maintain control of Nyal town and other key locations within Panyijiar County—a critical safety valve for the dispossessed of central Unity—could have led to a situation approaching the siege-like conditions of Greater Baggari and a substantial increase in civilian mortality

Table 7.3 South Sudan: Inferred objectives for the use of starvation as a weapon of war

	Price of Loyalty/ Disloyalty	Dispossession	Elimination
Central Unity	2014–2018: Northern Sub-ethnic Elites	2014–2018	Cannot be ruled out 2015: Hak and Dok Sub-groups
Greater Baggari	No co-ethnic counter-insurgency identified	2015–2018	Unlikely

Source: Chris Newton, 2022

In considering how starvation was brought about through organized violence, the cases highlight several clear pathways to the onset of famine conditions or famine. Most importantly, these cases demonstrate famine as a process, taking multiple years of organized violence at varying frequency and intensity to bring about starvation in different ways, as suggested by a consideration of *da̠k*. Across both pathways, key variables that contributed to the onset of starvation can be identified.

In central Unity, the collapse of a static frontline and a concomitant sharp decline in the military capacity of the armed opposition were instrumental in the rapid decline in food security. Shifts in sub-national politics brought related changes in the composition of counterinsurgency forces, closing the physical and social distance of the main perpetrating fighters with each successive government offensive. High cumulative restrictions on civilian movement and multiple periods of prolonged—at least three months, though longer in several cases, especially 2015 and 2016—denial of humanitarian access further reduced the coping capacity of the targeted civilian population. That civilians never completely lost the ability to engage in distress migration out of the targeted area was essential in avoiding exponentially greater loss of life during periods of extreme food insecurity and organized violence.

The frontline in Greater Baggari shifted over the course of government offensives, but never collapsed in the same way as those of Unity State, allowing the armed opposition to maintain rear areas to which civilians could flee and, after at least a season, begin to re-establish a minimum of agriculture. This is in part related to the ability of the Fertit Lions to maintain the military capacity to resist government offensives, especially through high-fatality ambushes. This may in part have also resulted from the high degree of physical and social distance between

among Hak and Dok Nuer civilians. It would need to be determined if not holding Nyal town and other locations was an actual policy failure and caused a change of objectives, as in away from elimination, or there never was any intent to hold such locations in the first place and their looting and destruction was only part of the wider livelihoods targeting.

Table 7.4 Some factors affecting the onset of famine conditions or famine

	Status of a Frontline	Armed Actor Capacity	Perpetrator Social and Physical Distance from Targeted Civilians	Cumulative Restriction on Civilian Movement	Civilian Ability to Engage in Distress Migration	3+ Months Loss of Humanitarian Access
Central Unity	Shift 2014	Conventional Symmetric 2014	High 2014	High	Yes	2015
	Collapse 2015		Moderate 2015–2016			2016
	Collapse 2018	Asymmetric 2015–2018	Minor 2018			2018
Greater Baggari	Shift 2016	Mixed case 2015–2018	High	Extreme	No	2017
	Shift 2017					2018
	Shift 2018					

▒ = Occurred in Pathway to Famine Conditions or Famine

Source: Chris Newton, 2022

counter-insurgent and targeted civilians, as the largely Fertit and other minority civilians were attacked by distant forces mostly from Dinka areas of Greater Bahr el Ghazal. Cumulative movement restrictions on civilians were even greater in Greater Baggari than in central Unity, however, with distress migration largely impossible for most civilians in the targeted area. When denied humanitarian access was prolonged, especially in 2017, the civilian population entered into famine conditions and potentially outright famine. Only the lifting of these conditions barely allowed the prevention, or possibly ending of, famine in Greater Baggari in 2017. Table 7.4 summarizes some of the characteristics common to each case, with highlighted cells indicating that some form of a characteristic was applicable to the pathways to mass starvation in each case.

In considering these and other possible pathways to famine conditions or famine through organized violence, it is clear that there is still much to improve regarding the analysis of the use of starvation as a weapon of war. Starting from the perspective of *dak*, the analysis presented here sought to consider historical legacies of conflict and weaponized starvation in South Sudan, general characteristics of the interaction of organized violence and rural livelihoods, and how mass starvation was inflicted in two rural areas of South Sudan during the current civil war. Although drawing on only two of what are likely many cases, specific mechanisms in how organized violence interacts with the objects, activities, and other elements of rural livelihoods can already be identified. The continuation of such work can support efforts in accountability for starvation crimes and humanitarian famine early warning, despite the persistent challenges to both within civil war and other situations of violence.

8

Starvation as Strategy in the Syrian Armed Conflict

Siege, Deprivation, and Detention

Mohammad Kanfash and Ali Aljasem

This chapter addresses the use of starvation as a weapon of war during the war in Syria including the possible goals and methods of the perpetrators, the outcomes for the victims, as well as the question of accountability. To provide a scope of the use of starvation during the war, as a tactic deployed by a variety of actors and across different geographies, this chapter includes four case studies: eastern Ghouta (in the Damascus suburbs), Aleppo, Deir Alzor and starvation in detention. It draws on the authors' interviews, previous research, and professional experience as humanitarian relief workers during the armed conflict in Syria, and an extensive review of media, human rights, and humanitarian reporting on conditions in the country throughout the civil war.

1. Background

Throughout the Syrian conflict the use of unprecedented violence captured the attention of the international community, however this focus on exceptional atrocities has seemingly crowded out comparable outrage against the violence perpetrated systematically and on a daily basis. Chief in this category was the weaponization of food and water[1] and the use of starvation to force surrender. This chapter explores the understudied use of starvation, which was perpetrated by all actors in the conflict including the Syrian regime[2] and its allies, the international coalition led by the United States and its Kurdish People's Protection Units (YPG) allies, and

[1] M. Daoudy, 'Water Weaponization in the Syrian conflict: Strategies of Domination and Cooperation', 96(5) *International Affairs* (2020) 1347–1366.

[2] Note that authors use the terms 'regime' and 'government' interchangeably in a solely descriptive manner devoid of judgement.

Mohammad Kanfash and Ali Aljasem, *Starvation as Strategy in the Syrian Armed Conflict* In: *Accountability for Mass Starvation.* Edited by: Bridget Conley, Alex de Waal, Catriona Murdoch, and Wayne Jordash QC, Oxford University Press.
 DOI: 10.1093/oso/9780192864734.003.0008

opposition forces and Islamist factions including the Islamic State of Iraq and the Levant (ISIL, also known as *Da'esh*) and affiliates of al-Qaida.

Prior to the war, Syria was a middle-income country with moderate urbanization and a diversified economy, including an important agricultural sector. Syrians engaged in small-scale and commercial farming, and Syria was a net food exporter. Agriculture was highly subsidized, accounted for up to one-third of gross domestic product (GDP), and the sector employed almost one-third of the working population.

During the decade preceding the conflict, the political and economic landscapes in Syria saw challenges and upheaval. These changes began when Bashar al-Assad assumed the presidency after the death of his father in 2000. Assad Junior had no previous history in party politics and was initially dependent on the incumbent elites to rule,[3] creating a balance of power between the presidency and the Ba'ath Party than had existed under Assad Senior.[4] Assad Junior's ascension to power created expectations of structural reforms.[5] This was reflected in the short-lived 'Damascus Spring', during which political forums flourished and intellectuals, secular actors, and liberal opposition were permitted to engage in public matters with new openness.[6]

The Damascus Spring faded as the Syrian economy stagnated, and the US war on terror and its occupation of Iraq put huge stresses on the economy and political elite. The US 'regime change' intervention in the region was vigorously opposed by the Syrian government. Iraq had been an important economic partner and a destination for Syrian goods, and its implosion was a large loss for the Syrian economy, to say nothing of the approximately 2 million Iraqi refugees and opposition members Syria hosted in the following years. In response to the Syrian position on Iraq, the United States retaliated with sanctions and political isolation.[7]

Internationally, pressure increased as the Syrian government was accused of assassinating the Lebanese prime minster, Rafiq al-Hariri. Subsequently, on 26 April 2005, the last Syrian troops left Lebanon after thirty years of contested presence. That exit meant losing a historical sphere of Syrian influence[8] and the further loss of

[3] R. Hinnebusch, 'President and Party in Post-Ba'athist Syria. From the Struggle for Reform to Regime Deconstruction', in R. Hinnebusch and R. Zintl (eds), *Syria from Reform to Revolt, Vol. 1: Political Economy and International Relations* (Syracuse: Syracuse University Press, 2015) 21–44, at 26–27

[4] Hinnebusch, see note 3.

[5] P. G. Pinto, 'God and Nation: The Politics of Islam under Bashar al-Assad', in Hinnebusch and Zintl (eds), see note 3, 154–175, at 154.

[6] T. Al-Om, 'Emergence of the political voice of Syria's civil society: The non-violent movements of the Syrian Uprising' in R. Hinnebusch and O. Imady (eds), *The Syrian Uprising. Domestic Origins and Early Trajectory* (London: Routledge/St. Andrews Syrian Studies Series, 2018) 159–172, at 159–160.

[7] B. Scheller, *The Wisdom of Syria's Waiting Game. Foreign Policy under the Assads* (London: Hurst & Company, 2013), at 121–149.

[8] L. Matar, *The Political Economy of Investment in Syria*, Studies in Political Economy of Public Policy (Houndmill: Palgrave Macmillan, 2016), at 97.

another key economic partner. Lebanon had played an important role facilitating Syrian businesses despite sanctions on the Syrian economy and banking system and provided a labour market for low-skilled Syrians. The damage to the relationship with Lebanon was damage to one lung through which the Syrian economy breathed.

Internally, socio-economic grievances were intensifying with rapid population growth, rural–urban migration, dwindling oil resources,[9] and widespread discontent at the corruption of the leadership.[10] The international and domestic pressures mounted to catalyse reforms intended to guarantee the survival of the regime. The old guard were not enthusiastic about reform and struggled against the new president until Assad brushed aside the old elites and replaced them with his own confidants.[11] Yet the old clientelist relationship retained power as the new reformers were just the younger generation of the old guard's families.[12]

In 2005, Assad Junior introduced his blueprint for a 'Social Market Economy'.[13] This model aimed to '(re)position [the State] as the guardian of social stability and welfare' and not their provider.[14] The private sector became a full partner with the state for economic development, and the market was accepted as the primary means of distributing resources.[15] These reforms entailed the 'silent privatization' of the Syrian economy—to the benefit of political interests of the state bourgeoisie.[16] The increased inequality resulting from these reforms festered hostility against the 'elites' and the ruling family.[17]

Assad Junior's structural adjustments and reduction in public subsidies led to the steady erosion of the decades-long welfarist social contract, which tragically collided with repeated droughts in Syria and the 2008 'world food crisis'. The result was greater hardship for most Syrians. During the drought, rampant mismanagement of underground water sources in rural areas contributed to an agricultural crisis, especially in the irrigated sector while the price of bread and animal fodders increased by 75 per cent, and fuel prices went up 350 per cent.[18]

[9] T. Zintl, 'The Co-option of Foreign-Educated Syrians: Between Legitimizing Strategy and Domestic Reforms', in Hinnebusch and Zintl (eds), see note 3, 113–132, at 113.

[10] Hinnebusch, see note 3

[11] R. Hinnebusch, 'Syria from Authoritarian Upgrading to Revolution?', 1 *International Affairs* (2012) 95–133, at 99.

[12] Zintl, see note 9, at 124

[13] Hinnebusch, 'Syria from Authoritarian Upgrading to Revolution?', see note 11, at 99.

[14] Hinnebusch, 'Syria from Authoritarian Upgrading to Revolution?', see note 11, at 49.

[15] S. N. Abboud and F. H. Lawson, 'Antinomies of Economic Governance in Contemporary Syria' in A. Khadim (ed.), *Governance in the Middle East and North Africa: A Handbook* (London: Routledge, 2013) 330–341, at 333.

[16] Matar, see note 8, at 109. See also, A. Fadilah, 'The Problem of Public–Private Partnerships and the Social Dimensions of Development' (in Arabic), *Syrian Economic Society*, 2010.

[17] Hinnebusch, 'Syria from Authoritarian Upgrading to Revolution?', see note 11, at 101–102.

[18] M. Ababsa, 'The End of a World. Drought and Agrarian Transformation in Northeast Syria (2007–2010)' in Hinnebusch and Zintl (eds), see note 3, 199–222, at 206.

These hardships combined to push farmers to migrate from their villages towards urban centres. Tens of thousands of peasants fled to main city suburbs in search of informal work.[19] According to the UN Office for the Coordination of Humanitarian Affairs (OCHA), some 300,000 families were driven to major cities which represented the 'largest internal displacement in the Middle East in recent years'[20] as Syria transformed from a middle-income economy to an aid recipient. Bashar al-Assad attempted to navigate these hazards with, Hinnebusch argues,[21] a weakened capacity to sustain power over society. Without a functioning social contract and with an increasing reliance on a small cabal surrounding him, Assad Junior's regime and the Syrian people were both experiencing political and economic vulnerability.

Although the country remained a highly centralized authoritarian and kleptocratic system during his first decade, his rhetoric and occasional implementation of reform led social actors in various realms to believe the dismantling of dictatorship was at hand.[22]

The conflict in Syria began in March 2011 as a wave of non-violent popular protests demanding democratic reforms. The protesters hoped that President Bashar al-Assad would either spearhead reforms himself or be forced from power. After initially offering and introducing a set of political and economic reforms, the regime resorted to violence. As (counter) violence and calls for the regime to step aside increased, the regime entrenched itself. It violently repressed protesters through arrests, torture, and extra-judicial killings. At this time, the uprising remained primarily non-violent and overwhelmingly non-sectarian. In July 2011, defectors from the military, including both officers and conscripts, announced the formation of the Free Syrian Army (FSA), aiming to overthrow the Assad regime by force. In addition to the FSA, a wide array of rebel groups with various religious and ethnic group emerged and took up arms against the regime. The regime escalated its security response and deployed the armed forces seeking a military solution to the conflict.[23]

Numerous external international actors quickly joined the conflict, intervening on behalf of different groups with funding and weaponry. The armed and political opposition groups were united in their position against Assad's government, but divided along ideological and political lines, and fragmented by diverse regional

[19] M. Ababsa, 'Agrarian Counter-Reform in Syria (2000–2010)' in R. Hinnebusch et al. (eds), *Agriculture and Reform in Syria* (Fife: University of St. Andrews Centre for Syrian Studies, 2011) 83–111, at 83.

[20] M. Ababsa, 'The End of a World', see note 18, at 199–207

[21] Hinnebusch, 'Syria from Authoritarian Upgrading to Revolution?', see note 11, at 99.

[22] C. Salamandra and L. Stenberg, 'A Legacy of Raised Expectations' in C. Salamandra and L. Stenberg (eds), *Syria from Reform to Revolt, Vol. 2: Culture, Society and Religion* (Syracuse: Syracuse University Press, 2015) 1–15.

[23] For an overview of the early stage of the Syrian conflict, see: J. Daher, *Syria After the Uprisings. The Political Economy of State Resilience* (Chicago: Haymarket Books, 2019), at 38–73.

and international alliances and backers. Meanwhile, the Syrian regime increased its dependence on paramilitary groups represented by the Shabbiha and later the National Defense Forces (NDF). International intervention escalated with the direct intervention of United States in 2014,[24] Russia in 2015,[25] and Turkey[26] in 2016.

The result has been widespread devastation. More than half of Syria's population is internally or externally displaced. After a decade of conflict, approximately 11 million people are in need of humanitarian assistance including 9.3 million people who are food insecure and another 2.2 million people at risk of food insecurity.[27] This number has continued to rise: the figures for 2020 were 42 per cent higher than 2019.[28] It is estimated that one in eight children has a stunted growth across the country, a rate that rises to one in six in the north-west.[29]

The conflict has dangerously corroded the Syrian economy. War economies have enabled warlords and cronies to dominate the scene at the expense of legitimate actors and businesses. The conflict has reduced export receipts, created a foreign currency crisis, inflation, and scarcity of basic goods. The real value of wages has contracted an astonishing 93 per cent over the last decade.[30] The economic deterioration has been compounded by US and EU sanctions.[31]

The deteriorating humanitarian situation, paralysis of the economy, and increased unemployment and poverty has led to an increased dependence on international aid, which currently sustains the lives of approximately 11 million Syrians, and its continuation is reliant on the political will of the various actors, particularly

[24] US Department of State, 'The Global Coalition to Defeat ISIS', available online at <https://www.state.gov/bureaus-offices/bureaus-and-offices-reporting-directly-to-the-secretary/the-global-coalition-to-defeat-isis/> (visited 19 September 2020).

[25] A. Osborn and P. Stewart, 'Russia begins Syria air strikes in its biggest Mideast intervention in decades', *Reuters*, 30 September 2015, available online at <https://www.reuters.com/article/us-mideast-crisis-russia/russia-begins-syria-air-strikes-in-its-biggest-mideast-intervention-in-decades-idUSKCN0RU0MG20150930> (visited 19 September 2020).

[26] E. Van Veen, 'Syria: foreign interventions and the revenge of realpolitik', *Clingendael Spectator*, 5 November 2019, available online at <https://spectator.clingendael.org/en/publication/syria-foreign-interventions-and-revenge-realpolitik> (visited 25 August 2020).

[27] WFP, *Syria Situation Report #7, July 2020*, 20 August 2020, available online at <https://reliefweb.int/report/syrian-arab-republic/wfp-syria-situation-report-7-july-2020> (visited 22 August 2020).

[28] Norwegian Refugee Council et al., *Syria Crisis: Hunger Spreading amid Covid and Economic Collapse*, 29 June 2020, available online at <https://reliefweb.int/report/syrian-arab-republic/syria-crisis-hunger-spreading-amid-covid-and-economic-collapse> (visited 22 August 2020).

[29] Save the Children, *Hidden Hunger in Syria, A look at malnutrition across Syria with a focus on under-twos*, September 2020, available online at https://resourcecentre.savethechildren.net/node/18284/pdf/hidden_hunger_in_syria-cc-2020.pdf (visited 22 August 2020).

[30] J. Daher, *Between Control and Repression: The Plight of the Syrian Labour Force*, Wartime and Post-Conflict in Syria (WPCS) at the European University Institute, 27 July 2020, available online at <https://cadmus.eui.eu/bitstream/handle/1814/67858/RSCAS_2020_11.pdf?sequence=1&isAllowed=y> (visited 27 August 2020), at 6.

[31] Z. Ghisn, 'How Economic Sanctions Negatively Affect the Health Sector in Syria: A Case Study of the Pharmaceutical Industry', London School of Economics Blog, 16 April 2020, available online at <https://blogs.lse.ac.uk/crp/2020/04/16/how-economic-sanctions-negatively-affect-the-health-sector-in-syria-a-case-study-of-the-pharmaceutical-industry/> (visited 20 September 2020).

the international ones. External control over the fate of humanitarian operations is most powerfully and destructively wielded by the United States and Russia, which have, respectively, used their influence to impose sanctions and reduce aid delivery.

2. Starvation During the War

Siege warfare was chief among the strategies and counter-insurgency tactics were deployed first by the Syrian regime and later by all other major actors. The military capability of the imposing actor determined the severity of the siege; the Syrian regime and US-led coalition imposed the harshest of the sieges, while the opposition forces and Islamists were comparatively less successful because they lacked the same level of military means.

Sieges were implemented using direct violence, including bombing of exit routes, deployment of snipers against civilians attempting to leave siege areas, massacres, the use of chemical weapons, as well as strategic and systematic use of starvation and deprivation of basic services. Irrespective of the deploying actors, siege tactics were used for the purposes of reducing enemy capacity to mount resistance and eventual seizure of territorial control. Sieges entailed sealing off areas, intentionally depriving civilians of objects indispensable to survival (OIS) such as electricity, running water, and garbage collection, and obstructing the entrance of aid. Targeted attacks on civilian centres such as hospitals, bakeries, and agricultural projects sought to undermine the resilience of opponents and besieged communities. Siege warfare was heavily employed by the Syrian regime and its Russian backers during their campaigns against Ghouta and Aleppo, as well as by the US-led coalition and its Kurdish-dominated Syrian Democratic Forces (SDF) during their campaign on Menbij, Raqqa, Deir Alzor, and Baghuz—the area where ISIL fought its last battles.

Siege tactics were first used by the regime forces in Dara'a province after the uprising, when a short and partial siege was imposed on the area. The tactic was then employed in Homs city in February 2012 when the regime deployed the army against an opposition stronghold in the Baba Amr neighbourhood. For a month, the area was surrounded and reduced to rubble by artillery attacks. During that siege, regime soldiers sprayed graffiti close to checkpoints calling on the opposition to 'surrender or starve'. This became known as the 'kneel or starve' strategy which used starvation to force surrender. By July 2012, the tactic was repeated in other opposition-dominated neighbourhoods. The 'starve' element included cutting off food supplies, water, electricity, and gas, waste services, medical care, as well as economic opportunities and access to banks. This was accompanied by indiscriminate attacks inside the area and attacks against any movement inward or outward. The situation was only relieved in 2014, following a series of negotiated surrenders that included ceding of territory and mass displacement.

The regime increased their use of siege warfare in late 2012 as their forces shrunk due to military losses and desertion, affecting its capacity to mount ground assaults or defend areas. The implementation of 'kneel or starve' was policed by troops and militias and combined with air raids and artillery bombardment. Throughout the conflict, siege warfare has been the most characteristic tactic of the regime and its allied forces, impacting hundreds of thousands of people in towns and cities across the country. Approximately 2.2 million Syrians have been victims of sieges to date.[32]

The end result of siege tactics has varied over time and geography.[33] In some instances, the regime gained control over both territory and population; in others, once territorial control was established, the entire population was displaced, and only small segments were allowed to return. However, as the regime's battlefield successes mounted, it increasingly aimed to consolidate control of both population and territory throughout the country.

The siege strategy of the Syrian regime was accompanied by a campaign of disinformation and denial that aimed to discredit the claims of victims and international opposition. The regime and its representatives never admitted the use of sieges as a counter-insurgency tactic and repeatedly claimed that people under siege were being held hostages by the rebels. Internationally, doctored videos and pictures were circulated by Russian, Lebanese, and Iranian media to show life in those areas as normal and to attempt to discredit the claims of the shortages of goods.[34] Propaganda and misinformation of this kind sought to minimize international pressure and repercussions, and also to confuse the affected peoples in making decisions whether to stay or flee.

While the opposition forces and Islamist groups also deployed sieges, it was only the US-led coalition and its local proxies—the Kurdish-dominated SDF—that matched or surpassed the level of violence employed by the Syrian regime. Siege tactics were deployed by the coalition in Menbij in the countryside of Aleppo, Raqqa, and Deir Alzor in 2016, 2017, and 2018–2019 respectively. In the battle for Raqqa, which lasted for four months, the coalition circled the city besieging approximately 50,000–100,000 civilians. Using incendiary and white phosphorus

[32] PAX Siege Watch, *Out of Sight, Out of Mind: The Aftermath of Syria's Siege*, 6 March 2019, available at <https://www.paxforpeace.nl/publications/all-publications/siege-watch-final-report> (visited 17 December 2020).

[33] In 2013–2015 as the regime was losing ground, it sought to establish areas of control along the border with Lebanon, to secure vital passageways. Although the Syrian regime always maintained a narrative of a national cause and the sanctity of the country's territorial integrity, some observers argue that this was a part of a plan to link Shi'ite territories in Lebanon with Alawite controlled areas in Syria should the regime need to retreat further and consolidate in an 'Alawistan' or a small part of Syria. In other areas, it sought to secure important Shi'ite religious shrines by homogenizing the sectarian identity of the surrounding population.

[34] L. Andriukaitis et al., *Breaking Ghouta*, 7 September 2018, available online at <https://www.atlanticcouncil.org/wp-content/uploads/2019/08/Breaking-Ghouta_English.pdf> (visited 17 March 2020).

ammunition,[35] the coalition destroyed much of the city, including civilian infrastructure.[36] During the siege, the city was reported to suffer from shortage of food, medicine, and fuel[37] and artillery and air attacks killed more than 1,600 civilians,[38] an equivalent of the number of civilians killed in the regime's assault in eastern Ghouta, which had more than four times the number of civilians.[39] Terrorist groups such as ISIL and al-Nusra Front[40] as well as Islamist and opposition groups also deployed sieges against their opponents; however, their efforts were undermined by their limited military means. The aims of these sieges differed in that these groups deployed sieges for the additional purposes of gaining political recognition and financial resources. In the prevailing polarized sectarian narratives in use at the time, besieging an area defined by its sectarian identity signalled a commitment to armed conflict defined along sectarian lines. Outcomes differed for the opposition forces, as will be shown in the case study on Aleppo, where the sectarian factor, especially in Nubl and Zahra, was salient.

Across communities, with high levels of unemployment and access to aid controlled directly or indirectly by armed groups, sieges allowed these groups to draw tactical advantages in their recruitment and allegiance building. In opposition-held areas, people whose support for the Assad's regime was not strong tended to consolidate their support for the rebels. Similarly, regime-held areas that were besieged by rebel and Islamist groups in Aleppo and Idlib showed an increased number of enlistment and support for (trans)national groups such as the Lebanese Shi'ite Party, Hezbollah, which claimed to be defending these areas. Meanwhile, local non-governmental organizations (NGOs) benefiting from the support of charity as well as national and international support focused their assistance at civilians, while the armed groups, including government forces, usually gave priority access to food and other supplies to their own troops, including recruits and

[35] Amnesty International, *Syria: Expert Analysis Shows US-Led Coalition Use of White Phosphorus May Amount to War Crime*, 16 June 2017, available online at <https://www.amnesty.org/en/latest/news/2017/06/syria-expert-analysis-shows-usled-coalition-use-of-white-phosphorus-may-amount-to-war-crime/> (visited 27 October 2021).

[36] Amnesty International, *'War of Annihilation': Devastating Toll on Civilians Raqqa—Syria*, 5 June 2018, available online at <https://www.amnesty.org.uk/files/reports/War%20of%20annihiliation%20report.pdf> (visited 22 August 2020).

[37] United Nations Office for the Coordination of Humanitarian Affairs, 'Syria: Fear for Civilians Mounts as Conflict in Ar-Raqqa Intensifies', June 2017, available online at <https://www.unocha.org/story/syria-fear-civilians-mounts-conflict-ar-raqqa-intensifies> (visited 22 August 2020).

[38] Amnesty International, *Syria: Unprecedented Investigation Reveals US-led Coalition Killed more than 1,600 Civilians in Raqqa 'Death Trap'*, 25 April 2019, available online at <https://www.amnesty.org/en/latest/news/2019/04/syria-unprecedented-investigation-reveals-us-led-coalition-killed-more-than-1600-civilians-in-raqqa-death-trap/> (visited 22 August 2020).

[39] Human Rights Watch, *Syria, Events of 2018* (2019), available online at <https://www.hrw.org/world-report/2019/country-chapters/syria#:~:text=Syrian%2DRussian%20Indiscriminate%20Attacks,-Indiscriminate%20attacks%20on&text=In%20February%2C%20government%20forces%20launched,February%2018%20until%20March%2021> (visited 22 August 2020).

[40] Currently known as Hay'at Tahrir al-Sham.

affiliates. There is no evidence, however, that defenders gained any strategic benefit from sieges, nor that they welcomed them.

Protracted siege warfare creates artificial scarcities and opportunities for windfall profits for those who can break the siege, and thus economic war generated a war economy. The war economy was associated with corruption, which allowed those with money or who controlled access and key commodities (fuel, medicine, food) to trade with the enemy, at times for enormous profit.[41] This underground economy meant that many people were able to survive who would otherwise have perished. However, it also represented a massive transfer of resources from ordinary Syrians to a mafia-like network of war profiteers on both sides of the conflict. At one point during the siege of eastern Ghouta, the price of a basic portion of bread cost eighty-five times more in east Ghouta than in Damascus, located just fifteen kilometres away.

Aid obstruction, as will be further shown in the case studies, was prevalent across the country. While government-held areas were usually supplied through the air, opposition-held areas were completely cut off and hence were mostly entirely dependent on international aid. A complex and often perilous humanitarian aid effort was mounted. International actors were frequently prevented from reaching the most vulnerable populations; specific examples are explored in the case studies later in this chapter, but there are chronicled patterns of obstruction by government and opposition forces.[42] A large network of local relief organizations sprang up during the war, some of which received assistance from international agencies and donors. Attacks against humanitarian aid workers and medical staff made the country top the list of the deadliest countries for humanitarian work.[43]

3. Case Studies

This chapter examines the use of sieges in five case studies. These case studies were selected to demonstrate the breadth of the actors employing starvation tactics, to demonstrate the impacts of those tactics in different geographies of the conflict, and to work to the strengths of the authors' experiences—allowing them to speak with authority on the details shared below. The first case documents patterns and distinguishing features of sieges directly impacting the capital of Damascus and its environs; an area of hundreds of thousands of people in some fifty towns

[41] The case of the war profiteer Hussam al-Qaterji facilitating oil trade between the regime and ISIS is just one example. For more details, see <http://www.levantnetworks.com/2020/06/04/syrian-businessmen-accused-of-oil-smuggling-linked-to-luxury-tourist-project/> (visited 16 December 2020).

[42] *Report of the Secretary-General on the implementation of Security Council resolution 2139* UN Doc. S/2014/208, 24 March 2014.

[43] A. Stoddard et al., *Aid Worker Security Report 2020*, Humanitarian Outcomes, August 2020, available online at <https://www.humanitarianoutcomes.org/AWSR2020> (visited 22 August 2020).

and villages, with a focus on eastern Ghouta. The second case study of Zabadani comes from along the border with Lebanon and demonstrates the role of strategic geographies and interlocking interests in determining the use of siege tactics. In Aleppo, in the north-west, and in Deir Alzor near the Iraqi border there are clear examples of the reciprocal use of siege warfare by rebel groups as well as the regime. Finally, a brief study of the use of starvation in prisons and detention centres under the control of the Syrian regime provides the clearest case of intention and culpability in the use of starvation and deprivation. Imposition of sieges and the use of starvation in Raqqa and Baghuz are worthy of further examination and so is the situation in the Al-Rukban camp, where despite being in control, the US forces have refused to relieve the shortages of food, water, and medicine,[44] which led to suicide cases among residents.[45]

A. Eastern Ghouta

The siege of eastern Ghouta was among the longest in history—two years longer than the siege of Leningrad in the Second World War, one year longer than the siege of Sarajevo—and was among the harshest in the Syrian context. It lasted between 2013 and 2018 and witnessed an intense use of all the weapons of siege warfare. The area is an agglomeration of towns and villages in the vicinity of Damascus. Historically, eastern Ghouta was an agricultural rural area, but in the 1980s urban growth saw agricultural land gradually shrinking to the benefit of residential and industrial complexes. The Assad regime and supporting transnational Shi'ite militias were exclusively responsible. Early on, during the beginning of civil unrest in March 2011, the residents of the area protested against the regime. The Assad forces responded with harsh oppression including arrests, which escalated to torture and extrajudicial killings as rebels started to employ violence on a small scale. Various rebel and FSA-affiliated groups began to emerge in eastern Ghouta in late 2011. In the spring of 2013, the regime cut off water and electricity to the area and began a siege; the following year, the Syrian regime banned civilian traffic into the enclave.

In the early stages, checkpoints were erected on the main entrances and roads leading to eastern Ghouta to prevent any significant movement of the rebels after

[44] J. Rogin, 'The United States won't feed 30,000 starving Syrians living under its protection', *The Washington Post*, 24 July 2019, available online at <https://www.washingtonpost.com/opinions/2019/07/24/united-states-wont-feed-starving-syrians-living-under-its-protection/#click=https://t.co/gdUTSWX8gI> (visited 22 August 2020).

[45] L. Al-Junid and A. H. M. Abo Rezeg, 'Hunger leads Syrian refugee to commit suicide', Anadolou Agency, 14 January 2019, available online at <https://www.aa.com.tr/en/middle-east/hunger-leads-syrian-refugee-to-commit-suicide/1364024> (visited 22 August 2020).

their attacks on the city of Damascus in July 2012.[46] Initially the movement of civilians and goods was not hindered. This changed as the rebel prowess increased and after multiple attacks on military bases and government institutions in the region of eastern Ghouta. Movement restriction was imposed and rationing of food supplies followed suit. Towards the end of 2012, under pressure from the rebels, the regime withdrew its forces and representatives from the region and a complete siege was fully imposed in April 2013. Eastern Ghouta was home to approximately 1.5 million people, as the siege progressed hundreds of thousands of civilians fled the area. With the withdrawal of the government institutions, basic services and provision were cut off by the regime or due to destruction as a result of military operations. At around the same time, although restriction on food provisions were introduced, the rebels, seemingly unaware of how harsh the impending siege would be, and in return for money, allowed local food traders and businessmen to empty their warehouses. This logic of the siege was military, and its aim seems to have been to contain the rebels and reduce their capacity to mount resistance or to attack the capital.

Initially, the region had several access routes. However, as the rebels attacked the checkpoints int their attempts to break the siege, the region was only left with two access routes to the outside world: al-Wafideen crossing, which only allowed the movement of civilians and a few selected cars, and a network of tunnels that lead to the Damascus suburbs, which developed during the siege. Al-Wafideen crossing was controlled by Syrian state forces on one side and Jaish al-Islam on the other. The other access route was a network of tunnels that ran out to the Damascus suburbs, al-Qaboun, and Barzeh, controlled by groups affiliated to the FSA. Several rounds of rebel infighting over control of these checkpoints and tunnels took place during the siege, as they represented a significant source of income from taxes on aid, food, and all other materials. Gradually, the regime regained controlled over eastern Ghouta; the regime focused on curtailing rebel access to crops and weapons, and one officer manning a checkpoint said that if the regime could cut off the oxygen supply, it would do the regime's bidding.[47]

Within the besieged areas, after several mergers and infighting rounds, control was eventually divided between two primary opposition armed groups: Islam Army (Arabic: *Jaysh al-Islam*) and al-Rahman Corps, an FSA affiliate group. Islam Army, an Islamist group mainly controlling Douma district, seized control over all aspects of life in the area under its control including policing, setting up courts, and distribution of aid under their direct control. This was an effort to consolidate control and gain allegiance from the people under its control. NGOs and groups

[46] I. Black and J. Borger, 'Syrian armed rebels take fight to government troops in Damascus', *The Guardian*, 17 July 2012, available online at <https://www.theguardian.com/world/2012/jul/17/syrian-armed-rebels-fight-damascus> (visited 22 August 2020).

[47] An officer manning the Maliha checkpoint, 2013, personal interview.

with different affiliation or political aspirations were harassed and had their work restricted or entirely banned. In the remaining part of eastern Ghouta, the FSA represented by al-Rahman Corps co-administered the area under its control with the civilian local councils and representatives of the Syrian interim government, which was recognized internationally. The FSA defended the area, while the municipal authority and Syrian interim government were left to arrange services such as water, healthcare, and waste disposal. Meanwhile, the FSA had a parallel services structure for its own affiliates.[48] Throughout the siege, initiatives to end the conflict were put forward by the regime and its allies, including Russia. Several rounds of negotiations took place in Damascus, eastern Ghouta, Geneva, and Egypt. However, the proposals of the regime were rejected as the rebels refused to surrender or reconcile.[49]

The impact of the siege differed throughout this period with the first few months being the harshest as the region was unprepared. During this time, the area was not yet on the radar of the international or national humanitarian aid community and no humanitarian aid was sent to the area. Additionally, no war economy had developed at the time to allow for the smuggling of food and other materials. Later on, as networks of mediators and war profiteers were established, a trickle of commercial food deliveries was allowed to enter the area, which were then sold by (rebel-affiliated) entities and individuals at hugely inflated prices. It is unknown if these food deliveries and other supplies such as medicine and gas cylinders were allowed by the general command or were due to the corruption of the officers in charge. Monopoly was common and several raids on commercial stores showed that food supplies were stockpiled to drive prices higher. Mohieddin Manfoush, a dairy magnate, had a near monopoly on big-scale trade between the besieged enclave and the outside world.[50] In addition to blocking food and basic services, medical supplies were stopped, and the besieged population had to make do with existing stocks and locally produced materials. With the government institutions departing the region, waste disposal also ceased in the area. The regime prohibited civilian movement out of the enclave by indiscriminately attacking any movement. Access was heavily restricted, and at times completely blocked and banned.

In addition to deprivation and siege, the regime and its allies subjected the population under siege in eastern Ghouta to air attacks including barrel bombs and an infamous chemical weapons attack in August 2013, the latter was said to be a pre-emptive attack to quell an assault by the rebels on the capital. Given the secrecy

[48] L. Andriukaitis et al., see note 34.

[49] S. Moutasem; head of negotiation committee in eastern Ghouta: southern sector, 1 March 2018, personal interview.

[50] Enab Baladi Investigative Unit, 'The Economic Map of Ghouta: Tunnels and "the Prince of Cheese"', *Syria Untold*, 26 July 2017, available online at <https://syriauntold.com/2017/07/26/the-economic-map-of-ghouta-tunnels-and-the-prince-of-cheese/> (visited 22 August 2020).

around the decision-making mechanism within the regime as well as its denial of such conduct, it is not possible to determine precise responsibility.

Additionally, military attacks, involving air raids, included a pattern of attacks on hospitals, bakeries, and communal kitchens, which may have been meant to reduce the capacity of a group to resist and to undermine the resilience of the local population. During the last push to conquer the enclave, bombs or missiles were targeted at locations where there was evidence of cooking (i.e. smoke rising from communal kitchens),[51] which would appear to be an effort at disrupting a bakery or kitchen. This pattern of attack was against all communal kitchens and bakeries and was always preceded by aerial reconnaissance. Once the majority of bakeries and communal kitchens were eliminated, the intensified attacks on hospitals and medical centres took place. This was a consistent pattern of depriving the inhabitants of eastern Ghouta of activities and objects essential to their survival.

As military action escalated, the siege tactics also continued. The regime tightly restricted international humanitarian aid and often blocked it entirely. Through the first half of 2017, no UN aid convoys entered eastern Ghouta. The 4 May 2017 'De-escalation Zone Agreement' was signed by Turkey, Iran, and Russia to reduce violence in four zones across the Syrian map including eastern Ghouta, and the 22 July 2017 Cairo ceasefire agreement that backed it up, both included detailed provisions for aid access, which were only partially honoured. There were UN aid convoys to Douma and Harasta between May and August 2017. Each time the amounts permitted and the people to whom the aid could be distributed were tightly regulated. For example, on 30 October 2017, supplies were allowed for 40,000 residents in the two towns of Kafr Batna and Saqba, but the regime stipulated the aid not be shared or distributed with residents of other areas in eastern Ghouta, which was estimated to be at 400,000 inhabitants.[52]

At the end of 2017, the regime further tightened its blockade and fewer goods were smuggled or allowed to the besieged area. After seventy-eight days without access to the enclave, a UN aid convoy was permitted access in February 2018. According to UN figures, the regime stripped the convoy of 3,810 units of medical equipment, including syringes, intravenous catheters, sterile surgical gloves, anaesthetics, adrenaline, and anti-asthma medicines.[53] The same happened to a UN convoy the following month, when regime forces removed most of the medical equipment, including surgical kits, insulin, dialysis equipment, and other supplies. Even the goods that were allowed to pass did not all make it into the hands

[51] E. Amer; humanitarian worker in Touba, a local NGO active in Ghouta, 20 February 2018, personal interview.

[52] H. Bashar; Head of Erbeen Local Council Humanitarian Committee, 29 November 2017, personal interview.

[53] *Report of Secretary General to the United Nations Security Council, Implementation of Security Council resolutions 2139 (2014), 2165 (2014), 2258 (2015), 2332 (2016), and 2393 (2017)*, UN Doc. S/2018/243, 20 March 2018.

of those who needed them so desperately. During the night, forty trucks pulled out of Douma after shelling on the town without fully unloading the supplies they had brought in. Ten trucks left the town still fully sealed, while four more had been partially unloaded. An indication of the level of scarcity is that, in November 2017, one kilogram of bread in eastern Ghouta cost 1,150 per cent more than in nearby Damascus.[54] From January 2017, bread and wheat flour prices increased by more than 174 per cent and 390 per cent, respectively, while sugar prices rose by more than 1,000 per cent. Boiling water to make it safe to drink often became impossible due to fuel shortages.

There is as yet no comprehensive assessment of the civilian impact of the siege and war in eastern Ghouta. A limited measure of the severity of the siege during the final year (2017), however, can be found in a humanitarian survey of the period from 29 October to 14 November 2017, which classified the situation as 'serious', having found a global acute malnutrition (GAM) rate of 11.9 per cent, a sharp increase from levels found in January 2017 (2.1 per cent). Chronic malnutrition levels were also classified as 'serious', with 36 per cent stunting rate, again an increase from January 2017 (30.5 per cent). The survey also found that residents were reduced to adapt negative coping mechanism including eating raw vegetables and consuming only one meal a day, with priority given to children.[55]

The siege was subsequently intensified with direct military action by Russian forces on behalf of the regime. This intervention was decisive in the fall of eastern Ghouta in March 2018. The final military assault resulted in the death of approximately 1,600 civilians. At the time the regime regained control, approximately 400,000 people were residing in the enclave. Upon surrender, affiliates of the armed and opposition groups as well as other citizens were given the choice to remain or be bussed to the north of the country. Approximately 60,000 people fled the area for fear of reprisals.[56] Despite the increased level of hunger during the last days of the attack, after their departure, warehouses full of food were found within the area that had been under the control of the rebels and local authorities.

B. Zabadani

In 2011, when protests against the Assad regime broke out in the city of Zabadani, which is located forty-five kilometres north of the capital Damascus, the regime

[54] Syrian American Medical Society, *The Daily Realities of East Ghouta: A Mother of 6 Struggles to Provide*, 26 October 2017, available online at <https://foundation.sams-usa.net/2017/10/26/daily-realities-east-ghouta-mother-6-struggles-provide/> (visited 4 June 2019).

[55] Physicians Across Continents—Turkey, *Nutrition SMART Survey Report: Eastern Ghouta*, November 2017, available online at <https://www.humanitarianresponse.info/sites/www.humanitarianresponse.info/files/documents/files/smart_survey_eastern_ghouta_november_2017_final_ .pdf> (visited 21 May 2019), at 12.

[56] L. Andriukaitis et al., see note 34.

responded harshly. The first death in Zabadani as a result of the Assad's forces crackdown was reported on 27 May 2011. Attacks against the regime forces had been reported earlier than this date and the government campaign retaliated by an arrest campaign, which targeted suspects between fifteen and sixty years old. By August 2011, re-armed with weapons smuggled from Lebanon, the opposition was able to take the military offensive.[57] During those attacks, regime associates and posts were attacked, prompting the former to leave and the latter to be evacuated. After the failure of local initiatives to restore peace, in November 2011, the regime forces attacked the town with heavy artillery and tanks. The campaign lasted for approximately one week, resulting in only partial achievement of regime aims, after which the regime resorted to indiscriminate bombardment. This resulted in the displacement of half the town's population of 26,285 (2004 census) from western neighbourhoods towards eastern neighbourhoods and Bludan town, and was followed by several military campaigns. Similar to other areas, local initiatives to end the conflict in the region were proposed on several occasions; however, they failed either due to their rejection by the rebels or later on due to being entangled in a regional deal that involved Iran, Qatar, the rebels, and Hezbollah.

The city remained under siege until it fell into the hands of the regime and its affiliated militias. During the siege, activists reported tens of deaths due to illnesses directly caused by deprivation of food and medical supplies,[58] lack of heating fuel through winter further exacerbated health impacts of the siege. Meanwhile, the city lacked all basic services including electricity, gas supplies, state education, and clean water. The regime attempts to break into az-Zabadani town started in July 2015 with the support of Lebanese Hezbollah, Iraqi militias of Abu Alfadl Alabbas, and Palestinian militias of Ahmed Jibril.

In late 2015, activists in the two cities of Madaya and Zabadani documented the death of forty-eight people in the last two months due to the siege of their cities. Among them, thirty-three died due to lack of food and medicine whilst seven died due to landmine explosions, and six were killed by snipers of the regime and its militias as they tried to run away from their besieged homes. Two were also killed by snipers as they attempted to smuggle food and medicine into besieged areas.[59] These deaths can be directly attributed to starvation tactics.

The siege of Zabadani by regime forces ended with the 'four towns deal' in 2017, negotiated among the regime, the opposition, Iran, and Qatar. The other three towns were Madaya, Foah, and Kefraya. The deal transferred civilian populations

[57] 'Wiretaps implicate Lebanon MP in arming Syrian rebels', *Agence France-Presse*, 4 December 2012, available online at <https://www.thenationalnews.com/world/mena/wiretaps-implicate-lebanon-mp-in-arming-syrian-rebels-1.401841> (visited 6 November 2020).

[58] Syrian American Medical Society, *Madaya: Starvation Under Siege*, September 2016, available online at <https://www.sams-usa.net/wp-content/uploads/2016/09/Report_Madaya_Starvation_Under_Siege_.pdf> (visited 4 June 2019), at 3.

[59] The Syrian Human Rights Committee, *Victims of Siege in Madaya and al-Zabadani*, 18 January 2016, available online at <http://www.shrc.org/en/?p=26517> (visited 18 April 2020).

with the effect of 'cleansing' along sectarian lines. It included a ransom paid by Qatar to release hostages taken by a Shi'ite armed group in a remote area of Iraq. The deal illustrates the many actors involved in and layers of interlocking interests that both helped to maintain and, finally, conclude this siege.

It is plausible to conclude that the process of negotiating the 'four towns deal' prolonged the siege, as it impacted local initiatives to end the siege earlier. Zabadani is strategically located on the route to Lebanon and had been an important smuggling route. As the war continued, the city became a pawn in a wider game of sectarian bargaining, used as a 'hostage' to trade against the siege that Islamists had imposed on Shi'ite towns in Idlib. Furthermore, initial talk of the deal began during a period when the regime was focused on consolidating areas of control along its border with Lebanon, which represented strategic depth for both Hezbollah and the Syrian regime which would have been crucial in the scenario of an Alawite-controlled enclave along the Lebanese border and Syrian coastal region. The siege ended with total population displacement. Gradually, and only after a process of reconciliation and security clearance, ex-residents are being allowed to return to their areas.

C. Aleppo

The use of starvation as a weapon of war in and around Aleppo is a more complex case due to the combination of different forms of siege tactics deployed alongside the regime's attacks on farms and agricultural areas. However, during the timespan of the armed conflict in Aleppo between 2012 and 2016, there were reciprocal sieges tried by the parties to the conflict: Assad's regime and rebel groups, mainly Islamists. In July 2012, a mix of armed groups, including the FSA, moved their troops into Aleppo and took control of almost half the city in less than a month. Thereafter, the city was divided into two parts: western Aleppo, under Assad's regime control, and eastern Aleppo, under a plethora of armed groups. Among the rebel groups were Jabhat al-Nusra and ISIL, which emerged as significant actors after mid-2013.[60]

Patterns of violence and deprivation mirrored those elsewhere, but distinct were the networks of relationships between armed forces that resulted in the imposition of severe restrictions on goods trafficking into regime-controlled areas. The Quadrilateral Committee of the opposition consolidated control over the crossing

[60] The Chemical Weapons Attack on eastern Ghouta was the most significant event in the Syrian conflict. The failure of the international community to deter and thereafter to hold Assad's use of chemical weapons contributed significantly to the radicalization of many moderate groups and facilitated the spread of and expansion of Da'esh across Syria.

to the regime's areas at Bustan al-Qaser neighbourhood.[61] However, by July 2016, the Assad regime tightened the screws on the opposition groups and laid siege to the areas under their control.[62] Aided by Russia, the regime followed a scorched-earth strategy to force the opposition to surrender its positions. In December 2016, all opposition affiliated groups and activists were bussed to the northern countryside of Aleppo, a recurrent scenario during the Syrian war.[63]

To the east, the countryside of Aleppo is a rich agricultural area with a comparatively good irrigation system. The regime launched targeted and systematic attacks on the infrastructure, fields, markets, and OIS.[64] The town of Maskana, 100 kilometres east of Aleppo, was the location of farms and water installations that provided water to the city. Regime rockets struck the state-owned cattle farm and sugar factory. Markets, bazaars, and trucks loaded with food were regularly attacked and destroyed. The large Wednesday market in Maskana was repeatedly attacked.[65]

Women customarily have the larger roles in agriculture around Aleppo, including planting, weeding, and harvesting vegetables and other crops. They also do the majority of buying and selling in food markets. The regime strategies directly impacted these activities. This began with army control over the power supply for the irrigation pumps and extended to firing shells at farms and markets, and preventing access to farms within a four-kilometre radius of Kweres military base. The result was a disastrous drop in the incomes of farming families as well as food shortages.

The town of Albab is a large commercial hub that links Aleppo, Idlib, and Turkey to the eastern part of Syria. It became a place of refuge for Aleppo inhabitants who fled the city. In the first two years of the conflict Albab was not attacked systematically.[66] It was targeted whenever there was a rebel military operation against the nearby Kweres Military Airbase, to put pressure on the armed groups factions to withdraw from the areas around the base. Thereafter, markets, bazaars, hospitals,

[61] After the increasing number of armed groups in Aleppo, the main four groups of the Free Syrian Army, Ahrar al-Sham, Daesh, and Jabhat al-Nusra created one umbrella body to coordinate the military operations and the governance of the city.

[62] 'The Syrian regime applies the siege on eastern Aleppo and western Aleppo celebrates', *al Quds al Arabi*, 30 July 2016, available online at <https://www.alquds.co.uk/%EF%BB%BF-الن ظام-السوري-يطبق-الحصار-على-حلب-ال/> (visited 3 January 2020).

[63] K. Shaheen, 'Hundreds leave besieged east Aleppo on first day of evacuation', *The Guardian*, 15 September 2016, available online at <https://www.theguardian.com/world/2016/dec/15/syria-ambulances-on-the-move-as-aleppo-evacuation-operation-begins> (visited 2 January 2020).

[64] Q. Abdullah; Head of Local Council Irrigation Office in Deir-Hafer, 15 January 2019, personal interview. Author's own observation during field visits in the eastern countryside of Aleppo.

[65] 'More than 50 people were killed in the Russian bombing of a popular market in the eastern countryside of Aleppo', *Arabi 21*, 15 December 2015, available online at <https://bit.ly/39IMuKr> (visited 2 January 2020).

[66] Y. Safwan; Interview with a paramedic from Al-Bab city, 12 February 2019, personal interview.

and bakeries were targeted by mortars, missiles, and barrel bombs.[67] This damaged the economy, pressured the inhabitants to leave, and made it difficult for businesspeople to reconstruct damaged houses, industries, farms, and markets. Henceforth, the food supply for the local people, the displaced people, and for the market in Aleppo suffered. As the war intensified in this area, these attacks continued. In April 2015, regime fighter jets targeted the main hospital in the city of Deir Hafer, killing around thirty people including medical staff of the city main hospital.[68] Until late 2013 and 2014, when ISIL gained momentum and obtained a foothold in Aleppo district, trade between different parts of Aleppo continued despite the conflict. Following the rise of ISIL, regime strongholds became surrounded, until a new military campaign mounted in mid-2013 from Hama reopened supply lines.[69] By early 2014, the regime forces managed to break through and secure a land supply line between Damascus through Hama to Aleppo.

North of Aleppo were areas controlled by armed groups affiliated with the Kurdish Democratic Union Party (PYD), which maintained relations with regime forces, a relationship that allowed the two Shi'a towns in the north to subvert total siege. Nubl and Zahraa, surrounded by opposition groups from three sides, were dependent on the supply line connecting them with Afrin, which was under the control of the YPG. Moreover, aerial supply never stopped into the two Shi'a towns until the regime-allied Shi'a militias opened the land supply line in February 2016 by ousting the opposition groups encircling the two towns.[70] During the time the opposition groups were putting pressure on the Shi'a towns, civilians were able to move into Afrin or use helicopters to be transferred into regime-controlled areas of western Aleppo. Considering the rebel groups' limited resources, the adverse impact on food supplies to the two Shi'a towns was low. However, intermittent attacks and shelling during military operations in rebel attempts to take control of the two towns damaged local markets and caused increases in the prices of essential goods.

D. Deir Alzor

Deir Alzor is another case of reciprocal siege tactics mounted by regime forces and ISIL over the period from July 2014 to September 2017.

[67] 'Aerial Barrel Bombing of Al-Bab in the countryside of Aleppo', *Ad-Dustour*, 2 December 2013, available online at <https://www.addustour.com/articles/210127--الطيران-يقصف-مدينة-الباب-في-ريف-حلب-بالبراميل-المتفجرة> (visited 3 January 2020).

[68] 'New massacre in Aleppo kills 30 people', *Zaman Alwasl*, 23 April 2015, available online at <https://www.zamanalwsl.net/news/article/60114> (visited 4 June 2019).

[69] B. Diop, 'The Syrian army lifts militants' siege of Aleppo', *Al-Akhbar*, 8 October 2013, available online at <https://al-akhbar.com/Syria/58705> (visited 4 June 2019).

[70] 'The regime cuts the supply road to Aleppo and ends the siege of Nubl and Zahra', *Al Jazeera*, 2 April 2020, available online at <https://www.aljazeera.net/news/arabic/2016/2/4/النظام-يقطع-طريق-إمداد-حلب-ويفك-حصار-نبل-الزهراء> (visited 4 June 2019).

Deir Alzor is the largest city in eastern Syria, in the oil-producing area of the country, close to the Iraqi border. As the conflict intensified, it was difficult for the regime to keep control over this large remote area. Hence, the regime forces started withdrawing from smaller towns, and consolidated its forces at the military airport of Deir Alzor, the Talaeá 'Vanguard' Camp, and Military Brigade 137 around the city. By 2013, the entire countryside was under the control of the opposition armed groups, whereas the city was divided between the opposition groups in the eastern part of the city and the regime in the western part. The regime adopted the same strategy that was being followed in other places: attacking food convoys, markets, bakeries, and hospitals. In this case, the control of bridges was particularly crucial.

For more than three years, ISIL besieged a regime-controlled enclave of 200,000 civilians, who were intermittently supplied by the UN. This regime-aligned population suffered enormously, both from the ISIL siege and attacks and also from the regime's military strategy.

By the end of 2014, ISIL entered Deir Alzor and took control of much of the city. The first ISIL action was to cut the supply lines to the regime-controlled areas, where 200,000 civilians lived. The Syrian regime responded by targeting the bridges which link the city with its eastern rural hinterland. This cut overland supply routes, intensifying the suffering of the population. ISIL used boats to supply the city, but the government garrison at Jabal al-Tharda in the southern part of the city fired on boats when it could. ISIL prioritized supplies for its fighters over those for the civilian population. The regime still controlled the airport, but ISIL attacks made it dangerous for aircraft to land. The UN used airdrops to provide humanitarian supplies, which could deliver only small amounts. By 2015, there were reports of civilians, mostly children under five, dying of starvation in Deir Alzor.[71] Very little aid reached the ISIL-controlled areas, apart from WFP airdrops, and it was not possible to conduct on-site assessments. Nonetheless, reports of deaths from starvation and related diseases persisted through 2019, as the remaining civilian population attempted to flee the final regime push to defeat ISIL.[72]

E. Starvation in Detention

The use of starvation in detention constitutes a strong case of the direct culpability of the Assad regime in systemic use of starvation. Almost without exception, detainees who were lucky to be released from Assad's prisons had suffered from the

[71] UN Office for the Coordinator of Humanitarian Affairs, 'Syria: Flash Update, Deir-Ez-Zor City—15 January 2016', 15 January 2016, available online at <https://reliefweb.int/report/syrian-arab-republic/syria-flash-update-deir-ez-zor-city-15-january-2016> (visited 4 June 2019).

[72] UN News, 'Syrians "exposed to brutality every day" as thousands continue fleeing ISIL's last stand', 1 March 2019, available online at <https://news.un.org/en/story/2019/03/1033882> (visited 4 June 2019).

systematic deprivation of food, clean water, and medicine.[73] What makes the use of starvation in detention distinct is that it was systematic. The regime had total control over the prisoners and there was no relief aid.

The regime, and its agencies and proxies, detained numerous people before and during the conflict. In clear cases of intention and culpability, the regime carried out starvation on a large scale against people in detention. Detainees were subjected to conditions in detention that involved the deprivation of objects indispensable for survival including food, water, and necessary clothing.[74] In January 2014, an official forensic photographer for the Military Police, codenamed 'Caesar', defected from the regime with a dossier of 53,275 files, including photographs taken between May 2011 and August 2013, that documented torture across five Syrian regime detention centres, under the control of Military Intelligence, Airforce Intelligence, 'Patrols' (military intelligence), and 'Palestine' (military intelligence).[75] The Syrian Network for Human Rights documented 14,129 people killed while being tortured by parties to the conflict (March 2011 to March 2019); 13,983 of these deaths occurred while detainees were held by the Syrian regime.[76]

Expert analysis of the photographs demonstrated evidence of violent blunt force trauma, suffocation, and starvation. A doctor working for the Syrian Association for Missing and Conscience Detainees (not a forensic expert) 'reviewed all 28,707 of the detainee photographs and found more than 40 percent of the bodies were emaciated, with sharply defined rib cages, prominent pelvic bones, and sunken faces'.[77] Reviewing a subset of the photographs representing nineteen victims, Physicians for Human Rights found that six showed evidence of starvation, and 'in four of the cases starvation is likely to have contributed to the victim's death'.[78]

4. Conclusion

This chapter addresses the use of siege and starvation as weapons of warfare Syria, a strategy that was used by different actors to the conflict, chief among them the

[73] At the outset of the uprising of 2011, Assad's regime started detaining activists, and those who are suspected of being so, widely and concentrating them in very small confinements. For elaborate accounts on the starvation strategies deployed by the regime in the notorious prison of Saydanaya, please see *Saydanaya Prison during the Syrian Revolution: Testimonies* (in Arabic), full text available online at <https://bit.ly/326xh3n> (visited 25 August 2021).

[74] Security officers, who ruled prisons as corrupt 'fiefdoms', were also known to be engaged in major deals relating to selling food contracts.

[75] Human Rights Watch, *If the Dead Could Speak: Mass Deaths and Torture in Syria's Detention Facilities*, December 2015, available online at <https://www.hrw.org/report/2015/12/16/if-dead-could-speak/mass-deaths-and-torture-syrias-detention-facilitiesm> (visited 4 June 2019), at 2.

[76] 'Death toll due to torture', Syrian Network for Human Rights, 24 September 2018, <http://sn4hr.org/blog/2018/09/24/death-toll-due-to-torture/> (visited 7 June 2019).

[77] Human Rights Watch see note 75, at 7-8.

[78] Y. Safwan; Interview with a paramedic from Al-Bab city, 12 February 2019, personal interview.

Syrian regime. The logic behind the imposition of sieges differed across actors with the majority aiming to reduce the capacity of opponents and to gain military victories. The use of these tactics and military actions that destroyed infrastructure has resulted in deaths and malnutrition and they continue to impact the lives and the future of the Syrian people.

Economic conditions in Syria immediately prior to the conflict had witnessed increased levels of malnutrition due to a combination of factors including the contraction of state welfare provision, drought, poor government response to drought, the world food crisis, and reduction of aid due to international pressures. Increased hunger was the outcome of a confluence of factors including official neglect. The situation was entirely different throughout the conflict, which witnessed unprecedented levels of malnutrition, starvation, and associated death. These were all the foreseeable outcomes of deliberate actions. During the conflict, the weaponization of food and water as well as targeting of OIS were used by all actors. The outcome of such strategies was widely reported, but rarely were actions taken to mitigate the use of starvation.

Culpability for such crimes is not only limited to local actors. A range of international actors became engaged in the Syrian war and shaped the ways in which it was fought. They undoubtedly share culpabilities. In some cases, the US-led Coalition, Iran, and Russia were active participants in starvation sieges, and their military involvement, including the use of internationally prohibited weapons and destruction of basic infrastructure, will continue to impede the recovery of the Syrian agricultural sector into the future. Furthermore, international actors continue to affect the conflict through their political engagement represented by sanctions and obstruction of aid, both of which impact the humanitarian operations in the country.

Furthermore, information control including censorship and communications blackouts, propaganda, and misrepresentation, were all weapons in the Syrian war. The importance of a free media in famine prevention is well-recognized in the academic literature.[79] The Syrian case also points to the importance of accurate information for people who are targeted by starvation crimes. Compelled to make day-to-day decisions crucial for their survival, they are compelled to act in informational fog. Meanwhile, existing food security reporting, monitoring, and analytical frameworks have failed to grapple properly with the Syrian case.

The aforementioned begs the questions of accountability for the starvation crimes committed. The extent of the crimes and multiplicity of actors that were engaged in these crimes may render criminal accountability unattainable, especially if it was to contribute to political deterioration leading to renewed conflict in the future. Accountability, if not targeted against individuals, could translate into new

[79] A. Sen, *Development as Freedom* (Oxford: Oxford University Press, 1999).

sanctions imposed on Syria as a whole, which would increase the hardships faced by victims. The difficulties of pursuing individual criminal accountability should not be an excuse for failing to pursue political accountability and provision of transitional justice including the restoring the dignity of victims, truth commissions, national reconciliation, and the adaptations of regulations that prevent new crimes and establish or strengthen the rule of law by introducing institutional and political reforms. Such initiatives, while unable to remedy the grievous harms inflicted upon Syrians, will hopefully contribute to communal peace and may help close the book on one of the most terrible chapters of the Syrian conflict.

9

'Once We Control Them, We Will Feed Them'

Mass Starvation in Yemen

Aditya Sarkar

1. Introduction

Mass starvation in contemporary Yemen has been caused by both structural and proximate factors. These include the precarious livelihoods of many Yemenis on account of the country's political economy, and crucially, the military and economic strategies used by the different belligerents in the conflict.

Yemen rank as probably the largest and most protracted episode of mass starvation of recent times. While there has been no official declaration of 'famine' by the United Nations on the basis of a food security assessment in accordance with the Integrated food security Phase Classification (IPC) scale, the data that do exist indicate a vast crisis, with some pockets of greater severity (resulting in an IPC level 5 'famine' being indicated) and many others that would have descended into famine were it not for humanitarian aid. Those data sets are often incomplete, partly due to the denial of access by the belligerent parties. There is good reason to fear that the poor quality of information conceals severe human deprivation including starvation.

Famine and mass starvation in Yemen[1] arise from both food availability decline and collapse in real demand (people's ability to purchase food). Even before the conflict began, Yemen was a poor country with a fragile economy dependent on labour migration and associated remittances, and oil revenues (which were declining). Yemen has been almost entirely dependent on food imports for its basic staples since the 1970s, and hunger was pervasive, especially in rural areas. Yemen's kleptocratic, patronage-based, transactional political system was characterized

[1] The author wishes to thank Sama'a al Hamdani, Martha Mundy, Helen Lackner, and the staff of the Mwantana Organization for Human Rights for reviews of earlier drafts.

See Introduction to this volume, for a discussion on the terms 'famine' and 'mass starvation', and section 2.B in this chapter on whether a famine has indeed occurred in Yemen.

Aditya Sarkar, *'Once We Control Them, We Will Feed Them'* In: *Accountability for Mass Starvation*. Edited by: Bridget Conley, Alex de Waal, Catriona Murdoch, and Wayne Jordash QC, Oxford University Press. © Aditya Sarkar 2022.
DOI: 10.1093/oso/9780192864734.003.0009

by pervasive rent-seeking behaviour among elites which created incentives for macro-economic mismanagement and disincentivized political and economic reform. However, none of these caused famine. This chapter argues that culpability for mass starvation in Yemen lies directly with the military and economic strategies used by belligerents to fight the war. By depriving citizens of their ability to earn livelihoods or obtain the things they need to survive, these war strategies have contributed to and exacerbated food insecurity in the country. They have made the food crisis wider, deeper, and more lethal.

First, the blockade (both in its complete and partial forms) imposed by the Saudi/United Arab Emirates (UAE)-led coalition (SLC)[2] significantly restricted the import of essential commodities and food and led to a drop in food supply in some areas and increased prices.[3] Second, the aerial bombing campaign by the SLC, and to a lesser extent, artillery and mortar attacks, and use of landmines near food and water points by the Houthis,[4] Yemeni armed forces and other militias resulted in the destruction of critical infrastructure including roads and bridges and agricultural facilities, as well as those related to the generation and supply of electricity and water. Agricultural areas and artisanal fishing have been attacked, as have markets and private businesses. Not only has this affected food supply, it has also led to bankruptcy and unemployment—in other words, a broader loss of livelihoods, which in turn has led to a collapse of real demand. It could be argued that these constitute attacks on 'objects indispensable to survival' (OIS)—which are a critical element in the war crime of starvation. The healthcare system too has been targeted by both air and artillery strikes and has all but collapsed, with only about half of all medical facilities still functional.

Economic policies, such as the decisions by the Internationally Recognized Government of Yemen (IRG) to shift the Central Bank of Yemen (CBY) from Sana'a to Aden, and restrictions on circulation of money and fuel imports have compounded existing economic crises and created new ones: public sector salaries and pensions have either not been paid or only paid irregularly since 2016, and welfare schemes have been suspended. The rapid depletion of currency reserves of the CBY (and after 2016, of the CBY in Aden) has led to spending cuts and made it even more difficult for traders to import essential commodities. The Houthis too have played a

[2] The SLC consists of Saudi Arabia, UAE, Kuwait, and Bahrain, with some non-Gulf Cooperation Council (GCC) countries having been induced to join and/or contribute forces. These include or have included Egypt, Jordan, Sudan, Morocco, and Senegal and later Somalia and Eritrea (though they have participated to different extents). Saudi Arabia is the primary financier and architect of the SLC, while the UAE is the other decision-maker and financier.

[3] S. Tandon and T. Vishwanath, 'Evolution of Poor Food Access over the Course of the Conflict in the Republic of Yemen', Policy Research Working Paper No. 8813 (The World Bank Group, 2019), available online at <https://openknowledge.worldbank.org/bitstream/handle/10986/31542/WPS8813.pdf?sequence=4&isAllowed=y> (visited 26 August 2021), at 3.

[4] We use the term Houthis to refer to the *de facto* government in Sana'a throughout this chapter, even though the Houthis adopted the name Ansarallah when they agreed to participate in the National Dialogue Conference in 2012. Not all those who fight on their side are part of the Houthi movement.

role in precipitating and intensifying these crises, through their policies on controlling fuel imports, payment of salaries, and monetary policy.

A war economy of profiteering from the trade in essential commodities has also emerged: this is characterized by corruption, pillage, smuggling, and the proliferation of taxes on movement of goods. All parties (including local armed groups) have engaged in this, but it is particularly noticeable during instances of siege warfare, such as the siege of Ta'izz by the Houthis. Finally, and critically, all sides to the conflict have impeded humanitarian supplies and operations—through blockade (imposed by the SLC), diversion of humanitarian aid and restricting access (most notably the Houthis, but also most local armed actors), and the imposition of onerous restrictions, levies, and fees. The humanitarian crises caused by these military and economic strategies (which include a protracted outbreak, or multiple outbreaks of cholera since 2016) have been compounded by floods and desert locust infestations across the region, as well as the COVID-19 pandemic and its consequences.

The actions of the belligerent parties are culpable to varying degrees. As a general rule, economic policies, however severe their outcomes may be for human well-being, are not subject to criminal sanction. In the case of Yemen, the selective and targeted imposition of economic policies, when their impact in causing starvation had already become clear, may demonstrate the use of starvation as a method of war by the belligerents. The case would be strengthened by the evidence of clearly prohibited military tactics (such as attacks on health facilities and fishing boats) and by evidence of systematic diversion of humanitarian aid and corruption. Together, they point to the sustained and repeated uses of starvation as a method of warfare.

This chapter is organized as follows. Section 2 outlines the history of the present conflict and examines whether famine has occurred in Yemen. Section 3 sets out the longer-term features of the political economy which have contributed to widespread food insecurity in Yemen. Sections 4 and 5 focus on the military and economic strategies which have contributed to starvation and famine in Yemen. These thematic discussions are supplemented by two short case studies on al-Hudaydah and Ta'izz.

Every famine has multiple causes. These include both the 'structural factors that determine vulnerability, and the proximate triggers of the crisis'.[5] Globally, over the last 150 years, the structural causes of famine have become less salient, and the proximate causes have become more important. Where a lack of administrative capacity and minor political miscalculations could create famine in poorer regions of the world in the nineteenth century, contemporary episodes of starvation and famine require more particular triggers, including specific politico-military

[5] A. de Waal, 'The End of Famine? Prospects for the Elimination of Mass Starvation by Political Action', 62 *Political Geography* (2018) 184–195, at 185.

decisions.[6] Further, the second decade of the twenty-first century has witnessed the emergence of 'compound crises': the convergence of multiple factors which can in combination lead to starvation and famine.[7] These trends include climate change (including the increase in extreme weather events) and turbulence in national economies associated with economic globalization which can lead to sudden and unexpected increases in the price of food, as well as the loss of employment and livelihoods. These risks are exacerbated by persistent political turmoil, the pursuit of political priorities by states and actors to the exclusion of humanitarian norms (counter-humanitarianism), globally and nationally entrenched systems of transactional politics, increase in conflict, and the global war on terror.

This chapter argues that even though Yemen can be understood as a compound crisis, and even though structural causes of hunger were important prior to the conflict, the most important drivers of starvation and famine are the actions of the belligerents. For a prosecutor seeking to prove criminal culpability, however, the challenge would be to clarify the chains of causation involving these actions and proximate drivers of hunger in a way that satisfies the evidentiary requirements of international criminal law.[8]

2. Conflict, Humanitarian Crisis, and the Curious Case of non-declaration of Famine in Yemen

A. Background: Cycles of Conflict and Crisis in Yemen

Yemen is no stranger to political crises or armed conflict. The modern-day Republic of Yemen was established in 1990 as a result of a hurried merger between the Yemen Arab Republic (YAR, and commonly known as North Yemen) and the People's Democratic Republic of Yemen (PDRY or South Yemen).[9] However, the political and state-building trajectories of YAR and PDRY were very different, and the fault-lines between the two, including grievances from the unification period and subsequent civil war remain salient today.

North Yemen achieved *de facto* independence with the withdrawal of the Ottoman authorities after the end of the First World War. In 1962, an Arab

[6] de Waal, 'The End of Famine?', see note 5.

[7] A. de Waal, *Mass Starvation: The History and Future of Famine* (Cambridge: Polity, 2018), at 200.

[8] See Chapter 5 of this volume for a discussion on the options for legal redress.

[9] This was due to, among other things, the collapse in superpower support to both countries following the end of the Cold War. The collapse of the Soviet Union, in particular, affected the PDRY more than the YAR, even though both received some support from the erstwhile USSR. This is also not to argue that the PDRY was merely a client state of the USSR. Aliboni argues that although the PDRY was influenced by the USSR and its growth was fostered by the USSR and other socialist 'Eastern Bloc' countries, it also drew on the movements of Arab nationalism. It was, therefore, dependent on the USSR, but also autonomous of it (R. Aliboni, *The Red Sea Region: Local Actors and the Superpowers* (Sydney: Routledge, 1985), at 44).

nationalist revolutionary movement led by army officers overthrew the ruler—the Zaydi Imam Mohammed al-Badr—and declared a republican state with Egyptian support.[10] Civil war broke out between the republicans and the royalists, who were backed by the United Kingdom, Saudi Arabia, and other world and regional powers, and only ended in 1970 with a republican victory. Although Saudi Arabia has a long history of exercising influence in Yemen, it was this 1962–1970 war which laid the foundations of its future policy on Yemen. Saudi policy is often opaque, and can appear contradictory, but it is overwhelmingly premised on security and containment. It has three major elements: (1) delineating and reinforcing the physical border with Yemen, using a combination of technology, buffer zones and military action;[11] (2) offering monetary support to the regime to stave off financial collapse; and (3) purchasing influence from sub-state actors (such as political parties, and some tribal groups) within Yemen and becoming financially entrenched in the patronage networks that form the basis of Yemeni politics.[12]

South Yemen remained a British colony (and was known as Aden and the Protectorates, later the Federation of South Arabia). It became independent in 1967 after a violent independence struggle.[13] By 1970 the country had been renamed PDRY, and over the next two decades, its socialist government pursued an agenda of broader social transformation and had some success in guaranteeing a reasonable measure of living standards to its population despite its 'abysmal' economic situation at independence.[14]

Factional and ideological conflicts persisted in both North and South Yemen: in the YAR, a series of assassinations and coups (with alleged Western involvement) culminated in Ali Abdullah Saleh taking power in 1978. Saleh went on to rule Yemen for thirty-three years and entrenched and presided over a system of kleptocratic, patronage-based politics, the basic structure and norms of which persists to date.[15] In the PDRY, civil war broke out in 1986; some displaced southern military

[10] M. Wenner, 'The Civil War in Yemen: 1962–1970', in R. Licklider (ed.), *Stopping the Killing: How Civil Wars End* (New York: NYU Press, 1993). See also P. Dresch, *A History of Modern Yemen* (Cambridge: Cambridge University Press, 2000), at 89–119.

[11] N. Obaid, 'A Saudi Arabian Defense Doctrine: Mapping the Expanded Force Structure the Kingdom Needs to Lead the Arab World, Stabilize the Region, and Meet its Global Responsibilities' (Belfer Center for Science and International Affairs, Harvard Kennedy School, 2014), available online at <https://www.belfercenter.org/sites/default/files/legacy/files/Saudi%20Strategic%20Doctrine%20-%20web.pdf> (visited 26 August 2021).

[12] S. Phillips, *Yemen and the Politics of Permanent Crisis* (Oxon: Routledge, 2011), at 76.

[13] The independence struggle was marked by violence and ideological conflict between different groups, and ended with a decisive victory for the National Liberation Front (NLF). C. Harrington, 'The Colonial Office and the Retreat from Aden: Great Britain in South Arabia, 1957–1967', 25 *Mediterranean Quarterly* (2014) 5–26, at 12. In fact, the principal liberation movements—the Front for the Liberation of Occupied Southern Yemen (FLOSY) and the NLF—fought each other almost as bitterly as they fought the British (see H. Lackner, *Yemen in Crisis: The Road to War* (London: Verso, 2019), at 97–100); see also S. Mawby, 'Workers in the Vanguard: the 1960 industrial relations ordinance and the struggle for independence in Aden', 57 *Labor History* (2016) 35–52.

[14] Lackner, *Yemen in Crisis*, see note 13, at 104 and 107.

[15] The basic settlement was an alliance, between tribal confederations in north YAR essentially steered by the late Abdullah al-Ahmar (which ensured that recruitment to the army was largely from

officers, among them Abd Rabbu Mansour Hadi (Yemen's future president and the current head of the IRG), fled to the YAR and joined the northern military.[16] The likelihood of economic collapse and the end of the Cold War created the short-term impetus for unification of the two states, but relations deteriorated rapidly after. In 1994, north–south tensions resulted in a brief and brutal civil war, with the northern army winning a decisive victory. This victory established and extended the dominance of a particular group of (predominantly) northern elites in Yemeni politics including in the former PDRY. This remained largely unchallenged for the next two decades.

The current conflict in Yemen has its roots in a series of recurrent political and economic crises, which culminated in mass popular uprisings against Saleh in 2011.[17] After coming to power in 1978, Saleh ruled Yemen through a patrimonial system. Although his initial priority was to 'coup-proof' his regime by appointing family and kin to powerful military-security positions, Saleh 'also worked to incorporate influential social elites, particularly tribal shaykhs, in networks of patronage through direct payment, the distribution of government posts, and later, access to the private sector'.[18]

Politics in Yemen changed substantially over the course of Saleh's rule, in response to the availability of resources (in the form of both domestic and international rents—predominantly related to oil, aid, and security cooperation), the presence of political competition, and shifting geopolitics. Until the mid-1980s, however, Saleh was only one of several sources of patronage in the broader Yemeni political system: remittances from workers in the oil states of the Arabian peninsula created an independent private sector with limited ties to the ruling regime in Sana'a, and Saudi Arabia was deeply imbricated in the tribal politics of the northern

the northern zones of the YAR), big landlords from the regions of Tihama and lower Yemen where such landholding exists, and intermediate traders. Gradually the top tribal shaykhs came to merge with trading and other 'modern' economic cartels. While the strengthening of internal security began earlier, the dramatic bloating of security and military institutions was achieved under Saleh. Further, from the 1970s onwards Western and Western-dominated international organizations determined 'development' policy in Yemen, for instance, by providing the bulk of the budget of the central state in the 1970s beyond direct transfers from Gulf countries. See A. B. Al-Saqqaf, اجلمهورية بني السلطنة والقبيلةيف اليمن الشماي, (2020, first published in Cairo, 1988) available online at <https://www.peacehorizons.net/ar/wp-content/uploads/2020/08/%D9%83%D8%AA%D8%A7%D8%A8-%D8%AF.-%D8%A3%D8%A8%D9%88%D8%A8%D9%83%D8%B1-%D8%A7%D9%84%D8%B3%D9%82%D8%A7%D9%81-.pdf> (visited 26 August 2021).

[16] P. Salisbury, 'Yemen: Stemming the Rise of a Chaos State', Middle East and North Africa Programme Research Paper (Chatham House, 2016), available online at <https://www.chathamhouse.org/sites/default/files/publications/research/2016-05-25-yemen-stemming-rise-of-chaos-state-salisbury.pdf> (visited 26 August 2021), at 7–8.

[17] Lackner, *Yemen in Crisis*, see note 13, at 35. See also T. Juneau, 'Yemen and the Arab Spring', in M. Kamrava (ed.), *Beyond the Arab Spring: The Evolving Ruling Bargain in the Middle East* (New York: Oxford University Press, 2014) 373–396.

[18] A. Longley-Alley, 'The Rules of the Game: Unpacking Patronage Politics in Yemen', 64 *Middle East Journal* (2010) 385–409, at 387.

governorates, distributing money directly to shaykhs. The fall of remittances after the mid-1980s[19] coincided with the discovery of oil—and Yemen's political economy shifted dramatically—as Saleh's ability to distribute economic largesse in the form of patronage increased even as the citizenry were rendered relatively economically dependent.[20] The primary tool for the distribution of patronage was the General People's Congress (GPC) which was established in 1982. As patronage networks in Yemen became more centralized and expansive, the GPC became an 'amalgam of all political tendencies within Saleh's regime', rather than operating on the basis of any distinguishing ideology.[21] Illustrating Yemen's elite compact, the GPC shared a close relationship with the main Islamist political party, the Yemeni Congregation for Reform, better known as *Islah*.[22] The two formed an alliance against the southern socialists between 1990 and 1994, and enjoyed a relatively cooperative relationship until 2007, even though Saleh was increasingly wary of *Islah*'s growing popularity.

Fissures in Yemeni politics began to widen in the mid-2000s. In 2006, Saleh was challenged for the national presidency in an election for the first time by the *Islah*-led Joint Meeting of Parties (JMP), the umbrella opposition alliance. The southern secessionist *Hirak* movement was formed in 2007, and though it was composed of groups pursuing divergent interests and agendas, campaigned for a referendum on southern independence. Between 2004 and 2010, Saleh also fought a series of wars with the Houthis (formally known as Ansarallah), a Zaydi Shia revivalist movement in the northern province of Sa'ada.[23] The regime also received substantial foreign/counter-terrorism assistance from external actors (and especially the United States), as part of the global war on terror, although Saleh was generally perceived to be an unreliable ally.[24]

[19] There were multiple reasons for this. The fall in the price of oil in the mid-1980s resulted in a decline of remittances and aid from Gulf countries and Saudi Arabia (see Dresch, see note 10, at 159–167). This was compounded by Saleh's decision to support Saddam Hussein after Iraq invaded Kuwait in August 1990. Angered by Yemen's vote in the Security Council, Saudi Arabia expelled between 800,000 and 1,000,000 Yemeni workers (see Phillips, see note 12, at 67–68).

[20] It was also at this time that the Yemeni state began to implement taxes on the private sector and introduce import licences; Sana'a's aim was to control, in some way, the country's merchant class, which continued to retain some power.

[21] P. Dresch and B. Haykel, 'Stereotypes and Political Styles: Islamists and Tribesfolk in Yemen', 27 *International Journal of Middle East Studies* (1995) 405–431, at 406–407. Dresch and Haykel note that the common view was caught by a political cartoon where one man asks another, 'Which party do you belong to?' and the second replies, 'I've told you twenty times—I'm in the GPC.' 'Yes, yes,' says the first, 'but which party?' (*aywah, aywah, bas aysh min hizb*), at 407.

[22] Lackner, *Yemen in Crisis*, see note 13, at 126 and 131. Islah included a variety of groups with varying ideological positions—ranging from the Muslim Brotherhood to hard-line Islamists, but within which the Al-Ahmar led tribal configuration was central.

[23] See Salisbury, see note 16, at 7–8. For a detailed analysis of the Houthi wars see M. Brandt, *Tribes and Politics in Yemen: A History of Houthi Conflict* (Oxford: Oxford University Press, 2017).

[24] S. W. Day, 'America's Role in the Yemen Crisis', in S. W. Day and N. Brehony (eds), *Global, Regional, and Local Dynamics in the Yemen Crisis* (London: Palgrave Macmillan, 2020) 51–68, at 55–56.

Matters came to a head in 2011. Macro-economic crisis and falling oil revenues meant that the inclusive/'big-tent' model of patronage which Saleh had relied on became increasingly unsustainable, even as tensions with the opposition increased over perceptions that Saleh was preparing his eldest son to succeed him.[25] Public protests (which were connected to but started earlier than the 'Arab Spring' protests in Egypt and Tunisia) accelerated the political crisis.[26] High-profile members of the regime defected and the opposition parties openly supported the protesters, arguably instrumentalizing the protests for their own ends.[27] After a protracted transition process mediated by the Gulf Cooperation Council (GCC), Saleh ceded power to his vice-president Hadi in November 2011. Hadi's presidency was confirmed in an election (where he was the sole candidate) in 2012.

The transition obscured the continuity of the principles underpinning Yemen's political economy before and after 2011.[28] In fact, some have argued that the transition in 2011 in Yemen was less a revolution and more an exchange of power.[29] By the time a National Dialogue Conference began in 2013, no significant redistribution of resources or hard power outside the traditional elite had occurred and the Salehs remained powerful actors in the process of political contestation.[30] The new transitional government was made up of a mix of GPC and JMP officials, and Hadi continued to govern through networks of patronage, although he sought to replace those he perceived as being close to Saleh (albeit with limited success).

Three broad points are worth noting at this juncture. First, the entrenched patterns of patrimonial politics and persistent and recurrent political crises created incentives for short-term, survival-focused politics among Yemeni elite, even as a long-term 'open-door' economic policy permitted them to move their money out of Yemen freely. This blocked essential economic and social reforms which could have ameliorated the structural drivers of food insecurity. This is, of course, not only a recent phenomenon: it has characterized Yemeni politics for nearly four decades. Second, these patterns of networked patronage politics have proved extremely difficult to dislodge or reform—especially in the direction of democracy and welfare/development. The GCC/UN mechanism for transition of 2011

[25] Phillips, see note 12. See also Lackner, *Yemen in Crisis*, see note 13, at 35; G. Hill et al., 'Yemen: Corruption, Capital Flight, and Global Drivers of Conflict', Chatham House Report, September 2013, available online at <https://www.chathamhouse.org/2013/09/yemen-corruption-capital-flight-and-global-drivers-conflict> (visited 26 August 2021).

[26] See H. Lackner, 'The Change Squares of Yemen: Civil Resistance in an Unlikely Context', in A. Roberts et al. (eds), *Civil Resistance in the Arab Spring: Triumphs and Disasters* (Oxford: Oxford University Press, 2016).

[27] Salisbury, see note 16, at 9.

[28] Hill et al., see note 25.

[29] A. Hamidaddin, 'Yemen: Negotiations with Tribes, States, and Memories', in W. Zartman (ed.), *Arab Spring: Negotiating in the Shadow of the Intifadat*, (Athens: University of Georgia Press, 2015), at 132. See also M. Transfeld, 'Political Bargaining and Violent Conflict: Shifting Elite Alliances as the Decisive Factor in Yemen's Transformation', 21 *Mediterranean Politics* (2016) 150–169.

[30] A. Longley-Alley, 'Tracking the "Arab Spring": Yemen Changes Everything . . . And Nothing', 24 *Journal of Democracy* (2013) 74–85, at 78–79.

illustrates this clearly—it failed to change the broader structures and patterns of elite Yemeni politics (in other words, the 'rules of the game') in a meaningful way. Finally, as the remainder of this chapter argues, transactional, patronage-based politics continues to shape contemporary political crisis and conflict, with implications for food insecurity.[31]

The transition government failed to address most of the demands which had led to the 2011 protests. The economy remained inequitable, job opportunities and services were scarce, and people's living conditions continued to deteriorate, even as the Houthis began to consolidate their control over Sa'ada and other northern governorates.[32] The GCC transition effectively ended in September 2014, when the Houthis took control of Sana'a, in an opportunistic coalition with forces loyal to Saleh. By March 2015, the Houthi-Saleh forces controlled the northern highlands, and the IRG had retreated to Aden. The SLC intervened militarily (through the unfortunately named Operation Decisive Storm) in Yemen on 26 March 2015. The SLC consists of Saudi Arabia, UAE, Kuwait, and Bahrain, with some non-GCC countries having been induced to join and/or contribute forces. These include or have included Egypt, Jordan, Sudan, Morocco, and Senegal and later Somalia and Eritrea. Some of these countries have been nominal participants, imposing sharp limits on their participation, while other, such as Eritrea, played a more active role by allowing the SLC to use its bases.[33] Sudan has provided a large contingent of ground forces. Saudi Arabia is the primary financier and architect of the SLC, while the UAE is the other decision-maker and financier (and for some time, had boots on the ground). The United States has supported the SLC directly and indirectly by providing weapons, intelligence, and training to its members as well as diplomatic cover. The United Kingdom and France and others have also continued providing weapons and other forms of military support.

Since 2015, multiple UN peace processes have been attempted, but none has succeeded in ending the war—although some temporary/local ceasefires have been negotiated. In the meantime, the coalition of convenience which existed at the beginning of the war has splintered. Saleh was killed by the Houthis in December 2017 and armed groups have proliferated, drawing sustenance from a war economy and external patronage. The impact of war on a fragile economy and a chronically food-insecure population have been ruinous.[34]

[31] For a discussion of the intersections between the transactional politics in Yemen and food insecurity, see A. al-Iryani and A. Nasser, 'Political Marketplace Framework and Humanitarian Crisis in Yemen', Paper presented at Workshop on Political Markets and Humanitarianism, Remote/Tufts University, 5–9 October 2020.

[32] Lackner, *Yemen in Crisis*, see note 13, at 48–57.

[33] B. Riedel, 'Saudi Arabia's Role in the Yemen Crisis', in Day and Brehony (eds), see note 24, at 115–130; A. de Waal, 'The Horn of Africa and the Yemen Crisis', in Day and Brehony (eds), see note 24, at 195–208. Qatar was a member of the coalition until 2017.

[34] See International Crisis Group, *Instruments of Pain (I): Conflict and Famine in Yemen, Crisis Group Middle East Briefing No 52* (2017), available online at <https://www.crisisgroup.org/middle-east-north-africa/gulf-and-arabian-peninsula/yemen/b052-instruments-pain-i-conflict-and-fam

B. Famine and Mass Starvation in Yemen

A year after the SLC started its military operations, humanitarian agencies began warning that food security conditions were sharply deteriorating, with some analysts predicting famine.[35] These assessments were based on worsening economic indicators, in a context of chronic humanitarian need and food insecurity.[36] In 2017, the UN issued a warning of impending famine, and the Under-Secretary-General for Humanitarian Affairs and Emergency Relief Coordinator, Stephen O'Brien, noted that Yemen was the largest humanitarian crisis in the world.[37] However, the UN system has been circumspect about using the word 'famine', and the criteria for declaring famine under the IPC scale (especially related to malnutrition and mortality) have not been met.[38] This begs the question: has famine actually occurred in Yemen? We argue that even though famine has not formally been declared in Yemen: (1) it is highly likely that famine has occurred, at least in some areas; (2) even without a famine declaration, widespread hunger and hunger-related mortality has occurred among populations designated as being in 'crisis' and 'emergency' phases. Most critically for the argument in this chapter, however, there is no requirement that famine be determined for a starvation crime to have occurred. Very large-scale and severe malnutrition and excess deaths are relevant for assessing the gravity of a starvation crime but are not required to determine that such a crime has been committed.

As Conley and de Waal have argued, there is no single definition of famine.[39] The IPC definition, which is used by the UN system to evaluate whether a famine has occurred, is an operational one. It is also quite restrictive. For a famine to be declared, there needs to be evidence of lack of food, elevated mortality, and increased

ine-yemen#:~:text=Instruments%20of%20Pain%3A%20Conflict%20and%20Famine,-Print&text=Shortfalls%20are%20not%20the%20only,crises%20are%20chronically%20underfunded%3B%20and> (visited 26 August 2021). The Crisis Group has argued: 'Yemenis are starving because of war. No natural disaster is responsible. No amount of humanitarian aid can solve the underlying problem', at 1.

35 F. Al-Muslimi and M. Rageh, *Yemen's Economic Collapse and Impending Famine: The Necessary Immediate Steps to Avoid Worst-case Scenarios*, Yemen in Crisis, Report No. 3, Sana'a Center for Strategic Studies and Friedrich Ebert Stiftung, October 2015, available online at <http://sanaacenter.org/wp-content/uploads/2015/11/files_yemens_economic_collapse_and_impending_famine_en.pdf> (visited 26 August 2021).

36 D. Maxwell, 'Famine Early Warning and Information Systems in Conflict Settings: Challenges for Humanitarian Metrics and Response', Occasional Paper (Conflict Research Programme, London School of Economics and Political Science, 2019), available online at <http://eprints.lse.ac.uk/102836/> (visited 26 August 2021), at 19.

37 UN Office for the Coordination of Humanitarian Affairs (UN-OCHA), 'USG/ERC Stephen O'Brien Statement to the Security Council on Missions to Yemen, South Sudan, Somalia and Kenya and an Update on the Oslo Conference on Nigeria and the Lake Chad Region', ReliefWeb, 10 March 2017, available online at <http://reliefweb.int/report/yemen/usgerc-stephen-o-brien-statement-security-councilmissions-yemen-south-sudan-somalia> (visited 26 August 201).

38 Maxwell, see note 36, at 21.

39 Introduction to this volume.

malnutrition among at least one-fifth of the population, despite the delivery of humanitarian aid.[40] As Maxwell observes in Chapter 11 in this volume, while the IPC scale is widely accepted and has become the standard method and metric for diagnosing 'famine', its findings are only as strong as the capacity of researchers to access affected areas, and the quality of the data used to inform the analysis. There has also been a general trend towards the politicization of information-gathering and analysis under the IPC Scale, and the IPC's biggest weakness is addressing cases of deliberate starvation perpetrated for political or military purposes; Yemen is no different.[41]

In Yemen, the IPC process suffers from several shortcomings: data collection is challenging, IPC reports are only produced annually (and are sometimes based on outdated data), and national authorities are closely involved in data collection, with implications for data quality and transparency.[42] The central conundrum for analysts, however, is that the indicators of food insecurity in Yemen have looked very severe for a long time but reported malnutrition figures and mortality rates have stayed fairly (or very) low.[43] Such nutritional resilience is extremely unusual: not only has the food security crisis been long-lasting, widespread, and severe, health facilities have been attacked and destroyed, a crisis of water and sanitation has led to a protracted outbreak of cholera (comprising multiple waves of outbreaks), and the destruction of livelihoods and shifting gender roles should have resulted in higher child mortality rates (often the most significant contributor to famine mortality).[44] The reasons for this discrepancy are not entirely clear. The issue may be with the quality of the data, the data collection methods, the IPC analytical model, political influence over either the data collection or analytical process, a

[40] IPC Global Partners, 'Integrated Food Security Phase Classification Technical Manual Version 3.0. Evidence and Standards for Better Food Security and Nutrition Decisions' (2019), available online at <http://www.ipcinfo.org/fileadmin/user_upload/ipcinfo/manual/IPC_Technical_Manual_3_Final.pdf> (visited 26 August 2021), at 9.

[41] D. Maxwell and P. Hailey, *The Politics of Information and Analysis in Famines and Extreme Emergencies: Synthesis of Findings from Six Case Studies* (Medford: Feinstein International Center, 2020), available online at <https://fic.tufts.edu/wp-content/uploads/PIA-Synthesis-Report_May-13.pdf> (visited 26 August 2021). at 18; Introduction to this volume; Chapter 11 of this volume.

[42] See D. Maxwell et al., *Constraints and Complexities of Information and Analysis in Humanitarian Emergencies: Evidence from Yemen* (Medford: Feinstein International Center, Tufts University, 2019).

[43] As in other cases, the most frequently missing information in food security analysis in Yemen are mortality data. As per the published data on crude mortality rates, remarkably, mortality (from all causes) has declined since the beginning of the war. These data are almost certainly, in the words of one observer, 'rubbish'. See Maxwell, see note 36, at 23. For a broader discussion on mortality data in the context of famine analysis in Yemen see J. J. Kim, E. McCloskey, and P. Hailey, 'Constraints and Complexities of Information and Analysis: Data Planning in Famine Risk Countries—Findings and Recommendations for Food Security Analysis: South Sudan, Somalia, Nigeria, and Yemen', MQSUN Report, March 2018, available online at <https://reliefweb.int/report/south-sudan/constraints-and-complexities-information-and-analysis-data-planning-famine-risk> (visited 26 August 2021).

[44] These can be described as the broader social ecology of nutrition—see S. Jaspars, 'A Role for Social Nutrition in Strengthening Accountability for Mass Starvation', Occasional Paper No. 18 (World Peace Foundation, 2019), available online at <https://sites.tufts.edu/wpf/files/2019/09/A-Role-for-Social-Nutrition-Susanne-Jaspers.pdf> (visited 26 August 2021).

combination of these factors, or indeed something else entirely.[45] The point, however, is that even though the data do not allow for a declaration of famine as per the IPC scale, *the data are simply not good enough to say that famine has not occurred.*

The IPC analyses paint a picture of a wide-ranging humanitarian disaster—where virtually the entire country is facing a food crisis, with possible famine to follow if food supplies are cut off to the worst hit areas. The IPC analysis for November/December 2018 concluded that 15.9 million people, or about 53 per cent of the population analysed were severely food insecure, despite ongoing humanitarian food assistance. Of these, about 5 million people were classified as falling in IPC Phase 4 (emergency) and 63,500 people were thought to be in Phase 5 (famine conditions). Without humanitarian assistance, 20.1 million people (67 per cent of the population) would have been severely food insecure, of whom 238,000 would have been in famine conditions.[46] Access restrictions meant that this assessment was based on outdated data, but the report concluded that food insecurity was highest in areas which had witnessed active fighting, with pockets of Al-Bayda, Al-Dhale'e, Al-Hudaydah, Al-Mahwit, Amran, Hajjah, Sa'ada, and Ta'izz facing famine.[47] The next IPC report was published in July 2019, but was based on data collected from only twenty-nine of the forty-five hardest-hit districts, with access denied by the authorities (mostly the Houthis) in the remaining districts.[48] Although it did not find evidence of famine in the assessed areas, it noted that eleven districts (including five across al-Hudaydah and Ta'izz governorates) were classified as facing IPC Phase 4 (emergency).[49]

Three IPC updates have been published since. Partial analyses based on 133 districts were published in July and October 2020. These did not analyse areas in the north of the country (under Houthi control) where the majority of the population live.[50] They concluded that, in the areas assessed, about one in every four persons was highly food insecure (IPC Phase 3 and above)—with the relatively modest improvements in food security being attributable largely to humanitarian aid. Lowland regions in al-Hudaydah and Ta'izz governorates continue to be classified as critical (IPC Phase 4) which, as we discuss later in the chapter, are closely

[45] Maxwell et al., see note 41, at 26.
[46] Integrated Food Security Phase Classification, 'Yemen—IPC Acute Food Insecurity Analysis: December 2018–January 2019' (2018), available online at <http://www.ipcinfo.org/fileadmin/user_upload/ipcinfo/docs/IPC_Yemen_AcuteFI_2018Dec2019Jan.pdf> (visited 26 August 2021).
[47] Integrated Food Security Phase Classification, see note 46.
[48] Maxwell, see note 36, at 22.
[49] Integrated Food Security Phase Classification, 'Yemen—IPC Acute Food Insecurity Analysis: July–September 2019' (2019), available online at <http://www.ipcinfo.org/fileadmin/user_upload/ipcinfo/docs/IPC_Yemen_AFI_Hotspot%20Analysis_2019JulySept.pdf> (visited 26 August 2021).
[50] Integrated Food Security Phase Classification, 'Yemen—IPC Acute Food Insecurity Analysis: July–December 2020' (2020), available online at <http://www.ipcinfo.org/fileadmin/user_upload/ipcinfo/docs/IPC_Yemen_AcuteFoodInsecurity_2020FebDec_Report_English.pdf> (visited 26 August 2021); Integrated Food Security Phase Classification, 'Yemen—IPC Acute Malnutrition Analysis: January–December 2020' (2020), available online at <http://www.ipcinfo.org/fileadmin/user_upload/ipcinfo/docs/IPC_Yemen_Acute_Malnutrition_2020JanDec.pdf> (visited 26 August 2021).

related to the specific ways in which the war has been fought in Yemen. The IPC update published in December 2020 (the most recent at the time of writing) found that the food security situation remained broadly unchanged from 2018. 13.5 million people (or about 45 per cent of the population remains acutely food insecure (IPC Phase 3 or above), of whom 3.6 million are in IPC Phase 4, and 16,500 are facing famine.[51] These numbers were projected to increase over the first half of 2021, with between 17 and 19 million people expected to be in need of humanitarian food assistance.[52] To sum up then, while there is no evidence that large-scale areas of famine developed, it is clear that pockets of famine or near-famine conditions have existed, and the areas most affected by hunger remain largely inaccessible and under-assessed.[53]

A second, and related point is that a non-declaration of famine (under the IPC scale) does not definitively indicate the scale of humanitarian crisis. When large populations suffer extended periods under conditions of extreme food insecurity or humanitarian emergency (IPC Phases 3 and 4), they can suffer elevated mortality rates.[54] Such excess deaths can rapidly accumulate to surpass the thresholds used for assessing historical famines. This is usually because of an overall deterioration in the social ecology of food, nutrition, and health.[55] As Conley and de Waal point out, there is a difference between starvation in the individual sense and in the population centric sense. The former refers to 'acute protein-energy malnutrition with heightened risk of death', while the latter 'is closest to the deterioration in the ecology of health and nutrition, that causes an increase in death rates'. Used in this latter sense, starvation does not just refer to the reduced intake of food, but includes other deprivations such as 'lack of health care, poor quality housing and shelter, contaminated water supplies and inadequate sanitation, the stresses of displacement, and reduced maternal care for young children—which separately and in combination contribute to higher risks of death'.[56] The point here is that mass starvation can occur irrespective of whether famine has been declared—and indeed, it is likely that mass starvation has taken place in Yemen.

Most critically, however, neither famine nor starvation need have occurred (or been declared) for a starvation crime to be made out. This is because there is a key

51 Integrated Food Security Phase Classification, 'Yemen—Integrated Food Insecurity Phase Classification Snapshot: October 2020–June 2021', *ReliefWeb*, 3 December 2020, available online at <https://reliefweb.int/sites/reliefweb.int/files/resources/IPC_Yemen_Acute_Food_Insecurity_2020Oct2021June_Snapshot.pdf> (visited 26 October 2021).

52 FEWSNET, *Yemen Food Security Outlook: October 2020–May 2021*, available online at <https://fews.net/sites/default/files/documents/reports/YEMEN_Food%20Security%20Outlook_102020_FINAL.pdf> (visited 26 August 2021).

53 Maxwell, see note 36, at 22.

54 See Maxwell, see note 42, where he notes that 43 per cent of the total mortality in the Somali famine of 2011 took place prior to reaching IPC Phase 5 (famine) levels or severity—or in locations that never reached Phase 5.

55 See Jaspars, see note 44.

56 See Introduction to this volume.

difference between the 'lay' and 'legal' meanings of starvation: in the legal sense, starvation is not confined solely to the deprivation of food but also includes OIS such as such as clean water, medicine, shelter, blankets, and arguably maternal care. This is reflected in the definitive articulation of the war crime of starvation, which is contained in Article 8(2)(b)(xxv) (international armed conflict) and Article 8(2)(e)(xix) (non-international armed conflict) of the Rome Statute. The crime has four elements: (1) the perpetrator deprived civilians of OIS; (2) the perpetrator intended to starve civilians as a method of warfare; (3) the conduct took place in the context of and was associated with an armed conflict; and (4) the perpetrator was aware of the existence of the armed conflict.[57] This means that while the crime requires the deprivation of OIS as both conduct and consequence, 'it does not appear to require proof that civilians did in fact starve'.[58]

To sum up, then, the non-declaration of famine in Yemen does not mean that famine has not occurred. Nor does it mean that a starvation crime has not been committed. All the parties to the conflict in Yemen have sought to weaponize access to food and objects indispensable for survival;[59] whether that has resulted in famine in the strict IPC sense of the term is perhaps less important. Instead, attributing responsibility for starvation crimes in Yemen requires a careful parsing of the structural and proximate drivers of food insecurity.

3. The Political Economy of Hunger and Vulnerability in Yemen

Prior to 2014, when the current wave of conflict broke out, Yemen was the poorest country in the Arab world with very low human development indicators. In 2014, it was ranked 159th (out of 188 countries) in the Human Development Index, with half of its estimated population of 30 million[60] living in poverty (defined as living on less than US$ 3.10 per day) and one-in-five people living in extreme poverty (less than US$ 1.90 per day).[61] Infant mortality and malnutrition rates were very

[57] W. Jordash, C. Murdoch, and J. Holmes, 'Strategies for Prosecuting Mass Starvation', 17 *Journal of International Criminal Justice* (2019) 849–879, at 853.

[58] Jordash, Murdoch, and Holmes, see note 57, at 855. Note that this proposition has not yet been tested before a tribunal.

[59] See *Final Report of the Panel of Experts on Yemen*, UN Doc. S/2018/68, 26 January 2018, at 53, fn. 194. The UNSC Panel of Experts in their 2018 report found that the blockade was 'essentially using the threat of starvation as a bargaining tool and an instrument of war'.

[60] There are conflicting estimates of Yemen's population. The WFP estimated that it was 26 million in 2014 (see later in this chapter), whereas the United Nations Development Programme (UNDP) estimated the population to be 30 million in the same year.

[61] For Yemen's HDI rank in 2014–2015, see UNDP, *Human Development Report 2016* (2016) available online at <http://hdr.undp.org/sites/default/files/2016_human_development_report.pdf> (visited 26 August 2021), at 200. Yemen's rank fell to 168 in 2015. For development data, see J. Moyer et al., *Assessing the Impact of War on Development in Yemen*, UNDP and Frederick S. Pardee Center for International Futures, University of Denver (2019) available online at <https://yemen.un.org/sites/defa

high and in 2014, the World Food Programme (WFP) estimated that over 40 per cent of the population was food insecure—this number having declined from about 46 per cent of the population in 2011.[62] Poverty and food insecurity were concentrated in rural areas where between 65 per cent and 70 per cent of the population lived. Nearly half of the rural population was food insecure (compared to just over 25 per cent of the urban population) and rates of poverty remained stubbornly high in rural areas, even when they fell in the rest of the country during the growth years of 1998–2005.[63] Unsurprisingly, the data are outdated and patchy but they point to the fact that the Yemeni economy had deep structural weaknesses, with significant disparities between rural and urban areas.

Yemen's economic history in the last three decades is one of astonishing volatility, repeatedly buffeted by major shocks and alternating cycles of boom and bust. A period of modest growth driven by emigration and remittances came to an abrupt halt in 1990, when Saudi Arabia expelled hundreds of thousands of Yemeni workers during the Iraq war.[64] In any event, the economic growth from this period was channelled into consumption of imported goods rather than longer-term investment for development. A decade later, Yemen's economy rebounded on the basis of oil exports—but the benefits of the oil boom were largely confined to the elite. When that bonanza ended, the economy crashed again. In the years immediately following the 2011 uprising, the economic crisis intensified and indicators for malnutrition worsened.

The drivers of food insecurity in Yemen are simultaneously agricultural, social, political, and environmental. Since 1968, the country[65] has been incorporated into the wider regional oil economy and has gradually adopted a series of economic and social policies which devalued local grain production, encouraged rural male labour out-migration, and neglected women's rights and family planning.[66] Agriculture (and those who worked in it) was marginal to the Saleh regime,

ult/files/2019-09/Assessing%20the%20Impact%20of%20War%20on%20Development%20in%20Yemen.pdf> (visited 26 August 2021), at 34.

62 World Food Programme (WFP), *Yemen: Comprehensive Food Security Survey* (2014) available online at <https://documents.wfp.org/stellent/groups/public/documents/ena/wfp269771.pdf?_ga=2.41003947.862677590.1606893566-2107303201.1606581506> (visited 26 August 2021). For the 2011 data, see WFP, *The State of Food Security and Nutrition in Yemen: Comprehensive Food Security Survey* (2012), available online at <https://documents.wfp.org/stellent/groups/public/documents/ena/wfp247832.pdf> (visited 26 August 2021).

63 WFP (2014), see note 62. See also Government of Yemen, World Bank and UNDP, *Yemen Poverty Assessment* Vol. 1, (The World Bank Group, 2007), available online at <https://documents.worldbank.org/en/publication/documents-reports/documentdetail/124931468334795087/main-report> (visited 26 August 2021).

64 Lackner, *Yemen in Crisis*, see note 13, at 274.

65 Prior to unification, the YAR and the PDRY.

66 M. Mundy, 'The Strategies of the Coalition in the Yemen War: Aerial Bombardment and Food War' (2018), available online at <https://sites.tufts.edu/wpf/files/2018/10/Strategies-of-Coalition-in-Yemen-War-Final-20181005-1.pdf> (visited 26 August 2021), at 8.

especially after the post-1995 consolidation of a military/security state around oil and security rents. It is therefore not surprising that this period was characterised by chronic underinvestment in agriculture and artisanal fishing, and the uncritical adoption of policies recommended by multilateral development institutions. The widespread installation of remittance-funded diesel fuel-based lift pumps, for instance, meant that traditional irrigation systems were no longer maintained,[67] and placed greater stress on Yemen's strained groundwater resources.[68]

In sum, agriculture, and more particularly rain-fed agriculture, which was already exposed to chronic water shortages and climate change, with high labour inputs, was left to fend for itself. Agricultural policy, driven by (dogmatic) neoliberal policy prescriptions of Western development institutions favoured the production of high-value market-oriented crops for export and Yemeni urban markets at the expense of traditional, homegrown grain crops.[69] Unsurprisingly, the sector suffered. Over time, national food production did not keep pace with a rising population, and the great majority of Yemenis came to rely on purchasing food that had been commercially imported.[70] In 2011, 55 per cent of food products consumed in the country were imported as was 90 per cent of wheat (the main staple).[71] In fact, Yemen depends almost entirely on imports to meet internal market demand for its staple foods, that is, wheat, rice, sugar, dairy products, and cooking oil.[72]

Yemeni elite profited from these changes: President Saleh's close relatives controlled the major food-grain import and distribution corporation, and smuggling of diesel fuel played a major role in the self-enrichment strategies of elites.[73] By 2011, agriculture contributed only about 10 per cent of GDP but continued to employ over 40 per cent of the labour force (especially when subsistence farmers were included).[74] While the majority of those living in rural areas continued to work

[67] For a detailed discussion, see M. Mundy and F. Pelat, 'The Political Economy of Agriculture and Agricultural Policy in Yemen', in N. Brehony and S. Al-Sarhan (eds), *Rebuilding Yemen: Political, Economic and Social Challenges* (Berlin: Gerlach Press, 2015) 98–122; M. Mundy, A. Al-Hakimi, and F. Pelat, 'Neither Security nor Sovereignty: The Political Economy of Food in Yemen', in Z. Babar and S. Mirgani (eds), *Food Security in the Middle East* (New York: Oxford University Press, 2014) 136–158.

[68] D. Varisco, 'Pumping Yemen Dry: A History of Yemen's Water Crisis', 47 *Human Ecology* (2019) 317–329, at 323.

[69] Mundy and Pelat, see note 57, at 100.

[70] C. Breisinger et al., 'Impacts of the Triple Global Crisis on Growth and Poverty: The Case of Yemen', 29 *Development Policy Review* (2011) 155–184, at 158.

[71] Bressinger at al., see note 70.

[72] 'In 2014, one year before the outbreak of the current war, Yemen imported a record 3.3 million tonnes of wheat grains, 433 thousand tonnes of rice, a record 1.2 million tonnes of sugar—more than twice the annual average for the previous ten years—a record 109 thousand tonnes of milk and cheese, and some 322 thousand tonnes of cooking oil. Combined, these five commodities alone amounted to an all-time high import volume of 5.4 million tonnes for a total import value of $2.7 billion, which represented 23 percent of the value of Yemen's total merchandise imports for that year.' See Z. A. Basha, 'Arabia Felix: The Rapid and Costly Transformation from Food Self-Sufficiency to Insecurity', unpublished working paper for the 'Yemeni Voices for Sustainable Agriculture' programme (London School of Economics, Middle East Centre).

[73] Mundy and Pelat, see note 57 at 104; Phillips, see note 12, at 34–35.

[74] See Central Statistical Organization, Republic of Yemen and International Labour Organization, *Yemen Labour Force Survey 2013–14* (2015), available online at <https://www.ilo.org/wcmsp5/gro

in agriculture, male cyclical migration and informal employment in urban labour markets also became increasingly important to household livelihood strategies. This is relevant to our analysis because the military and economic strategies of the belligerents have either directly targeted or indirectly impacted these livelihood strategies, leading to a collapse in households' ability to purchase food.

Two other points are worth noting about the political economy of pre-war Yemen. The first relates to the expansion of the public sector under Saleh and Hadi. Even as the rentier-security state used its patronage networks to allow elites selective access to land and property, access to business licenses, and aid flows, it also expanded the size of the public sector. Between 2000 and 2014 the public sector grew from 432,351 state employees to 1.2 million, distributed across 1,450 state institutions—this amounts to about 30 per cent of Yemen's workforce.[75] Assuming that each civil servant is attached to a household, this means that between 5 million and 6 million Yemenis were dependent on civil service salaries.[76] As discussed later in this chapter, the economic policies of the IRG which resulted in the suspension of these salary payments have had a direct impact on the food security of this group.

The Yemeni economy was also vulnerable because it had very few sources of foreign exchange. From 2000–2010, oil dominated exports, and the government budget: almost 75 per cent of the government's revenues came from oil, leaving it highly vulnerable to global price shifts. At the same time the government imported almost all oil for domestic consumption, ostensibly due to a lack of domestic refining capacity. Oil revenue underpinned the government's patronage system, which it distributed by expanding the public payroll, giving elites access to lucrative project contracts, and by licensing/facilitating fuel smuggling networks. The critical point, however, is that the focus of the regime was the maintenance of this expansive patronage system to retain power—it was not to improve the living conditions of most of the country's citizens. As a result, the oil boom did not result in increased development for the vast majority of the population (in fact, rates of poverty may have actually increased), and the structural determinants of food insecurity were never addressed.[77]

ups/public/---arabstates/---ro-beirut/documents/publication/wcms_419016.pdf> (visited 26 August 2021), at 22.

[75] Lackner, *Yemen in Crisis*, see note 13, at 247. It is worth noting that as many as one-third of these 1.2 million may actually have been ghostworkers, or workers who never actually turned up to work. See P. Salisbury, 'Corruption in Yemen: Maintaining the Status Quo?', in Brehony and Al-Sarhan (eds), see note 67, at, 61–77, at 66.

[76] M. Rageh, A. Nasser, and F. Al-Muslimi, 'Yemen Without A Functioning Central Bank: The Loss of Basic Economic Stabilization and Accelerating Famine', *Open Democracy*, 22 November 2016, available online at <https://www.opendemocracy.net/en/north-africa-west-asia/yemen-without-functioning-central-bank-los/> (visited 26 August 2021).

[77] Lackner, *Yemen in Crisis*, see note 13—see the chapter 'The Economy: Neoliberal Policies and Worsening Poverty' in that volume.

The other major source of foreign exchange in Yemen is remittances from migrant workers in Saudi Arabia, other GCC countries, and beyond. These are a lifeline for poorer and middle-income households, are outside the purview of government finances, but remain subject to significant variations due to economic conditions in the 'sending' countries.[78] For instance, the COVID-19 pandemic has had a disproportionate impact on the price of oil, and on the informal sector in which Yemeni emigrants work: as a result, remittances are estimated to have dropped by 80 per cent in 2020, with knock-on effects on household well-being.[79]

Despite these structural weaknesses, it is worth noting that in modern times Yemen has never witnessed outright famine prior to the outbreak of war in 2014–2015. Responsibility for that lies with the belligerents and the military and economic strategies used to fight the war, which have fundamentally transformed both the nature and the scale of food insecurity.

4. Military Strategies and Mass Starvation

> 'Once we control them, we will feed them'[80]

Aerial bombardment in Yemen has led to thousands of casualties among civilians (though in the last two years higher casualties have been caused by other forms of attack such as shelling). Alongside these violations, Yemenis have been subject to a slow, tortuous form of suffering caused by belligerents imposing blockades, besieging cities, and targeting essential civilian and economic infrastructure and services (including agricultural infrastructure such as farms and water facilities which support the economy and also sustain civilians), undermining the economy and people's livelihoods. It is worth bearing in mind that the separation between military and economic strategies in the Yemeni conflict is an artificial one. Most of the strategies used to fight the war in Yemen have clear economic motivations and/or impacts. For instance, a blockade is a military strategy, but it is usually intended to alter the political calculus of those in the blockaded areas, and to reduce their capacity for resistance by depriving them of resources. This section and the next analyse these military and economic strategies in greater detail.

[78] The World Bank estimates that remittances have been in the region of US$ 3.3 billion between 2012–2015 and averaged around US$ 3.7 billion annually between 2016–2019. See World Bank Open Data, available online at <https://data.worldbank.org/indicator/BX.TRF.PWKR.CD.DT?locations=YE> (visited 26 August 2021).

[79] Oxfam Press Release, 'Remittances to Yemen plummet as needs surge amid war and coronavirus', 1 June 2020, available online at <https://www.oxfam.org/en/press-releases/remittances-yemen-plummet-needs-surge-amid-war-and-coronavirus> (visited 26 August 2021).

[80] Anonymous Saudi diplomat, quoted in Mundy, see note 66, at 7.

A. Blockade

Shortly after it began airstrikes in Yemen on 26 March 2015, the SLC imposed a *de facto* naval blockade on the ports of Hudaydah, Aden, Saleef, and Ras Issa. Ostensibly, this was to ensure compliance with the arms embargo provisions of Security Council Resolution 2216 (April 2015), but its effect was to severely restrict the flow of food, fuel, and medicine to the civilian population.[81] Ships seeking entry into Yemeni ports required authorization following an inspection carried out by the SLC through its Evacuation and Humanitarian Operations Committee.[82] This delayed or prevented goods from entering—and in particular, vessels trying to reach Hudaydah port (the primary source of imports for areas under Houthi control and for wider swathes of Yemen) had to wait for up to four to six weeks before receiving entry permits.[83] The delays and uncertainties, increased demurrage costs and insurance premiums for shipping companies further reduced the number of vessels shipping goods to Yemen.[84] Following complaints about the severity of these restrictions, the United Nations Verification and Inspection Mechanism was established to facilitate commercial shipping to Red Sea ports not under the control of the IRG/SLC. It only began operations in May 2016, almost a year after discussions in the UN Security Council on the need for the mechanism. The coalition continued to maintain an additional and onerous inspection process, however, and denied entry to vessels on 'a seemingly arbitrary basis'.[85]

The airspace around Sana'a airport was closed to commercial flights by the IRG and the SLC in August 2016. This effectively resulted in the closure of Sana'a airport (except to flights for humanitarian organizations), and meant that thousands of Yemeni civilians were prevented from evacuations and access to life-saving healthcare and humanitarian supplies were constrained.[86] The airport was reportedly reopened for very limited humanitarian purposes from 3 February 2020, however, these exceptions have been insufficient to address the overwhelming humanitarian need.[87] In November 2017, the SLC also imposed a total blockade on Yemen for

[81] International Crisis Group, *Instruments of Pain (I)*, see note 34, at 2.

[82] *Situation of human rights in Yemen, including violations and abuses since September 2014: Report of the detailed findings of the Group of Eminent International and Regional Experts on Yemen*, UN Doc. A/HRC/42/CRP.1, 3 September 2019, at 184–185, §768–772.

[83] Security Council Report, 'In Hindsight: The Story of the UN Verification and Inspection Mechanism in Yemen', *Monthly Forecast*, 1 September 2016, available online at <https://www.securitycouncilreport.org/monthly-forecast/2016-09/the_story_of_the_un_verification_and_inspection_mechanism_in_yemen.php?pri%E2%80%A6> (visited 26 August 2021).

[84] *Letter dated 27 January 2017 from the Panel of Experts on Yemen addressed to the President of the Security Council*, UN Doc. S/2018/193, 31 January 2017, at 57, §157.

[85] Human Rights Council, *Situation of human rights in Yemen*, see note 82.

[86] *Situation of human rights in Yemen, including violations and abuses since September 2014: Report of the detailed findings of the Group of Eminent International and Regional Experts on Yemen*, UN Doc. A/HRC/39/43, 17 August 2018, at 9, §56.

[87] *Situation of human rights in Yemen, including violations and abuses since September 2014: Report of the detailed findings of the Group of Eminent International and Regional Experts on Yemen*, UN Doc. A/HRC/45/6, 14 September 2020, at 9, §57.

sixteen days, after the Houthis fired a ballistic missile into Saudi Arabia. At least 500,000 tonnes of food and fuel imports, some of which spoiled, as well as large amounts of humanitarian aid were locked out of Yemen as a result.[88] Delays continue to affect imports of humanitarian aid at the time of writing.[89] For instance, in 2020, the Panel of Experts[90] on Yemen noted that medical and nutritional shipments continued to be delayed by between 16 and 169 days at the port of Aden, outside Houthi control.[91] During the total blockade, heavy airstrikes also occurred throughout Houthi controlled territories, damaging several markets.

The blockade of Yemen has had several major impacts. First, it impacted the availability and prices of essential items—food, fuel, and medicines. While it is difficult to quantify this impact with precision (and separately from the effects of other concurrent shocks such as violence and war), reports have suggested that immediately after the beginning of the blockade, imports to al-Hudaydah declined to between 15 per cent and 40 per cent of pre-war levels.[92] Given that around 80 per cent of all imports for Yemen passed through the port prior to the war, WFP has stated that the import restrictions had a significant impact on the availability of essential goods and affected the functioning of Yemeni markets.[93] Further, analysis

[88] 'Humanitarian assistance struggling to reach affected population in Yemen as blockade continues', Logistics Cluster Blog, 22 November 2017, available online at <https://logcluster.org/blog/humanitarian-assistance-struggling-reach-affected-population-yemen-blockade-continues> (visited 26 August 2021).

[89] As of 2020, the process for clearance of goods is as follows: Imports to Red Sea ports of al Hudaydah and Salif involves a three-step process. First, the importer applies for clearance through UNVIM which is usually delivered within forty-eight hours allowing the vessel to proceed to a holding area about 140 nautical miles (260 kilometres) north-west of al-Hudaydah. The vessel stays in the holding area until it receives a clearance from the SLC Evacuation and Humanitarian Operations Cell in Riyadh, through a SLC vessel, to proceed to the anchorage area (AA) at the entrance of al Hudaydah or Salif port. Delays in the holding area remain unpredictable. Finally, the vessel waits in the anchorage area until it receives clearance from port authorities under Houthi control. The IRG, SLC, and the Houthis each wield significant leverage over importers by delaying their chartered vessels, forcing them to pay extra charges for demurrage. *Letter dated 27 January 2020 from the Panel of Experts on Yemen addressed to the President of the Security Council*, UN Doc. S/2020/70, 27 January 2020, Annex 21, at 129.

[90] Note that the Panel of Experts on Yemen is distinct from the Group of Eminent International and Regional Experts appointed by the Human Rights Council. The former, among other things, monitors compliance with sanctions imposed under Resolution 2140 (2014) by the Security Council, while the latter reports on the situation of human rights in Yemen, including violations and abuses since September 2014. In this chapter we refer to the former as the Panel of Experts and to the latter as the Group of Experts.

[91] Security Council 2020, see note 89, at 45, §122.

[92] There is some dispute about the precise level of imports; see differing reports in: International Crisis Group, *Instruments of Pain (I)*, see note 34, at 2; S. Gebrekidan and J. Saul, 'In blocking arms to Yemen, Saudi Arabia squeezes a starving population', *Reuters*, 11 October 2017, available online at <https://www.reuters.com/article/us-yemen-saudi-blockade-specialreport/special-report-in-blocking-arms-to-yemen-saudi-arabia-squeezes-a-starving-population-idUSKBN1CG16C> (visited 26 August 2021). The disparity could be because analysts were comparing imports over different periods of time after the escalation of conflict.

[93] WFP, *State of Food Insecurity in Yemen based on the Emergency Food Security and Nutrition Assessment (EFSNA)*, April 2017, available online at <https://www.wfp.org/publications/yemen-state-food-insecurity-emergency-food-security-nutrition-assessment-april-2017#:~:text=27%20April%202017-,Yemen%20%2D%20State%20of%20Food%20Insecurity%20in%20Yemen%20based%20on%20the,Assessment%20(EFSNA)%2C%20April%202017&text=Over%20two%2Dfifth%20of%20Yemeni,day%20and%20night%20without%20eating> (visited 26 August 2021), at 9.

of the effects of the *total* blockade of all ports in November 2017 show that, despite being in place for only a short period, it resulted in a decline in access to food and basic services, an increase in negative coping mechanisms (such as distress sales of household assets and livestock), and an increase in the number of households facing multiple deprivation *across the country*.[94] Much of this was due to the shortage-induced increase in fuel prices, affecting electricity generation, agriculture, and the availability of other services, such as pumping of water and supply through water tankers.

Prior to the closure of the airport and tight restrictions on flights, around one-third of all passengers on Yemenia Airways (the main commercial carrier) were estimated to be travelling outside the country to access healthcare, and in 2017, the Ministry of Health in Sana'a reported that more than 13,000 people had died of conditions that could have been treated abroad.[95] With the partial collapse of the healthcare system, the blockade further constrained the ability of Yemenis to access healthcare.

A third major consequence which appears to be emerging is a general shift of shipping traffic away from Red Sea ports (under Houthi control) to the Indian Ocean/Gulf of Aden ports of Mukalla and Aden (under the control of IRG and SLC), since the imposition of the 2017 blanket blockade.[96] The reasons for this are the increased costs associated with risks of conflict around the Red Sea ports as well as the uncertainties around the import mechanism. Finally, the blockade has also played into the dynamics of the war economy in Yemen—with fuel shortages being instrumentalized by both sides (this is discussed in the next section). The key point here is that the blockade has played, and continues to play a key role in restricting civilian access to objects indispensable for survival—food, fuel, medicines, and humanitarian aid.

B. Aerial Bombardment

According to data collected by the Yemen Data Project (YDP), the SLC undertook 22,360 air raids in Yemen between March 2015 and October 2020.[97] The YDP classifies air raids into categories based on the objects struck—targeting cultural

[94] S. Tandon and T. Vishwanath, 'The evolution of poor food access over the course of the conflict in Yemen', 130 *World Development* (2020) 1–16, at 12–13.

[95] Human Rights Council, *Situation of human rights in Yemen*, see note 86, at 32, §28.

[96] *Letter dated 25 January 2019 from the Panel of Experts on Yemen addressed to the President of the Security Council*, UN Doc. S/2019/83, 25 January 2019, at 43, §119, and at 56, §166.

[97] Data as of 31 October 2020. See 'Yemen Data Project' available at <https://yemendataproject.org/ > (visited 22 March 2022). Note, however, that YDP classifies object based on use/function pre conflict, not at time of strike. This means that it may be difficult to make claims under international criminal law or international humanitarian law on this basis. The point of this data is not to make those claims—but to point to the broader patterns of aerial bombardment and its impacts.

heritage, educational facilities, media, international community, civilians, economic infrastructure, infrastructure, political and tribal, military and security targets, and finally raids where the target is unknown. For the purposes of this analysis, we have reorganized this dataset as follows. Air raids targeting:

(i) cultural heritage, educational facilities, media, international community, and civilians have been re-classified as affecting 'Civilians',
(ii) economic infrastructure and infrastructure have been re-classified as impacting 'Infrastructure (including economic infrastructure)', and
(iii) political and tribal, and military and security targets, have been reclassified as affecting 'Military, Security, and other political'.

The reclassified data is presented in Figure 9.1, and is clear that until the end of 2018, a significant proportion of all air raids were hitting either civilian or infrastructure targets (although it is difficult to draw more precise conclusions because of the high number of air raids which hit 'unknown' targets). Particularly notable is the spike in attacks on civilian and infrastructure targets around November 2017, the time at which the SLC had imposed a total blockade of all Yemeni ports.

SLC air strikes have targeted and destroyed critical infrastructure which include electricity facilities, port facilities, water bottling factories and pumping plants, health facilities and hospitals, food processing factories, markets, businesses, and essential irrigation infrastructure. Air strikes have also destroyed farmland and targeted artisanal fishing and related facilities on the Red Sea Coast. These can all be considered as attacks on OIS and are in addition to the attacks on 'purely'

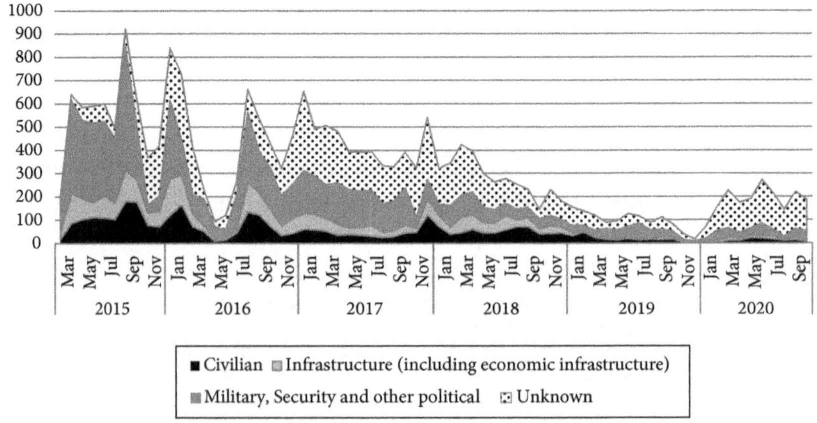

Figure 9.1 Number of air raids by target (data from 26 March 2015 to 31 October 2020)
Source: A. Sarkar, 2022. Data: Yemen Data Project.

civilian targets (such as residential complexes, houses, and funeral halls). The latter are most likely in violation of humanitarian law, but are not the direct focus of this chapter.

Between 2015 and 2019, the Group of Eminent Experts on Yemen appointed by the UN Human Rights Council noted that a number of coalition airstrikes attacked indispensable food and water facilities, mainly in the governorates of al-Hudaydah, Saa'dah, Hajjah, and Sana'a.[98] They also noted a systematic pattern of attacks on facilities for food production, processing or storage: including fourteen attacks on crowded marketplaces, nineteen air strikes on farms and agricultural workers, eight incidents where the SLC targeted food processing or storage facilities, and twelve airstrikes on food transports (for civilians).[99] Other scholars have also documented the systematic pattern of attacks against farms, agricultural land, and irrigation infrastructure, as well as the authorities responsible for maintaining this infrastructure.[100] Given that agriculture covers a very small proportion of Yemen's land surface (about 3 per cent), and arable land and permanent crops cover only about 6 per cent of all agricultural land, it is unlikely that these targets were hit accidentally.[101]

Before the war began in 2015, fisheries were a key export, and contributed around 2 per cent of Yemen's GDP. The sector was also a key source of food, income, and employment—providing job opportunities to around 500,000 people (and indirectly supporting around 1.7 million individuals), with artisanal fishing dominating the Red Sea coast.[102] The conflict has devastated the sector. Fishermen are unable to afford fuel for their boats, but most critically, the aerial campaign

[98] Human Rights Council 2019, *Report of the detailed findings of the Group of Eminent International and Regional Experts on Yemen*, see note 82, at 180–181, §755. An assessment produced for DFID Yemen noted: 'in all 18 governorates water and sanitation infrastructure has been affected by war—either by the direct impact of the war or the inability to carry out maintenance. From the data available in the period 2014–2016, a total of 962 WASH facilities (including healthcare facilities) were damaged, of which 39% were totally destroyed. This included 438 water facilities, 21,497 health units, and 27 sanitation installations. In order of impact, most damage was caused by air strikes, combat, and conflict-related non-availability of spare parts or fuel. Sa'ada governorate experienced the highest rate of completely destroyed WASH facilities projects (145) followed by Taiz (137), Al-Hudaydah (127), Al-Byadah (116), and Hajjah (77)—i.e. in Houthi controlled areas and areas in the frontline of the conflict'. See ICED Facility, *Effects of war on water security in Yemen: Stocktaking study*, June 2019, available online at <http://icedfacility.org/wp-content/uploads/2019/07/190618-Yemen-Stocktaking.pdf> (visited 26 August 2021), at 15.

[99] ICED Facility, see note 98. According to an NRC report of 24 September 2020, on data collected by the Civilian Impact Monitoring Project, there were 348 airstrikes and 570 cases of shelling affecting farms since January 2018, and that the overwhelming majority of the incidents have targeted farmland in Hodeidah (392) and Sa'ada (337) governorates. See Norwegian Refugee Council, *Yemen: Airstrike and Shelling Hits on Farms in Three Years*, 24 September 2020, available online at <https://www.nrc.no/news/2020/september/yemen-900-airstrike-and-shelling-hits-on-farms-in-three-years/> (visited 26 August 2021).

[100] Mundy, see note 66.

[101] Mundy, see note 66, at 12.

[102] A. M. Al-Fareh, *The Impact of the War in Yemen on Artisanal Fishing of the Red Sea*, LSE Middle East Centre (2018), available online at <http://eprints.lse.ac.uk/91022/1/Al-Fareh_The-impact-of-war_Author.pdf> (visited 26 August 2021), at 7.

has destroyed fish landing areas and fish markets, and scores of fishermen have been killed. One report estimated that 146 fishermen had been killed, fifty-seven had been wounded, and 222 fishing boats had been destroyed between March 2015 and December 2017.[103] Fearing for their lives, fewer fishermen are willing to venture out to sea, causing a crisis of livelihoods. Paradoxically, the food crisis has also meant that coastal communities are more reliant than ever on fish for their nutrition, resulting in overfishing.

The final point worth touching on has been a persistent pattern of attacks on health centres and clinics by the SLC (even as Houthis and other armed groups have attacked health centres and used them for military operations).[104] Médecins sans Frontières, for instance, has reported that a number of its sites have been struck by aerial bombardment despite being clearly marked.[105] The responsibility for destruction of medical facilities does not lie with the SLC alone: between 2015 and 2018, the UN Secretary General reported that 119 attacks (by all parties to the conflict) had targeted hospitals in Yemen.[106] In a context marked by inadequate healthcare before the war, the effects have been crippling. Barely half of the country's public healthcare facilities are fully functional.[107] The collapse of incomes has also meant that where medical facilities are functional, most people are no longer able to afford the transport costs to go to them.[108] This means that curable health conditions often become severe or deadly.

In the face of criticism for violations of international law, the SLC established the Joint Incidents Assessment Team (JIAT) in August 2016. It consists of members from the coalition, and was intended to investigate, among other things, alleged violations committed by the SLC during the aerial campaign in Yemen and provide insights into patterns of civilian harm.[109] It has failed to conduct credible, impartial, and transparent investigations into violations of the laws of war. Not only has the JIAT delayed starting its work and conducted investigations extremely slowly, it has also not made many of its findings/reports publicly available (even though it has released press statements on its conclusions). Further, it has consistently

[103] Al-Fareh, see note 102, at 21.

[104] Human Rights Council, *Situation of human rights in Yemen*, see note 82, at 169, §709.

[105] Médecins Sans Frontières, *Yemen: No True Accountability in Bombing of MSF-Supported Hospital*, 30 October 2019, available online at <https://www.doctorswithoutborders.org/what-we-do/news-stories/news/yemen-no-true-accountability-bombing-msf-supported-hospital> (visited 26 August 2021).

[106] *Children and Armed Conflict in Yemen: Report of the Secretary General*, UN Doc. S/2019/453, 3 June 2019, at 10, §43.

[107] K. Garber et al., 'Estimating Access to Health Care in Yemen, A Complex Humanitarian Emergency Setting: A Descriptive Applied Geospatial Analysis', 8 *Lancet Global Health* (2020) e1435–e1443, at e1435.

[108] Médecins Sans Frontières, *Yemen, a Country in Crisis*, available online at <https://www.msf.org/yemen-depth> (visited 26 August 2021).

[109] Human Rights Watch, *Hiding Behind the Coalition: Failure to Credibly Investigate and Provide Redress for Unlawful Attacks in Yemen* (2018), available online at <https://www.hrw.org/report/2018/08/24/hiding-behind-coalition/failure-credibly-investigate-and-provide-redress-unlawful> (visited 26 August 2021).

absolved the SLC of responsibility, relying on dubious and flawed understandings of factual circumstances and international law.[110] This has been noted by human rights organizations, as well as the UN Panel of Experts, and the Group of Eminent Experts on Yemen appointed by the UN Human Rights Council.[111] Critically, the JIAT has sought to argue that failure to place a target on the SLC's 'no-strike' list, absolves the coalition of its responsibility to distinguish between civilian and military targets, and to ensure strikes are 'proportional'.[112] This is a clear inversion of the responsibility under relevant customary international law, which requires the military to exercise due care in its attacks, rather than placing that burden on the targets.[113]

The United States, the United Kingdom, and to some extent other countries which supply arms to the SLC, such as France[114] and Italy,[115] are complicit in the harms caused by the aerial campaign (though their legal liability lies outside the scope of this chapter).[116] The United States, in particular, has contributed intelligence and logistical support in addition to being a long-time supplier of weapons to the Saudi Army and Air Force, and US contractors have helped maintain Saudi planes. It has also provided refuelling assistance to Saudi and Emirati aircraft, and in 2018 Secretary of State Mike Pompeo certified to Congress that the SLC had taken adequate measures to protect civilians.[117] Refuelling support ended in November 2018, and a bipartisan measure to end US involvement in the Yemeni

[110] Human Rights Watch, *Hiding Behind the Coalition*, see note 109.

[111] See for instance, *Letter dated 26 January 2018 from the Panel of Experts on Yemen mandated by Security Council resolution 2342 (2017) addressed to the President of the Security Council*, UN Doc. S/2019/594, 26 January 2018, Annex 58 ('Case Studies of Air Strikes in Yemen (2017)'), at 233.

[112] According to the principle of proportionality, international humanitarian law requires that expected incidental civilian casualties or damage to civilian objects should not be excessive in relation to the concrete and direct anticipated military advantage. Accordingly, armed forces should weigh the military advantage that an attack is anticipated to give against the expected civilian casualties or damage and make sure that a specific attack does not lead to excessive civilian loss.

[113] Human Rights Council, *Situation of human rights in Yemen*, see note 82, at 214, §895.

[114] K. Roth and B. Jeannerod, *France Should Stop Fueling Saudi War Crimes in Yemen*, Human Rights Watch, 17 May 2019, available online at <https://www.hrw.org/news/2019/05/17/france-should-stop-fueling-saudi-war-crimes-yemen> (visited 26 August 2021). See also 'La France et le Yémen: cartographie d'un mensonge d'État', *Mediapart*, 15 April 2019, available online at <https://www.mediapart.fr/journal/international/150419/la-france-et-le-yemen-cartographie-d-un-mensonge-d-etat?utm_content=buffer5e34b&utm_medium=social&utm_source=Facebook_Page&utm_campaign=CM> (visited 26 August 2021).

[115] Mwatana for Human Rights, *Made in Italy, Bombed in Yemen*, 27 October 2020, available online at <https://mwatana.org/en/made-in-italy-bombed-in-yemen/> (visited 26 August 2021).

[116] For a discussion of the possible legal liability of the United States and the United Kingdom for aiding and abetting alleged war crimes in Yemen, see R. Goodman, 'The Law of Aiding and Abetting (Alleged) War Crimes: How to Assess US and UK Support for Saudi Strikes in Yemen', *Just Security*, 1 September 2016, available online at <https://www.justsecurity.org/32656/law-aiding-abetting-alleged-war-crimes-assess-uk-support-saudi-strikes-yemen/> (visited 26 August 2021).

[117] The US administration declined to provide this certification in early 2019, after it had stopped providing refuelling assistance to SLC aircraft. See International Crisis Group, *Ending the Yemen Quagmire: Lessons for Washington from Four Years of War* (2019), available online at <https://www.crisisgroup.org/united-states/003-ending-yemen-quagmire-lessons-washington-four-years-war> (visited 26 August 2021).

war (passed in April 2019) was vetoed by President Trump.[118] In its final days, the outgoing Trump administration also sought to designate the Houthis a 'foreign terrorist organization'—a decision which could have made the humanitarian situation in Yemen even worse by making it more difficult for humanitarian organizations to operate in Houthi-controlled areas. The Biden administration has, however, suspended 'relevant' arms sales to Saudi Arabia and the UAE (at the time of writing), citing its commitment to helping end the war in Yemen, and has also revoked the designation of the Houthis as a terrorist organization.[119] The United Kingdom, on the other hand, has provided (and continues to provide) weapons, as well as some logistical and intelligence support to the SLC, despite a legal campaign to stop the supply of weapons.[120] In fact, UK and US officials were reported to have access to the list of targets to be attacked by the SLC, but did not play a role in selecting them.[121] Some analysts have speculated that the support of the United Kingdom and the United States to the SLC campaign in Yemen stemmed, at least in part, from a desire to ensure compliance with international humanitarian law.[122] If this is true, the strategy has been a resounding failure.

C. Siege Warfare, Indiscriminate Bombing/Attacks on Civilians, and Impeding Essential Commodities, Humanitarian Supplies, and Operations

Over the course of the war, the Houthis (and in some cases, other armed groups, including some affiliated with the SLC and backed by the UAE) have attacked or taken over medical facilities, indiscriminately shelled and launched sniper attacks against civilians, markets, and shops, and laid landmines without regard to the

[118] E. Wong, 'U.S. rationale for military aid to Saudis in Yemen war is fraying', *New York Times*, 23 September 2020, available online at <https://www.nytimes.com/2020/09/23/us/politics/yemen-us-weapons-saudi-arabia.html> (visited 26 August 2021).

[119] See J. Borger and P. Wintour, 'Biden announces end to US support for Saudi-led offensive in Yemen', *The Guardian*, 4 February 2021, available online at <https://www.theguardian.com/world/2021/feb/04/us-end-support-saudi-led-operations-yemen-humanitarian-crisis> (visited 26 August 2021). On the revocation of the designation of the Houthis as a foreign terrorist organization, see US Department of State, 'Revocation of the Terrorist Designation of Ansarallah', 12 February 2021, available online at <https://www.state.gov/revocation-of-the-terrorist-designations-of-ansarallah/> (visited 26 August 2021).

[120] Campaign Against Arms Trade (CAAT), 'CAAT Files New Judicial Review Application Against Decision to Renew Arms Sales to Saudi Arabia', 27 October 2020, available online at <https://caat.org.uk/news/caat-files-new-judicial-review-application-against-decision-to-renew-arms-sales-to-saudi-arabia/> (visited 26 August 2021). See also P. Wintour, 'UK declines to follow US in suspending Saudi arms sales over Yemen', *The Guardian*, 8 February 2021, available online at <https://www.theguardian.com/world/2021/feb/08/uk-declines-to-follow-us-in-suspending-saudi-arms-sales-over-yemen> (visited 26 August 2021).

[121] E. Graham-Harrison, 'British and US military "in command room" for Saudi strikes on Yemen', *The Guardian*, 15 January 2016, available online at <https://www.theguardian.com/world/2016/jan/15/british-us-military-in-command-room-saudi-strikes-yemen> (visited 26 August 2021).

[122] International Crisis Group, *Ending the Yemen Quagmire*, see note 117.

consequences for civilians.[123] Some of the most egregious examples of these attacks occurred during the siege of Ta'izz city by the Houthis (discussed in greater detail later in this chapter), but also in Hajour in Hajjah governorate.[124] In addition, the war has been characterized by moving frontlines, enforced disappearances, arbitrary detentions, and extrajudicial executions. Yemeni armed forces as well as armed groups affiliated with the SLC have used similar tactics against Houthi-controlled areas (such as al-Durayhimi district) in al-Hudaydah governorate.[125]

Sieges have been accompanied by significant restrictions on the flow of humanitarian supplies, including food, water, and fuel. In some cases, supplies have been looted at checkpoints. Humanitarian workers have also been arbitrarily detained or killed. The Houthis are primarily (but not solely) responsible for these violations. The blocking or diversion of humanitarian aid is among the most high-profile actions contributing to starvation, alongside restrictions imposed in the form of preconditions, delays, and levies on such assistance. These actions by parties to the conflict contributed to the starvation of civilians; they are a reason why the risk of and actual starvation due to other factors was not sufficiently relieved. Sieges also provide the perfect conditions for the development of war economies centred around licit and illicit goods as well as the diversion of humanitarian aid. This is dealt with in the next section.

5. Economic Policies and Mass Starvation

Shortly after the outbreak of the war, its calamitous economic impacts became clear. Business confidence collapsed, government revenue declined sharply, and government spending increased as both the IRG and the Houthis put more civil servants and soldiers on the payroll, causing a haemorrhage of foreign exchange reserves, and a spike in the prices of essential commodities including food and fuel.[126] The hikes in the prices of food and fuel were felt, more-or-less equally, in

[123] For a discussion, see Human Rights Council, *Situation of human rights in Yemen*, see note 82, at 69–90, §300–370. Human Rights Watch have noted that '[l]andmines have also left at least three western coast water facilities inaccessible, two aid groups said. In addition, mines have made it more difficult for villagers to feed themselves and maintain their income. Five people said that they had been injured or that relatives had been killed when landmines detonated in farmlands or grazing lands; many displaced people said mines prevented safe harvesting and killed valuable livestock. Landmines have prevented humanitarian organizations from reaching communities in need along the western coast, Human Rights Watch said. These included villages and towns in the Tuhayta and Mawza'a districts, as well as the major port city of Hodeida. Three aid groups said they could not reach key places or provide services to areas because landmines were planted there or along the route.' See Human Rights Watch, *Yemen: Houthi Landmines Kill Civilians*, Block Aid, 22 April 2019, available online at <https://www.hrw.org/news/2019/04/22/yemen-houthi-landmines-kill-civilians-block-aid> (visited 26 August 2021).

[124] Human Rights Council, *Situation of human rights in Yemen*, see note 82, at 114, §457.

[125] Human Rights Council, *Situation of human rights in Yemen*, see note 82, at 124, §503.

[126] Sana'a Center for Strategic Studies, *The Yemen Review: War's Elusive End*, (2019), available online at <https://sanaacenter.org/files/TYR_Annual_2019_en.pdf (visited 26 August 2021), at 76–77.

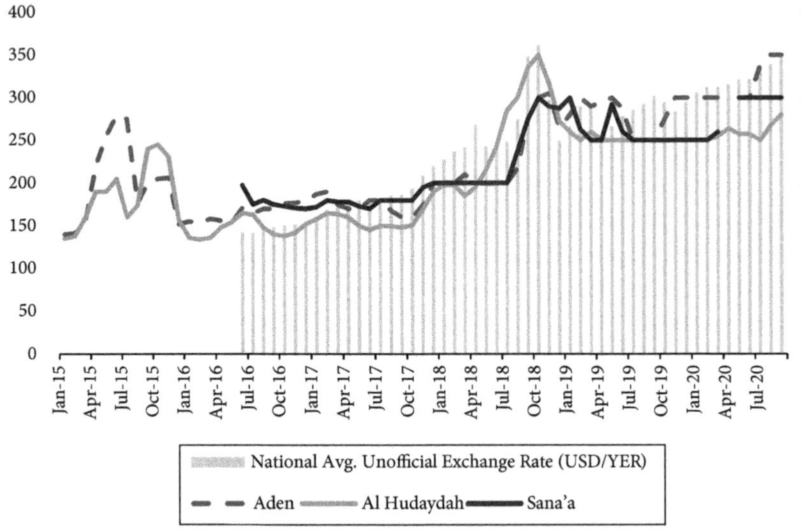

Figure 9.2 Prices of wheat flour in Aden, al-Hudaydah and Sana'a (YER/Kg), and unofficial exchange rate (USD-YER): Jan-2015—Oct-2020

Source: A. Sarkar, 2022. Data: World Food Programme (data available at <https://dataviz.vam.wfp.org/economic_explorer/prices> (visited 26 August 2021)).

Aden, Hudaydah, and Sana'a. Figure 9.2 shows the change in prices of wheat flour against the average national unofficial exchange rate and is drawn from monthly price data collected by the WFP.[127] It illustrates that until mid-2018, the crisis of hunger was caused partly by an increase in food prices, but much more so by the collapse of people's purchasing power.

In fact, until the beginning of 2018, food prices fluctuated and overall rose modestly, less than the devaluation of the Yemeni Rial—that is, not increasing in real terms. There was significant variation between different regions—for instance, wheat flour was less expensive in al-Hudaydah and most expensive in Tai'zz (not shown in the graph). However, most food crises are characterized by sharp rises in food prices: this occurred in Yemen, but later and not to the extent it occurs in other famines. At this juncture, the key problem was not price inflation but the collapse in people's abilities to purchase the food available. As the conflict over the central bank became more acute, many public sector salary payments were either suspended or became infrequent, and social security and other welfare programmes

[127] We are using fluctuations in the prices of wheat flour as a proxy for fluctuations in food prices—this is because around 74 per cent of Yemen's cereal consumption consisted of wheat by 2009, and is only likely to have increased since (see Mundy and Pelat, see note 57, at 104). Two notes of caution when interpreting these data: first, the average national USD/YER exchange rate masks significant national disparity, especially after mid-2019, when the exchange rates in the south and the north began to diverge; second, there were significant price differences in Ta'izz, as noted in the case study.

also ceased. For instance, the Social Welfare Fund, which provided unconditional cash transfers to around 1.5 million people suspended operations in 2014. This meant that, along with the broader collapse in economic activity caused by conflict, there was simply not enough real demand to buy the available food.[128] Food prices spiked again in mid-2018, alongside rapid depreciation of the Yemeni Riyal (YER), which exacerbated the crisis. The increased demand for foreign exchange to fund imports, and market speculation which caused the depreciation is a symptom of the broader fragmentation of Yemen's economic system and the struggle over control of monetary policy.[129]

In addition to the collapse in purchasing power and the central bank crisis, the war in Yemen has been characterised by ferocious contestation over control of economic resources. A war economy has emerged, generating significant profits for military business cartels. These outcomes are not surprising. Yemen's political system is a paradigmatic example of a 'political marketplace':[130] a system of governance where monetized transactional politics has become systematic.[131] In these political systems politics is run on the basis of personal transactions, and political loyalties and services are sold to the highest bidder according to the laws of supply and demand, and the role of formal institutions or the rule of law is secondary.[132] In Yemen, the Houthis, the IRG, and an ever-proliferating group of belligerents have fought over the shifting networks of key institutions, foreign patronage (especially from regional actors), private sector players, and licit and illicit actors which comprise Yemen's wartime economy; this has allowed them to sustain the conflict,

[128] World Food Programme, *What Does the Conflict Induced Public Sector Crisis Mean for Food Security in Yemen?*, November 2016, available online at <http://wfp.org/publications/yemen-special-focus-conflict-public-sector-crisis-food-security-november-2016> (visited 26 August 2021).

[129] Sana'a Center for Strategic Studies, *The Yemen Review: August 2018* (2018), available online at <https://sanaacenter.org/publications/the-yemen-review/6394> (visited 26 August 2021), at 7.

[130] al-Iryani, and Nasser, see note 31.

[131] The concept was first developed by Alex de Waal, in the context of elite politics in the Horn of Africa. See A. de Waal, *The Real Politics of the Horn of Africa* (Cambridge: Polity, 2015). A succinct explanation of the framework is set out in A. de Waal, 'Introduction to the Political Marketplace for Policymakers', JSRP Policy Brief 1 (London School of Economics and Political Science, 2016), available online at <https://www.lse.ac.uk/ideas/Assets/Documents/Conflict-Research-Programme/policy-reports/JSRP-Brief-1.pdf> (visited 26 August 2021).

[132] The exact functioning and organization of a political marketplace depends on a few key elements: (1) the goals and strategies of the key players—that is, whether they are interested in self-enrichment, holding on to power, or have broader ideological motivations; (2) the structure of the political system in which they operate—this includes the degree and nature of political competition, the ease with which new actors can enter and establish themselves in the political system, and the durability of agreements and 'deals' being entered into between the key political actors; and (3) the ways in which violence and resources are used by politicians to exercise control of the political system—this depends on the funds (or means) that politicians can access to purchase or rent loyalties, and the extent to which politicians control the means of violence and coercion, and are willing to use them. For a discussion, see A. de Waal, A. Sarkar, and B. Spatz, *A Political Marketplace Framework Methodology: A Process Toolkit*, Conflict Research Programme and the World Peace Foundation (2019), available online at <http://eprints.lse.ac.uk/111009/1/CRP_the_political_marketplace_framework_and_toolkit_published.pdf> (visited 26 August 2021).

pursue their ideological and strategic goals, and enrich themselves at the same time.[133]

A. Conflict over the Central Bank of Yemen and its (Continuing) Fallout

In the early months of the war, the CBY managed to maintain a remarkable level of technocratic proficiency and political impartiality under exceptionally adverse conditions, maintaining a tight monetary policy, sustaining credit to businesses for importing food, servicing the domestic debt by issuing government bonds, and paying salaries for approximately 1.2 million people on the state payroll.[134] The CBY maintained neutrality between Houthi-controlled Sana'a and IRG-controlled Aden to the extent of paying salaries to soldiers fighting on both sides. However, these measures only postponed the financial crisis, as the CBY spent its reserves in the process, which declined from US$ 4.6 billion in 2014 to US$ 700 million in September 2016.[135] Consequently in August 2016, the CBY was compelled to suspend payments to civil servants across the country.[136]

Beginning in 2016, the IRG began to depart from a tacit agreement to respect the neutrality of the central bank. It claimed that the CBY had funnelled US$ 4 billion of support to the Houthi movement which contributed to broader efforts by the Houthis to siphon funds from ministries to support the war effort. While this allegation is difficult to prove, it is undoubtedly the case that the Houthis benefited from the neutrality of the CBY: they are reported to have added thousands of militiamen to the Ministry of Defence roster and imposed a war tax on the salaries of civil servants, a majority of whom lived in Houthi-controlled areas.[137] Finally, in September 2016, President Hadi issued a decree replacing the CBY governor and ordering the headquarters of the CBY to be moved to Aden from Sana'a. He acknowledged that the action would result in hardship to millions of Yemenis but argued that the move was necessary to apply additional pressure on the Houthis. This move also reflected the stated willingness of IRG officials to 'wage economic war on areas in Yemen under Houthi control'.[138] The transfer itself was carried out

[133] T. Eaton et al., *Conflict Economies in the Middle East and North Africa*, Chatham House Report, June 2019, available online at <https://www.chathamhouse.org/2019/06/conflict-economies-middle-east-and-north-africa> (visited 26 August 2021), at 18–19.

[134] Rageh, Nasser, and al-Muslimi, see note 76.

[135] A. Biswell, *Yemen Economic Bulletin: The War for Monetary Control Enters a Dangerous New Phase*, Sana'a Center for Strategic Studies, 21 January 2020, available online at <http://sanaacenter.org/files/The_War_for_Monetary_Control_en.pdf> (visited 26 August 2021).

[136] Biswell, see note 136, at 5.

[137] Rageh, Nasser, and al-Muslimi, see note 76.

[138] Rageh, Nasser, and al-Muslimi, see note 76. Notably, this step appears to have been taken without consulting western partners, who were nonetheless unwilling to criticize the IRG after having argued for its legitimacy.

in a piecemeal manner. The new Aden-based CBY had the legal authority to print money (though notes are physically printed in Russia), and has access to global financial systems, while the Sana'a based branch has continued to operate under Houthi control, having retained most of the staff, documentary archives, and control over Yemen's major population and commercial centres. At the same time, branches of the CBY in Hadramawt and Marib have been operating as *de facto* independent central banks.[139] Yemen has therefore been partitioned in practice into a set of connected but distinct financial systems where central bankers are competing for control over monetary and financial policies and occasionally enriching themselves in the process.[140]

The operations of the CBY in Aden (and by extension the IRG) have been funded by a combination of sources, which include receipts from customs and other trade related taxes, some oil and gas revenue, a US$ 2 billion deposit by Saudi Arabia placed with the Aden CBY to support imports and the YER, and finally, by printing money. The Houthis, on the other hand, have run an alternate financial system. In an effort to increase financial liquidity, they have resorted to the control of and smuggling of fuel and putting financial strains on the population under their control through imposition of additional taxes and levies.[141] Since 2018, the Houthis have also restricted the circulation of new banknotes printed by the Aden CBY in areas under their control, though enforcement has varied in the frontline regions such as al-Hudaydah, Ta'izz, and al-Jawf.

After the CBY was transferred from Sana'a to Aden, it initially failed to pay salaries and pensions to public officials in the Houthi-controlled areas. Many still do not receive regular and full payments, with significant implications for their food security. Since late 2016, however, some salary payments were resumed by the IRG to officials not associated with the military and security services—these include some workers in health, judiciary, and higher education sectors, as well as around 40,000 pensioners.[142] By October 2020, almost all of the Saudi cash deposit had been used up and salaries were suspended once again. Further, in April 2020, the UAE-supported Southern Transitional Council (STC) declared emergency self-rule across all southern Yemen in a direct challenge to the authority of the IRG and seized control of shipments of newly printed banknotes which had arrived in

[139] The UN Panel of experts noted that revenues 'collected by the Governorates of Marib, Mahrah and Hadramawt continue to be appropriated by officials without any effective control by the Central Bank of Yemen in Aden', and that local leaders were being enriched from sales of local oil and gas and receipts from customs checkpoints. See Security Council, see note 89, at 28, §76.

[140] H. Lackner, 'Yemen's hopes and expectations—Part 3: living conditions and humanitarian aid', Open Democracy, 7 February 2020, available online at <https://www.opendemocracy.net/en/north-africa-west-asia/yemens-hopes-and-expectations-part-3-living-conditions-and-humanitarian-aid/> (visited 26 August 2021).

[141] See generally, Sana'a Center for Strategic Studies, *The Yemen Review: Starvation, Diplomacy, and Ruthless Friends* (2018), available online at <http://sanaacenter.org/files/TYR_Annual_2018_en.pdf> (visited 26 August 2021).

[142] Biswell, see note 136, at 13.

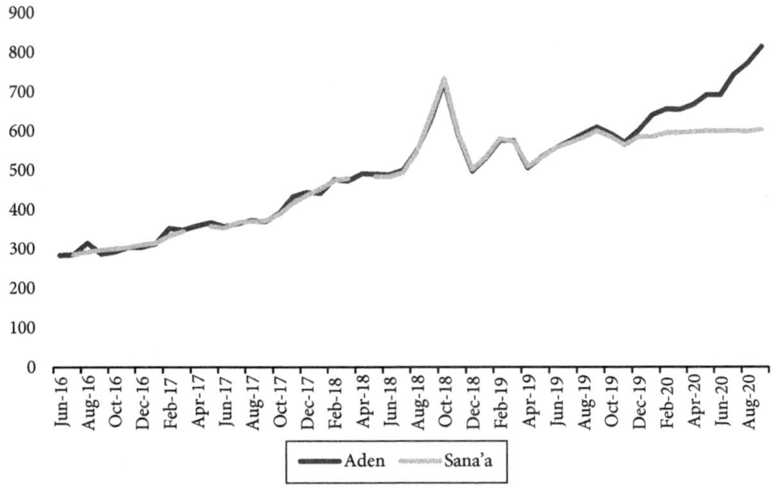

Figure 9.3 USD-YER unofficial exchange rate
Source: A. Sarkar. Data: World Food Programme (data available at: <https://dataviz.vam.wfp.org/economic_explorer/prices> (visited 26 August 2021)).

Aden (they handed it back later). Together, the depletion of the deposit and the diversion of money has meant that even fewer traders can access the letters of credit essential for importing food, fuel, and medicines. For some time, the CBY in Aden was under siege from the STC, and the STC ordered all payments to be made to a local bank, under their control rather than the CBY.

The efforts by the Houthis to control the circulation of banknotes in northern Yemen has led to the divergence of YER-USD exchange rates in Sana'a and Aden (Figure 9.3), increased smuggling and trafficking of foreign exchange (since it is profitable to buy dollars and Saudi rials in Houthi-controlled areas, and sell them in IRG-controlled areas), and led to the creation of a parallel exchange market for new and older YER notes. The result is a shortage of banknotes in the North—constraining commercial and trading activity, and rapid depreciation of YER in the south, with direct (and negative) implications for household food access.[143]

In sum, the conflicts over the control of the CBY have resulted in: (1) massively reduced cash incomes and savings through interruption in salaries, welfare payments and pensions, unemployment, and disruption of commerce; (2) degradation of both official and informal welfare service provision; (3) disruption of existing import mechanisms; and (4) the creation of incentives for currency speculation.

[143] Biswell, see note 136, at 13. On the impact on household food access in IRG controlled areas, see FEWSNET, *Yemen Food Security Outlook Update: September 2020* (2020), available online at <https://fews.net/sites/default/files/documents/reports/YEMEN_Food_Security_Outlook_Update_September_2020_FINAL.pdf> (visited 26 August 2021), at 2.

These consequences, which have resulted in higher prices of commodities, and more critically, in a fall in people's purchasing power, were clearly foreseeable. In choosing to fight the war on these terms, the belligerents appear to have acted with recklessness, if not direct culpability.

B. Fuel Imports

One of the major drivers of food price increases in Yemen in recent periods has been fuel shortages. This has been caused by the *de facto* blockade, profiteering, the difficulties faced by the IRG in sustaining the letter of credit import financing mechanism, localized protests around non-payment of salaries which have affected Aden port, and, crucially, competition over control of revenues from fuel imports.[144] The last of these is worth exploring in greater detail because it illustrates how competition over economic resources can directly cause food-price increases.

The IRG has enacted two laws, Decree 75 and Decree 49, to consolidate its control over revenue from fuel imports. The former outlines several regulations with which importers need to comply, the most important being to provide documentation that shows that importers intend on paying the exporter using the formal banking system (which is controlled by the IRG). Decree 75 effectively disqualified several Houthi-affiliated traders from importing fuel, and a number of tankers were held up in March and April 2019, when the Houthis allegedly urged importers not to comply with the law.[145] Decree 49 is even more egregious from the Houthi perspective: it mandates that all fuel importers have to pay fuel import taxes and customs to the government in order to import fuel into Yemen. This resulted in another stand-off as fuel imports stalled in September 2019.[146] The impacts of these crises, especially on fuel prices in Sana'a can be clearly seen in Figure 9.4, which plots the market price of diesel fuel against the unofficial YER–USD exchange rate.

It is clear that in the recent context, these decrees formed part of the IRG's broader war efforts and they probably bear primary responsibility for the fuel crisis, though the Houthis are also guilty of exacerbating the crisis for their political and strategic goals. Decree 75 was enacted in response to allegations that the Houthis had diverted large sums of money collected from fuel imports in aid of their war efforts. This remains difficult to prove but it is clear that the Houthis have benefited from creating monopolies over the distribution of fuel.[147] The Houthis have also reportedly exploited the fuel shortages by extracting revenue from the local

[144] FEWSNET, *Yemen Food Security Outlook: October 2020–May 2021*, see note 52, at 2–3.
[145] Human Rights Council, *Situation of human rights in Yemen*, see note 82, at 192, § 799.
[146] Sana'a Center for Strategic Studies, Economic Unit, *Yemen Economic Bulletin: Another Stage-Managed Fuel Crisis*, July 2020, available online at <https://sanaacenter.org/files/Another_Stage_Managed_Fuel_Crisis_en.pdf> (visited 26 August 2021), at 4–5.
[147] Sana'a Center for Strategic Studies, Economic Unit, *Yemen Economic Bulletin*, see note 148.

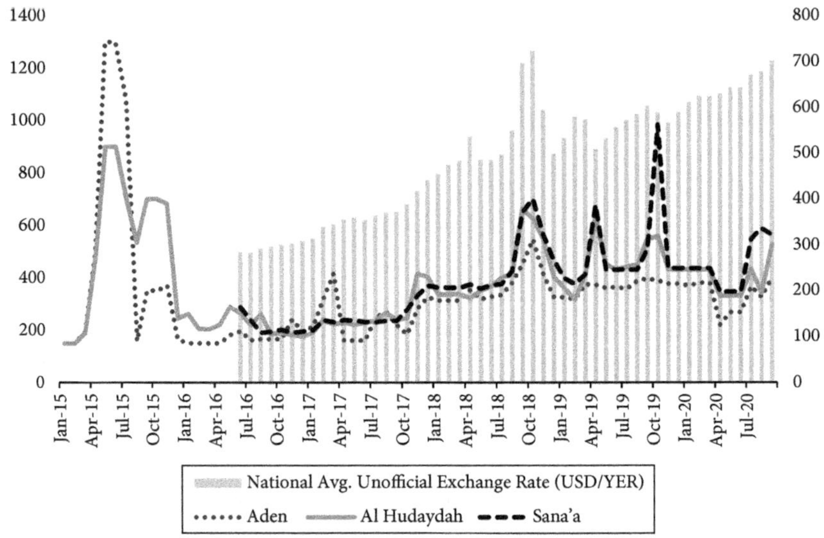

Figure 9.4 Prices of diesel fuel in Aden, al-Hudaydah and Sana'a (YER/Litre): Jan 2015–Oct 2020

Source: A. Sarkar, 2022. Data: World Food Programme.

market through black-market fuel sales.[148] Market speculation by traders has also contributed to price increases. For instance, the spike in fuel prices in September and October 2018, which affected both Houthi and IRG controlled areas, occurred to the backdrop of increasing global oil prices. Yemeni traders acted as a cartel to drive up fuel prices so as to maintain profits in the face of increased import costs and a depreciating currency.[149] This type of profiteering has become endemic in Yemen's war economy.

C. War Economy, and the Diversion and Control of Humanitarian Aid

The war economies of 'new wars' are characterized by the important role played by clandestine commercial networks, which dominate not only formal institutions but also cross political and military lines, leading to collusive profiteering by leading members of groups that are ostensibly enemies. They emerge in protracted wars, usually with multiple sides and a proliferation of state and non-state armed groups, hybridized with criminal gangs and transnational smuggling operations.

[148] Sana'a Center for Strategic Studies, *Yemen Review: Battle for Marib*, September 2020, available online at <https://sanaacenter.org/files/TYR_September_2020_en.pdf> (visited 26 August 2021), at 6.

[149] Sana'a Center for Strategic Studies, *The Yemen Review*, see note 142, at 34.

A highly precarious gig economy for militarized male labour emerges to supply the workforce for these armed groups, and with much reduced domestic production, the war effort begins to depend on pillage, extractive taxation and shakedowns, and external patronage.[150] Aid and humanitarian resources are often taxed, diverted, or looted.[151] As interests in the war economy become more entrenched, battles become rarer, frontlines crystallize, and cooperation between warring factions becomes common. Armed operations may be undertaken more for commercial purposes than in pursuit of military victory. War economies are also typified by what Peer Schouten calls 'roadblock politics'—where actors and armed groups impose themselves on strategic points of passage on trade routes, to derive power—primarily financial but also political—from the capacity to disrupt trade flows.[152]

Yemen's war economy has all of these characteristics. While it is difficult to ship goods into Yemen, and into the port in Hudaydah in particular, land routes through Oman and Saudi Arabia have remained largely open, with goods taking two to three days to reach their intended destinations across the country. Essential commodities are taxed multiple times—by the IRG and the Houthis, but also by the armed groups which control different territories and checkpoints. Salisbury notes, for instance, that even while basic goods cross internal borders with relative ease, they are taxed at as many as fifteen to twenty-five checkpoints, which drives up prices by 10–15 per cent.[153] This is of course not the case for besieged areas (such as Ta'izz), where the flow of goods was even more restricted. The fragmentation of financial systems between the different belligerents has created additional opportunities for corruption—especially around the compliance with administrative requirements for imports, and in accessing credit. As traders have passed these 'costs' on to customers, the price of essential goods has increased.

Weapons have moved freely across the frontlines alongside essential commodities, and commanders of armed groups have made profits using the time-honoured technique of collecting payment and materials (primarily from Saudi Arabia and the UAE) for 'ghost-soldiers'.[154] Analysts report that arms (such as Austrian Steyr rifles, for example) which could only have been provided by Saudi Arabia and UAE

[150] See M. Kaldor, *New and Old Wars: Organized Violence in a Global Era* (3rd edn., Cambridge: Polity Press, 2012), at 94–96.

[151] See for instance, the discussion on the famine in Somalia in 1991–1992 in A. de Waal, *Famine Crimes: Politics and the Disaster Relief Industry in Africa* (Oxford: James Currey, 1997), at 163–178. More generally, see D. Maxwell and K. H. Gelsdorf, *Understanding the Humanitarian World* (New York: Routledge, 2019).

[152] P. Schouten, 'Roadblock Politics in Central Africa', *Environment and Planning D: Society and Space* (2019) 1–18, at 2.

[153] P. Salisbury, *Yemen: National Chaos, Local Order*, Chatham House Research Paper, December 2017, available online at <https://www.chathamhouse.org/2017/12/yemen-national-chaos-local-order> (visited 26 August 2021), at 24–25.

[154] Sana'a Center for Strategic Studies, *Corruption in Yemen's War Economy*, Policy Brief: Rethinking Yemen's Economy, 5 November 2018, available online at <http://sanaacenter.org/files/Rethinking_Yemens_Economy_policy_brief_9.pdf> (visited 26 August 2021), at 4.

are available for openly available for sale in Sana'a.[155] The fragmentation of Yemen into territories controlled by different political groups/authorities is therefore a source of significant profit for some, as they exploit price differences between the different regions. This may not be a direct cause of starvation, but it has certainly helped sustain the broader drivers of privation and hunger.

The Houthis have diverted and attempted to control the distribution of humanitarian aid, and of restricting access to humanitarian agencies.[156] Though all parties to the conflict have been found to have interfered in the distribution of humanitarian aid, the Houthis, in particular, have arrested and intimidated humanitarian workers, restricting access to already imported humanitarian supplies, creating administrative and bureaucratic impediments, and illegally seizing the property of humanitarian organizations and workers.[157] Humanitarian supplies have been looted, and both the IRG and the Houthis have sought to ensure that humanitarian relief is diverted to loyalists.[158] In fact, restrictions on access resulted in suspension of humanitarian operations in Houthi-controlled areas. For instance, USAID suspended aid to Houthi-controlled areas in March 2020, and shortly thereafter, the WFP announced that it would cut humanitarian food assistance to those areas by 50 per cent, impacting an estimated 8.5 million beneficiaries.[159] The crisis in humanitarian funding threatens to exacerbate these impacts.[160] The diversion of humanitarian aid is not the primary cause of mass starvation but it certainly means that existing suffering is not alleviated, and may be a violation of international humanitarian and human rights law. Wilfully impeding relief supplies can also point to the commission of a starvation crime.

D. Humanitarian Support

One of the characteristics of the Yemeni war is that the most important protagonists in the SLC, Saudi Arabia, and the UAE are also the most significant contributors to the humanitarian effort. In 2019, for instance, they contributed about 54

155 Eaton et al., see note 133, at 19.

156 See *Situation of human rights in Yemen, including violations and abuses since September 2014: Report of the detailed findings of the Group of Eminent International and Regional Experts on Yemen*, UN Doc. A/HRC/45/6, 14 September 2020, at 9, §53–55.

157 Security Council, see note 89, at 45–46, §123-127.

158 *Situation of human rights in Yemen*, see note 156, at 9, §54.

159 Sana'a Center for Strategic Studies, *Yemen's Accelerating Economic Woes During the Covid-19 Pandemic*, Policy Brief Rethinking Yemen's Economy, October 2020, available online at <https://sanaacenter.org/files/Rethinking_Yemens_Economy_No7_En.pdf> (visited 26 August 2021), at 18.

160 UN-Office for the Coordination of Humanitarian Affairs (UN-OCHA), 'Under Secretary-General for Humanitarian Affairs and Emergency Relief Coordinator, Mark Lowcock: Briefing to the Security Council on the humanitarian situation in Yemen', 11 November 2020, available online at <https://reliefweb.int/sites/reliefweb.int/files/resources/201111-Yemen%20SECCO%20statement%20Final.pdf> (visited 26 August 2021).

per cent of the total amount raised under the humanitarian response plan, and in fact the vast pledges of humanitarian aid by some members of the SLC appear to indicate awareness of levels of malnutrition in Yemen. Their overall contributions to the humanitarian programme, of about US$ 4 billion are considerable, but insignificant when compared to the broader costs of waging the war—in military materiel, salaries for their national military personnel, for the Yemeni military and militias, and for various mercenaries, primarily the Sudanese.[161] In 2020, however, with COVID-19, and the fall in global energy prices, these countries have been fiscally 'squeezed', and the contributions to the humanitarian programme have fallen drastically. As of November 2020, the Yemen humanitarian response plan had received only about US$ 1.5 billion, or 45 per cent of the amount sought.[162] Notably, other than Saudi Arabia, none of the SLC member countries have pledged funds for humanitarian programmes.[163]

6. Case Study: Al-Hudaydah—Yemen's Primary Food Pipeline

The last two substantive sections of this chapter consist of brief case studies, of al-Hudaydah and Ta'izz, which illustrate the complexities of ascertaining both intent and culpability for mass starvation in Yemen.

Al-Hudaydah was the poorest governorate in Yemen prior to the outbreak of conflict.[164] The war's most significant toll was exacted on the already suffering population: the IPC assessment in 2018 found that 57 per cent of the population ranked at IPC Phase 3 or higher (with 6,000 facing risk of famine) and would be worse without humanitarian assistance.[165] In 2020, nearly two years after the ceasefire (which resulted in, at best, a tenuous peace), the IPC noted that 4 per cent of the population was still in IPC Phase 3 and above.[166] In addition, the (ongoing) cholera outbreak has resulted in scores of deaths in the governorate. Al-Hudaydah

[161] Lackner, see note 141.

[162] UN OCHA, 'Under Secretary-General for Humanitarian Affairs and Emergency Relief Coordinator, Mark Lowcock', see note 160.

[163] Sana'a Center for Strategic Studies, *Yemen's Accelerating Economic Woes During the Covid-19 Pandemic*, see note 159, at 15.

[164] Part of the reason for this was the shift in land ownership patterns in the Tihama region, of which al-Hudaydah governorate is a part, with large land holdings owned by absentee landowners and being given over for mechanized agriculture. A consequence of this was the impoverishment of the majority of people who became sharecroppers and labourers. This has led to the paradox of the Tihama being simultaneously known as the 'breadbasket' of Yemen, and the region with the highest poverty levels. See H. Lackner, 'The Future of Yemeni Agriculture and Water', in A. al Alim Alsoswa and N. Brehony (eds.), *Building a New Yemen: Recovery, Transition and the International Community* (London: Bloomsbury Collections, 2022), 175 – 190.

[165] IPC, see note 46, at 2.

[166] Integrated Food Security Phase Classification, 'Yemen: Acute Food Insecurity Situation October–December 2020 and Projection for January–June 2021', available online at <http://www.ipcinfo.org/ipc-country-analysis/details-map/en/c/1152947/> (visited 26 August 2021).

City and its surroundings hold a population of more than 600,000, making it one of the country's most densely populated areas; the impacts of war and a humanitarian crisis on the population were therefore eminently foreseeable.[167]

As discussed earlier in this chapter, al-Hudaydah and nearby Salif ports are the point of entry for more than 70 per cent of the country's basic commodities, including staple foods, medical supplies, and fuel. The *de facto* naval blockade from 2015 onward meant that these ports witnessed significant declines in commercial imports. In addition, critical infrastructure was targeted by the SLC as part of its air campaign. Coalition aircraft destroyed four port cranes and several food warehouses at the beginning of the conflict. This paralysed the port until WFP, with US funding, procured replacements, which finally arrived in 2018 after having been held up deliberately by the IRG and the SLC. The air campaign also destroyed the critical Al-Darjah bridge on the al-Hudaydah-Sana'a route in August 2016, and the Al-Qasbah bridge in January 2017. These damaged bridges, along with two others, were not reconstructed, and bypasses were put in place as a temporary fix. Finally, air strikes targeted agricultural land, affecting the farming communities along the Tihama coast but specifically those living in Wadi Zabid and Wadi Siham, and artisanal fishing.

From January 2018, Yemeni armed forces and affiliated UAE-backed armed groups advanced through Ta'izz governorate from the south toward al-Hudaydah city, claiming (with no real basis) that Iran was smuggling weapons to the Houthis through al-Hudaydah port. The logic for the campaign was the belief that the loss of al-Hudaydah would deprive the Houthis of a significant source of income and force them to the negotiating table.[168] In June 2018, the coalition began 'Operation Golden Victory', and fighting continued in the whole governorate throughout the second half of 2018, even as the UN repeatedly warned of catastrophic consequences.[169]

Fighting among and within armed groups on the ground, and airstrikes caused even more damage to al-Hudaydah's food infrastructure. Humanitarian operations too, were disrupted, especially near the shifting frontlines on the outskirts of the city. More critically though, the offensive caused an increase in prices for essential commodities (see Figure 9.5, which shows a clear spike in commodity prices tracking the fiercest fighting). At around the same time, Oxfam noted that even as prices of rice, wheat, and cooking oil had increased dramatically, household incomes were affected by the conflict-related closure of factories and businesses.[170] Costs for transportation for leaving al-Hudaydah also increased.

[167] Sana'a Center for Strategic Studies, *The Yemen Review*, see note 141, at 24.

[168] International Crisis Group, *How to Halt Yemen's Slide into Famine*, Crisis Group Middle East Report No 193 (2018), available online at <https://www.crisisgroup.org/middle-east-north-africa/gulf-and-arabian-peninsula/yemen/193-how-halt-yemens-slide-famine> (visited 26 August 2021), at 6–11.

[169] Human Rights Council, *Situation of human rights in Yemen*, see note 82, at 123, §499.

[170] Oxfam International Press Release, 'Yemen: Hodeidah cannot be allowed to become a graveyard', 4 July 2018, available online at <https://www.oxfam.org/en/press-releases/yemen-hodeidah-cannot-be-allowed-become-graveyard> (visited 26 August 2021).

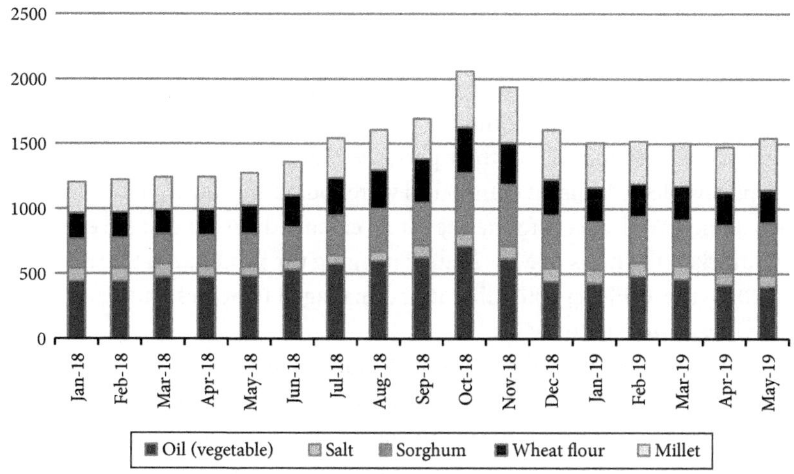

Figure 9.5 Prices of commodities in al-Hudaydah, January 2018–May 2019 (YER/Kg)
Source: A. Sarkar, 2022. Data: World Food Programme.

The fighting displaced around 455,000 people from or within the governorate, and most of the internally displaced moved to other urban centres in the governorate putting additional pressure on already strained water and sanitation services.[171] Attacks on medical centres in al-Hudaydah and al-Durayhimi affected the ability of Yemenis to receive adequate medical care. For instance, airstrikes destroyed a newly-constructed cholera treatment centre run by Médecins Sans Frontiéres in Abs (which is in Hajja, also in the Tihama region, but not administratively in al-Hudaydah governorate) as well as the only maternal and neonatal hospital in al-Durayhimi, while the Houthis took over and destroyed the 22nd May Hospital in al-Hudaydah city (after using it for military purposes).[172] Al-Durayhimi district in the governorate was besieged by the UAE-backed armed groups and witnessed fierce fighting, with its main water tank destroyed by shelling, and severe restrictions being placed on the movement of goods in and out of the district. The fighting in the governorate only ended with the signing of the Stockholm Agreement in December 2018—which appears to have largely held since, despite some violations.[173]

For their part, and as already noted, the Houthis have been guilty of indiscriminate use of landmines which have severely affected livelihoods of farming and fishing communities. They have also been responsible for denying humanitarian

[171] Human Rights Council, *Situation of human rights in Yemen*, see note 82, at 123, §502.
[172] Human Rights Council, *Situation of human rights in Yemen*, see note 82, at 123, §502.
[173] *The situation in the Middle East: Briefing by Mr. Martin Griffiths, Special Envoy of the Secretary-General for Yemen; and Mr. Mark Lowcock, Under-Secretary-General for Humanitarian Affairs and Emergency Relief Coordinator*, UN Doc. S/PV.8757, 15 September 2020.

access—most notably to the Red Sea Flour Mills. Before the fighting began in al-Hudaydah, the mills contained an estimated 51,000 tonnes of wheat, enough to feed 3.7 million people for one month.[174] When the mills were controlled by Houthi forces, mortar shells thought to be fired by Yemeni armed forces landed in and around the compound. On their part, the Houthis planted mines and improvised explosive devices inside compound warehouses and yards. Subsequently, the Houthis denied WFP access to the site for an extended period and are even alleged to have attacked the mills in May 2020, damaging the production line and silos.[175] In July 2020, the WFP reported that it had managed to access and save a massive stock of wheat stored at the Mills.[176]

The tactics used by the belligerents in al-Hudaydah demonstrate that all parties made systematic efforts to destroy and deprive civilians of objects indispensable for their survival. Given their likely awareness about the humanitarian situation, it is likely that the belligerents (and especially the SLC) were aware of the possible consequences for the civilian population that proceeded from their deliberate targeting of OIS. At the very least, they have shown reckless disregard for the impact of their actions on the population.

7. Case Study: Ta'izz—Yemen's Perennial Frontline

Ta'izz governorate was at the centre of the 2011 uprising. In the conflict, however, it has been the perennial frontline as different anti-Houthi militias vie for control of key areas and external patronage while battling the Houthis. In 2015, joint Houthi-Saleh forces took over the city and tried to consolidate power by integrating their forces into Yemen's military. The fight against Houthi–Saleh forces in the city was led by groups and individuals who were affiliated with the *Islah* party. Later, Salafist militias entered the city, seizing some territory and clashing with existing resistance groups. Heavy fighting also took place in the city in 2015, as Houthi-Saleh forces clashed with the fragmented forces opposing them (which were supported by SLC airstrikes). More generally, across Ta'izz governorate (and as in al-Hudaydah), the aerial campaign targeted essential infrastructure such as agricultural offices, animal farms, markets, and transportation centres.

The siege of Ta'izz began in August 2015, as the Houthis imposed a tight but incomplete blockade of the city, allowing in far too little food to sustain the population and causing a rise in severe and acute malnutrition. The blockade was

[174] *Situation of human rights in Yemen*, see note 156, at 8, §49.
[175] *Situation of human rights in Yemen*, see note 156, at 8, §49.
[176] See A. Symington, *WFP saves a Massive Stock of Wheat from Yemen's Frontline*, World Food Programme, 28 July 2020, available online at <https://www.wfp.org/stories/wfp-saves-massive-stock-wheat-yemens-frontline> (visited 26 August 2021).

accompanied by indiscriminate shelling/rocket attacks and mortar attacks on civilian targets as well as sniper attacks against civilians (including when they were attempting to buy food or seek shelter). The restrictions affected access to food such as vegetables, flour, sugar, and even drinking water, as well as medicines. At Houthi-Saleh checkpoints, merchants were stopped from entering with goods, and civilians were only allowed to carry in amounts sufficient for their own households. The inability to access wells, the unavailability of cooking gas, and arbitrary attacks on civilians at checkpoints all contributed to the dire humanitarian situation in the city. The health system in the city collapsed, with hospitals only partially open. By October 2015, it is estimated that over two-thirds of the original population of about 600,000 had fled the city.[177] Unsurprisingly, therefore, about 30 per cent of all IDPs in Yemen are from the governorate of Ta'izz. The siege finally ended in March 2016, with the opening of a road to Aden. Prior to the conflict, Ta'izz governorate was the location of some of Yemen's major food industries, but only about 10 per cent of the population obtained their food through farming, with 90 per cent reliant on the market. The siege of Ta'izz therefore deepened food insecurity by affecting the functioning of markets.

From late 2014 to 2017, Ta'izz experienced several bloody battles between the Houthi-Saleh militia all while being targeted by the SLC air campaign. Equally important since, have been the clashes between the different groups opposed to the Houthis. For instance, intense clashes have broken out between *Islah*-affiliated armed groups, and those supported by the UAE (which sees *Islah*, with its ties to the Muslim Brotherhood, as a terrorist organization).[178] Critically for food security, the carving up of the city into competing fiefdoms has meant that the costs of business have gone up, with numerous informal taxes and shakedowns, as fighters turn to roadblocks and extortion as a form of sustenance or enrichment. This adds to the broader collapse in purchasing power, driven by damage to businesses, and high rates of inflation.

By August 2018, 57 per cent of the population of Ta'izz governorate was ranked as being at IPC Phase 3 or higher, with 10,500 facing famine.[179] IPC estimated that the numbers would have been higher without humanitarian assistance. Even the December 2020 IPC assessment found that 41 per cent of the population were still in IPC Phase 3 or higher, with nearly 12 per cent, or 379,000, in IPC Phase 4.[180] Similar to the case of Al-Hudaydah, the belligerents in Ta'izz have generally

[177] Human Rights Council, *Situation of human rights in Yemen*, see note 82, at 82, §347.

[178] Sana'a Center for Strategic Studies, *The Yemen Review: War's Elusive End* (2019), available online at <https://sanaacenter.org/files/TYR_Annual_2019_en.pdf> (visited 26 August 2021), at 54.

[179] IPC, 'Yemen—IPC Acute Food Insecurity Analysis: December 2018–January 2019', see note 46, at 2.

[180] IPC, 'Yemen: Acute Food Insecurity Situation October–December 2020 and Projection for January–June 2021', see note 168.

disregarded the effect of their actions on the civilian population, while the Houthis have specifically targeted the civilian population through their siege.

8. Conclusion

Determining intent and assigning culpability for mass starvation is rarely straightforward. In most famines, the intent of protagonists shifts over time, and multiple motives and degrees of culpability may co-exist.[181] This exercise is especially complicated and imprecise in the context of the economic strategies utilized for waging war. First, war brings economic pressures and distortions, which in themselves demand exceptional policy responses. For example, war expenditure demands either borrowing or forced savings, often in the form of cutbacks in expenditure by states/governments, though this holds true for households as well. This has redistributive and/or inflationary impacts and which can increase inequality and/or poverty. Choosing where these burdens fall is a political choice, but one not normally regarded as potentially criminal. Second, there are direct economic weapons of war such as blockade (which is not unlawful *per se*) or the collateral destruction of objects necessary/essential for subsistence (which may include OIS). Third, restrictions on trade (such as trade in arms and other military supplies) can have knock-on effects on civilian well-being, for example by slowing down normal commerce. Fourth, tools of economic warfare such as blockade, currency manipulation, or the expropriation of assets generate secondary effects, such as the emergence of shadow economies of smugglers and profiteers, freelance mercenaryism, and collusion of commanders across frontlines—economic war creates a war economy. The combination of economic warfare and a war economy creates winners as well as losers; it not only impoverishes but redistributes. In the process it creates immense human suffering.

In this context, it is necessary to take into account the overall circumstances of the conflict and the economy, in order to determine what economic actions may be regarded as unlawful. Notably, when a belligerent party with control over economic and financial institutions (in the Yemen case, the IRG and SLC's control over one of the Central Banks of Yemen) makes economic policy choices that target the suffering on a particular population, which is also at the same time being targeted by other more direct measures such as military blockade and aerial bombardment targeting OIS, then it is probably fair to conclude that general economic policy is being designed and implemented to starve a population. There are also strong indications that the SLC has used the destruction of OIS as a specific way of conducting

[181] de Waal, see note 7 at 107.

hostilities, suggestive of the intentional use of starvation of civilians. For their part, the Houthis have used siege warfare (and adopted other tactics of war) without regard to the impact on civilians. They have also diverted and sought to control humanitarian aid while being aware of the humanitarian situation in areas under their control.

In addition to these, cases of bombing hospitals, and of the brief total maritime blockade prohibiting humanitarian aid are arguably the clearest cases of unlawful actions. They are likely to demonstrate the criminal intent of the perpetrators and some are clear cases of violations of international humanitarian law. Grave though they are as crimes, they only form part of the broader context of actions which have caused mass starvation in Yemen.

In closing, it is worth touching on the question we asked at the beginning of the chapter: how and to what extent are the different actors in Yemen responsible for famine and mass starvation? The answer, unequivocally, is that all the primary protagonists in the war are culpable (albeit to different degrees) of pursuing policies which are responsible for causing famine. More importantly, the belligerents are guilty of ignoring the evidence that their policies have created, inflicted, and prolonged the starvation of significant numbers of Yemenis.

10

Prosecution of Starvation in South Sudan

Wayne Jordash QC and Uzay Yasar Aysev

1. Introduction

Despite its relatively longstanding prohibition under conventional and customary international humanitarian law (IHL), the war crime of starvation has never been charged and prosecuted as a distinct crime internationally. This is mostly due to the purported complexity of the crime and the perceived challenges related to establishing its elements. Indeed, proving beyond reasonable doubt that an accused deprived civilians of objects indispensable for their survival (OIS) as a method of warfare with the intention to starve them may be a daunting task for a prosecutor. Starvation often takes place in multi-causal environments where alternative viable explanations may coexist as to why and how the deprivations occurred. Accused may claim that the deprivation of OIS occurred due to proportional collateral damage caused by a lawful attack on military objectives or was justified by military necessity since the objects in question were used by enemy combatants. They may even deny responsibility altogether by referring to the inevitable effects of warfare on food security, the co-occurrence of natural disasters or macro-economic realities as the reasons behind the ensuing starvation. Put simply, the prosecutor's task of disproving alternative explanations and removing reasonable doubt may well seem more formidable than for other crimes.

This chapter will examine strategies for prosecuting the war crime of starvation, building upon IHL prohibition against deliberate starvation[1] and the subject matter jurisdiction that the International Criminal Court (ICC) has over the war crime of starvation under Article 8 of the Rome Statute. Notwithstanding the available legal framework, there is no international jurisprudence on the war crime of starvation, meaning that developing strategies for prosecuting it remains a matter of foresight, not precedent. In situations of starvation, it is, thus, understandable that prosecutors opt for more familiar charges, crimes whose legal contours have

[1] Protocol Additional to the Geneva Conventions of 12 August 1949, and relating to the Protection of Victims of International Armed Conflicts (8 June 1977) 1125 UNTS 3 (hereafter AP I) Art. 54; Protocol Additional to the Geneva Conventions of 12 August 1949, and relating to the Protection of Victims of Non-International Armed Conflicts (8 June 1977) 1125 UNTS 609 (hereafter AP II) Art. 14.

Wayne Jordash QC and Uzay Yasar Aysev, *Prosecution of Starvation in South Sudan* In: *Accountability for Mass Starvation*. Edited by: Bridget Conley, Alex de Waal, Catriona Murdoch, and Wayne Jordash QC, Oxford University Press.
 DOI: 10.1093/oso/9780192864734.003.0010

been established in the jurisprudence (such as, *inter alia*, genocide, murder, other inhumane acts, cruel and inhuman treatment, deportation/forcible transfer, persecution, pillage)[2] rather than adventurously attempting to pursue a novel and, so far, unprecedented prosecution of the war crime of starvation.

With the aim of shifting this perspective and placing the war crime of starvation within the charging repertoire of domestic and international prosecutors, in this chapter we will explore how the war crime of starvation could be prosecuted, drawing on analogy, principle, and experience. Our focus, for context, is on South Sudan. Our view is that while pleading starvation as a war crime does indeed present a complex set of legal and evidentiary challenges, they do not necessarily go above and beyond those posed by other similarly complex crimes (such as persecution, genocide, and forced displacement). In examining this, we will assess the potential issues that may arise in proving the war crime of starvation in South Sudan in light of the documented facts and will discuss how prosecutors may address these issues. In trying to foresee the way ahead, we will examine issues of scale and whether for practical reasons, rather than a technical legal requirement, it will be easier to prove the *mens rea* to starve where starvation is widespread. Although in many cases this will be true, viable prosecutions for starvation are by no means confined to large-scale and widespread occurrences of starvation. In demonstrating this, we set out some examples where the intention to starve might be established in incidents involving discrete, individualized, or relatively small-scale starvation.

International criminal courts and tribunals are by and large mandated to investigate and prosecute those most responsible for atrocity crimes. As such, we will also examine how the application of appropriate modes of liability can enable prosecutors to pursue not just the ground-level perpetrators but the decision-makers responsible for deliberately starving civilian populations, including senior military and political leaders. Specifically, we will discuss important considerations and challenges which might arise in building a viable starvation prosecution, and possible approaches thereto, including:

(i) Identifying the instances of deprivation of OIS in South Sudan, that is the *actus reus* of the offence. This will involve predominantly a 'crime-base' analysis;

[2] See for instance Judgment, *Seromba*, (ICTR-2001-66-I), Trial Chamber, 13 December 2006, § 327 (hereafter *Seromba*); Closing Order, *Nuon Chea, Ieng Sary, Khieu Samphan, and Thirith Ieng*, (Case 002), D427, Office of the Co-Investigating Judges, 15 September 2010, §§ 338–342 (hereafter *Nuon Chea et al.*); Judgement, *Delalić et al.*, (IT-96-21-T), Trial Chamber, 16 November 1998, §§ 1113–1119 (hereafter *Delalić et al.*); Judgement, *Tolimir*, (IT05-88/2-T), Trial Chamber, 12 December 2012, § 830 (hereafter *Tolimir*); Judgment, *Krnojelac*, (IT-97-25-T), Trial Chamber II, 15 March 2002, §§ 442–443 (hereafter *Krnojelac*); Judgement, *Hadzihasanović & Kubura*, (IT-01-47-A), Appeals Chamber 22 April 2008, § 1875 (hereafter *Hadzihasanović & Kubura*).

(ii) Establishing a perpetrator's intention to starve civilians as a method of warfare through direct and indirect evidence in South Sudan; and
(iii) Pinpointing the modes of liability that might be the most suitable in pursuing senior and remote defendants for the commission of the war crime of starvation in South Sudan. This is what is well known in International Criminal Law (ICL) as the 'linkage' component of the case.

This chapter will tie legal and evidentiary considerations to facts, demonstrate how the challenges of proving starvation may be met, and illustrate how the various components of a case can be meshed together to form a single viable prosecution. To meet these aims, we have found it more constructive to focus on a single conflict: the recent civil war in South Sudan. Our focus on South Sudan is for the following reasons. First, at the time of writing, South Sudan is facing one of the most acute situations of food insecurity in the world, which *prima facie* evidence suggests has been caused amongst other things by the use of starvation as a method of warfare in the course of the civil war.[3] The situation in South Sudan shares features with food insecurity in other contexts such as the variety of causes for it, both natural and deliberate, whilst at the same time exhibiting features that are less common amongst other situations of food insecurity, such as the pastoral livelihoods system upon which many rural South Sudanese communities depend, which appear to have been targeted as a method of warfare. This makes South Sudan an interesting case study to ascertain the potential challenges that prosecutors may face in prosecuting starvation as a war crime in other contexts where there are credible allegations regarding its commission, such as Yemen and Syria.[4] Furthermore, there is an ongoing impetus for transitional justice in South Sudan. In September 2018, the Transitional Government renewed its commitment to the establishment of the Hybrid Court of South Sudan with the cooperation of the African Union which will have jurisdiction over international crimes, including war crimes.[5] With the governmental approval of January 2021,[6] the Hybrid Court represents a realistic chance for the investigation and prosecution of the commission of the war

[3] *Report of the Commission on Human Rights in South Sudan*, UN Doc. A/HRC/43/56, 31 January 2020, §§ 69–71 (hereafter HRC 'January 2020 Report of the Commission on Human Rights in South Sudan'); see Chapter 8 in this volume.

[4] Human Rights Council, 'Situation of human rights in Yemen, including violations and abuses since September 2014' in *Report of the Group of Eminent International and Regional Experts as submitted to the United Nations High Commissioner for Human Rights*, A/HRC/42/17, 9 August 2019, (hereafter HRC 'Situation of human rights in Yemen'), §§ 96(b)–(d); Independent International Commission of Inquiry on the Syrian Arab Republic, 'Sieges as a Weapon of War: Encircle, Starve, Surrender, Evacuate', 29 May 2018, hereafter OHCRC 'Siege Policy Paper'), §7.

[5] Human Rights Council, *'There is nothing left for us': starvation as a method of warfare in South Sudan', Conference room paper of the Commission on Human Rights in South Sudan*, A/HRC/45/CRP.3, 5 October 2020 (hereafter HRC 'Conference room paper'), § 43.

[6] N. Tut Pur, *A Glimmer of Hope for South Sudan's Victims*, Human Rights Watch (2021), available online at <https://www.hrw.org/news/2021/01/31/glimmer-hope-south-sudans-victims> (visited 9 September 2021).

crime of starvation in South Sudan before an internationalized tribunal. Whilst acknowledging the weighty political obstacles still standing in the way of meaningful accountability in South Sudan, it is our hope that through our input into how a viable prosecution might work, the way ahead will become easier to foresee. Notwithstanding the focus on South Sudan, however, we have endeavoured, where possible, to draw comparisons with other situations in order to assist prosecutors looking to address instances of deliberate starvation in different contexts.

2. Identifying Instances of Deprivation of OIS in South Sudan

The first step of any prosecution of the war crime of starvation in South Sudan should be to establish its *actus reus*, that is the crime base. In order to do this, prosecutors must be able to prove beyond reasonable doubt that '[t]he perpetrator deprived civilians of [OIS]'.[7] Generally speaking, OIS include 'foodstuffs, agricultural areas for the production of foodstuffs, crops, livestock, drinking water installations and supplies and irrigation works'[8] as well as medical supplies,[9] means of shelter,[10] fuel and electricity.[11] In principle, however, any object that is required for sustenance of civilians in a particular context may qualify as OIS.[12] In rural or urban contexts, and across the range of livelihood systems of civilians (e.g. smallholder farming, pastoralism, fishing, wage labour), and the fall-back coping options open to people in times of crisis, the factors threatening survival, and, thus, the objects that may qualify as OIS differ. Accordingly, in establishing this element, prosecutors should first focus on understanding and demonstrating the livelihood systems and coping strategies of civilians, as well as the principal factors which threaten their survival in the relevant context. This contextual assessment will underpin the contours of the definition of OIS in a given fact pattern.

Having established that the objects in question constituted OIS, the next step is to prove that the perpetrators deprived civilians of such objects. Deprivation occurs if civilians are restricted from accessing/using OIS, for instance, by acts such as attacking, destroying, removing objects, rendering them useless for the civilians,

7 Art. 8(2)(b)(xxv), Element 1, Elements of Crimes (2011).

8 AP I (n 1), Art. 54(2).

9 K. Dörmann, L. Doswald-Beck, and R. Kolb, *Elements Of War Crimes Under The Rome Statute Of The International Criminal Court* (Cambridge: Cambridge University Press, 2003), at 475; see also Geneva Convention Relative to the Protection of Civilian Persons in Time of War, 12 August 1949, 75 UNTS 287 Art. 59, which is considered to be part of customary international law applicable also in NIACs (ICRC Customary International Law Study, Rule 55: Access to Humanitarian Relief to Civilians in Need); see also GC IV, Art. 23 which includes 'clothing and tonics intended for children under fifteen, expectant mothers and maternity cases'.

10 AP I, Art. 69.

11 C. Pilloud et al., *Commentary on The Additional Protocols Of 8 June 1977 to the Geneva Conventions of 12 August 1949* (Geneva: International Committee of the Red Cross, 1987), § 2101.

12 ICRC, *Commentary on The Additional Protocols*, see note 11, §§ 2102–2103.

restricting access to them,[13] or omitting to ensure that civilians have access to such objects.[14] One specific way that perpetrators may deprive civilians of OIS which often draws a high level of international attention is by wilfully impeding relief supplies. This is expressly provided for in the Rome Statute definition of the crime, as an illustrative way in which deprivations of OIS may be established.[15] Given the range of ways in which these deprivations may be perpetrated, the war crime of starvation (similar, for instance, to genocide, forced displacement, or persecution) is an 'open conduct' or 'umbrella' crime, where various acts or omissions that ultimately deprive civilians of OIS may satisfy the *actus reus* of the crime.[16] Accordingly, prosecutors should be open to the possibility that perpetrators may have used a range of different methods in depriving civilians of OIS, which is also likely to be context-specific. In Yemen, for instance, airstrikes have commonly been used to target OIS, whereas in South Sudan, in the absence of an airborne capability, the preferred method has been to burn agricultural fields and pillage/destroy foodstuffs and livestock and water facilities.

There is *prima facie* evidence that indicates that access to food and other vital OIS has been undermined in South Sudan by the actions and strategies of the government forces (including the Sudan People's Liberation Army (SPLA)[17] and affiliated militia) as well as, to a lesser extent, opposition forces.[18] The available information reveals that civilians were deprived of OIS by government forces during the attacks that took place in various parts of South Sudan in the course of the 2013 civil war, including the Western Bahr el-Ghazal State, Jonglei State, and Unity State. This was done through the destruction and pillaging of villages, food supplies (including agricultural produce and livestock), agricultural fields, markets, water pumps, and hospitals and medicine stores belonging to civilians.[19] Such acts may constitute the war crime of starvation or be prosecuted separately as war crimes of pillaging and destruction/seizing of property of an adversary.[20]

[13] OIS may be rendered useless if the activities that utilize them are inhibited, such as farming, movement to and from agricultural land, markets, and pastoral camps, livestock migrations, and movement for collecting natural resources like cooking fuel and wild foods. See Chapter 8 in this volume.

[14] Art. 8(2)(b)(xxv) ICC Rome Statute (last amended 2010) (1998)

[15] Art. 8(2)(b)(xxv) Rome Statute.

[16] Decision on the Confirmation of Charges Pursuant to Article 61(7)(a) and (b) of the Rome Statute, c.f. *Ruto et al.*, (ICC-01/0910/11), Pre-Trial Chamber II, 4 February 2012, § 244; Decision on the Prosecution's Request for a Ruling on Jurisdiction under Article 19(3) of the Statute (ICC-RoC46(3)-01/18), Pre-Trial Chamber I, 6 September 2018, § 61.

[17] Through the Republican Order No. 18/2018 issued on 2 October 2018, SPLA's name was changed to South Sudan People's Defence Forces (SSPDF). For the sake of consistency, the authors will refer to the government forces as SPLA. HRC 'Conference room paper', see note 5, § 9, fn. 15.

[18] HRC 'January 2020 Report of the Commission on Human Rights in South Sudan', see note 3, Annex II, § 40.

[19] HRC 'January 2020 Report of the Commission on Human Rights in South Sudan', see note 3, § 42 and § 97; OHCHR *The State of Human Rights in the Protracted Conflict in South Sudan*, 4 December 2015, (hereafter OHCHR, UNMISS Report), at 1; *Report of the Commission on Human Rights in South Sudan*, A/HRC/40/CRP.1, 21 February 2019, (hereafter HRC 'February 2019 Report the Commission on Human Rights in South Sudan'), §§ 145–146.

[20] See Art. 8(2)(e)(v) and (xii) Rome St.

Another manner in which civilians were deprived of OIS was through rural besiegement. During their operations in the Greater Baggari (Wau County, Western Bahr el Ghazal State), government forces imposed extreme movement restrictions on the civilian population, effectively preventing their return to the areas from which they were displaced and, thus, their livelihood systems.[21] Further, government forces imposed arbitrary, unjustified, and systematic restrictions on the movement and activities of humanitarian organizations (including by attacking and pillaging their facilities and supplies)[22] and traders who transported vital foodstuffs and medicine into areas where tens of thousands of civilians were in dire need of humanitarian supplies.[23] There is also evidence indicating that the opposition forces (i.e. Sudanese Liberation Movement in Opposition led by Riek Machar—SPLA-IO (RM)) interfered with the activities of international humanitarian aid organizations that delivered vital nutrition and health services to communities in need in Central Equatoria.[24] As discussed above, this is expressly provided in the Rome Statute as a means by which the deprivation of OIS may be completed, (echoing the position in IHL).[25] The cumulative effect of all these policies and attacks was the displacement of hundreds of thousands of civilians into the bush where they remained for months without access to adequate food, potable water, or medicine.[26] Since the overwhelming majority of its population depend on farming, fishing, or herding to meet their food and income needs, the consequences of the displacement were catastrophic in terms of food security in South Sudan.[27]

Deprivation of OIS manifests itself somewhat differently in more urbanized contexts where significant parts of the population are dependent upon the formal cash economy. For instance, in Yemen, where agricultural production covers a relatively smaller proportion of the livelihood of civilians,[28] deprivations of OIS have been perpetrated through targeted attacks directed against urban civilian objects (rather than looting/destruction of villages and agricultural produce and economic warfare in the form of blockades). In relation to the former, the underlying criminal acts there included indiscriminate shelling, aerial bombardment, and mortar attacks against markets or shops, medical facilities,[29] food processing factories, and infrastructure related to generation and supply of electricity and water, as well as agricultural objects (including farmlands, irrigation facilities, and artisanal fishing establishments).[30] Furthermore, blockades and restrictions imposed

[21] See Chapter 7, this volume.
[22] HRC 'Conference room paper', see note 5, §§ 99–100.
[23] HRC 'Conference room paper', §§ 68, 101, and 107; see Chapter 8 in this volume.
[24] HRC 'Conference room paper', see note 5,§§ 128–129.
[25] Art. 8(2)(b)(xxv) Rome St.; ICRC Customary International Law Study, Rule 53: Starvation as a Method of Warfare.
[26] HRC 'Conference room paper', see note 5, §§ 59–60, 96
[27] HRC 'Conference room paper', § 15; HRC 'February 2019 Report the Commission on Human Rights in South Sudan', see note 19, §§ 152–157.
[28] See Chapter 9 in this volume.
[29] See Chapter 9 in this volume at 217.
[30] See Chapter 9 in this volume at 217.

by the Saudi-led coalition on naval and airports in Yemen appear to have also led to significant disruptions in the supply of food and medical supplies, humanitarian aid, and fuel imports.[31]

In Syria, on the other hand, the war crime of starvation manifested itself during the sieges laid by the governmental forces and armed opposition groups to various urban population centres.[32] During these sieges, approximately 2.2 million civilians were encircled, trapped, and routinely deprived of vital foodstuffs, health items, other essential supplies such as gas, water, and electricity, and humanitarian aid.[33] The besieged civilians experienced deprivation from two directions. On the one hand, sieging forces cut supply flow into the sieged areas and carried out targeted attacks against hospitals, medical facilities, bakeries, and communal kitchens.[34] On the other hand, the armed forces within the sieged areas 'confiscated or hid food items to distribute them preferentially to those within their ranks, their family members and confidants rather than the civilian population at large'.[35] These variations in the manner in which civilians have been deprived of OIS in rural South Sudanese civilian populations compared with the urban Syrian and Yemeni populations underscores the significance of understanding the context, particularly the livelihood systems, in demonstrating how the deprivation of OIS occurred.

3. Proving the Intention to Starve as a Method of Warfare in South Sudan

The second element of the war crime of starvation requires prosecutors to prove that '[t]he perpetrator intended to starve civilians as a method of warfare'. To satisfy this element, prosecutors must prove beyond reasonable doubt that the perpetrator (1) used starvation as a method of warfare,[36] and, in doing so, (2) either directly intended to starve civilians *or* was aware that his/her conduct, in the ordinary course of events, would lead to the starvation of civilians.[37]

A. The Use of Starvation as a Method of Warfare in South Sudan

To prove that the perpetrator used starvation as a method of warfare, prosecutors must prove that he/she deprived civilians of OIS as part of the overall military

[31] See Chapter 9 in this volume at 217.
[32] *Report of the Independent International Commission of Inquiry on the Syrian Arab Republic*, A/HRC/46/54, 21 January 2021, § 45.
[33] See Chapter 8 in this volume, at; OHCRC 'Siege Policy Paper', see note 4, § 9.
[34] OHCRC 'Siege Policy Paper', see note 4, § 9; and Chapter 8 in this volume, 195.
[35] OHCRC 'Siege Policy Paper', see note 4, § 2.
[36] Chapter 5 in this volume, at 107.
[37] Chapter 5 in this volume, at 107.

endeavour and as 'a specific, tactical or strategic way of conducting hostilities'.[38] In establishing this element, as demonstrated in Chapter 5, it would be sufficient, though not necessary, to prove that the perpetrator used starvation with the purpose of overwhelming and weakening the adversary. This would be the case, for instance, if the perpetrators deprived civilians of OIS in the course of their military operations with the purpose of improving their military capabilities or gaining military advantage.[39] Conversely, deprivations of OIS that do not qualify as a method of warfare will not suffice to establish this element. For instance, certain factors such as flooding and other forms of climatic adversity, poor macro-economic conditions, economic crimes,[40] and the consequent socio-economic inequality, extreme levels of poverty, and lack of access to essential services have significantly contributed to some instances of starvation in South Sudan.[41] While these factors or the failure to respond to hardship caused by these factors could potentially be considered within the remit of the individual responsibility of South Sudanese government officials and might be relevant for determining the existence, nature or scope of any acts alleged to constitute a method of warfare, they are likely not to be considered themselves as a method of warfare.

Indeed, macro-economic decisions taken in the ordinary course of state governance that led to deprivations of OIS could not be considered as methods of warfare, unless a sufficient nexus between such decisions and the conduct of hostilities could be established. If it can be proven that the perpetrator weaponized macro-economic processes as a strategic/tactical way of conducting hostilities to deprive civilians of OIS, the actions of the decision-makers may arguably qualify as starving civilians as a method of warfare. Suspending the provision of essential services (such as the provision of food assistance or medical services) in opposition-controlled areas in order to put pressure on their military may be such an example. For instance, the cutting of gas, electricity, and water in the besieged cities and towns of Syria may be regarded as depriving fighters and civilians alike of OIS as a method of warfare,[42] rather than *bona fide* economic measures necessitated by the war.

There are a number of reports that provide *prima facie* evidence indicating that starvation was used as a method of war in the course of the civil war in South Sudan.[43] They indicate that between January 2017 and November 2018, government forces carried out a series of attacks to dislodge the SPLA-IO forces from the

[38] Chapter 5 in this volume, at 107.
[39] Chapter 5 in this volume, at 107.
[40] That is, corruption in the form of tax evasion, money laundering, bribery, using one's position to influence decisions in the allocation of state resources, using public funds for personal gain and advantage.
[41] HRC 'Conference room paper', see note 5, § 14; HRC 'January 2020 Report of the Commission on Human Rights in South Sudan', see note 3, § 33.
[42] Chapter 8 in this volume, at 195; OHCRC 'Siege Policy Paper', see note 4, § 9.
[43] HRC 'January 2020 Report of the Commission on Human Rights in South Sudan' see note 3, § 54.

Wau Triangle in the Western Bahr el Ghazal State, moving from one opposition-controlled town/village to another, murdering civilians, carrying out sexual violence, destroying and pillaging OIS, and, consequently, forcing the civilian population to flee.[44] In Wau, the commission of atrocities appears to have increased considerably following the arrival of the new 5 Division SPLA Commander on 5 June 2018 to lead government forces.[45] Government forces systematically deprived civilians living in these areas of critical resources by raiding villages, and pillaging and destroying OIS including civilian homes and agricultural produce, and blocking the provision of vital humanitarian aid.[46] The areas attacked by government forces comprised primarily Fertit and Luo minority groups deemed by the government as being aligned with the opposition.[47]

Similar patterns can be observed in the Jonglei State during government attacks against opposition-controlled areas. According to reports, in February 2017, governmental forces led by a Lieutenant General of the SPLA Division 1 'embarked on a brutal campaign in Yuai Town [in Uror County, Jonglei State], attacking the civilian population and destroying the town including through the pillaging and destruction of civilian property'.[48] Reportedly, government forces set fire to civilian homes, razed crops that civilians had harvested and stored, and looted cattle.[49] As a consequence, civilians fled towards nearby towns.[50] As they fled, government forces chased and fired at them.[51] Only those who were willing to side with the government remained behind.[52] In the same month, government forces attacked opposition-controlled Waat village in Uror County, opening fire on civilians and forcing them to flee.[53] Government forces also destroyed hospitals, medicine stores and beds, civilian houses, crop stocks, and pillaged the compounds of four international non-governmental organizations (NGOs), stealing their generators, vehicles, and food stores.[54] By April 2017, government forces had established control in the area. In Akobo County, Jonglei State, government forces (SPLA Eighth Division) systematically and arbitrarily denied access to humanitarian actors as

[44] Starting with the Wau Town (June 2016) and then moving to Wadhalelo payam Jur County (January 2017–June 2018), Mboro Town and Ngozili (June–September 2018), Ngo Pere (September 2018), Ngoko Village (October 2018), Tagoti Vimoi Village (November 2018). See HRC 'Conference room paper', note 5, § 56.

[45] HRC 'February 2019 Report the Commission on Human Rights in South Sudan', see note 19, §§ 811–813.

[46] HRC 'Conference room paper', see note 5, §§ 9, 74, and 79.

[47] HRC 'January 2020 Report of the Commission on Human Rights in South Sudan', see note 3, Annex II, § 49; HRC 'Conference room paper', see note 5, § 53.

[48] HRC 'Conference room paper', see note 5, para. 97.

[49] HRC 'January 2020 Report of the Commission on Human Rights in South Sudan', see note 3, Annex II, § 49; HRC 'Conference room paper', see note 5, § 97.

[50] HRC 'Conference room paper', see note 5, § 98.

[51] HRC 'Conference room paper', see note 5, § 98.

[52] HRC 'Conference room paper', see note 5, § 98.

[53] HRC 'Conference room paper', see note 5, § 99.

[54] HRC 'Conference room paper', see note 5, § 100.

well as traders who attempted to bring vital foodstuffs and medicine into the area, in some instances looting such objects.[55]

Lastly, in Unity State, the government forces (SPLA Fourth Division) launched several military offensives between 2014 and 2018 against opposition-controlled areas.[56] During the 2015 offensive, the government appears to have pursued a scorched-earth policy designed to displace the civilian population in parts of the Unity State permanently and forcibly.[57] The UN characterized the situation as follows:

> From the middle of 2015, a new pattern emerged, particularly in central and southern countries of Unity, with entire villages being burned down, food crops destroyed and livestock looted. There are indications that this may have been a deliberate strategy by the government or the SPLA aimed at depriving civilians of any source of livelihood with a view to force their displacement.[58]

The UN assessed that the fundamental purpose of these military operations was to 'retake geographic areas considered critical to the survival of the incumbent regime, including the state capital and oil installations'.[59] This was to be achieved by 'annihilating ... the opposition's support base [through the] systematic destruction of villages and towns, forcing people into the [UN Protection of Civilians] sites and creating an "empty area" across the main transport axes in Central and Southern Unity'.[60] During the 2018 offensive (which lasted during the cultivation season from mid-April to June), government forces were reported to have employed the same scorched-earth tactics, through 'complete village destruction, stripping whatever assets remained to be found ... killing a large number of civilians and displacing others'.[61] The United Nations Commission on Human Rights in South Sudan (UNCHRSS) reported a 'pervasive pattern of armed forces and armed groups attacking villages, looting people's crops and animals' in Leer and Mayendit Counties.[62] Government forces, including the SPLA Fourth Division, SPLA-IO (TD),[63] and militia from Koch County attacked at least forty towns and villages,

[55] HRC 'Conference room paper', see note 5, §§ 103–107.

[56] HRC 'February 2019 Report the Commission on Human Rights in South Sudan', see note 19, § 693.

[57] Chapter 8 in this volume, at 195; HRC, 'February 2019 Report the Commission on Human Rights in South Sudan', see note 19, § 734.

[58] Chapter 8 in this volume, at 195; OHCHR, UNMISS Report, see note 19, at 1.

[59] Chapter 8 in this volume, at 195.

[60] Chapter 8 in this volume, at 195; *Letter dated 21 August 2015 from the Panel of Experts on South Sudan established pursuant to Security Council resolution 2206 (2015) addressed to the President of the Security Council*, S/2015/656, 21 August 2015, at 37.

[61] Chapter 8 in this volume, at 195.

[62] HRC 'February 2019 Report the Commission on Human Rights in South Sudan', see note 19, § 145.

[63] SPLA-IO (TD) is an armed group formed under Taban Deng Gai's leadership after it split from Riek Machar's SPLA-IO (henceforth SPLA-IO (RM)) after Deng Gai was appointed as First Vice President of South Sudan following the ceasefire of 11 July 2016. From then on, SPLA-IO (TD) fought forces loyal to Riek Machar and carried out operations in Western Bahr el Ghazal and Jonglei States.

targeting civilians with 'astonishing brutality'[64] and carrying out killings, rapes, beatings, abductions, looting, and destruction of property.[65]

These are the type of factual patterns that any putative prosecutor could use as means of establishing the use of starvation as a method of warfare in South Sudan, at least by the government forces, (and maybe also the opposing forces).[66] The incidents described above appear to reveal a pattern of conduct that suggests that government forces specifically and deliberately deprived civilians of OIS (through the destruction and pillage of civilian property and the blocking of humanitarian access) during their military operations against opposition-controlled areas. Assessing a range of these incidents, UNCHRSS concluded that '[d]enying access to food was used as an instrument to target and punish communities perceived to be non-aligned and supportive of the opposition while rewarding Government soldiers by allowing them to retain provisions stolen and looted from these communities'.[67] This was a result of deliberate policies 'envisaged and implemented as part of a wider strategy to deprive enemy communities of resources and thus force their capitulation, allow soldiers and militias to reward themselves ... or simply to compel individuals to join different factions engaged in the conflict'.[68] The context in which civilians were deprived of OIS (including to reward troops, to conscript recruits, and to weaken or displace communities perceived as enemies) is highly likely to be sufficient to establish that deprivations of OIS were linked to the hostilities and, thus, used as a method of warfare by government forces.

B. Demonstrating the Intention to Starve

The most challenging aspect of the prosecution of the war crime of starvation in South Sudan (or more generally) will likely be proving the perpetrator's intention to starve civilians. As discussed in Chapter 5, the intent requirement of the war crime of starvation can be established either by proving that the perpetrator directly intended to starve civilians *or* was aware that starvation would occur in the ordinary course of events due to his/her conduct.[69] Depending on the availability of evidence, this can either be done by direct or indirect (circumstantial) evidence (not to be confused with direct and indirect intent, which are alternative legal standards both amounting to intent).

[64] *Report of the Commission on Human Rights in South Sudan*', A/HRC/40/69, 12 March 2019 (hereafter HRC 'March 2019 Report of the Commission on Human Rights in South Sudan'), § 69.

[65] HRC 'March 2019 Report of the Commission on Human Rights in South Sudan', see note 64, § 73; HRC 'February 2019 Report the Commission on Human Rights in South Sudan', see note 19, §§ 714–715.

[66] See also HRC 'January 2020 Report of the Commission on Human Rights in South Sudan', see note 3, § 70, and Annex II, § 42.

[67] HRC 'Conference room paper' see note 5, § 88 and § 123.

[68] HRC 'January 2020 Report of the Commission on Human Rights in South Sudan', see note 3, § 70 and Annex II, § 42.

[69] See Chapter 5 in this volume, at 107.

For instance, insider witnesses (those who once operated within the political or military/security forces) could provide direct evidence of the accused's intention to execute a plan/policy to starve civilians and/or his/her knowledge that their conduct would cause civilians to starve in the ordinary course of events. Such evidence may encompass the oral orders passed or words uttered by the perpetrator during meetings or otherwise in the execution of their functions. Documentary or digital evidence in the form of written orders, meeting notes, internal memorandums, or transcripts/audio-visual recordings of speeches may also be relied on as direct evidence. For instance, in Syria the images of regime soldiers spraying graffiti close to checkpoints calling on the opposition to 'surrender or starve' in numerous areas that they laid siege to (known as the 'kneel or starve' strategy) amounts to direct evidence of an intention to starve. While, for the time being, there does not appear to be any similar direct evidence in the public domain capable of proving an intent to starve civilians in South Sudan, such evidence may be expected to surface during investigations conducted by professional investigators and/or after the conflict has ended.

Indirect evidence could also be relied on to prove the perpetrator's intention or knowledge. Such evidence could be gathered through an examination of the circumstances surrounding the deprivations of OIS. Through such examination, prosecutors may be able to piece together the perpetrator's intention to starve civilians or knowledge that it would happen in the ordinary course of events if certain conduct was pursued or repeated. This is likely to pose certain investigative challenges. The evidence is likely to include alternative viable explanations, which sit somewhat at odds with evidence tending towards establishing an intention to starve. This is especially so in multi-causal environments such as South Sudan where various military purposes (lawful or unlawful) are likely to coexist and overlap.[70] For instance, deprivations could have occurred as a collateral consequence of otherwise lawful military activity or during the pursuit of other objectives, criminal or lawful, that led to starvation.[71] The perpetrator may also claim that the appropriation of OIS was necessary for provisioning the armed forces, which is permissible under IHL if certain strict conditions are met.[72] Dispelling these justifications in South Sudan will require an analysis of the factual patterns and a grasp of the competing narratives so that any intention to starve on the part of the perpetrator can be disentangled and properly tracked and evidenced. As detailed in

[70] See Chapter 5 in this volume, at 107.

[71] It should be noted that perpetrators may harbour a range of objectives or intentions simultaneously, some criminal others lawful. As long as it can be shown, however, that an intention to starve civilians as a method of warfare was present, the existence of other intentions is immaterial. See Chapter 5 in this volume; W. Jordash, C. Murdoch, and J. Holmes, 'Strategies or Prosecuting Mass Starvation', 17 *Journal of International Criminal Justice* (2019) 849–879, at 871–872.

[72] IHL allows for the appropriation of property if it is justified by military necessity. For instance, according to the Hague Regulations, forcible contribution of money requisition for the needs of the occupying army and seizure of material obviously related to the conduct of military operations, though restricted, are lawful in principle. Further, a party to the conflict may also seize enemy military equipment captured or found on the battlefield or private property that could be used directly for military purposes as war booty. For the latter, the appropriating party must give out receipts in exchange for the

Chapter 5, this should be done in a systematic way, including by showing: (1) that the perpetrator's acts or omissions caused the deprivation of OIS; (2) the manner in which the deprivations of OIS occurred; (3) the lack of any respect for positive IHL obligations and any failure to take concrete steps to alleviate civilian suffering; and (4) the suspect's awareness of the risk that the deprivations of OIS would likely lead to starvation in the ordinary course of events.[73] An evaluation of the available evidence in South Sudan in line with these considerations appears to be indicative (on *prima facie* basis) of the existence of an intention to starve on the part of the perpetrators. Repeated direct attacks, destruction, theft, and blockages of OIS with no obvious justification or attempt to ameliorate obvious harm and widespread suffering speaks eloquently to relevant intent. Other essentials and/or indications are discussed in the following sections.

1. Proving that the Acts of the Perpetrator Caused the Deprivations of OIS

As noted in Chapter 5, whilst there is no legal requirement to prove that deprivations of OIS, in fact, caused a civilian population to starve, linking deprivations of OIS to the starvation of the population will be indicative of the intention to starve on the part of the perpetrators.[74] Accordingly, prosecutors should look to establish that deprivations of OIS did in fact cause starvation, even though it is not a legal requirement. In doing this, prosecutors will first have to distinguish between deliberate deprivation and starvation perpetrated by the perpetrators and that which occurred due to factors beyond their control, including natural causes. Whilst destroying agricultural facilities belonging to civilians who are already food insecure due to natural causes may very well imply an intention to starve on the part of the perpetrators, it will be important to establish that the destruction constitutes a significant cause of the starvation. A granular analysis is required: the destruction of agricultural facilities of little import is one thing; quite another if they are the sole source of food for a village.[75]

In various parts of South Sudan, significant loss of agricultural produce occurred towards the latter parts of the civil war due to abnormally heavy rains, high levels of seasonal flooding (in Jonglei), and droughts.[76] These natural disasters, partly

property and return it/provide compensation for it to the owner upon the termination of the conflict. Judgment, *Martić*, (IT-95-11-T), Trial Chamber I, 12 June 2007, (hereafter *Martić*), § 102; Judgment, *Hadzihasanović and Kubura*, (IC-01-47-T), Trial Chamber, 15 March 2006 (hereafter *Hadzihasanović & Kubura*), § 1875; Judgment, *Simić et al.*, (IT-95-9-T), Trial Chamber II, 17 October 2003 (hereafter *Simić et al.*), § 100.

[73] See Chapter 5 in this volume, at 107.

[74] See Chapter 5 in this volume, at 107.

[75] See Chapter 5 in this volume, at 107.

[76] *Detailed Findings of the Commission on Human Rights in South Sudan*, A/HRC/46/CRP.2, 18 February 2021, (hereafter HRC, 'Detailed Findings'), § 48; HRC 'January 2020 Report of the Commission on Human Rights in South Sudan', see note 3, Annex II, § 39.

coinciding with the COVID-19 pandemic which further inflated the prices for staple foods and basic commodities, have significantly contributed to starvation in South Sudan in the course of the civil war.[77] The facts set out earlier in this chapter, however, suggest that the deprivations of OIS reportedly perpetrated by the governmental forces operated in parallel with these natural causes and were one of the major factors in the ensuing starvation of the South Sudanese civilian population. These natural causes of starvation do not exclude liability for deliberate starvation, particularly where perpetrators have taken advantage of pre-existing food insecurity and have caused or exacerbated it. However, these competing chains of causation must be understood and established on the evidence as a step towards the identification of intent.

2. Scale and Manner of Deprivations of OIS

An important factor that will also provide indications of an intention to starve is the manner in which the deprivations of OIS were perpetrated. The frequency, proximity, and similarity in the *modus operandi* of the deprivations of OIS may well be the most significant indicator of an intention to starve. Repetitive attacks that are close in time and space to one another carried out against similar types of OIS resulting in the starvation of civilians without mitigating steps may well amount to dispositive proof.

However, it is also important to underscore those viable prosecutions for starvation are by no means confined to widespread or systematic occurrences of starvation. Indeed, smaller or more discrete deprivations where the chain of causation is short, direct, and clear, and the consequences more immediate may well prove fertile ground. For example, in a detention setting, where one or more detained person is deliberately starved by a prison guard, the task of proving that he acted with an intention to starve may be achieved relatively straightforwardly. Outside of a detention setting, it is also foreseeable that where, for example, an acutely food-insecure and vulnerable community relies upon a single source of water or food and that essential source of sustenance is destroyed without lawful justification, that intent could be inferred solely upon that (relatively) small-scale or singular incident. Similarly, large-scale but self-contained and discrete acts such as besieging a civilian community might clearly evince an intention to starve on the part of the perpetrators.

As for South Sudan, the available evidence indicates that the deprivations of OIS may have occurred in the context of a widespread and systematic attack by government forces against the civilian population[78] with routine disregard of IHL and ICL norms, resulting in the commission of numerous crimes against humanity and war crimes across South Sudan. As discussed, government forces appear to

[77] HRC 'Conference room paper', see note 5, §§ 12–14.
[78] HRC 'Conference room paper', see note 5, §§ 93, 123; See later in this chapter at 274.

have systematically attacked numerous civilian cities/towns/villages located in Western Bahr el Ghazal, Jonglei and the Unity States resulting in significant numbers of deaths, rapes and other forms of sexual violence, and the destruction, arson, and looting of civilian property.[79] As also already discussed, in the course of these attacks, government forces may have systematically deprived civilians belonging to ethnic groups perceived as hostile of OIS in order to pursue certain military objectives.[80] Due to resultant physical and food insecurity many women, men, and children have been forcibly displaced.[81] Although the exact number of victims is unknown, a 2018 study estimated the death toll of the civil war to be approximately 383,000, half of which is attributable to deaths occurring due to displacement, the disruption of health services, and a lack of food.[82] Undoubtedly, these factual patterns will be critical in demonstrating a particular individual's (or group's) intention to starve civilians as a method of warfare.

As for more discrete deprivations, certain specific acts carried out by the government forces during their attacks could be seen as particularly indicative of a direct intention to starve. After the eruption of the conflict in Wau Town in June 2016, for instance, government forces erected checkpoints to prevent citizens from selling foodstuffs (such as sorghum and groundnuts) in the market.[83] During the attack on Mboro which started in June 2018, SPLA soldiers systematically destroyed or dismantled the vast majority of the pumps 'that were used by locals to pump water from boreholes, depriving them of access to water for both consumption and sanitation'.[84] It is difficult to fathom an alternative explanation for such conduct other than a direct intention to starve civilians.

The timing of the attacks may also be highly relevant to establishing the perpetrators' intention to starve civilians. There is evidence indicating that the offensives that occurred in the Unity State (Leer and Mayendit Counties) and Western Bahr el Ghazal (Wau County) coincided with the planting and growing seasons.[85] The displacement that occurred during these seasons has had a particularly catastrophic effect on food security in South Sudan.[86] In some areas, government forces imposed movement restrictions for months which prevented civilians from cultivating their lands to produce agricultural products at time periods that are crucial for agricultural activities.[87] According to one witness, following the launch of the

[79] HRC 'Conference room paper', see note 5, § 93.
[80] See later in this chapter, at 276.
[81] HRC 'February 2019 Report the Commission on Human Rights in South Sudan', see note 19, § 158; HRC 'Conference room paper', see note 5, § 93.
[82] See F. Checchi et al., 'Estimates of Crisis-Attributable Mortality in South Sudan, December 2013–April 2018' (London School of Hygiene and Tropical Medicine, 2018) available online at <https://www.lshtm.ac.uk/south-sudan-full-report> (visited 9 September 2021).
[83] HRC 'Conference room paper', see note 5, § 53.
[84] HRC 'Conference room paper', see note 5, § 69.
[85] Chapter 8 in this volume, at 195.
[86] HRC 'February 2019 Report the Commission on Human Rights in South Sudan', see note 19, §§ 143–144.
[87] Chapter 8 in this volume, at 195.

southern Unity offensive in April 2018, an SPLA commander in Leer told women sheltering in the Temporary Protection Area that 'nobody should cultivate this year'.[88] When placed in context, this may constitute compelling evidence of an intention to starve on part of government forces. No one in South Sudan could have been unaware of the consequences of such punitive and unnecessary restrictions.

Overall, the systematic and widespread nature of the deprivations of OIS that took place in South Sudan presents a persuasive set of facts for showing that the perpetrators intended to starve civilians. There appears to be no obvious or discernible lawful purpose behind the deprivations that occurred in the incidents outlined here. Further, deprivations of OIS do not appear to have been a secondary consequence of otherwise lawful military operations or wanton, random, and spontaneous criminality that occurs during armed conflicts. Rather, the perpetrators appear to have focused on depriving civilians of OIS by pillaging and destroying homes, agricultural lands and produce, livestock and water facilities in an organized, coordinated, and deliberate manner. These facts are somewhat distinct from those in Syria and Yemen where siege or blockade is the primary cause of deprivations and where competing explanations may need to be properly parsed and understood.

In Syria, for instance, an argument could be made that starvation occurred in the course of otherwise lawful sieges laid with the purpose of weakening the enemy rather than starving civilians. The same could be argued for the sieges in Yemen. Similarly, the blockade imposed by the Saudi-led coalition which led to a drop in food supply in some areas in Yemen could be characterized as an attempt to ensure compliance with the arms embargo set up by the UN Security Council.[89] Furthermore, the destruction of OIS which occurred in the course of the aerial bombing campaign by the SLC and the artillery/mortar attacks by the Houthis could be deemed as proportional collateral damage or lawful strikes justified by military necessity. Whilst many of these explanations dissipate upon closer examination, they do not even arise for consideration in South Sudan. There is no evidence suggesting that the destroyed or pillaged OIS were used solely by the opposition armed forces, or that the destruction was carried out because the items were used in direct support of military action, or that there was any imperative military necessity that required their destruction. On the contrary, the evidence appears to reveal that the attacks carried out against civilians and the destruction and pillaging of OIS were widespread, systematic, targeted, and prolonged. They also occurred in the midst of other attacks consisting of serious violations of IHL ranging from murder, sexual violence, unlawful destruction and appropriation of property, pillage, forcible displacement, and other attacks directed against civilians

[88] HRC 'February 2019 Report the Commission on Human Rights in South Sudan', see note 19, § 144.
[89] See Chapter 9 in this volume, at 217.

and civilian objects suggesting that there was method in the attacks on civilians and the OIS.

3. Implementation (or Lack Thereof) of IHL Obligations

Implementation of IHL obligations and concrete steps taken by the perpetrator to alleviate civilian suffering caused by the deprivation of OIS occurred in the course of the conflict may stand as solid rebuttals of any indications of an intention to starve civilians. Indeed, it will be difficult to prove an intention to starve in situations where the perpetrator could demonstrate that he/she genuinely tried to avoid/minimize the infliction of damage to OIS in the course of military operations or facilitated the access of humanitarian aid to the areas where civilians were deprived of OIS.[90] However, such steps would need to be linked to the deprivations alleged to indicate intent. A warring party cannot offset or trade deprivations (or intent) in one location or community by providing OIS in others.

(a) *Measures taken to avoid/minimize the infliction of damage to OIS and concrete steps taken to alleviate civilian suffering*

Article 8 of the Rome Statute criminalizes grave breaches of the Geneva Conventions and other serious violations of the laws and customs applicable in international and non-international armed conflicts, within the established framework of international law.[91] The prohibition of the war crime of starvation as a war crime under this provision is founded upon principles of IHL, meaning that for particular conduct to amount to a war crime, it must be a violation of IHL in the first place.[92] It follows that if the conduct that led to a deprivation of OIS adheres with the fundamental principles of IHL (i.e. distinction, proportionality, and precaution),[93] it cannot be said to have constituted the war crime of starvation. In other words, attacks on civilian objects, including OIS, cannot form the basis of a starvation charge where the attack in question was carried out in line with these three principles. If an attack was carried out against food supplies solely used by the adverse party to provide for the members of its armed forces, it would be in line

[90] See Chapter 5 in this volume, at 107.

[91] Art. 8(2)(a), (b), and (e) Rome Statute.

[92] D. Akande and E. Gillard, 'Conflict Induced Food Insecurity and the War Crime of Starvation of Civilians as a Method of Warfare', 17 *Journal of International Criminal Justice* (2019) 753–779, at 759.

[93] The principle of distinction requires the parties to the conflict to distinguish between civilians and combatants at all times and only direct attacks against combatants, and not civilians. The principle of proportionality in attack requires parties to refrain from launching attacks that may be expected to cause incidental loss of civilian life, injury to civilians, damage to civilian objects, or a combination thereof, which would be excessive in relation to the concrete and direct military advantage anticipated. The principle of precautions against the effects of attacks parties to a conflict to take all feasible precautions to protect the civilian population and civilian objects under their control against the effects of the attacks. See ICRC Customary IHL Study, Rule 1: The Principle of Distinction between Civilians and Combatants, Rule 14: Proportionality in Attack, Rule 22: Principle of Precautions against the Effects of Attacks.

with the principle of distinction.[94] However, where the OIS in question was used both by civilians and members of the armed forces in direct support of military action, it cannot be targeted if it is expected to leave the civilian population with inadequate food or water as to cause its starvation or force its movement.[95] Such an attack would be in contravention of the principle of proportionality. The principle of precaution on the other hand requires an attacking party to take all feasible measures to protect the civilian population and civilian objects under their control against the effects of the attack.[96]

During conflicts where military and civilian objects/targets are proximate to each other and difficult to distinguish, compliance with these foundational IHL principles will need to be considered as stepping-stones to disentangling intent. The ICTY followed a similar approach in adjudicating charges of attacks on civilians as a violation of the laws and customs of war at Koševo Hospital in the Galić case. Despite frequent protests by the UN, the Koševo Hospital in Sarajevo was shelled on numerous occasions by SRK[97] between 1992 and 1994, resulting in damage to its building as well as deaths and injury to its staff and patients.[98] The Defence argued that the hospital was a legitimate military target at the time it was attacked since the Army of Bosnia and Herzegovina launched mortar attacks from the hospital grounds or its vicinity.[99] In its final judgment, applying the principle of precaution, the Appeals Chamber reiterated that civilian objects, including hospitals, lose their protection and may be legitimately targeted when used for hostile/harmful purposes, only, however, 'after a warning has been given, setting, whenever appropriate, a reasonable time-limit, and after such warning has remained unheeded'.[100] Such loss of protection persists only as long as it remains a military target (i.e. for as long as the harmful acts continue) and to the extent that it is reasonably necessary for the opposing side to respond to the military activity originating from therein.[101]

Further, applying the principle of proportionality, the Appeals Chamber held that any attack carried out on the hospital must be specifically aimed at military objects in its vicinity, meaning that only weaponry reasonably necessary for neutralizing such objects can be used.[102] In line with these considerations, the Appeals Chamber found that some of the SRK attacks were carried out against mortar positions in the vicinity of the Koševo hospital within a reasonable

[94] AP I, Art. 54(3)(a).
[95] AP I, Art. 54(3)(b).
[96] See AP I, Arts 51(5)(b), 57 and 58; Akande and Gillard, see note 92, at 767.
[97] SRK stands for Sarajevo Romanija Corps of the Army of Republika Srpska (VRS), i.e. the Bosnian Serb Army during the civil war in former Yugoslavia.
[98] Judgment, *Galić*, (IT-98-29-T), Trial Chamber I, 5 December 2003 (hereafter *Galić*), §§ 498–503.
[99] Judgment, *Galić*, §§ 501, 504–508
[100] Judgment, *Galić*, (IT-98-29-A), Appeals Chamber, 20 November 2006, (hereafter *Galić Appeal*), §§ 344-346; See AP I, Arts 11(2) and 13(1).
[101] *Galić Appeal*, § 346.
[102] *Galić Appeal*, § 346.

time after mortars were fired from the hospital and, as such, were lawful.[103] The Appeals Chamber also found, however, that certain other SRK attacks on the Koševo Hospital were carried out in circumstances where there were no discernible legitimate military targets in the area (for instance, while vehicles were arriving and leaving from the hospital and people were being carried on stretchers from building to building) and by using weaponry that was not suitable for addressing the military threat.[104] Ultimately, the Appeals Chamber came to the conclusion that 'some, but not all, of the attacks on the hospital by the SRK constituted examples of the campaign of attack on civilians. Other attacks were attacks on a legitimate military target'.[105]

Of course, there may well be situations or instances, including many in South Sudan, where the evidence suggests deliberate targeting of civilians and civilian objects, in clear violation of the principles of distinction, proportionality, and precautions. However, in many other cases, respect (or lack thereof) for the principles of distinction, proportionality, and precaution will need to be closely examined. Adherence, on a macro or granular level, will provide a window into the mind of the alleged perpetrator and will often prove to be an essential step in determining relevant intent.

(b) Attempts to suppress IHL violations involving deprivation of OIS

Another relevant consideration, particularly in relation to senior-level perpetrators, is whether there were any attempts to suppress violations of IHL that deprived civilians of OIS. If it can be shown that an individual genuinely attempted to prevent, investigate, or punish deprivations of OIS committed by his/her subordinates, this will be powerful evidence of his/her lack of intent to starve civilians.

While some investigations and prosecutions appear to have been carried out in South Sudan in relation to certain incidents that occurred during the civil war, their outcomes have not been published to allow for an assessment as to whether potential suspects might be able to point to such action as indicators of their lack of intent.[106] Overall, there is no information on any state investigations or prosecutions against the direct or high-level perpetrators for the commission of the war crime of starvation.[107] On the contrary, there is information available that indicates

[103] *Galić Appeal*, § 347.

[104] *Galić Appeal*, § 348.

[105] *Galić Appeal*, § 351.

[106] HRC, 'Transitional justice and accountability: a roadmap for sustainable peace in South Sudan' in *Conference room paper of the Commission on Human Rights in South Sudan*, A/HRC/45/CRP.4, 5 October 2020 (hereafter HRC 'Transitional justice and accountability: a roadmap for sustainable peace in South Sudan'), §§ 50–52

[107] See, for instance, HRC 'February 2019 Report the Commission on Human Rights in South Sudan', see note 19, §§ 744, 870, 872; Regarding the ongoing impunity for other war crimes and crimes against humanity in South Sudan, see HRC *Detailed findings of the Commission on Human Rights in South Sudan* A/HRC/46/CRP.2, 18 February 2021, § 148. HRC 'Transitional justice and accountability: a roadmap for sustainable peace in South Sudan', see note 106, § 51,

that individuals implicated in attacks on civilians and OIS have been rewarded with promotions and government appointments, rather than being held criminally accountable.[108]

(c) *Ensuring humanitarian access*

IHL requires the parties to an armed conflict to allow and facilitate rapid and unimpeded passage of humanitarian relief for all civilians in need.[109] This rule, the same as for all IHL rules, must be applied by the warring parties without any adverse distinction based on race, colour, sex, language, religion or belief, political or other opinion, national or social origin, wealth, birth, or other status, or any other similar criteria.[110] Not only restricting humanitarian access is prohibited under IHL, it is also specifically indicated as one of the ways in which the actus reus of the war crime of starvation may be perpetrated.[111] Accordingly, demonstrating that the perpetrators systematically restricted humanitarian aid from reaching civilians, especially in situations where their acts deprived them of OIS, would provide compelling evidence of an intention to starve them.

Due to its dismal history of mass starvation and famine, humanitarian access has been particularly crucial for civilian sustenance in South Sudan. Indeed, international humanitarian operations have been continuously operated in some form in South Sudan for well over three decades. Operation Lifeline Sudan (OLS), which began its operations in 1989, for instance, was the largest-ever coordinated humanitarian programme at the time.[112] Under the coordination of the UN, aid agencies engaged the government and military of Sudan as well as armed groups like the SPLA in an effort to gain access to the Sudanese most affected by armed conflict. Despite efforts to assist those in need, however, OLS was frequently manipulated and interfered with by the parties to the conflict and consequently failed to prevent mass starvation.[113] This effort, like so many others, ran into the political and

[108] HRC 'February 2019 Report the Commission on Human Rights in South Sudan', see note 19, § 950. For instance, the political reappointment of the Gany County Commissioner who, according to the UNHRCSS, was found to be among those who bear the greatest responsibility for war crimes in southern Unity between April and May 2018 may be taken as indicative in this regard. See HRC 'February 2019 Report the Commission on Human Rights in South Sudan', see note 19, § 55–745.

[109] ICRC, J-M. Henckaerts and L. Doswald-Beck, *Customary International Humanitarian Law* Vol. 1, (Cambridge: Cambridge University Press, 2005) (hereafter ICRC, *Customary International Humanitarian Law*), at 193.

[110] Henckaerts and Doswald-Beck, note 109, at 308.

[111] Art.8(2)(b)(xxv) Rome Statute.

[112] See A. Karim, *OLS Operation Lifeline Sudan. A Review* (UNICEF 1996); D. Maxwell, M. Santschi, and R. Gordon, 'Looking back to look ahead? Reviewing key lessons from Operation Lifeline Sudan and past humanitarian operations in South Sudan', Working Paper 24, (Secure Livelihoods Research Consortium, 2014) available online at <https://securelivelihoods.org/wp-content/uploads/Reviewing-key-lessons-from-Operation-Lifeline-Sudan-and-past-humanitarian-operations-in-South-Sudan.pdf> (visited 9 September 2021).

[113] L. B. Deng, *Famine in the Sudan: Causes, Preparedness and Response—A Political, Social and Economic Analysis of the 1998 Bahr el Ghazal Famine* (London: Institute for Development Studies, 1999), available online at <https://www.ids.ac.uk/publications/famine-in-the-sudan-causes-preparedness-and-response-a-political-social-and-economic-analysis-of-the-1998-bahr-el-ghazal-famine/>

economic logic of the civil war. Humanitarian aid was regarded by the parties to the conflict as another resource, the denial of which in some areas and concentration in others could be used to advance a wide range of military, political, and economic objectives.[114] With the signing of the Comprehensive Peace Agreement that ended the 1983–2005 war and the establishment of the SPLA's control in southern Sudan, the humanitarian operations in Sudan expanded. The access to humanitarian aid of millions of displaced South Sudanese seeking to return their homes improved.[115] Organized violence remained pervasive across much of the country, however, as a wide range of South Sudanese armed groups competed for power under the new regime.[116] The combination of the needs of the returnees, spikes in different forms of violence, and the lingering devastation of the war ensured that humanitarian operations become further embedded in South Sudan's political, social, and economic systems.[117]

The newly independent South Sudan plunged into a civil war in this humanitarian context. In the aftermath of the war, humanitarian operations expanded, eventually becoming more extensive compared to the situation under the OLS. As in the previous war, widespread denial of humanitarian access created mass starvation. Indeed, the available evidence suggests that in South Sudan, the government and, to a lesser extent, opposition forces have denied humanitarian access to areas where tens of thousands of civilians deprived of OIS were displaced. The UN Office for the Coordination of Humanitarian Affairs reported a total of 5,910 humanitarian access incidents since the conflict broke out in 2013.[118] These include

(visited 9 September 2021); REACH Initiative, *Now the Forest Is Blocked: Shocks and Access to Food—South Sudan*, April 2018, available online at reliefweb.int/report/south-sudan/now-forest-blocked-shocks-and-access-food> (visited 27 October 2021).

[114] For instance, humanitarian access was often limited to towns garrisoned by the Sudanese Armed Forces and, when severely affected rural areas were reached, the levels of assistance were often grossly insufficient. D. Keen, *The Benefits of Famine: A Political Economy of Famine and Relief in Southwestern Sudan 1983–9* (Athens: Ohio University Press, 2008).

[115] S. Pantuliano and I. Mosel, *The Long Road Home: Opportunities and Obstacles to the Reintegration of IDPs and Refugees Returning to Southern Sudan and the Three Areas*, Humanitarian Policy Group (2008).

[116] M. Schomerus and T. Allen, *Southern Sudan at Odds with Itself: Dynamics of Conflict and Predicaments of Peace* (London: DESTIN Development Institute, 2010).

[117] Notably, the delivery of in-kind food assistance increased in the interim period between the Comprehensive Peace Agreement and the independence of South Sudan in 2011. See B. Sharp, 'Food Aid and Development in Southern Sudan: Implications of the Comprehensive Peace Agreement for Response Planning', 31 *Disasters* (2007) S104–S1223.

[118] See United Nations Office for the Coordination of Humanitarian Affairs, '2014 Humanitarian Needs Overview South Sudan (September 2013)', *ReliefWeb* (2013), available online at <https://reliefweb.int/sites/reliefweb.int/files/resources/HNO_South_Sudan_2014.pdf> (visited 9 September 2021); United Nations Office for the Coordination of Humanitarian Affairs, 'South Sudan: Humanitarian access situation snapshot (January–December 2015)', *ReliefWeb*, (2016), available online at <https://reliefweb.int/sites/reliefweb.int/files/resources/access_snapshot_jan-dec2015.pdf> (visited 9 September 2021); United Nations Office for the Coordination of Humanitarian Affairs, 'South Sudan: Humanitarian Access Situation Snapshot (Jan–Dec 2016)', *ReliefWeb* (2017), available online at <https://reliefweb.int/sites/reliefweb.int/files/resources/170125_january_december_2016_accesssnapshot.pdf> (visited 9 September 2021); United Nations Office for the Coordination of Humanitarian

direct violence perpetrated against humanitarian personnel, assets, and facilities (including by murder, arbitrary detention, robbery/burglary/looting, threats, and harassment), operational interference in the implementation of humanitarian activities, restriction on the movement of organizations, personnel and goods within and into the country, as well as bureaucratic administrative impediments (through illegal taxation, cumbersome accreditation processes, and extortion of fees to access areas in need).[119]

For instance, reportedly, the humanitarian organizations operating in and around the Wau Triangle area of Western Bahr el Ghazal had extremely limited access to civilians in need due to the intricate web of checkpoints erected by the government forces.[120] According to UNHRCSS, '[d]irect operational interference was particularly notable in Baggari, Bisselia, Bazia and Gedi where SPLA forces turned back humanitarian convoys at checkpoints for more than two months between mid-June and late August 2018, depriving up to 28.000 people [who were in dire need of food, water, health, sanitation and hygiene facilities] of humanitarian aid'.[121] In Jonglei State, it was reported that '[g]overnment forces systematically denied humanitarian actors access to Akobo and Pibor Counties ... between 2017 and 2019, depriving thousands of civilians living under opposition control of [OIS] and denying them access to food'.[122] In Waat village (Uror County, Unity State) in April 2017, government forces reportedly looted the properties, including the generators, vehicles, and food stores from humanitarian compounds and international NGOs.[123] Similarly, in Akobo in 2017–2018, government forces appear to have systematically restricted humanitarian actors from bringing food, blocking roads, stopping convoys that were transporting food, and looting the food on board and turning the convoys around.[124] Across South Sudan, at least 117 humanitarian

Affairs, 'South Sudan: Humanitarian Access Overview (January–December 2017)', *ReliefWeb* (2018), available online at <https://reliefweb.int/sites/reliefweb.int/files/resources/SS_20180213_Annual_Access_Snapshot_Final.pdf> (visited 9 September 2021); United Nations Office for the Coordination of Humanitarian Affairs, 'South Sudan: Annual Humanitarian Access Review (January–December 2018)', *ReliefWeb* (2019), available online at <https://reliefweb.int/report/south-sudan/south-sudan-annual-humanitarian-access-review-january-december-2018> (visited 9 September 2021); United Nations Office for the Coordination of Humanitarian Affairs, 'South Sudan: 2019 Humanitarian Access Overview (January to December 2019)', *ReliefWeb* (2020), available online at <https://reliefweb.int/report/south-sudan/south-sudan-2019-humanitarian-access-overview-january-december-2019> (visited 9 September 2021); United Nations Office for the Coordination of Humanitarian Affairs, 'South Sudan: 2020 Humanitarian Access Overview (January to December 2020)', *ReliefWeb* (2021), available online at <https://reliefweb.int/sites/reliefweb.int/files/resources/south_sudan_2020_access_annual_overview.pdf> (visited 9 September 2021).

[119] United Nations Office for the Coordination of Humanitarian Affairs, '2014 Humanitarian Needs Overview South Sudan (September 2013)', see note 118; HRC 'February 2019 Report the Commission on Human Rights in South Sudan', see note 19, § 153.

[120] HRC 'Conference room paper', see note 5, § 74.

[121] HRC 'Conference room paper', see note 5, § 74.

[122] HRC 'Conference room paper', see note 5, § 11.

[123] HRC 'Conference room paper', see note 5, § 100.

[124] HRC 'Conference room paper', see note 5, § 107.

actors were detained for prolonged periods in 2018 by both government and the opposition forces. Further, since 2013, a total of 126 humanitarians, mostly South Sudanese, have been killed while providing critical assistance to people across the country, including by the opposition non-state armed groups.[125]

Accordingly, in line with the patterns observed in the previous armed conflicts in Sudan, 'humanitarian aid has continued to be a political tool in South Sudan, used by all parties to the conflict.' strategically and deliberately have obstructed the access of communities perceived to support the opposing party to humanitarian aid whilst allowing and indeed redirecting humanitarian aid towards themselves or supportive civilian communities.[126] Clearly, such a partial approach to the provision of aid cannot comply with IHL.[127] As such, humanitarian organizations have once again found themselves manipulated or leveraged in furtherance of diverse aims, often to the detriment of a civilian population that depended on humanitarian aid.[128] These strategies appear to correspond with the tactics deployed in Syria, especially by the Assad regime. As reported, government forces in Syria have also 'instrumentalized aid by restricting, impeding, and diverting humanitarian assistance to their benefit'.[129] In both conflicts, this instrumentalization of vital aid—without which populations can be expected to starve—provides clear indications of relevant intent.

Moreover, in the context of South Sudan, these violations occurred in 'complete violation of the obligation under the Cessation of Hostilities Agreement of December 2017, which required parties to facilitate unfettered access for humanitarian assistance and to guarantee the safety and security of all humanitarian personnel,[130] and the reiteration of these commitments in the Revitalised Agreement

[125] HRC 'Conference room paper', see note 5, § 129; United Nations Office for the Coordination of Humanitarian Affairs, 'South Sudan: UN condemns killing of one aid worker and attack against humanitarian convoy in Unity State', *ReliefWeb* (2021), available online at <https://reliefweb.int/report/south-sudan/south-sudan-un-condemns-killing-one-aid-worker-and-attack-against-humanitarian#:~:text=At%20least%20two%20aid%20workers,broke%20out%20in%20late%202013> (visited 9 September 2021).

[126] HRC 'February 2019 Report the Commission on Human Rights in South Sudan', see note 19, § 152.

[127] See ICRC, *Customary International Humanitarian Law*, Rule 55: Access for Humanitarian Relief to Civilians in Need in combination with Rule 88: Non-Discrimination.

[128] See D. Sullivan, *Displaced Nations: The Dangerous Implications of Rushed Returns in South Sudan*, Refugees International, 29 November 2018, available online at <https://www.refugeesinternational.org/reports/2018/11/29/displaced-nation-the-dangerous-implications-of-rushed-returns-in-south-sudan> (visited 30 October 2021), at 17–20; HRC 'Conference room paper', see note 5, § 110.

[129] N. Hall and W. Todman, *Lessons Learned from a Decade of Humanitarian Operations in Syria*, Center for Strategic and International Studies, 22 April 2021; See, for instance, *Reuters*, 'UN worried about the reported diversion of aid in Syria', 21 May 2015, available online at <https://www.reuters.com/article/syria-crisis-un-aid/u-n-worried-about-reported-diversion-of-aid-in-syria-idINKBN0O62M520150521> (visited 29 October 2021); Human Rights Watch, *Rigging the System: Government Policies Co-Opt Aid and Reconstruction Funding in Syria*, 28 June 2019, available online at <https://www.hrw.org/report/2019/06/28/rigging-system/government-policies-co-opt-aid-and-reconstruction-funding-syria#> (visited 29 October 2021) .

[130] Agreement on Cessation of Hostilities, Protection of Civilians and Humanitarian Access (signed 21 December 2017), Art. 8.

on the Resolution of the Conflict in South Sudan of September 2018'.[131] The signing of the agreements may serve as a double-edged sword: on the one hand, the agreements may indicate an awareness of the need for OIS *and* an intention to ensure their provision; on the other, their violation despite this awareness may provide cogent evidence of an intent to deprive.

If there are patterns of restricting humanitarian access, prosecutors must seek to understand the underlying purpose with a view to ascertaining whether it suggests an intention to starve the civilian population, while keeping in mind the lawful grounds for restricting humanitarian aid.[132] There is no indication that the narrow exceptions which would allow for warring parties to block humanitarian aid lawfully were present in the incidents discussed earlier in this chapter. As found by the UNCHRSS, 'the denial of humanitarian access and displacement brought about by unlawful tactics have significantly exacerbated famine in different parts of the country, depriving hundreds of thousands of civilians of vital needs, including access to food'.[133] Yemen may provide another example. Over the course of the war, sieges laid down by the adversaries 'have been accompanied by significant restrictions on the flow of humanitarian supplies, including food, water and fuel'. Additionally, there are documented instances in which perpetrators looted humanitarian supplies and arbitrarily detained or killed humanitarian workers.[134] Such acts, if proven through sufficient evidence, may not only constitute the war crime of starvation but also of attacking personnel or objects involved in humanitarian assistance.[135]

4. The Perpetrator's Awareness that the Deprivations of OIS Would Lead to Starvation

As outlined in Chapter 5, demonstrating that the perpetrator knew that the deprivations of OIS would lead to starvation of civilians 'in the ordinary course of events', and continuing to pursue that course of action, is sufficient to lay the foundation for establishing the relevant intent.[136] Importantly, regardless of what the perpetrator's original *purpose* was for depriving civilians of OIS, an intention to starve could still be found if it can be proven beyond reasonable doubt that the perpetrator knew that continuing along that path would almost certainly lead to starvation of civilians.[137] In order to demonstrate the perpetrator's knowledge in

[131] HRC 'Conference room paper', see note 5, § 101.

[132] Jordash et al., 'Strategies for Prosecuting', see note 70, at 874; that is, lack of impartiality or humanitarian character on the part of the humanitarian organization; the existence of a military necessity to restrict humanitarian activities; imposition of reasonable technical/bureaucratic arrangement (searches, imposition of conditions for delivery, or temporary limitations of movement of relief personnel) in cases of urgent necessity and in the interest of the civilian population concerned.

[133] HRC 'January 2020 Report of the Commission on Human Rights in South Sudan', see note 3, § 70.

[134] See Chapter 9 in this volume, at 195.

[135] Arts 8(2)(b)(iii) and 8(2)(e)(iii) Rome Statute.

[136] Art. 30 Rome Statute.

[137] See Chapter 5 in this volume, at 107.

this respect, prosecutors first need to show that the deprivations of OIS would certainly lead to starvation of civilians, and second that the perpetrator was aware of the existence of such risk.

Despite, in most areas, being fertile and agriculturally productive, South Sudan is and has been one of the most acutely food-insecure areas of the world in recent history. This is mostly due to the armed conflicts that occurred in the last three decades that have repeatedly led to incidents of starvation, including two major famines in 1987–1988 and 1997–1998 that caused a massive loss of human life.[138] Even before the beginning of the civil war of 2013, 'there were already more than one and a half million people in South Sudan (17 percent of the population) categorised as being Phase 3 (Crisis) or above of the IPC system'.[139] This was caused, amongst other things, by the armed conflict that took place in Pibor (Jonglei State) in mid/late-2013, as well as localized armed conflicts and natural calamities (such as floods) that took place between 2006 and 2013. Expectedly, the civil war significantly exacerbated these precarious circumstances,[140] culminating in a declaration of famine in 2017 by humanitarian agencies and the government of South Sudan.[141] As of July 2021, South Sudan is experiencing the most extreme levels of food insecurity since its independence in 2011, with almost 7 million people (60 per cent of the population) struggling to find enough food each day.[142] As already indicated, in the course of the civil war, various other contributory factors ranging from natural disasters such as floods and droughts to unfavourable macroeconomic conditions and prevalent poverty have exacerbated the situation of food security in the country. Prosecutors could use these and similar facts related to the persistent state of food insecurity in South Sudan in proving that any major interference with OIS would have almost certainly led to the starvation of civilians in the ordinary course of events.

As already outlined, prosecutors must also establish that the perpetrator was aware of this likely risk. This requires demonstrating that any suspect was sufficiently aware of these facts. Since starvation is a condition that develops gradually over time, arguably, individuals, whether political or military leaders or further down the chains of command, are likely to become aware of them over time, even if they lacked initial awareness of the prevailing food insecurity and starvation.

138 See Chapter 8 in this volume, at 195; see J. Millard Burr, *Quantifying Genocide in Southern Sudan and the Nuba Mountains* (Washington, DC: US Committee for Refugees, 1998).

139 HRC 'February 2019 Report the Commission on Human Rights in South Sudan', see note 19, § 142.

140 HRC 'February 2019 Report the Commission on Human Rights in South Sudan', see note 19, § 143.

141 'South Sudan declares famine in Unity State' *BBC*, 20 February 2017, available online <https://www.bbc.com/news/world-africa-39025927> (visited 9 September 2021).

142 WFP, 'South Sudan emergency', available online at <https://www.wfp.org/emergencies/south-sudan-emergency#:~:text=Food%20insecurity%20in%20South%20Sudan,levels%20since%20independence%20in%202011.&text=However%2C%20the%20situation%20remains%20dire,find%20enough%20food%20each%20day> (visited 9 September 2021)

Of course, this inference is all the more readily drawn where, as in South Sudan, famine and/or deprivation is widespread and consistently reported by the international governmental and non-governmental organizations (such as the World Food Programme (WFP), Médecins Sans Frontières (MSF), etc.) as well as the domestic and foreign media. In this sense, the widespread nature of the food insecurity in South Sudan and the consequent flows of displaced persons, in itself, as well as the fact that the government of South Sudan declared famine in February 2017, stands as strong, if not irrefutable, evidence of the awareness of the senior political and military leaders of the government as well as, potentially, any armed group operating in the country.

Even in cases where international access to affected populations is extremely limited (as in South Sudan, Yemen, and areas of siege in Syria), humanitarian information networks are sufficiently robust to inform international policy-makers, humanitarians, and the media who are mandated to publicize these facts and communicate their concerns to the parties of the conflict. Consequently, as with South Sudan, the widespread publicity in Yemen of the starvation of the population would make it very difficult for any government or non-state actor to claim that they were not aware of the consequences of the military strikes being carried out against OIS.[143] This, in turn, is a solid departure point for establishing their awareness of the virtual certainty that the civilian population in Yemen would starve due to their conduct and the critical framework for assessing their intent.

Furthermore, South Sudanese leaders as well as, conceivably, the younger participants in the civil war are informed by their own personal experiences of the current conflict and similar episodes in the past. There is a long history of starvation being used as a method of warfare in the various armed conflicts that transpired in South Sudan over the last three decades. Coming from similar livelihood systems and living their whole lives in South Sudan, it could be argued that they knew exactly how certain military tactics that interfere with these livelihood systems (such as attacks against livestock herds, agricultural production, market access, and various other coping strategies) would bring about deprivation leading to mass starvation.[144] Indeed, it is indisputable that the SPLA leaders themselves must have observed first-hand the effectiveness of weaponized starvation during the 1983–2005 war.[145] As discussed in Chapter 8, there is cogent evidence showing that the Sudanese Armed Forces and their allies, including a series of southern Sudanese armed actors, engineered several famines among the civilian population in areas under SPLA control over the course of that war.[146] As acknowledged by its first leader John Garang, the SPLA used starvation as a method of warfare. As also

[143] See Chapter 9 in this volume, at 217.
[144] See Chapter 8 in this volume, at 195.
[145] See Chapter 8 in this volume, at 195.
[146] See Chapter 8 in this volume, at 195.

noted in Chapter 8, Garang explicitly stated '[SAF] garrison towns in the South are famine-stricken and are real disaster areas, and this is good; it means our military strategy is working'.[147] Leaders on both sides during the Second Sudanese Civil War made similarly damning statements about their own awareness and intent.[148] One may even say that its recurrent use as a method of warfare over the decades embedded starvation in the oral culture and memory of the South Sudanese society. In the face of the history of conflict and famine in South Sudan, any future accused seeking to argue that they, or others, who deprived civilians of OIS were unaware that their conduct would cause starvation, is going to face an uphill struggle.

4. Linking the Senior Leaders to the Commission of the War Crime of Starvation

Once the commission of the war crime of starvation is established, the next step is to link it to specific perpetrators through the applicable modes of liability. For these purposes, we will focus on accomplice liability, known variously to ICL as joint criminal enterprise or (indirect or direct) co-perpetration. As will be further explained, this liability framework is likely to suit a prosecution of starvation. We also deal briefly at the end of this chapter with the command responsibility mode of liability, which may also serve as a practical tool for any future court process.

A. Accomplice Liability (Joint Criminal Enterprise/Co-perpetration)

Joint Criminal Enterprise (JCE) and co-perpetration are often pleaded in the prosecution of high-level perpetrators who were far removed from the crimes on the ground but nevertheless played a significant role in the commission of the crimes through their role in a group/organization acting pursuant to a common plan. At the ICTY, for instance, JCE was the preferred mode of liability charged against many of the Serbian accused. Forcible transfer or 'ethnic cleansing' was the central crime with which several alleged JCE members were charged. Prosecutors argued that the common purpose and shared intention of the alleged JCE members were to ethnically cleanse parts of Bosnia and Herzegovina and/or Croatia of non-Serbs. While forcible transfer was the principal legal prohibition at the centre of these trials, a vast array of crimes (such as murder, looting, sexual violence, arbitrary detention, cruel treatment, torture, etc.) were introduced into the

[147] See Chapter 8 in this volume, at 195.
[148] See Africa Watch Committee, *Denying the Honor of Living: Sudan, a Human Rights Disaster* (New York: Africa Watch Committee, 1990).

courtroom by the prosecution as underlying coercive acts (the means) that ultimately led to the non-Serb civilian population being forcibly displaced from their homes and villages.

Starvation may similarly lend itself to being charged as the pivotal, or ultimate, crime at the apex of a common plan, since, as discussed earlier, whereas the *actus reus* legally only requires proof of one or more acts or omissions depriving a civilian population of OIS, an essential and arguably defining element that qualifies such conduct as the war crime of starvation is the intention to starve.[149] It may be difficult to establish this intent with only isolated or one-off incidents where OIS have been destroyed, even where the intent to destroy is apparent. In order to meet the beyond reasonable doubt standard, the evidence would need to exclude all other reasonable inferences. A court may be reluctant to reach such a conclusion without some additional proof that the intent went beyond mere destruction for mischievous or punitive reasons and was aimed at starvation as commonly understood. Moreover, even the intent to destroy the OIS may be difficult to establish in such circumstances. The accused may, for instance, argue that there were military targets in the vicinity of the targeted OIS or otherwise that a mistake had been made. Of course, such defences, are more difficult to sustain in circumstances where the 'mistake' or 'accident' occur repeatedly and amount to a course of conduct, policy, or plan. This suggests that JCE or co-perpetration is likely to prove a more apt liability framework with which to prosecute starvation.

A fundamental aspect common to JCE and (both direct and indirect) co-perpetration is the existence of a plurality of persons who acted pursuant to a common plan.[150] To prove indirect co-perpetration, more stringent requirements apply; that is, the existence of an organized and hierarchical apparatus of power over which the co-perpetrators exercise joint control and, thus, gives them the ability to secure the commission of the crime in question through the automatic compliance of their subordinates with their orders.[151] In contrast, neither JCE nor direct co-perpetration requires the plurality of persons to be organized in a military, political, or administrative structure.[152] Additionally, prosecutors must

[149] An analogy can be drawn with genocide in this respect. Genocide can similarly be committed through various acts such as killing, causing serious bodily or mental harm, inflicting on conditions of life calculated to bring about physical destruction, preventing births, and forcibly transferring children. Such acts, however, must be committed with the specific intent to destroy a national, ethnical, racial, or religious group. Art. 6 Rome Statute.

[150] Judgment, *Karadžić*, (IT-95-5/18-T), Trial Chamber, 24 March 2016, (hereafter *Karadžić*), §§ 561–563; Appeal Judgment, *Bemba et al.*, (ICC-01/05-01) Appeals Chamber, 8 March 2018 (hereafter *Bemba et al.*), §§ 818–821.

[151] Decision on the Confirmation of Charges, *Katanga*, (ICC-01/04-01//07-717) Pre-Trial Chamber I, 14 October 2008; Decision on the Confirmation of Charges, *Kenyatta et al.*, (ICC-01/09-02/11) Pre-Trial Chamber II, 29 January 2012, §§ 297; Judgment, *Katanga*, (ICC-01/04-01/07), Trial Chamber II, 17 March 2014, §§ 1399, 1403–1405.

[152] *Karadžić*, see note 153 §562; Judgment, *Lubanga*, (ICC-01/04-01/06) Trial Chamber I, 13 July 2012 (hereafter *Lubanga* Trial Judgment), §§ 980.

establish that the accused furthered the common plan in a way that lent a significant contribution to the crimes (JCE)[153] or made an essential contribution to the common plan (co-perpetration).[154] Such contribution may be made at any stage of the commission of the crime, including its planning, preparation, attempt, or intent stage (i.e. when the agreement is conceived).[155]

The first step of linking senior South Sudanese leaders to the commission of the war crime of starvation through JCE or co-perpetration is to identify the common plan that the perpetrators acted in accordance with and intended to effect. Such common plan need not be explicit, previously arranged, or formulated and may materialize extemporaneously.[156] In the absence of direct evidence—for instance, the statements of insider witnesses—the existence of a common plan can be inferred from circumstantial evidence.[157] The concerted (i.e. systematic and organized and not random) actions of the JCE members or co-perpetrators that led to the commission of the war crime of starvation would be highly probative of this plan.[158] Any prosecutor would need to piece together the plan from a wide variety of circumstantial evidence, including contacts or meetings between alleged JCE members or co-perpetrators where the commission of crimes, or military action associated with the deprivation of OIS, was discussed, their subsequent conduct in the field pursuant to those meetings/actions, failures to prevent starvation harm to civilians, failures to punish direct perpetrators, etc.[159]

In proving the existence of a common plan, context is everything. Prosecutors will be required to build a compelling narrative from which the only reasonable inference is a common plan to starve the civilian population.[160] This involves ruling out all reasonable alternatives.[161] This task should not be underestimated since the presumption of innocence rightly, but firmly, stacks the odds in favour of the defence. However, this is standard practice for international prosecutions where common purposes are routinely alleged.

In this respect, there may be little in the South Sudanese context to distinguish a common plan to forcibly transfer civilian populations—a plan routinely prosecuted in international courts—and a plan to starve them. In other words, it may well be argued that by destroying/pillaging their homes, food supplies, water infrastructure, and medical facilities, and by obstructing the provision of humanitarian

[153] *Karadžić*, see note 155, § 561.
[154] *Bemba et al.*, see note 155, §§ 181–820; Appeal Judgment, *Lubanga*, (ICC-01/04-01/06), Appeal Chamber, 1 December 2014, §§ 445 and 469.
[155] *Bemba et al.*, see note 155, §§ 8179, 8170; *Karadžić* see note 153, § 564.
[156] *Karadžić*, see note 155, § 563.
[157] *Lubanga* Trial Judgment, § 988; Decision on the Confirmation of Charges *Ruto et al.*, § 301; *Karadžić*, see note 155, § 3447.
[158] *Lubanga* Trial Judgment, § 988.
[159] *Kenyatta*, see note 156, § 400.
[160] Appeal Judgment, *Šainović et al.*, (IT-05-87-A), Appeals Chamber, 23 January 2014, § 654; Appeal Judgment, *Delalić et al.*, (IT-96-21-A) 20 February2001, § 458; *Karadžić*, see note 155, § 10; *Bemba et al.*, see note 155, § 868.
[161] Appeal Judgment, *Šainović et al.*, (IT-05-87-A), Appeals Chamber, 23 January 2014, § 654.

aid to them, government forces effectively compelled civilian populations deemed hostile to leave their homes,[162] forcing them out of their lands and country and into internationally displaced persons camps or inhospitable areas such as forests or swamps.[163] Through their consecutive and repeated attacks on various towns across Western Bahr el Ghazal and the Unity State, the government forces displaced civilians deeper into the bush or swamplands.[164] Indeed, '[o]ne effective means of forcing civilian movement is to deprive them of objects and activities indispensable to survival, rendering them destitute'.[165] In this sense, the intent to starve becomes part of the overall intent to transfer forcibly, both equally compelling and concomitant intents.

There is some evidence that may go to prove the existence of this common plan and its execution by the government forces in South Sudan, leading to the commission of the war crime of starvation. In Western Bahr el Ghazal, for instance, over the course of a five-month offensive starting in mid-June 2018, it has been reported that the 'SPLA engaged in a concerted campaign against the civilian population in Wau Triangle [i.e. Baggari], attacking at least 10 towns and villages' and driving the civilians from their land.[166] These attacks appear to have been carried out in a systematic fashion in the sense that they followed a consistent pattern in terms of their execution[167] and recurrence over time.[168] As discussed earlier in this chapter, numerous criminal acts, among which deliberately depriving civilians of OIS figured prominently, were perpetrated by the SPLA soldiers during these attacks and a large number of civilians were displaced.[169] The offensive appears to have been planned and coordinated between the SPLA Fifth Division Commander (who acted as the overall commander of the operation)[170] and the State Security Committee in Wau.[171]

[162] HRC 'January 2020 Report of the Commission on Human Rights in South Sudan', see note 3, § 70 and Annex II, § 42.

[163] See Chapter 8 in this volume, at 195.

[164] HRC 'Conference room paper', see note 5, §§ 60, 62, 66, 68, 69, 73–74, 77, 79, 84; HRC 'February 2019 Report the Commission on Human Rights in South Sudan', see note 19, §§ 712, 832.

[165] See Chapter 8 in this volume, at 195.

[166] HRC 'March 2019 Report of the Commission on Human Rights in South Sudan', see note 63, § 86.

[167] Government attacks generally occurred following an ambush by SPLA-IO forces against their forces. As retaliation for their losses, SPLA would then launch attacks against the civilian population perceived as supportive of the opposition. The attack would start in the morning with the government forces arriving in military vehicles and firing into the village as inhabitants fled, killing, beating, and raping civilians, looting their possessions, and setting their homes on fire. HRC 'March 2019 Report of the Commission on Human Rights in South Sudan', see note 64, § 87–92; HRC 'February 2019 Report the Commission on Human Rights in South Sudan', see note 19, § 810.

[168] For instance, Ngoko was attacked multiple times by the SPLA soldiers where they repeatedly destroyed and pillaged civilian houses and property, including OIS. HRC 'February 2019 Report the Commission on Human Rights in South Sudan', see note 19 § 818–825.

[169] HRC 'February 2019 Report the Commission on Human Rights in South Sudan', see note 19 § 818–825.

[170] HRC 'February 2019 Report the Commission on Human Rights in South Sudan', see note 19, §§ 867

[171] State Security Committee in Wau met weekly and included the SPLA, the National Security Service, the Governor of Wau (who wielded significant influence), and a number of state Ministers

One incident is particularly relevant for understanding the contours of the alleged common plan. At the close of the operations in Mboro, government forces declared peace in the area and announced that displaced civilians were returning. In reality, however, this appears to have been a ploy staged by the Government to transfer the ethnic Dinka population (some of whom were relatives of government-aligned politicians or military forces) to Mboro, an area that was historically populated by the Fertit community.[172] Government officials then started exerting pressure on humanitarian organizations to assist the staged population movement and to provide the new arrivals with food. In combination, such conduct could be deemed as evidence of 'a clear intent to displace and dispossess local Fertit communities and reengineer the ethnic demographics of the town'[173] and 'a broader systematic strategy to prioritise the economic, social, and cultural rights of populations politically aligned with the Government at the expense of those displaced'.[174] The systematic pillaging/destruction of OIS suggests that deliberate starvation was one of the principal methods used by the perpetrators to force the civilians in Mboro to flee and to ensure that they do not return so that government supporters could be settled on their lands.

Similarly, the evidence suggests that deprivations of OIS that occurred during the April–June 2018 government offensive in Unity State were perpetrated in a widespread and systematic manner by state agents and forces under their control.[175] Government forces attacked more than forty villages in the Leer and Mayendit Counties, some of them multiple times,[176] looting or destroying countless civilian property, including homes, foodstuffs, and livestock, and causing massive displacement.[177] The offensive appeared to have been organized and systematic in the sense that government forces, led by particular commanders, were involved across multiple fronts.[178] Witness evidence suggests that the Southern Unity offensive was planned and coordinated at the highest levels of the government of South Sudan with the participation of SPLA, the SPLA-IO (TD), Gany County Commissioner,

such as Minister of Local Government and Finance. HRC 'February 2019 Report the Commission on Human Rights in South Sudan', see note 19, § 866.

[172] HRC 'Conference room paper', see note 5, § 70.

[173] HRC 'Conference room paper', see note 5, § 71.

[174] HRC 'Conference room paper', see note 5, 72.

[175] HRC 'February 2019 Report the Commission on Human Rights in South Sudan', see note 19 §§ 725.

[176] For instance, the village of Gandor was attacked four times between 29 May and 3 July 2018, resulting in the killing of 232 civilians, raping 120 women and girls, looting and destruction of civilian property. HRC 'February 2019 Report the Commission on Human Rights in South Sudan' see note 19, § 710–716

[177] HRC 'February 2019 Report the Commission on Human Rights in South Sudan', see note 19, § 714–718.

[178] HRC 'February 2019 Report the Commission on Human Rights in South Sudan', see note 19, § 741.

and government officials at the national state and county levels in Juba, Bentiu, and Northern and Southern Liech States[179] who may have been instrumental in the delivery of weapons and ammunition to the armed groups.[180]

Reports suggest that the armed groups that carried out the attacks on the ground included the SPLA 4 Division led by a Brigadier General, SPLA-IO (TD) under the command of the Commander of Unity, and the youth militia under the control of the Gany County Commissioner.[181] One of the aims of this offensive was to drive out the SPLA-IO(RM) forces from southern Unity and 'to clear the area of civilians who could potentially provide support to the SPLA-IO (RM) and prevent their return by burning and destroying their homes and making them too scared of the brutal attacks'.[182] This was agreed during a meeting in mid-April held in Leer County with the participation of the Governor of Southern Liech State and the SPLA Commander in Leer.[183] A part of the plan was to clear the area of civilians 'on the premise that if civilians were driven out of the area, the SPLA-IO (RM) would not return'.[184] The ensuing offensive in Leer and Mayendit Counties by SPLA and SPLA-IO (TD) and affiliated militias ultimately led to the displacement of half the population of Leer County, as well as thousands from Mayendit and Koch Counties.[185] Overall, the attacks carried out by government forces in Leer and Mayendit Counties 'have formed part of a planned attack against the civilian population... [S]uperiors encouraged pillage of goods as compensation for their services ... [and] part of the aim of the attack was to displace and terrorize the civilian population.'[186]

Similar patterns could be observed during the government attacks in the Jonglei State. As reported, in Yuai Town, '[g]overnment forces embarked on a brutal campaign... attacking the civilian population destroying the town including through the pillage and destruction of civilian property'[187] and 'deliberately and systematically attack[ing], destroy[ing] and render[ing] useless [OIS]'.[188] Reportedly, the

[179] HRC 'February 2019 Report the Commission on Human Rights in South Sudan', see note 19, §§ 737–738.

[180] HRC 'February 2019 Report the Commission on Human Rights in South Sudan', see note 19, § 706–708.

[181] The Gany County Commissioner was specifically involved in recruited and controlled the militia forces active during the offensive. HRC 'February 2019 Report the Commission on Human Rights in South Sudan', see note 19, § 704.

[182] HRC 'February 2019 Report the Commission on Human Rights in South Sudan', see note 19, § 704, § 734.

[183] HRC 'February 2019 Report the Commission on Human Rights in South Sudan', see note 19, § 705.

[184] HRC 'February 2019 Report the Commission on Human Rights in South Sudan', see note 19, § 705.

[185] HRC 'February 2019 Report the Commission on Human Rights in South Sudan', see note 19, § 734.

[186] HRC 'February 2019 Report the Commission on Human Rights in South Sudan', see note 19, § 722, 724, 728, 743.

[187] HRC 'Conference room paper', see note 5, § 97.

[188] HRC 'Conference room paper', see note 5, § 123.

SPLA soldiers did not differentiate between the humanitarians, civilians, or soldiers in their attack, destroyed homes, harvested and stored agricultural produce, looted cattle, killed civilians, and raped women, leading to mass displacement of a high number of civilians.[189] In Waat village as well, '[g]overnment forces entered the village in vehicles and opened fire on residents, forcing fearful civilians to flee'[190] and, over the course of two months, 'destroyed everything' including all houses and crops in the village.[191]

B. Command Responsibility

Importantly, military commanders and civilian superiors may also incur liability for the crimes committed by forces under their effective command, control, or authority pursuant to the doctrine of command/superior responsibility.[192] This mode of liability may be particularly useful in prosecuting military commanders or civilian superiors who may personally have lacked the requisite intention to starve civilians, or where the existence of an overarching common plan or policy cannot be proven but where the defendant, nonetheless, knew or should have known that the forces under his/her effective control committed the war crime of starvation and where he/she failed to take the necessary and reasonable measures within his/her power to repress its commission or to submit the matter to the authorities for investigation and prosecution.[193] As noted earlier, there are some indications that some individuals belonging to the government forces may incur liability for the war crime of starvation under the doctrine of command/superior responsibility.[194]

5. Conclusion

The prosecution of the war crime of starvation would be an important step towards its deterrence. While the prosecution of starvation is yet to be seen in an international jurisdiction and only a handful of times has anything resembling the war crime of starvation been prosecuted domestically, the broadening of the Rome Statute's jurisdiction by the Assembly of States Parties may well signal a change in attitude towards a desire to label starvation appropriately. The challenges involved in prosecuting starvation will, in most cases, be considerable: prosecutors are most

[189] HRC 'Conference room paper', see note 5, § 97–98.
[190] HRC 'Conference room paper', see note 5, § 99.
[191] HRC 'Conference room paper', see note 5, § 100.
[192] Art. 28 Rome St.
[193] Note that different standards apply to command and superior responsibility under the Rome Statute. See Rome Statute, Art. 28.
[194] See Rome Statute, Art. 28.

likely to need to prove intention to starve where concurrent natural or otherwise lawful causes of starvation may be competing causes; they may well wish to hold remote commanders responsible for actions perpetrated by their subordinates thousands of miles away; and they may also need to attach appropriate relevance to the compliance with IHL principles. However, precedents for dealing with most of these challenges can be found in the prosecution of other similar crimes and can be met by drawing from the practices that have developed over time at various international tribunals and courts in relation to the prosecution of other equally complex crimes.

In this chapter, we have attempted to demonstrate how some of these challenges will be navigated. No doubt future trials will throw up different or unforeseen challenges. Indeed, each conflict in which starvation as a method of warfare has been deployed bears its own characteristics. In South Sudan, those seeking to leverage benefit from the starvation of civilians have done so, *inter alia*, by attacking the agro-pastoralist livelihood system. Here the challenge of ruling out possible inferences as to the perpetrators' state of mind which might be present as alternatives to an intention to starve, particularly where 'scorched-earth policies' can be attributed to perpetrators, may not be so difficult. Although establishing an evidential nexus capable of imputing criminal responsibility to remote decision-makers, within a disorganized and often malfunctioning military chain of command and where there is a multitude of different armed groups with undefined and varying links to pro-government and rebel forces, will be a challenge.

Attacks on subsistence farming are less prevalent in Syria, where some of the most significant assaults on civilian life were the sieges of Homs and Aleppo which resulted in widespread food insecurity and loss of life. In that context, prosecutors will need to consider the lawfulness of the sieges and whether principles of IHL were followed. In Yemen, agricultural facilities, fishing boats, and water sources have been destroyed through airstrikes which the Saudi-led Coalition argue were directed towards military targets. The naval blockade, preventing supplies from entering Yemen, combined with the obstruction and manipulation of humanitarian aid, has also undoubtedly caused extensive human starvation. Again, any future defendants alleged to be responsible for these attacks will likely seek to rely on the presence of military targets in each case as excluding criminal responsibility, because of their purported compliance with the principles of distinction, proportionality, and precaution. In these circumstances, even where there is an arguable case of some compliance with these principles on a case-by-case basis, where prosecutors can prove patterns of attacks against OIS that are proximate in time, space, and modus operandi, and recurring over time, a strong case can nevertheless be built. Many of the modern prosecutions in which JCE has been alleged have built upon similar patterns of conduct. Each of these conflicts, therefore, creates different challenges. However, in most cases support from analogous preceding prosecutions can be found.

So far, meaningful accountability has had little to do with the use of starvation as a method of warfare, for a variety of rational and irrational reasons. However, a legal framework is now in place for the prosecution of starvation as a war crime in the form of the Rome Statute. Representatives of the international community expanded that jurisdiction through an inclusive, consultative, and democratic process to cover both non-international as well as international armed conflicts. The man-made cause of deliberate starvation as a tactic of war, which has been used for centuries to weaken the adversary and punish its supporters, has thus far been hidden from view, masquerading and excused as natural causes. However, the mask seems finally to be slowly but surely lifting. Whilst starvation has been a contextual feature of other prosecutions, this is in our view an inadequate forensic examination of its causes, consequences, and culpability. Indeed, in modern conflicts such as South Sudan, Syria, most recently in the Tigray region of Ethiopia, and perhaps most notoriously in Yemen, mass starvation has become synonymous with the conflicts being waged on their territories. There are similarities here with the ethnic cleansing that occurred in Bosnia and Herzegovina and Croatia in the early 1990s. In those cases, prosecuted at the ICTY, ethnic cleansing—charged as forcible transfer—became the crime at the centre of the joint criminal enterprise, and thus the vehicle for the Prosecution's central thesis. Through the prosecution of forcible transfer in this way, the campaigns of ethnic cleansing received an extensive forensic examination, a judicial determination, and public understanding and recognition. The adjudication and labelling of this conduct and the sentences imposed for it reinforced the prohibition and contributed towards rendering the crime toxic.

The track record of international criminal justice tells us that accountability will not by itself deter future instances of deliberate starvation, nor is it a system that consistently delivers justice for the victims of atrocities.[195] However, as public understanding of the causes of starvation appears to be growing, criminal accountability in the form of prosecutions for the war crime of starvation can play an important expressive role in rendering starvation morally toxic.

[195] Although this is a problem that is predominantly caused by operational issues, rather than fundamental issues that undermine the concept of international criminal justice.

PART IV
BROADER PERSPECTIVES

The work of preventing and responding to starvation crimes includes a much broader range of issues than just prosecutions. This section introduces key issues that inform policy response and engagement, including the potential and pitfalls of famine early warning systems and the imposition of sanctions as a response to the creation of starvation conditions. It also introduces nuance to how we understand starvation crimes. Like other crimes, deliberate starvation entails differentiated vulnerabilities, demanding that attention be paid to how sex, gender and age play significant roles in the experience of harms. Changing the public understanding of intentional starvation requires that we also pay attention to the question, who tells the stories of mass starvation—both as they occur and long after, when survivors struggle to make sense of what they have suffered.

11

Humanitarian Challenges and Implications for Famine Early Warning Systems

Daniel Maxwell

1. Introduction

Famine early warning systems (EWS) began with support from international donors in the aftermath of the Sahelian famine of the 1970s, though in some ways they trace their origins back as far as the Indian Famine Codes of the nineteenth century. The information systems that track humanitarian conditions and inform decision-makers have expanded substantially in the past two decades and in many cases have reached a degree of unprecedented sophistication. These systems—and the analytical outputs they produce—are intended to provide timely information to decision-makers about the coming three to six months to enable timely mitigation and response measures (the *early warning* function), and provide information about the severity of the crisis as it is occurring (the *resource allocation* function).

These systems predict and classify famine that is imminent or occurring, vital for informing early humanitarian action—and which therefore have a limited but crucial role to play in holding parties to account for the question of starvation crimes (as defined by Conley and de Waal in this volume). However, while these systems can be generally predictive, they are weak with regard to linking specific causes to the occurrence of famine or crises of lesser severity.[1] They are especially weak with regard to conflict analysis, or linking specific conflict acts to specific famine or crisis-related outcomes. And the analysis of the intent of conflict actors—presumably critical to the prosecution of starvation crimes—is unheard of in either the analytical protocols or outputs of these systems. Causal analysis in EWS is slowly being improved but distinct risks are involved in taking on questions about intent.

[1] In fact, despite the fact that the word garners so much attention, the term 'famine' may be counterproductive in a discussion about 'starvation crimes' because famine, as it is currently defined, may be too restrictive a term. So the term needs to be understood broadly in this context, not just in the narrow technical definition. To put it bluntly, 'starvation crimes' can occur even if there is no 'famine' *per se* (by current definitions).

Daniel Maxwell, *Humanitarian Challenges and Implications for Famine Early Warning Systems* In: *Accountability for Mass Starvation*. Edited by: Bridget Conley, Alex de Waal, Catriona Murdoch, and Wayne Jordash QC, Oxford University Press.
 DOI: 10.1093/oso/9780192864734.003.0011

These systems have become increasingly sophisticated in the past decade but they still tend to be based on several assumptions that are important to understand. This chapter briefly describes existing famine or food security EWS and outlines some of the assumptions on which they are based—both in theory and in practice. Then it gives four brief case studies of recent famine or 'near-famine' events and pieces together the formal analysis process with an attempt to reconstruct events on the ground from a conflict analysis perspective—highlighting the extent to which the formal famine analysis did or did not deal with conflict analyses and the political kryptonite around the discussion of 'intent'. It closes with a summary of gaps in the current system and an assessment of the risks of trying to address those gaps through famine early warning (EW) or alternative means.

2. Early Warning and Information Systems

Several global initiatives constitute the bulk of the early warning and analysis capacity related to famine and starvation. The goal of an EWS specifically for starvation crimes would be to account not only for factors predicting famine itself but also those concerned with the larger context of conflict and fragility, and to be able to assess specific threats to civilian groups. These factors broadly speak to the means starvation crimes (access to food), the motives (for conflict), and the victims (specific civilian groups). No single existing EWS does all of these things. Currently famine early warning systems, are distinct from political fragility/atrocity EWS.

A. Famine Early Warning/Information Systems

Integrated Food Security Phase Classification (IPC). IPC was devised in Somalia in the early 2000s to provide a graphic representation of current-status information related to the severity of food insecurity—and therefore the allocation of international aid. IPC developed the now ubiquitous maps that depict the severity of current status from 'minimal current food insecurity' (Phase 1), through progressively more crisis-prone phases all the way to 'famine' (Phase 5).[2] Given that 'famine' is the most severe of the classification phases, the IPC definition for that phase has become the *de facto* definition for famine globally. Briefly, IPC's definition of famine requires the simultaneous breaching of three

[2] The Integrated Food Security Phase Classification (IPC) Global Partners, *Technical Manual Version 3.0: Evidence and Standards for Better Food Security and Nutrition Decisions* (2018), available online at: <http://www.ipcinfo.org/fileadmin/user_upload/ipcinfo/manual/IPC_Technical_Manual_3_Final.pdf> (visited 24 November 2020).

thresholds for the severity of current status: food insecurity (at least 20 per cent of the population with no access to food), malnutrition (at least 30 per cent of children under five years of age moderately or severely wasted—low weight for height), and mortality (at least two people per 10,000 dying per day from famine-related causes).[3] IPC analysis is now undertaken in some thirty-five chronically food-insecure countries; a nearly identical protocol known as 'Cadre Harmonisé' is conducted in West African countries. As such, IPC is the biggest provider of current-status information about food security crises globally. It is made up of a group of donors, humanitarian agencies, and research institutes. It is hosted and managed by the UN Food and Agriculture Organization (FAO) with a small Global Support Unit in Rome and teams in various countries attached to FAO field offices.

FEWS NET. The Famine Early Warning System Network (FEWS NET) is a global project that provides early warning information about food security to its funder, the United States Agency for International Development (USAID), but whose information is broadly available through a public website and a 'data warehouse' containing the historic records of past food security crises. It covers thirty-eight chronically food-insecure countries, either by actually having staffed field offices in-country, or through remote monitoring from a regional office. FEWS NET has adopted IPC classification for both its current-status updates and the projections it makes for early warning analysis, but it has a more detailed approach to the early warning function. As a result, FEWS NET is probably the biggest single provider of food security early warning information globally. Though FEWS NET is part of the IPC consortium, and works very closely with IPC analysis teams in the field, they maintain an independent analysis, which doesn't always agree with IPC analyses.

The World Food Programme. WFP is the world's largest humanitarian agency, responsible for frontline response to food security crises. As such, it has enormous internal information requirements that may not be met by FEWS NET or IPC (though WFP, like FEWS NET, is a member of the IPC consortium). The Vulnerability Assessment and Mapping Unit both conducts current-status assessments and serves some early warning functions—indeed WFP-led assessments are a major source of information for both IPC and FEWS NET analyses.

Global Food Security Cluster and Global Nutrition Cluster. Since the humanitarian response mechanism was reorganized into sectoral 'clusters' in the mid-2000s, both the food security and nutrition clusters have been major sources of famine-related information. National nutrition clusters—led by UNICEF—typically organize the annual schedule of Standardized Monitoring and Assessment

[3] IPC, see note 2. There is considerable controversy as to what is considered 'famine-related causes'—an important consideration in this discussion. This point will be brought up later.

of Relief and Transitions (SMART) surveys that enumerate information on child and maternal nutrition, health, and mortality (and sometimes a range of other outcomes). The actual surveys are often carried out by non-governmental organizations (NGOs), sometimes by local government.

Other existing systems. Other national early warning and information systems exist—usually, but not always, led by national governments. Additionally, many non-governmental humanitarian organizations operating regional or local EWS—sometimes intentionally community-based systems. The extent to which these inform national systems varies, and even where they exist, their coverage is localized and patchy. Other global mechanisms that track hunger—such as the Global Hunger Index—exist, but these tend to amalgamate data from disparate sources to make a combined index. They don't track crises in real time and certainly do not do forecasting or early warning.

Recent developments. In the past two or three years, several novel attempts have been launched to completely change famine analysis and prediction from empirical, field-assessment-based analyses to computational or econometric modelling, artificial intelligence, or some combination of these. The Modeling Early Risk Indicators to Anticipate Malnutrition (MERIAM) project, led by Action Against Hunger, combines econometric and computational modelling to forecast the prevalence of malnutrition three to six months out.[4] A similar initiative is underway at the London School of Hygiene and Tropical Medicine—forecasting both malnutrition and mortality rates.[5] Lentz and colleagues developed a forecasting model for food security indicators.[6] The World Bank Famine Action Mechanism (FAM) initiative attempts to harness both econometric modelling and artificial intelligence to forecast IPC phase classifications and population numbers within phases.[7] What all these have in common is that they use publicly available data in real time to model an independent forecast. To date, all of these are prototypes, still being fine-tuned using one or two specific countries' data. None of them is up and running in terms of providing real-time forecasts, and some of them face the inevitable challenge of being very 'data hungry' modelling approaches in very 'data scarce' contexts. But several of them do incorporate conflict data, and while the need for on-the-ground data collection is unlikely to disappear in the near future, these methods offer a distinctly different approach to forecasting famine, food insecurity, malnutrition, and mortality.

[4] Action Against Hunger, *Modeling Early Risk Indicators to Anticipate Malnutrition*, available online at <https://knowledgeagainsthunger.org/research/prevention/meriam-modelling-early-risk-indicators-to-anticipate-malnutrition/> (visited 24 November 2020).

[5] F. Checchi, personal communication.

[6] E. Lentz et al., 'A Data-Driven Approach Improves Food Insecurity Crisis Prediction', 122 *World Development* (2019) 399–409.

[7] Z. Carmichael, personal communication.

B. Fragility and Atrocity Early Warning Indices

Fragility indices. Of several indices of fragility, the two best known include the Fund for Peace *Fragile States Index*[8] and the Organisation for Economic Co-operation and Development (OECD) *States of Fragility Report*.[9] They compile data on a range of indicators (economic, political, demographic, social) to provide an assessment of risk of crisis in the coming year. Using measures of past or ongoing state failure, the Fragile States Index does not have any independent predictive value[10] (in other words, it reports current status but does not function as an EWS).

Atrocity early warning and risk assessment lists. In the field of atrocity prevention and response several institutionalized efforts are being made to monitor countries at a global level[11] for the likelihood that atrocities would occur.[12] These include qualitative analysis frameworks, for example, as deployed by the UN Office on the Prevention of Genocide[13] (which is very unwieldy at present, containing 143 underlying and proximate factors to assess the risk of genocide, crimes against humanity, and war crimes); quantitative analysis, like the CIA-managed Political Instability Task Force (PITF, which employs political scientists in universities and which also maintains a separate dataset focused on atrocity risk assessment) and the Atrocity Forecasting Project (Australian National University);[14] and mixed methodology lists, like the Sentinel Project[15] and the Early Warning Project (US Holocaust Memorial Museum).[16]

[8] Fund For Peace (FFP), *Fragile States Index Annual Report* (2019), available online at: <https://fundforpeace.org/2019/04/10/fragile-states-index-2019/> (visited 24 November 2020).

[9] Organization for Economic Cooperation and Development, *States of Fragility Framework* (2018), available online at <http://www.oecd.org/dac/conflict-fragility-resilience/statesoffragilityframework2018.htm> (visited 24 November 2020).

[10] H. Mueller, 'Fragility in the Data', background paper for P. Collier, T. Besley, and A. Khan (eds), *Escaping the Fragility Trap*, Commission on State Fragility, Growth and Development, London School of Economics and University of Oxford's Blavatnik School of Government (2018).

[11] There are also a number of regional and national endeavours to undertake this work, by coordinating across several countries and focusing on monitoring and coordination within countries (across government and with civil society actors). This summary focuses on global systems; note, these models tend to focus on direct killing, rather than conditions of increased mortality, including those that might be included as starvation crimes.

[12] B. Harff, and T. R. Gurr, *Risk Assessments 2015: Potential State Perpetrators of Genocide and Politicide*, Genocide Prevention Advisory Network (2015). The list from 2015 includes the note: 'The hazards, or relative risks, in all countries will not change significantly in the near future unless any of their driving variables change. So these assessments can be expected to be valid through, say 2020, and quite possibly beyond.'

[13] The UN Office on Genocide Prevention and the Responsibility to Protect, *Framework of Analysis for Atrocity Crimes* (2014), available online at: <https://www.un.org/en/genocideprevention/documents/our-work/Doc.1_Framework%20of%20Analysis%20for%20Atrocity%20Crimes_EN.pdf> (visited 24 November 2020).

[14] Australian National University, *Atrocity Forecasting Project*, available online at: <https://politicsir.cass.anu.edu.au/research/projects/atrocity-forecasting> (visited 24 November 2020). This is a forecasting list; it attempts to predict where atrocities will occur.

[15] The Sentinel Project, *Early Warning System*, available online at: <https://thesentinelproject.org/what-we-do/early-warning-system/> (visited 24 November 2020).

[16] United States Holocaust Memorial Museum (USHMM), *Early Warning Project*, available online at <https://earlywarningproject.ushmm.org/> (visited 24 November 2020).

C. Discussion of EWS

In the context of today's famine-risk countries, the existing systems described usually work well to highlight food security crises, both predictively and in real time, but they do not aim to predict conflict, and they are mostly not very good at predicting and rationally analysing the consequences of conflict. Conflict and fragility systems aren't very good at this either. While food security systems assess current status and predict future conditions, several concerns arise with regard to these tasks in the context of conflict-driven crises: their organization and independence, their data and methods, their assumptions, issues of politics and access, and the alignment of atrocity/fragility and food security EW.

Organization and independence. FEWS NET is an independent project, funded by USAID. WFP's information systems are deliberately built to serve internal information needs. IPC is a consortium, but in-country it is a government-led analysis, organizationally housed within an FAO country office. So it is often perceived as linked to the political interests of government and the organizational interests of FAO. In many cases, this works fine, but where the government is party to a conflict leading to food insecurity, IPC has difficulty functioning independently from political influences.[17]

Data and methods. Conflict data are not collected by these systems. There are some publicly available datasets on conflict, but these have limited predictive ability. These data can be used to predict the food security consequences of violent conflict. But even with publicly available data, analysts face serious constraints in utilizing these in government-led analysis processes.

Assumptions. The timing of information collection and analysis is driven by assumptions about the causes of food insecurity. Almost without exception, the timing of analysis is driven by the assumption that hunger fluctuates seasonally and any shocks to food access are driven primarily by environmental and economic factors. In some cases, there may be a seasonal connection to conflict—dry season offensives, etc. But in many cases where conflict is a significant causal factor in food insecurity, it may be delinked from seasonal considerations—such that seasonally based analysis may actually miss the greatest spikes in food insecurity. Conflict analysis is at best weak and generic; analysis of starvation crimes is unheard of in these analyses.

Politics and access. Even given efforts to maintain an independent analysis, information is often missing—making for, at best, an incomplete analysis. When information is missing because of access constraints on assessment teams in the field,

[17] D. Maxwell, and P. Hailey, *The Politics of Information and Analysis in Famines and Extreme Emergencies: Synthesis of Findings from Six Case Studies* (Medford: Feinstein International Center, 2020), available online at <https://fic.tufts.edu/wp-content/uploads/PIA-Synthesis-Report_May-13.pdf> (visited 26 August 2021).

ascertaining the difference between security constraints and political constraints is difficult. Nowhere is this a bigger problem than in conflict-induced food security crises or famines.

Atrocity and fragility EW. Most of the fragility and atrocity EWS are risk assessments: drawing on statistical models that rely on annually produced national-level data. They attempt to calculate the probability of atrocities (defined variably across datasets) occurring. Several verge on 'early warning' by incorporating information about more fast-moving factors and potential triggers for new episodes of mass violence—such as elections, coups, or assassinations—or by incorporating expert opinion. However, these systems remain of limited policy-making value. For instance, at present, the US Holocaust Memorial Museum early warning project notes that it 'considers countries ranked in the top 30 to be at high risk'.[18] This number of countries at risk suggests that the rankings have some distance to go to be valuable for identifying when and how policy attention should be focused.

Alignment of atrocity/fragility EW and food security EW. It is perhaps worth noting that the country case studies offered here (Somalia, South Sudan, Syria, and Yemen) are the four countries at the absolute highest level of fragility on the current Fund for Peace *Fragile States Index*, and three of them (Somalia, South Sudan, and Yemen) are in the top four on the OECD *States of Fragility Report* for 2018. However, while this underlines the convergence of conflict, fragility, and food insecurity, it doesn't necessarily mean much in terms of early warning.

In May 2018, at least partly in response to the 'four famines' scenario experienced in 2017, the UN Security Council (SC) unanimously adopted Resolution 2417 that highlights the link between armed conflict and the threat of famine. Much of the resolution was about respecting international humanitarian law (IHL) and refraining from attacking the infrastructure that supports civilian access to adequate food and water, but it also calls for unimpeded humanitarian access to conflict-affected populations and urges prompt investigation into violations of IHL that may have resulted in human starvation. This provides some basis for improving conflict analysis and prediction in food security information and early warning systems. The resolution is mostly silent about the issue of information, except for requiring the Secretary General to report annually to the Security Council on the implementation of the resolution. Article 11, however, does request the Secretary General to 'provide information on the risk of famine and food insecurity in countries with armed conflict'.[19]

The information that the Secretary General is obliged to provide will have to come from the systems described earlier here—as well as synthesizing outputs of different systems. However, despite internationally agreed priorities about the

[18] USHMM, see note 16, *Ranking of All Countries*, available online at: <https://earlywarningproject.ushmm.org/ranking-of-all-countries> (visited 24 November 2020).

[19] SC Res. 2417 24 May 2018, Art. 11.

links between armed conflict and extreme hunger, the question of deliberately inflicted hunger is rarely if ever addressed by these systems. This is partly for reasons noted earlier in this chapter—because they are either government-owned systems (and governments are, without contemporary exception, parties to the conflicts that cause famines or extreme food security crises) or they are managed by UN agencies that have to negotiate access to affected populations and who are reluctant to anger parties to the conflict (not to mention having budgetary interests).

3. Case Studies

Several recent cases of famine or near-famine crises demonstrate that—despite international consensus statements like UNSCR 2417—even analysing the impact of conflict on food security can be difficult; analysing the use of hunger as a weapon of war is even more difficult. Cases include Somalia 2011, in which a well-documented famine clearly occurred but in which mitigation and response were constrained both by armed non-state actors and the counter-terrorism measures of donor governments; South Sudan in 2017 in which government leadership of the process made analysis of the causes virtually impossible; Syria in 2015–2018, which probably did not amount to a famine by contemporary definitions, and where famine EWS mostly do not exist; and Yemen in 2018—a near-famine case. Several of these cases have been described extensively elsewhere in this volume; Somalia will be explored in more detail here.

A. Somalia (2011)

Areas of south-central Somalia experienced famine in 2011, with a formal declaration of famine in July. The crisis affected over 3 million people; over half a million children were malnourished, and though no absolute number was given at the time of the declaration, tens of thousands of people were assumed to have already died from malnutrition and disease. Hundreds of thousands of additional people were displaced—both internally and outside the country. Although the famine was declared in real time, numerous critics at the time and since have noted that ample warnings of the impending disaster were given, but the attempts to mitigate the crisis, or even to respond to the acute suffering in real time, were under-funded and inadequate—and in some ways deliberately restricted—until the time of the declaration.[20]

[20] D. Maxwell, and N. Majid, *Famine in Somalia: Competing Imperatives and Collective Failures, 2010–2012* (New York: Oxford University Press, 2016).

The famine declaration galvanized the international community to respond. Overnight, donor funding for Somalia doubled and within months tripled. New and innovative forms of response—notably relying on cash transfers rather than in-kind food aid—were launched. Agencies scaled up, negotiations over access were stepped up, and a large-scale response throughout the second half of 2011 helped to bring the crisis under control.[21]

The crisis was caused by a combination of factors. A drought of significant proportion swept through the whole of the Horn of Africa. This badly affected agricultural production in the grain growing areas of Somalia and caused significant loss of livestock in pastoral areas. But equally importantly, the drought lowered river levels bringing irrigated farming to a halt, causing demand for rural labour to plummet at a time when people typically took refuge in these areas in search of wage labour. At the same time, global prices of basic food grains spiked dramatically. Somalia imports most of its basic food grains, even in 'good' years. This combination of events led to a dramatic collapse in purchasing power for the hardest hit groups.[22]

Somalia effectively had no central state apparatus at the time of the famine—most of the country was ruled by armed groups. The famine-affected area was controlled by *Al-Shabaab*, an Islamist group with ties to *Al-Qaeda*, labelled by the United States and other Western countries as a terrorist group. The Africa Union, with support from Western countries, had troops in Somalia fighting *Al-Shabaab*, along with the limited armed forces of the Transitional Federal Government. The fighting displaced people, along with the drought and the collapse of livelihood options. *Al-Shabaab* did little to prevent the onset of the famine and its repressive policies had done much to exacerbate the problem—including severe limitations on access. *Al-Shabaab* threats against humanitarian agencies, and in some cases, killing of staff, meant humanitarian agencies (including the World Food Programme) that could have mitigated the crisis had pulled out of southern Somalia.[23]

But equally important, for much of the period leading up to the declaration of famine, Western donors put severe restrictions on funding for anything in south central Somalia for fear that such resources might end up in the hands of terrorist groups like *Al-Shabaab*. Aid diversion was rampant in Somalia at the time: a UN report in 2010 suggested that up to half of all food aid in Somalia, for example, was ending up in the wrong hands (often, but not always, *Al-Shabaab*).[24] The counterterrorism measures put in place by Western donors and agencies, combined with the general policies of *Al-Shabaab* with regard to aid, led to severe constraints on

[21] Maxwell and Majid, see note 20.
[22] Maxwell and Majid, see note 20.
[23] Maxwell and Majid, see note 20.
[24] UN Monitoring Group on Somalia and Eritrea, *Report of the Monitoring Group on Somalia Pursuant to Security Council Resolution 1853* (2010).

humanitarian action as the crisis spiralled out of control—indeed were significant causes of it spiralling out of control. Throughout the period leading up to the declaration, inadequate funding available for humanitarian work in south central Somalia, the risk of criminal liability for diverted aid, and the reputational damage of being accused of 'aiding terrorists' combined to preclude the kind of early intervention needed to avert the crisis. While the situation was clearly dramatically worsening on the ground, not enough was done to mitigate the crisis until it was far too late.

This was not by any means the first time that the international humanitarian community had seen a crisis coming and failed to act in time, but it was probably the most tragic instance of this kind of 'early warning/late response' failure.[25] Eventually the death toll from the famine would be estimated at nearly 260,000 people—disproportionately young children.[26]

This crisis was well predicted. The drought was caused by the well-known progression of the La Niña-related drought in the Horn of Africa and there were warnings about drought from August 2010 onwards. The collapse in purchasing power was also noted as early as late 2010, and of course the conflict with *Al-Shabaab* was ongoing and had gradually been leading to tighter and tighter restrictions to access on the ground. The absence of the World Food Programme and other frontline agencies was noted by both donors and the UN leadership in Somalia in 2010. But few contingency plans were put in place.[27]

Between mid-2010 and the declaration of famine in July 2011, the FEWS NET and Food Security and Analysis Unit (FSNAU) produced sixteen special bulletins or early warning flash alerts (beyond their regular reporting). These alerts became more specific and more alarming over time.[28] The real-time evaluation of the crisis early 2012 noted that early warning information was 'accurate and timely' across the region.[29] However, what was not predicted—because it has never been part of any humanitarian information system—was the way in which *Al-Shabaab* restrictions on access would combine with donor sanctions on aid diversion to complicate and delay action to mitigate the crisis. This became abundantly clear as the crisis deepened in the first half of 2011. US contributions to the humanitarian

[25] R. Bailey, *Famine Early Warning and Early Action: The Cost of Delay* (London: Chatham House, 2012). A. Seal, and R. Bailey, 'The 2011 Famine in Somalia: Lesson Learnt from a Failed Response?' 7 *Conflict and Health* (2013) 1–5.

[26] F. Checchi and C. Robinson, *Mortality among Populations of Southern and Central Somalia Affected by Severe Food Insecurity and Famine During 2010–2012*, London School of Hygiene and Tropical Medicine, Famine Early Warning System Network and Food and Agriculture Organization (2013).

[27] J. Darcy, P. Bonard, and S. Dini, *IASC Real Time Evaluation of the Humanitarian Response to the Horn of Africa Drought Crisis: Somalia 2011–2012*, Inter-Agency Standing Committee Somalia (2012), available online at: https://reliefweb.int/sites/reliefweb.int/files/resources/IASC-RTE%20Somalia%202012.pdf (visited 24 November 2020).

[28] C. Hillbruner, and G. Moloney, 'When Early Warning Is Not Enough—Lessons Learned from the 2011 Somalia Famine', 1(1) *Global Food Security* (November 2012) 20–28.

[29] Darcy, Bonard, and Dini, see note 27.

effort declined sharply in 2010–2011 (until the famine was declared). While some agencies had the contacts and the capacity to work in in the famine-affected area, some refrained out of fear of the possible legal consequences—effectively basing their decisions on legal and reputational considerations, not humanitarian need. To be sure, some agencies were on the ground but not enough, and some individuals and agencies were struggling behind the scenes to develop an effective work-around for Somalia, but it took a long time.

The stand-off over counter-terrorism policy was a major factor preventing the scale up that might have mitigated the worsening crisis. Seal and Bailey, writing in 2013, noted, 'Inadequate funding was a direct and inevitable consequence of donor anti-terror legislation. So was the failure to provide an enabling legal environment for humanitarian agencies to operate without the threat of prosecution. This strategy also had serious consequences for the presence, operational capacity and access of agencies on the ground.'[30]

No early warning or information system has ever been set up to predict these kinds of complicating factors in a famine. And yet it was without doubt these complicating factors (*Al-Shabaab*'s restrictions on access, the donors' restrictions and the associated legal and reputational risks, and the absence of WFP) that tipped an otherwise very bad year in Somalia over into an actual, full-blown famine. A drought shock of relatively similar magnitude in 2016–2017 was met with earlier and more decisive intervention, but it is not clear whether this meant that the 'system' has taken the lessons of 2011 on board or simply that a handful of committed individuals saw to it that earlier actions were taken in 2017. In any case, the threat of legal and reputational retribution against intervening agencies was lower in 2017.

What is clear is that it was politics—more than drought, prices, or *even armed conflict*—that effectively prevented early action in Somalia in 2011. While the actions of both *Al-Shabaab* and Western donors were not directly intended to cause a famine, in retrospect they clearly contributed significantly to it. The course of the conflict was not specifically tracked but even if it had been, it would not have changed anything about either the early warning or the blockages to early action.

Since 2011, most of the solutions to the constraints on early intervention in famine have been technical in nature, but the biggest constraints in 2011 were political. The security and counter-terrorism imperative clearly took precedence over the humanitarian imperative in 2011, and while the exact circumstances are perhaps unlikely to recur, politics and security concerns, together with restrictions on access by conflict actors, will certainly outweigh humanitarian concerns again under different circumstances. So, who was accountable for famine in Somalia? Unfortunately, the blame can be spread to many parties, but no-one has

[30] Seal and Bailey, see note 25, at 3.

ever faced any sanction. A 2013 report by the UN Office for the Coordination of Humanitarian Affairs (OCHA) and the Norwegian Refugee Council concludes:

> In Somalia, the restrictions placed upon humanitarian actions through sanctions and counter-terrorism measures are considered by many in the humanitarian community to have compounded the already difficult operating environment in the Al-Shabaab controlled areas ... While it is impossible to determine the extent to which the abrupt decrease in aid [observed in the 18 months running up to the declaration] contributed to the famine that followed in mid-2011, some relationship cannot be discounted. Certainly, the severity of the food crisis and the publicity around it prompted a reversal of donor policy.[31]

B. South Sudan (Greater Baggari, 2016–2018)

Between 2015 and the end of 2017, a series of military offensives in Western Bahr al Ghazal, South Sudan, led to a situation described elsewhere as a blatant case of ethnic cleansing and large-scale displacement of civilians in an area known as 'Greater Baggari'. Trapped behind a frontline, this population was unable to access food, markets, or means of livelihood and were mostly inaccessible to humanitarian actors. This gave rise to serious concerns about the possibility of localized famine.[32]

The Greater Baggari case came to the attention of famine analysts in South Sudan, but not until August 2017, after eight months of denied access. The famine declared in Unity State in early 2017 consumed all attention during the first half of the year, when most of the forced displacement and siege-like conditions of blocked access were occurring in Wau County. When a field assessment team was finally granted access to Greater Baggari in August 2017, an estimated 10 per cent of the population was found to be in Phase 5 conditions—meaning they were experiencing famine conditions, but the proportion of the population was too low to permit a declaration of famine.[33] The standard famine analysis, overwhelmingly focused on humanitarian outcomes rather than causes, did not make clear that ethnic cleansing was the reason for the displacement in the first place or that the blocked access was a deliberate military strategy. When a report was finally issued in September, it stated:

[31] K. Mackintosh, and P. Duplat, *Study of the Impact of Donor Counter Terrorism Measures on Principled Humanitarian Action*, OCHA and Norwegian Refugee Council (2013), at 102–103.

[32] See Chapter 5 of the current volume.

[33] This brief summary of the analysis is reconstructed from Integrated Phase Classification (IPC) reports and narratives from observers on the ground.

> of great concern is Greater Baggari, a sub-area of former Wau County, with an estimated population of 25,000, where 10 percent of the population is in Humanitarian Catastrophe (IPC Phase 5) … as a result of *sustained insecurity, sporadic humanitarian access since 2016, lack of freedom of movement and extreme depletion of livelihoods*. Should these very limited access conditions persist, the food security situation is expected to deteriorate and widen further.[34]

Clearly, such a statement was not inaccurate, but it revealed very little about what was actually occurring. References to 'sustained insecurity' and 'sporadic access' betrayed little notion of ethnic cleansing, or tactical operations that amounted to a siege, or the deliberate blockage of humanitarian access that amounted to the use of food as a weapon. So why the watered down and depoliticized language and recommendations in the analysis?

IPC analysis in South Sudan, as everywhere, was a government-led process, and building government capacity for analysis is a major part of IPC. While that is good development policy, it is clearly fraught with possibilities for political manipulation of the analysis where conflict is the dominant factor driving food insecurity or famine.[35] In the South Sudan analysis, even a discussion of famine was a near-taboo topic. International agencies feared reprisals, denial of work permits, and programme stoppage if the analysis became too 'political'.[36] Several government civil servants had been sacked from their jobs (and feared for their lives for a period of time) after the famine was declared in central Unity State earlier in 2017. There was a general sense that discussion of population in Phase 5 was about as far as anyone could go unless there was overwhelming evidence for discussing famine. Conflict analysis was relegated to, at best, a secondary role in the analysis. Given the lack of skills and the political influences, there was every reason to keep the language in the analysis and recommendation very generic.

C. Syria (2012–2018)

Prior to the Arab Spring in 2011, Syria was an extremely unlikely place to be talking about famine or starvation. It was a middle-income country and, while having

[34] IPC Technical Working Group, *Key IPC Findings: September 2017–March* 2017, at 1. Emphasis added.

[35] D. Maxwell et al., *Constraints and Complexities of Information and Analysis in Humanitarian Emergencies: Evidence from South Sudan* (Medford: Feinstein International Center, Tufts University, 2018), available online at <https://fic.tufts.edu/assets/SouthSudan-Case-Study-Report.pdf (22 October 2021).

[36] One analyst who had the temerity not only to speak out about but actually measure mortality in a conflict zone in a different part of the country at the time was attacked and badly beaten up. While no-one was ever apprehended or prosecuted for that crime, the widespread suspicion was that government soldiers were responsible for the attack.

an arid climate in parts of the country, it was generally listed as a food-exporting country, with a strong irrigated agriculture sector in its diverse economy. Peaceful protests associated with the 'Arab Spring' soon turned into an outright civil war.[37] Siege warfare quickly became the hallmark of the Syrian war. Altogether, at least eighteen separate siege events have been noted during the conflict. By late 2018, OCHA noted that more than a million people were still in 'hard to reach' areas (a polite way of saying besieged areas).[38] By 2019, the UN Humanitarian Response Plan (HRP) for Syria estimated that more than 6.5 million people within Syria were in need of food assistance, and more than 11 million in need of some form of humanitarian assistance to survive. The HRP is notable for its elucidation of needs but very weak on analysis of why those needs persist.[39]

Despite myriad reports referencing siege warfare with names like 'Starvation by Siege,' and 'Encircle, starve, surrender, evacuate',[40] there has never been a formal analysis of famine or starvation in Syria. Neither FEWS NET nor IPC operate in Syria. The 2018 HRP was based on an IPC-like analysis,[41] and makes references to 'interruption or restriction of humanitarian assistance', but provides little evidence on food insecurity or malnutrition. It proved impossible to collect data necessary for the analysis in 136 sub-districts (out of a total of 284).[42]

This is partly due to the extremely limited access that humanitarian actors have in Syria, for either assessment or response, and partly due to a deep reluctance to endanger the little access they do have by crossing the regime (or some of the non-state conflict actors).[43] The limited analysis of the impact of sieges has been conducted completely outside 'normal' channels of famine analysis,[44] and indeed, it isn't clear how standard famine analysis would apply in sieges. IPC analysis can apply to any population with a minimum size of 10,000 people. Certainly at least some of the besieged areas had populations many times that size,[45] but the inability to access the besieged areas repeatedly meant that there are little data on which to base any such judgement.

[37] See Chapter 8 in the current volume.

[38] OCHA Syria, *Humanitarian Response Plan 2019 for Syria* (2019), available online at: <https://reliefweb.int/sites/reliefweb.int/files/resources/2019_hrp_syria.pdf> (visited 24 November 2020).

[39] OCHA Syria, see note 38.

[40] S. Power, 'Starvation by Siege: Applying the Law of Armed Conflict in Syria', 8 (2) *Amsterdam Law Forum* (2016) 1–22; Independent International Commission of Inquiry on the Syrian Arab Republic, *Sieges as a Weapon of War: Encircle, Starve, Surrender, Evacuate: Sieges as a Weapon of War*, 29 May 2018, available online at: <https://www.ohchr.org/Documents/HRBodies/HRCouncil/CoISyria/PolicyPaperSieges_29May2018.pdf> (visited 21 March 2022).

[41] Food Security Sector, *Food Security Situation in Syria: Expanded version of the Food Security Sector Humanitarian Needs Overview 2018* (2018), available online at <https://fscluster.org/syria/document/food-security-situation-syria-expanded> (visited 30 October 2021).

[42] Food Security Sector, see note 41.

[43] K. Howe, *No End in Sight: A Case Study of Humanitarian Action and the Syrian Conflict* (Medford: Feinstein International Center, Tufts University, 2015).

[44] M. Kanfash, and A. Aljasem, *Accountability for Starvation Crimes: Syria* (Medford: Global Rights Compliance/World Peace Foundation, 2019); and Kanfash and Aljasem, see note 37.

[45] Independent International Commission of Inquiry on the Syrian Arab Republic, see note 40.

Perhaps more important to the understanding starvation crimes would be intensive assessment of, and interviews with, people escaping or being forced to leave besieged enclaves—an attempt to piece together what happened. The question arising from sieges and starvation crimes, however, is whether standard measures of 'famine' apply at all? Do famine thresholds matter—or are they even applicable to—a context like Homs or Eastern Ghouta? If the starvation is a deliberate tactic of warfare, does it matter how many people or what proportion of the population was affected?

D. Yemen (2015–2019)

Modern-day Yemen is a relatively new country, formed in 1990. Despite its semi-arid landscape, Yemen is fairly heavily populated with an estimated population of 28.7 million people in 2018. Since 2014, Yemen has been in a civil war between *Ansar Allah* (Partisans of God, known informally as 'the Houthis') and the internationally recognized government. *Ansar Allah* began as a peaceful protest movement but took up arms after government forces killed their leader. A civil war broke out in September 2014 that shortly saw the Houthis taking control much of the populated northern highlands. The Houthis took control the capital of Sana'a, but their regime is not recognized by the international community.[46] A year after a Saudi-led coalition (SLC) started its military operations in support of the internationally recognized government, humanitarian agencies began warning that food security conditions were sharply deteriorating. At the height of the crisis in 2018, UN Secretary General Antonio Guterres referred to Yemen as 'the world's worst man-made humanitarian crisis'[47] and there were significant fears of famine in Yemen. A variety of factors came together, all of which were related to the conduct of the conflict, and included widespread internal displacement of people and the rapid decline of purchasing power by average Yemeni citizens.

Yemen had a relatively limited food security information system prior to the war. IPC analysis was begun in 2011 but has not conducted regularly, so do not represent comparable findings over time. Despite years of attempting, FEWS NET has never secured legal registration. As a result, there are special challenges relate to both capacity and bureaucratic constraints.[48] Access poses even greater challenges. Despite warnings of famine in 2018, data collection teams were unable to assess conditions in the hardest hit areas. Because permission to visit was not granted, much of the analysis was based on out-of-date

[46] See Chapter 9 in the current volume.

[47] OCHA, *Humanitarian Response Plan 2018: Yemen*, January 2018, available online at: <https://reliefweb.int/sites/reliefweb.int/files/resources/20180120_HRP_YEMEN_Final.pdf> (visited 24 November 2020).

[48] Maxwell et al., see note 35.

information. The 2018 IPC estimated that, in the absence of humanitarian assistance, 20.1 million or 67 per cent of the population would face severe food insecurity, including 238,000 people projected to be in IPC Phase 5 (famine conditions).[49] The UN Country Team took extraordinary political and macro-economic interventions, but these were in spite of—not because of—the formal famine analysis.

Groups completely outside the traditional early warning or food security information community have independently monitored the impact of the war.[50] But these sources only report the incidents of attack—they cannot convey the impact on peoples' access to adequate food. More recently, Houthi attempts to take control of humanitarian food aid and divert it to their own purposes has led to threats of cutting off aid to the north altogether. All the major parties to the Yemen conflict have attempted to weaponize access to food—and whether or not this has led to famine in the strict definition of the word may not be important. But several points are worth noting.

First, if humanitarian access to respond to the food needs of conflict-affected people is contingent on the decisions of both state and non-state authorities, humanitarian agencies are reluctant to put that limited degree of access at risk by pushing too hard on the analysis—particularly regarding any link between conflict and famine or starvation. Thus, while an analysis of the conflict is very helpful to the overall understanding of need in a complex humanitarian emergency like Yemen, that conflict analysis is best conducted outside Yemen, and by non-humanitarians.

Second, there are international standards for access and information even in warfare, and donor governments—as well as humanitarian agencies themselves—could have pushed harder for access, independence, and adherence to international standards regarding data transparency. This will require greater leadership at the highest levels of the humanitarian community—it cannot be left to the technical teams tasked with undertaking the analysis.

Third, while it is relatively easy to blame authorities for blocking access or trying to control information, in this case some of the donors were also implicated. Saudi Arabia and the United Arab Emirates are two of the three largest donors to the UN Humanitarian Response Plan for Yemen in 2019—as they were in 2018.[51] These actors clearly also have an interest in controlling the narrative on the humanitarian impact of the war.

[49] IPC, *Yemen: IPC Acute Food Insecurity Analysis December 2018–January 2019* (2018).

[50] M. Mundy, *The Strategies of the Coalition in the Yemen War: Aerial Bombardment and Food War*, World Peace Foundation, available online at <https://reliefweb.int/sites/reliefweb.int/files/resources/Strategies%20of%20Coalition%20in%20Yemen%20War.pdf> (visited 19 September 2019).

[51] OCHA, *Humanitarian Response Plan 2019: Yemen*, March 2019.

4. Discussion

Several key points emerge from the case studies. First, food insecurity EWS are not very good at conflict analysis or incorporation of conflict data, but there is no need to collect additional conflict data to draw necessary conclusions. Such data are available from multiple local and global sources,[52] so the paucity of data isn't the reason for the absence of conflict analysis in famine EWS. Existing conflict datasets and state fragility indices are not predictive of conflict, but the important point is mostly about predicting future food insecurity resulting from *already observed* conflict or its immediate consequences (displacement or entrapment).

Second, incorporating conflict analysis into a consensus-based analysis of food insecurity and famine is nearly impossible when that analysis is led by government in the context of a civil war in which the government is a party to the conflict. While it is logical to speculate on the conditions of people in conflict-affected or besieged areas, it has proven difficult to conduct analyses of famine or starvation in those areas.

Third, none of these systems capture the element of intentionality inherent in the concept of starvation crimes. If government-led systems have a difficult time even acknowledging famine and mostly do not incorporate conflict analysis, it is not hard to see that these systems would be totally unable to assess the question of intentionality with regard to famine or starvation-related deaths. Any assessment of that question would clearly need to be undertaken independently and outside the context of the analysis of the humanitarian situation.

In some ways, innovative technology could be helpful to address this challenge: for instance, remote sensing to track human population movement and displacement, or even to count graves in the case of mass mortality (both are not only demonstrably possible—actual examples exist). The Ushahidi platform, used to great success in the Haiti earthquake search and rescue mission, actually had its roots in the post-election violence in Kenya in 2007–2008, where it was useful in alerting the authorities to places where one local group was being threatened by another. Artificial intelligence is increasingly capable of accessing and digesting multiple and disparate sources of conflict information and amalgamating it with other, more conventional forms of EW (some version of this is already being done by initiatives like MERIAM or FAM initiatives—the difference is that MERIAM and FAM are being tested in places with at least some accessibility).

In all the cases examined here (and virtually all others in which there is a demonstrable link between violent conflict and famine or severe food insecurity—Nigeria, Afghanistan, Central African Republic, Sudan, parts of Ethiopia, Democratic Republic of Congo, Myanmar, etc.), the ability to access affected areas lies with

[52] The Armed Conflict Location and Event Data Project (ACLED), the Uppsala Conflict Data Program Georeferenced Event Dataset (UCDP-GED), as well as country-specific sources.

controlling authorities—both state and non-state—who have every reason to deny access for either assessment or the prevention of starvation if the latter is part of, or even just a by-product of, their war strategy.[53] So inevitable trade-offs must be made between the completeness of the analysis on the one hand and access on the other (recalling the humanitarian imperative—access is more for prevention of starvation, not just the analysis of it).

Ultimately, however, while incorporating more conflict analysis into more independent analytical process would be ideal, simply establishing *whether* a famine occurred is useful information, even if the causal links to human intentionality can only be weakly inferred. For the objective of prosecuting starvation as a crime against humanity (which requires that the crime is systematic and large scale), demonstrating that some threshold of severity and magnitude have been surpassed would be necessary. Simply establishing the fact of famine (i.e. the current-status analysis conducted by IPC) is in itself, important for establishing the level of gravity necessary to suggest that famine is a crime against humanity. The severity threshold for starvation crimes as violations of international humanitarian law is not as high as it is for famine: starvation-related mortality at lesser levels of severity or magnitude than that implied by IPC thresholds for 'famine' could still qualify as violations on the prohibition against using starvation as a method of war. This occurs frequently and rarely attracts much attention.[54]

Proceeding too far down the road of pushing for more conflict analysis or analysis of intentionality could be counterproductive. The one thing that current analysis is still partially able to do is to establish the fact that famine (or crisis of a lesser severity, but still of devastating dimensions in humanitarian terms) is occurring, which of course is itself necessary if prosecution is the objective. To insert the element of demonstrating intentionality is likely to be impossible and attempting to do so might further complicate the analysis that is currently done.

In the end, to be able to make any statement about 'starvation crimes', information would be needed for at least four factors: the outcome (mortality), the causes (conflict or acts of war), the motives (intentions of the conflict actors), and some evidence that directly links cause and motivation to the outcome. That is a high bar to set for verifiable information in a conflict/complex humanitarian emergency.

Even if better conflict analysis was incorporated into early warning, would action to prevent and mitigate the impact of conflict be possible? Clearly having governments as one partner engaged in the analysis, much less leading it, is problematic in

[53] Indeed, one official let slip at an IPC analysis in South Sudan that one of the reasons he feared IPC analysis was that 'it might be collecting information for the ICC' (confidential personal communication).

[54] For example, even though the mortality in the Somalia famine of 2011 received a lot of attention, 43 per cent of the total mortality took place prior to reaching IPC Phase 5 (famine) levels or severity—or else in locations that never reached Phase 5 (F. Checchi, personal communication). If the crisis hadn't breached famine thresholds, it would have gone down as just 'another bad year in the Horn of Africa', and doubtless, no one would have even thought to calculate the number of people killed.

a context where conflict is the main driver of food insecurity and the government is party to the conflict. In such cases (South Sudan and Yemen are both clearly good examples) there needs to be a way for making early warning and analysis independent of—and yet still permitted to operate by—governments. That is a tall order in today's political environment. Conflict analysis might need to take place in parallel with—rather than being incorporated into—the food security/nutrition analysis processes. While this might not enable changes in humanitarian access or response, it might help to address macro-economic or political drivers—as indeed seems to have been the case in Yemen in 2018.

Famine experts have long been discussing the issue of accountability for famine.[55] The discussion among technical famine experts needs to be merged with the legal discussion, and needs to go beyond just 'famine' as defined by IPC. Levels of food security-related mortality can actually reach higher levels in crises of lower severity than famine if they are greater in magnitude and duration.[56] So, much remains to be done. But clearly the possibility of prosecution offers one solution to the dilemma of accountability, and improving conflict analysis and incorporating it into (or alongside of) existing EWS is one critical step along this path.

[55] N. Haan, S. Devereux, and D. Maxwell, 'Global Implications for Famine Prevention, Mitigation and Response', 1(1) *Global Food Security, Special Edition on the Somalia Famine 2011–2012* (2012) 74–79.

[56] See note 15.

12

Sanctions as a Mechanism for Accountability for Starvation Crimes

Benjamin J. Spatz, Oliver Windridge, and Catriona Murdoch

1. Introduction

United Nations Security Council Resolution S/RES/2417 (UNSC 2417) on armed conflict and hunger, adopted on 24 May 2018, includes reference to one specific action that the Council might take in response to violations: sanctions. Paragraph 9 '[r]ecalls that the Council has adopted and can consider to adopt sanction measures, where appropriate and in line with existing practice, that can be applied to individuals or entities obstructing the delivery of humanitarian assistance, or access to, or distribution of, humanitarian assistance'. Existing practices by the UN and North American and European states for targeted sanctions against individuals or entities deemed responsible for human rights violations or international crimes have also occasionally extended to crimes of starvation, and could do so more in future.

Less noticed, are the four examples of where sanctions have been used to respond to crimes of starvation. First, on 13 July 2018, the Security Council adopted resolution 2428 on South Sudan. In that resolution the UN imposed sanctions (travel ban and asset freeze) on two South Sudanese individuals. One of them, General Paul Malong, was singled out for, *inter alia*, 'the obstruction of the activities of international peacekeeping, diplomatic, or humanitarian missions in South Sudan, including ... the delivery or distribution of, or access to, humanitarian assistance'.[1] This targeted sanction was pursuant to previous UNSC resolutions concerned with achieving peace and preventing violations of international humanitarian law in South Sudan, rather than the implementation of the provisions of UNSC 2417. Less than a week later the UK also listed Malong for, amongst other things, the preventing 'the transport of humanitarian supplies'.[2] Second, on 24 December 2018, an unnamed major general of the Myanmar army was listed

[1] SC Res. 2428, 13 July 2018, Annex 1, p. 8.

[2] 'Consolidated List of Financial Sanctions Targets in the UK', Office of Financial Sanctions Implementation HM Treasury (updated 20 August 2021), available online at <https://www.gov.uk/government/publications/the-uk-sanctions-list> (visited 27 August 2021).

Benjamin J. Spatz, Oliver Windridge, and Catriona Murdoch, *Sanctions as a Mechanism for Accountability for Starvation Crimes* In: *Accountability for Mass Starvation.* Edited by: Bridget Conley, Alex de Waal, Catriona Murdoch, and Wayne Jordash QC, Oxford University Press.
DOI: 10.1093/oso/9780192864734.003.0012

(financial restrictions) by the UK 'for serious human rights violations' including 'the systematic burning and clearing of civilian villages [and] the obstruction of humanitarian relief to civilians in Kachin, in particular the blocking of food transports'.[3] Third, on 15 March 2021, Ibrahim Yassar, a Syrian businessperson and financier to President Assad, operating across multiple sectors of the Syrian economy, was listed (financial restrictions) under the Syria (Sanctions) (EU Exit) Regulations 2019 for his association with the Assad regime, in particular that he and his family business 'act as a front for Bashar and Asma Assad's personal hold on the Syrian economy, whilst millions of Syrians are food insecure'. Last, on 23 May 2021, the United States issued sanctions (visa restrictions) on any current or former Ethiopian or Eritrean government officials, members of the security forces, or other individuals—to include Amhara regional and irregular forces and members of the Tigray People's Liberation Front (TPLF)—responsible for, or complicit in, undermining resolution of the crisis in Tigray. It specifically highlighted and condemned amongst other violations, the destruction of objects indispensable to survival, including civilian property, water sources, hospitals and medical facilities, alongside the denial of humanitarian access.[4]

These four examples demonstrate practical avenues for using sanctions in response to armed conflict and hunger. The naming of Malong was momentous. He, alongside the other named and unnamed alleged perpetrators, enter the historical record as the first individuals ever targeted for sanctions for a starvation crime, alongside other violations. The four cases listed show the under-realized potential of using sanctions to bring pressure to bear on individuals and entities responsible for starvation crimes *per se*.[5]

This chapter asks, what might sanctions such as this be expected to achieve if imposed more often and more consistently?

In addressing this question, it is necessary first to place sanctions in context. As coercive policy tools short of military force, sanctions have a mixed record. While their use as a proposed remedy for starvation crimes has emerged over recent years, sanctions also have a record of contributing to hunger and impeding humanitarian

[3] 'Consolidated List of Financial Sanctions Targets in the UK', see note 1.

[4] The United States imposed travel restrictions under Section 212(a)(3)(C) of the Immigration and Nationality Act 1952 on Ethiopia and Eritrean government officials' and members of the security forces, or other individuals—including Amhara regional and irregular forces and members of the TPLF—condemning, amongst other violations, the destruction of OIS including civilian property, water sources, hospitals and medical facilities and the denial of humanitarian access. restrictions. See US Department of State Press Release, 'United States' Actions to Press for the Resolution of the Crisis in the Tigray Region of Ethiopia', 23 May 2021, available online at <https://www.state.gov/united-states-actions-to-press-for-the-resolution-of-the-crisis-in-the-tigray-region-of-ethiopia/> (visited 28 August 2021).

[5] See, Global Rights Compliance, 'Starvation Sanctions Digest', 28 January 2021, available online at <https://starvationaccountability.org/news-and-events/starvation-related-sanctions-digests-january-2021> (visited 27 August 2021). The Digest outlines relevant country-based UN, EU, and US sanctions measures dealing peripherally with starvation, objects indispensable to survival, and humanitarian access-related issues since 2017.

responses while not often achieving their stated objectives. The problematic history includes blanket economic embargoes that not only failed to achieve their policy goals but contributed to major humanitarian emergencies in Iraq and Haiti in the early 1990s. Countries including Cuba, North Korea, and Sudan have also blamed economic hardship on sanctions, though major factors in the deprivations experienced by their populations were mismanagement, corruption, and conflict. Subsequently the sanctions toolbox has been refined and today almost all UN and unilateral sanctions are targeted on individuals and specific entities within states or armed groups, deployed with the goals of affecting the material capacity and reputations of those actors. Like all such instruments, the actual impacts of sanctions need to be distinguished from their success or otherwise in achieving policy goals. It is particularly important to develop the analytical tools needed to assess the impacts of the current generation of sanctions which are quite different from previous sanctions regimes.

This chapter describes the historical, legal, humanitarian, and political context surrounding the potential use of sanctions as a tool to pursue accountability for starvation crimes. It is organized around the following sections. First is a review of the evolution of sanctions practices (blanket and targeted) including their rationales, how they are decided upon and evaluated. This also includes a discussion of the role of terrorism designations in humanitarian outcomes and policy measures adopted to mitigate those adverse impacts. Second, we turn to contemporary instruments for targeted sanctions utilized against individuals and entities deemed responsible for violations, focusing on the scope and jurisdiction of sanctions programmes at the UN and by North American and European governments. This includes a brief analysis of the UN panels of experts for Yemen and South Sudan and their unique roles in highlighting starvation and humanitarian issues. Last, we examine the ways in which sanctions can support pathways to justice for starvation crimes.

2. Modern Context of Sanctions: General Issues of Theory and Practice

A. What Are Sanctions?

Sanctions are a coercive policy tool, short of military force, whereby the sender temporarily places restrictions on the target. Senders of contemporary sanctions are most commonly the UN, the United States, western European states, and the European Union (EU), with the US being the most active sender by many measures.[6] The United States often—and increasingly—acts unilaterally, but by virtue of

[6] J. Gordon, 'The Hidden Power of the New Economic Sanctions', 118 *Current History* (2019) 3–10.

the structure of the UNSC it supports all UN sanctions measures. Regional entities such as Economic Community of West African States (ECOWAS) and the African Union have, at times, imposed various sanctions on their members (usually consisting of suspension of membership) outside of the context of UN or EU sanctions, but this has been limited.

Targets can be any entity or individual. They have included states and entities of the state (e.g. specific military units or parastatals, etc.) and non-state entities (e.g. armed actors, political groups, corporate entities, etc.). Sanctioned individuals have been members of governments (usually leadership figures or their deputies), terrorist groups, and individuals involved in terrorist activity, armed groups (e.g. rebel factions) and their leaders, parties to a conflict, and the family members of the aforementioned individuals, their associates, supporters, and facilitators, and associated business partners.[7]

The actual sanctions are Often called 'measures' and typically fall into five categories. (1) Diplomatic sanctions: restrictions on the activities of political entities and governments, such as by banning or limiting the travel or number of diplomatic personnel, closing embassies/offices of representation, and other visa policy restrictions. (2) Individual sanctions: asset freezes and travel bans applied to individuals and corporate entities. (3) Sectoral sanctions: arms embargos, restrictions on material or technology related to nuclear proliferation, and transportation restrictions, such as restrictions of aviation and maritime activity. (4) Commodity sanctions: bans or limits on the trade in commodities and resources, such as oil, timber, diamonds, charcoal, luxury goods, etc. (5) Financial sector sanctions: investment bans, sovereign wealth fund restrictions, and restrictions on engagement with certain financial markets.[8] Our concern in this chapter is almost entirely with individual sanctions.

It is common to assume that sanctions are imposed to change target behaviour, but this is actually just one of many goals. Some of these objectives are very specific, others generic; most relate to the targeted country, individual, or entity but others are more associated with the politics of the sender. Sanctions are also imposed to punish, weaken, constrain, or distract adversaries; signal preferences (to allies, foes, and domestic constituencies); placate domestic constituencies; support allies; and deter actors that are not party to the sanctions. Modern sanctions regimes have additional aims, including to encourage democracy; stop human rights violations and the suppression of internal opposition; enforce peace agreements;

[7] T. Biersteker et al., 'UN Targeted Sanctions Datasets (1991–2013)', 55 *Journal of Peace Research* (2018) 404–412.

[8] B. J. Spatz, *Sanctions in the Political Market*, Conflict Research Programme, London School of Economics and Political Science, 26 November 2019, available online at <https://www.lse.ac.uk/ideas/Assets/Documents/Conflict-Research-Programme/crp-memos/Sanctions-Memo-261119.pdf> (visited 27 August 201).

assist in the pursuit of individuals for prosecution before international courts; ensure compliance with treaty obligations; promote a sender's reputation domestically and internationally; maintain international norms and structures; prevent and contain armed conflict; achieve compliance with international law; counter conflicting parties' military aggression; express outrage; build support for military action; assist in negotiations; prevent the export of sensitive technologies; embarrass the targets; limit the spread of weapons; constrain international rogue actors; or bring suspected terrorists to justice.[9]

These multiple goals often overlap, and, at times, conflict. Sanctions may work at cross-purposes when there are multiple senders (e.g. the United States, EU, UN) pursuing different political objectives, but it can be the case even with only a single sender. For example, within a single state bureaucracy there are often multiple constituencies for sanctions that use them for different tactical and strategic ends. It is for this reason, among others, that seeking to untangle whether sanctions 'work' is a fraught question. Additionally, the purposes for why sanctions are imposed are often not fully known and/or are often contested. Moreover, since it is common for there to be multiple, simultaneous (at times conflicting) purposes of sanctions, it is possible—indeed likely—for there to be successes, failures, and areas of non-impact along multiple dimensions of a single use of sanctions.[10]

B. Evolution of the Use of Sanctions

The design of contemporary sanctions regimes and instruments has been strongly shaped by the experience of the blanket economic embargoes imposed by the UN on Iraq and Haiti in the early 1990s. These caused and exacerbated humanitarian emergencies, compelling senders to respond to these devastating unintended consequences.

The story of UN sanctions—and really all contemporary sanctions—begins with the end of the Cold War when bipolarity and the relative lack of integration between the sides meant that unilateral measures—sanctions imposed by the United States, for example, on a state allied with the Soviet Union—could have been easily evaded, if they had any impact at all. At the same time, before 1990, UNSC consensus on such coercive measures was essentially impossible and so sanctions were only used twice: against Southern Rhodesia (economic sanctions from 1965–1979) and South Africa (arms embargo in 1977–1994).[11] However, the dissolution of the Soviet Union cleared the way for the UNSC—led by the United States, Britain, and

[9] Spatz, see note 8. M. Eriksson, *Targeting Peace: Understanding UN and EU Targeted Sanctions* (Farnham: Ashgate, 2011), at 2.

[10] Spatz, see note 8.

[11] Eriksson, see note 9.

France—to employ sanctions in nearly every major challenge to peace and security in the 1990s, which was dubbed the 'sanctions decade'.[12]

The enthusiasm was short lived. The earliest sanctions, such as those imposed on Iraq and Haiti (and elsewhere), were poorly conceived, blanket economic measures that cut off all trade with those countries. While the elite could withstand the pain, there were 'intolerable consequences for innocents'.[13] In Haiti, sanctions caused severe malnourishment and drove 'child mortality increases of up to 64 per cent'.[14] One year into the Iraq sanctions, in March 1991, the sanctions had such a negative humanitarian impact that UN Under-Secretary-General Martti Ahtisaari called the situation 'near-apocalyptic'.[15] In those first few years in Iraq, sanctions led to a loss of US$ 250 billion in oil revenues, a 250-times increase in a household's monthly food costs, and between 100,000 and 227,000 additional child deaths.[16] The UN attempted to increase humanitarian aid but need outstripped relief. Relief supplies, too, while exempted from sanctions, still had to pass through a review process, further slowing the humanitarian response.[17] In 1996, then-US Ambassador to the United Nations, Madeleine Albright, voiced the implicit—and flawed—logic that the people's pain would lead to political gain. When a reporter asked her whether an estimated 500,000 children who died as a consequence of sanctions was 'worth it', Albright responded, 'I think it is a very hard choice, but the price—we think, the price is worth it'.[18] She later regretted the remark.

[12] D. Cortright and G. A. Lopez, *The Sanctions Decade: Assessing UN Strategies in the 1990s* (Boulder: Lynne Rienner Publishers, 2000).

[13] E. Carisch, L. Rickard-Martin, and S. R. Meister, *The Evolution of UN Sanctions: From a Tool of Warfare to a Tool of Peace, Security and Human Rights* (New York: Springer, 2017), at 56.

[14] Carisch, Rickard-Martin, and Meister, see note 12, at 56.

[15] *Report to the Secretary-General on Humanitarian Needs in Kuwait and Iraq in the Immediate Post-crisis Environment by a Mission to the Area Led by Mr. Martii Ahtisaari, Under-Secretary-General for Administration and Management*, UN Doc S/22366, 20 March 1991, §8.

[16] D. W. Drezner, 'Sanctions Sometimes Smart: Targeted Sanctions in Theory and Practice', 13 *International Studies Review* (2011) 96–108, at 97; E. Hoskins, 'Humanitarian Impacts of Sanctions and War in Iraq', in T. Weiss et al. (eds), *Political Gain and Civilian Pain* (New York: Rowman & Littlefield, 1997) 91–147; A. Alnasrawi, 'Iraq: Economic Sanctions and Consequences, 1990–2000', 22 *Third World Quarterly* (2001) 205–218; M. O'Sullivan, *Shrewd Sanctions* (Washington, DC: Brookings Institution, 2003); R. Garfield, 'Morbidity and Mortality Among Iraqi Children from 1990 through 1998', March 1999, available online at <http://www.casi.org.uk/info/garfield/dr-garfield.html> (visited 27 August 2021).

[17] Weiss et al. (eds), see note 16 at 225.

[18] The figure of 500,000 children's lives was an estimate at the time; as referenced above, the figure was later determined to be between 100,000 and 227,000. Albright has apologized repeatedly for the statement and said that 'back then I was trying to say that basically it was due to the fact that Saddam Hussein was not fulfilling what was required of him. But we learned in many ways that comprehensive sanctions often hurt the people of the country and don't really accomplish what is wanted in order to change the behavior of the country being sanctioned ... What I said was totally stupid. I use it in my class as an example of how thinking through what you're going to say is important. I regret it. I have apologized for it I can't tell you how many times ... I do not think the sanctions were worth any children's lives, frankly, because I don't believe in that ... It was just the worst possible thing I could've said.' D. Marchese, 'Madeleine Albright thinks it's good when America gets involved', *The New York Times*, 20 April 2020, available online at <https://www.nytimes.com/interactive/2020/04/20/magazine/madeline-albright-interview.html> (visited 27 August 2021).

Alive to the tragic irony that they were responding to crises of their own creation, the UNSC and member states scrambled to devise ways to limit humanitarian impacts. In a prominent case, this meant breaking one's own embargo: later in the decade, Andrew Natsios successfully advocated to provide North Korea emergency food aid despite sanctions prohibiting such assistance, based on the logic that maintaining a strict sanctions regime during famine conditions wouldn't lead to mass revolt but just mass death.[19] During this period, targeted, or so-called smart sanctions replaced full-scale blanket embargoes. Targeted sanctions are measures that apply 'coercive pressures on specific individuals and entities and that restricts selective products or activities, while minimizing unintended economic consequences for vulnerable populations and innocent bystanders'.[20] The last comprehensive sanctions imposed by the UN were on Haiti in 1994.[21]

For almost three decades, all UN sanctions have been targeted on individuals and entities. Current practice is that, on a case-by-case basis, the UNSC imposes measures on individuals, entities, and groups. North American and European governments have meanwhile developed sanctions programmes that provide the legal basis to target individuals and entities deemed responsible for human rights violations. With a growing technical capacity to track illicit financial transactions (drawing in part from counter-terror measures), targeted sanctions have expanded in reach and intrusiveness. By their nature, the implementation of measures such as asset freezes work without publicity and are therefore difficult to monitor, making their effectiveness even harder to measure using established political science metrics. While the switch to targeted measures does not eliminate the problem of adverse unintended consequences, it does raise a hard empirical question about how their intended impacts are to be assessed. It is necessary to develop new methodologies that can monitor the behaviour of those individuals and entities within the existing political systems and provide transparent processes for de-listing individuals and entities. Until this is done, both academic literature and political commentary on the empirical outcomes of sanctions will remain dominated by the now-outdated paradigm of country-level sanctions and by the persistent observation that sanctions don't 'work'.[22]

[19] See, S. K. Afesorgbor, 'Sanctioned to Starve? The Impact of Economic Sanctions on Food Security in Targeted States', *Social Sciences Research Network*, 25 July 2020, available online at <http://dx.doi.org/10.2139/ssrn.3660536> (visited 27 August 2021), at 1. For criticisms levied at sanctions impeding the flow of humanitarian aid see, 'The Question of Humanitarian Exceptions from UN Sanctions Regimes', *Old Dominion University Model United Nations Society, Issue Brief Security Council* (2019), available online at <https://www.odu.edu/content/dam/odu/offices/mun/issue-brief-2019/ib-sc-humanitarian-exceptions-from-sanctions.pdf> (visited 27 August 2021), at 1.

[20] Cortright and Lopez, see note 12, at 25.

[21] Somewhat confusing the point that no comprehensive UN sanctions were imposed after 1994, is the fact that the UNSC more or less maintained the comprehensive sanctions on Iraq that it had imposed in 1990 until 2003. See Biersteker et al., see note 7.

[22] See e.g. S. Jenkins, 'Sanctions are imposed by the sanctimonious, and achieve nothing', *The Guardian*, 28 May 2021, available online at <https://www.theguardian.com/commentisfree/2021/may/27/sanctions-achieve-nothing-belarus-lukashenko> (visited 27 August 2021).

C. Measuring Sanctions' Impacts

Sanctions vary in their goals, targets, and the assumptions about how they should work. Three models dominate the political science literature. The first theory is that if sanctions impose costs broadly on a society, then the population will rise up and force leaders to change. This is sometimes called the naïve theory and, as was made painfully clear in Iraq and Haiti, there is no evidence that this logic chain holds true.[23] The second assumes that if sanctions impose costs on a broadly defined class of social, economic, political, or military elites broadly, then this class will, through politicking and coalition shifts, force the leadership to change behaviour. In a more targeted variation, the third posits that if sanctions impose sufficient costs directly on individual leaders responsible for policies, then they will change behaviour.

In each, the pathway to political change rests on the assumption 'that economic pain will (somehow) produce political gain'.[24] Here lies a disconnect: 'an oversimplified causal chain, which equates harm to the target's macroeconomy with the incentives its leaders have to change policies'.[25] Indeed, 'there is very little empirical evidence as to whether this is what actually occurs on the ground'.[26] Yet the assumption has been entrenched in the literature as scholars of sanctions regimes have chiefly used country-level economic data to assess the impacts of targeted sanctions. Two obvious problems arise: there is mismatch between macro-economic effects and measures imposed on individuals (even if those individuals control or disproportionately benefit from the macroeconomy) and also targeted sanctions are often designed precisely so as to minimize macro-economic impacts.

We believe it is more fruitful to consider sanctions in relation to how they might interact with existing political systems. The situations we are concerned with are those characterized by violence and hunger; they are typically countries in which institutionalized states never existed or have collapsed completely or in part, and where transactional politics based on the trifecta of coercion, cash rewards and personal connections are constitutive of 'real politics'.[27] Members of the political elite in such countries are primarily driven by material factors—access to money and the means of violence. Sanctions, then, have multiple potential entry points to impact the elite political bargaining that forms the basis of their dealings, provided of

[23] J. Galtung, 'On the Effects of International Economic Sanctions: With Examples from the Case of Rhodesia', 19 *World Politics* (1967) 378–416.

[24] L. Jones, *Societies Under Siege: Exploring How International Economic Sanctions (Do Not) Work* (Oxford: Oxford University Press, 2015), at 1.

[25] R. A. Brooks, 'Sanctions and Regime Type: What Works, and When?' 11 *Security Studies* (2002) 1–50, at 12.

[26] S. H. Allen, 'The Domestic Political Costs of Economic Sanctions', 52 *The Journal of Conflict Resolution* (2008) 916–44, at 916.

[27] Spatz, see note 8; B. J. Spatz, 'Cash Violence: Sanctions and the Politics of Power, and Peace', (PhD Thesis on file at The Fletcher School, Tufts University, Medford, MA, 2020).

course that sanctions can meaningfully limit material access to weapons or money. From this perspective, whilst sanctions are unlikely to change a political system's fundamental rules, they can disrupt the political *status quo* among elite actors by pinching the political players' capabilities and the tools that are at their disposal.[28] That is, sanctions interact with domestic logics of political power to restructure elite power dynamics, which in turn shapes bargaining incentives, strategies, and political outcomes.[29] Sanctions, when imposed in a targeted manner against specific individuals and accompanied by clear messaging from the sanctioning party, can upend an elites' cost-benefit analysis of continuing with a particular pattern of behaviour or policy.[30]

In the case of operationalizing UNSC 2417, paragraph 9, or utilizing another sanctions regimes for similar ends, the key, then, is to determine what political currents might lead elite actors to pursue political strategies that incorporate, or otherwise lead to, starvation crimes or failure to prevent humanitarian crises and food emergencies.

D. Terrorism Designations

Terrorism designations, such as those made by the United States, although not always understood as sanctions in a strict sense, have structural similarities to targeted sanctions. The older mechanism of designating a country as a 'state sponsor of terror' could lead to far-reaching embargoes. This was the case for Sudan (1993–2020) and Syria (1979–present). Current mechanisms focus on entities and individuals. These too can have societal impacts well beyond the designated targets, while the metrics of success (terrorist attacks prevented and activities impeded) are both kept secret and are intrinsically hard to measure.

Terrorism designations prohibit third parties—individuals, businesses including financial entities, non-governmental organizations (NGOs), states, etc.—from engaging in trade and providing material support, broadly defined, to the designated individuals and entities. This could cover humanitarian assistance or other basic items, or could even come from having conversations that could be construed as having material value to those designated. Violations expose third parties to legal jeopardy in the United States even if violations are not uniformly enforced. As in

[28] Spatz, see note 8.

[29] Spatz, 'Cash Violence', see note 27.

[30] For example, South Sudan. Following a period of increased violence, targeted network sanctions imposed by the United States from 2017 onwards has been credited with playing a significant role in bringing warring parties back to the negotiating table, the revival of the peace process and the creation of a new unity government. Whilst progress in South Sudan remains very slow, the use of targeted network sanctions has, at the very least, appeared to support the resumption of that progress. See B. Brooks-Rubin, *The Global Magnitsky Human Rights Accountability Act: Taking Stock*, 24 March 2021, available online at <https://humanrightscommission.house.gov/sites/humanrightscommission.house.gov/files/documents/GloMag_TheSentry_BBrooksRubin_final.pdf> (visited 27 August 2021).

all cases, exemptions can be built into the system and waivers can be obtained. However, these processes can be opaque and onerous (and at times arbitrary); some entities might view continued engagement as being too time-consuming, costly, or risky, and therefore choose to disengage, which can have unintended civilian consequences. A case in point is the US designation of Al-Shabaab as a terrorist group: after the designation in 2010, humanitarian organizations that allowed for any assistance to reach Al-Shabaab—including 'access taxes' to operate in Al-Shabaab-controlled territory—were open to US prosecution. When the US government would not give assurances to humanitarian actors that they would not pursue prosecutions, many stopped operating in Somalia, which was a significant factor in the collapse of humanitarian assistance to Somalia in the months leading up to the 2011 famine.[31] The same logic has significantly complicated humanitarian operations in Syria and was the basis for criticism of the outgoing Trump administration's designation of the Houthis in Yemen as a terrorist organization.

Subsequently, humanitarian workarounds have been built into terrorism-related designations and targeted sanctions regimes with the aim of enabling essential humanitarian activities to continue. These, however, remain fraught with difficulties and act as a significant constraint on humanitarian aid. For example, screening procedures for staff mean that host country professionals—whose contacts and cultural skills are particularly needed in these complex crises—are often not employed, and less suitable foreign nationals are taken on. Similar considerations inhibit partnering with local NGOs or organizations formed among diaspora groups.

These examples show how sanctions, particularly US sanctions, however 'targeted', often have a wider effective perimeter than the stated measures, such as a travel ban on an individual or the freezing of a personal bank account.

3. The Scope and Jurisdiction of Current Sanctions Programmes

This section briefly describes the scope and jurisdiction of sanctions programmes that are potentially relevant to starvation crimes.

A. United Nations

UN sanctions have unique power and reach since they are legally binding on all 193 UN member states. In theory, and in the best cases of implementation, this means they have a truly global impact with the least room for evasion. The UNSC derives

[31] D. Maxwell, and N. Majid, *Famine in Somalia: Competing Imperatives and Collective Failures, 2010–2012* (New York: Oxford University Press, 2016); Chapter 11 in this volume.

its power to impose sanctions under Chapter VII (Article 41) of the UN Charter regarding threats to peace and acts of aggression in conjunction with Article 25 of the UN Charter that states that all member states are obliged to 'agree and carry out the decisions of the Security Council'.[32] The UN Charter does not outline specific technical standards for sanctions designations. In a sense, the only true criterion for imposing UN sanctions is political—that the five Permanent Members (P-5) agree, or more specifically, that no P-5 member state issues a veto, since Chapter VII requires consensus for action. Abstentions, however, do not count against consensus and, in practice, sanctions imposition has at times hinged on convincing reluctant P-5 members, particularly Russia and China, to abstain from votes on sanctions resolutions. The designation criteria of many UNSC sanctions regimes often provide for violations of human rights law, International Humanitarian Law (IHL), and the obstruction of humanitarian aid or access[33]—which can be understood to include starvation-related and humanitarian access-related crimes, even if not explicitly stated. To date it is rare for designations to be based solely on these grounds. At the time of writing, sanctions under UNSC 2417 have yet to be imposed.

The UN has built extensive political, administrative, and technical architecture to support its ability to impose and implement sanctions effectively. Each UNSC sanctions regime is overseen by a sanctions committee composed of the fifteen UNSC member states, chaired by a non-permanent member of the UNSC, and supported by staff from the Security Council Affairs Division of the Department of Political and Peacebuilding Affairs. Committees as such have no technical capacity to gather information on the sanctions they oversee, aside from information that might be gathered by individual members states' diplomatic corps and intelligence services. However, states are often reluctant to share such information and even when shared the credibility of the information and the political motivations of the member states can be questioned by other UNSC members. Therefore, in the UN resolution imposing sanctions, the UNSC typically calls for the Secretary-General to establish a small group—a UN Panel of Experts—to monitor and investigate sanctions and related issues.[34]

[32] Chapter VII of the United Nations Charter covers 'Actions with Respect to Threats to the Peace, Breaches of the Peace, and Acts of Aggression'. Art. 39 states that the UNSC 'shall determine the existence of any threat to the peace, breach of the peace, or act of aggression and shall make recommendations, or decide what measures shall be taken ... to maintain or restore international peace and security'. Art. 41, the basis of sanctions imposition in the UN Charter, states that '[t]he Security Council may decide what measures not involving the use of armed force are to be employed to give effect to its decisions, and it may call upon the Members of the United Nations to apply such measures. These may include complete or partial interruption of economic relations and of rail, sea, air, postal, telegraphic, radio, and other means of communication, and the severance of diplomatic relations.' UN Charter, 24 October 1945.

[33] See e.g. SC Res. 2140, 26 February 2014, at §18(c); SC Res. 2216, 15 April 2015, at § 19; SC Res. 2521, 29 May 2020, at §15(c) and (d); SC Res. 1844, 20 November 2008, at §8 (c); SC Res. 2002, 29 July 2011, at §1 (c); SC Res. 2093, 6 March 2013, at §43 (c).

[34] These are variously referred to as Groups of Experts or Monitoring Groups. Naming conventions aside, their roles and structures are essentially the same. Panels of Experts report directly to UN Sanctions Committees, through an administrative mechanism supported by the UN Security

Panel of Experts' mandates are provided by UN resolution and their roles have evolved over time from an initial, somewhat narrow, focus on sanctions monitoring 'to include detailed analysis of regional conflicts and recommendations for solving them'.[35] Panels have routinely documented sanctions violations, tracked arms traffickers, diamond and timber smugglers, investigated mercenary and militia groups, followed financial flows tied to conflict, conducted impact assessments, analysed ways to build state capacity to address these issues, and provided attendant recommendations to the UNSC. The UNSC relies on this reporting and analysis to 'to help determine which actors bear responsibility for violating sanctions and perpetuating conflict'.[36]

Panels also regularly monitor and investigate issues related to human rights and humanitarian concerns, including famine and humanitarian access at the express request of the UNSC. This reflects lessons learned from the UNSC's early missteps with sanctions and continued interest in the issues, and is visible through the appointment of the individual experts. Experts are appointed to fit the technical specifications of measures outlined in the sanctions resolution. For example, if the sanctions regime includes an arms embargo, an 'arms expert' is appointed, it is increasingly common for a humanitarian affairs expert to be appointed. Of the thirteen current UN sanctions regimes, ten have panels of experts.[37] Of these ten, seven include humanitarian experts: Somalia, Democratic Republic of the Congo, Sudan, South Sudan, Central African Republic, Mali, and Yemen.[38]

Council Affairs Division of the Department of Political Affairs. The experts are consultants—not UN staff—giving them, in theory, the ability to provide information to the UNSC objectively without the prejudices and fears of retribution that might come from being permanent employees. The sizes of various panels have ranged from one expert to over ten, but are typically between four and six. The duration of each panel's mandate typically runs approximately one year, matching the duration set out for the sanctions regime itself in the specific UN resolution.

[35] A. J. Boucher, *UN Panels of Experts and UN Peace Operations: Exploiting Synergies for Peacebuilding*, (Washington, DC: The Henry L. Stimson Center, 2010), available at <https://www.stimson.org/2010/un-panels-experts-and-un-peace-operations-0/> (visited 29 October 2021), at ix.

[36] A. J. Boucher, and V. K. Holt, *Targeting Spoilers: The Role of United Nations Panels of Experts* (Washington, DC: The Henry L. Stimson Center, 2009), available at <https://www.stimson.org/2009/targeting-spoilers-role-united-nations-panels-experts/#:~:text=Targeting%20Spoilers%3A%20The%20Role%20of%20United%20Nations%20Panels%20of%20Experts,-By%20Victoria%20K&text=United%20Nations%20Panels%20of%20Experts%20are%20small%2C%20civilian%2C%20fact%2D,peace%20in%20war%2Dtorn%20regions> (visited 29 October 2021), at 11.

[37] The thirteen current UN sanctions regimes are: Democratic People's Republic of Korea, Yemen, Iraq, Libya, Mali, Guinea-Bissau, Sudan, Somalia, South Sudan, Central Africa Republic, Democratic Republic of the Congo, the sanctions regime related to the assassination of Lebanese Prime Minister Rafik Hariri, and the sanctions regime that covers terrorism/terrorism financing and is specifically geared to address al-Qaida, ISIS, and the Taliban. The three sanctions regimes that do not have panels of experts are: Iraq (an arms embargo); Guinea-Bissau (travel ban); and the sanctions regime related to the assassination of Lebanese Prime Minister Rafik Hariri. For current UN sanctions regimes see, 'Sanctions', United Nations Security Council, available online at <https://www.un.org/securitycouncil/sanctions/information> (visited 27 August 2021).

[38] The three that do not are the sanctions regime focused on terrorism and terrorism financing (originally imposed on actors affiliated with Al-Qaida, the Taliban, and later extended to include ISIS), the nuclear non-proliferation sanctions regime imposed on North Korea, and Libya

In some of these cases it is becoming common for Panels to acknowledge and report on humanitarian access-related issues and to a lesser degree to track the extent of food insecurity and starvation violations. Given that the legal frameworks around starvation are still untested, there appears to remain some hesitation in tackling these issues head on, and instead these violations, and references to them, are sometimes subsumed under humanitarian access issues, rather than as direct violations.

Examples from Yemen and South Sudan illustrate how the UNSC integrates issues of human rights into sanctions regimes and how, in turn, Panels with a humanitarian mandate consider famine, starvation, and issues of humanitarian access, in their monitoring, investigation, and reporting.[39] UNSC Resolution 2140 (2014), that first imposed sanctions on Yemen, explicitly referred to the humanitarian challenges. In paragraphs 17 and 18, the resolution specified the designation criteria to include acts that violate IHL. These criteria were further sharpened in UNSC resolution 2216 (2015) paragraph 19 that specifies 'additional criteria' for the potential designation of individuals and entities to sanction. In this resolution, the UNSC 'underscores that acts that threaten the peace, security, or stability of Yemen may also include the violations of the arms embargo imposed ... or obstructing the delivery of humanitarian assistance to Yemen or access to, or distribution of, humanitarian assistance in Yemen'. The Yemen Panel's reports have emphasized grave issues of siege, the use of starvation as a method of war, and obstruction of humanitarian access and the resulting food insecurity. While no individual or entity has been designated based solely on these criteria,[40] the Yemen Panel has played an important role in investigating and reporting upon starvation crimes in their reports to the UNSC. Its January 2016 report the Panel 'noted that civilians are disproportionately affected by the conduct of hostilities owing to the widespread and systematic use of tactics that practicably, and in certain cases directly, constitute the prohibited use of starvation as a method of warfare'.[41] The Panel went on to specify:

[39] The UNSC Panel of Experts on Yemen in their latest report (2020) investigated and found numerous accounts regarding the obstruction of humanitarian assistance, including arrests and intimidation of humanitarian workers, illegal seizures of property belonging to humanitarian workers or belonging to humanitarian organizations in Sana'a and numerous bureaucratic and administrative hurdles have been imposed on humanitarian organizations (*Final Report of the Panel of Experts on Yemen*, UN Doc S/2020/70, 28 April 2020, at 45–46. Other examples include *Final Report of the Panel of Experts on Somalia*, UN Doc S/2020/949, 28 September 2020, at 31–33; *Interim Report of the Panel of Experts on South Sudan Submitted Pursuant to Resolution 2521 (2020)*, UN Doc S/2020/1141, 25 November 2020, at 9. See also Global Rights Compliance, see note 5.

[40] 'Narrative Summaries of Reasons for Listing', United Nations Security Council (UNSC), available online at <https://www.un.org/securitycouncil/sanctions/2140/materials/summaries> (visited 27 August 201).

[41] *Final Report of the Panel of Experts on Yemen Established Pursuant to Security Council Resolution 2140 (2014)* UN Doc S/210/192, 26 January 2016.

> In this context, the systematic blockade of a city or country, as a form of military siege, to prevent goods from entering and people from leaving, raises serious implications from the perspective of international humanitarian law. When a city or a country's access to food, water and/or medicine is cut off or steps are taken to deprive access to such basic necessities of human life, the principle of discrimination becomes to all practicable means and purposes effectively inverted—where not only is there no special protection for the civilian population, but civilians also become the population that will inevitably bear the brunt of the measures imposed.[42]

This potentially expands the list of individuals and entities that could be sanctioned to a very high level. In its 2018 and 2019 reports, the Panel explored (amongst other violations) the blockade of 2017, the routine obstruction of humanitarian aid, and attacks on objects indispensable to survival, and the consequential effect of these apparent violations on access to food.[43]

South Sudan provides a more concrete example because eight individuals have been sanctioned on account of their involvement in violations of IHL, among other reasons.[44] The listing of two individuals were justified specifically with reference to the designation criteria, outlined in UNSC resolution 2206 (2015), covering 'the obstruction of ... the delivery or distribution of, or access to, humanitarian assistance'. The designations were supported by reporting provided by the Panel of Experts, who continuously kept the Sanctions Committee updated on the starvation and humanitarian access-related issues. This highlights what can be a Panel's most important function: providing an evidentiary fact base and an 'analytical context'[45] for policy decisions that is grounded by credible documentary evidence. This is particularly true given the complex, at times inaccessible or opaque and often rapidly evolving situations where Panels operate.

No fewer than eleven pages of the Panel's 2017 report to the UNSC (almost one-quarter of the text) were concerned with humanitarian crisis and famine.[46] In that report, the panel noted that it had provided evidence concerning individuals 'complicit in actions and policies' that violated international humanitarian law 'including those responsible for the conditions that have resulted in

[42] *Final Report of the Panel of Experts on Yemen Established Pursuant to Security Council Resolution 2140 (2014)*, see note 41, at §167.

[43] *Final Report of the Panel of Experts on Yemen*, UN Doc S/2019/83, 25 January 2019, at 56–57; *Final Report of the Panel of Experts on Yemen*, UN Doc S/2020/70, 28 April 2020, at 45–46. Specifically, in Appendix 33.D. 'Airstrike of 23 July 2018, Noshour, Sa'adah (water borehole)', the Panel reports that '[t]he water borehole and the solar panels are civilian objects protected against direct attack by IHL. Furthermore, a water supply system providing drinking water to the civilian population is an object indispensable to the survival of the civilian population. It is therefore prohibited to attack, destroy or remove it or to render it useless.'

[44] UNSC, see note 40.

[45] Boucher, see note 35, at 3.

[46] *Final Report of the Panel of Experts on South Sudan*, UN Doc. S/2017/326, 13 April 2017.

the unprecedented humanitarian crisis, including famine'.[47] Subsequently, one of the two individuals placed under sanctions by UNSC resolution 2428 (2018) is General Paul Malong. The Annex to the resolution notes specifically, 'information indicates that Malong ordered Sudan People's Liberation Army (SPLA) units to prevent the transport of humanitarian supplies across the Nile River, where tens of thousands of civilians were facing hunger, claiming that food aid would be diverted from civilians to militia groups. As a result of Malong's orders, food supplies were blocked from crossing the Nile for at least two weeks.'[48] As noted at the beginning of this chapter, this set important precedent: the first explicit sanctioning of an individual for a starvation crime.

The UN sanctions' architecture currently contains the institutional capacity for bringing sanctions to bear on starvation crimes and the mandates of many current sanctions regimes already consider issues of humanitarian concern (including famine) while sanctions monitoring groups issuing reports that include information on such issues. The relevant information needed for accountability for starvation crimes is often already provided to the key political actors at the UN. All the dots are connected regarding sanctions and starvation.

B. National Human Rights Sanctions Programmes

Alongside the established UN sanctions programme are several recently added state-specific human rights sanctions programmes. These are unilateral programmes, and insofar as their purpose is targeting individuals and entities deemed responsible for human rights violations or international crimes, they are in principle complementary to the UN sanctions discussed. Legal powers derive from domestic legislation. The most significant are the US Global Magnitsky Act, the Canadian 'Sergei Magnitsky Law' programme, the UK's Global Human Rights Sanctions programme,[49] and the European Union Global Human Rights Sanction regime. These sanctions programmes act in parallel to states' international obligations but often go further than UN programmes. They are also more detailed in their focus on issues of humanitarian concern and have greater legal specificity in designation criteria. This represents a frontier in sanctions practice and a potential tool of particular import in relation to starvation crimes and human rights.

The US Global Magnitsky Act is the most significant. Its programme is not only a shift in US sanctions policy but also represents a global shift in human rights

[47] *Final Report of the Panel of Experts on South Sudan*, see note 46, at 16(a).

[48] SC Res 2428, 13 July 2018, Annex 1, at 8.

[49] National programs also exist in Lithuania, Latvia, and Estonia. Whilst other states and regional bodies are actively contemplating the possibility of enacting similar programmes, e.g. Australia and the European Union.

sanctions policy, moving from a country-by-country focus to a thematic one, in this case human rights and corruption. In late 2016, US Congress passed the Global Magnitsky Human Rights Accountability Act, named after Russian whistle-blower and lawyer Sergei Magnitsky, who was tortured and died in prison in Russia in 2009 (Global Magnitsky Act).[50] At first, the Global Magnitsky Act allowed the US President to block or revoke US visas and to block all US-based property and interests in property of foreign persons, whether individuals or entities, who had engaged in extrajudicial killings, torture, or other gross violations of human rights against individuals who sought to either 'to expose illegal activity carried out by government officials' or 'to obtain, exercise, defend, or promote internationally recognized human rights and freedoms, such as the freedoms of religion, expression, association, and assembly, and the rights to a fair trial and democratic elections'.[51] Subsequently, in 2017 President Trump signed Executive Order 13818, which significantly expanded the scope of the Act. This expansion was due to important amendments to the wording of the Global Magnitsky Act, moving from 'gross violations of international recognized human rights' to simply 'serious human rights abuse'.[52] This has been seen as a significant move to widen the scope of the programme to include both governmental and non-governmental actors, in singular cases with a generally accepted broader range of violations that the original law's 'gross violations' standard.[53] The Executive Order also removed the need for victims to be working to 'expose illegal activity carried out by government officials' or to 'obtain, exercise, defend, or promote internationally recognized human rights and freedoms,' meaning human rights violations against any victim could fall within the programme's scope.

The scope of conduct covered is also broad, allowing sanctions to be issued on any foreign person who is responsible for or complicit in, or to have directly or indirectly engaged in serious human rights abuses, or to be or have been a leader or official of an entity, including any government entity, that has engaged in, or whose members have engaged in serious human rights abuse. In addition, any person—not necessarily foreign—can be sanctioned who has materially assisted, sponsored, or provided financial, material, or technological support for, or goods or services

[50] The 'Global Magnitsky Human Rights Accountability Act' was signed into law on 23 December 2016, as Sections 1261–1265, Subtitle F, Public Law 114-328, of the FY17 National Defense Authorization Act.

[51] The Global Magnitsky Act also contained a corruption limb, allowing sanctions against government officials or senior associates of such officials who are engaged in or responsible for acts of significant corruption. Individuals who have acted as agents of or on behalf of human rights abusers or who have materially assisted corrupt officials can also be sanctioned.

[52] Executive Order 13818 also expanded the scope of the corruption limb, from 'significant acts of corruption' to 'corruption'; and eliminating the requirement that 'the facilitation or transfer of the proceeds of corruption' only apply to transfers to foreign jurisdictions. Executive Order 13818 as of 20 December 2017, 82 Federal Register (26 December 2017), 60839–60842.

[53] 'Global Magnitsky Act FAQ', Human Rights First, available online at <https://www.humanrightsfirst.org/sites/default/files/hrf-global-magnitsky-faq.pdf> (visited 27 August 2021).

to, or in support of serious human rights abuses conducted by a foreign person.[54] It borrows tools used to track and block terrorist financing for application to human rights abusers.

The Global Magnitsky Act does not specify a particular burden of proof or evidentiary standard, but in practice relevant US departments have adopted a 'reason to believe' based on 'credible information' minimum standard in order to be satisfied it can defend designations against challenges brought in US courts.[55]

Canada has a parallel measure, commonly known as the 'Sergei Magnitsky Law'. Passed unanimously by the Canadian House of Commons in 2017, Canada's Justice for Victims of Corrupt Foreign Officials Act 2017 allows for travel bans and the freezing of Canadian assets and the restrictions of transactions with any Canadian person.[56] Sanctions can only be authorized against foreign nationals. The programme has jurisdiction to sanction those 'responsible for, or complicit in extrajudicial killings, torture or other gross violations of internationally recognized human rights committed against individuals in any foreign state who seek (i) to expose illegal activity carried out by foreign public officials, or (ii) to obtain, exercise, defend or promote internationally recognized human rights and freedoms, such as freedom of conscience, religion, thought, belief, opinion, expression, peaceful assembly and association, and the right to a fair trial and democratic elections'.[57] It is closer to the original US Global Magnitsky Act before the broadening of the scope under Executive Order 13818.

The United Kingdom has also created its own national human rights sanctions programme. Launched in July 2020, the UK's Global Human Rights Sanctions regime (UK GHRS) is the first time the United Kingdom has the ability to authorize its own human rights based sanctions, and is established under the Sanctions and Anti-Money Laundering Act 2018[58] (SAMLA) and subsequent Global Human Rights Sanctions Regulations 2020 (2020 Regulations).[59] The UK GHRS regime allows the United Kingdom to act unilaterally to apply sanctions measures to deter, and provide accountability for activities which, if carried out by or on behalf of a state within the territory of that state, would amount to a serious violation by that State of an individual's human rights.[60] Similar to the US and Canadian

[54] Executive Order, see note 52.

[55] Human Rights First, see note 53.

[56] Justice for Victims of Corrupt Foreign Officials Act, Section 4(3) and Section 18, Canadian government, available online at <https://laws.justice.gc.ca/eng/acts/J-2.3/FullText.html> (visited 27 August 2021).

[57] Justice for Victims of Corrupt Foreign Officials Act, see note 56, Section 4(2)(a). The other freedoms mentioned are 'freedom of conscience, religion, thought, belief, opinion, peaceful assembly and association, and democratic elections', Sections 4(2)(a)(ii).

[58] Sanctions and Anti-Money Laundering Act 2018, UK government, available online at <https://www.legislation.gov.uk/ukpga/2018/13/contents/enacted> (29 October 2021).

[59] *The Global Human Rights Sanctions Regime*, Foreign, Commonwealth & Development Office, UK government, 6 July 2020, available online at <https://www.gov.uk/government/collections/uk-global-human-rights-sanctions> (visited 27 August 2021).

[60] *The Global Human Rights Sanctions* Regime, see note 59.

programmes, the UK GHRS allows for travel bans and asset freezes. The UK GHRS regime is currently limited however to three human rights: (1) torture, inhuman and degrading treatment, (2) human trafficking and forced labour, and (3) the right to life,[61] leaving a number of recognized international human rights (freedom of expression, freedom of association, right to fair trial, right not to be discriminated, right to food and water) outside its jurisdiction. Starvation crimes could adequately fall within grounds (1) and (3).[62]

While the roster of human rights abuses under the UK GHRS is limited, the conduct that can be sanctioned under the programme is more widely drawn. Sanctions can be imposed on an 'involved person' who is not a direct perpetrator, particularly important in cases of corruption.

C. European Union Human Rights Sanctions

In January 2021 the European Union launched its Global Human Rights Sanctions Regime (EU GHRS). The EU GHRS can target individuals and entities, and those associated with them, who are responsible for or involved in serious human rights violations or abuses worldwide. EU GHRS sanctions include EU travel bans, EU asset freezes, and also prohibiting any EU person from making funds and economic resources available to perpetrators.[63]

Whilst the EU GHRS covers 'serious human rights violations and abuses', in common with national human rights sanctions programmes, importantly it explicitly includes genocide and crimes against humanity within its jurisdiction in addition to torture and other cruel, inhuman, or degrading treatment or punishment; slavery; extrajudicial, summary, or arbitrary executions and killings; enforced disappearance of persons; arbitrary arrests or detentions.[64] This gives the EU GHRS explicit jurisdiction over not only a wide array of human rights abuses but also international crimes, something that similar domestic programmes lack.[65]

[61] *The Global Human Rights Sanctions* Regime, see note 59, at Part 1, Regulation 4.

[62] See Chapter 5 in this volume; W. Jordash, C. Murdoch, and J. Holmes, 'Strategies for Prosecuting Mass Starvation' 17 *Journal of International Criminal Justice* (2019) 849–879; *The Crime of Starvation and Methods of Prosecution and Accountability*, Global Rights Compliance, World Peace Foundation, Policy Paper (2019), available online at <https://sites.tufts.edu/wpf/files/2019/06/The-Crimes-of-Starvation-and-Methods-of-Prosecution-and-Accountability.pdf> (visited 27 August 2021).

[63] 'Concerning Restrictive Measures Against Serious Human Violations and Abuses', Council Regulation (EU) 2020/1998, 7 December 2020, available online at <https://eur-lex.europa.eu/legal-content/EN/TXT/?uri=uriserv%3AOJ.LI.2020.410.01.0001.01.ENG&toc=OJ%3AL%3A2020%3A410I%3ATOC> (visited 27 August 2021), Art. 3; Council Decision (CFSP) 2020/1999, available online at <https://eur-lex.europa.eu/legal-content/EN/TXT/?uri=CELEX:32020D1999> (visited 27 August 2021), Art. 3.

[64] Council Regulation (EU) 2020/1998, see note 63, Art. 2; and CFSP, Art. 1.

[65] The EU Global Human Rights Sanctions (GHRS) jurisdiction also includes other acts, including but not limited to the following, in so far as those violations or abuses are widespread, systematic or are otherwise of serious concern as regards the objectives of the common foreign and security policy set

It extends to covering persons and entities that provide financial, technical, or material support for or are 'otherwise involved in acts' including planning, directing, ordering, assisting, preparing, facilitating, or encouraging such acts.[66]

All of these measures do not confine targets for investigation and sanctioning to within the boundaries of the country in question. Nationals of other countries, who are engaged directly in violations or who play a role in facilitating these violations, or who may benefit from them, can also potentially be identified and become the target of sanctions.

4. Utilizing Sanctions for Accountability for Starvation Crimes

Senders have the legal and practical ability to impose sanctions on individuals and entities—with measures that restrict essentially any good or service they wish—for violations related to starvation crimes. The UN Security Council set a precedent in the case of the South Sudanese general Paul Malong and the United States in relation to Ethiopia and Eritrea. UNSC 2417 reaffirms that this could become standard practice. The sanctions programmes of the EU and individual countries provide complementary openings for this, either through the lens of human rights violations or, for the EU GHRS specifically, crimes against humanity or indeed genocidal starvation. There are several questions that arise. What are the relevant legal considerations on which sanctions can be invoked? How can sanctions and sanctions-related investigations serve as a pathway to other forms of accountability? What considerations regarding potentially adverse humanitarian consequences must be taken into account? What are the methodologies for measuring whether they 'work'? And finally, how practically can sanctions programmes support the strengthening of the norm prohibiting starvation?

A. Legal Considerations

One of the reasons why targeted sanctions are an attractive policy tool is that they permit measures to be taken without specifying precisely the legal regime under which the violations have been perpetrated and without requiring the criminal standards of

out in Art. 21 of the Treaty on European Union: trafficking in human beings, as well as abuses of human rights by migrant smugglers as referred to in this answer, sexual and gender-based violence, violations or abuses of freedom of peaceful assembly and of association, violations or abuses of freedom of opinion and expression, violations or abuses of freedom of religion or belief.

[66] EU GHRS, see note 63, Art. 3.3; and CFSP, see note 63, Art. 2.1.

proof that would be required in court proceedings. This was the case for resolution 2428 under which Malong was sanctioned. National sanctions programmes such as the Global Magnitsky Act make reference to human rights law, while the EU includes a reference to international criminal law (specifically, crimes against humanity). UN sanctions programmes generally refer to violations of IHL, specifically obstruction of humanitarian assistance. This aligns with an emerging policy approach in relation to action to prevent conflict induced hunger or famine, articulated most clearly by the United Kingdom, which pledged to 'act early on a "no regrets" basis to prevent excess mortality, even when robust data is not yet available'.[67] Sanctions could, if used cautiously and in a targeted circumscribed manner, offer an interim punitive and preventative tool, whilst documentation and investigations are ongoing.

Under the Global Magnitsky Act, the United States is authorized to issue sanctions for 'serious human rights abuses'. This could include violations of the right to food, an umbrella term which includes the right to adequate food and the right to be free from hunger.[68] There are also relevant prohibitions on rape and other forms of sexual and gender-based violence torture and other ill-treatment that may be applicable to starvation situations.[69] Also, the deprivation of food and water has been regarded as constituting torture.[70] This means that we can look to at least three human rights when considering application to the US programme: (1) right to food, (2) right to life, and (3) prohibition on torture, cruel, inhumane, or degrading treatment.

[67] *G7 Famine Prevention and Humanitarian Crises Compact*, Foreign, Commonwealth & Development Office, available online at <https://www.gov.uk/government/publications/g7-foreign-and-development-ministers-meeting-may-2021-communique/g7-famine-prevention-and-humanitarian-crises-compact> (visited 27 August 2021).

[68] See Chapter 6 in this volume; S. Hutter, *Starvation as a Weapon* (Geneva: Martinus Nijhoff Publishers, 2015); S. Hutter, 'Starvation In Armed Conflicts—An Analysis Based on the Right to Food', 17 *Journal of International Criminal Justice* (2019),723–752.

[69] *Convention Against Torture*, A/RES/39/46 10 December 1984, Arts 2 and 16; *International Covenant on Civil and Political Rights*, A/RES/2200A(XXI) 16 December 1966, (Arts 7 and 4(2)), and as a fundamental principle of customary international law and a *jus cogens* norm, see HRC, *General Comment No. 24: Issues Relating to Reservations Made upon Ratification or Accession to the Covenant or the Optional Protocols thereto, or in Relation to Declarations under Article 41 of the Covenant*, UN Doc. CCPR/C/21/Rev.1/Add.6, 4 November 1994, at 8; *Convention against Torture and Other Cruel, Inhuman or Degrading Treatment or Punishment, General Comment No. 2*, UN Doc CAT/C/GC/2, 24 January 2008, §§ 1 and 3.

[70] Closing Order, *Kaing Guek Eav alias Duch*, Trial Chamber, (001/18-07-2007/ECCC/TC), 26 July 2010, §§ 1435–1438; Judgment, *Nuon Chea and Khieu Samphan*, Trial Chamber, (002/19-09-2007/ECCC/TC), 7 August 2014, §§ 457, §§ 644–645, § 648; Judgment, *Kaing Guek Eav alias Duch*, Trial Chamber, (001/18-07-2007/ECCC/TC), 26 July 2010, §§ 3339, 372; Judgment, *Prlić et al.* (IT-04-74-A), Trial Chamber, 29 May 2013, §§ 1159, 1162; the DPRK Report, whereby: 'decisions and policies violating the right to food, which were applied ... in full awareness that such decisions would exacerbate starvation and related deaths' amounted to CAH, *Report of the Commission of Inquiry on Human Rights in the Democratic People's Republic of Korea*, UN Doc. A/HRC/25/63, 7 February 2014, §§ 78, at 1115–1137; See, e.g. other inhumane acts; Judgement, *Blaškić*, (IT-95-14-A) Appeal Chamber 29 July 2004, § 155; Judgment, *Stanisić and Župljanin*, (IT-08-91-T)Trial Chamber, 27 March 2013, §§ 203,

The UK GHRS regime has jurisdiction over a much narrower set of human rights than the United States, however, importantly the right to life and torture, cruel, inhuman, or degrading treatment are included. This means, at least in theory, there is scope for the UK GHRS to issue sanctions for incidences of starvation through the lens of right to life and/or prohibition of torture, as and when the evidence adequately demonstrates this.

The EU provides for perhaps the widest jurisdictional reach in which to seek sanctions against those involved in starvation related incidences. The EU GHRS's jurisdictional scope includes 'serious human rights abuses or violations' and explicitly lists crimes against humanity and genocide, opening a new jurisdictional door that links starvation to these crimes.

B. Pathways to Justice

Sanctions can contribute to accountability for starvation crimes in several ways. First, measures such as travel bans and asset freezes, and the reputational consequences of being named by the UN or a government as a target of sanctions, are themselves a form of calling to account. Second, the investigations undertaken by a UN panel of experts or similar group are an important source of information. They can be regarded as a preliminary assessment of the factual matrix, which can serve as an important informational foundation for criminal investigators and prosecutors. Relatedly, third, this investigation and documentation is itself a crucial step towards recognizing the crime. It is the first crucial element in the exercise of truth-telling and is a gesture towards the humanity and dignity of the victims and survivors. The straightforward acknowledgement that starvation is a crime perpetrated by political and military leaders, and not a fact of nature or a personal or communal failing of those who suffer, is very important. Fourth, sanctions could potentially support other transitional justice measures such as compensation and restitution. Finally, sanctions could be used as a measure to press for states and entities to comply with international tribunals.

224, 226, 678–679, 681, 683, 701, 928, 930, 936–937, 969, 984–985, 1120-1121, 1191–1192, 1249–1250, 1286–1288, 1341, 1256–1358, 1484, 1498–1500, 1553–1555; Judgment, *Blagojević and Jokić*, (IT-02-60-T), Trial Chamber I, 17 January 2005, §§ 606, 610, 620–621; Judgment, *Sikirica et al.*, (IT-95-8-S) Trial Chamber, 13 November 2001, §§ 127, 161, 203; *Ireland v. the United Kingdom*, ECtHR, Application No. 5310/71, Judgment of 18 January 1978, § 167 ('deprivation of food and drink: subjecting the detainees to a reduced diet during their stay at the centre and pending interrogations'); *Weinberger v. Uruguay*, HRC Communication No. 28/1978, Views of 29 October 1980, §§ 2 and 16 ('Food was scarce (a piece of bread and thin soup twice a day without any meat). When his family was allowed to visit him after 10 months, serious bodily harm (one arm paralysed, leg injuries, infected eyes) could be seen. He had lost 25 [kilograms]').

C. Humanitarian Considerations

Sanctions have had a bad press. One of the most adverse impacts of blanket sanctions was to limit legitimate economic activities and push commerce into the illicit grey zone, empowering the more ruthless and criminal elements in a country at the expense of moderates and those engaged in licit commerce. The risks of this are reduced by the use of targeted sanctions and associated financial tools aimed at individuals and entities, especially those involved in corrupt activities. However, all coercive tools are likely to have unintended humanitarian consequences, some of which are foreseeable. Humanitarian operations will inevitably be impeded, the question is to what extent. Members of a targeted political elite will seek to insulate themselves against the impact of sanctions and will also try to manipulate sanctions for their own ends. They will try to rally a spirit of nationalism against sanctions, blame hardships that they have themselves caused on foreign sanctions and supposed international conspiracies,[71] and may shift the burden of sanctions onto civilians or even use sanctions as a pretext for imposing measures such as increased taxation or reduced welfare spending.

Since the calamitous impacts of sanctions on Haiti and Iraq, and the role of anti-terrorism legislation on impeding humanitarian assistance in Somalia, senders have developed mechanisms intended to tailor sanctions to reduce their contribution to the deprivation of civilians. However, the risk of such adverse outcomes cannot be entirely eliminated. Better methods for measuring impacts are required.

D. Measuring 'Success'

Methods for measuring the success or failure of targeted sanctions are woefully under-developed. As discussed earlier, much of the scholarly literature assesses the impacts of sanctions according to the metrics of whether they achieved their stated goals. Such analyses cannot easily capture reality: there are many types of sanctions measures (arms embargoes, travel bans, asset freezes, etc.) bundled into single sanctions regimes, each with potentially separate or overlapping purposes, imposed to address multiple goals that are rarely, if ever, all explicitly stated. Unilateral targeted financial sanctions are a particularly stealthy tool, often deployed without publicity and with only the most general references to intended purposes. Furthermore, the purposes for imposition change over time and may even vary from one sanctioned individual or entity to another within a single sanctions' regime. The challenges of

[71] As seen in the protests in Ethiopia in response to the US sanctions, see O. Oshin, 'Ethiopians protest US sanctions over atrocities in Tigray', *The Hill*, 30 May 2021, available online at <https://thehill.com/policy/international/middle-east-north-africa/556161-ethiopians-protest-us-sanctions-over-atrocities> (visited 27 August 2021).

defining and measuring success are amplified when the tools are used for new purposes, such as preventing and punishing starvation crimes.

Another angle of assessment is whether sanctions caused undue suffering to the population of the targeted country, and whether they had other unintended humanitarian consequences. Unlike evaluating slippery metrics like 'success' this has the benefit that humanitarian impact of a certain scale is often quite visible. However, these assessments are complicated by contexts in which the targeted regimes manipulate the sanctions regimes for their own ends and also by the array of other economic, diplomatic and military instruments used by senders alongside sanctions. Sanctions are never deployed in isolation of other tools; understanding how the various tools interact represents a frontier of sanctions research that is only beginning to be explored.[72]

Focusing on 'success' or other predetermined outcomes is valuable insofar as scholars are confident they know what they're looking for, but often these analyses miss the mark. Analysing sanctions' political impacts is a more valuable undertaking. However, it may be too much to expect that we can determine them precisely and in real time. Deploying targeted sanctions demands detailed information about the targets and the context—their true interests, calculations, and circumstances, all of which can change. This requires a granular behind-the-scenes understanding of what is driving elite behaviour in violent, opaque political systems. Rarely is this visible or legible to outsiders.[73] Accessing and analysing such information challenges the most capable state intelligence services (whose assessments remain out of public view), let alone individual researchers and advocates. The UN, however, provides the leading example: sanctions information collection is systematized in the mechanism of panels of experts. Those panels have the very important primary effect of gathering and publishing information about the situation under consideration, generating transparency and deepening understanding, which are important benefits irrespective of any actions taken, such as imposing sanctions. Panels provide high-quality and publicly available raw data regarding ongoing sanctions situations, which can feed into political analyses or other accountability efforts, including those related to starvation crimes. Documentation of crimes is essential for accountability in any form; this intermediary step is particularly worthwhile to consider when taking on questions of 'success'.

[72] T. Biersteker, R. Brubaker, and D. Lanz, 'UN Sanctions and Mediation: Establishing Evidence to Inform Practice', United Nations University Centre for Policy Research (18 February 2019), available online at <https://cpr.unu.edu/research/projects/un-sanctions-and-mediation-establishing-evidence-to-inform-practice-2.html#outline> (visited 27 August 2021).

[73] Although note the commendable and rigorous analysis of the use of sanctions in South Sudan by The Sentry and Oliver Windridge. More of this investigative work is needed to measure the true impact of sanctions, <https://thesentry.org/reports/taking-south-sudan/

E. Ethics and Norms

Perhaps the most important, if least easy to measure, outcome of sanctions programmes is the way in which they help consolidate a norm against starvation crimes. The inclusion of language regarding starvation crimes in UN resolutions, UN reports, documents, and testimony is a way to consolidate the recognition that starvation is an act that can be prohibited, and thereby to institutionalize accountability. Since the adoption of UNSC 2417 in May 2018, we have seen the language of starvation crimes and humanitarian access violations creeping into other resolutions and mandates,[74] in addition to two White Papers on UNSC 2417 by the UN Office for the Coordination of Humanitarian Affairs (OCHA) in 2018 relating to South Sudan and Yemen whereby sanctions were subsequently issued.[75] As starvation enters into the multilateral zeitgeist the more likely it is that tolerance for repeated violations will decrease. Analogous to the way in which sexual and gender-based violence (SGBV) has become a focus for international outrage, crystallized in the landmark UNSC resolution 1325 and international prosecutions for SGBV crimes, so too there is growing intolerance of starvation crimes.

Sanctions will not end starvation crimes, but they are a useful tool to expose and confront those perpetrating starvation crimes with impunity and to rally support for the principle that such crimes cannot be tolerated.

[74] Global Rights Compliance, see note 5. See e.g. SC Res. 2568, 12 March 2021, § 38; *Letter dated 12 March 2021 from the President of the Security Council addressed to the Secretary-General and the Permanent Representatives of the members of the Security Council*, S/2021/255, 12 March 2021; SC Res. 2567, 12 March 2021; SC Res. 2567, 12 March 2021, at 2; SC Res. 2520, 29 May 2020; *Letter dated 29 May 2020 from the President of the Security Council addressed to the Secretary-General and the Permanent Representatives of the members of the Security Council*, S/2020/459, 29 May 2020; *Letter dated 29 May 2020 from the President of the Security Council addressed to the Secretary-General and the Permanent Representatives of the members of the Security Council*, S/2020/466, 1 June 2020, § 35; SC Res. 2474, 11June 2019; SC Res. 2472, 31 May 2019, §31.

[75] Both White Papers were confidential, see 'South Sudan Consultations', What's in Blue, 9 August 2018, available online at <https://www.whatsinblue.org/2018/08/south-sudan-consultations-10.php> (visited 27 August 2021); UN Security Council Report, Yemen, October 2018, available online at <https://www.securitycouncilreport.org/chronology/yemen.php> (visited 27 August 2021).

13

Sex, Gender, Age, and Mass Starvation

Dyan Mazurana, Bridget Conley, and Kinsey Spears

1. Introduction

The concept of 'starvation crimes'[1] draws attention to how policies, systems, and practices can intentionally increase the risk of starvation. Indeed, in contexts where sexual and gender-based violence (SGBV) inhibits maternal care, SGBV might be considered as a specific starvation crime. Starvation in this context includes acts that are prohibited under various international laws that intentionally deprive civilians of 'objects indispensable to their survival'.[2] These 'objects' are not exhaustively defined and are not limited to food, but may include access to potable water, shelter, medicine, non-food items, and maternal care, among other necessities.[3] In this chapter, we examine how and why mass starvation impacts people of different sexes, genders, and ages, as well as how these factors influence 'objects indispensable' to people's survival. We explore what this means for prevention, protection, accountability for, and response to starvation crimes and conflict-induced mass starvation.

During times of mass starvation,[4] sex, gender, and age matter. These factors impact who dies, who lives, and how people suffer. They inform the lives and livelihoods before, during, and after crises.[5] But, precisely how and why sex, gender, and age factors intersect with deprivation and mass starvation have been largely overlooked within scholarly and legal arenas, and require further investigation.

Globally, across their lifespan, women and girls experience hunger—chronically and endemically—more than men and boys. Multiple factors shape this reality: laws

[1] See Chapter 2 of this volume.

[2] The term 'objects indispensable to survival' is found within Art. 8(2)(b)(xxv) and Art. 8(2)(e)(xix), of the Rome Statute. See, UN General Assembly, *Rome Statute of the International Criminal Court (last amended 2010)*, 17 July 1998, ISBN No. 92-9227-227-6, available at <https://www.refworld.org/docid/3ae6b3a84.html (accessed 22 October 2021).

[3] Chapters 5 and 6 in this volume.

[4] In this chapter, we use 'mass starvation' to describe conditions of extreme deprivation of objects indispensable for life. 'Mass' references deprivation of a targeted population, and 'starvation' implies a policy intended to or with the outcome of starving others. Throughout, we draw on studies of historical famines to inform our presentation of what is known about the intersection of gender, sex and age, and extreme deprivation. When researchers reference famine, we have kept their language. For more detail on definitions of 'famine', 'mass starvation, and 'starvation crimes', Chapter 2 in this volume.

[5] D. Mazurana and K. Proctor, 'Gender and Humanitarian Action,' in R. Mac Ginty and J. H. Peterson (eds), *Handbook on Humanitarian Action* (New York: Routledge, 2014) 49–61.

Dyan Mazurana, Bridget Conley, and Kinsey Spears, *Sex, Gender, Age, and Mass Starvation* In: *Accountability for Mass Starvation*. Edited by: Bridget Conley, Alex de Waal, Catriona Murdoch, and Wayne Jordash QC, Oxford University Press.
 DOI: 10.1093/oso/9780192864734.003.0013

and practices that discriminate against females, patriarchal norms that value males over females, lower pay for female labour, fewer property rights for females, biological factors that increase the impacts of hunger (e.g. menstruation, pregnancy, childbirth, and lactation), and females' reduced access to educational, financial, political, and social resources.[6] Gender, according to a widely used definition, refers to 'culturally expected behaviours of men and women based on roles, attitudes and values ascribed to them on the basis of their sex'.[7] Sex refers to 'biological and physical characteristics'. As argued by Cohn, gender can be further understood as: (1) embodied and performed identity (roles, relations, expectations, performance) and (2) structural power relations with deep symbolic significance and institutionalized forms.[8] Gender differences are learned and, while deeply rooted in every culture, and are changeable over time. There is also wide variation within and among cultures, as gender intersects with and is shaped by ethnicity, race, religion, class or caste, sexual orientation, and disability. Mazurana writes:

> Gender is a way of categorizing, ordering and symbolizing power, of hierarchically structuring relationships among different categories of people and different human activities in a manner symbolically associated with masculinity and femininity. Gender, at its heart, is a structural power relation that rests upon a central set of distinctions among categories of people, valuing some over others.[9]

Biology plays an unquestionably important role in survival and long-term outcomes for individuals affected by mass starvation. At the same time, gender and age intersect with violent acts that can increase the risk of mass starvation for different groups. Additionally, the gendered impacts of starvation crimes are also strongly affected by, and difficult to disentangle from, localized political, social, cultural, and economic factors.

In applying analysis of sex, gender, and age to issues related to mass starvation, including risks, protection, and accountability, we make contributions in four areas. First, we address how SGBV interacts with the perpetration of starvation crimes, creating deadly risks for girls, women, their children, and families. We find that

[6] World Food Program USA, *Women and Hunger*, available online at <https://www.wfpusa.org/women-hunger/>> (visited 5 August 2021). Despite these disadvantages, globally, female life expectancy is higher than that of males, see, World Health Organization, *Mortality and Global Health Estimates*, World Health Data Platform, available online at <https://www.who.int/data/gho/data/themes/mortality-and-global-health-estimates#:~:text=Global%20life%20expectancy%20at%20birth,men%20all%20around%20the%20world> (visited October 21, 2020).

[7] The International Committee of the Red Cross (ICRC), *Addressing the Needs of Women Affected by Armed Conflict: An ICRC Guidance Document*, March 2004, available online at < https://www.icrc.org/en/publication/0840-addressing-needs-women-affected-armed-conflict-icrc-guidance-document> (visited 5 August 2021), at 7.

[8] C. Cohn, 'Women and Wars: Towards a Conceptual Framework', in C. Cohn (ed.), *Women and Wars: Contested Histories, Uncertain Futures* (Cambridge: Polity Press, 2013) 1–35.

[9] Mazurana and Proctor, see note 5, at 53.

mass starvation and SGBV are mutually reinforcing atrocity crimes. Widespread conditions of deprivation and starvation can increase the risk of SGBV. At the same time, SGBV, and in some cases even the threat of SGBV, can increase the risk of starvation, in ways that differ by sex, gender, age, and context.

Second, we discuss the evidence for how sex, gender, and age impact outcomes for populations affected by mass starvation in terms of mortality. Third, we document and analyse the long-term, intergenerational gender- and age-influenced health and socio-cultural risks associated with exposure to mass starvation. There is strong and clear evidence of lifetime and intergenerational impacts of exposure to even short periods of starvation. The chapter concludes with several recommendations, including the need for more sex and age-disaggregated data collection and gender analysis from and research about contexts of mass starvation; increased understanding of SGBV at the nexus with starvation crimes; the need for medical, psychological, and socio-economic support specifically targeted to women-headed households and female breadwinners in the immediate wake of mass starvation; and the need for gender-just remedy and reparation for victims, including incorporating a long-term, intergenerational view of the impacts of starvation crimes.

2. Sexual and Gender-Based Violence in the Context of Starvation Crimes

In this section, we focus on patterns and examples of the perpetration of 'starvation crimes'. Across historical and contemporary cases of mass starvation, women and girls, and to a lesser extent boys and men,[10] have been subjected to SGBV, including transactional sex, forced prostitution, rape, sexual slavery, sexual torture, forced marriage, child marriage, forced abortion, forced impregnation, forced childbearing, and infanticide. As we demonstrate, two causal relationships become clear: SGBV can increase the likelihood of starvation, and starvation can increase the likelihood of SGBV.

A. When SGBV Increases the Risk of Starvation Crimes

Many forms of SGBV are already criminalized under international law.[11] In some instances, we argue, these acts may also be considered starvation crimes. It is

[10] The authors recognize that the terminology 'men, women, girls, and boys' does not capture many persons of diverse sexual orientation, gender identity and expression, or sex characteristics (SOGIESC) who are not included in the scope of this study. The lack of gender, sex, and age disaggregated data has impacted the ability to fully capture the broad ways in which SOGIESC individuals are uniquely harmed by crimes of mass starvation, SGBV, and famine. This gap further highlights the importance of accurate gender sensitive data in order to better understand how all genders are impacted by mass starvation and famine.

[11] L. Ullrich, '"But What About Men?" Gender Disquiet in International Criminal Justice', 25 *Theoretical Criminology* (2021) 209–227, at 211–212. Ullrich discusses advances in including SGBV crimes in international law and points to areas of continued contention.

imperative to study the nexus between SGBV and starvation crimes, as rape, forced marriage, sexual enslavement, and other forms of sexual and gender-based violence are prevalent features throughout contemporary instances of mass starvation, including in South Sudan (2013–present), Yemen (2015–present), Somali (2010–2011; 2017–present), Nigeria (2009–present) and Ethiopia (2020–present). This is an emerging area of research and requires additional investigation. One area where we find direct evidence linking the perpetration of SGBV to starvation crimes is when SGBV reduces the possibility for young children to receive maternal care, which can be indispensable for life.[12]

When females are intentionally separated from their young children over a duration of time for the purposes of perpetrating SGBV, including rape, forced marriage, and sexual enslavement, this may constitute a starvation crime. Separation can significantly elevate risks for children's survival, especially in the context of ongoing mass starvation. To illustrate, in the mass starvation in Ethiopia which began in 2021 and continues to this day, a Tigrayan woman carrying her infant child was abducted by the Ethiopian army and held as a sex slave for two weeks. She reported that members of the Ethiopian and Eritrea army, recognizable by their uniforms, tied her hand to a tree to prevent her escape and repeatedly raped her. She said the men stood in a line to rape her and that they would hand her child to the next man in line while the other man would take his turn raping her. She said she was raped continuously and could not breastfeed her baby. When her rapists decided that her baby was starving to death, she was untied to breastfeed the child. At this point, she escaped with her child. She is now in hiding in a safe house inside of the Tigray region and has not returned to her family for fear that her family will reject her and her child. She said that many other Tigrayan women and girls were held in the same area (an abandoned construction site) with her and that they were also subjected to gang rape in a similar manner.[13]

In South Sudan, Pinaud documented examples of violent attacks that had destructive impacts on maternal care. During assaults on villages, families often made split-second decisions to flee in different directions in an attempt to ensure that at least some will survive. The desperate flight to escape belligerents was often extremely difficult for pregnant women and mothers who fled with the youngest, especially nursing children.[14] Pinaud documented instances of attacks that appeared to target pregnant and breastfeeding mothers intentionally. These included examples of mothers were separated from infants, who were left to die, and of belligerents who raped and killed mothers in front of their children and then gloated that the children would not survive the long treks to camps for refugees or internally displaced people.[15]

[12] The authors wish to thank Alex de Waal for suggesting this avenue of research.
[13] Phone interview with medical care provider from Tigray, Dyan Mazurana, 18 June 2021.
[14] C. Pinaud, *War and Genocide in South Sudan* (Ithaca: Cornell University Press, 2021), at 176.
[15] Pinaud, see note 14, at 178–179, and 206.

SGBV was ubiquitous in the war in South Sudan: in a 2015 survey of four Protection of Civilians Sites across the country, the United Nations Population Fund found that 72 per cent of women had been raped, largely by soldiers or police officers, since the outbreak of the war.[16] Rape, as psychologist and psychotherapist Josse finds, can significantly deteriorate a mother's ability to care for her children:

> Rape victims may no longer be able to look after or meet the needs of their children, whether for physical reasons (long convalescence from the injuries sustained, disability caused by the rape, etc.), psychological reasons (trauma, clinical depression, psychotic delirium) or cultural reasons (in some societies, rape victims are not allowed to nurse or prepare food for their children). Even when they are allowed to fulfil their duties as parents, they often become irritable or aggressive towards their children.[17]

While not all of those who are raped are mothers, nor are all mothers rendered incapable of caring for their children after rape, a cross-case study of the physical impacts of rape in conflict zones found high prevalence of severe physical wounds from rape, including new pregnancies, traumatic genital injuries/tears, fistulae, and sexual problems/dysfunction.[18] The mental impacts of rape can also impede maternal care and include post-traumatic stress disorder (PTSD), anxiety, and depression.[19] These impacts have been studied primarily in terms of the harms done directly to victims, but when viewed through the lens of starvation crimes, their impact on maternal care raises additional concerns for the lives of their children.

The SGBV suffered by these girls and women constitute war crimes and potentially crimes against humanity, without reference to starvation. But when SGBV interrupts a girls' or woman's ability to care for herself and/or her children—especially in a context of actual or threatened famine when resources are stretched to their limits—it becomes a life-threatening deprivation that could constitute a starvation crime.

B. When Mass Starvation Increases the Risk of SGBV

Addressing contexts in which SGBV increases the risks of starvation is a largely unexplored area. There is research that can inform our understanding of how mass

[16] See Chapter 7 in this volume and Amnesty International, '*Do Not Remain Silent*': *Survivors of Sexual Violence in South Sudan Call for Reparations and Justice*, (24 July 2017) available online at <https://www.amnesty.org/en/documents/afr65/6469/2017/en/> (visited 5 August 2021).

[17] E. Josse, '"They Came with Two Guns": The Consequences of Sexual Violence for the Mental Health of Women in Armed Conflict', 877 *International Review of the Red Cross* (2010) 176–195, at 180.

[18] Josse, see note 17, at 128.

[19] Josse, see note 17, at 128.

starvation can increase the risks of SGBV, including the sale of girls and women during times of famine, forced marriage, child marriage, sexual exchange practices, and survival practices that expose females to rape. Depending on context, some of these acts may fit legal definitions of the crimes of rape, sexual slavery, enforced prostitution, and so forth.

One of the most robust studies on female sexual violence during a period of mass starvation is Edgerton-Tarpley's analysis of the Northern Chinese Famine of 1876–1879.[20] Edgerton-Tarpley discusses the sale of women and girls for sex as a key reason that females survived at higher rates than males. A large portion of Edgerton-Tarpley's discussion around 'prostitution' and survivability comes from Westerners who were in China during that time and reported their observations. One key observation made by a missionary stated that 'women would be purchased before they starved since wives were scarce, this shortage created a market for women that expanded during hard times'.[21] In her book *Beautiful Merchandise: Prostitution in China*, Gronewold further explored the economic system that developed during and after the period of mass starvation, in which 'women and young girls were regularly bought, sold, traded, pawned', or taken as slaves, forced brides, or foster children.[22] In China prior to this period, the buying and selling of women, girls, and boys for sex was not common, but during this period of severe deprivation, the practice became common and public.

More recently, in Syria and Yemen, there was a rise in forced marriage of girls as families sought ways to keep themselves and their daughters fed and alive.[23] Additionally, the Lake Chad Basin region has some of the highest prevalence of child marriage in the world—an increase that is due to the ongoing armed violence and deteriorating economic conditions that are resulting in extreme food insecurity and mass starvation.[24]

Another important study on SGBV and mass starvation focuses on North Korea from 1994 to 1998. Robinson et al. investigate forced marriage and the so-called bride trade on the border of North Korea and China as a means for thousands of unmarried North Koreans female migrants to reduce their families' economic

[20] K. Edgerton-Tarpley, 'Family and Gender in Famine: Cultural Responses to Disaster in North China, 1876–1879', 16 *Journal of Women's History* (2004) 119–147.

[21] Edgerton-Tarpley, see note 20, at 139.

[22] S. Gronewold, *Beautiful Merchandise: Prostitution in China, 1840–1936* (New York: Harrington Park Press, 1985).

[23] K. Howe et al., *The Wages of War: Learning from How Syrians Have Adapted Their Livelihoods Through Seven Years of Conflict*, Mercy Corps (2018), available online at <https://reliefweb.int/sites/reliefweb.int/files/resources/RD_SyriaReport_dl_0118_FINAL-A4-web.pdf> (visited 5 August 2021); United Nations Population Fund, *Child Marriage on the Rise*, (1 September 2016) available online at <https://yemen.unfpa.org/en/news/child-marriage-rise> (visited 30 October 2020).

[24] Plan International, *Adolescent Girls in Crisis: Voices from the Lake Chad Basin*, (2018), available online at <https://plan-international.org/publications/adolescent-girls-crisis-lake-chad-basin> (visited 24 August 2021).

burdens and as a survival mechanism during the period of mass starvation.[25] The demographics of those crossing the border between North Korea and China show that 46.6 per cent of women crossing the border were single, as compared to 34.6 per cent of men.[26] This disparity speaks not only to the pressure women felt to migrate if they were deemed a burden on their families but to the potential for becoming part of the 'bride trade'. In the early 1990s, many of the women crossing the border went in search of food, shelter, and employment. They often ended up purchased by and married to 'ordinary Korean Chinese farmers and businesses peddlers'.[27] However, as mass starvation intensified in the late 1990s, traffickers kidnapped women crossing the Chinese–North Korean border or within North Korea and sold them to men in China.[28] These examples from the China–North Korean border speak to the complexity of using terms like 'prostitution' or 'transaction sex' as catch-alls without factoring in sexual and gender-based violence to analyse how much agency women and girls have and whether or not they even made a decision to engage in 'survival sex' or 'prostitution'. It also calls for more attention to starvation-related forced marriage, rape, human trafficking, sexual enslavement, and child marriage.

Importantly, both Edgerton-Tarpley and Robinson et al. discuss what these sexual actions during mass starvation meant for the women's and girls' future in their societies. During and after the Northern Chinese Famine, songs and statues were created to celebrate women who chose to adhere to strict Confucian norms of morality and self-sacrifice. Women were praised for giving up their food and even committing suicide to free up food to preserve the lives of their husbands, sons, and mothers-in-law.[29] Alternatively, those that experienced starvation-related sexual violence were resoundingly criticized and ostracized by their communities as allegedly 'promiscuous' women. These women and their immoral behaviour were also blamed and persecuted as causing the famine.[30]

Furthermore, Davis. found that North Korean women and girls who fled to the Chinese border and were forced into the illicit sex trade were not welcome back. Those who returned or were forced back to North Korea after engaging in sex were often imprisoned and sent into labour camps. Chillingly, at times their so-called mixed race pregnancies were forcibly terminated and the resulting children killed.[31]

25 W. C. Robinson et al., 'Famine, Mortality, and Migration: A Study of North Korean Migrants in China', in H. Reed and C. Keely (eds), *Forced Migration & Mortality* (Washington, DC: National Academies Press, 2001) 69–85.

26 Robinson et al., see note 25.

27 Robinson et al., see note 25.

28 E. Kim et al., 'Cross Border North Korean Women Trafficking and Victimization between North Korea and China: An Ethnographic Case Study', 37 *International Journal of Law, Crime and Justice* (2009) 154–169.

29 Edgerton-Tarpley, see note 20.

30 Edgerton-Tarpley, see note 20.

31 K. Davis, 'Brides, Bruises and The Border: The Trafficking of North Korean Women into China', 26 *SAIS Review of International Affairs* (2006) 131–141

During conflict-caused mass starvation, it is often women and girls who must venture into areas controlled by armed forces and groups to collect wild foods and gather firewood for cooking and heating. Females may engage in these activities due to gendered labour roles or because of well-founded fear that if the males in their families undertake this work, they are likely to be murdered by armed actors. While their knowledge of wild foods might help females survive periods of extreme deprivation, it also exposes them to harms.[32] Such violence results in women and girls having to make choices between searching for food to eat and firewood to cook and facing rape, or not venturing out to avoid rape and facing starvation of their children, the elderly, and themselves.[33] This phenomenon has been documented in mass starvation periods in Darfur, Sudan, Somalia, and South Sudan, among other locations.[34]

As illustrated by these examples, SGBV directly impacts women's and girls' ability to survive mass starvation as well as negatively shaping their life chances in the post-famine context. For some women and girls, starvation-related vulnerabilities led to rape, sexual enslavement, a range of forms of sexual violence, forced marriage, forced pregnancy, child marriage, forced termination of pregnancies, undergoing dangerous abortions, infanticide, and the outright killing of their 'undesirable' children by the state. Of particular risk is during and after flight from areas with extreme scarcity of objects indispensable for life, especially when these areas overlap with conflict zones, as we discuss below.

C. SGBV, Displacement, and Starvation Crimes

Flight to camps for refugees and internally displaced persons in search of food and assistance during mass starvation can increase females' exposure to SGBV. During forced displacement, they can be subjected to rape by civilians and armed actors. When they encounter checkpoints and roadblocks manned by various

[32] J. El Bushra and E. Piza-Lopez, 'Gender, War and Food', in J. Macrae and A. Zwi (eds), *War and Hunger: Rethinking International Responses to Complex Emergencies* (London: Zed Books, 1994) 180–193; L. Cliggett, *Grains from Grass: Aging, Gender, and Famine in Rural Africa* (Ithaca: Cornell University Press, 2005); L. Deng, *Famine in the Sudan: Causes, Preparedness and Response—A Political, Social and Economic Analysis of the 1998 Bahr el Ghazal Famine* (London: Institute for Development Studies, 1999),, available online at <https://www.ids.ac.uk/publications/famine-in-the-sudan-causes-preparedness-and-response-a-political-social-and-economic-analysis-of-the-1998-bahr-el-ghazal-famine/> (visited 3 August 2021) at 18; A de Waal, *Famine that Kills: Darfur, Sudan, 1984–1985* (Oxford: Clarendon Press, 1989).

[33] A. Raven-Roberts, 'Women and the Political Economy of War', in Cohn (ed.), see note 8 36–53.

[34] E. Patrick, 'Sexual Violence and Firewood Collection in Darfur', 27 *Forced Migration Review* (2007) 40–41; Amnesty International, see note 16, at 32; Danish Refugee Council, *A Sexual and Gender-based Violence Rapid Assessment*, July 2012, available online at <https://reliefweb.int/sites/reliefweb.int/files/resources/sexual_gender_based_violence_south_sudan.pdf> (visited 5 August 2021), at 3; United Nations High Commissioner for Refugees, *Evaluation of the Dadaab firewood project, Kenya*, June 2001, available at <https://www.unhcr.org/3b33105d4.pdf> (visited 5 August 2021).

armed actors and criminal groups, they can face rape, sexual enslavement, and other forms of SGBV. Civilians travelling among those fleeing may also take advantage of the situation and commit SGBV in exchange for food, water, security, and/or shelter. At internally displaced or refugee camps, those in charge of camp security (including international forces mandated to protect civilians)[35] or in control of resources, both formally and informally, can use their power to commit sexual violence against women and girls through requiring sex or forced marriage in exchange for food and other items necessary for survival. Instances of requiring sexual favours for resources were reported recently in, for example, South Sudan, Somalia, and Ethiopia.[36]

In Ethiopia (2020–present), women and girls from Tigray living in displaced camps said they feared becoming an 'outcast in the community' if they were to talk about the rape and sexual violence they experienced at the hands of the Ethiopian and Eritrean armies. One displaced girl told researchers, '[e]ven if I and the women and girls experience rape, we would not seek help due to the fear of stigma and shame'.[37] Women and men from the Daabat displaced camp housing Tigraians explained that the widespread sexual violence perpetrated by Ethiopian and Eritrean armed forces and Amhara militias against Tigraian women and girls is the greatest risk that females face, next to shortage of food.[38]

As noted in the cases in this section, the longer-term gendered, socio-cultural, and economic impacts of SGBV, including disability, stigma, rejection, and children born of rape, among others, often severely damage females' status within their own community. This damaged status can result in long-term, negative economic, social, and emotional outcomes for both them and their children, sending them into deepening—and often lifelong—experiences of violence, poverty, and hunger.[39] For example, Tigraian women and girls during the conflict-induced famine that began in 2020 were living in hiding because they were afraid of

[35] S. Wheeler, *UN Peacekeeping has a Sexual Abuse Problem*, Human Rights Watch (11 January 2020), available online at <https://www.hrw.org/news/2020/01/11/un-peacekeeping-has-sexual-abuse-problem#> (visited 5 August 2021).

[36] W. Giles, 'Women Forced to Flee: Refugees and Internally Displaced Persons', in Cohn (ed.), see note 8, 80–101; Human Rights Watch, *'The Power These Men Have Over Us': Sexual Exploitation and Abuse by African Union Forces in Somalia* (2014) available online at <https://www.hrw.org/report/2014/09/08/power-these-men-have-over-us/sexual-exploitation-and-abuse-african-union-forces> (visited 5 August 2021); International Rescue Committee, *Gender Analysis Key Findings: Women's exploitation and gender-based violence across Ethiopia's Tigray crisis* (4 May 2021) available online at <https://www.rescue.org/sites/default/files/document/5868/irctigraygenderanalysiskeyfindingsmay.pdf> (visited 5 August 2021).

[37] A. Habte and M. Afework, *CARE Rapid Gender Analysis [Ethiopia] – [Tigray Crisis]*, CARE (4 April 2021) available online at <https://careevaluations.org/wp-content/uploads/Rapid-Gender-Analysis-RGA-Tigray-Conflict-V.1.pdf> (visited 4 August 2021).

[38] Habte et al., see note 37.

[39] Mazurana and Proctor, see note 5; E. von Joeden-Forgey, 'Gender and the Future of Genocide Studies and Prevention', 7 *Genocide Studies and Prevention* (2012) 89–107; H. Slim, *Killing Civilians: Method, Madness and Morality in War* (New York: Columbia University Press, 2008), at 37–119.

retribution for reporting rape and sexual enslavement. They reported being in desperate need of medical care. In some cases, they were shunned by their families because they had been raped. The family of one woman told the staff of a safe house where she was recovering that they would not like to see or speak to her because she had been raped.[40]

D. Declining Birthrates

Birthrate reductions during periods of mass starvation is another factor that could be considered through the intersection of starvation crimes and SGBV. Two caveats are needed. First, such a reduction is not consistently noted across studies of famine and mass starvation. Second, reaching a legal threshold for holding perpetrators accountable for reductions in birthrates is extremely unlikely. Imposing measures intended to prevent births within a national, ethnic, racial, or religious group, is recognized as a genocidal act only when there is a clear genocidal intent to destroy the group, in whole or in part. Nonetheless, given the depth of harm in such losses, it is important to consider the impact of starvation on birthrates.

When birthrates decrease during periods of extreme deprivation, both physiological and socio-cultural reasons must be factored in to the decline.[41] Biological explanations for declines in pregnancies include declines in fertility, caused by loss of menstruation due to severe stress, malnutrition and/or low body weight that causes the hypothalamus and pituitary gland not to function properly, increased miscarriages, and physiological sterility.[42] Socio-cultural explanations include the abortion of pregnancies, decrease in marriage rates, separation of the sexes during times of conflict, intensive migration (discussed later in the chapter in greater depth), and decreased sexual desire.[43]

[40] H. Murdock, 'Hundreds of women, girls brutalized by soldiers in Tigray war', *Voice of America* (7 July 2021) available online at <https://www.voanews.com/ethiopia-tigray/hundreds-women-girls-brutalized-soldiers-tigray-war-0> (visited 5 August 2021).

[41] K. Macintyre, 'Famine and the Female Mortality Advantage', in T. Dyson and C. Ó Gráda (eds), *Famine Demography: Perspectives from the Past and Present* (Oxford: Oxford University Press, 2002) 240–259; P. Boyle, and C. Ó Gráda, 'Fertility Trends, Excess Mortality, and the Great Irish Famine', 23 *Demography* (1986) 543–562; V. G. Valaoras, 'Some Effects of Famine on the Population of Greece', 24 *The Milbank Memorial Fund Quarterly* (1946) 215–234; T. Dyson, 'On the Demography of South Asian Famines: Part I', 45 *Population Studies* (1991), 5–25; T. Dyson, 'On the Demography of South Asian Famines: Part II', 45 *Population Studies* (1991) 279–297; R. Akresh et al., 'War and Stature: Growing up during the Nigerian Civil War', 102 *American Economic Review* (2012) 273–277; S. G. Elias et al., 'Menstruation during and after Caloric Restriction: The 1944–1945 Dutch famine', 88 *Fertility and Sterility* (2007) 1101–1107; J. Trussell and R. E. Frisch, 'Menarche and Fatness: Reexamination of the Critical Body Composition Hypothesis', 200 *Science* (1978) 1506–1513; J. Delaney, M. J. Lupton, and E. Toth, *The Curse: A Cultural History of Menstruation* (Champaign: University of Illinois Press, 1988).

[42] Dyson (1991, Part II), see note 41.

[43] A. Razzaque, 'The Effect of Famine on Fertility in a Rural Area of Bangladesh', 20 *Journal of Biosocial Science* (1988) 287–294, at 292–293.

In most cases, biological and socio-cultural factors appear simultaneously and may have long-lasting consequences. In both the Great Irish Famine[44] and the 1984–1985 Ethiopian famine fertility rates declined by approximately 25 per cent.[45] In the early 1940s in famine in Bengal there was a clear decline in conception rates with approximately five years of lower-than-normal conception rates from 1941 to 1946. Valaoras describes abortion as a decision that Greek women made in order to survive during the 1941–1942 Greek famine.[46] Cai and Feng document how Chinese women spoke openly about using abortion during the Great Leap Forward to keep themselves alive.[47] In these instances, females are forced to make exceptionally difficult decisions about how to preserve scarce resources required to survive.

Even if a challenge for the law, creating the conditions that increase miscarriages and abortions and force women to make decisions not to have children are horrendous and too often effective weapons of war and domination.

Mass starvation and SGBV are mutually reinforcing atrocity crimes. Widespread conditions of deprivation and starvation can increase the risk of SGBV. At the same time, SGBV, and in some cases even the threat of SGBV, can increase the risk of starvation in ways that differ by sex, gender, age, and context. Whilst SGBV prosecutions and investigations on the international level have increased, there remains a lacuna in how these crimes intersect and mutually reinforce others. This chapter reveals the investigative and prosecutorial need for a more nuanced and holistic view of the factual scenarios on the ground. Too often SGBV is viewed narrowly, with rape as the paradigmatic crime, and a cascading flow of reduced interest and attention to other forms of SGBV. Starvation-related SGBV inevitably falls outside the prosecutorial wheelhouse. This can—and ought to—change; it requires increased research, investigative work, and prosecutorial vision.

3. Mortality: Gender, Sex, and Age Differentials

In this section, our focus shifts from the perpetration of starvation crimes to understanding outcomes for populations that suffer mass starvation. Here we hone in on one key measure: mortality. While starvation crimes hinge on an *intent* to starve rather than death as an outcome, for both legal and common understanding, the

[44] There is some dispute about this. Fitzpatrick says Parish data were unreliable and thus we cannot conclude the actual rate of decreased conception, see D. Fitzpatrick, 'Women and the Great Famine', in M. Kelleher and J. H. Murphy (eds), *Gender Perspectives in Nineteenth-Century Ireland: Public and Private Spheres* (Dublin: Irish Academic Press, 1997) 50–69.

[45] A. Kidane, 'Demographic Consequences of the 1984–1985 Ethiopian Famine', 26 *Demography* (1989) 515–522.

[46] Valaoras, see note 41.

[47] Y. Cai, and W. Feng, 'Famine, Social Disruption, and Involuntary Fetal Loss: Evidence from Chinese Survey Data', 42 *Demography* (2005) 301–322.

ability to document that deprivations of objects indispensable for life caused actual starvation or widespread increased mortality bolsters the case.[48] The preponderance of what is known today about how gender, sex, and age impact mortality during periods of mass starvation emerges mostly from study of historical famines. One of the most curious insights of these studies is that despite high instances of chronic hunger among females and patterns of directly targeting females, as demonstrated earlier, there appears to be in many (although not all) cases a female mortality advantage (FMA). This finding means that relying on death rates to determine that there is a 'famine' or that starvation crimes have occurred or are occurring, misses how sex and gender affect mortality.

The FMA consists of females dying at lower rates than males, notably among adolescents and adults in their prime. In one of the few cross-national case studies of gender and famine, Macintyre (2002) surveyed the existing literature on famine. She found that while gender analyses are infrequently applied to demographic analyses, in most cases there is FMA.[49] However, Macintyre finds that the famine researchers rarely 'take the time to analyse why there might be a female advantage, nor do they address what specific factors might explain it'.[50] Macintyre calls for more gender-sensitive famine research, including greater attention to the timing and cause of death, immunological differences, the severity and duration of starvation, long-term versus short-term impacts, policy responses, and multidisciplinary research examining the intersection of cultural and biological factors.

Macintyre's call remains salient today. Almost twenty years later, there continues to be inadequate sex and age-disaggregated data collected during and after periods of mass starvation and there is a lack of gender analysis brought to bear to understand how mass starvation targets and is experienced among different populations. Yet, these data and analysis are essential for understanding who is affected, where, when, why, and how, and the effects for the future. To illustrate, there was no widespread or consistent collection of sex- and age-disaggregated data for the threatened five famines in recent years: South Sudan (2013–present), Yemen (2015–present), Somali (2010–2011; 2017–present), Nigeria (2009–present), and Ethiopia (2020–present). This failure occurs despite repeated calls by the United Nations and governments for sex- and age-disaggregated data and increased attention to the specific needs of women and girls as relates to malnutrition and hunger.[51]

Lacking such data, blanket statements are frequently made about the FMA, including that sexual exchange practices can explain gendered morality differentials.

[48] See Chapter 10 in this volume.

[49] Macintyre, see note 41.

[50] Macintyre, see note 41, at 240.

[51] D. Mazurana et al., *Sex and Age Matter: Improving Humanitarian Response in Emergencies* (OCHA, Care International, Feinstein International Center: New York, 2011).

For example, statements exclaim that 'through prostitution women are able to get extra resources'.[52] These claims are founded in dubious assumptions about why and how females survive famines. They can also serve to undermine the seriousness of the SGBV that women and girls are subjected to during and after mass starvation and infer a degree of autonomy and agency which cannot be assumed.

Similarly, the singular focus on mortality can obscure more complex interactions, including maternal care, that are hampered or damaged through starvation crimes. Nonetheless, mortality is a defining measure of famine and a relevant indicator of seriousness for starvation crimes. Thus, mortality rates require investigation. In this section, we review research related to FMA, asking what do we know about gender, age, and mortality during periods of mass starvation? We focus on three major areas: cause of death, biology, and migration.[53]

A. Cause of Death

To understand the perpetration and impact of starvation crimes, it is important to analyse gender, sex, and age dimensions of causes of death. In the context of mass starvation, deaths are sometimes caused by starvation, but they overwhelmingly result from infectious diseases that attack malnourished bodies with lowered immune systems. These diseases spread through migration, displacement, or disruptions in access to clean water, basic healthcare, and good hygiene.[54] Historically, natural disasters played a large role in triggering famines. However, over the past 150 years, famines overwhelmingly coincide and are causally associated with the violence of armed conflict and political repression.[55] Thus, in addition to disease and malnutrition, 'direct violence' is a significant, contemporaneous cause of increased mortality and suffering during periods of mass starvation.

In some historical studies of famine, the data clearly indicate cause of death.[56] However, since the end of the Second World War, both conflicts and mass starvation tend to occur in poorer countries where baseline demographic data collection is weak and new data collection is further complicated by widespread displacement. During periods of repression and conflict, state authorities charged with

[52] V. Zarull et al., 'Women live longer than men even during severe famines and epidemics', 115(4) *Proceedings of the National Academy of Sciences* (2018) 832–840; at 838.

[53] For a more complete discussion of the female mortality advantage see K. Spears, B. Conley, and D. Mazurana, 'Is there a female mortality advantage in famine?', World Peace Foundation and the Feinstein International Center (2021), available online at <https://sites.tufts.edu/wpf/new-occasional-paper-gender-famine-and-mortality/> (visited 27 January 2022).

[54] Chapters 2 and 3 in this volume..

[55] de Waal, see note 32.xyz

[56] The International Classification of Diseases (1938), which was used to categorize causes of death for the Second World War cases of The Netherlands and Greece, groups malnutrition and violent death in the same category, deaths from external causes, but further subdivides causes into malnutrition, cold,

data collection may have interests in skewing how causes of deaths are recorded, or if deaths are recorded at all. The Ukrainian famine, the Holodomor, is a signature example: state authorities outright forbade references to famine and the coterminous typhus epidemic, which was likely to have been the leading cause of death, to silence potential critics of state policies.[57]

We highlight three insights related to sex, gender, age, and cause of death based on examination of existing research on historical famines.[58] First, researchers found that the more severe the food crisis, the more females survive compared to males. This is especially true when the cause of death is starvation, understood in the narrow biological sense, as opposed to infectious disease interacting with undernutrition. Second, deaths for both male and female children appear to be more sensitive to variations in social norms and in the disease profile. Third, where FMA manifests, it is proportionately greatest for adolescents and adults in their prime, seemingly regardless of cause of death.

A key case in which starvation was the primary cause of death and the data are of high quality was Greece during the Second World War. A study by Hionidou (2006) demonstrates that disease contributed little to excess mortality and, due to restrictions on movement by the German and Italian occupying forces, migration played a minimal role.[59] She finds that Greek children benefited from school soup kitchens that bolstered survival rates across this age cohort. However, among both adults and the elderly, Greek females not only died in lower numbers than males but they also died at later stages of the crisis.[60] Discussing the literature on gender and famine, Hionidou agrees with those that posit a female physiological advantage, which appears to be greatest when starvation (versus disease) is the primary cause of death. Nonetheless, cultural explanations also play a role.[61] Hionidou's findings resonate with other studies that find adult FMA increases as food deprivation becomes more extreme.[62]

More frequently, disease is the leading cause of death—and disease profile matters for understanding variations in sex and gendered mortality outcomes. To illustrate, diarrhoeal diseases have greater incident rates for males (ages 1–5) but higher

military service, civilian war-related death, and executions (see P. Ekamper et al., 'War-related Excess Mortality in The Netherlands, 1944–45: New Estimates of Famine- and Nonfamine-related Deaths from National Death Records', 50 *Historical Methods: A Journal of Quantitative and Interdisciplinary History* (2017)113–128, at 117; and V. Hionidou, *Famine and Death in Occupied Greece, 1941–1944* (Cambridge: Cambridge University Press, 2006), at 172–173.

[57] M. Livi-Bacci, 'On the Human Costs of Collectivization in the Soviet Union', 19 *Population and Development Review* (1991) 743–766, at 757.

[58] Spears et al., see note 53.

[59] Hionidou, see note 56 at 172–173.

[60] Hionidou, see note 56, at 169 and 176.

[61] Hionidou, see note 56, at 177.

[62] Deng, see note 32, at 17; K. J. Pitkänen, 'Famine Mortality in 19th Century Finland: Is There a Sex Bias?' in Dyson and Gráda (eds), see note 41, 240–259, at 81.

mortality rates for females at the same age.[63] Acute lower respiratory and infectious pneumonia tend to have higher mortality rates for males.[64] Typhus has been shown to more severely impact males.[65] Cholera does not have a clear sex differential, but in many cases, the activities that expose an individual to the disease are disproportionately undertaken by girls and women.[66] Tuberculosis impacts males at higher rates and with greater severity than females.[67] These realities mean that a sex, gender, and age lens needs to be applied to treating people during disease outbreaks, and in particular during mass starvation.[68] For example, in an examination of five famines in south-east Asia (between 1896–1975), where malaria and/or cholera were the primary causes of death, found that mortality increased the most among those in late childhood and adulthood, particularly among males.[69] In the Darfur famine of 1984–1985, de Waal found that excess male mortality was most marked among adolescents, especially members of pastoralist communities.[70]

However, findings are not consistent across or even within country studies. In a study of three Finnish famines, all of which cited the leading causes of death as typhoid fever, dysentery, or relapsing fever, Pitkänen found one famine with FMA and two famines without.[71] Scholars likewise found no evidence of FMA in studies of Bangladesh (1971) and Ethiopia (1984–1985).[72] There may not have been FMA in these cases but other factors might be at play. In the Finnish case, soldiers are excluded from the data. In this case, the primary cause of civilian deaths was infectious disease with highest intensity in conflict-affected areas and where soldiers were quartered by civilians.[73] The intermingling of mixed-sex civilian and primarily male military populations during an epidemic might suggest that these two groups be studied together to understand gender patterns of famine-related

[63] World Health Organization (WHO), *Addressing Sex and Gender in Epidemic Prone Infectious Diseases* (2007), available online at <<https://www.who.int/csr/resources/publications/SexGenderInfectDis.pdf>> (visited 5 August 2021), at 9.

[64] WHO, see note 63, at 10.

[65] M. Khan, 'A Plausible Explanation for Male Dominance in Typhoid Ileal Perforation', 5 *Clinical and Experimental Gastroentology* (2012) 213–217.

[66] N. Rancourt, *Gender and Vulnerability to Cholera in Sierra Leone*, Oxfam Research Report (June 2013), available online at <https://oxfamilibrary.openrepository.com/bitstream/handle/10546/293965/rr-gender-cholera-vulnerability-sierra-leone-170613-en.pdf;jsessionid=6107C555D6E3D17CBE7C56EA7230D9BE?sequence=4> (visited 5 August 2021).

[67] K. Horton, R. White, and R. Houben, 'Systematic Neglect of Men as a Key Population in Tuberculosis', 113 *Tuberculosis* (2018) 249–253.

[68] WHO, see note 63, at 1.

[69] Dyson (1991, Part II), see note 41, at 294.

[70] de Waal, see note 32, at 178–179.

[71] Pitkänen, see note 62.

[72] A. K. M. Chowdhury and L. C. Chen, *The Dynamics of Contemporary Famine*, The Ford Foundation Report 47 (January 1977), available online at <http://dspace.icddrb.org/jspui/bitstream/123456789/3306/1/1977-FordFoundation-1-ChowdhuryAKMA.pdf> (visited 5 August 2021); Kidane, see note 45.

[73] K. J. Pitkänen and J. H. Mielke, 'Age and Sex Differentials in Mortality During Two Nineteenth Century Population Crises', 9 *European Journal of Population/Revue Européenne de Démographie* (1993) 1–32, at 7.

diseases. This might result in higher male deaths, even if only counting those who died from famine-related diseases.

Armed conflict is likely to increase male deaths due to direct violence, but other factors related to soldiering may play a role in gender mortality differentials. Hionidou documents an example related to Greek soldiers during the Second World War. Predominately male Greek soldiers stationed in the Albanian mountains were inadequately clothed, fed, and supplied, and many suffered frostbite. After the defeat by Axis forces in 1941, many returned on foot to Greece in a weakened state. A significant number of these returning soldiers found themselves among the urban unemployed, a group that died at higher rates when the famine struck later that year.[74]

The Netherlands (1944–1945) illustrates another complexity of examining causes of death during overlapping crises within a single country. Over the course of several months, the country experienced high-intensity war and famine, known as the *Hongerwinter.* War-related deaths during this period accounted for 70 per cent of all excess mortality from September through December 1944. Famine took over as the major cause of death from January through May 1945, concentrated in the urban west and including some rural western areas, though war deaths remained at 30 per cent. Throughout the entire period, males experienced higher mortality rates than females experiencing the same conditions, but the causes of death varied geographically and temporally.[75]

Male vulnerability to direct violence in most contexts of conflict and repression often means that males are killed at higher rates than females.[76] Deng's study of the 1998 famine in southern Sudan[77] produced a survey with women in 1999, after the peak of famine, who were asked about household aggregate deaths from 1998.[78] This survey found that many more females had survived compared to males. However, given that there was ongoing violence within the study area at the same time as the famine, and that the survey did not ask women to specify cause of death, it is likely that some deaths of adolescent and adult males (although not exclusively a male issue) resulted from direct violence, rather than from disease or starvation.

Finally, suicide is referenced in several famine studies, but without much detail. Dyson and Ó Gráda propose that suicide increases during the worst parts of famine and is more likely among men. Similar spikes in suicides during famine are

[74] Hionidou, see note 56, at 175.
[75] Ekamper et al., see note 56.
[76] C. Ormhaug, P. Meier, and H. Hernes, *Armed Conflict Deaths Disaggregated by Gender*, International Peace Research Institute (23 November 2009) available online at <<https://www.files.ethz.ch/isn/109997/Armed%20Conflict%20Deaths%20Disaggregated%20by%20Gender.pdf>> (visited 5 August 2021).
[77] Deng, see note 32, at 32.
[78] Deng, see note 32, at 18.

discussed by Dyson in India[79] and Garenne in Madagascar[80] where, overall, males died at higher rates than females. Unfortunately, neither scholar provides gender-disaggregated data specifically related to this cause of death so it is unclear how they reach their conclusions regarding male suicide rates.

The ultimate cause of death during a famine—violence, disease, depravation, starvation, and or suicide— cannot explain all sex, gender, and age differences with any single famine case, and certainly not the variations across cases. However, an awareness of who is dying (or at greater risk from dying) from what, when, and why is important to shaping response to prevent and respond to famine and mass starvation. Paying attention to these patterns may also inform knowledge about, and responses to, starvation crimes.

B. Biology and Mortality during Mass Starvation

Examining the cause of death is central to understanding age, sex and gender differences in mortality rates. In this section, we take a closer look at research on the role played by biological differences. Biological factors that we examine include body fat, the immune system, and fertility.

1. Sex and Body Fat

The body fat or body mass index (BMI) and famine survival hypothesis was developed by Rivers (1988) and advanced in later famine scholarship. The premise is that, on average, compared to adult males of their group, adult females (over 18 years of age) have naturally higher BMI, less muscle, are physically smaller, and thus have fewer caloric needs to sustain their internal organs. Several authors claim that adult females' higher BMI enables them to draw on fat resources and protect vital organ functions for longer than males and that this is one of the most important biological factors in the FMA during a famine.[81] Rivers also argued that women need lower fat and protein intake, have lower energy needs, and can withstand on average temperatures two degrees lower than men.[82]

Yet the data are not clear cut. Indeed, sex-disaggregated anthropometric data from famines and mass starvation are rare, and when analysed are inconsistent in supporting female BMI as the reason for FMA in famine. In the Dutch famine

[79] T. Dyson, 'Famine in Berar, 1896–1897 and 1899–1900: Echoes and Chain Reactions', in Dyson and Gráda (eds), see note 41, 240–259, at 109.

[80] M. Garenne et al., 'The Demographic Impact of a Mild Famine in an African City: The Case of Antananarivo, 1985–7', in Dyson and Gráda (eds), see note 41, 204–217, at 216.

[81] J. P. Rivers, 'Women and Children Last: Essay on sex discrimination in disasters', 6 *Disasters* (1982) 259–263; J. P. Rivers 'The Nutritional Biology of Famine', in G. A. Harrison (ed.), *Famine* (Oxford: Oxford University Press, 1988) 57–106; Dyson, see note 41; Livi-Bacci, see note 57; de Waal, see note 32; Deng, see note 32.

[82] Rivers, see note 81.

of 1945, Henry concluded that women have a lower minimum BMI level needed to survive compared to men. In the Madras famine of 1877, Aykroid found no difference in weights of people who died.[83] However, we suggest that the timing of deaths disaggregated by gender might provide further insight if women lived longer than males, despite dying at similar weights. Perhaps the most robust study is Collins'[84] investigation of severe adult malnutrition and famine oedema during the 1992–1993 famine in Somalia. He found that among adults, adult males had higher rates of severe famine oedema and a worse prognosis at any grade of severity in comparison to females.[85] However, Collins concluded that it was unclear whether there is a sex difference in the lowest level of BMI compatible with life. He flagged a potential data bias in that men who were so ill and weak that they could no longer walk were often carried into the clinics where his study was conducted. In contrast, most women in the clinics had walked in under their own power and hence, may have been in better health upon entry to the clinic.[86]

Macintyre's gendered analysis of the literature on famine discussed the body fat hypothesis and found no actual cases of research on famines in which adult females' higher BMI is shown to contribute to their survival advantage.[87] She discussed Collins' research and concluded, as does he, that the survival advantage attributed to body fat is questionable given the gender bias of who was able to reach the clinic where he was conducting the research and in what condition. She argues that any such impact of body fat and caloric needs are likely, if at all, to be only two factors amongst many other gendered socio-cultural and political factors that contribute to a female survival advantage in a famine (if and when one occurs).[88]

Finally, using a validated mathematical survival model for total starvation to compare adult males and females to test the body fat hypothesis, Speakman further questioned the body fat hypothesis.[89] Running a model with sex-disaggregated data from forty-eight countries at the low end of the obesity spectrum, he predicted that in the complete absence of food adult females would survive for ninety-eight days and males sixty-eight days, thus females survived 40 percent or one month longer than adult males. This is due to females' lower resting metabolic rates, lower muscle composition, and smaller body stature. Interestingly, Speakman used the same model to test his hypothesis that older adults should live longer than young adults, but the model did not find this. Speakman concludes that body fat may be a factor, but it cannot explain the range of outcomes in actual famines: 'These data emphasize the complex nature of famine mortality and suggest that a simple

[83] W. R. Aykroid, *The Conquest of Famine* (London: Chatto & Windus, 1974).
[84] S. Collins, 'The Limit of Human Adaptation to Starvation', 1 *Nature Medicine* (1995) 810–814.
[85] Collins, see note 84, at 812.
[86] Collins, see note 84, at 246.
[87] Macintyre, see note 41.
[88] Macintyre, see note 41, at 248.
[89] J. Speakman, 'Sex- and Age-related Mortality Profiles during Famine: Testing the "Body Fat" Hypothesis', 45 *Journal of Biosocial Medicine* (2013) 823–840.

model of energy utilization alone is inadequate to explain the major aspects of this phenomenon.'[90]

2. Sex, Gender, Age, and the Immune System

Human males' immune systems are disadvantaged as compared to females and this may handicap them during mass starvation and under other stressful conditions. The male sex hormone testosterone has an adverse effect on the body's immune system. In men, this results in a weaker immunologic response and more difficulty fighting pathogens and resulting diseases. Furthermore, the X chromosome, of which females have two (XX) and males have only one (XY), are encoded with the most 'immune-related' genes, which is likely to contribute to females' overall stronger and better coordinated immune responses.[91]

Age is also a crucial factor. Among neonatals, when the mothers are under stress from crisis conditions, political upheaval, and armed violence, male foetuses are more likely than females to spontaneously abort.[92] Overall death rates in famines are almost always highest for children under five years of age and the elderly. Young children die from birth complications and common childhood illnesses that are exacerbated by malnutrition and poor hygiene. At a biological level, older people often have a combination of multiple chronic diseases that make them more susceptible to malnutrition and disease.[93]

Sex and gender are closely connected, and gendered behaviour has biological and physiological effects. Worldwide, men's greater likelihood to participate in health-impairing behaviour such as smoking and drinking alcohol can suppress their immune systems and contribute to a variety of diseases. Men are also significantly less likely to seek medical care compared to women. Women are more likely to be the primary providers of caregiving and ensuring the health of their families, and are more likely to engage in health-seeking and health-maintaining activities. These sex- and gender-related behaviours help shape and explain what appear as solely biological disadvantages for males in surviving famine.

Other factors commonly cited in the literature on famine and FMA include migration patterns (which variably are posited to benefit either males or females, depending on the case); females' knowledge of famine foods;[94] especially harsh labour requirements imposed on males;[95] customary gendered division of labour

[90] Speakman, see note 89, at 823.

[91] L. A. Walter and A. J. McGregor, 'Sex- and Gender-specific Observations and Implications for COVID-19', 21 *Western Journal of Emergency Medicine: Integrating Emergency Care with Population Health* (2020) 507–509.

[92] R. Catalano and T. Bruckner, 'Secondary Sex Ratios and Male Lifespan: Damaged or Culled Cohorts', 103 *Proceedings of the National Academy of Sciences of the United States of America* (2006) 1639–1643.

[93] M. Hickson, 'Malnutrition and Ageing,' 82 *Postgraduate Medical Journal* (2006), 2 – 8.

[94] See this chapter, section I.B.

[95] A Sen, *Poverty and Famines: An Essay on Entitlement and Deprivation* (Oxford: Clarendon Press, 1981); A Sen, *Gender and Cooperative Conflicts*, World Institute for Development Economics Research

whereby women and girls work for wages paid in food, often in domestic settings where they can also eat their employers' leftovers, while men and boys work for cash wages distant from food preparation;[96] and charity and relief practices that favour females.[97] Lower birthrates, both for physiological and socio-cultural reasons, during periods of famine and mass starvation are also cited by several scholars as a potential explanation for FMA, given that in normal times pregnancy and childbirth impose increased risks for females.[98] However, none of these factors are consistent across cases nor can they account for variations in whether and how FMA appears. Across the board, these studies require us to look closely at gendered vulnerabilities and coping strategies that entail increased risks—all of which interact with local practices and biases to produce mortality risks that may shift over time and across contexts.

Overall, we find that male's biology and socio-cultural behaviour put them at greater risk of death at all ages than females. Actors that induce famine and mass starvation as part of their war and repression tactics and strategies seek to destroy a targeted groups' ability to physically and politically to sustain life. Mass starvation means that a population is made sick, weak, and dies *en masse*—often males in greater numbers than females, with high risks for the very young and the elderly. Further, as discussed later in this chapter, it renders those who survive—usually a larger number of females (and their offspring) than males—sicker and worse off in the long term.

4. Surviving Mass Starvation: Long-term Outcomes

The enormity of the negative physical and mental health, social, educational, and economic costs of mass starvation on survivors, their children, and grandchildren make clear that a focus on mortality alone misrepresents the true toll.[99] Indeed, the effects of surviving mass starvation last well beyond the end of severe deprivation

Working Papers (July 1987), available online at <https://www.wider.unu.edu/sites/default/files/WP18.pdf> (visited 5 August 2021), at 37; M. Davis, *Late Victorian Holocausts: El Niño Famines and the Making of the Third World* (New York: Verso, 2001), at 37; and L. Sami, 'Gender Differentials in Famine Mortality: Madras (1876–78) and Punjab (1896–97)', 37 *Economic and Political Weekly* (2002) 2593–2600.

[96] de Waal, see note 32, at 181.

[97] Fitzpatrick see note 44, at 60–62; Sen (1987), see note 95, at 34, footnote 47; Sami see note 95, at 2599; B. Lindtjørn and T. Alemu, 'Intra-household correlations of nutritional status in rural Ethiopia', 26 *International Journal of Epidemiology* (1997) 160–165; at 160; Deng see note 32, at 12; Pitkänen and Mielke see note 73, at 8.

[98] Macintyre, see note 41; Boyle, and Ó Gráda, see note 41; Valaoras, see note 41; Dyson (1991, Part I) see note 41, at 25; Akresh et al., see note 41.

[99] Z. Luo, R. Mu, and X. Zhang, 'Famine and Overweight in China', 28 *Applied Economic Perspectives and Policy* (2006) 296–304.

and vary for different ages, sexes, and genders. These factors should be figured into both prevention of and accountability for those who induce mass starvation.

A. Long-term Health Effects

Scholars of famine describe two patterns resulting from exposure to famine that may also help us understand the sex differences in long-term outcomes: culling and scarring. The male 'culling effect', attributed to environmental and nutritional stressors, describes higher incidents of miscarriage or spontaneous abortion of weaker males (but not females) *in utero*. This results in the births of fewer, but more vigorous, males. While fewer males survive, those who do often show a greater range of health advantages in their later life compared to their female cohort.[100]

Research also shows more significant long-term health effects of mass starvation and other shocks for females than for males. The effects of severe deprivation and mass starvation in early life are more harmful over time to surviving women than men.[101] This is due to what is referred to as 'scarring', in which those who survive birth or early infancy, while obviously healthier than those that perish, carry with them effects that can permanently impair their health as they age.[102]

Regardless of sex, undernutrition in foetal and infant life may result in the human body making adaptions that can manifest as chronic disease in adulthood.[103] Multiple in-depth studies of two famines provide insight into the lifelong impact of exposure to famine conditions.

Due to its brief duration, the Dutch famine (1944–1945) provides a compelling example where data are strong and it is relatively easy to separate famine-impacted populations from those that were not impacted. Scholars have found that people exposed to starvation in early life suffered an increased risk of being overweight and having diabetes, coronary heart disease, chronic obstructive pulmonary disease,

[100] C. Huang et al., 'Malnutrition in Early Life and Adult Mental Health: Evidence from a Natural Experiment', 97 *Social Science & Medicine* (2013) 259–266; Catalano and Bruckner, see note 92; R. Mu and X. B. Zhang, 'Why Does the Great Chinese Famine Affect the Male and Female Survivors Differently?: Mortality Selection Versus Son Preference', 9 *Economics and Human Biology* (2011) 92–105.

[101] C. Huang et al., 'Early Life Exposure to the 1959–1961 Chinese Famine Has Long-term Health Consequences', 140 *The Journal of Nutrition* (2010) 1874–1878; S. Maccini and D. Yang, 'Under the Weather: Health, Schooling, and Economic Consequences of Early-life Rainfall', 99 *American Economic Review* (2009) 1006–1026; A. C. J. Ravelli et al., 'Obesity at the Age of 50 in Men and Women Exposed to Famine Prenatally', 70 *American Journal of Clinical Nutrition* (1999) 811–816.

[102] C. Bozzoli, A. Deaton, and C. Quintana-Domeque, 'Adult Height and Childhood Disease', 46 *Demography* (2009) 647–669; Mu and Zhang, see note 100; S. H. Preston, M. E. Hill, and G.L. Drevenstedt, 'Childhood Conditions that Predict Survival to Advanced Ages Among African-Americans', 47 *Social Science and Medicine* (1998) 1231–1246; S. G. Song, W. Wang, and P. F. Hu, 'Famine, Death, and Madness: Schizophrenia in early adulthood after prenatal exposure to the Chinese Great Leap Forward Famine', 68 *Social Science and Medicine* (2009) 1315–1321.

[103] D. J. Barker, 'The Fetal and Infant Origins of Adult Disease', 301 *British Medical Journal* (1990) 1111.

and asthma.[104] Studies of the Dutch famine also found that prenatal exposure to starvation was associated with antisocial personality disorder in adolescence,[105] major affective disorders,[106] and schizophrenia[107] in adulthood, and higher BMI in adult women.[108] Fransen's study of the Dutch famine found that being exposed to famine as a girl resulted in those females as adults adopting unhealthy behaviours, including increased smoking and being physically inactive.[109] The association was dose-dependent: the greater the exposure to famine of the girl, the higher levels of smoking and inactivity when she became a woman. These unhealthy behaviours are known to contribute to many non-communicable diseases.[110] Several studies find that the relationships between exposure to famine and being overweight as an adult is more pronounced in female famine survivors then males.[111]

Researching the health outcomes of the Great Famine in China (1959–1962), several scholars[112] found significant stunting in infants and children exposed to the famine. Stunting is associated with underdevelopment of the brain and the resulting reduced mental ability and learning aptitude, poor school performance, increases of malnutrition-related chronic disease, including diabetes, hypertension, and obesity. Studies on mental health and the Great Famine in China also found prenatal exposure to famine significantly increased the risk of developing schizophrenia in both adolescence and adulthood.[113] Females who were exposed to the Great Famine in China while they were *in utero* or infants were more likely to

[104] A. F. van Abeelen et al., 'Famine Exposure in the Young and the Risk of Type 2 Diabetes in Adulthood', 61 *Diabetes* (2012) 2255–60; A. F. van Abeelen et al., 'Cardiovascular Consequences of Famine in the Young', 33 *European Heart Journal* (2012) 538–45; A. F. van Abeelen et al., 'Postnatal Acute Famine and Risk of Overweight: The Dutch *Hungerwinter* study', *International Journal of Pediatrics* (2012) 1–9; A. F. van Abeelen et al., 'Famine in the Young and Risk of Later Hospitalization for COPD and Asthma', 8 *PloS One* (2013) 1–8; H. P. Fransen, 'Exposure to Famine at a Young Age and Unhealthy Lifestyle Behavior Later in Life', 11 *PLoS One* (2016) 1–11.

[105] R. Neugebauer, H. W. Hoek, and E. Susser, 'Prenatal Exposure to Wartime Famine and Development of Antisocial Personality Disorder in Early Adulthood', 281 *Journal of the American Medical Association* (1999) 455–62.

[106] A. S. Brown et al., 'Further Evidence of Relation Between Prenatal Famine and Major Affective Disorder', 157 *American Journal of Psychiatry* (2000) 190–5.

[107] H. E. Hulshoff Pol, et al., 'Prenatal Exposure to Famine and Brain Morphology in Schizophrenia', 157 *American Journal of Psychiatry* (2000)1170–2.

[108] Ravelli et al., see note 101; Luo et al., see note 99.

[109] Fransen, see note 104.

[110] M. Ezzati and E. Riboli, 'Behavioral and Dietary Risk Factors for Noncommunicable Diseases', 369 *New England Journal of Medicine* (2013) 954–964; G. Ferrara et al., 'Risk Factors Associated with Pulmonary Tuberculosis: Smoking, diabetes and anti-TNFα drugs', 18 *Current Opinion in Pulmonary Medicine* (2012) 233–240.

[111] Luo et al., see note 99.

[112] Y. Chen and L. Zhou, 'The Long-term Health and Economic Consequences of the 1959–1961 Famine in China', 26 *Journal of Health Economics* (2007) 659–681; T. Gørgens, X. Meng, and R. Vaithianathan, 'Stunting and Selection Effects of Famine: A case study of the Great Chinese Famine', 97 *Journal of Development Economics* (2012) 99–111; X. Meng and N. Qian, *The Long-term Consequences of Famine on Survivors: Evidence from a unique natural experiment using China's great famine*. National Bureau of Economic Research (2009), available online at <https://www.nber.org/system/files/working_papers/w14917/w14917.pdf> (visited 25 August 2021).

[113] D. St Clair et al., 'Rates of Adult Schizophrenia Following Prenatal Exposure to the Chinese Famine of 1959–1961', 294 *Jama* (2005) 557–562

miscarry and experience stillbirths as adults than women who were not exposed to famine in their early years.[114] Compared to their male counterparts, women born during the Great Chinese Famine are more likely to be stunted, obese, illiterate, and under- or unemployed.[115] These women also have fewer years of schooling and are less likely to have completed secondary school than their male counterparts. These effects are stronger based on their mothers' exposure to famine, as compared to their fathers' famine exposure.[116]

These case study examples direct our attention to a potential higher disease burden in female survivors of mass starvation compared to males. Yet again, the research points to the need for more sex- and age-disaggregated data and gender analysis for other cases of mass starvation. The studies suggest significant and important implications in shaping post-crisis gender-equitable provision of public health policy, programming, health insurance, and care. Policy interventions that promote adequate nutrition for girls and women, and pre-natal, maternal, and postnatal health will be essential to disrupt the intergenerational effects of poor health on future generations' developmental, educational, economic, and social outcomes.[117]

B. Long-term Social and Economic Harm

More research is required to examine the long-term social, economic, and health challenges at the intersection of starvation crimes and gender, sex, and age. However, we can extract some findings from the gender-focused conflict research, which suggests serious, detrimental long-term harms. We surmise that the experience of mass starvation, especially given what we know about the health impacts (see section 3.A), is likely to present further detrimental impacts for many survivors.

Research in Uganda[118] finds that compared to other war affected populations, in the post-conflict period survivors of war crimes and crimes against humanity are statistically significantly more likely to have worse outcomes in several key

[114] Huang et al., see note 101; Cai and Feng, see note 47.

[115] Gorgens et al., see note 112, at 106; Meng and Qian, see note 112; Luo et al., see note 99; D. Almond et al., *Long-term Effects of the 1959–1961 China Famine: Mainland China and Hong Kong*, National Bureau of Economic Research (2007), available online at <https://www.nber.org/papers/w13384> (visited 24 August 2021); Chen and Zhou, see note 112; X. Shi, 'Famine, Fertility, and Fortune in China', 22 *China Economic Review* (2011) 244–259.

[116] W. Fung and W. Ha, 'Intergenerational Effects of the 1959-61 China Famine', in R. Fuentes-Nieva and P. A. Seck (eds), *Risk, Shocks, and Human Development* (London: Palgrave Macmillan, 2010) 222–254.

[117] R. Mu and X. Zhang, *Gender Difference in the Long-Term Impact of Famine*, International Food Policy Research Institute Discussion Paper #00760 (2008) available online at <http://cdm15738.contentdm.oclc.org/utils/getfile/collection/p15738coll2/id/9449/filename/9450.pdf> (visited 5 August 2021).

[118] A. Marshak et al., *Tracking change in livelihoods, service delivery and governance: Evidence from a 2013-2015 panel survey in Uganda*, Working paper 59, Overseas Development Institute, London (2017),

measures of socio-economic well-being: food security, access to healthcare and clean water, and children out of school. And they are significantly more likely to be in the bottom quartile of households (i.e. the poorest households). Outcomes are even more troubling for households that include survivors of sexual violence that constitutes war crimes or crimes against humanity. In the post-conflict period, they are significantly more likely to become victims of additional crimes, including violent crimes and property crimes. Individual victims of sexual war crimes and crimes against humanity are also significantly more likely to experience more sexual crimes in the post-conflict than their war affected counterparts.

Most contexts of mass starvation produce populations in which many adolescent boys and adult men in their prime have died (see section 2) or been violently killed. They leave behind young families that struggle economically and socially in their absence. Many families are now headed by women who themselves are physically, emotionally, socially, and culturally weakened due to the conflict and mass starvation. In many cases, they are also in disadvantaged positions due to patriarchy and other discriminatory formal and informal systems and practices.[119]

Mortality is an inadequate record of harms during periods of conflict. The so-called indirect consequences of armed conflict shapes people's lives and livelihoods during and after conflict, often with a multi-generational impact. Evidence finds that women and girls often bear the brunt of these indirect consequences. Neumayer and Plümper (2006) found that both the direct and indirect consequences of armed conflict combine to kill more women, and/or kill them at a younger age, than their male counterparts.[120] The indirect effects of war are, in fact, the deadliest. These indirect effects include limited food and water access; poor sanitation and hygiene; weak or collapsed health services; and increased displacement, family dislocation, family stress, and domestic violence. For example, women are more affected by declines in health services due to conflict because of their reproductive and caring roles, reduction in obstetrical care, and increase in child and maternal mortality. In societies where women already face discrimination in terms of accessing food, resources, and health services, the aftermath of violent conflict exacerbates such discrimination and can make it even more deadly.[121] How these documented experiences of females in the post-conflict context intersect with additional harms imposed by exposure to mass starvation during conflict is a question that urgently requires additional research.

available online at <https://securelivelihoods.org/wp-content/uploads/2.-Tracking-change-in-livelihoods-service-delivery-and-governance-panel-survey-in-Uganda-2.pdf> (visited 5 August 2021).

[119] Raven-Roberts, see note 33.

[120] E. Neumayer and T. Plümper, 'The Unequal Burden of War: The Effect of Armed Conflict on the Gender Gap in Life Expectancy', 60 *International Organization* (2006) 723–754.

[121] Neumayer and Plumper, see note 120.

What is clear, however, is that in the aftermath of armed conflict and mass starvation, the short- and long-term and intergeneration harm caused by those responsible for starvation crimes demands accountability and justice mechanisms. This may include criminal proceedings and remedy and reparation for survivors and their current and future family members.

5. Conclusion: Towards Protection and Accountability

Those responsible for famines are complicit in crimes whose harm is inter- and multi-generational. At the national, regional, and international level, strong and sustained political, health, educational, and economic efforts are needed to prevent states and armed groups from using mass starvation as a weapon against civilian populations. Where that fails, accountability and assistance efforts are needed on the behalf survivors and their offspring.

We offer five recommendations to inform gender-just protection and accountability for victims of mass starvation.

First, it is unacceptable that in the five most recent famines, there continues to be a lack of sex- and age-disaggregated data on the victims, and this is inexplicable, given high-level calls for such data. As we have shown, human suffering and responses to suffering are influenced by sex, gender, and age. Thus, sex, gender, and age data and analyses are key tools for informing policy and response, and we argue that governments and agencies cannot adequately understand or respond to mass starvation without such analyses. Thus, governments and international and national organizations must require the strong collection, analysis, and operational use of sex- and age-disaggregated data and gender analysis in shaping all responses. Better understanding how the various forms of violence within mass starvation are orchestrated, by whom, when, where, and against whom, and with what affects will be essential to protecting lives and ensuring accountability for crimes.

Second, in this chapter we have begun to develop the intersection between SGBV and starvation crimes. As we have argued, SGBV can increase risks of starvation, and starvation crimes can cause increases in SGBV. Being sold for sex, being used as a sex slave, preventing mothers from caring for their children, being forced into marriage, being exposed to rape and sexual enslavement in order to meet survival needs, decisions about who eats and who does not, and undertaking sexual activities in order to keep oneself and children alive, violate the rights of (primarily) women and girls. Displacement caused by mass starvation exposes women and girls to a wide range of SGBV. Trying to combat starvation and access items indispensable to survival while in the camps can lead women and girls to experience more forms of SGBV. The women and girls who survive these crimes then face enormous amounts of stigma and rejection from their families and communities that can lead to their future violence, deprivation, and impoverishment. Women and girls suffer lost pregnancies and heart-wrenching decisions about how best to preserve scarce resources. It is crucial that SGBV starvation crimes be recognized for what they are and that perpetrators be held accountable. Finally, gender analyses of the starvation crimes suffered should inform gender-just remedy and reparation programmes for victims.[122]

Third, mass starvation is a highly gendered crime that causes the living to suffer increased morbidity and mortality across populations now and into the future. Mass starvation causes families to be violently and irrevocably torn apart. It causes the unborn, particularly males, to be spontaneously aborted. It causes the females that are born to suffer serious health conditions that will plague them and their family members for the rest of their lives. The children of the original victims then become adults who are more likely to pass on their chronic health problems to their own children. These negative long-term, intergenerational impacts should be factored into prevention, accountability, and response policies and mechanisms.

National leaders, humanitarian actors and policy-makers need to direct substantial resources towards survivors of mass starvation and their children's long-term health and educational needs. The higher chronic disease burden in female survivors of mass starvation compared to males has important implications in shaping post-crisis, gender-responsive healthcare. Policy interventions that promote adequate nutrition for girls and women, and prenatal, maternal and postnatal health will be essential to disrupt the intergenerational effects of poor health on future generations'—and particularly girls'—developmental, educational, economic, and social outcomes. Extra attention and support should be provided to children and affected pregnant mothers. The type of support would depend on the identified need but could include complementary feeding, micronutrient supplementation (for children and pregnant mothers), zinc supplementation, vitamin A supplementation, folic iron supplementation for pregnant mothers, and maternal calcium supplementation. Psychological support to victims of SGBV and their children is needed to help them overcome traumatic impacts that may limit their longer-term prospects. Without directed and sustained efforts the harmful intergenerational effects of mass starvation will continue to be felt through future generations of the survivors' families.

Fourth, in the aftermath of conflict and mass starvation, efforts are needed to enable the many women-headed households and female breadwinners and their families to rebuild their lives and livelihoods. These efforts should range from

[122] R. Rubio (ed.), *The Gender of Reparations: Unsettling Gender Hierarchies while Addressing Human Rights Violations* (Cambridge: Cambridge University Press, 2009); M. U. Walker, 'Transformative Reparations? A Critical Look at a Current Trend in Thinking about Gender-Just Reparations', 10 *International Journal of Transitional Justice* (2016) 108–125; D. Mazurana et al., *Making Gender Just Remedy and Reparation Possible: Upholding the Rights of Women and Girls in Northern Uganda*, Feinstein International Center and Isis WICCE (2013), available online at <http://reliefweb.int/sites/reliefweb.int/files/resources/Gender-Just-Remedy-and-Reparation-final-June-2013.pdf> (visited 5 August 2021).

updating inheritance and property laws to enable women to inherit and own property (especially important in places where male heads of household are dead/missing) to offering free legal services to women to enable them legally to remain in their homes, on their land, and to keep their children. Efforts should also include access to mental and physical healthcare and rehabilitation, and programmes for their children to attend school for free with no hidden fees, as these responses are crucial to help pull their families out of cycles of poverty.

Starvation crimes inflict harmful, longlasting, intergenerational impacts on survivors. The perpetration of these crimes and their impacts on a targeted population vary depending on gender, sex, and age. Where prevention fails, accountability is required. Neither prevention, response nor accountability is complete without attention to the victims' gender, sex, and age.

14
Reporting Famine

Jane Ferguson

In one of the main hospitals of Yemen's capital, Sana'a, a little baby girl with a medical tube down her nostril winced and cried as milk finally reached her stomach. She was a toddler's age, but shrivelled into nearly the size of a baby. Severe malnutrition keeps children's bodies suspended in time. For this little girl, the rarity of drinking milk was a painful experience. Her cries were weak, soft squeals. The children's ward of the Republican Hospital had become a *de facto* malnutrition ward, with skeletal babies and children each bundled up inside a pile of blankets placed on beds. Anxious parents sat next to their bundle of cloth, enduring complete powerlessness. The nurses were astonished to see me, a reporter, enter the hospital with TV cameras.

The conflict between the Saudi Arabia-led coalition that backs the internationally recognized government of Abd-Rabbuh Mansour Hadi, against what they refer to as the 'Houthi rebels', the 'Salvation/Rescue Government' of Ansarallah, and its allies based in Sana'a, brought the country to the brink of famine by 2018, when I arrived to report on the war. Yemen was 'the world's worst humanitarian crisis',[1] but few people really knew what that meant. Those four words were repeatedly used to describe a catastrophe befallen on millions, but about which people around the world had no real idea. Actual reporting from rebel-held Yemen was practically non-existent. Save for a few pictures sent out by aid agencies and frantic press releases from the United Nations filled with numbers of those at risk, there were no stories, people, or explanations as to what was happening and why, and what it was like for the people experiencing it.

By the summer of 2018, attempts to get inside rebel-held parts of Yemen had become a go-to topic of conversation between any and all foreign correspondents, from across the Middle East and in news headquarters from New York to Washington DC to London. The first hurdle, and the one that kept most journalists out, was securing a visa from the Yemeni government based in Aden and backed by

[1] *Yemen—The World's Worst Humanitarian Crisis*, World Food Programme, available online at <https://www.wfp.org/yemen-crisis (visited 27 August 2021); 'Humanitarian crisis in Yemen remains the worst in the world, warns UN', *UN News*, 14 February 2019, available online at <https://news.un.org/en/story/2019/02/1032811> (visited 27 August 2021).

Jane Ferguson, *Reporting Famine* In: *Accountability for Mass Starvation*. Edited by: Bridget Conley, Alex de Waal, Catriona Murdoch, and Wayne Jordash QC, Oxford University Press. © Jane Ferguson 2022.
DOI: 10.1093/oso/9780192864734.003.0014

a Saudi-led coalition. Visas were difficult to get, they involved waiting for months, often hiring a local Yemeni 'fixer' to help speed along the process. If and when a visa finally arrived, it was only the first step, security clearance was arbitrarily given and denied.

The only way to fly into Houthi-held territory was on a UN humanitarian flight. The Saudi-led coalition banned all but United Nations planes from landing into Sana'a airport, enforced by their control of the air, land, and sea around Yemen. From August 2016 to the time of writing, UN humanitarian staff in charge of taking bookings for their Humanitarian Air Service (UNHAS) flights refused to acknowledge that Saudi officials were checking the manifest of UN planes and expelling reporters. However, in December 2016, a senior UN official with direct knowledge of the situation wrote to me via email when I complained: 'I have been very dismayed that a party to the conflict can interfere in the use of a UN humanitarian asset. KSA [Kingdom of Saudi Arabia] state that media are not humanitarians. This comes in spite of us pointing out (in writing and consultations) that we need to raise Yemen humanitarian profile, public awareness, advocacy and resource mobilization.'[2]

Some journalists had made it to Aden, a city in the south of the country that was not controlled by the Saudi-backed government, via small boats from Djibouti. The fishermen who regularly made a living on their traditional wooden Dhows in the Gulf of Aden were happy to make good money ferrying the odd journalist and crew across to Aden city. But this pathway was closed beginning in January 2018, when the coalition bombs made it too dangerous for the fishermen to make their normal living, let alone ferry reporters across. Even Yemen's West Coast fishing communities—as self-sufficient as any in the country—began to face deadly hunger. Crossing by boat had become a no-go. Journalists had to fly. The only way was to fly into Aden on flights chartered through Yemenia Airways. Buying a ticket was no guarantee. Many reporters were suddenly kicked off planes around boarding time by airline staff, with no explanation other than that they didn't have 'permission'.

In December 2018, I was about to leave my hotel room in Cairo to head to the airport to catch a Yemenia Airways flight to Aden when my fixer called from Sana'a. He was a travel agent before the war and had for decades been booking tickets with the state carrier. 'They said you have been removed from the manifest, Jane, and not to come to the airport', he told me. I flew to Jordan a couple of days later and managed to get onto a Yemenia flight from there, after much discussion at check in between myself and airline staff. Most journalists flying to Yemen would have to call their editors from Amman or Cairo airport to let them know if they were being allowed to board. It wasn't until the plane took off that you knew you were really on the flight and heading to Yemen.

[2] Email exchange, 15 December 2020.

Landing into Aden airport involved questions about permits that rarely existed anywhere else in the world. Fixers could smooth out disputes by arguing and showing paperwork that proved you were a reporter working in Aden, but frequently, journalists would be turned around and put on the next plane out. Even if you got out of the airport and to your hotel, as I did, there would be men hanging out in the lobby to monitor your movements, making little effort to be subtle. At least one major US broadsheet correspondent told me their team had to sneak out of the hotel and drive off in the middle of the night to start their journey to rebel-held northern areas.

Less difficult to come by were visas issued by the Sana'a-based Houthi government, which ran a Ministry of Information as though it was the country's central government. However, journalists attempting to get this visa would have to hire another fixer, based in rebel-controlled areas.

After all that was the greatest challenge to reporters: the checkpoints between Aden and Sana'a. Driving north from Aden involved dozens of them, for the first half of the journey the checkpoints were manned by soldiers affiliated with the Saudi-coalition backed and internationally recognized government. An unwritten rule was that journalists were not allowed to travel to rebel territory, so getting through those checkpoints meant disguising yourself, or taking lesser-known mountain passes.

These logistical nightmares placed enormous hurdles in the way of reporters trying to shed light on the war in Yemen and its ruinous impact on the people there. They explain how, between 2016 and 2018, there were only a handful of news cover stories covering Yemen from reporters who had been inside the country. In June 2018, I was the first Western TV reporter to get into rebel-controlled northern Yemen in two years, and since my last trip to the country in December 2018, I have been unable to return because visas have been repeatedly denied.

The journey was dangerous, about as challenging as they come, and very expensive. In reality, news organizations had taken massive risks recently to cover the fighting in Mosul against Islamic State of Iraq and Syria (ISIS) and the crackdown on rebel-held areas of north-western Syria, so being in Yemen didn't present much more physical danger. But security experts hired by major news networks and papers argued escape routes—getting out of Yemen—were impossible to find should reporters need to quickly leave rebel-held territory. Interest from media organizations to send teams of reporters, despite the expense and danger, was very low.

The Saudi-led coalitions' extreme limitation on access was a tactic that worked well. Few news outlets could do the kind of reporting about the conflict and humanitarian crisis that would garner attention. The reality of TV news is that without their own correspondent and team there, no news network is likely to give the story much coverage, if they report on the story at all. Newspaper reporters could talk to aid workers by phone and use photographs sent to them by the non-governmental organizations (NGOs), but even then, Yemen was not a story that led most paper's international news sections.

The limited access to rebel-held parts of Yemen, where the vast majority of the population live and where the much of the widespread hunger existed, had clear impacts. The top three US TV networks—ABC, NBC, and CBS—dedicated a combined twenty minutes of airtime to the war in Yemen for the entire year of 2018.[3] That, incidentally, equalled a third of the amount of airtime the Royal Wedding in London received. Royal weddings will always attract TV lenses, but Yemen's war would have undoubtedly drawn more coverage if the work of journalists had not been purposefully hindered and blocked at every turn. It was clear that the blockade on journalists was to prevent the reporting of one undeniable fact: that Yemen's humanitarian catastrophe was being caused not only directly by the war but by the way it was being fought, in particular by the tactics used by the Saudi-led coalition. I had never experienced such a comprehensive, overt push to block journalists from an entire conflict in my career, and have not since. The Saudi-led coalition were aware that reports that shed light on the levels and causes of suffering amongst Yemen's people could raise further questions in Washington DC. The stories and images could help generate political pressure on the Saudis and their Emirati partners in this war.

That is exactly what happened when reporters did start sneaking past the barriers placed in front of them. After I and my camera crew safely returned from rebel-held Yemen in the summer of 2018, other news organizations decided to risk sending their people in. The results were some extremely high-profile reporting highlighting the devastating cost of the war in an up close and personal manner that only real field reporting can achieve. In October of 2018, the front page of the *New York Times* carried a now famous picture that Tyler Hicks took of a skeletal seven-year-old girl, Amal Hussein, her head turned to the side in what seems like profound sadness and exhaustion.[4] Her tiny arms are crossed over a rib cage that pushes painfully through her skin. The picture deeply shocked the American public. The next week, Declan Walsh, the *New York Times* journalist, reported that Amal had died.[5] Around the same time, a series of reports came out from a BBC team, led by correspondent Orla Guerin, bringing the level of suffering to TV screens globally. The 2019 Pulitzer Prize for photography went to Lorenzo Tugnoli of the *Washington Post* for pictures taken in Yemen of the crisis.[6] The explosion

[3] 'Year in Review 2018', Tyndall Report, available online at <http://tyndallreport.com/yearinreview2018/war/ (visited 27 August 2021).

[4] D. Walsh, 'The tragedy of Saudi Arabia's War in Yemen', *The New York Times*, 26 October 2018, available online at <https://www.nytimes.com/interactive/2018/10/26/world/middleeast/saudi-arabia-war-yemen.html> (visited 27 August 2021).

[5] D. Walsh, 'Yemen girl who turned world's eyes to famine is dead' *The New York Times*, 1 November 2018, available online at <https://www.nytimes.com/2018/11/01/world/middleeast/yemen-starvation-amal-hussain.html> (visited 27 August 2021).

[6] The 2019 Pulitzer Prize Winner in Feature Photography, *The Pulitzer Prizes*, available online at <https://www.pulitzer.org/winners/lorenzo-tugnoli-washington-post> (visited 27 August 2021).

of reports was exactly what the Saudi-led coalition and its allies in Washington DC were trying to avoid and managed to do so very effectively in the years prior to 2018.

The media coverage prompted renewed discussion of the moral and legal implications of the US and European countries' support for the war, with voices like Senator Bernie Sanders leading the charge to end US involvement. His measure to enact the War Powers Act to stop US support for the coalition gained surprisingly wide bipartisan support, but was eventually vetoed by President Trump.[7] A belated and ultimately unsuccessful attempt to limit the war, it came after years of repressed media coverage as the humanitarian catastrophe grew. Of course, as reporters it is not our job or our aim to affect political decisions, but instead to help the general public become fully aware of the realities of what is happening in wars and why, so they can take decisions based on reliable information. Sometimes that means we must thwart attempts to hide aspects of the truth from the public, be they images of starving children or the destruction of hospitals by air strikes.

The year before in 2017, in South Sudan, my reporting from another man-made humanitarian crisis and recently declared famine was not blocked in such a concerted way. There was no US or European military involvement at risk of public pressure. The government of South Sudan was precariously balancing its culpability in causing the famine through counter-insurgency measures, and their desperate need for aid to keep the country from falling into a deeper crisis. Journalists were welcomed but closely monitored for how they were explaining the hunger to their readers and viewers.

In 2013 a rift between South Sudan's President Salva Kiir and his Vice President, Riek Machar, dragged the country into a civil war, with divisions often drawn along tribal lines.[8] Kiir's Dinka fighters, battling for whatever remained of the Juba-based government, fought an insurgency by Machar's mainly Nuer fighters and their allies. Both sides committed atrocities against communities they associated with their enemies, often making civilians and their home villages the target of attacks. By the spring of 2017, the United Nations had declared famine in Leer and Mayendit county in Unity State, saying starvation had begun and 100,000 people were in immediate danger of dying, with 1 million more also slipping into deep hunger.[9] The starvation in Leer was the result of government offensives against rebels, which in reality meant attacks on civilian communities affiliated with rebel

[7] M. Landler, and P. Baker, 'Trump vetoes measure to force end to U.S. involvement in Yemen war', *The New York Times*, 16 April 2019, available online at <https://www.nytimes.com/2019/04/16/us/politics/trump-veto-yemen.html> (visited 27 August 2021).

[8] J. Williams, 'The Conflict in South Sudan, Explained', Vox, 8 December 2016, available online at <https://www.vox.com/world/2016/12/8/13817072/south-sudan-crisis-explained-ethnic-cleansing-genocide> (visited 27 August 2021).

[9] 'Famine declared in region of South Sudan—UN', *UN News* (February 2017), available online at <https://news.un.org/en/story/2017/02/551812-famine-declared-region-south-sudan-un> (visited 27 August 2021).

groups.[10] Counter-insurgency tactics involved decimating communities that were viewed as providing shelter and logistical support to rebels, such as food.[11] Women and children considered family members of the rebels were killed and raped during attacks.[12]

On a brutally hot and dusty day in Leer town in April 2017, we stopped briefly on our way from the dirt landing strip into rebel-controlled areas seemingly in the middle of nowhere, where UN agencies had made food drops. The town had been ransacked by government troops. Few buildings were left standing, mostly some shacks made of corrugated tin. The remains of other buildings lay scattered around as yellow grass grew up and over it. Whatever small trees had grown there had been mostly hacked down to their stumps, as those who fled took whatever was left, including precious firewood for cooking. A church still stood on the edge of the town, from the outside it looked untouched—save for the front door hanging half off its hinges. Random attacks by government soldiers who aid organizations had accused of looting their supplies remained a threat, and we—a small group of reporters on a rare trip to the area—had to quickly climb into our 4 × 4 vehicles and move on. There were no people around to interview.

A short drive down the road, through a checkpoint manned by government soldiers, and on into rebel-held areas, we arrived at the drop site. Several dozen civilians sat under a tree waiting patiently as aid workers unloaded boxes of farming equipment. Hoes, spades, and seeds were being handed out to people. A neat queue of women waited for their turn to be given a satellite phone for a few minutes to call loved ones they had lost in the chaos of the war, if they owned a phone. A thin, middle-aged man called Ruot Machar approached me and through a local translator we began to talk. Before answering questions about what had happened there, he asked: 'Can you give me a fishing rod?' He had snuck out of swamps to come here when he heard that food was being distributed, but had left hungry family members in the swamps, waiting for him to return with something to sustain them. He, like the rest of the group, was deeply traumatized. When I asked people to describe what the recent weeks had been like for them, they described running from government fighters with their children into the swamps nearby and hiding for days. One woman crouched low to the ground, showing me how they had hidden below the reeds for days, terrified they would be seen and shot. Or worse. The man who had asked for a fishing rod later told me he had not fled his village in time before government soldiers came to his home, murdered his two-year-old daughter,

[10] J. Pedneault, *Starving under the Bullets in South Sudan*, Human Rights Watch, April 2017, available online at <https://www.hrw.org/news/2017/04/11/starving-under-bullets-south-sudan#> (visited 27 August 2021).

[11] Pedneault, see note 10.

[12] 'How rape is used as a weapon in South Sudan's war', *PBS NewsHour*, May 2017, available online at <https://www.pbs.org/newshour/show/rape-used-weapon-south-sudans-war (visited 27 August 2021).

and then chopped up her body before forcing him to eat pieces of her corpse. Attempts to terrify these people into leaving their homes for good had been brutally effective.

When people fled into the wilderness, there was nothing to eat. The swamps provided protection from military vehicles that couldn't follow them, but many had then faced a slower death from starvation. This area was a restive place with a population seen by government troops as providing shelter for rebels, and the government's response had been to punish them by getting rid of them entirely.

As we talked, we stood next to charred stumps of wood that had, according to aid workers, once been stalls in a market. This remote spot had been a place where rural communities bought and sold livestock and meat before soldiers burned it to the ground. A few bare sheep and cow skulls were piled up in the grass nearby. The fact that we, journalists from PBS and the main agencies, were able to make it to this spot to interview these people was only through risks taken by one particular NGO. They had managed to get us on one of their propeller plane flights from the government-controlled capital Juba and then drove us out to meet victims of the violence. 'Please, if you are going to focus on how the starvation happened and what caused these people to flee, then don't mention our organization in your reporting', asked the NGO's media manager. This became a common request throughout our assignment.

Aid agencies are dependent upon the good graces of the government to operate in South Sudan and faced constant intimidation and threats from the government. They would not go on camera to talk about what had happened here nor would they specifically finger government troops. All they could do was bring us to such places and let us see for ourselves. I saw this predicament in both South Sudan and Yemen, where hunger crises and famines were a direct result of the tactics of war. Around the world, aid agencies often face the dilemma of speaking out about the reasons behind the hunger and potentially losing their ability to access those most in need or keeping a diplomatic silence to maintain their ability to work.

Without reporters on the ground, news organizations rely on statements and interviews with aid workers who are there; in these conditions, the information provided and interviews focus on the scale of the hunger and the dire need for help, not the causes of famine. There is much less emphasis on the crime than the resulting hunger. In South Sudan, even more so than in Yemen, few international news organizations came to the country to report during the famine. The danger and the expense of operating in South Sudan had put many off, alongside the typical lack of reporting resources devoted to African news. The year before we travelled to South Sudan, government troops had attacked a hotel in the capital, executing a local journalist and gang-raping five foreign aid workers.[13] For news

[13] J. Beaubien, 'U.N. report addresses gang rape of aid workers in South Sudan', *National Public Radio*, 23 August 2016, available online at <https://www.npr.org/sections/goatsandsoda/2016/08/23/491057541/gang-rape-of-aid-workers-in-south-sudan-is-a-turning-point> (visited 27 August 2021).

organizations, South Sudan was now perceived as one of the most dangerous places on earth to send their people and few were taking the risk.

The story told through news reports focused on a hunger crisis in the midst of a war and less on the specifics of what was happening and why people were going hungry. Stories painted a vague picture of general chaos, hunger, and war, with a sense of inevitability that all too often accompanies African crises—South Sudan was a country that could not feed itself and was wracked with violence. The general public around the world remained largely unaware of exactly why and how the world's latest famine in this new country was happening and who was behind the conduct of hostilities deliberately targeting food and other indispensable items.

Aid organizations faced the same issue in Yemen. Speaking out publicly on the record about who is responsible for specific attacks, who is causing the hunger and why, can endanger their access. They still rely on the Saudi-led coalition to provide permits to bring food and essential humanitarian supplies into the country. Also, attacks and intimidation by the Houthi rebels were making the professional realities of aid workers in the north of the country particularly difficult. The rebel government used permits and visas for international workers to enter the area as leverage when they attempted to coerce control over how and to whom food and medical supplies were provided. 'They tried to get us to give them the food to distribute themselves', explained one senior level UN official in Sana'a, astonished.[14] They refused. Another major international aid agency[15] had to abandon a multi-million-dollar initiative to bring in medical equipment when the rebel's commanders demanded they decide what equipment and who they buy it from. The NGO returned the money to its donors instead. Intimidation at Houthi checkpoints led many aid organizations to stop their international staff from travelling out of the capital city, while people in the countryside were starving.

During my trip to Yemen in 2018, we travelled to a refugee camp close to the border with Saudi Arabia to witness one major aid organization distributing food and cash to people who had fled their homes that had become engulfed in the fighting. The workers who planned to join us at the camp arrived late because they were repeatedly turned back at the checkpoints, they told us, with gun-wielding rebels demanding more paperwork. At the same time, Médecins Sans Frontières was packing up its international workers in a town a couple of hours away because a coalition airstrike had just destroyed one of their hospitals. They had ordered their staff back to the capital Sana'a for their own safety, leaving only government hospital workers, many of whom were not receiving salaries and often didn't come to work, to fend for themselves. Half of the country's medical facilities had shut and hospitals were overwhelmed. So, in a cruel double-edged sword, those who had been driven to malnutrition and disease by the tactics of this war were further

[14] Communicated to the author in person, June 2018.
[15] Communicated to the author in person, July 2018.

impeded from getting decent medical attention at hospitals that were understaffed, lacked basic supplies and equipment, or were closed or destroyed altogether.

With international aid workers hindered from reaching rural areas, they could often only help the lucky people who could afford a cab into towns and cities to reach a hospital. We drove out to tiny villages and found stories of parents who had already taken a weakened child, sick with malnutrition to the hospital once. When the child got sick again—a sure thing when there was still no nutritious food in the home—parents didn't have the resources to return to the hospital. They simply had to sit in their houses and watch their children waste away. In the Yemeni city of Hajja, nurses in the main hospital said they tend to see the same children several times. The children would get better under intensive feeding in the hospital but then fall ill again when they returned home. The nurses suspect many children die at home, but they have no way of knowing who survived. The increase in fuel prices and lack of incomes due to economic collapse meant no-one could afford the small buses that once transported Yemen's poor around the country. Culturally, it is rare for a woman to travel from her rural home into a town without a male escort, making it necessary for men to accompany their wives to the hospitals, adding to the costs of transport and potentially causing them to miss work. For families where the male breadwinner is a soldier or rebel fighter, women left alone at home have less access to a suitable male escort to bring a child to a hospital or clinic.

When reporting from somewhere like Yemen does produce pictures and visual elements—as I did as part of the PBS' TV stories featuring malnourished children clinging to life or the *New York Times*' photographs of those like little Amal—the impact is felt in newsrooms across the country. News is often a visual medium and there is a sense of urgency to send reporters to areas where the hunger is so visually apparent, drawing more journalists to cover such crises. In South Sudan, however, despite the formal declaration of famine (unlike in Yemen), there were few if any images of starving children. Images of skeletal babies were rarely seen because the starvation was happening quickly, in the remote countryside, quickly claiming its victims away from the world's cameras. Those left to film were the survivors, explaining why their family members had vanished. Everyone I interviewed who had lost loved ones to hunger had buried them in the swamps long before. Only those who had made it to a food source lived to tell their tale. The impact of those stories in terms of attracting further media interest as a result was clearly less than in Yemen where journalists had access to hospitals and clinics and homes where children were wasting away. In Yemen, millions were malnourished, everywhere you turned; in South Sudan, accessing those worst-affected was tough and many of the most vulnerable populations died by the time journalists were able to get to them.

In another area of South Sudan, Unity State, I met teenager Rebecca Riak Chol in a village on an archipelago of islands in the midst of vast swamps. She was living with her mother in the rebel-controlled village and attending a nearby school funded by Mercy Corps while her Mum sold tea in the local market to make some money. Her ordeal was typical of the experiences of those caught up in the famine. A government military offensive caused her family and fellow villagers to run, suddenly, terrified, and with no food. 'When we fled our village, we were twenty-eight people; when we got here, we were twenty-four', she told me. 'Two were shot and two died of hunger.' Her thirteen-year-old sister died. They had walked for weeks and stayed in the swamps, growing weak with hunger.

At the same school I also met Marco Nuer, who was sixteen years old. Visibly traumatized, he said he saw around twenty people shot dead when the soldiers reached his village. On the road, his brother, sister, and father all succumbed to starvation, he told me, nervously fingering his face and staring into space. Neither Marco nor Rebecca fulfilled stereotypical images of famine victims or survivors. Their family members who perished were buried in the swamps, not clinging to life in hospitals. When starving South Sudanese people were in the swamps, they had largely no access to help at all. Their deaths were much faster. As a result, there were no TV images of skeletal children, akin to Ethiopia 1984 or Somalia in 1991 and 2011, or Yemen today. Editors expressed surprise that there were no images that would shock and stir viewers and readers.

Added to this was the ever-constant logistical challenge of reaching rebel-held areas. For several days we took propeller planes, a helicopter, a wooden canoe, and eventually walked on foot to reach Rebecca and Marco. It took help and coordination with aid agencies and much time. Getting into the country involved hiring a logistics company to handle the myriad paperwork requested by the government, and the constant threat of violence, harassment, and arrest at the hands of the South Sudanese security forces. Our cameraman was detained twice for filming in the street, despite having all permits necessary. We were followed and intimidated by armed soldiers when filming with UN peacekeepers in the street in Juba. By the time we left the country the government had stationed plain-clothed security officials in our hotel lobby. We had requested an interview with the government's Information Minister, which he accepted and then at the last minute cancelled. Feeling that officials were aware that our reporting was focusing on how the famine was caused by government military offensives and perpetration of atrocities, we decided to leave South Sudan and edit our stories in Kenya. Just days after we flew out of Juba, the National Public Radio East Africa correspondent, Eyder Peralta, was arrested in the same hotel we had stayed in and held in prison for four days before being released.[16]

Despite these challenges, the news that famine was declared in South Sudan was a big story. Famines were meant to be something fading out of existence in a world where aid agencies were able to step in quickly during hunger crises. No famine had

[16] E. Peralta, 'NPR reporter recounts detention in South Sudan', *National Public Radio*, 16 June 2017, available online at <https://www.npr.org/2017/06/16/533176641/npr-reporter-recounts-detention-in-south-sudan> (visited 27 August 2021).

been declared since 2011 in Somalia and before that it had been the early 1990s. Plenty of newspapers were reporting from afar on the news, but there was little follow-up with extensive field reporting. And yet, when we returned from South Sudan at the end of April 2017, and our stories aired shortly afterwards, I was surprised to find only a few media teams followed after us—unlike in Yemen the year after, when my phone rang constantly with reporters asking for advice and contacts on how to get into and across Yemen to report on that crisis. I believe the lack of shocking images of skeletal, starving people contributed to the muted response.

Furthermore, the fleeting, superficial approach that many media outlets take towards foreign news reports rarely lends itself to complex, man-made famines. Covering famine caused by war takes real airtime, at a time when news networks in the United States in particular are reducing the length of their reports to a matter of seconds. Investigating the causes of the hunger, the reason people were fleeing their homes in South Sudan, the historical context of the civil war takes more than seventy or ninety seconds to explain. A preference for English-speaking, often Western aid workers in TV reporting also added to the cloudy explanations of what is happening, as few wish to point fingers at those responsible for the hunger and prefer to explain simply the proportions of the crisis. Little reporting takes on the important work of humanizing those directly affected, hearing their stories, in whatever language they speak. These witness accounts are crucial to help uncover why man-made famines are happening and how. Their voices also push back against dated, racist stereotypes that accompany impressions of African famines and conflict.

Similarly, in Yemen, in-depth reporting was needed to explain that the war was being fought was causing the starvation, with economic pressures placed deliberately on rebel-held areas, such as the cutting off of government salaries for bureaucrats and slowing food imports upon which Yemen is highly dependent. The crisis in Yemen reached further into families than just those who lost children to hunger. It challenged the social norms and structures in a highly conservative, organized tribal society at which family was the centre. The implications of such breakdowns can last for generations. One such example is how many widows are increasingly pressured to remarry, as extended families are less and less able to help them feed their children and instead look to hand them over to a new family through remarriage. In some cases, the new husbands do not accept children from the previous marriage, and they end up at in orphanages.

In the largest and oldest orphanage in Yemen, Dar Riayat Al Aytam, hundreds of little boys eat, sleep, and play football between classes at their own school. The facility opened in 1925 and had moved to a more modern campus in the city in the 1970s. Many of the boys in the orphanage have living mothers. 'I'm going to go and see my mother soon, in a few weeks', one little boy told me. It is common for children in Yemen who have lost a father to be considered orphans and to be sent away rather than cared for by extended families. Growing poverty contributes to the swelling number of children in the orphanage, its manager told me. In a hospital a few miles away a mother cried as she stood next to her four-year-old daughter Ikram. Ikram looked like a standing skeleton, her malnutrition was so severe. Her mother Ayesha explained that her husband's family had refused to help. 'They say Allah will take care of her', she said, through her tears. In Yemen's deeply traditional society, family remains a central part of its culture. When families start to break apart as a result of famine, the means to cope diminish.

Those fighting wars go to great lengths to prevent reporting on the needless, sometimes criminal, loss of civilian life. There are concerted efforts to separate and compartmentalize humanitarian crises and the conflict at hand that causes them. Yemen's war has been the starkest example of this I have ever seen, and South Sudan also saw such attempts to compartmentalize, therefore excusing actions that one way or another killed many. Those of us who have reported on hunger, fighting, and the devastating link between the two have done so in a hope that the world comes to understand the far-reaching impacts war can have on the innocent, even when they die many miles away from the fighting.

15
Truth, Memory, and Starvation

Alex de Waal

1. Introduction

The first and most significant element in the agenda of recognizing starvation as a crime is the act of recognition itself. Naming the crime can be an act of emancipation for its victims and survivors: helping to lift the dark shadow of shame and humiliation that invariably hangs over the memory of famine.

It is common for the generation that experienced an atrocity not to speak about it. In the case of mass starvation, the cruelties and privations are particularly deep, personal, and stripping of dignity. In his exploration of Irish culture in the aftermath of Ireland's Great Famine of 1845–1851, Breandán Mac Suibhne provides neither any description of the starvation itself nor any oral histories of the years of utter deprivation. Rather, starvation is an unacknowledged but ubiquitous presence, a totem and taboo imprinted on every element of life. A clue to this consensual silence is found in a rare direct allusion to the Famine itself as it was experienced: a 'grey zone' of 'the demimonde of soupers and grabbers, moneylenders and mealmongers, and those among the poor who had a full pot when neighbours starved, and the poorhouse bully who took the biscuit from the weak'.[1] For the term and the framework 'grey zone', Mac Suibhne draws on Primo Levi's *Survival in Auschwitz*.[2] Even in a concentration camp, the ultimate perpetrator can seem remote and obscure, while those who commit petty offences are immediate and evident, and many people are both victims and offenders.

With the important exception of small children, famine victimhood is neither clean nor clear. To obtain food and other items essential to sustain life, people will sell their possessions and engage in degrading activities. The hungry deny food from the hungry, the shivering do not share their blankets. The pains of famine are

[1] B. Mac Suibhne, *The End of Outrage: Post-Famine Adjustment in Rural Ireland* (Oxford: Oxford University Press, 2017), at 17.

[2] P. Levi, *The Drowned and the Saved* (New York: Simon and Schuster, 2017). (Original work published 1986).

Alex de Waal, *Truth, Memory, and Starvation* In: *Accountability for Mass Starvation*. Edited by: Bridget Conley, Alex de Waal, Catriona Murdoch, and Wayne Jordash QC, Oxford University Press.
DOI: 10.1093/oso/9780192864734.003.0015

filtered through the web of social and economic relations, revealing every contour and gradient of local hierarchies of power. Those who are already poorest suffer first and most; those who are excluded are further exploited. Death, life, and dignity depend on the tiniest increments of resources and standing among the dispossessed and destitute.

For those who have emerged from this protracted and degrading ordeal, it is the intimate abuses and violations, suffered and perpetrated, within the family and among neighbours, that are most vivid in the memory, and least spoken about. The sale of one's small plot of land, inherited from great-grandfathers, for a pittance; the sale of one's body for another's sexual gratification, for less than a pittance; the failure to extend the basic rituals of respect to the dead—these are the memories that haunt the survivors which they most want to banish. Even more discomforting are those small but cruel acts of gain on account of others' misfortune: the hard bargain struck to buy that piece of land, the chance taken to exploit a neighbour's daughter's body, the market calculation to profit from the high price for a sack of grain, or the simple everyday act of cooking and eating a meal—while the starving look on. Starvation survivor's guilt was, perhaps, what ultimately killed Levi. Mona Simpson writes:

> For many of his readers, the end of Levi's life has been particularly hard to bear. In 1987, after a debilitating bout of major depression (in which, according to his biographer Carole Angier, he 'dwelt obsessively' over the 'drops of water he had not shared' with his fellow prisoner in Auschwitz), while his mother suffered through an agonizing illness, he was found dead on the lobby floor of his own apartment building. Though some doubt remains, there's unanimity among those closest to him in believing that he committed suicide.[3]

Too rarely are the political causes of mass starvation recognized for what they are: the transitivity of the verb 'to starve' is forgotten. The survivors silently cry out for a 'me, too' movement to liberate them from the shame that dogs their memories, like a persistent beggar whose disfigurement one doesn't want to look in the face. Conceiving of mass starvation as a crime, as a wrong inflicted by powerful men situated far away, as suffering for which blame should be directed outward, should be an act of emancipation. The message conveyed to the victims and survivors, by naming and memorializing famine as an atrocity, is elementary but compelling: *it wasn't your fault.*

[3] M. Simpson, 'If This Is a Man,' *The Atlantic*, June 2007, available online at https://www.theatlantic.com/magazine/archive/2007/06/if-this-is-a-man/305897/ (visited 14 December 2020).

2. Memorializing Famine in Ireland

An Gorta Mór, the Great Irish Famine—or, as it might more accurately be named, the Great English Famine in Ireland[4]—is the most thoroughly documented and most extensively memorialized of all famines. The long and painful process whereby the physical memorials to that famine came to be constructed, alongside the historical and literary reconstruction of the famine, is instructive.

In monuments across the hills of the west of Ireland, the lives lost to starvation, and the communities lost to emigration in its aftermath, are carved in stone. Many of the memorials are traditional Celtic crosses. Almost all were erected in the last generation: it took two lifespans before even the simplest memorials to be erected. In simple demographic terms the famine was a calamity without modern parallel: Ireland is one of the very few places on earth where there are fewer people today than 175 years ago. A million died, more than another million emigrated, and entire counties were depopulated. But the great hunger did more than these numberless individual tragedies: it destroyed the old landholding system, the clustered villages with their communal traditions of dancing and storytelling. It was followed by the 'Great Silence' in which the Irish language all but vanished from the public realm. The famine made modern Ireland, in the sense of a country remade in the image of its oppressor, the paragon of modernity. As Seamus Deane writes, the previous communities died of their injuries:

> What had been [their] vivid internal life withered and hardened into a rabid Catholicism (of a reactionary, baroque kitsch form imported from anti-revolutionary France) and, simultaneously, dissolved into the Anglophone capitalist modernity that continues its wild Atlantic ways to the present.[5]

Another infamous perpetrator of starvation, Josef Stalin, is credited with the remark that 'if only one man dies of hunger, that is a tragedy; if millions die, that's only statistics'. His pithy words are commonly used to encapsulate the scale of his inhumanity—on that occasion in Ukraine—and by extension to make the point that those who kill on a truly grand scale are exempt from ordinary moral calculations and instead sanctified as national heroes. But there is another reading too: the obliteration of a people in this manner writes them out of history in a manner that makes meaningless the grief of the survivors, and may even make the descendants of those survivors thankful for the progress that was wrought from the wreckage of their destroyed society.

[4] A. de Waal, 'Monuments to Famine', 41 *London Review of Books*, 7 March 2019, at 30.
[5] S. Deane, 'Expunged', *Dublin Review of Books*, 1 March 2018, available online at www.drb.ie/essays/expunged (visited 14 December 2020).

So too in Ireland. The first generation of Irish nationalists was outraged at the British government's cruel and inhumane administration of relief. Notoriously, the Gregory Clause of 1847 required the poor to give up all but a quarter acre of land as a precondition for being eligible for relief. Poor houses were designed to humiliate. Relief was apportioned in rigorously tiny quanta on the premise that unwarranted public spending was a greater evil than mass starvation—not least because, under Malthusian dogma, the poor collectively had only themselves to blame for having been born in the first place.

But the *causes* of the famine were rarely exposed to the same critique. Many among the Irish middle class despised the hungry villagers; when Queen Victoria visited Cork at the very nadir of the hunger, the bunting was strung up and brass bands welcomed the monarch, while the town authorities shipped the destitute and starving to a safe distance away. President Michael D. Higgins was at pains to point out this uncomfortable fact in his 2018 speech at the famine commemoration ceremony in Cork. He noted the absence of solidarity and empathy for human suffering by citizens while hungry ghosts, spectres, and phantoms wandered the city.[6] Indeed, early nationalists shared much of the political economy analysis of the British, blaming the backwardness of Irish society, especially smallholder agriculture and a culture that, it was claimed, did not value industry and frugality. They conceded that Providence was remedying a deep fault in Irish society, dragging it into a modern era of hygiene and improved agriculture. Whitehall was blamed for failings of food relief. Only much later—in solidarity with Indian nationalists—did Irish nationalists raise their polemical gunsights and start blowing holes in the colonial project itself. And even then, it took another two generations for public remembrance of the famine to begin, at the time when '[t]hose people, who, in youth, read the lined faces of those who had seen it all' were gone.[7] What the departing generation had witnessed was not just the famine, but the shaming betrayals of the 'grey zone'. As Mac Suibhne notes, the 'famine pot looms large' in oral history,[8] and as the generations passed, the betrayals of the 'grey zone' could be occluded and the simpler story of the oppression of the Irish people as a whole could be remembered. Perhaps not coincidentally, the Irish public also realized that their starvation was not something unique, and that they could extract dignity from collective outrage at what was happening elsewhere.

Ireland's first famine memorial was erected in St Stephen's Green, Dublin in 1967.[9] The artist was Edward Delaney. He sculpted three emaciated people, one

[6] M. Higgins, 'Address by President Michael Higgins at the National Famine Commemoration', University College Cork, 12 May 2018, available online at <https://www.rte.ie/player/ie/show/rte-news-special-1516/10878577/> (visited 14 December 2020).

[7] Mac Suibhne, see note 1, at 257.

[8] B. Mac Suibhne, 'A Jig in the Poorhouse', *Dublin Review of Books* (2013), available online at <http://www.drb.ie/essays/a-jig-in-the-poorhouse> (visited 14 December 2020).

[9] M. Kelleher, 'Hunger and History: Monuments to the Great Irish Famine', 16 *Textual Practice* (2002) 249–276.

giving water to another. Just apart from the human figures is a dog. Shadowing the sick and dying, the scavenging dog is a reminder of how starvation reduces human beings to bone and flesh. Some were offended by Delaney's dog and in fact it was stolen shortly afterwards (and then found and restored).

Within a year of Delaney's monument there was an awakening of Irish public humanitarianism. Irish nationalism had long had an internationalist bent, making common cause with those struggling against colonial oppression in India, Latin America, the Belgian Congo, and South Africa (among others), but in 1968 this impulse fastened upon famine for the first time. The occasion was Biafra, the separatist war waged in south-east Nigeria, which resulted in a famine that gained unprecedented attention in the news media. It was the stimulus for the founding of Concern, the Irish relief agency that grew over the subsequent half century to be the largest Irish non-governmental humanitarian organization. Biafra had its own resonant echoes, not only of starvation but of deprivation cruelly endorsed by a British government whose neo-colonial interests (specifically Nigeria's oil) made it indifferent to human suffering. In the last months of 1968, Concern's campaign for public contributions for famine relief exceeded all expectations and awoke a popular consciousness that an independent and newly prosperous Ireland could play a special role as an aid donor animated by a spirit of solidarity with the oppressed.

But it took another twenty-five years before memorials became common. More than a hundred were constructed in the ten years after the sesquicentenary in 1995. Most are Celtic crosses, some of them standing in picture-postcard landscapes that our romantic aesthetic reflexively identifies as 'unspoilt'—reminding us that they are not so much empty, as emptied. Others are figurative, representing human beings reduced to their simplest forms. The principal Dublin memorial was commissioned as part of the 150-year anniversary in 1997. The sculptor Rowan Gillespie created six gaunt, Giacometti-like figures, one carrying a dead child. There is also a dog.[10] It is a monument not just to death but to emigration: it is located on Custom House Quay, from where people boarded ships to leave Ireland forever, and five are carrying pitifully small bundles of their possessions. Many more 'coffin ships' sailed from the ports on the western and southern coasts of Ireland, where the famine struck hardest. Many perished on the voyage (hence the name), some in the quarantine centres where they first disembarked in the New World. The Irish national famine memorial, by John Behan, in Murrisk in County Mayo takes the form of a ship, its rigging consisting of skeletal figures.

Why this sudden, belated explosion of memory? Was it due to Mary Robinson who, as President, represented a new, fresh, national self-confidence, and who campaigned for emergency aid to Somalia? Was it the maturing of Ireland's own

[10] The iconography of famine often includes dogs and birds: a 1943 drawing by the Bengali artist Zainul Abedin shows two hungry children, one licking the last scraps from a bowl, and three crows.

international aid policies, which combine a consistent ranking as the best value for money with unmatched cultural champions in the form of Bob Geldof and Bono? Or with the imminence of the Good Friday Agreement that ended the conflict in Northern Ireland and the prospect that there would be no more IRA prisoners starving themselves to death? Or can it best be seen as part of the fast-expanding wave of memorialization of the Holocaust and other egregious human rights abuses? Certainly, British sensitivities remained: Prime Minister John Major vetoed a proposal to hold a commemorative event in Liverpool on the occasion of President Robinson's visit in 1996 on the grounds that it would ignite demands for an apology from London.[11]

Most of the memorials are in the Republic; a dozen or so are in North America, the destination of a million or so Irish emigrants; a few are in Australia, and just three are on the British mainland—in Liverpool, Cardiff, and Carfin, Lanarkshire. The Celtic cross is the most common, the simplest, and least controversial choice for a community leader wishing to raise funds and erect a stone monument. This was the choice for the 2019 memorial on Deer Island in Boston harbour, a place of quarantine for the sick and starving when they arrived in America, and where dozens, sick and exhausted from the ocean crossing, perished within sight of the mainland. Other monuments follow Delaney and Gillespie and are figurative; most reproduce Victorian imagery of the emaciated mother and child. In her comprehensive critical survey of monuments to the Irish famine, Emily Mark-Fitzgerald notes, 'the construction of several extraordinarily expensive and historically blinkered works (including Boston and Philadelphia) indicates that a retrograde, bombastic visual vocabulary of Famine continues to hold sway in some quarters'.[12]

The first memorial in the United States, by Maurice Harron on Cambridge Common which was erected in 1997, shows two adults, each holding a child, parting from one another. The plinth has the words 'Never again should a people starve in a world of plenty'. Note the choice of '*a* people'—a signal of famine potentially as genocide, not hunger as generic poverty. The downtown Boston memorial by Robert Shure has two parts; one with near-skeletal drooped figures representing the suffering in Ireland, the other with energetic, upright figures striding ashore in Massachusetts. It has been much mocked by critics who ask, how come the emigrants were implausibly restored to health and optimism during the transatlantic voyage, and why is the adult man the spitting image of John F. Kennedy?

There is no sufficient way of representing loss and atrocity on this scale. The abstract, minimalist representations of absence that are the favoured form of Holocaust memorials are also a convention. But the nineteenth-century imagery of

[11] S. Hickey, 'Ex-British PM John Major Shelved Famine Commemoration', *Irish Times*, 13 January 2020, available online at https://www.irishtimes.com/news/politics/ex-british-pm-john-major-shelved-famine-commemoration-1.4137492 (visited 14 December 2020).

[12] E. Mark-Fitzgerald, *Commemorating the Irish Famine: Memory and the Monument* (Liverpool: Liverpool University Press, 2013), at 279.

the pitiful starving is peculiarly jarring. People in famine-affected countries, along with reflective aid workers and journalists, have become discomfited with famine imagery that dwells on helpless, emaciated people, especially when juxtaposed with foreign saviours. In 2007, the Dóchas (the Irish Association of non-governmental aid agencies) adopted a code of conduct for images and messages, aiming to replace the erstwhile standard fare of fundraising with 'images and related messages based on values of respect equality, solidarity and justice'.[13] Their problem was that pitiful pictures do their work: people donate, and famine is put in a politically safe space where it can more easily be defended from those who would aid only the deserving poor on the condition that they are grateful and know their place.

War and genocide memorials have also evolved over the last generation. Most monuments become unnoticed shortly after they have been erected—it is the debate over their form, and whether they should exist at all, that generates public attention.[14] Contemporary memorials tend to be stripped of overt imagery and directives, challenging the visitor to reflect and contribute their own meaning. Examples are Berlin's memorial to the murdered Jews of Europe, which takes the form of a field of blocks of polished stone of uneven size, and Vietnam war memorial in Washington DC, which is a wall inscribed with the names of the US soldiers who died.

Three other memorials to the Irish famine exemplify this. In downtown Manhattan there is a quarter acre of grass with a ruined croft. It is a picturesque emptiness, across which the visitor wanders. Around its exterior wall are inscriptions, which evoke its complicated place in history. Among them is a quotation from Elihu Burritt, following his visit to Skibbereen in 1847: 'Let Ireland's extremity be America's opportunity to teach the nations a magnificent lesson in human brotherly love.' Another is from Mary Robinson, following her visit to Somalia: 'Grief and silence are luxuries which we in the west cannot indulge if men and women and children in Somalia are to survive. They need our action not our tears; our practical downright problem-solving help and not our wordless horror.'[15] The geographical location of the quarter acre, amidst some of the most expensive real estate in the world, between an upscale shopping mall and an Au Bon Pain, and a block from the grandeur of the 9/11 memorial, also needs no commentary. However, Mark-Fitzgerald observes that even this post-modern conceptual work

[13] 'The Dóchas Code of Conduct on Images and Messages', Dóchas (2007), available online at <https://www.dochas.ie/assets/Files/Code_of_Conduct_on_Images_and_Messages.pdf> (visited 14 December 2020).

[14] An alternative reminder of their significance would be to propose removing them—as demonstrated by the confrontation over an American Civil War memorial statue in Charlottesville, Virginia, in 2017.

[15] The quotation can be found in M. Robinson, *A Voice for Somalia* (Dublin: O'Brien Press, 1993), at 12–13.

is appreciated by the public mostly for 'its mimetic accuracy and nostalgic reification of the 'pieces of Ireland' it presents'.[16]

In Toronto, there are huge granite slabs that look like the cliffs of Galway's Atlantic coast, with names inscribed in the crevices. A more conventional figurative memorial is nearby. In Sydney, where the British shipped famine orphans, a memorial, overlooked by the stern façade of the colonial barracks, takes the form of a table with an empty plate.

What purpose do these memorials serve? As David Lloyd asked in a seminal essay, are they no more than 'an issueless tribute of remembrance'?[17] The discomfiting debates over the appropriate form of a memorial testifies to the lack of closure, the failure to reconcile with the past. Adequate redress is impossible, not just because the dead cannot be brought back to life but because the famine was an act of obliterating a way of life. In a parallel universe in which the Irish peasantry had not been erased, different ways of being a person, of living in a community, would have persisted. The 'Green Atlantic', within which the diaspora Irish have played a central but ambiguous role,[18] would have been very different. These diverse memorials at least pose these questions.

3. Famine Memorialization Elsewhere

Over the last 150 years, more than 100 million people have perished in famines.[19] The vast majority of these deaths occurred in famines with clear political or military culpability. Several of the episodes of mass starvation were also instances of genocide, for example in German South-West Africa, Armenia, German operations in the Second World War, and the Khmer Rouge Year Zero, in all of which the numbers of fatalities due to hunger matched or exceeded those due to direct acts of violence. Yet memorials to the victims of starvation are rare in comparison to those that commemorate those who died from bullets, blades, or poison gas. Nonetheless, there is a sufficient number of famine memorials to attempt a cursory survey. There is a span from official monuments set up by states, to secret memorials, with many forms in between.

There is a short but intriguing list of memorials in the former USSR. After the Second World War, the Soviet Union built numerous and vast heroic monuments to the fallen of the Great Patriotic War. Among them was the Monument to the

[16] Mark-Fitzgerald, see note 12, at 279.

[17] D. Lloyd, 'The Indigent Sublime: Specters of Irish Hunger', 92 *Representations* (2005) 152–158.

[18] P. O'Neill and D. Lloyd (eds), *The Black and Green Atlantic: Cross-Currents of the African and Irish Diasporas* (London: Palgrave Macmillan, 2009).

[19] A. de Waal, *Mass Starvation: The History and Future of Famine* (Cambridge: Polity Press, 2018), at 55–67.

Heroic Defenders of Leningrad. It was, however, commissioned only in 1958, after the death of Stalin. While Stalin was alive, the Soviet authorities were sensitive to the charge that they had failed to do enough to relieve the siege. Among the tableaux of soldiers, sailors, pilots, partisans, and citizen volunteers building defences is a sculptural form of a starving family.[20] There is also a much more modest monument at the Piskarevskoye Memorial Cemetery, the site of 186 mass graves of 420,000 civilians who starved to death and soldiers who died in the city's hospitals. This was constructed later, at the behest of survivors, as a testament to the tragedy of the siege rather a tribute to heroism. It has a wall inscribed with the words of the poet and broadcaster Olga Berggolts, herself a survivor, identifying the anonymous dead as:

> Leningraders, citydwellers—men, women, and children
> And next to them, Red Army soldiers... We cannot list their noble names here
> There are so many of them under the eternal protection of granite
> But know this, those who regard these stones
> No one is forgotten, nothing is forgotten.[21]

During Communist rule there was, of course, nothing to commemorate to those who died during Stalin's forced famines in Ukraine, southern Russia, and Kazakhstan, nor the vast numbers who starved in the immediate aftermath of the revolution and the civil war, nor the starvation in the wake of the advancing Red Army at the close of the Second World War.

The Ukrainian famine of 1932–1934 was first instigated by a programme of collectivization of agriculture including dispossession of the assets of richer peasants, affecting both Ukraine, nearby areas of southern Russia, and Kazakhstan. It was a reckless and counterproductive economic policy carried out very brutally. It appears that when Stalin realized the disastrous impact of these programmes, he scaled them back in Russia but intensified them in Ukraine as a punitive measure. This famine—known as the Holodomor—was depicted by Raphael Lemkin as a case of using starvation as a tool of genocide.[22] Unfortunately, the genocide label has obscured as much as it has revealed, fostering singular narratives on the nationalist Ukrainian side, and denials on the Russian side.

[20] 'Monument to the Heroic Defenders of Leningrad', Saint-Petersburg.com, available online at <http://www.saint-petersburg.com/monuments/heroic-defenders/> (visited 14 December 2020).

[21] H. Klavin, 'Who is Forgotten? Memory of the Siege of Leningrad', William & Mary in St. Petersburg, n.d., available online at <http://petersburg.blogs.wm.edu/who-is-forgotten-memory-of-the-siege-of-leningrad-helena-klavin/> (visited 14 December 2020).

[22] R. Lemkin, 'Soviet Genocide in Ukraine,' in R. Serbyn, 'Lemkin on the Ukrainian Genocide', 7 *Journal of International Criminal Justice* (2009) 123–130.

The Holodomor as an act of genocide has become part of Ukrainian nationalist discourse, but it is contested.[23] Memorialization began locally with crosses set up in cemeteries by surviving relatives who for decades had been unable properly to mourn. One such memorial was established outside a church in Kiev, after which the process of memorialization was co-opted by the Ukrainian state, which established a 'national candle of memory' in the capital. A second monument was erected in Kharkiv, which had been the capital during the famine, and is a mainly Russian-speaking city. These official monuments have old-fashioned aesthetics with conventional statues of distressed figures; they were initiated by the nationalist leadership without public debate over function and form. The Holodomor narratives are vigorously challenged by Russian nationalists. In May 2018, a Kiev memorial dedicated to the victims of the Holodomor was burned down.[24]

The blatant co-option of the Holodomor memorials for political purposes has detracted from the possibility that they might serve as a stimulus to reflection on the tragedy and the crime. As they exist today, they encourage truth-telling only in the limited sense of refusing to forget this massive crime.

The 1932–1933 famine has also been belatedly recognized in Kazakhstan. At least three memorials to famine victims have been erected, the largest in May 2017 near the former building of the People's Commissariat for Internal Affairs in Alma Ata.[25] The 1946–1947 famine in Moldova—the last to date in Europe, which struck due to a harsh winter and the harsh extractions of Soviet commissars—is also now being memorialized, with one village monument erected in 2017.[26]

Africa is almost entirely devoid of famine memorials, and those that exist are in the context of commemorating the victims of massacre and war. There is a modest gravestone in the Namibian desert to mark the Herero and Nama who were forced into the desert by the colonial forces in 1904 and died en masse of hunger and thirst. Heroic bronze statues of the German soldiers who inflicted that atrocity still stand in Namibian towns, albeit moved amid controversy to less prominent places. In the northern Ethiopian city of Mekelle (Tigray), the towering memorial to the fighters who lost their lives in the war against the military dictatorship from 1975–1991, includes figures of a group of civilians trekking to find food and safety,

[23] T. Zhurzhenko, 'Commemorating the Famine as Genocide: The Contested Meanings of Holodomor Meanings in Ukraine', in S. Buckley-Zistel and S. Schäfer (eds), *Memorials in Times of Transition* (Cambridge: Intersentia, 2014) 221–242.

[24] 'Monument to the "Holodomor" Burned by Unknown Persons in the Kiev Region', *Regnum*, 15 March 2018, available online at <https://regnum.ru/news/2415054.html> (visited 14 December 2020).

[25] 'A Monument to The Victims of the Holodomor Was Erected in Kazakhstan. Its Discoveries Have Been Waiting for A Quarter Century', *Current Time TV*, 31 May 2017, available online <https://www.currenttime.tv/a/28520949.html> (visited 14 December 2020).

[26] 'Monument to the Victims of Hunger in Gagauzia', *Moldovenii*, 11 May 2016, available online at <http://www.moldovenii.md/ru/news/view/taxon/1673/id/22453/from/noi> (visited 14 December 2020).

helped by soldiers, among the tableaux.[27] Members of Biafra's Igbo diaspora community meet to commemorate their war and the human losses that it entailed, but there is no starvation memorial as such. The recurrent famines in Somalia, Sudan, and South Sudan have yet to be memorialized.

Given the scale of the historic famines in Asia, it is remarkable how little recognition is extended to their tens of millions of victims. Villages across China have local memorials to the millions who perished during Mao Zedong's Great Leap Forward, the worst famine on record that cost perhaps 30 million dead. There is no official monument. The Chinese Communist Party has reversed its collectivist economic policies but it remains the same party that presided over the greatest single demographic calamity of the century. The numerous famines in China during the late nineteenth century and early twentieth century—which the Communists could at least attribute to imperial aggression—are also not formally commemorated.

The four years of Khmer Rouge rule in Cambodia cost 1.75 million lives, of which 69 per cent were deaths through starvation.[28] Hunger was the most pervasive, overpowering experience for the great majority of the Cambodian population, and it appropriately figures prominently in memoirs and artistic representations of the period, such as the films of Rithy Panh. In common with other population-scale mass atrocities, there is an unstated but nonetheless clear hierarchy of victimhood, with those who perished from hunger, disease or exposure at the bottom. Cambodia's most visited atrocity sites are the S21 'Tuol Sleng' prison and the Choueng Ek 'killing field', thirty minutes' drive from Phnom Penh, where the bodies of 8,895 people were exhumed after the Khmer Rouge was driven from power. Neither site gives prominence to starvation, which is unsurprising as each of the two sites was chosen because it had played a specific role in the apparatus of torture and killing, and few if any were starved to death in these places. Those who died of hunger died one by one, scattered throughout the country, in work camps or communal farms, on forced marches, or in their own homes, sometimes in hospitals, or when trying to flee. Also, when the Vietnamese-led forces defeated the Khmer Rouge in 1979, and made these two places into memorial sites, it was partly with the aim of showing to the world that mass atrocities had indeed taken place, which would justify the invasion and the claim to forming a legitimate government. In the case of Tuol Sleng, the evidence included photographic documentation of people tortured to death, chained to their beds, as discovered by the liberating troops. For Choueng Ek, this entailed sorting the human remains that had been unearthed into neat piles, categorizing the skulls by the types of fatal injuries inflicted. Even had starvation been a major killer in these sites, death from the infliction of hunger is harder to show in this graphic way.

[27] B. Conley, *Memory from the Margins: Ethiopia's Red Terror Martyrs Memorial Museum* (Cham: Palgrave Macmillan, 2019) at 99–102.

[28] B. Kiernan, 'The Demography of Genocide in Southeast Asia: The Death Tolls in Cambodia, 1975–79, and East Timor, 1975–80', 35 *Critical Asian Studies* (2003) 585–597.

There are no public memorials to famine in India. This is an intriguing omission as British rule created many famines in the subcontinent, and this became a subject on which nationalist politicians berated the imperial rulers. In the 1940s, the young communist poet Sukanta Bhattacharya, wrote 'starvation days gradually build an empire'.[29]

Barely a decade after the Battle of Plassey in 1757, after which British troops occupied Bengal, the East India Company's ruinous taxation policies were without question the single most important reason for a calamity of a scale that is still hard to comprehend. Between 1769 and 1773, as many as 10 million people died of hunger and disease in Bengal, reducing a province that formerly possessed wealth and industry comparable to Britain itself, to abject penury. The East India Company was at worst directly culpable for the calamity and at minimum showed an astonishing indifference to human life. The devastation contributed to the attempt to impeach Warren Hastings for crimes committed in his tenure as Governor General, the one and only attempt to bring criminal charges against a colonial officer during all the centuries of British imperial rule.

The hundred years of East India Company rule in India was accompanied by a drumbeat of famines. So too were the decades after the Company was wound up and the British Raj took over. By the 1870s even the most doctrinaire colonial officials had learned that even modest efforts, such as price controls on basic grains, could stave off mass deaths. Nonetheless, deprivation reached a crescendo with what Mike Davis aptly called the 'late Victorian Holocausts' of the 1890s, in which at least 12.9 million died.[30] Famine was an instrument the more effective because its provenance could be disguised, and as it rampaged through the subject peoples, it co-opted many—such as landowners and merchants, who could profit from others' distress—and demoralized all.

The very last episode of colonial starvation, again in Bengal, in the middle of the Second World War, killed at least 2 million people. Seventy-five years on, its causes are still controversial. Economists and historians cannot agree on the relative importance of British economic policies, wartime measures to stem the advance of the Japanese armies, food production shortfalls, hoarding by grain merchants, and the failure to divert food shipments to break the price spiral in the market, in causing the famine. Without question, the famine was readily preventable, the greatest betrayal of the 'anti-famine political contract' forged between the British Raj and the Indian political class some forty years earlier.[31] The famine rent Bengal's social fabric, contributing to the 1946 inter-communal riots and pogroms

[29] S. Bhattacharya, 'To Rabindranath', (c. 1945), *The Daily Star*, 4 March 2017, available online at <https://www.thedailystar.net/literature/rabindranath-1370521> (visited 29 October 2021).

[30] M. Davis, *Late Victorian Holocausts: El Niño Famines and the Making of the Third World* (London: Verso, 2002).

[31] A. de Waal, *Famine Crimes: Politics and the Disaster Relief Industry in Africa* (London: International African Institute in association with James Currey, 1997), at 13–14.

that in turn did so much to prompt partition. In this context, we might have expected nationalist leaders to unite in condemning the famine and elevating it in the narrative of liberation. No such thing occurred. Most likely this is because the famine also served as a spike that levered open the fault lines of Indian resistance to British rule: some sided with Britain, others with Japan; many of the Calcutta business class were profiting from the expansion in manufacturing associated with the war and the inflationary policy that rewarded war capitalists, at the expense of the labourers, fishermen, and artisans who starved en masse; and those class divisions took on a Hindu–Muslim dimension as well. The Bengal famine's 'grey zone' enveloped the bourgeois nationalists, who understandably preferred for those mists to hang in the air for as long as possible. If the Irish case is any guide, Bengal is at least half a century away from the kind of honest reckoning of complicities provided by President Higgins.

In the meantime, India's memory of famine is subaltern, often private, and in poetry and art. It is pervasive, imprinted in ways that are easily unnoticed, but ubiquitous once the signs are legible. The sculptor Somnath Hore has spoken of the way in which the 'wounds' of that famine engraved themselves on his style.[32] For the poet Bhattacharya, interleaved with rage at the inhumanity of empire and the profiteering of grain traders is evocation of the simple empty misery of starvation. Of Bengal in 1943, he wrote:

> Poetry, we do not need you any more.
> A world devastated by hunger
> is rendered so prosaic,
> The full moon looks like grilled bread.[33]

'The Famine and after it' by Vaidyanath Mishra 'Nagarjun' is even more elemental:

> For many days the oven was crying, the mill was sad
> For many days the one-eyed dog slept beside him
> For many days the lizard's patrol was stuck on the wall
> For many days the condition of the rats was desperate.
> Grain came into the house after many days
> Smoke rose up from the courtyard after many days
> The eyes of the whole house started to shine after many days
> The crow shook his wings after many days.[34]

[32] N. Sarkar, *A Matter of Conscience: Artists Bear Witness to the Great Bengal Famine of 1943* (Calcutta: Punascha, 1998).

[33] S. Bhattacharya, 'He Mahajiban (O Great Life)' trans O. Gani, *All Poetry*, available online at <https://allpoetry.com/poem/12815378-O-GREAT-LIFE--%E0%A6%B9%E0%A7%87-%E0%A6%AE%E0%A6%B9%E0%A6%BE%E0%A6%9C%E0%A7%80%E0%A6%AC%E0%A6%A8---Written-by-Sukanta-Bhattacharya---Tran-by-Osman-Gani> (visited 29 October 2021).

[34] V. 'Nagarjun' Mishra, 'Akaal aur Usake Baad (Famine and after it)'tr. Dimitrios Vassiliades (1952), available online at <https://elinepa.org/the-famine-and-after-it/> (visited 14 December 2020).

Recently the Indian diplomat and parliamentarian, Shashi Tharoor, has suggested that Britain's temple of empire, the Victoria Monument in Calcutta, be transformed into a museum of the experience of colonialism.[35] If this were acted upon it would be the first step towards a public memorial. However, the most appropriate place to memorialize Britain's famines in India—and in Ireland, South Africa, and a host of other formerly conquered territories—is in the imperial metropolis itself. There is no shortage of suitable places: in Leadenhall Street, where the site of the headquarters of the East India Company is now occupied by the appropriately skeletal Lloyds Building, or in St James's Park, opposite the India Office, now the Foreign, Commonwealth and Development Office and the neighbouring Treasury, from where the famine in Ireland was administered. Unlike post-war Germany and post-Algeria France, Britain has never been forced to confront its past. Few Britons are aware that their country, too, was made by famine; or that—contrary to the rosy dementia of too many politicians and newspaper editors—the infliction of these outrages was intrinsic to empire. Like the International Slavery Museum in Liverpool and the memorial to the murdered Jews of Europe in Berlin, a famine memorial would remind those who live in the countries that perpetrated great historic crimes, of what was done in their name.

4. Conclusion

The wider topic of transitional justice for acts of starvation has been neglected by scholarship, law, and human rights activism. This is a field wide open for exploration. This chapter begins to map just one part of this conceptual terrain, namely memory and truth-telling.

A further exploration would undoubtedly identify many other famines that are remembered—or not—in different ways. This chapter has not, for example, touched on the extensive memorialization of the 1866–1868 famine in Finland,[36] or the hunger-driven dispossession of Native American peoples,[37] and nor has it delved into music or drama. Hidden in the silenced, subaltern annals of colonialism are the stories of the 'mad', including religious prophets incarcerated in lunatic asylums who had inflamed millenarian movements in the wake of famine and other ravages.[38] In the obscured lineage of cuisine we find the origins story of Jamaican jerk, which was first invented as a means of cooking wild pigs without

[35] S. Tharoor, *Inglorious Empire: What the British Did to India* (London: Hurst and Co., 2017).

[36] A. Newby, 'Finland's "Great Hunger Years" Memorials', available online at <https://katovuodet1860.wordpress.com/about>/ (visited 14 December 2020).

[37] J. Daschuk, *Clearing the Plains: Disease, Politics of Starvation, and the Loss of Aboriginal Life* (Regina: University of Regina Press, 2013).

[38] M. Vaughan, *Curing Their Ills: Colonial Power and African Illness* (Stanford: Stanford University Press, 1991), at 102.

using fire (and hence smoke) by fugitive Maroons hiding in the forests during the slave wars of the seventeenth century.[39]

The intent of memorializing famine crimes can, however, be stated clearly. It aims to recognize the crime of starvation for what it is, and thereby to help emancipate the victims of the crime from the otherwise pervasive feelings of worthlessness and self-blame, to lift the fog that obscures the ultimate culpability for these atrocities. In doing so, this exercise should also dismantle the hierarchy of victimhood, so that those who perished of starvation, thirst, exposure, and exhaustion can properly be recognized on par with those murdered by violent means.

[39] A. Lee, 'Jerk, an Authentic Taste of Jamaican Liberty' 69 *History Today* (May 2019) 84–88.

Bibliography

'A monument to the victims of the Holodomor was erected in Kazakhstan. its discoveries have been waiting for a quarter century', *Current Time TV*, 31 May 2017, available online <https://www.currenttime.tv/a/28520949.html> (visited 14 December 2020).

'Aerial barrel bombing of Al- Bab in the countryside of Aleppo', *Ad-Dustour*, 2 December 2013, available online at <https:// www.addustour.com/ articles/ 210127--يقصف-الطي ران-المتفجرة-بالبراميل-حلب-ريف-في-الباب-مدينة> (visited 3 January 2020).

'As famines of "biblical proportion" loom, Security Council urged to "act fast"', *UN News*, 21 April 2020, available online at <https://news.un.org/en/story/2020/04/1062272> (visited 1 October 2021).

'Concerning Restrictive Measures Against Serious Human Violations and Abuses,' Council Regulation (EU) 2020/1998, 7 December 2020, available online at <https://eur-lex.europa.eu/legal-content/EN/TXT/?uri=uriserv%3AOJ.LI.2020.410.01.0001.01.ENG&toc=OJ%3AL%3A2020%3A410I%3ATOC> (visited 27 August 2021).

'Concerning restrictive measures against serious human rights violations and abuses', Council Decision (CFSP) 2020/1999, Consolidated version 13 December 2021, available online at <https://eur-lex.europa.eu/legal-content/EN/TXT/?uri=CELEX:32020D1999> (visited 27 August 2021).

'Consolidated List of Financial Sanctions Targets in the UK', Office of Financial Sanctions Implementation HM Treasury (updated 20 August 2021), available online at <https://ofsistorage.blob.core.windows.net/publishlive/ConList.html> (visited 27 August 2021).

'Death toll due to torture', Syrian Network for Human Rights, 24 September 2018, <http://sn4hr.org/blog/2018/09/24/death-toll-due-to-torture/> (visited 7 June 2019).

'Ethiopia: video of Tigray massacre lifts lid on "war without photos"', *France24*, 10 March 2021, available online at <https://observers.france24.com/en/africa/20210312-ethiopia-tigray-video-massacre-war-mai-harmaz-investigation> (visited 5 August 2021).

'Famine Action Mechanism (FAM)', Washington, DC: The World Bank, available online at <http://www.worldbank.org/en/programs/famine-early-action-mechanism> (visited 18 July 2019).

'Famine declared in region of South Sudan—UN', *UN News* (February 2017), available online at <https://news.un.org/en/story/2017/02/551812-famine-declared-region-south-sudan-un> (visited 27 August 2021).

'G7 Famine Prevention and Humanitarian Crises Compact', Foreign, Commonwealth & Development Office, May 2021, available online at <https://www.gov.uk/government/publications/g7-foreign-and-development-ministers-meeting-may-2021-communique/g7-famine-prevention-and-humanitarian-crises-compact> (visited 27 August 2021).

'Global Magnitsky Human Rights Accountability Act', Sections 1261–1265, Subtitle F, Public Law 114-328, of the FY17 National Defence Authorization Act, 23 December 2016.

Global Magnitsky Act FAQ, Human Rights First, available online at <https://www.humanrightsfirst.org/sites/default/files/hrf-global-magnitsky-faq.pdf> (visited 27 August 2021).

'How rape is used as a weapon in South Sudan's war', *PBS NewsHour* (May 2017), available online at <https://www.pbs.org/newshour/show/rape-used-weapon-south-sudans-war> (visited 27 August 2021).

'Humanitarian assistance struggling to reach affected population in Yemen as blockade continues', Logistics Cluster Blog, 22 November 2017, available online at <https://logcluster.org/blog/humanitarian-assistance-struggling-reach-affected-population-yemen-blockade-continues> (visited 26 August 2021).

'Humanitarian crisis in Yemen remains the worst in the world, warns UN', *UN News*, 14 February 2019, available online at <https://news.un.org/en/story/2019/02/1032811> (visited 27 August 2021).

'International community must act to stop catastrophic famine in Yemen, top humanitarian affairs official tells Security Council', UN Press Release, 23 October 2018, available online at <https://www.un.org/press/en/2018/sc13550.doc.htm> (visited 5 August 2021).

'Justice for Victims of Corrupt Foreign Officials Act, Sections 4(3) and Section 18', Canadian Government, available online at <https://laws.justice.gc.ca/eng/acts/J-2.3/FullText.html> (visited 27 August 2021).

'La France et le Yémen: cartographie d'un mensonge d'État', *Mediapart*, 15 April 2019, available online at <https://www.mediapart.fr/journal/international/150419/la-france-et-le-yemen-cartographie-d-un-mensonge-d-etat?utm_content=buffer5e34b&utm_medium=social&utm_source=Facebook_Page&utm_campaign=CM> (visited 26 August 2021).

'Law on the Establishment of the Extraordinary Chambers in the Courts of Cambodia for the Prosecution of Crimes Committed during the Period of Democratic Kampuchea (with amendments)', doc. no. NS/RKM/1004/006, 27 October 2004.

'Monument to the heroic defenders of Leningrad', *Saint-Petersburg.com*, available online at <http://www.saint-petersburg.com/monuments/heroic-defenders/> (visited 14 December 2020).

'Monument to the "Holodomor" burned by unknown persons in the Kiev region', *Regnum*, 15 March 2018, available online at <https://regnum.ru/news/2415054.html> (visited 14 December 2020).

'Monument to the victims of hunger in Gagauzia', *Moldovenii*, 11 May 2016, available online at <http://www.moldovenii.md/ru/news/view/taxon/1673/id/22453/from/noi> (visited 14 December 2020).

'More than 50 people were killed in the Russian bombing of a popular market in the eastern countryside of Aleppo', *Arabi 21*, 15 December 2015, available online at <https://bit.ly/39IMuKr> (visited 2 January 2020).

'Narrative Summaries of Reasons for Listing', United Nations Security Council (UNSC), available online at <https://www.un.org/securitycouncil/sanctions/2140/materials/summaries> (visited 27 August 201).

'New massacre in Aleppo kills 30 people', *Zaman Alwasl*, 23 April 2015, available online at <https://www.zamanalwsl.net/news/article/60114> (visited 4 June 2019).

'Note to Correspondents: Statement by Adama Dieng, United Nations Special Adviser on the Prevention of Genocide, on the situation in Hudaydah, Yemen', UN Secretary General, 14 June 2018, available online at <https://www.un.org/sg/en/content/sg/note-correspondents/2018-06-14/note-correspondents-statement-adama-dieng-united-nations> (visited 5 August 2021).

'Nutrition causal analysis study. South and Central Somalia', *SNS Consortium* (2015), available online at <https://www.wfp.org/publications/nutrition-causal-analysis-study> (visited 25 August 2021).

'Overview of the present working methods of the Committee', Committee on Economic, Social and Cultural Rights, available online at <https://www.ohchr.org/EN/HRBodies/CESCR/Pages/WorkingMethods.aspx> (visited 28 November 2019).

'Report of a workshop on the improvement of the nutrition of refugees and displaced people in Africa, University of Nairobi, Machakos, Kenya' (United Nations Administrative Committee on Coordination/Standing Committee on Nutrition (UN SCN), 1994).

'Sanctions', United Nations Security Council, available online at <https://www.un.org/securitycouncil/sanctions/information> (visited 27 August 2021).

'Sanctions and Anti-Money Laundering Act' (the Sanctions Act), 2018, c. 13, Parliament of the United Kingdom, available online at <https://www.legislation.gov.uk/ukpga/2018/13/contents/enacted> (visited 29 October 2021).

'Statement by Acting Under-Secretary-General for Humanitarian Affairs and Emergency Relief Coordinator, Ramesh Rajasingham—Briefing to the Security Council on the humanitarian situation in Ethiopia', *ReliefWeb*, 2 July 2021, available online at <https://reliefweb.int/report/ethiopia/statement-acting-under-secretary-general-humanitarian-affairs-and-emergency-relief-1> (visited 5 August 2021).

'Statement by Thomas Andrews, UN Special Rapporteur on the Situation of Human Rights in Myanmar', Human Rights Council, 7 July 2021, available online at <https://www.ohchr.org/en/NewsEvents/Pages/DisplayNews.aspx?NewsID=27283&LangID=E> (visited 29 September 2021).

'South Sudan consultations', *What's in Blue*, 9 August 2018, available online at <https://www.whatsinblue.org/2018/08/south-sudan-consultations-10.php> (visited 27 August 2021).

'South Sudan declares famine in Unity State' *BBC*, 20 February 2017, available online <https://www.bbc.com/news/world-africa-39025927> (visited 9 September 2021).

'Syrians "exposed to brutality every day" as thousands continue fleeing ISIL's last stand', *UN News*, 1 March 2019, available online at <https://news.un.org/en/story/2019/03/1033882> (visited 4 June 2019).

'The 2019 Pulitzer Prize Winner in Feature Photography', *The Pulitzer Prizes*, available online at <https://www.pulitzer.org/winners/lorenzo-tugnoli-washington-post ((visited 27 August 2021).

'The Dóchas Code of Conduct on Images and Messages', *Dóchas*, 2007, available online at <http://www.dochas.ie/images-and-messages> (visited 14 December 2020).

'The Global Human Rights Sanctions Regime', Foreign, Commonwealth & Development Office, UK Government, 6 July 2020, available online at <https://www.gov.uk/government/collections/uk-global-human-rights-sanctions> (visited 27 August 2021).

'The Nobel Peace Prize for 2020', *Nobel Peace Prize Committee*, 9 October 2020, available online <https://www.nobelprize.org/prizes/peace/2020/press-release/> (visited 25 August 2021).

'The question of humanitarian exceptions from UN sanctions regimes', *Old Dominion University Model United Nations Society, Issue Brief Security Council* (2019), available online at <https://www.odu.edu/content/dam/odu/offices/mun/issue-brief-2019/ib-sc-humanitarian-exceptions-from-sanctions.pdf> (visited 27 August 2021).

'The regime cuts the supply road to Aleppo and ends the siege of Nubl and Zahra', *Al Jazeera*, 2 April 2020, available online at <https:// www.aljazeera.net/ news/ arabic/ 2016/ 2/ 4/النظام-يقطع-طريق-إمداد-حلب-ويفك-حصار-نبل-والزهراء> (visited 4 June 2019).

'The social and economic consequences of malnutrition in ACP countries', Background document (European Parliament), available online at <http://www.europarl.europa.eu/meetdocs/2009_2014/documents/acp/dv/background_/background_en.pdf> (visited 20 March 2019).

'The Syrian regime applies the siege on eastern Aleppo and western Aleppo celebrates', *al Quds al Arabi*, 30 July 2016, available online at <https:// www.alquds.co.uk/%EF%BB%BFالنظام-السوري-يطبق-الحصار-على-حلب-ال/> (visited 3 January 2020).

'Tigray crisis: Ethiopia region at risk of huge "humanitarian disaster"', *BBC*, 2 February 2021, available online at <https://www.bbc.com/news/world-africa-55905108> (visited 5 August 2021).

'Under Secretary-General for Humanitarian Affairs and Emergency Relief Coordinator, Mark Lowcock: Briefing to the Security Council on the humanitarian situation in Yemen', *ReliefWeb*, 11 November 2020, available online at <https://reliefweb.int/sites/reliefweb.int/files/resources/201111-Yemen%20SECCO%20statement%20Final.pdf> (visited 26 August 2021).

'UN worried about the reported diversion of aid in Syria', *Reuters*, 21 May 2015, available online at <https://www.reuters.com/article/syria-crisis-un-aid/u-n-worried-about-reported-diversion-of-aid-in-syria-idINKBN0O62M520150521> (visited 29 October 2021).

'UN gravely concerned at South Sudan's "food security crisis"', *Associated Press*, 10 August 2018, available online at <https://apnews.com/article/c3091aa26df24f9f85eae8d7e375c7e3> (visited 5 August 2021).

'U.N. report addresses gang rape of aid workers in South Sudan', *National Public Radio*, 23 August 2016, available online at <https://www.npr.org/sections/goatsandsoda/2016/08/23/491057541/gang-rape-of-aid-workers-in-south-sudan-is-a-turning-point> (visited 27 August 2021).

'U.S. Executive Order 13818 as of December 20, 2017', 82 *Federal Register*, 26 December 2017, 60839–60842.

'United Nations Special Representative of the Secretary-General on Sexual Violence in Conflict, Ms. Pramila Patten, urges all parties to prohibit the use of sexual violence and cease hostilities in the Tigray region of Ethiopia', UN Press Release, 21 January 2021, available online at <http://bit.ly/2NiLx55> (visited 5 August 2021).

'Wiretaps implicate Lebanon MP in arming Syrian rebels', *Agence France-Presse*. 4 December 2012, available online at <https://www.thenationalnews.com/world/mena/wiretaps-implicate-lebanon-mp-in-arming-syrian-rebels-1.401841> (visited 6 November 2020).

'WFP Chief warns of hunger pandemic as COVID-19 spreads (Statement to UN Security Council)', United Nations World Food Programme, 20 April 2021, available online at <https://www.wfp.org/news/wfp-chief-warns-hunger-pandemic-covid-19-spreads-statement-un-security-council> (visited 1 October 2021).

'Year in Review 2018', *Tyndall Report*, available online at <http://tyndallreport.com/yearinreview2018/war/> (visited 27 August 2021).

'Yemen—The world's worst humanitarian crisis', World Food Programme, available online at <https://www.wfp.org/yemen-crisis> (visited 27 August 2021).

M. Ababsa, 'The End of a World. Drought and Agrarian Transformation in Northeast Syria (2007–2010)', in R. Hinnebusch and R. Zintl (eds), *Syria from Reform to Revolt Vol. 1: Political Economy and International Relations* (Syracuse: Syracuse University Press, 2015) 199–222.

M. Ababsa, 'Agrarian Counter-Reform in Syria (2000–2010)', in R. Hinnebusch et al. (eds), *Agriculture and Reform in Syria* (Fife: University of St. Andrews Centre for Syrian Studies, 2011) 83–111.

S. N. Abboud and F. H. Lawson, 'Antinomies of Economic Governance in Contemporary Syria', in A. Khadim (ed.), *Governance in the Middle East and North Africa: A Handbook* (London: Routledge, 2013) 330–341.

Action Against Hunger, *Modeling Early Risk Indicators to Anticipate Malnutrition*, available online at <https://knowledgeagainsthunger.org/research/prevention/meriam-modelling-early-risk-indicators-to-anticipate-malnutrition/> (visited 24 November 2020).

Action Contre La Faim (ACF), *Link-NCA. Nutrition Causal Analysis* (2017), available online at <https://linknca.org> (visited 22 October 2021).

S. K. Afesorgbor, 'Sanctioned to Starve? The Impact of Economic Sanctions on Food Security in Targeted States', *Social Science Research Network* 25 July 2020, available online at <http://dx.doi.org/10.2139/ssrn.3660536> (visited 27 August 2021).

Africa Watch Committee, *Denying the Honor of Living: Sudan, a Human Rights Disaster* (New York: Africa Watch Committee, 1990).

African Charter on Human and Peoples' Rights on the Rights of Women in Africa, Assembly of the African Union, 11 July 2003 (hereafter the 'Maputo Protocol').

African Commission on Human and Peoples Rights, *Resolution on the Fact-Finding Mission to the Tigray Region of the Federal Democratic Republic of Ethiopia*, 12 May 2021, ACHPR/ Res. 482, available online at <https://www.achpr.org/sessions/resolutions?id=513> (visited 6 August 2021).

African Globe, 'ICC shelves Darfur case for lack of UN support',13 December 2014, available online at <https://www.africanglobe.net/africa/icc-shelves-darfur-case-lack-support/> (visited 8 January 2015).

African Rights, *Land Tenure, the Creation of Famine, and Prospects for Peace in Somalia* (1993).

African Rights, *Food and Power in Sudan: A Critique of Humanitarianism* (1997), available online at <https://www.sudanarchive.net/> (visited 27 October 2021).

International Panel of Eminent Personalities, *Rwanda: The Preventable Genocide* (Addis Ababa, Ethiopia: African Union, July 2000).

Agreement between the United Nations and the Royal Government of Cambodia Concerning the Prosecution Under Cambodian Law of Crimes Committed During the Democratic Kampuchea Period, 6 June 2003, available online at <https://www.eccc.gov.kh/sites/default/files/legal-documents/Agreement_between_UN_and_RGC.pdf> (visited 27 January 2022).

D. Akande and E.-C. Gillard, 'Conflict Induced Food Insecurity and the War Crime of Starvation of Civilians as a Method of War', 17 *Journal of International Criminal Justice* (2019) 753–779.

R. Akresh et al., 'War and Stature: Growing up during the Nigerian Civil War', 102 *American Economic Review* (2012) 273–77.

A. M. Al-Fareh, *The Impact of the War in Yemen on Artisanal Fishing of the Red Sea*, LSE Middle East Centre (2018), available online at <http://eprints.lse.ac.uk/91022/1/Al-Fareh_The-impact-of-war_Author.pdf> (visited 26 August 2021).

A. Al-Iryani and A. Nasser, 'Political Marketplace Framework and Humanitarian Crisis in Yemen', Paper presented at Workshop on Political Markets and Humanitarianism, Remote/Tufts University, 5–9 October 2020.

L. Al-Junid and A. H. M. Abo Rezeg, 'Hunger Leads Syrian Refugee to Commit Suicide', Anadolou Agency, 14 January 2019, available online at <https://www.aa.com.tr/en/middle-east/hunger-leads-syrian-refugee-to-commit-suicide/1364024> (visited 22 August 2020).

F. Al-Muslimi and M. Rageh, *Yemen's Economic Collapse and Impending Famine: The Necessary Immediate Steps to Avoid Worst-case Scenarios* Yemen in Crisis, Report No. 3, Sana'a Center for Strategic Studies and Friedrich Ebert Stiftung, October 2015, available online at <http://sanaacenter.org/wp-content/uploads/2015/11/files_yemens_economic_collapse_and_impending_famine_en.pdf> (visited 26 August 2021).

T. Al-Om, 'Emergence of the Political Voice of Syria's Civil Society: The Non-violent Movements of the Syrian Uprising', in R. Hinnebusch and O. Imady (eds), *The Syrian*

Uprising. Domestic Origins and Early Trajectory (London: Routledge/St. Andrews Syrian Studies Series, 2018) 159–172.

A. B. Al-Saqqaf, 2020) اجلمهورية بني السلطنة والقبيلةيف اليمن الشماي, first published in Cairo, 1988), available online at <https://www.peacehorizons.net/ar/wp-content/uploads/2020/08/ %D9%83%D8%AA%D8%A7%D8%A8- %D8%AF.- %D8%A3%D8%A8%D9%88%D8%A8%D9%83%D8%B1-%D8%A7%D9%84%D8%B3%D9%82%D8%A7%D9%81-.pdf> (visited 26 August 2021).

R. Aliboni, *The Red Sea Region: Local Actors and the Superpowers* (Sydney: Routledge, 1985).

C. A. Allen, 'Civilian Starvation and Relief During Armed Conflict: The Modern Humanitarian Law', 19 *Georgia Journal of International & Comparative Law* 31 (1989) 1–85.

S. H. Allen, 'The Domestic Political Costs of Economic Sanctions', 52 *The Journal of Conflict Resolution* (2008) 916–44, at 916.

D. Almond et al., *Long-term Effects of the 1959–1961 China Famine: Mainland China and Hong Kong*, National Bureau of Economic Research (2007), available online at <https://www.nber.org/papers/w13384> (visited 24 August 2021).

A. Alnasrawi, 'Iraq: Economic Sanctions and Consequences, 1990–2000', 22 *Third World Quarterly* (2001) 205–218.

K. Ambos, 'Karadzic's genocidal intent as the "only reasonable inference"?', EJIL: Talk! Blog of the European Journal of International Law, 1 April 2016, available online at <https://www.ejiltalk.org/karadzics-genocidal-intent-as-the-only-reasonable-inference/> (visited 2 May 2019).

Amnesty International, *'We Are Still Running': War Crimes in Leer, South Sudan*, 2016, available online at <https://reliefweb.int/report/south-sudan/we-are-still-running-war-crimes-leer-south-sudan#:~:text=%E2%80%9CWe%20are%20still%20running%E2%80%9D%3A,between%20August%20and%20December%202015> (visited 27 October 2021).

Amnesty International, *'Do Not Remain Silent': Survivors of Sexual Violence in South Sudan Call for Reparations and Justice*, 2017, available online at <https://www.amnesty.org/en/latest/news/2017/07/south-sudan-sexual-violence-on-a-massive-scale-leaves-thousands-in-mental-distress-amid-raging-conflict/> (visited 27 October 2021).

Amnesty International, *Syria: Surrender or Starve Strategy Displacing Thousands of Amounts to Crimes Against Humanity*, 2017, available online at <https://www.amnesty.org/en/latest/news/2017/11/syria-surrender-or-starve-strategy-displacing-thousands-amounts-to-crimes-against-humanity/> (visited 23 September 2019).

Amnesty International, *Syria: Expert Analysis Shows US-Led Coalition Use of White Phosphorus May Amount to War Crime*, 16 June 2017, available online at <https://www.amnesty.org/en/latest/news/2017/06/syria-expert-analysis-shows-usled-coalition-use-of-white-phosphorus-may-amount-to-war-crime/> (visited 27 October 2021).

Amnesty International, *'We Will Destroy Everything': Military Responsibility for Crimes Against Humanity in Rakhine State, Myanmar*, 26 June 2018, available online at <https://www.amnesty.org/en/documents/asa16/8630/2018/en/> (visited 4 October 2021).

Amnesty International, *'War of Annihilation': Devastating Toll on civilians Raqqa—Syria'*, 5 June 2018, available online at <https://www.amnesty.org.uk/files/reports/War%20of%20annihiliation%20report.pdf> (visited 22 August 2020).

Amnesty International, *Syria: Unprecedented Investigation Reveals US-led Coalition Killed More than 1,600 Civilians in Raqqa 'Death Trap'*, 25 April 2019, available online at <https://www.amnesty.org/en/latest/news/2019/04/syria-unprecedented-investigation-reveals-us-led-coalition-killed-more-than-1600-civilians-in-raqqa-death-trap/> (visited 22 August 2020).

N. Andersson et al., 'Childhood Malnutrition During the Bosnian Conflict: Four Linked Cross-Sectional Studies', 5(3) *Vulnerable Children and Youth Studies* (2019) 197–207.

L. Andriukaitis et al., *Breaking Ghouta*, 7 September 2018, available online at <https://www.atlanticcouncil.org/wp-content/uploads/2019/08/Breaking-Ghouta_English.pdf> (visited 17 March 2020).

G. A. Aneme, 'Apology and Trials: The Case of the Red Terror Trials in Ethiopia', *African Human Rights Law* (2006) 64–84.

G. A. Aneme, 'The Anatomy of Special Prosecutor v. Colonel Mengistu Hailemarriam et al. (1994–2008)', 4(1/2) *International Journal of Ethiopian Studies* (2009) 1–53.

S. Annys et al., *Tigray: Atlas of the Humanitarian Situation*, Research Gate, July 2021, available online at <https://www.arcgis.com/apps/webappviewer/index.html?id=e7538a480f004487927852d75a90bb69 2021).

Y. Arai-Takahashi, *The Law of Occupation: Continuity and Change of International Humanitarian Law, and its Interaction with International Human Rights Law* (Leiden: Brill/Nijhoff, 2009).

Assembly of States Parties to the Rome State, Resolution ICC-ASP/18/Res.5, 6 December 2019.

Australian National University, *Atrocity Forecasting Project*, available online at <https://politicsir.cass.anu.edu.au/research/projects/atrocity-forecasting> (visited 24 November 2020).

W. R. Aykroid, *The Conquest of Famine* (London: Chatto & Windus, 1974).

R. Bailey, *Famine Early Warning and Early Action: The Cost of Delay* (London: Chatham House, 2012).

L. Balcells and S. N. Kalyvas, 'Does Warfare Matter? Severity, Duration, and Outcomes of Civil Wars', 58 *Journal of Conflict Resolution* (2014) 1390–1418.

A. A. Balema, *Economic Development and Democracy in Ethiopia* (Rotterdam: Erasmus University, 2003).

D. J. Barker, 'The Fetal and Infant Origins of Adult Disease', 301 *British Medical Journal* (1990) 1111.

Z. A. Basha, 'Arabia Felix: The Rapid and Costly Transformation from Food Self-Sufficiency to Insecurity', unpublished working paper for the 'Yemeni Voices for Sustainable Agriculture' programme (London School of Economics, Middle East Centre).

J. Beaubien, 'U.N. report addresses gang rape of aid workers in South Sudan', *National Public Radio*, 23 August 2016, available online at <https://www.npr.org/sections/goatsandsoda/2016/08/23/491057541/gang-rape-of-aid-workers-in-south-sudan-is-a-turning-point> (visited 27 August 2021).

A. Bellal, *Human Rights Obligations of Armed Non-State Actors: An Exploration of the Practice of the UN Human Rights Council*. Geneva Academy of International Humanitarian Law and Human Rights, Academy Briefing No. 7, December 2016, available online at <https://www.geneva-academy.ch/joomlatools-files/docman-files/InBrief7_web.pdf> (visited 11 February 2020).

S. Bhattacharya, 'To Rabindranath' (c. 1945), *The Daily Star* (4 March 2017), available online at <https://www.thedailystar.net/literature/rabindranath-1370521> (visited 29 October 2021).

S. Bhattacharya, 'He Mahajiban (O Great Life)' trans. O. Gani, *All Poetry*, available online at <https://allpoetry.com/poem/12815378-O-GREAT-LIFE--%E0%A6%B9%E0%A7%87-%E0%A6%AE%E0%A6%B9%E0%A6%BE%E0%A6%9C%E0%A7%80%E0%A6%AC%E0%A6%A8---Written-by-Sukanta-Bhattacharya---Tran-by-Osman-Gani> (visited 29 October 2021).

Z. Bhutta et al., 'What Works? Interventions for Maternal and Child Undernutrition and Survival', 371 *Lancet* (2008) 417–40.

T. Biersteker, R. Brubaker, and D. Lanz, *UN Sanctions and Mediation: Establishing Evidence to Inform Practice*, United Nations University Centre for Policy Research (18 February 2019), available online at <https://cpr.unu.edu/research/projects/un-sanctions-and-mediation-establishing-evidence-to-inform-practice-2.html#outline> (visited 27 August 2021).

T. Biersteker et al., 'UN Targeted Sanctions Datasets (1991–2013)', 55 *Journal of Peace Research* (2018) 404–12.

A. Biswell, *Yemen Economic Bulletin: The War for Monetary Control Enters a Dangerous New Phase*, Sana'a Center for Strategic Studies, 21 January 2020, available online at <http://sanaacenter.org/files/The_War_for_Monetary_Control_en.pdf> (visited 26 August 2021).

I. Black and J. Borger, 'Syrian armed rebels take fight to government troops in Damascus', *The Guardian*, 17 July 2012, available online at <https://www.theguardian.com/world/2012/jul/17/syrian-armed-rebels-fight-damascus> (visited 22 August 2020).

R. Black et al., 'Maternal and Child Undernutrition: Global and Regional Exposures and Health Consequences', 371 *Lancet* (2008) 243–246.

R. Black et al., 'Maternal and Child Undernutrition and Overweight in Low-income and Middle-income Countries', 382 *Lancet* (2013) 427–451.

J. Borger and P. Wintour, 'Biden announces end to US support for Saudi-led offensive in Yemen', *The Guardian*, 4 February 2021, available online at <https://www.theguardian.com/world/2021/feb/04/us-end-support-saudi-led-operations-yemen-humanitarian-crisis> (visited 26 August 2021).

M. Bothe, K. J. Partsch, and W. A. Solf, *New Rules for Victims of Armed Conflicts: Commentary on the Two 1977 Protocols Additional to the Geneva Conventions of 1949* (2nd edn., Leiden: Martinus Nijhoff Publishers, 2013).

A. J. Boucher, *c* (Washington, DC: The Henry L. Stimson Center, 2010), available online at <https://www.stimson.org/2010/un-panels-experts-and-un-peace-operations-0/>> (visited 29 October 2021).

A. J. Boucher, and V. K. Holt, *Targeting Spoilers: The Role of United Nations Panels of Experts* (Washington, DC: The Henry L. Stimson Center, 2009), available online at <https://www.stimson.org/2009/targeting-spoilers-role-united-nations-panels-experts/#:~:text=Targeting%20Spoilers%3A%20The%20Role%20of%20United%20Nations%20Panels%20of%20Experts,-By%20Victoria%20K&text=United%20Nations%20Panels%20of%20Experts%20are%20small%2C%20civilian%2C%20fact%2D,peace%20in%20war%2Dtorn%20regions> (visited 29 October 2021).

P. Bowbrick, 'The Causes of Famine: A Refutation of Professor Sen's Theory', 11 *Food Policy* (1986) 105–124.

P. Boyle, and C. Ó Gráda, 'Fertility Trends, Excess Mortality, and the Great Irish Famine', 23 *Demography* (1986) 543–562.

C. Bozzoli, A. Deaton, and C. Quintana-Domeque, 'Adult Height and Childhood Disease', 46 *Demography* (2009) 647–669.

M. Brandt, *Tribes and Politics in Yemen: A History of Houthi Conflict* (Oxford: Oxford University Press, 2017).

R. Brauman, 'The ICC's Bashir Indictment: Law Against Peace', *World Politics Review*, 23 July 2008, available online at <https://www.worldpoliticsreview.com/articles/2471/the-iccs-bashir-indictment-law-against-peace> (visited 25 August 2021).

R. Brauman, 'Darfur: The International Criminal Court is Wrong', *MSF Crash*, 10 September 2010, available online at <https://www.msf-crash.org/en/publications/rights-and-justice/darfur-international-criminal-court-wrong> (visited 25 August 2021).

C. Breen, *Economic and Social Rights and the Maintenance of International Peace and Security* (London: Routledge, 2017).

C. Breisinger et al., 'Impacts of the Triple Global Crisis on Growth and Poverty: The Case of Yemen', 29 *Development Policy Review* (2011) 155–184.

Campaign Against Arms Trade (CAAT), *CAAT Files New Judicial Review Application Against Decision to Renew Arms Sales to Saudi Arabia*, 27 October 2020, available online at <https://caat.org.uk/news/caat-files-new-judicial-review-application-against-decision-to-renew-arms-sales-to-saudi-arabia/> (visited 26 August 2021).

R. A. Brooks, 'Sanctions and Regime Type: What Works, and When?' 11 *Security Studies* (2002) 1–50.

B. Brooks-Rubin, *The Global Magnitsky Human Rights Accountability Act: Taking Stock*, 24 March 2021, available online at <https://humanrightscommission.house.gov/sites/humanrightscommission.house.gov/files/documents/GloMag_TheSentry_BBrooksRubin_final.pdf> (visited 27 August 2021).

A. S. Brown et al., 'Further Evidence of Relation Between Prenatal Famine and Major Affective Disorder', 157 *American Journal of Psychiatry* (2000) 190–195.

J. M. Burr, *Quantifying Genocide in Southern Sudan and the Nuba Mountains* (Washington, DC: US Committee for Refugees, 1998).

Y. Cai and W. Feng, 'Famine, Social Disruption, and Involuntary Fetal Loss: Evidence from Chinese Survey Data', 42 *Demography* (2005) 301–322.

C. Cambrezy, *Nutrition Surveys In Somalia. 1980–1996* (Rome: World Food Programme, 1997).

P. J. Cameron, 'The Limitations on Methods and Means of Warfare', 9 *Australian Yearbook of International Law* (1980) 247–226.

E. Carisch, L. Rickard-Martin, and S. R. Meister, *The Evolution of UN Sanctions: From a Tool of Warfare to a Tool of Peace, Security and Human Rights* (New York: Springer, 2017).

S. Casey-Maslen and S. Haines, *Hague Law Interpreted: The Conduct of Hostilities under the Law of Armed Conflict* (Oxford: Hart Publishing, 2018).

A. Cassese and P. Gaeta (eds), *Cassese's International Criminal Law* (3rd edn., Oxford: Oxford University Press, 2013).

R. Catalano and T. Bruckner, 'Secondary Sex Ratios and Male Lifespan: Damaged or Culled Cohorts', 103 *Proceedings of the National Academy of Sciences of the United States of America* (2006) 1639–1643.

Centers for Disease Control (CDC), 'Famine-affected, Refugee and Displaced Populations: Recommendations for Public Health Issues', 41(13) *Morbidity and Mortality Weekly Report* (1992).

Central Statistical Organization, Republic of Yemen and International Labour Organization, *Yemen Labour Force Survey 2013–14* (2015), available online at <https://www.ilo.org/wcmsp5/groups/public/---arabstates/---ro-beirut/documents/publication/wcms_419016.pdf> (visited 26 August 2021).

F. Checci et al., *Estimates of Crisis-attributable Mortality in South Sudan, December 2013–April 2018: A Statistical Analysis*, London School of Hygiene and Tropical Medicine, September 2018, available online at <https://www.lshtm.ac.uk/south-sudan-full-report> (visited 9 October 2019).

P. Chandler, B. Kiernan, and C. Boua (eds and trans), *Pol Pot Plans the Future: Confidential Leadership Documents from Democratic Kampuchea* (New Haven: Yale University Press, 1988).

D. Chandler, *Voices from S-21: Terror and History in Pol Pot's Secret Prison* (Berkeley: University of California Press, 1999).

C. Chanda Pheakdey, 'Five Sons in the Khmer Rouge Butchery', 2nd Quarter *Searching for the Truth: Magazine of the Documentation Center of Cambodia* (2007) 56–57.

A. Chapman, A 'Violations Approach' for Monitoring the International Covenant on Economic, Social and Cultural Rights, 18 *Human Rights Quarterly* (1996) 23–66.

K. Cheam aka Kosal, 'My Life During the Pol Pot Regime', 2nd Quarter *Searching for the Truth: Magazine of the Documentation Center of Cambodia* (2005) 53–58.

Y. Chen and L. Zhou, 'The Long-term Health and Economic Consequences of the 1959–1961 Famine in China', 26 *Journal of Health Economics* (2007) 659–681.

E. Chole, *Underdevelopment in Ethiopia* (Addis Ababa: Organisation for Social Science Research in Eastern and Southern Africa, 2004).

A. K. M. Chowdhury and L. C. Chen, *The Dynamics of Contemporary Famine*, The Ford Foundation Report 47 (January 1977), available online at <http://dspace.icddrb.org/jspui/bitstream/123456789/3306/1/1977-FordFoundation-1-ChowdhuryAKMA.pdf> (visited 5 August 2021).

L. Chutel, 'Will Sudan Send Bashir to the Hague?', *Foreign Policy*, 18 August 2021, available online at <https://foreignpolicy.com/2021/08/18/sudan-bashir-icc-hague-justice-darfur-hemeti/> (visited 6 March 2021).

I. Cismas, 'The Intersection of Economic, Social, and Cultural Rights and Civil and Political Rights', in E. Riedel, G. Giacca, and C. Golay (eds), *Economic, Social, and Cultural Rights in International Law: Contemporary Issues and Challenges* (Oxford: Oxford University Press, 2014) 448–472.

Civil Society Forum, 'Social Movements Statement on Nutrition', 57(2) *Development* (2014) 305–309.

H. Clark and R. Kyte, 'In Tigray, Sexual Violence Has Become a Weapon of War', *Foreign Policy*, 27 April 2021, available online at <https://foreignpolicy.com/2021/04/27/in-tigray-sexual-violence-has-become-a-weapon-of-war/> (visited 5 August 2021).

J. Clay and B. H. Holcomb, *Politics and the Ethiopian Famine 1984–1985* (Cambridge: Cultural Survival Inc., 1986).

L. Cliggett, *Grains from Grass: Aging, Gender, and Famine in Rural Africa* (Ithaca: Cornell University Press, 2005).

A. Coco, J. Hemptinne, and B. Lander (eds), 'Special Issue on Starvation in International Law', 17 *Journal of International Criminal Justice* (2019) 673–931.

C. Cohn, 'Women and Wars: Towards a Conceptual Framework', in C. Cohn (ed.), *Women and Wars: Contested Histories, Uncertain Futures* (Cambridge: Polity Press, 2013) 1–35.

S. Collins, 'The Limit of Human Adaptation to Starvation', 1 *Nature Medicine* (1995) 810–814.

Commission on the Responsibility of the Authors of the War and on Enforcement of Penalties, 'Report Presented to the Preliminary Peace Conference, 29 March 1919', 14 *American Journal of International Law* (1920) 95–154.

B. Conley (ed.), *How Mass Atrocities End: Studies from Guatemala, Burundi, Indonesia, the Sudans, Bosnia-Herzegovina, and Iraq* (New York: Cambridge University Press, 2016).

B. Conley, *Mass Atrocity Endings*, World Peace Foundation (2017), available online at <https://sites.tufts.edu/atrocityendings/> (visited 8 July 2019).

B. Conley, *Memory from the Margins: Ethiopia's Red Terror Martyrs Memorial Museum* (Cham: Palgrave Macmillan, 2019).

B. Conley and A. de Waal, 'The Purposes of Starvation: Historical and Contemporary Uses', 17 *Journal of International Criminal Justice* (2019) 699–722.

D. Cortright and G. A. Lopez, *The Sanctions Decade: Assessing UN Strategies in the 1990s* (Boulder: Lynne Rienner Publishers, 2000).

M. Cottier, 'War Crimes—Para. 2(b)(xxv) Starvation of Civilians as a Method of Warfare', in O. Triffterer (ed.), *Commentary on the Rome Statute of the International Criminal Court* (Baden-Baden: Nomos, 1999).

L. Cotula and M. Vidar, *The Right to Adequate Food in Emergencies*, FAO-Legislative Study No. 77, FAO (2002), available online at <http://www.fao.org/3/a-y4430e.pdf> (visited 3 February 2020).

J. Craze and J. Tubiana with C. Gramizzi, *A State of Disunity: Conflict Dynamics in Unity State, South Sudan, 2013–15*, Small Arms Survey (2016), available online at <http://www.smallarmssurveysudan.org/fileadmin/docs/working-papers/HSBA-WP42-Unity-Dec-2016.pdf> (visited 27 October 2021).

M. Cutts, *The Humanitarian Operation in Bosnia, 1992–1995: Dilemmas of Negotiating Humanitarian Access*, UNHCR Working Paper No. 8, Policy Research Unit, 21 May 1999.

D. F. da Costa, S. Hutchinson, and N. Pendle, *Pastoralism in Greater Upper Nile: Socio-political Report*, VISTAS and Vétérinaires Sans Frontières-Suisse (2015).

J. Daher, *Syria After the Uprisings. The Political Economy of State Resilience* (Chicago: Haymarket Books, 2019).

J. Daher, *Between Control and Repression: The Plight of the Syrian Labour Force*, Wartime and Post-Conflict in Syria (WPCS) at the European University Institute, 27 July 2020, available online at <https://cadmus.eui.eu/bitstream/handle/1814/67858/RSCAS_2020_11.pdf?sequence=1&isAllowed=y> (visited 27 August 2020).

Danish Refugee Council, *A Sexual and Gender-based Violence Rapid Assessment*, July 2012, available online at <https://reliefweb.int/sites/reliefweb.int/files/resources/sexual_gender_based_violence_south_sudan.pdf> (visited 5 August 2021).

T. Dannenbaum, 'Famine in Tigray, Humanitarian Access, and the War Crime of Starvation' *Just Security*, 26 July 2021, available online at <https://www.justsecurity.org/77590/famine-in-tigray-humanitarian-access-and-the-war-crime-of-starvation/> (visited 6 August 2021).

T. Dannenbaum, 'Encirclement, Deprivation, and Humanity: Revising the *San Remo Manual* Provisions on Blockade', 97 *International Legal Studies* (2021) 307–394.

T. Dannenbaum, 'Siege Starvation: A War Crime of Societal Torture', 22 *Chicago Journal of International Law* (2022) 1–73.

T. Dannenbaum (ed.), 'Criminalizing Starvation in an Age of Mass Deprivation in War: Intent, Method, Form, and Consequence', *Vanderbilt Journal of Transnational Law* (forthcoming).

M. Daoudy, 'Water Weaponization in the Syrian Conflict: Strategies of Domination and Cooperation', 96(5) *International Affairs* (2020) 1347–1366.

J. Darcy, P. Bonard, and S. Dini, *IASC Real Time Evaluation of the Humanitarian Response to the Horn of Africa Drought Crisis: Somalia 2011–2012*, Inter-Agency Standing Committee Somalia (2012), available online at <https://reliefweb.int/sites/reliefweb.int/files/resources/IASC-RTE%20Somalia%202012.pdf> (visited 24 November 2020).

J. Daschuk, *Clearing the Plains: Disease, Politics of Starvation, and the Loss of Aboriginal Life* (Regina: University of Regina Press, 2013).

K. Davis, 'Brides, Bruises and the Border: The Trafficking of North Korean Women into China', 26 *SAIS Review of International Affairs* (2006) 131–141.

M. Davis, *Late Victorian Holocausts: El Niño Famines and the Making of the Third World* (New York: Verso, 2001).

S. W. Day, 'America's Role in the Yemen Crisis', in S. W. Day and N. Brehony (eds), *Global, Regional, and Local Dynamics in the Yemen Crisis* (London: Palgrave Macmillan, 2020) 51–68.

R. C. DeFalco, 'Justice and Starvation in Cambodia: International Criminal Law and the Khmer Rouge Famine', LLM Thesis, *University of Toronto TSpace* (2013) 32–34.

R. C. DeFalco, 'The Uncertain Relationship between International Criminal Law Accountability and the Rule of Law in Post-Atrocity States: Lessons from Cambodia', 42(1) *Fordham International Law Journal* (2018), 1–60.

A. de Waal, *Evil Days: Thirty Years of War and Famine in Ethiopia* (New York: Africa Watch, 1991).

A. de Waal, 'Starving out the South', in M. Daly and A. Alsikainga (eds), *Civil War in Sudan* (London: IB Taurus, 1994).

A. de Waal, *Famine Crimes: Politics and the Disaster Relief Industry in Africa* (London: African Rights & the International African Institute in association with James Currey, Oxford & Indiana University Press, Bloomington, 1997).

A. de Waal, 'Counter-Insurgency on the Cheap', 26 *London Review of Books*, 5 August 2004, 716–725.

A. de Waal, *Class and Power in a Stateless Somalia*, Social Science Research Center (2007), available online at <https://items.ssrc.org/crisis-in-the-horn-of-africa/class-and-power-in-a-stateless-somalia/> (visited 25 August 2021).

A. de Waal, *A Critique of the ICC Prosecutor's Case against President Bashir*, Making Sense of Darfur/African Arguments, 27 January 2009, available online at <https://sites.tufts.edu/wpf/files/2020/12/Bashir-public-application-critique-d6-250109.pdf> (visited 25 August 2021).

A. de Waal, *The Real Politics of the Horn of Africa: Money, War and the Business of Power* (Cambridge: Polity, 2015).

A. de Waal, 'Patterns of Violence and Imperfect Endings', in B. Conley-Zilkic (ed.), *How Mass Atrocities End: Studies from Guatemala, Indonesia, the Sudans, Bosnia-Hercegovina and Iraq* (Cambridge: Cambridge University Press, 2016).

A. de Waal, *Introduction to the Political Marketplace for Policymakers*, JSRP Policy Brief 1 (London School of Economics and Political Science, 2016), available online at <https://www.lse.ac.uk/ideas/Assets/Documents/Conflict-Research-Programme/policy-reports/JSRP-Brief-1.pdf> (visited 26 August 2021).

A. de Waal, *Mass Starvation: The History and Future of Famine* (Cambridge: Polity, 2017).

A. de Waal, 'Social Nutrition and Prohibiting Famine', 9(1) *World Nutrition* (2018).

A. de Waal, 'The End of Famine? Prospects for the Elimination of Mass Starvation by Political Action', 62 *Political Geography* (2018) 184–195.

A. de Waal, 'Monuments to Famine', 41 *London Review of Books* (7 March 2019).

A. de Waal, 'The Horn of Africa and the Yemen Crisis', in S. W. Day and N. Brehony (eds), *Global, Regional, and Local Dynamics in the Yemen Crisis* (London: Palgrave Macmillan, 2020) 195–208.

A. de Waal and B. Conley, 'What Justice for Starvation Crimes?', in J. Bhabha and M. Matache (eds), *Time for Reparation? Addressing State Responsibility for Collective Injustice* (Philadelphia: University of Pennsylvania Press, 2021), 272–290.

A. de Waal, A. Sarkar, and B. Spatz, *A Political Marketplace Framework Methodology: A Process Toolkit*, Conflict Research Programme and the World Peace Foundation (2019), available online at <http://eprints.lse.ac.uk/111009/1/CRP_the_political_marketplace_framework_and_toolkit_published.pdf> (visited 26 August 2021).

S. Deane, 'Expunged', *Dublin Review of Books* (1 March 2018), available online at www.drb.ie/essays/expunged> (visited 14 December 2020).

J. Delaney, M. J. Lupton, and E. Toth, *The Curse: A Cultural History of Menstruation* (Champaign: University of Illinois Press, 1988).

L. Deng, *Famine in the Sudan: Causes, Preparedness and Response—A Political, Social and Economic Analysis of the 1998 Bahr el Ghazal Famine* (London: Institute for Development Studies, 1999), available online at <https://www.ids.ac.uk/publications/famine-in-the-sudan-causes-preparedness-and-response-a-political-social-and-economic-analysis-of-the-1998-bahr-el-ghazal-famine/> (visited 27 October 2021).

L. Deng, 'Increased Rural Vulnerability in the Era of Globalization: Conflict and famine in Sudan in the 1990s', in S. Devereux (ed.), *The New Famines: Why Famines Persist in an Era of Globalization* (London: Routledge, 2007) 245–268.

L. Deng, 'Are Non-Poor Households Always Less Vulnerable? The Case of Households Exposed to Protracted Civil War in Southern Sudan', 32 *Disasters* (2008) 377–398.

L. Deng, 'Social Capital and Civil War: The Dinka Communities in Sudan's Civil War', 109 *African Affairs* (2010) 231–250.

I. Desportes, 'The Humanitarian Theatre: Drought Response during Ethiopia's Low-Intensity Conflict of 2016', 57 *Journal of Modern African Studies* (2019) 31–59.

S. Devereux, *Theories of Famine* (London: Harvester Wheatsheaf, 1993).

S. Devereux, *Famine in the Twentieth Century, IDS Working Paper 105* (Brighton: University of Sussex, 2000).

S. Devereux, 'Sen's Entitlement Approach: Critiques and Counter-critiques', 29 *Oxford Development Studies* (2001) 245–263.

S. Devereux and R. Sabates-Wheeler, 'Editorial Introduction: Debating Social Protection', 38 *IDS Bulletin* (2007).

F. Dews, *No Peace without Development, No Development without Peace*, Brookings Institution, 17 October 2013, available online at <https://www.brookings.edu/blog/brookings-now/2013/10/17/un-deputy-secretary-general-jan-eliasson-no-peace-without-development-no-development-without-peace/> (visited 7 February 2020).

B. Diop, 'The Syrian army lifts militants' siege of Aleppo', *Al-Akhbar*, 8 October 2013, available online at <https://al-akhbar.com/Syria/58705> (visited 4 June 2019).

R. Donia, *Sarajevo: A Biography* (Ann Arbor: University of Michigan Press, 2006).

K. Dörmann, L. E. Doswald-Beck, and R. Kolb, *Elements of War Crimes under the Rome Statute of the International Criminal Court: Sources and Commentary* (Cambridge: Cambridge University Press, 2003), online publication 2009.

K. Dörmann, L. E. Doswald-Beck, and R. Kolb, *Elements of War Crimes under the Rome Statute of the International Criminal Court: Sources and Commentary* (Cambridge: Cambridge University Press, 2003).

L. Doswald-Beck, *Human Rights in Times of Conflict and Terrorism* (Oxford: Oxford University Press, 2011).

L. Doswald-Beck (ed.), *San Remo Manual on International Law Applicable to Armed Conflicts at Sea* (Cambridge: Cambridge University Press, 1995).

M. Duffield, 'The Political Economy of Internal War: Asset Transfer, Complex Emergencies and International Aid', in J. Macrae and A. Zwi (eds), *War and Hunger: Rethinking International Responses to Complex Emergencies* (London: Zed Books, 1995) 50–69.

P. Dresch and B. Haykel, 'Stereotypes and Political Styles: Islamists and Tribesfolk in Yemen', 27 *International Journal of Middle East Studies* (1995) 405–431.

P. Dresch, *A History of Modern Yemen* (Cambridge: Cambridge University Press, 2000).

P. Drew, 'Can We Starve the Civilians?: Exploring the Dichotomy between the Traditional Law of Maritime Blockade and Humanitarian Initiatives', 95 *International Law Studies* (2019) 302–321.

J. Drèze, 'Democracy and the Right to Food', in P. Alston and M. Robinson (eds), *Human Rights and Development: Towards Mutual Reinforcement* (Oxford: Oxford University Press, 2005) 45–64.

D. W. Drezner, 'Sanctions Sometimes Smart: Targeted Sanctions in Theory and Practice', 13 *International Studies Review* (2011) 96–108.

T. Dyson, 'On the Demography of South Asian Famines: Part I', 45 *Population Studies* (1991), 5–25.

T. Dyson, 'On the Demography of South Asian Famines: Part II', 45 *Population Studies* (1991) 279–297.

T. Dyson, 'Famine in Berar, 1896–1897 and 1899–1900: Echoes and Chain Reactions', in T. Dyson and C. Ó Gráda (eds), *Famine Demography: Perspectives from the Past and Present* (Oxford: Oxford University Press, 2002) 240–259.

T. Eaton et al., *Conflict Economies in the Middle East and North Africa*, Chatham House Report, June 2019, available online at <https://www.chathamhouse.org/2019/06/conflict-economies-middle-east-and-north-africa> (visited 26 August 2021).

T. Eatwell, *State Responsibility for Human Rights Violations Committed in the State's Territory by Armed Non-state Actors*, Geneva Academy of International Humanitarian Law and Human Rights, Academy Briefing No. 13, December 2018, available online at <https://www.geneva-academy.ch/joomlatools-files/docman-files/Academy%20Briefing%2013.pdf> (visited 7 February 2020).

Economic Community of West African States, 'Charter for Food Crisis Prevention and Management in the Sahel and West Africa', November 2011.

K. Edgerton-Tarpley, 'Family and Gender in Famine: Cultural Responses to Disaster in North China, 1876–1879', 16 *Journal of Women's History* (2004) 119–147.

J. Edkins, 'The Criminalisation of Mass Starvations; from Natural Disaster to Crime Against Humanity', in S. Devereux (ed.), *The New Famines: Why Famines Persist in an Era of Globalisation* (Abingdon: Routledge, 2007).

J. Edkins, *Whose Hunger? Concepts of Famine, Practices of Aid* (Minneapolis: University of Minnesota Press, 2008).

P. Ekamper et al., 'War-related Excess Mortality in The Netherlands, 1944–45: New Estimates of Famine- and Nonfamine-related Deaths from National Death Records', 50 *Historical Methods: A Journal of Quantitative and Interdisciplinary History* (2017) 113–128.

J. El Bushra and E. Piza-Lopez, 'Gender, War and Food', in J. Macrae and A. Zwi (eds), *War and Hunger: Rethinking International Responses to Complex Emergencies* (London: Zed Books, 1994) 180–193;

F. Elgesem and G. A. Aneme 'The Rights of the Accused', in K. Tronvoll, C. Schaefer, and G. A, Aneme (eds), *The Ethiopian Red Terror Trials* (Suffolk: James Currey, 2009) 33–50.

S. G. Elias et al., 'Menstruation During and After Caloric Restriction: The 1944–1945 Dutch Famine', 88 *Fertility and Sterility* (2007) 1101–1107.

S. Em, 'Female Patients', 33 *Searching for the Truth: Magazine of the Documentation Center of Cambodia* (September 2002).

Enab Baladi Investigative Unit, 'The economic map of Ghouta: tunnels and "the Prince of Cheese"', *Syria Untold*, 26 July 2017, available online at <https://syriauntold.com/2017/07/26/the-economic-map-of-ghouta-tunnels-and-the-prince-of-cheese/> (visited 22 August 2020).

P. Engle, S. Castle, and P. Menon, 'Child Development: Vulnerability and Resilience', 43(5) *Social Science and Medicine* (1996) 621–635.

M. Eriksson, *Targeting Peace: Understanding UN and EU Targeted Sanctions* (Farnham: Ashgate, 2011).

European Social Charter, 2151 UNTS 277, Art. 30, 1 July 1999.

M. Ezzati and E. Riboli, 'Behavioral and Dietary Risk Factors for Noncommunicable Diseases', 369 *New England Journal of Medicine* (2013) 954–964.

A. Fadilah, 'The Problem of Public–Private Partnerships and the Social Dimensions of Development' (in Arabic), Economic Tuesday Seminar 23, *Syrian Economic Society*, 2010, available online at <http://www.mafhoum.com/syr/articles_10/fadila.pdf> (visited 20 April 2022).

B. Feleke et al., ' "Two bullets is enough": Analysis of Tigray massacre video raises questions for Ethiopian Army', *CNN*, 2 April 2021, available online at <https://www.cnn.com/2021/04/01/africa/tigray-mahibere-dego-massacre-video-cmd-intl/index.html> (visited 5 August 2021).

FEWSNET, *Yemen Food Security Outlook Update: September 2020* (2020), available online at <https://fews.net/sites/default/files/documents/reports/YEMEN_Food_Security_Outlook_Update_September_2020_FINAL.pdf> (visited 26 August 2021).

FEWSNET, *Yemen Food Security Outlook: October 2020–May 2021*, available online at <https://fews.net/sites/default/files/documents/reports/YEMEN_Food%20Security%20Outlook_102020_FINAL.pdf> (visited 26 August 2021).

G. Ferrara et al., 'Risk Factors Associated with Pulmonary Tuberculosis: Smoking, Diabetes and Anti-TNFα drugs', 18 *Current Opinion in Pulmonary Medicine* (2012) 233–240.

D. Fitzpatrick, 'Women and the Great Famine', in M. Kelleher and J.H. Murphy (eds), *Gender Perspectives in Nineteenth-Century Ireland: Public and Private Spheres* (Dublin: Irish Academic Press, 1997) 50–69.

J. Flint and A. de Waal, *Darfur: A New History of a Long War* (London: Zed Books, 2008).

Food and Agriculture Organization of the United Nations, *The State of Food and Agriculture 1983* (1984), available online at <http://www.fao.org/3/a-ap663e.pdf> (visited 28 September 2018).

Food and Agricultural Organization the United Nations, *Voluntary Guidelines to Support the Progressive Realization of the Right to Adequate Food in the Context of National Food Security* (2004), available online at <https://www.fao.org/publications/card/en/c/cceef08f-0627-5ec9-a8e2-63d7c0b608c2/> (visited 28 January 2022).

Food and Agricultural Organization et al., *The State of Food Security and Nutrition in the World 2019: Safeguarding against Economic Slowdowns and Downturns* (2019), available online at <http://www.fao.org/3/ca5162en/ca5162en.pdf> (visited 6 February 2020).

Food and Agricultural Organization, *Sustainable Development Goals—Indicators*, available online at <http://www.fao.org/sustainable-development-goals/indicators/211/en/> (visited 6 February 2020).

Food Security Sector, *Food Security Situation in Syria: Expanded version of the Food Security Sector Humanitarian Needs Overview 2018* (2018), available online at <https://fscluster.org/syria/document/food-security-situation-syria-expanded> (visited 30 October 2021).

H. P. Fransen, 'Exposure to Famine at a Young Age and Unhealthy Lifestyle Behavior Later in Life', 11 *PLoS One* (2016) 1–11.

Fund For Peace (FFP), *Fragile States Index Annual Report* (2019), available online at <https://fundforpeace.org/2019/04/10/fragile-states-index-2019/> (visited 24 November 2020).

W. Fung and W. Ha, 'Intergenerational Effects of the 1959-61 China Famine', in R. Fuentes-Nieva and P. A. Seck (eds), *Risk, Shocks, and Human Development* (London: Palgrave Macmillan, 2010) 222–254.

J. Galtung, 'On the Effects of International Economic Sanctions: With Examples from the Case of Rhodesia', 19 *World Politics* (1967) 378–416.

K. Garber et al., 'Estimating Access to Health Care in Yemen, a Complex Humanitarian Emergency Setting: A Descriptive Applied Geospatial Analysis', 8 *Lancet Global Health* (2020) e1435–e1443.

R. Garfield, 'Morbidity and Mortality Among Iraqi Children from 1990 through 1998', March 1999, available online at <http://www.casi.org.uk/info/garfield/dr-garfield.html> (visited 27 August 2021).

M. Garenne et al., 'The Demographic Impact of a Mild Famine in an African City: The Case of Antananarivo, 1985–7', in T. Dyson and C. Ó Gráda (eds), *Famine Demography: Perspectives from the Past and Present* (Oxford: Oxford University Press, 2002) 204–217.

S. Gebrekidan and J. Saul, 'In blocking arms to Yemen, Saudi Arabia squeezes a starving population', *Reuters*, 11 October 2017, available online at <https://www.reuters.com/article/us-yemen-saudi-blockade-specialreport/special-report-in-blocking-arms-to-yemen-saudi-arabia-squeezes-a-starving-population-idUSKBN1CG16C> (visited 26 August 2021).

Z. Ghisn, 'How Economic Sanctions Negatively Affect the Health Sector in Syria: A Case Study of the Pharmaceutical Industry', London School of Economics Blog, 16 April 2020, available online at <https://blogs.lse.ac.uk/crp/2020/04/16/how-economic-sanctions-negatively-affect-the-health-sector-in-syria-a-case-study-of-the-pharmaceutical-industry/> (visited 20 September 2020).

G. Giacca, *Economic, Social, and Cultural Rights in Armed Conflicts* (Oxford: Oxford University Press, 2014).

W. Giles, 'Women Forced to Flee: Refugees and Internally Displaced Persons', in C. Cohn (ed.), *Women and Wars: Contested Histories, Uncertain Futures* (Cambridge: Polity Press, 2013) 80–101.

S. Gillespie and J. Harris, 'How Nutrition Improves: Half a Century of Understanding And Responding to the Problem of Malnutrition', in S. Gillespie et al. (eds), *Nourishing Millions: Stories of Change in Nutrition* (Washington, DC: International Food Policy Research Institute, 2016).

Global Rights Compliance, *Starvation Sanctions Digest* (28 January 2021), available online at <https://starvationaccountability.org/news-and-events/starvation-related-sanctions-digests-january-2021> (visited 27 August 2021).

Global Rights Compliance, *Starvation Digests*, 12 July 2021, available online at <https://starvationaccountability.org/news-and-events/starvation-jurisprudence-digest-december-2020> (visited 29 September 2021).

Committee on World Food Security, 'Global Strategic Framework for Food Security and Nutrition (GSF)' (2017), available online at <http://www.fao.org/cfs/home/activities/gsf/en/> (visited 7 February 2020).

Government of Ethiopia, Ministry of Information, 'The Federal Democratic Republic of Ethiopia Foreign Affairs and National Security Policy and Strategy' (Addis Ababa, 2002).

R. Goodman, 'The law of aiding and abetting (alleged) war crimes: how to assess US and UK support for Saudi strikes in Yemen', *Just Security*, 1 September 2016, available online at <https://www.justsecurity.org/32656/law-aiding-abetting-alleged-war-crimes-assess-uk-support-saudi-strikes-yemen/> (visited 26 August 2021).

J. Gordon, 'The Hidden Power of the New Economic Sanctions', 118 *Current History* (2019) 3–0.

T. Gørgens, X. Meng, and R. Vaithianathan, 'Stunting and Selection Effects of Famine: A Case Study of the Great Chinese Famine', 97 *Journal of Development Economics* (2012) 99–111.

Government of Yemen, World Bank, and UNDP, *Yemen Poverty Assessment* Vol. 1 (Washington, DC: The World Bank Group, 2007), available online at <https://docume

nts.worldbank.org/en/publication/documents-reports/documentdetail/12493146833 4795087/main-report> (visited 26 August 2021).

E. Graham-Harrison, 'British and US military "in command room" for Saudi strikes on Yemen', *The Guardian*, 15 January 2016, available online at <https://www.theguardian.com/world/2016/jan/15/british-us-military-in-command-room-saudi-strikes-yemen> (visited 26 August 2021).

S. Gronewold, *Beautiful Merchandise: Prostitution in China, 1840–1936* (New York: Harrington Park Press, 1985).

D. Guha-Sapir and O. Degomme, *Darfur: Counting the Deaths: Mortality Estimates from Multiple Surveys*, Brussels: Centre for Research on the Epidemiology of Disasters (2005), available online at <http://hdl.handle.net/2078.1/179719> (visited 25 August 2021.

N. Haan, S. Devereux, and D. Maxwell, 'Global Implications for Famine Prevention, Mitigation and Response', 1(1) *Global Food Security, Special Edition on the Somalia Famine 2011–2012* (2012) 74–79.

A. Habte and M. Afework, *CARE Rapid Gender Analysis [Ethiopia]—[Tigray Crisis]*, CARE (4 April 2021), available online at <https://careevaluations.org/wp-content/uploads/Rapid-Gender-Analysis-RGA-Tigray-Conflict-V.1.pdf> (visited 4 August 2021).

S. Haggard, M. Noland, and E. Weeks, *North Korea on the Precipice of Famine* (New York, Peterson Institute for International Economics, 2008), at 746–747.

F. Haldemann and R. Kouassi, 'Transitional Justice Without Economic, Social, and Cultural Rights?', in E. Riedel, G. Giacca, and C. Golay (eds), *Economic, Social, and Cultural Rights in International Law: Contemporary Issues and Challenges* (Oxford: Oxford University Press, 2014), 498–516.

N. Hall and W. Todman, *Lessons Learned from a Decade of Humanitarian Operations in Syria*, Center for Strategic and International Studies, 22 April 2021.

A. Hamidaddin, 'Yemen: Negotiations with Tribes, States, and Memories', in W. Zartman (ed.), *Arab Spring: Negotiating in the Shadow of the Intifadat* (Athens: University of Georgia Press, 2015).

K. Hampshire et al., 'The Social Context of Childcare Practices and Child Malnutrition in Niger's Recent Food Crisis', 33 (1) *Disasters* (2009) 132–151.

B. Harff, and T. R. Gurr, *Risk Assessments 2015: Potential State Perpetrators of Genocide and Politicide* (Genocide Prevention Advisory Network, 2015).

C. Harrington, 'The Colonial Office and the Retreat from Aden: Great Britain in South Arabia, 1957–1967', 25 *Mediterranean Quarterly* (2014) 5–26.

J-M. Henckaerts and L. Doswald-Beck (eds), *Customary International Humanitarian Law* (Cambridge: Cambridge University Press, 2005).

S. Hickey, 'Ex-British PM John Major shelved famine commemoration', *Irish Times* (13 January 2020), available online at <https://www.irishtimes.com/news/politics/ex-british-pm-john-major-shelved-famine-commemoration-1.4137492> (visited 14 December 2020).

M. Hickson, 'Malnutrition and Ageing', 82 *Postgraduate Medical Journal* (2006), 2–8.

M. Higgins, 'Address by President Michael Higgins at the National Famine Commemoration', University College Cork (12 May 2018), available online at <https://www.rte.ie/player/ie/show/rte-news-special-1516/10878577/> (visited 14 December 2020).

G. Hill et al., *Yemen: Corruption, Capital Flight, and Global Drivers of Conflict*, Chatham House Report, September 2013, available online at <https://www.chathamhouse.org/2013/09/yemen-corruption-capital-flight-and-global-drivers-conflict> (visited 26 August 2021).

C. Hillbruner, and G. Moloney, 'When Early Warning Is Not Enough—Lessons Learned from the 2011 Somalia Famine', 1(1) *Global Food Security* (November 2012) 20–28.

R. Hinnebusch, 'Syria from Authoritarian Upgrading to Revolution?', 1 *International Affairs* (Oxford: Oxford University Press, 2012) 95–133.

R. Hinnebusch, 'President and Party in Post-Ba'athist Syria. From the Struggle for Reform to Regime Deconstruction', in R. Hinnebusch and R. Zintl (eds), *Syria from Reform to Revolt, Vol. 1: Political Economy and International Relations* (Syracuse: Syracuse University Press, 2015) 21–44.

V. Hionidou, *Famine and Death in Occupied Greece, 1941–1944* (Cambridge: Cambridge University Press, 2006).

K. Horton, R. White, and R. Houben, 'Systematic Neglect of Men as a Key Population in Tuberculosis', 113 *Tuberculosis* (2018) 249–253

E. Hoskins, 'Humanitarian Impacts of Sanctions and War in Iraq', in T. Weiss et al. (eds), *Political Gain and Civilian Pain* (New York: Rowman & Littlefield, 1997) 91–147.

K. Houreld, 'Medical official: air strike kills at least 43 in Ethiopia's Tigray', *Reuters*, 23 June 2021, available online at <https://www.reuters.com/world/africa/witness-airstrike-kills-dozens-ethiopias-tigray-region-2021-06-23/> (visited 5 August 2021).

R. Howard-Hassmann, *State Food Crimes* (Cambridge: Cambridge University Press, 2016).

K. Howe, *No End in Sight: A Case Study of Humanitarian Action and the Syrian Conflict* (Medford: Feinstein International Center, Tufts University, 2015).

K. Howe et al., *The Wages of War: Learning from How Syrians Have Adapted Their Livelihoods Through Seven Years of Conflict*, Mercy Corps (2018), available online at <https://reliefweb.int/sites/reliefweb.int/files/resources/RD_SyriaReport_dl_0118_FINAL-A4-web.pdf> (visited 5 August 2021).

P. Howe, 'Priority Regimes and Famine', in S. Devereux (ed.), *The New Famines: Why Famines Persist in an Era of Globalization* (London: Routledge, 1994).

P. Howe, 'Famine Systems: A New Model for Understanding the Development of Famines', 105 *World Development* (2018) 144–155.

P. Howe and S. Devereux, 'Famine Intensity and Magnitude Scales: A proposal for an instrumental definition of famine', 28 *Disasters* (2004) 353–372.

C. Huang et al., 'Early Life Exposure to the 1959–1961 Chinese Famine Has Long-term Health Consequences', 140 *The Journal of Nutrition* (2010) 1874–1878.

C. Huang et al., 'Malnutrition in Early Life and Adult Mental Health: Evidence from a Natural Experiment', 97 *Social Science & Medicine* (2013) 259–266.

H. E. Hulshoff Pol et al., 'Prenatal Exposure to Famine and Brain Morphology in Schizophrenia', 157 *American Journal of Psychiatry* (2000) 1170–1172.

Human Rights Watch Africa, *Ethiopia: Reckoning under the Law*, 1 December 1994, available online at <https://www.hrw.org/sites/default/files/reports/ethiopia94d.pdf> (visited 30 October 2018).

Human Rights Watch, *'The Power These Men Have Over Us;: Sexual Exploitation and Abuse By African Union Forces in Somalia*, (2014), available online at <https://www.hrw.org/report/2014/09/08/power-these-men-have-over-us/sexual-exploitation-and-abuse-african-union-forces> (visited 5 August 2021).

Human Rights Watch, *If The Dead Could Speak: Mass Deaths and Torture in Syria's Detention Facilities*, December 2015, available online at <https://www.hrw.org/report/2015/12/16/if-dead-could-speak/mass-deaths-and-torture-syrias-detention-facilitiesm> (visited 4 June 2019).

Human Rights Watch, *'They Burned It All,' Destruction of Villages, Killings, and Sexual Violence in Unity State South Sudan*, (2015), available online at <https://www.hrw.org/rep

ort/2015/07/22/they-burned-it-all/destruction-villages-killings-and-sexual-violence-unity-state> (visited 19 September 2019).

Human Rights Watch, *Hiding Behind the Coalition: Failure to Credibly Investigate and Provide Redress for Unlawful Attacks in Yemen*, (2018), available online at <https://www.hrw.org/report/2018/08/24/hiding-behind-coalition/failure-credibly-investigate-and-provide-redress-unlawful> (visited 26 August 2021).

Human Rights Watch, *Syria, events of 2018*, (2019), available online at <https://www.hrw.org/world-report/2019/country-chapters/syria#:~:text=Syrian%2DRussian%20Indiscriminate%20Attacks,-Indiscriminate%20attacks%20on&text=In%20February%2C%20government%20forces%20launched,February%2018%20until%20March%2021> (visited 22 August 2020).

Human Rights Watch, *Yemen: Houthi Landmines Kill Civilians, Block Aid*, 22 April 2019, available online at <https://www.hrw.org/news/2019/04/22/yemen-houthi-landmines-kill-civilians-block-aid> (visited 26 August 2021).

Human Rights Watch, *Rigging the System: Government Policies Co-Opt Aid and Reconstruction Funding in Syria*, 28 June 2019, available online at <https://www.hrw.org/report/2019/06/28/rigging-system/government-policies-co-opt-aid-and-reconstruction-funding-syria#> (visited 29 October 2021) .

Humanitarian Aid Commission, *Humanitarian Situation in Sudan* (Khartoum: Ministry of Humanitarian Affairs, 2009).

Humanitarian Policy and Conflict Research (eds), *Commentary on the Humanitarian Policy and Conflict Research Manual on International Law Applicable to Air and Missile Warfare* (Cambridge: Harvard University, 2010).

Humanitarian Policy Group at the Overseas Development Institute (ODI), *Conflict and Hunger: Breaking A Vicious Cycle*, December 2017, available online at <https://www.permanentrepresentations.nl/latest/news/2017/12/14/release-report-conflict-and-hunger> (visited 11 February 2020).

S. Hutter, *Starvation as a Weapon: Domestic Policies of Deliberate Starvation as a Means to an End under International Law* (Leiden: Brill-Nijhoff International Humanitarian Law Series, 2015).

S. Hutter, 'Starvation in Armed Conflicts—An Analysis Based on the Right to Food', 17 *Journal of International Criminal Justice (JICJ)* (2019) 723–752.

International Commission of Inquiry on Darfur, 'Report of the International Commission of Inquiry on Darfur to the UN Secretary-General', 25 January 2005, available online at <https://www.un.org/ruleoflaw/files/com_inq_darfur.pdf> (visited 22 January 2022).

Independent International Commission of Inquiry on the Syrian Arab Republic, 'Sieges as a Weapon of War: Encircle, Starve, Surrender, Evacuate: Sieges as a Weapon of War', 29 May 2018, available online at <https://www.ohchr.org/Documents/HRBodies/HRCouncil/CoISyria/PolicyPaperSieges_29May2018.pdf> (visited 30 October 2021).

Infrastructure and Cities for Economic Development, *Effects of War on Water Security in Yemen: Stocktaking Study*, June 2019, available online at <http://icedfacility.org/wp-content/uploads/2019/07/190618-Yemen-Stocktaking.pdf> (visited 26 August 2021).

Integrated Food Security Phase Classification, 'Technical Manual Version 2.0: Evidence and Standards for Better Food Security Decisions' (2012), available online at <http://www.fews.net/sites/default/files/uploads/IPC-Manual-2-Interactive.pdf> (visited November 10, 2020).

The Integrated Food Security Phase Classification, Technical Working Group, 'Key IPC Findings: September 2017–March 2017'.

Integrated Food Security Phase Classification, 'South Sudan IPC Full Report for January 2017', available online at <http://www.ipcinfo.org/ipcinfo-website/resources/resources-details/en/c/1151919/> (visited 27 October 2021).

Integrated Food Security Phase Classification, 'Yemen—IPC Acute Food Insecurity Analysis: December 2018–January 2019' (2018), available online at <http://www.ipcinfo.org/fileadmin/user_upload/ipcinfo/docs/IPC_Yemen_AcuteFI_2018Dec2019Jan.pdf> (visited 26 August 2021).

Integrated Food Security Phase Classification (IPC), 'Technical Manual Version 3.0. Evidence and Standards for Better Food Security and Nutrition Decisions', The Integrated Food Security Integrated Food Security Phase Classification (IPC), 'Global Partners (2019)', available online at <http://www.ipcinfo.org/fileadmin/user_upload/ipcinfo/manual/IPC_Technical_Manual_3_Final.pdf> (visited 25 August 2021).

Integrated Food Security Phase Classification, 'Yemen—IPC Acute Food Insecurity Analysis: July–September 2019' (2019), available online at <http://www.ipcinfo.org/fileadmin/user_upload/ipcinfo/docs/IPC_Yemen_AFI_Hotspot%20Analysis_2019JulySept.pdf> (visited 26 August 2021).

Integrated Food Security Phase Classification, 'Yemen—IPC Acute Food Insecurity Analysis: July–December 2020' (2020), available online at <http://www.ipcinfo.org/fileadmin/user_upload/ipcinfo/docs/IPC_Yemen_AcuteFoodInsecurity_2020FebDec_Report_English.pdf> (visited 26 August 2021).

Integrated Food Security Phase Classification, 'Yemen—IPC Acute Malnutrition Analysis: January–December 2020' (2020), available online at <http://www.ipcinfo.org/fileadmin/user_upload/ipcinfo/docs/IPC_Yemen_Acute_Malnutrition_2020JanDec.pdf> (visited 26 August 2021).

Integrated Food Security Phase Classification, 'Yemen—Integrated Food Insecurity Phase Classification Snapshot: October 2020–June 2021' *ReliefWeb*, 3 December 2020, available online at <https://reliefweb.int/sites/reliefweb.int/files/resources/IPC_Yemen_Acute_Food_Insecurity_2020Oct2021June_Snapshot.pdf (visited 26 October 2021).

Integrated Food Insecurity Phase Classification, 'Yemen: Acute Food Insecurity Situation October–December 2020 and Projection for January–June 2021', available online at <http://www.ipcinfo.org/ipc-country-analysis/details-map/en/c/1152947/> (visited 26 August 2021).

Integrated Phase Classification (IPC), 'Ethiopia: Acute Food Insecurity Situation May–June 2021 and Projection for July–September 2021,' June 2021, available online at <http://www.ipcinfo.org/fileadmin/user_upload/ipcinfo/docs/IPC_Ethiopia_Acute_Food_Insecurity_2021MaySept_national.pdf> (visited 6 August 2021).

International Committee of the Red Cross, Commentary of 1858 to Art. 59 GC IV, at 322, available online at <https://ihl-databases.icrc.org/applic/ihl/ihl.nsf/Comment.xsp?action=openDocument&documentId=15B5740DF2203BE4C12563CD0042C966> (visited 18 July 2019).

International Committee of the Red Cross, Customary IHL Study, Rule 5: Definition of Civilians, available online at <https://ihl-databases.icrc.org/customary-ihl/eng/docs/v1_rul_rule5.

International Committee of the Red Cross, *Geneva Convention Relative to the Protection of Civilian Persons in Time of War (Fourth Geneva Convention)*, 12 August 1949, 75 UNTS 287, available online at <https://www.refworld.org/docid/3ae6b36d2.html> (visited 22 October 2021).

International Committee of the Red Cross, *Geneva Convention for the Amelioration of the Condition of the Wounded and Sick in Armed Forces in the Field*, 12 August 1949.

International Committee of the Red Cross, *Geneva Convention for the Amelioration of the Condition of Wounded, Sick and Shipwrecked Members of Armed Forces at Sea*, 12 August 1949.

International Committee of the Red Cross, *Geneva Convention relative to the Treatment of Prisoners of War*, 12 August 1949.

International Committee of the Red Cross, *Protocol Additional to the Geneva Conventions of 12 August 1949, and relating to the Protection of Victims of International Armed Conflicts (Protocol I)*, 8 June 1977, 1125 UNTS 3, available online at <https://www.refworld.org/docid/3ae6b36b4.html> (visited 22 October 2021).

International Committee of the Red Cross, *Protocol Additional to the Geneva Conventions of 12 August 1949, and relating to the Protection of Victims of Non-International Armed Conflicts (Protocol II)*, 8 June 1977, 1125 UNTS 609, available online at <https://www.refworld.org/docid/3ae6b37f40.html> (visited 22 October 2021).

International Committee of the Red Cross, *War Crimes: Working Paper Prepared by the ICRC for the United Nations Preparatory Committee for the Establishment of an International Criminal Court* (1997), available online at <https://www.icrc.org/en/doc/resources/documents/misc/57jngx.htm> (visited 29 September 2021).

International Committee of the Red Cross (ICRC), *Addressing the Needs of Women Affected by Armed Conflict: An ICRC Guidance Document*, March 2004, available online at <https://www.icrc.org/en/doc/assets/files/other/icrc_002_0840_women_guidance.pdf> (visited 5 August 2021).

International Committee of the Red Cross, *Customary IHL Database* (2005), available online at <https://www.icrc.org/en/doc/assets/files/other/customary-international-humanitarian-law-i-icrc-eng.pdf

International Committee of the Red Cross, *South Sudan: ICRC Forced to Withdraw from Leer County Following Threats and Looting*, 5 October 2015, available online at www.icrc.org/en/document/south-sudan-conflict-leer-looting-icrc-forced-withdrawal#:~:text=In%20May%202015%2C%20the%20ICRC,from%20carrying%20out%20its%20activities> (visited 27 October 2021).

International Committee of the Red Cross, *Commentary on the Additional Protocols*, 9 June 2020.

International Rescue Committee, *Gender Analysis Key Findings: Women's Exploitation and Gender-based Violence across Ethiopia's Tigray Crisis*, 4 May 2021, available online at <https://www.rescue.org/sites/default/files/document/5868/irctigraygenderanalysiskeyfindingsmay.pdf> (visited 5 August 2021).

International Criminal Court, Rome Statute, 1998, available online at <https://www.icc-cpi.int/resource-library/documents/rs-eng.pdf> (visited 22 January 2022).

International Crisis Group, *Ending the Yemen Quagmire: Lessons for Washington from Four Years of War*, 2019, available online at <https://www.crisisgroup.org/united-states/003-ending-yemen-quagmire-lessons-washington-four-years-war> (visited 26 August 2021).

International Crisis Group, *How to Halt Yemen's Slide into Famine, Crisis Group Middle East Report No. 193*, 2018, available online at <https://www.crisisgroup.org/middle-east-north-africa/gulf-and-arabian-peninsula/yemen/193-how-halt-yemens-slide-famine> (visited 26 August 2021).

International Crisis Group, *Instruments of Pain (I): Conflict and Famine in Yemen, Crisis Group Middle East Briefing No. 52* (2017), available online at <https://www.crisisgroup.org/middle-east-north-africa/gulf-and-arabian-peninsula/yemen/b052-instruments-pain-i-conflict-and-famine-yemen#:~:text=Instruments%20of%20Pain%3A%20Confl

ict%20and%20Famine,-Print&text=Shortfalls%20are%20not%20the%20only,crises%20 are%20chronically%20underfunded%3B%20and> (visited 26 August 2021).

International Organization for Migration Displacement Tracking Matrix, *Conflict and Displacement Timeline: Bentiu/Unity 2014–2016* (Geneva: International Organization for Migration, 2016).

International Rescue Committee, *Gender Analysis Key Findings: Women's Exploitation & Gender-Based Violence across Ethiopia's Tigray Crisis*, 4 May 2021, available online at <https://www.rescue.org/sites/default/files/document/5868/irctigraygenderanalysiskey findingsmay.pdf> (visited 5 August 2021).

S. Jaspars, *Solidarity and Soup Kitchens: A Review of Principles and Practice for Food Distribution in Conflict*, Humanitarian Policy Group, Report 17, Overseas Development Institute (2000), available online at <https://cdn.odi.org/media/documents/301.pdf> (visited 25 August 2021).

S. Jaspars, *Food Aid in Sudan. A History of Power, Politics and Profit, Politics and Development in Contemporary Africa* (London: Zed Books, 2018).

S. Jaspars, 'A Role for Social Nutrition in Strengthening Accountability for Mass Starvation', Occasional Paper No. 18 (World Peace Foundation, 2019), available online at <https://sites.tufts.edu/wpf/files/2019/09/A-Role-for-Social-Nutrition-Susanne-Jaspers.pdf> (visited 26 August 2021).

S. Jaspars, G. Adan, and N. Majid, *Food and Power in Somalia: Business as Usual? A Scoping Study on the Political Economy of Food Following Shifts in Food Assistance and in Governance*, London School of Economics and Political Science (2020), available online at <https://eprints.lse.ac.uk/103138/7/Food_and_Power_in_Somalia_business_as_usual_v5.pdf> (visited 25 August 2021).

S. Jaspars and D. Maxwell, *Targeting in Complex Emergencies: Somalia Country Case Study*, Feinstein International Center (2008), available online at <https://fic.tufts.edu/publication-item/targeting-in-complex-emergencies-2/> (visited 25 August 2021).

S. Jaspars, T. Scott-Smith, and E. Hull, *Contested Evolution of Nutrition for Humanitarian and Development Ends. Report of an International Workshop*, Refugee Studies Centre Working Paper Series No. 125. (2018), available online at <https://www.rsc.ox.ac.uk/publications/contested-evolution-of-nutrition-for-humanitarian-and-development-ends> (visited 25 August 2021).

S. Jenkins, 'Sanctions are imposed by the sanctimonious, and achieve nothing', *The Guardian*, 28 May 2021, available online at <https://www.theguardian.com/commentisfree/2021/may/27/sanctions-achieve-nothing-belarus-lukashenko> (visited 27 August 2021).

D. H. Johnson, 'Political Ecology in the Upper Nile: The Twentieth Century Expansion of the Pastoral "Common Economy"', 30 *The Journal of African History* (1989) 463–486.

L. Jones, *Societies Under Siege: Exploring How International Economic Sanctions (Do Not) Work* (Oxford: Oxford University Press, 2015).

W. Jordash QC, C. Murdoch, and J. Holmes, 'Strategies for Prosecuting Mass Starvation' 17 *Journal of International Criminal Justice* (2019) 849–879.

E. Josse, '"They Came with Two Guns": The Consequences of Sexual Violence for the Mental Health of Women in Armed Conflict', 877 *International Review of the Red Cross* (2010) 176–195.

T. Juneau, 'Yemen and the Arab Spring', in M. Kamrava (ed.), *Beyond the Arab Spring: The Evolving Ruling Bargain in the Middle East* (New York: Oxford University Press, 2014) 373–396.

M. Kaldor, *New and Old Wars: Organized Violence in a Global Era* (3rd edn., Cambridge: Polity Press, 2012).

W. Kälin and J. Künzli, 'Das Recht auf Nahrung', *Jusletter* 6 January/13 January 2003, Part 1.

S. N. Kalyvas, 'Ethnic Defection in Civil War', 41 *Comparative Political Studies* (2008) 1043–1068.

P. E. Kamper, 'Independent and Additive Association of Prenatal Famine Exposure and Intermediary Life Conditions with Adult Mortality between Age 18–63 Years', 119 *Social Science & Medicine* (2014) 232–239.

M. Kanfash and A. Aljasem, *Accountability for Starvation Crimes: Syria* (Medford: Global Rights Compliance/World Peace Foundation, 2019).

R. Kaplan, *Surrender or Starve: The Wars Behind the Famine* (London: Routledge, 1988).

A. Karim, *OLS Operation Lifeline Sudan. A Review* (New York, UNICEF, 1996).

L. Kassa '"A Tigrayan womb should never give birth": rape in Tigray', *Al Jazeera*, 21 April 2021, available online at <https://www.aljazeera.com/news/2021/4/21/a-tigrayan-womb-should-never-give-birth-rape-in-ethiopia-tigray> (visited 5 August 2021).

C. Kaufmann and M. Grosz, 'Poverty, Hunger and International Trade: What's Law Got to Do with It?', 51 *German Yearbook of International Law* (2008) 75–110.

D. Keen, *The Benefits of Famine: Political Economy of Famine and Relief in Southwestern Sudan, 1983–1989* (Princeton: Princeton University Press, 1994).

M. Kelleher, 'Hunger and History: Monuments to the Great Irish Famine', 16 *Textual Practice* (2002) 249–276.

A. Keys et al., *The Biology of Human Starvation* (2 vols, Minneapolis: University of Minnesota Press, 1950).

M. Khan, 'A Plausible Explanation for Male Dominance in Typhoid Ileal Perforation', 5 *Clinical and Experimental Gastroentology* (2012) 213–217.

A. Kidane, 'Demographic Consequences of the 1984–1985 Ethiopian Famine', 26 *Demography* (1989) 515–522.

B. Kiernan, 'The Demography of Genocide in Southeast Asia: The Death Tolls in Cambodia, 1975–79, and East Timor, 1975–80', 35 *Critical Asian Studies* (2003) 585–597.

B. Kiernan, *Blood and Soil: A World History of Genocide and Extermination from Sparta to Darfur* (New Haven: Yale University Press, 2007).

B. Kiernan, *The Pol Pot Regime: Race, Power and Genocide in Cambodia under the Khmer Rouge, 1975–19* (New Haven: Yale University Press, 2008).

E. Kim et al., 'Cross Border North Korean Women Trafficking and Victimization between North Korea and China: An Ethnographic Case Study', 37 *International Journal of Law, Crime and Justice* (2009) 154–169.

J. J. Kim, E. McCloskey, and P. Hailey, 'Constraints and Complexities of Information and Analysis: Data Planning in Famine Risk Countries—Findings and Recommendations for Food Security Analysis: South Sudan, Somalia, Nigeria, and Yemen', MQSUN Report, March 2018, available online at <https://reliefweb.int/report/south-sudan/constraints-and-complexities-information-and-analysis-data-planning-famine-risk> (visited 26 August 2021).

H. Klavin, 'Who is Forgotten? Memory of the Siege of Leningrad', William & Mary in St. Petersburg, n.d., available online at <http://petersburg.blogs.wm.edu/who-is-forgotten-memory-of-the-siege-of-leningrad-helena-klavin/> (visited 14 December 2020).

P. Knopf et al., *Letter dated 21 August 2015 from the Panel of Experts on South Sudan established pursuant to Security Council resolution 2206 (2015) addressed to the President of the Security Council*, United Nations Security Council, 21 August 2015, available online at <https://reliefweb.int/report/south-sudan/letter-dated-21-august-2015-panel-experts-south-sudan-established-pursuant> (visited 27 October 2021).

M. Kohut and I. Herrera, 'As Venezuela collapses, children are dying of hunger', *The New York Times*, 17 December 2017, available online at <https://www.nytimes.com/interactive/2017/12/17/world/americas/venezuela-children-starving.html> (visited 5 February 2020).

D. Korn, *Ethiopia, the United States, and the Soviet Union* (Illinois: Southern Illinois University Press, 1986).

J. Kraska and S. Power, 'Siege Warfare in Syria: Prosecuting the Starvation of Civilians', 8 *Amsterdam Law Forum* (2016) 1–22.

G. Kumar, *Ethiopian Famines 1973–1985: A Case Study*, Working Paper 26, United Nations University World Institute for Development Economics Research (1987).

N. Kulish, 'New estimate sharply raises death toll in South Sudan', *The New York Times*, 9 January 2014, available online at <https://www.nytimes.com/2014/01/10/world/africa/new-estimate-sharply-raises-death-toll-in-south-sudan.html> (visited 27 October 2021).

H. Lackner, 'The Change Squares of Yemen: Civil Resistance in an Unlikely Context', in A. Roberts et al. (eds), *Civil Resistance in the Arab Spring: Triumphs and Disasters* (Oxford: Oxford University Press, 2016).

H. Lackner, *Yemen in Crisis: The Road to War* (London: Verso, 2019).

H. Lackner, 'Yemen's Hopes and Expectations—Part 3: Living Conditions and Humanitarian Aid', *Open Democracy*, 7 February 2020, available online at <https://www.opendemocracy.net/en/north-africa-west-asia/yemens-hopes-and-expectations-part-3-living-conditions-and-humanitarian-aid/> (visited 26 August 2021).

H. Lackner, 'The Future of Yemeni Agriculture and Water', in A. Al Alim Alsoswa and N. Brehony (eds), *Building a New Yemen: Recovery, Transition and the International Community* (London: Bloomsbury Collection, 2022), 175–190.

M. Landler and P. Baker, 'Trump vetoes measure to force end to U.S. involvement in Yemen war', *The New York Times* (16 April 2019), available online at <https://www.nytimes.com/2019/04/16/us/politics/trump-veto-yemen.html> (visited 27 August 2021).

T. Lang, 'Food Control or Food Democracy? Re-engaging Nutrition with Society and the Environment', 8 (6A) *Public Health Nutrition* (2005) 730–737.

T. Lang, D. Barling, and M. Caraher, 'Nutrition', in T. Lang, D. Barling, and M. Caraher (eds), *Food Policy: Integrating Health, Environment and Society* (Oxford: Oxford University Press, 2009) 101–142.

M. Langford, 'Closing the Gap? An Introduction to the Optional Protocol to the International Covenant on Economic, Social and Cultural Rights', 27 *Nordic Journal of Human Rights* (2009) 1–28, available online at <https://www.jus.uio.no/ior/english/people/aca/malcolml/NTMR109-1.pdf> (visited 28 November 2019).

M. Langford et al., *Global Justice, State Duties: The Extra-Territorial Scope of Economic, Social and Cultural Rights in International Law* (Cambridge: Cambridge University Press, 2013).

M. Lattimer, 'Enforcing Human Rights through International Criminal Law', in M. Lattimer and P. Sands (eds), *Justice for Crimes against Humanity* (Oxford: Hart Publishing, 2003).

A. Lee, 'Jerk, an Authentic Taste of Jamaican Liberty', 69 *History Today* (May 2019) 84–88.

R. S. Lee, *The International Criminal Court: The Making of the Rome Statute: Issues, Negotiations, Results* (Leiden: Brill, 1999).

R. Lemkin, *Axis Rule in Occupied Europe* (Washington, D.C.: Carnegie Endowment for International Peace, 1944).

R. Lemkin, 'Soviet Genocide in Ukraine', in R. Serbyn (ed.), 'Lemkin on the Ukrainian Genocide', 7 *Journal of International Criminal Justice* (1 March 2009) 123–130.

E. Lentz et al., 'A Data-Driven Approach Improves Food Insecurity Crisis Prediction', 122 *World Development* (2019) 399–409.

P. Levi, *If This is a Man and The Truce* (London: Abacus, 1987).

P. Levi, *The Drowned and the Saved* (New York: Simon and Schuster, 2017).

C. Levinson, 'UN Aid Group: Israel deliberately hampering West Bank, Gaza relief efforts', *Haaretz*, 30 May 2010, available online at <https://www.haaretz.com/1.5126675> (visited 18 July 2019).

B. Lindtjørn and T. Alemu, 'Intra-household Correlations of Nutritional Status in Rural Ethiopia', 26 *International Journal of Epidemiology* (1997) 160–165.

M. Livi-Bacci, 'On the Human Costs of Collectivization in the Soviet Union', 19 *Population and Development Review* (1991) 743–766.

D. Lloyd, 'The Indigent Sublime: Specters of Irish Hunger', 92 *Representations* (Fall 2005) 152–158.

H. Locard, *Pol Pot's Little Red Book: The Sayings of Angkar* (Chiang Mai: Silkworm Books, 2005).

A. Longley-Alley, 'The Rules of the Game: Unpacking Patronage Politics in Yemen', 64 *Middle East Journal* (2010) 385–409.

A. Longley-Alley, 'Tracking the "Arab Spring": Yemen Changes Everything ... And Nothing', 24 *Journal of Democracy* (2013) 74–85.

S. C. Lubkemann, 'Involuntary Immobility: On a Theoretical Invisibility in Forced Migration Studies', 21 *Journal of Refugee Studies* (2008) 454–475.

Z. Luo, R. Mu, and X. Zhang, 'Famine and Overweight in China', 28 *Applied Economic Perspectives and Policy* (2006) 296–304.

J. Lyall, 'Are Coethnics More Effective Counterinsurgents? Evidence from the Second Chechen War', 104 *American Political Science Review* (2010) 1–20.

K. Mackintosh and P. Duplat, *Study of the Impact of Donor Counter Terrorism Measures on Principled Humanitarian Action* (OCHA and Norwegian Refugee Council, 2013), available online at <https://www.nrc.no/globalassets/pdf/reports/study-of-the-impact-of-donor-counterterrorism-measures-on-principled-humanitarian-action.pdf> (visited 17 April 2022).

Maastricht Principles on Extraterritorial Obligations of States in the Area of ESCR, 28 September 2011, available online at <https://www.etoconsortium.org/nc/en/main-navigation/library/maastricht-principles/?tx_drblob_pi1%5BdownloadUid%5D=23> (visited 4 February 2020).

B. Mac Suibhne, 'A Jig in the Poorhouse', *Dublin Review of Books* (2013), available online at www.drb.ie/essays/a-jig-in-the-poorhouse> (visited 14 December 2020).

B. Mac Suibhne, *The End of Outrage: Post-Famine Adjustment in Rural Ireland* (Oxford: Oxford University Press, 2017).

S. Maccini and D. Yang, 'Under the Weather: Health, Schooling, and Economic Consequences of Early-life Rainfall', 99 *American Economic Review* (2009) 1006–1026.

K. Macintyre, 'Famine and the Female Mortality Advantage', in T. Dyson and C. Ó Gráda (eds), *Famine Demography: Perspectives from the Past and Present* (Oxford: Oxford University Press, 2002) 240–259.

J. L. Maclean et al. (eds), *Rice Almanac: Source Book for the Most Important Economic Activity on Earth* (3rd edn., Wallingford: CABI Publishing, 2002).

J. Macrae and A. Zwi (eds), *War and Hunger. Rethinking international responses to complex emergencies* (London: Zed Books, 1994).

M. Mamdani, 'AUCISS, Respondent XY to the African Union Commission of Inquiry on South Sudan', African Union Commission of Inquiry on South Sudan, 29 July 2014, available online at <https://www.peaceau.org/uploads/auciss.separate.opinion.pdf> (visited 16 April 2022).

A. Marshak et al., *Tracking Change in Livelihoods, Service Delivery and Governance: Evidence from a 2013–2015 Panel Survey in Uganda*, Working paper 59, Overseas Development Institute, London (2017), available online at <https://securelivelihoods.org/wp-content/uploads/2.-Tracking-change-in-livelihoods-service-delivery-and-governance-panel-survey-in-Uganda-2.pdf> (visited 5 August 2021).

D. Marchese, 'Madeleine Albright thinks it's good when America gets involved', *The New York Times*, 20 April 2020, available online at <https://www.nytimes.com/interactive/2020/04/20/magazine/madeline-albright-interview.html> (visited 27 August 2021).

D. Marcus, 'Famine Crimes in International Law', 97 *The American Journal of International Law* (2003) 245–281.

E. Mark-Fitzgerald, *Commemorating the Irish Famine: Memory and the Monument* (Liverpool: Liverpool University Press, 2013).

P. Martell, 'South Sudan is dying, and nobody is counting', *Agence-France Presse*, 10 March 2016, available online at <https:/sg.news.yahoo.com/south-sudan-dying-nobody-counting-045835128.html> (visited 5 October 2021).

J. C. Martinez and B. Eng, 'The Unintended Consequences of Emergency Food Aid: Neutrality, Sovereignty and Politics in the Syrian Civil War, 2012–15', 92(1) *International Affairs* (2016) 153–173.

L. Matar, *The Political Economy of Investment in Syria*, Studies in Political Economy of Public Policy (Basingstoke: Palgrave Macmillan, 2016).

S. Mawby, 'Workers in the Vanguard: The 1960 Industrial Relations Ordinance and the Struggle for Independence in Aden', 57 *Labor History* (2016) 35–52.

D. Maxwell, *Famine Early Warning and Information Systems in Conflict Settings: Challenges for Humanitarian Metrics and Response*, Occasional Paper (Conflict Research Programme, London School of Economics and Political Science, 2019), available online at <http://eprints.lse.ac.uk/102836/> (visited 26 August 2021).

D. Maxwell and K. H. Gelsdorf, *Understanding the Humanitarian World* (New York: Routledge, 2019).

D. Maxwell and P. Hailey, *The Politics of Information and Analysis in Famines and Extreme Emergencies: Synthesis of Findings from Six Case Studies* (Medford: Feinstein International Center, 2020), available online at <https://fic.tufts.edu/wp-content/uploads/PIA-Synthesis-Report_May-13.pdf> (visited 26 August 2021).

D. Maxwell and S. Lautze, 'Why Do Famines Persist in the Horn of Africa? Ethiopia 1999–2003', in S. Devereux (ed.), *The New Famines: Why Famines Persist in an Age of Globalization* (New York: Routledge, 2007) 222–244.

D. Maxwell and N. Majid, *Famine in Somalia. Competing Imperatives, Collective Failures, 2011–12* (Oxford: Oxford University Press, 2016).

D. Maxwell, M. Santschi, and R. Gordon, *Looking Back to Look Ahead? Reviewing Key Lessons from Operation Lifeline Sudan and Past Humanitarian Operations in South Sudan*, Working Paper 24 (Secure Livelihoods Research Consortium, 2014), available online at <https://securelivelihoods.org/wp-content/uploads/Reviewing-key-lessons-from-Operation-Lifeline-Sudan-and-past-humanitarian-operations-in-South-Sudan.pdf> (visited 9 September 2021).

D. Maxwell et al., *Constraints and Complexities of Information and Analysis in Humanitarian Emergencies: Evidence from South Sudan* (Medford: Feinstein International Center, Tufts University, 2018), available online at <https://fic.tufts.edu/assets/SouthSudan-Case-Study-Report.pdf (22 October 2021).

D. Maxwell et al., *Constraints and Complexities of Information and Analysis in Humanitarian Emergencies: Evidence from Yemen* (Medford: Feinstein International Center, Tufts University, 2019).

D. Maxwell et al., 'Viewpoint: Determining Famine: Multi-dimensional Analysis for the Twenty-first Century', 92 *Food Policy* (2020) 1–13.

D. Mazurana and K. Proctor, 'Gender and Humanitarian Action', in R. Mac Ginty and J. H. Peterson (eds), *Handbook on Humanitarian Action* (London: Routledge, 2014) 49–61.

D. Mazurana et al., *Sex and Age Matter: Improving Humanitarian Response in Emergencies* (New York, OCHA, Care International, Feinstein International Center, 2011).

D. Mazurana et al., *Making Gender Just Remedy and Reparation Possible: Upholding the Rights of Women and Girls in Northern Uganda*, Feinstein International Center and Isis WICCE (2013), available online at <http://reliefweb.int/sites/reliefweb.int/files/resources/Gender-Just-Remedy-and-Reparation-final-June-2013.pdf> (visited 5 August 20 (29 October 2021).

Médecins Sans Frontières, *Yemen, a Country in Crisis*, available online at <https://www.msf.org/yemen-depth> (visited 26 August 2021).

Médecins Sans Frontières, *Yemen: No True Accountability in Bombing of MSF-Supported Hospital*, 30 October 2019, available online at <https://www.doctorswithoutborders.org/what-we-do/news-stories/news/yemen-no-true-accountability-bombing-msf-supported-hospital> (visited 26 August 2021).

X. Meng and N. Qian, *The Long-term Consequences of Famine on Survivors: Evidence from a Unique Natural Experiment using China's Great Famine* (Cambridge, MA, USA: National Bureau of Economic Research, 2009), available online at <https://www.nber.org/system/files/working_papers/w14917/w14917.pdf> (visited 25 August 2021).

Mercy Corps, *Emergency Market Mapping and Analysis (EMMA): Livestock Off-take and Sorghum Market Systems in Leer County, Unity, South Sudan*, January 2015, available online at <https://www.emma-toolkit.org/report/emma-livestock-take-and-sorghum-market-systems> (visited 27 October 2021).

N. Melzer and G. Gaggioli, 'Methods of Warfare', in D. Akande and B. Saul (eds), *Oxford Guide to International Humanitarian Law* (Oxford: Oxford University Press, 2019).

M. Mezgebu, *In Search of Truth*, World Peace Foundation, 8 May 2012, available online at <https://sites.tufts.edu/reinventingpeace/2012/05/08/in-search-of-truth/> (visited 15 July 2019).

V. 'Nagarjun' Mishra, 'Akaal aur Usake Baad (Famine and after it)'tr. Dimitrios Vassiliades (1952), available online at <https://elinepa.org/the-famine-and-after-it/> (visited 14 December 2020).

G. Moloney et al., 'Malnutrition and Mortality—Southern Somalia, July 2011', 60(30) *Morbidity and Mortality Weekly Report* (2011) 1026–1027.

J. Moore, *Humanitarian Law in Action within Africa* (Oxford: Oxford University Press, 2012).

E. Mottershawa, 'Economic, Social and Cultural Rights in Armed Conflict: International Human Rights Law and International Humanitarian Law', 12 *The International Journal of Human Rights* (2008) 449–470.

J. Moyer et al., *Assessing the Impact of War on Development in Yemen*, UNDP and Frederick S. Pardee Center for International Futures, University of Denver (2019), available online at <https://yemen.un.org/sites/default/files/2019-09/Assessing%20the%20Impact%20of%20War%20on%20Development%20in%20Yemen.pdf> (visited 26 August 2021).

R. Mu and X. Zhang, *Gender Difference in the Long-Term Impact of Famine*, International Food Policy Research Institute Discussion Paper #00760 (2008), available online at <http://cdm15738.contentdm.oclc.org/utils/getfile/collection/p15738coll2/id/9449/filename/9450.pdf> (visited 5 August 2021).

R. Mu and X. B. Zhang, 'Why Does the Great Chinese Famine Affect the Male and Female Survivors Differently?: Mortality Selection Versus Son Preference', 9 *Economics and Human Biology* (2011) 92–105.

E. Muchomba and B. Sharp, *Southern Sudan Livelihood Profiles*, Southern Sudan Commission for Census, Statistics and Evaluation/Livelihoods Analysis Forum (2006), available online at <http://www.sudanarchive.net> (visited 27 October 2021).

H. Mueller, 'Fragility in the Data', background paper for P. Collier, T. Besley, and A. Khan (eds), *Escaping the Fragility Trap*, Commission on State Fragility, Growth and Development, London School of Economics and University of Oxford's Blavatnik School of Government (2018).

N. Mulder and B. van Dijk, 'Why Did Starvation Not Become the Paradigmatic War Crime in International Law?', in K. J. Heller and I. Venzke (eds), *Contingency and the Course of International Law* (Oxford: Oxford University Press, 2021) 370–388.

A. Müller, *The Relationship between Economic, Social and Cultural Rights and International Humanitarian Law, An Analysis of Health-Related Issues in Non-International Armed Conflicts* (Leiden: Martinus Nijhoff Publishers, 2013).

M. Mundy, 'The Strategies of the Coalition in the Yemen War: Aerial Bombardment and Food War' (2018), available online at <https://sites.tufts.edu/wpf/files/2018/10/Strategies-of-Coalition-in-Yemen-War-Final-20181005-1.pdf> (visited 26 August 2021).

M. Mundy, *The Strategies of the Coalition in the Yemen War: Aerial Bombardment and Food War*, World Peace Foundation, available online at <https://reliefweb.int/sites/reliefweb.int/files/resources/Strategies%20of%20Coalition%20in%20Yemen%20War.pdf> (visited 19 September 2019).

M. Mundy and F. Pelat, 'The Political Economy of Agriculture and Agricultural Policy in Yemen', in N. Brehony and S. Al-Sarhan (eds), *Rebuilding Yemen: Political, Economic and Social Challenges* (Berlin: Gerlach Press, 2015) 98–122.

M. Mundy, A. Al-Hakimi, and F. Pelat, 'Neither Security nor Sovereignty: The Political Economy of Food in Yemen', in Z. Babar and S. Mirgani (eds), *Food Security in the Middle East* (New York: Oxford University Press, 2014) 136–158.

H. Murdock, 'Hundreds of women, girls brutalized by soldiers in Tigray war', *Voice of America* (7 July 2021), available online at <https://www.voanews.com/ethiopia-tigray/hundreds-women-girls-brutalized-soldiers-tigray-war-0> (visited 5 August 2021).

K. A. S. Murshid, *Food Security in an Asian Transitional Economy: The Cambodian Experience*, UNRISD, Working Paper 6 (1998), available online at <https://www.unrisd.org/unrisd/website/document.nsf/(<httpPublications)/06D24C68979175DF80256B67005B708D?OpenDocument> (visited 20 November 2020).

Mwatana for Human Rights, *Made in Italy, Bombed in Yemen*, 27 October 2020, available online at <https://mwatana.org/en/made-in-italy-bombed-in-yemen/> (visited 26 August 2021).

H. J. Nesbitt (ed.), *Rice Production in Cambodia* (Manila: International Rice Research Institute, 1997).

R. Neugebauer, H. W. Hoek, and E. Susser, 'Prenatal Exposure to Wartime Famine and Development of Antisocial Personality Disorder in Early Adulthood', 281 *Journal of the American Medical Association* (1999) 455–462.

E. Neumayer and T. Plumper, 'The Unequal Burden of War: The Effect of Armed Conflict on the Gender Gap in Life Expectancy', 60 *International Organization* (2006) 723–754.

Editorial Board, 'The well-fed dead in Bosnia', *New York Times*, 15 July 1992, available online at <https://www.nytimes.com/1992/07/15/opinion/the-well-fed-dead-in-bosnia.html> (visited 25 August 2021).

A. Newby, 'Finland's "Great Hunger Years" Memorials', available online at <https://katovuodet1860.wordpress.com/about/> (visited 14 December 2020).

C. Newton, 'Pandemic of Hunger Symposium: Famine in a NIAC's shadow—other situations of violence and a challenge for UNSCR 2417', Opinio Juris, 20 May 2021, available online at <http://opiniojuris.org/2021/05/20/pandemic-of-hunger-symposium-famine-in-a-niacs-shadow-other-situations-of-violence-and-a-challenge-for-unscr-2417/> (visited 5 August 2021).

C. Newton and K. Rickard, *Living Memory of Famine in South Sudan: Using Local Knowledge to Inform Famine Early Warning*, Humanitarian Practice Network of Overseas Development Institute, 10 October 2018, available online at odihpn.org/blog/living-memory-famine-south-sudan-using-local-knowledge-inform-famine-early-warning/> (visited 27 October 2021).

M. Nijs, 'Humanizing Siege: Applying the Principle of Proportionately to Sieges', 102 *International Review of the Red Cross* (2020) 683–704.

N. Nisbett, 'Understanding the Nourishment of Bodies at the Centre of Food and Health Systems—Systemic, Bodily and New Materialist Perspectives on Nutritional Inequity', 228 *Social Science and Medicine* (2019) 9–16.

A. Nolan, 'Budget Analysis and Economic and Social Rights', in E. Riedel, G. Giacca, and C. Golay (eds), *Economic, Social, and Cultural Rights in International Law: Contemporary Issues and Challenges* (Oxford: Oxford University Press, 2014).

A. Nolan and E. Schmid, 'Do No Harm'?: Exploring the Scope of Economic and Social Rights in Transitional Justice, 8 *International Journal of Transitional Justice* (2014) 362–382.

Norwegian Refugee Council, *Briefing on Protecting Civilians Affected by Conflict-induced Hunger*, 21 April 2020, available online at <https://www.nrc.no/resources/briefing-notes/briefing-on-protecting-civilians-affected-by-conflict-induced-hunger/> (visited 1 October 2021).

Norwegian Refugee Council et al., *Syria Crisis: Hunger Spreading amid Covid and Economic Collapse*, 29 June 2020, available online at <https://reliefweb.int/report/syrian-arab-republic/syria-crisis-hunger-spreading-amid-covid-and-economic-collapse> (visited 22 August 2020).

Norwegian Refugee Council, *Yemen: 900 Airstrike and Shelling Hits on Farms in Three Years*, 24 September 2020, available online at <https://www.nrc.no/news/2020/september/yemen-900-airstrike-and-shelling-hits-on-farms-in-three-years/> (visited 26 August 2021).

C. Ó Gráda, *Famine: A Short History* (Princeton: Princeton University Press, 2009).

P. O'Neill and D. Lloyd (eds), *The Black and Green Atlantic: Cross-Currents of the African and Irish Diasporas* (London: Palgrave Macmillan, 2009).

M. O'Sullivan, *Shrewd Sanctions* (Washington, DC: Brookings Institution, 2003).

N. Obaid, *A Saudi Arabian Defense Doctrine: Mapping the Expanded Force Structure the Kingdom Needs to Lead the Arab World, Stabilize The Region, and Meet Its Global Responsibilities* (Belfer Center for Science and International Affairs, Harvard Kennedy School, 2014), available online at <https://www.belfercenter.org/sites/default/files/legacy/files/Saudi%20Strategic%20Doctrine%20-%20web.pdf> (visited 26 August 2021).

O. Obasanjo et al., *Final Report of the African Union Commission of Inquiry on South Sudan*, African Union, 15 October 2014, available online at <https://www.peaceau.org/en/article/final-report-of-the-african-union-commission-of-inquiry-on-south-sudan> (visited 27 October 2021).

Organization for Economic Cooperation and Development, *States of Fragility Framework* (2018), available online at <http://www.oecd.org/dac/conflict-fragility-resilience/statesoffragilityframework2018.htm> (visited 24 November 2020).

C. Ormhaug, P. Meier, and H. Hernes, *Armed Conflict Deaths Disaggregated by Gender*, International Peace Research Institute (23 November 2009), available online <https://www.files.ethz.ch/isn/109997/Armed%20Conflict%20Deaths%20Disaggregated%20by%20Gender.pdf> (visited 5 August 2021).

A. Osborn and P. Stewart, 'Russia begins Syria air strikes in its biggest Mideast intervention in decades', *Reuters*, 30 September 2015, available online at <https://www.reuters.com/article/us-mideast-crisis-russia/russia-begins-syria-air-strikes-in-its-biggest-mideast-intervention-in-decades-idUSKCN0RU0MG20150930> (visited 19 September 2020).

O. Oshin, 'Ethiopians protest US sanctions over atrocities in Tigray', *The Hill*, 30 May 2021, available online at <https://thehill.com/policy/international/middle-east-north-africa/556161-ethiopians-protest-us-sanctions-over-atrocities> (visited 27 August 2021).

T. Owen and B. Kiernan, 'Bombs over Cambodia', *The Walrus* (2006).

Oxfam International Press Release, *Remittances to Yemen Plummet as Needs Surge Amid War and Coronavirus*, 1 June 2020, available online at <https://www.oxfam.org/en/press-releases/remittances-yemen-plummet-needs-surge-amid-war-and-coronavirus> (visited 26 August 2021).

Oxfam International Press Release, 'Yemen: Hodeidah cannot be allowed to become a graveyard', 4 July 2018, available online at <https://www.oxfam.org/en/press-releases/yemen-hodeidah-cannot-be-allowed-become-graveyard> (visited 26 August 2021).

A. Pacey and P. Payne, *Agricultural Development and Nutrition* (London: Hutchinson & Co., 1985).

R. Pankhurst, 'The Ethiopian Famine: Cultural Survival's New Report', 2(3) *Anthropology Today* (1986) 4–5.

S. Pantuliano and I. Mosel, *The Long Road Home: Opportunities and Obstacles to the Reintegration of IDPs and Refugees Returning to Southern Sudan and the Three Areas*, Humanitarian Policy Group (2008).

I. Park, *The Right to Life in Armed Conflict* (Oxford: Oxford University Press, 2018).

R. Patel et al., 'Cook, Eat, Man, Woman: Understanding the New Alliance for Food Security and Nutrition, Nutritionism and its Alternatives from Malawi', 42(1) *The Journal of Peasant Studies* (2015) 21–44.

E. Patrick, 'Sexual Violence and Firewood Collection in Darfur', 27 *Forced Migration Review* (2007) 40–41.

PAX Siege Watch, *Out of Sight, Out of Mind: The Aftermath of Syria's Siege*, 6 March 2019, available online at <https://www.paxforpeace.nl/publications/all-publications/siege-watch-final-report> (visited 17 December 2020).

J. Pedneault, *Starving under the Bullets in South Sudan*, Human Rights Watch, April 2017, available online at <https://www.hrw.org/news/2017/04/11/starving-under-bullets-south-sudan#> (visited 27 August 2021).

D. Pelletier and U. Jonnson, 'The Use of Information in the Iringa Nutrition Programme: Some Global Lessons for Nutrition Surveillance', 19 *Food Policy* (1994) 301–313.

J. Pejic, 'The Right to Food in Situations of Armed Conflict: The Legal Framework', 83(844) *International Review of the Red Cross* (2001) 1097–1109.

E. Peralta, 'NPR reporter recounts detention in South Sudan', *National Public Radio*, 16 June 2017, available online at <https://www.npr.org/2017/06/16/533176641/npr-reporter-recounts-detention-in-south-sudan> (visited 27 August 2021).

S. Phillips, *Yemen and the Politics of Permanent Crisis* (Oxford: Routledge, 2011).

Physicians Across Continents—Turkey, *Nutrition SMART Survey Report: Eastern Ghouta*, November 2017, available online at <https://www.humanitarianresponse.info/sites/

www.humanitarianresponse.info/files/documents/files/smart_survey_eastern_ghouta_november_2017_final_.pdf> (visited 21 May 2019).

N. Piacente, 'Importance of the Joint Criminal Enterprise Doctrine for the ICTY Prosecutorial Policy', 2 *Journal of International Criminal Justice* (2004) 446–454.

C. Pilloud et al., *Commentary on The Additional Protocols of 8 June 1977 to the Geneva Conventions of 12 August 1949* (Geneva: International Committee of the Red Cross, 1987).

N. Tut Pur, *A Glimmer of Hope for South Sudan's Victims*, Human Rights Watch (2021), available online at <https://www.hrw.org/news/2021/01/31/glimmer-hope-south-sudans-victims> (visited 9 September 2021).

C. Pinaud, 'Genocidal Rape in South Sudan: Organization, Function, and Effects', 42 *Human Rights Quarterly* (2020) 667–694.

C. Pinaud, *War and Genocide in South Sudan* (Ithaca: Cornell University Press, 2021).

P. G. Pinto, 'God and Nation: The Politics of Islam under Bashar al-Asad', in R. Hinnebusch and R. Zintl (eds), *Syria from Reform to Revolt, Vol. 1: Political Economy and International Relations* (Syracuse: Syracuse University Press, 2015) 154–175.

K. J. Pitkänen, 'Famine Mortality in 19th Century Finland: Is There a Sex Bias?', in T. Dyson and C. Ó Gráda (eds), *Famine Demography: Perspectives from the Past and Present* (Oxford: Oxford University Press, 2002) 240–259.

K. J. Pitkänen and J. H. Mielke, 'Age and Sex Differentials in Mortality during Two Nineteenth Century Population Crises', 9 *European Journal of Population/Revue Européenne de Démographie* (1993) 1–32.

A. Pitzer, *One Long Night: A Global History of Concentration Camps* (Boston: Little, Brown and Company, 2017).

Plan International, *Adolescent Girls in Crisis: Voices from the Lake Chad Basin* (2018), available online at <https://plan-international.org/publications/adolescent-girls-crisis-lake-chad-basin> (visited 24 August 2021).

B. Porter, 'The Reasonableness of Article 8(4)—Adjudicating Claims from the Margins', 27 *Nordic Journal of Human Rights* (2009) 39-53.

S. Power, 'Starvation by Siege: Applying the Law of Armed Conflict in Syria', 8(2) *Amsterdam Law Forum* (2016) 1–22.

S. Prato and N. Bullard, 'Editorial: Re-embedding Nutrition in Society, Nature and Politics', 57(2) *Development* (2014) 129–134.

S. H. Preston, M. E. Hill, and G. L. Drevenstedt, 'Childhood Conditions that Predict Survival to Advanced Ages Among African-Americans', 47 *Social Science and Medicine* (1998) 1231–1246.

R. Provost, 'Starvation as a Weapon: Legal Implications of the United Nations Food Blockade Against Iraq and Kuwait', 30 *Columbia Journal of Transnational Law* (1992) 577–639.

M. Rageh, A. Nasser, and F. Al-Muslimi, 'Yemen without a Functioning Central Bank: The Loss of Basic Economic Stabilization and Accelerating Famine', *Open Democracy*, 22 November 2016, available online at <https://www.opendemocracy.net/en/north-africa-west-asia/yemen-without-functioning-central-bank-los/> (visited 26 August 2021).

S. Ramet, *The Three Yugoslavias: State-Building and Legitimation, 1918–2005* (Bloomington: Indiana University Press, 2006).

N. Rancourt, *Gender and Vulnerability to Cholera in Sierra Leone*, Oxfam Research Report (June 2013), available online at <https://oxfamilibrary.openrepository.com/bitstream/handle/10546/293965/rr-gender-cholera-vulnerability-sierra-leone-170613-en.pdf;jsessionid=6107C555D6E3D17CBE7C56EA7230D9BE?sequence=4> (visited 5 August 2021).

A. C. J. Ravelli et al., 'Obesity at the Age of 50 in Men and Women Exposed to Famine Prenatally', 70 *American Journal of Clinical Nutrition* (1999) 811–816.

A. Raven-Roberts, 'Women and the Political Economy of War', in C. Cohn (ed.), *Women and Wars: Contested Histories, Uncertain Futures* (Cambridge: Polity Press, 2013) 36–53.

A. Razzaque, 'The Effect of Famine on Fertility in a Rural Area of Bangladesh', 20 *Journal of Biosocial Science* (1988) 287–294.

REACH Initiative, *Now the Forest Is Blocked: Shocks and Access to Food—South Sudan*, April 2018, available online at reliefweb.int/report/south-sudan/now-forest-blocked-shocks-and-access-food> (visited 27 October 2021).

Regulations concerning the Laws and Customs of War on Land (The Hague, 18 October 1907), available online at <https://ihl-databases.icrc.org/ihl/INTRO/195> (visited 4 October 2019).

Report of the General Secretariat of the Organization of American States (OAS) and the Panel of Independent International Exerts on the Possible Commission of Crimes against Humanity in Venezuela, 29 May 2018.

Report of the Working Group on Amendments, Annex IV Non-paper submitted by Switzerland: proposed amendments to article 8 of the Rome Statute on the inclusion of starvation as a war crime in non-international armed conflicts, ICC-ASP/17/3520, 29 November 2018.

Research and Documentation Center Sarajevo, *Human Losses in Bosnia and Herzegovina 1991–1995* (2008).

B. Riedel, 'Saudi Arabia's Role in the Yemen Crisis', in S. W. Day and N. Brehony (eds), *Global, Regional, and Local Dynamics in the Yemen Crisis* (London: Palgrave Macmillan, 2020) 115–130.

J. Rivers et al., 'Lessons for Epidemiology from the Ethiopian Famines', 56(4–5) *Annales Societe Beige de Medecine Tropicale* (1976) 345–360.

J. P. Rivers, 'Women and Children Last: Essay on Sex Discrimination in Disasters', 6 *Disasters* (1982) 259–263.

J. P. Rivers, 'The Nutritional Biology of Famine', in G. A. Harrison (ed.), *Famine* (Oxford: Oxford University Press, 1988) 57–106.

M. Robinson, *A Voice for Somalia* (Dublin: O'Brien Press, 1993).

M. Robinson, 'Preface', *Draft Guidelines: A Human Rights Approach to Poverty Reduction Strategies*, UN Office of the High Commissioner for Human Rights, 10 September 2002, available online at <https://www.refworld.org/pdfid/3f8298544.pdf> (visited 27 October 2021).

W. C. Robinson et al., 'Famine, Mortality, and Migration: A Study of North Korean Migrants in China', in H. Reed and C. Keely (eds), *Forced Migration & Mortality* (Washington, DC: National Academies Press, 2001) 69–85.

J. Rogin, 'The United States won't feed 30,000 starving Syrians living under its protection', *The Washington Post*, 24 July 2019, available online at <https://www.washingtonpost.com/opinions/2019/07/24/united-states-wont-feed-starving-syrians-living-under-its-protection/#click=<https://t.co/gdUTSWX8gI> (visited 22 August 2020).

E. Rosenblad, 'Starvation as a Method of Warfare, Conditions for regulation by Convention', 7 *International Lawyer* (1973) 252–270.

K. Roth and B. Jeannerod, *France Should Stop Fueling Saudi War Crimes in Yemen*, Human Rights Watch, 17 May 2019, available online at <https://www.hrw.org/news/2019/05/17/france-should-stop-fueling-saudi-war-crimes-yemen> (visited 26 august 2021).

R. Rubio (ed.), *The Gender of Reparations: Unsettling Gender Hierarchies while Addressing Human Rights Violations* (Cambridge: Cambridge University Press, 2009).

M. Ruel and H. Alderman, 'Nutrition-sensitive Interventions and Programmes: How Can They Help to Accelerate Progress in Improving Maternal and Child Nutrition?', 382 *Lancet* (2013) 536–551.

K. Ryan et al., *Letter dated 13 April 2017 from the Panel of Experts on South Sudan established pursuant to Security Council resolution 2206 (2015) addressed to the President of the Security Council*, United Nations Security Council, 13 April 2017, available online at <https://reliefweb.int/report/south-sudan/letter-dated-13-april-2017-panel-experts-south-sudan-established-pursuant> (visited 27 October 2021).

J. Ryle and M. Amuom, *Peace Is the Name of Our Cattle-Camp*, Rift Valley Institute (2018), available online at <http://riftvalley.net/publication/peace-name-our-cattle-camp#:%7E:text=Following%20the%202005%20Comprehensive%20Peace,and%20cycles%20of%20revenge%20killing> (visited 27 October 2021).

P. Salama et al., 'Famine in Somalia: Evidence for a Declaration', 1 *Global Food Security* (2012) 13–19.

C. Salamandra and L. Stenberg, 'A Legacy of Raised Expectations', in C. Salamandra and L. Stenberg (eds), *Syria from Reform to Revolt, Vol. 2: Culture, Society and Religion* (Syracuse: Syracuse University Press, 2015) 1–15.

P. Salisbury, 'Corruption in Yemen: Maintaining the Status Quo?', in N. Brehony and S. Al-Sarhan (eds), *Rebuilding Yemen: Political, Economic and Social Challenges* (Berlin: Gerlach Press, 2015) 61–77.

P. Salisbury, *Yemen: Stemming the Rise of a Chaos State*, Middle East and North Africa Programme Research Paper (Chatham House, 2016), available online at <https://www.chathamhouse.org/sites/default/files/publications/research/2016-05-25-yemen-stemming-rise-of-chaos-state-salisbury.pdf> (visited 26 August 2021).

P. Salisbury, *Yemen: National Chaos, Local Order*, Chatham House Research Paper, December 2017, available online at <https://www.chathamhouse.org/2017/12/yemen-national-chaos-local-order> (visited 26 August 2021).

L. Sami, 'Gender Differentials in Famine Mortality: Madras (1876–78) and Punjab (1896–97)', 37 *Economic and Political Weekly* (2002) 2593–2600.

Sana'a Center for Strategic Studies, 'Corruption in Yemen's War Economy', *Policy Brief: Rethinking Yemen's Economy*, 5 November 2018, available online at <http://sanaacenter.org/files/Rethinking_Yemens_Economy_policy_brief_9.pdf> (visited 26 August 2021).

Sana'a Center for Strategic Studies, *The Yemen Review: Starvation, Diplomacy, and Ruthless Friends*' (2018), available online at <http://sanaacenter.org/files/TYR_Annual_2018_en.pdf> (visited 26 August 2021).

Sana'a Center for Strategic Studies, *The Yemen Review: August 2018* (2018), available online at <https://sanaacenter.org/publications/the-yemen-review/6394> (visited 26 August 2021).

Sana'a Center for Strategic Studies, *The Yemen Review: War's Elusive End* (2019), available online at <https://sanaacenter.org/files/TYR_Annual_2019_en.pdf> (visited 26 August 2021).

Sana'a Center for Strategic Studies, Economic Unit, *Yemen Economic Bulletin: Another Stage-Managed Fuel Crisis*, July 2020, available online at <https://sanaacenter.org/files/Another_Stage_Managed_Fuel_Crisis_en.pdf> (visited 26 August 2021).

Sana'a Center for Strategic Studies, *Yemen Review: Battle for Marib*, September 2020, available online at <https://sanaacenter.org/files/TYR_September_2020_en.pdf> (visited 26 August 2021).

Sana'a Center for Strategic Studies, *Yemen's Accelerating Economic Woes During the Covid-19 Pandemic*, Policy Brief Rethinking Yemen's Economy, October 2020, available online at <https://sanaacenter.org/files/Rethinking_Yemens_Economy_No7_En.pdf> (visited 26 August 2021).

Y. Sandoz, C. Swinarski, and B. Zimmermann (eds), *Commentary on the Additional Protocols of 8 June 1977 to the Geneva Conventions of 12 August 1949* (Leiden: Martinus Nijhoff Publishers, 1987).

C. Sathyamala, *Nutrition: contested meanings. A theoretical and empirical enquiry* (PhD thesis on file at Erasmus University, Rotterdam, 2016).

C. Sathyamala, 'Nutritionalizing Food: A Framework for Capital Accumulation', 47(4) *Development and Change* (2016) 818–839.

C. Sathyamala, 'Assessment: Global Nutrition Report: Towards a Global Governance in Nutrition', 48(5) *Development and Change* (2017) 1227–1242.

N. Sarkar, *A Matter of Conscience: Artists Bear Witness to the Great Bengal Famine of 1943* (Calcutta: Punascha, 1998).

Save the Children, *Hidden Hunger in Syria: A look at malnutrition across Syria with a focus on under-twos*, September 2020, available online at <https://resourcecentre.savethechildren.net/node/18284/pdf/hidden_hunger_in_syria-cc-2020.pdf> (visited 22 August 2020).

Save the Children, *Six Months on: Almost 5,000 Children Separated from Parents by Conflict in Tigray*, 4 May 2021, available online at <https://reliefweb.int/report/ethiopia/six-months-almost-5000-children-separated-parents-conflict-tigray> (visited 5 August 2021).

Saydanaya Prison during the Syrian Revolution: Testimonies (in Arabic), full text available online at <https://bit.ly/326xh3n> (visited 25 August 2021).

W. Schabas, *Genocide in International Law: The Crime of Crimes* (2nd edn., Cambridge: Cambridge University Press, 2009).

W. Schabas, *The International Criminal Court: A Commentary to the Rome Statute* (2nd edn., Oxford: Oxford University Press, 2010).

D. J. Scheffer, 'Genocide and Atrocity Crimes', 1 *Genocide Studies and Prevention* (2006) 229–250.

B. Scheller, *The Wisdom of Syria's Waiting Game. Foreign Policy under the Assads* (London: Hurst & Company, 2013) 121–149.

P. Schouten, 'Roadblock Politics in Central Africa', *Environment and Planning D: Society and Space* (2019) 1–18.

L. Schubert et al., 'Re-imagining the "Social" in the Nutrition Sciences', 15(2) *Public Health Nutrition* (2011) 352–359.

T. Scott-Smith, *On an Empty Stomach: Two Hundred Years of Hunger Relief* (Ithaca: Cornell University Press, 2020).

A. Seal and R. Bailey, 'The 2011 Famine in Somalia: Lesson Learnt from a Failed Response?', 7(22) *Conflict and Health* (2013) 1–5.

Security Council Report, 'In Hindsight: The Story of the UN Verification and Inspection Mechanism in Yemen', *Monthly Forecast*, 1 September 2016, available online at <https://www.securitycouncilreport.org/monthly-forecast/2016-09/the_story_of_the_un_verification_and_inspection_mechanism_in_yemen.php?pri%E2%80%A6> (visited 26 August 2021).

Security Council Report, 'What's in Blue: South Sudan Consultations', 9 August 2018, available online at <https://www.securitycouncilreport.org/whatsinblue/2018/08/south-sudan-consultations-10.php> (visited 5 August 2021).

Security Council Report, 'What's in Blue: Yemen: Briefing on the Humanitarian Crisis', 22 October 2018, available online at <https://www.securitycouncilreport.org/whatsinblue/2018/10/yemen-briefing-on-the-humanitarian-crisis.php> (visited 5 August 2021).

Security Council Report, 'What's in Blue: Videoconference on Conflict-induced Hunger', 16 September 2020, available online at <https://www.securitycouncilreport.org/whatsinblue/2020/09/videoconference-on-conflict-induced-hunger.php> (visited 5 August 2021).

Security Council Report, 'What's in Blue: Ethiopia (Tigray): Informal Interactive Dialogue on the Humanitarian Situation', 14 June 2021, available online at <https://www.securitycouncilreport.org/whatsinblue/2021/06/ethiopia-tigray-informal-interactive-dialogue-on-the-humanitarian-situation.php> (visited 5 August 2021).

A. Sen, *Poverty and Famines: An Essay on Entitlement and Deprivation* (Oxford: Clarendon Press, 1981).

A. Sen, *Gender and Cooperative Conflicts*, World Institute for Development Economics Research Working Papers (July 1987), available online at <https://www.wider.unu.edu/sites/default/files/WP18.pdf> (visited 5 August 2021).

A. Sen, *Development as Freedom* (New York: Random House, 1999).

The Sentinel Project, *Early Warning System*, available online at <https://thesentinelproject.org/what-we-do/early-warning-system/> (visited 24 November 2020).

M. Sepulveda, *The Nature of the Obligations under the International Covenant on Economic, Social and Cultural Rights* (Cambridge: Intersentia, 2003).

E. Schmid, 'War Crimes Related to Violations of Economic, Social and Cultural Rights', 71 *Heidelberg Journal of International Law* (2011) 523–540.

E. Schmid, *Taking Economic, Social and Cultural Rights Seriously in International Criminal Law* (Cambridge: Cambridge University Press, 2015).

M. Schomerus and T. Allen, *Southern Sudan at Odds with Itself: Dynamics of Conflict and Predicaments of Peace* (London: DESTIN Development Institute, 2010).

K. Shaheen, 'Hundreds leave besieged east Aleppo on first day of evacuation', *The Guardian*, 15 September 2016, available online at <https://www.theguardian.com/world/2016/dec/15/syria-ambulances-on-the-move-as-aleppo-evacuation-operation-begins> (visited 2 January 2020).

B. Sharp, 'Food Aid and Development in Southern Sudan: Implications of the Comprehensive Peace Agreement for Response Planning', 31 *Disasters* (2007) S104–S1223.

X. Shi, 'Famine, Fertility, and Fortune in China', 22 *China Economic Review* (2011) 244–259.

B. A. Simmons, 'Should States Ratify? Process and Consequences of the Optional Protocol to the ICESCR', 27 *Nordic Journal of Human Rights* (2009) 64–81, available online at <https://www.jus.uio.no/ior/english/people/aca/malcolml/NTMR109-1.pdf> (visited 28 November 2019).

M. Simpson, 'If This Is a Man', *The Atlantic* (June 2007), available online at <https://www.theatlantic.com/magazine/archive/2007/06/if-this-is-a-man/305897/> (visited 14 December 2020).

O. Skoog, 'Swedish Statement at the UN Security Council Briefing on Yemen', Swedish Ministry of Foreign Affairs, 23 October 2018, available online at <https://www.government.se/statements/2018/10/swedish-statement-at-the-un-security-council-briefing-on-yemen/> (visited 5 August 2021).

E. Skrgic Mikulic, '600 Wartime Detention Sites Identified in Bosnia', *Balkan Investigative Reporting Network*, 13 December 2016, available online at <https://balkaninsight.com/2016/12/13/600-wartime-detention-sites-identified-in-ex-yugoslavia-12-13-2016/> (visited 25 August 2021).

H. Slim, *Killing Civilians: Method, Madness and Morality in War* (New York: Columbia University Press, 2008).

South Sudan Protection Cluster, *Protection Situation Update: Southern and Central Unity (April–September 2015)* (2015), available online at <https://reliefweb.int/report/south-sudan/protection-situation-update-southern-and-central-unity-april-september-2015> (visited 27 October 2021).

South Sudan Protection Cluster, *Protection Situation Update: Leer County, Southern Unity (October–December 2015)* (2015), available online at <https://reliefweb.int/report/

south-sudan/protection-situation-update-leer-county-southern-unity-october-december-2015> (visited 27 October 2021).

South Sudan Protection Cluster, *Protection Situation Update: Leer County, Southern Unity State (May 2016)* (2016), available online at <https://reliefweb.int/report/south-sudan/protection-situation-update-leer-county-southern-unity-state-may-2016> (visited 27 October 2021).

I. R. Smith and A. Stucki, 'The Colonial Development of Concentration Camps (1868–1902)', 39 *The Journal of Imperial and Commonwealth History* (2011) 417–437.

S. G. Song, W. Wang, and P. F. Hu, 'Famine, Death, and Madness: Schizophrenia In Early Adulthood after Prenatal Exposure to the Chinese Great Leap Forward Famine', 68 *Social Science and Medicine* (2009) 1315–1321.

B. J. Spatz, *Sanctions in the Political Market*, Conflict Research Programme, London School of Economics and Political Science, 26 November 2019, available online at <https://www.lse.ac.uk/ideas/Assets/Documents/Conflict-Research-Programme/crp-memos/Sanctions-Memo-261119.pdf> (visited 27 August 2021).

B. J. Spatz, 'Cash Violence: Sanctions and the Politics of Power, and Peace' (PhD Thesis on file at the Fletcher School, Tufts University, Medford, MA, 2020).

K. Spears, B. Conley, and D. Mazurana, 'Is there a female mortality advantage in famine?', World Peace Foundation and the Feinstein International Center (2021), available online at <https://sites.tufts.edu/wpf/new-occasional-paper-gender-famine-and-mortality/> (visited 27 January 2022).

J. Speakman, 'Sex- and Age-related Mortality Profiles during Famine: Testing the "Body Fat" Hypothesis', 45 *Journal of Biosocial Medicine* (2013) 823–840.

M. Ssenyonjo, *Economic, Social and Cultural Rights in International Law* (Oxford: Hart Publishing, 2016).

D. St Clair et al., 'Rates of Adult Schizophrenia Following Prenatal Exposure to the Chinese Famine of 1959–1961', 294 *Journal of the American Medical Association* (2005) 557–562.

P. Staniland, 'Between a Rock and a Hard Place: Insurgent Fratricide, Ethnic Defection, and the Rise of Pro-State Paramilitaries', 56 *Journal of Conflict Resolution* (2012) 16–40.

A. Stoddard et al., *Aid Worker Security Report 2020*, Humanitarian Outcomes, August 2020, available online at <https://www.humanitarianoutcomes.org/AWSR2020> (visited 22 August 2020).

S. Straus, *Making and Unmaking Nations: War, Leadership, and Genocide in Modern Africa* (Ithaca: Cornell University Press, 2015).

A. Street, 'Food as Pharma: Marketing Nutraceuticals to India's Rural Poor', 25(3) *Critical Public Health* (2015) 361–372.

D. Sullivan, *Displaced Nations: The Dangerous Implications of Rushed Returns in South Sudan*, Refugees International, 29 November 2018, available online at <https://www.refugeesinternational.org/reports/2018/11/29/displaced-nation-the-dangerous-implications-of-rushed-returns-in-south-sudan> (visited 30 October 2021) 17–20.

A. Symington, *WFP saves a Massive Stock of Wheat from Yemen's Frontline*, World Food Programme, 28 July 2020, available online at <https://www.wfp.org/stories/wfp-saves-massive-stock-wheat-yemens-frontline> (visited 26 August 2021).

Syrian American Medical Society, *Madaya: Starvation Under Siege*, September 2016, available online at <https://www.sams-usa.net/wp-content/uploads/2016/09/Report_Madaya_Starvation_Under_Siege_.pdf> (visited 4 June 2019).

Syrian American Medical Society, *The Daily Realities of East Ghouta: A Mother of 6 Struggles to Provide*, 26 October 2017, available online at <https://foundation.sams-usa.net/2017/10/26/daily-realities-east-ghouta-mother-6-struggles-provide/> (visited 4 June 2019).

A. Szakola, 'Syrian businessmen accused of oil smuggling linked to luxury tourist project', Levant Networks, 4 June 2020. <http://www.levantnetworks.com/2020/06/04/syrian-businessmen-accused-of-oil-smuggling-linked-to-luxury-tourist-project/> (visited 16 December 2020).

S. Tandon and T. Vishwanath, *Evolution of Poor Food Access over the Course of the Conflict in the Republic of Yemen*, Policy Research Working Paper No. 8813 (The World Bank Group, 2019), available online at <https://openknowledge.worldbank.org/bitstream/handle/10986/31542/WPS8813.pdf?sequence=4&isAllowed=y> (visited 26 August 2021).

S. Tandon and T. Vishwanath, 'The Evolution of Poor Food Access over the Course of the Conflict in Yemen', 130 *World Development* (2020) 1–16.

M. T. Tessema, *Prosecution of Politicide in Ethiopia: The Red Terror Trials* (Berlin: Springer, 2018).

S. Tharoor, *Inglorious Empire: What the British Did to India* (London: Hurst and Co., 2017).

The Crime of Starvation and Methods of Prosecution and Accountability, Global Rights Compliance, World Peace Foundation, Policy Paper (2019), available online at <https://sites.tufts.edu/wpf/files/2019/06/The-Crimes-of-Starvation-and-Methods-of-Prosecution-and-Accountability.pdf> (visited 27 August 2021).

The Syrian Human Rights Committee, 'Victims of Siege in Madaya and al-Zabadani', 18 January 2016, available online at <http://www.shrc.org/en/?p=26517> (visited 18 April 2020).

M. Transfeld, 'Political Bargaining and Violent Conflict: Shifting Elite Alliances as the Decisive Factor in Yemen's Transformation', 21 *Mediterranean Politics* (2016) 150–169.

O. Triffterer and K. Ambos (eds), *The Rome Statute of the International Criminal Court: A Commentary* (3rd edn., Munich: C.H. Beck, 2016).

K. Tronvoll, C. Schaefer, and G. Alemu Aneme, *The Ethiopian Red Terror Trials* (New York: Boydell & Brewer Inc., 2009).

J. Trussell and R. E. Frisch, 'Menarche and Fatness: Reexamination of the Critical Body Composition Hypothesis', 200 *Science* (1978) 1506–1513.

J. A. Tyner, *The Politics of Lists: Bureaucracy and Genocide under the Khmer Rouge* (Morgantown: West Virginia University Press, 2018).

L. Ullrich, '"But What About Men?" Gender Disquiet in International Criminal Justice', 25 *Theoretical Criminology* (2021) 209–227.

United Nations Children's Fund (UNICEF), *Strategy for Improved Nutrition of Children and Women in Developing Countries* (New York: UNICEF, 1990).

United Nations Development Programme, *Human Development Report 2016* (2016) available online at <http://hdr.undp.org/en/content/human-development-report-2016> (visited 26 August 2021).

United Nations High Commissioner for Refugees, *Evaluation of the Dadaab firewood project, Kenya* (June 2001), available online at <https://www.unhcr.org/3b33105d4.pdf> (visited 5 August 2021).

United Nations Mission in South Sudan Human Rights Division, *The State of Human Rights in the Protracted Conflict in South Sudan*, 4 December 2015, available online at <https://unmiss.unmissions.org/sites/default/files/human_rights_update_report_of_4_december_2015_final.pdf> (visited 27 October 2021).

United Nations Office for the Coordination of Humanitarian Affairs, '2014 Humanitarian Needs Overview South Sudan (September 2013)', *ReliefWeb* (2013), available online at<https://reliefweb.int/sites/reliefweb.int/files/resources/HNO_South_Sudan_2014.pdf> (visited 9 September 2021).

United Nations Office for the Coordination of Humanitarian Affairs, 'South Sudan: Humanitarian access situation snapshot (January–December 2015)' *ReliefWeb*

(2016) available online at <https://reliefweb.int/sites/reliefweb.int/files/resources/access_snapshot_jan-dec2015.pdf> (visited 9 September 2021).

United Nations Office for the Coordinator of Humanitarian Affairs, 'Syria: Flash Update, Deir-Ez-Zor City—15 January 2016', 15 January 2016, available online at <https://reliefweb.int/report/syrian-arab-republic/syria-flash-update-deir-ez-zor-city-15-january-2016> (visited 4 June 2019).

United Nations Office for the Coordination of Humanitarian Affairs, 'South Sudan: Humanitarian Access Situation Snapshot (Jan–Dec 2016)', *ReliefWeb* (2017) available online at <https://reliefweb.int/sites/reliefweb.int/files/resources/170125_january_december_2016_accesssnapshot.pdf> (visited 9 September 2021).

United Nations Office for the Coordination of Humanitarian Affairs, 'USG/ERC Stephen O'Brien Statement to the Security Council on Missions to Yemen, South Sudan, Somalia and Kenya and an Update on the Oslo Conference on Nigeria and the Lake Chad Region', *ReliefWeb*, 10 March 2017, available online at <http://reliefweb.int/report/yemen/usgerc-stephen-o-brien-statement-security-councilmissions-yemen-south-sudan-somalia> (visited 26 August 201).

United Nations Office for the Coordination of Humanitarian Affairs, 'Syria: Fear for Civilians Mounts as Conflict in Ar-Raqqa Intensifies', June 2017, available online at <https://www.unocha.org/story/syria-fear-civilians-mounts-conflict-ar-raqqa-intensifies> (visited 22 August 2020).

United Nations Office for the Coordination of Humanitarian Affairs, 'South Sudan: Humanitarian Access Overview (January–December 2017)', *ReliefWeb* (2018), available online at <https://reliefweb.int/sites/reliefweb.int/files/resources/SS_20180213_Annual_Access_Snapshot_Final.pdf> (visited 9 September 2021).

United Nations Office for the Coordination of Humanitarian Affairs, 'South Sudan: Annual Humanitarian Access Review (January–December 2018)', *ReliefWeb* (2019), available online at <https://reliefweb.int/report/south-sudan/south-sudan-annual-humanitarian-access-review-january-december-2018> (visited 9 September 2021).

United Nations Office for the Coordination of Humanitarian Affairs, 'South Sudan: 2019 Humanitarian Access Overview (January to December 2019)', *ReliefWeb* (2020), available online at <https://reliefweb.int/report/south-sudan/south-sudan-2019-humanitarian-access-overview-january-december-2019> (visited 9 September 2021).

United Nations Office for the Coordination of Humanitarian Affairs, 'South Sudan: 2020 Humanitarian Access Overview (January to December 2020)', *ReliefWeb* (2021), available online at <https://reliefweb.int/sites/reliefweb.int/files/resources/south_sudan_2020_access_annual_overview.pdf> (visited 9 September 2021).

United Nations Office for the Coordination of Humanitarian Affairs, 'South Sudan: UN condemns killing of one aid worker and attack against humanitarian convoy in Unity State', *ReliefWeb* (2021), available online at <https://reliefweb.int/report/south-sudan/south-sudan-un-condemns-killing-one-aid-worker-and-attack-against-humanitarian#:~:text=At%20least%20two%20aid%20workers,broke%20out%20in%20late%202013> (visited 9 September 2021).

United Nations Office of the Deputy Humanitarian Coordinator in South Sudan, *Crisis Impacts on Households in Unity State, South Sudan, 2014–2015* (2016), available online at <https://reliefweb.int/report/south-sudan/crisis-impacts-households-unity-state-south-sudan-2014-2015-initial-results> (visited 27 October 2021).

United Nations Office of the High Commissioner for Human Rights, *Principles and Guidelines for a Human Rights Approach to Poverty Reduction Strategies*, UN Doc. HR/PUB/06/12, 2006.

United Nations Office of the High Commissioner for Human Rights/Food and Agricultural Organization, 'Fact Sheet No. 34', *The Right to Adequate Food* (2010), available online at <https://www.ohchr.org/Documents/Publications/FactSheet34en.pdf> (visited 27 October 2021)

United Nations Office of the High Commissioner for Human Rights, *International Legal Protection of Human Rights in Armed Conflict*, (2011), available online at <https://www.ohchr.org/Documents/Publications/HR_in_armed_conflict.pdf> (visited 12 February 2020).

United Nations Office of the High Commissioner for Human Rights, *Living Under Siege: The Syrian Arab Republic*, February 2014.

United Nations Office of the High Commissioner for Human Rights, *The State of Human Rights in the Protracted Conflict in South Sudan*, 4 December 2015, available online at <https://www.ohchr.org/Documents/Countries/SS/UNMISS_HRD4December2015.pdf> (visited 30 October 2021).

United Nations Office of the High Commissioner for Human Rights, *Humanitarian Response Plan 2018: Yemen*, January 2018, available online at <https://reliefweb.int/sites/reliefweb.int/files/resources/20180120_HRP_YEMEN_Final.pdf> (visited 24 November 2020).

United Nations Office of the High Commissioner for Human Rights, Syria, *Humanitarian Response Plan 2019 for Syria* (2019), available online at <https://reliefweb.int/sites/reliefweb.int/files/resources/2019_hrp_syria.pdf> (visited 24 November 2020).

United Nations Office of the High Commissioner for Human Rights, *Humanitarian Response Plan 2019: Yemen*, March 2019.

United Nations Office of the High Commissioner for Humanitarian Affairs, *Venezuela: Situation Report*, 18 February 2020, available online at <https://reliefweb.int/sites/reliefweb.int/files/resources/Situation%20Report%20-%20Venezuela%20-%2018%20Feb%202020.pdf> (visited 26 October 2021).

United Nations Office on Genocide Prevention and the Responsibility to Protect, *Framework of Analysis for Atrocity Crimes* (2014), available online at <https://www.un.org/en/genocideprevention/documents/our-work/Doc.1_Framework%20of%20Analysis%20for%20Atrocity%20Crimes_EN.pdf> (visited 24 November 2020).

United Nations Population Fund, *Child Marriage on the Rise* (1 September 2016), available online at <https://yemen.unfpa.org/en/news/child-marriage-rise> (visited 30 October 2020).

United Nations Security Council Report, Yemen (October 2018), available online at <https://www.securitycouncilreport.org/chronology/yemen.php> (visited 27 August 2021).

US Department of State, 'The Global Coalition to Defeat ISIS', available online at <https://www.state.gov/bureaus-offices/bureaus-and-offices-reporting-directly-to-the-secretary/the-global-coalition-to-defeat-isis/> (visited 19 September 2020).

US Department of State, 'Revocation of the Terrorist Designation of Ansarallah', 12 February 2021, available online at <https://www.state.gov/revocation-of-the-terrorist-designations-of-ansarallah/> (visited 26 August 2021).

US Department of State, Press Release, 'United States' Actions To Press for the Resolution of the Crisis in the Tigray Region of Ethiopia', 23 May 2021, available online at <https://www.state.gov/united-states-actions-to-press-for-the-resolution-of-the-crisis-in-the-tigray-region-of-ethiopia/> (visited 28 August 2021).

US General Accountability Office, 'Darfur Crisis: Death estimates demonstrate severity of crisis, but their accuracy and credibility could be enhanced' (2006), available online at <https://www.gao.gov/products/GAO-07-24> (visited 25 August 2021).

United States Holocaust Memorial Museum (USHMM), *Early Warning Project*, available online at <https://earlywarningproject.ushmm.org/> (visited 24 November 2020).

United States Institute of Peace, *Ethiopia: Report of the Office of the Special Prosecutor*, February 1994, available online at <https://www.usip.org/sites/default/files/Ethiopia-SPODossier-2.pdf> (visited 23 October 2018).

C. Urquhart, 'Gaza on brink of implosion as aid cut-off starts to bite', *The Guardian*, 15 April 2006, available online at <https://www.theguardian.com/world/2006/apr/16/israel> (visited 5 August 2021).

V. G. Valaoras, 'Some Effects of Famine on the Population of Greece', 24 *The Milbank Memorial Fund Quarterly* (1946) 215–234.

A.F. van Abeelen et al., 'Cardiovascular Consequences of Famine in the Young', 33 *European Heart Journal* (2012) 538–545.

A. F. van Abeelen et al., 'Famine Exposure in the Young and the Risk of Type 2 Diabetes in Adulthood', 61 *Diabetes* (2012) 2255–2260.

A.F. van Abeelen et al., 'Postnatal Acute Famine and Risk of Overweight: The Dutch *Hungerwinter* Study', *International Journal of Pediatrics* (2012) 1–9.

A.F. van Abeelen et al., 'Famine in the Young and Risk of Later Hospitalization for COPD and Asthma', 8 *PloS One* (2013) 1–8.

L. van den Herik, 'Economic, Social, and Cultural Rights International Criminal Law's Blind Spot?', in E. Riedel, G. Giacca, and C. Golay (eds), *Economic, Social, and Cultural Rights in International Law: Contemporary Issues and Challenges* (Oxford: Oxford University Press, 2014).

E. Van Veen, 'Syria: foreign interventions and the revenge of realpolitik', *Clingendael Spectator*, 5 November 2019, available online at <https://spectator.clingendael.org/en/publication/syria-foreign-interventions-and-revenge-realpolitik> (visited 25 August 2020).

D. Varisco, 'Pumping Yemen Dry: A History of Yemen's Water Crisis', 47 *Human Ecology* (2019) 317–329.

M. Vaughan, *Curing Their Ills: Colonial Power and African Illness* (Stanford: Stanford University Press, 1991).

S. Vaughan, 'The Role of the Special Prosecutor's Office', in K. Tronvoll, C. Schaefer, and G. A. Aneme (eds), *The Ethiopian Red Terror Trials* (Suffolk: James Currey, 2009) 51–67.

M. Ventura, 'Prosecuting Starvation under International Criminal Law: Exploring the Legal Possibilities', 17 *Journal of International Criminal Justice* (2019) 881–906.

I. Venzke, 'Situating Contingency in the Path of International Law', in K. J. Heller and I. Venzke (eds), *Contingency and the Course of International Law* (Oxford: Oxford University Press, 2021) 3–19.

J. Vespa and F. Watson, 'Who is Nutritionally Vulnerable in Bosnia-Hercegovina?' 311 *British Medical Journal* (1995) 652–654.

Vienna Convention on the Law of Treaties, 1155 UNTS 331, 23 May 1969.

E. von Joeden-Forgey, 'Gender and the Future of Genocide Studies and Prevention,' 7 *Genocide Studies and Prevention* (2012) 89–107.

M. U. Walker, 'Transformative Reparations? A Critical Look at a Current Trend in Thinking about Gender-Just Reparations', 10 *International Journal of Transitional Justice* (2016) 108–125.

D. Walsh, 'The tragedy of Saudi Arabia's war in Yemen', *The New York Times* (26 October 2018), available online at <https://www.nytimes.com/interactive/2018/10/26/world/middleeast/saudi-arabia-war-yemen.html> (visited 27 August 2021).

D. Walsh, 'Yemen girl who turned world's eyes to famine is dead', *The New York Times* (1 November 2018), available online at <https://www.nytimes.com/2018/11/01/world/middleeast/yemen-starvation-amal-hussain.html> (visited 27 August 2021).

D. Walsh, 'Ethiopia's war leads to ethnic cleansing in Tigray Region, U.S. report says,' *New York Times*, 26 February 2021, available online at <https://www.nytimes.com/2021/02/26/world/middleeast/ethiopia-tigray-ethnic-cleansing.html> (visited 5 August 2021).

L. A. Walter and A. J. McGregor, 'Sex- and Gender-specific Observations and Implications for COVID-19', 21 *Western Journal of Emergency Medicine: Integrating Emergency Care with Population Health* (2020) 507–509.

F. Watson, 'Why Are There No Longer "War Famines" in Contemporary Europe?', in S. Devereux (ed.), *The New Famines: Why Famines Persist in an Era of Globalization* (London: Routledge, 2007) 269–289.

S. Watts, *Under Siege: International Humanitarian Law and Security Council Practice concerning Urban Siege Operations*, Harvard Law School: Counterterrorism and Humanitarian Engagement Project, May 2014, available online at <http://blogs.harvard.edu/cheproject/files/ 2013/10/CHE-Project-IHL-and-SC-Practice-concerning-Urban-Siege-Operations.pdf> (visited 18 July 2019).

P. Webb and A. Thorne-Lyman, *Entitlement Failure from a Food Quality Perspective: The Life and Death Role of Vitamins and Minerals in Humanitarian Crises*, UNU-WIDER, Research Paper No. 2006/140 (2006).

T. Weiss et al. (eds), *Political Gain and Civilian Pain* (New York: Rowman & Littlefield, 1997).

M. Wenner, 'The Civil War in Yemen: 1962–1970', in R. Licklider (ed.), *Stopping the Killing: How Civil Wars End* (New York: NYU Press, 1993).

S. Wheeler, *UN Peacekeeping has a Sexual Abuse Problem*, Human Rights Watch (11 January 2020), available online at <https://www.hrw.org/news/2020/01/11/un-peacekeeping-has-sexual-abuse-problem#> (visited 5 August 2021).

S. Wilkinson, *Standards of Proof in International Humanitarian and Human Rights Fact-Finding and Inquiry Missions* (Geneva Academy of International Humanitarian Law and Human Rights), available online at <https://www.geneva-academy.ch/joomlatools-files/docman-files/Standards%20of%20Proof%20in%20Fact-Finding.pdf> (visited 27 November 2019).

J. Williams, 'The conflict in South Sudan, explained', Vox (8 December 2016), available online at <https://www.vox.com/world/2016/12/8/13817072/south-sudan-crisis-explained-ethnic-cleansing-genocide> (visited 27 August 2021).

P. Wintour, 'UK declines to follow US in suspending Saudi arms sales over Yemen', *The Guardian*, 8 February 2021, available online at <https://www.theguardian.com/world/2021/feb/08/uk-declines-to-follow-us-in-suspending-saudi-arms-sales-over-yemen> (visited 26 August 2021).

D. Woldegiorgis, *Red Tears: War, Famine, and Revolution in Ethiopia* (Trenton: The Red Sea Press, 1988).

E. Wong, 'U.S. rationale for military aid to Saudis in Yemen war is fraying', *New York Times*, 23 September 2020, available online at <https://www.nytimes.com/2020/09/23/us/politics/yemen-us-weapons-saudi-arabia.html> (visited 26 August 2021).

World Bank, 'Personal remittances, received (current US$)—Yemen, Rep.', Open Data, available online at <https://data.worldbank.org/indicator/BX.TRF.PWKR.CD.DT?locations=YE> (visited 26 August 2021).

World Bank, *Poverty and Hunger: Issues and Options for Food Security in Developing Countries* (Washington, DC: World Bank,1986).

World Bank Group, *Who Are the Poor in the Developing World?* (Washington, DC: World Bank, 2016), available online at <http://documents.worldbank.org/curated/en/187011475416542282/pdf/WPS7844.pdf> (visited 6 February 2020).

World Food Programme, *Economic Explorer*, VAM Food Security Analysis, available online at <https://dataviz.vam.wfp.org/economic_explorer/prices> (visited 26 August 2021).

World Food Programme, *South Sudan Emergency*, available online at <https://www.wfp.org/emergencies/south-sudan-emergency#:~:text=Food%20insecurity%20in%20South%20Sudan,levels%20since%20independence%20in%202011.&text=However%2C%20the%20situation%20remains%20dire,find%20enough%20food%20each%20day> (visited 9 September 2021).

World Food Programme, *The State of Food Security and Nutrition in Yemen: Comprehensive Food Security Survey*, 2012, available online at <https://documents.wfp.org/stellent/groups/public/documents/ena/wfp247832.pdf> (visited 26 August 2021).

World Food Programme, *Yemen: Comprehensive Food Security Survey*, 2014, available online at <https://documents.wfp.org/stellent/groups/public/documents/ena/wfp269771.pdf?_ga=2.41003947.862677590.1606893566-2107303201.1606581506> (visited 26 August 2021).

World Food Programme, *What Does the Conflict Induced Public Sector Crisis Mean for Food Security in Yemen?*, November 2016, available online at wfp.org/publications/yemen-special-focus-conflict-public-sector-crisis-food-security-november-2016> (visited 26 August 2021).

World Food Programme, *State of Food Insecurity in Yemen based on the Emergency Food Security and Nutrition Assessment (EFSNA)*, April 2017, available online at <https://www.wfp.org/publications/yemen-state-food-insecurity-emergency-food-security-nutrition-assessment-april-2017#:~:text=27%20April%202017-,Yemen%20%2D%20State%20of%20Food%20Insecurity%20in%20Yemen%20based%20on%20the,Assessment%20(EFSNA)%2C%20April%202017&text=Over%20two%2Dfifth%20of%20Yemeni,day%20and%20night%20without%20eating> (visited 26 August 2021).

World Food Programme, *Global Report on Food Crisis*, 2 April 2019, available online at <https://www.wfp.org/publications/2019-global-report-food-crises)visited 28 January 2022).

World Food Program, *Syria Situation Report #7, July 2020*, 20 August 2020, available online at <https://reliefweb.int/report/syrian-arab-republic/wfp-syria-situation-report-7-july-2020> (visited 22 August 2020).

World Food Programme and UNICEF, *Emergency Food Security and Nutrition Assessment* (Rome: World Food Programme, 2005).

World Food Program USA, *Women and Hunger*, available online at <https://www.wfpusa.org/women-hunger/> (visited 5 August 2021).

World Health Organization, *Nutrition in Times of Disaster. Report of an International Conference held at the World Health Organisation Headquarters* (Geneva: UN SCN, 1988).

World Health Organization, *Mortality and Global Health Estimates*, World Health Data Platform, available online at <https://www.who.int/data/gho/data/themes/mortality-and-global-health-estimates#:~:text=Global%20life%20expectancy%20at%20birth,men%20all%20around%20the%20world> (visited October 21, 2020).

World Health Organization, *Addressing Sex and Gender in Epidemic Prone Infectious Diseases* (Geneva: World Health Organization, 2007), available online at <https://www.who.int/csr/resources/publications/SexGenderInfectDis.pdf> (visited 5 August 2021).

World Health Organization, *The Management of Nutrition in Major Emergencies* (Geneva: World Health Organization, 2000).

World Peace Foundation, *Starving Tigray: How Armed Conflict and Mass Atrocities Have Destroyed an Ethiopian Region's Economy and Food System and Are Threatening Famine*, April 2021, available online at <https://sites.tufts.edu/wpf/starving-tigray/> (visited 5 August 2021).

L. Yanev, 'Joint Criminal Enterprise', in J. De Hemptinne, R. Roth, and E. van Sliedregt (eds), *An Introduction to International Criminal Law and Procedure* (Cambridge: Cambridge University Press, 2019) 121–170.

H. Young, 'Public Nutrition in Emergencies: An Overview of Debates, Dilemmas and Decision-Making', 23(4) *Disasters* (1999) 277–291.

H. Young and S. Jaspars, 'The Meaning and Measurement of Acute Malnutrition in Emergencies. A Primer for Decision-makers', 56 *Humanitarian Practice Network Paper* (2006).

H. Young and A. Marshak, *Persistent Global Acute Malnutrition: A Discussion Paper on the Scope of the Problem, Its Drivers, and Strategies for Moving Forward for Policy, Practice, and Research*, Feinstein International Center, January 2018, available online at <https://fic.tufts.edu/publication-item/persistent-global-acute-malnutrition-discussion-paper/> (visited 22 October 2021).

H. Young and S. Jaspars, *Review of Nutrition and Mortality Indicators for the Integrated Food Security Phase Classification (IPC): Reference Levels and Decision-making*, SCN Task Force on Assessment, Monitoring and Evaluation, and The Integrated Food Security Phase Classification (IPC) Global Partners (2009).

H. Young et al., 'Public Nutrition in Complex Emergencies', 364 *The Lancet* (2004) 1899–1909.

J. Young, *Peasant Revolution in Ethiopia: The Tigray People's Liberation Front, 1975–1991* (New York: Cambridge University Press, 2006).

N. M. Zagre and G. Quince, 'Child hunger and its long-term effects', UNICEF connect, 24 September 2014, available online at <https://blogs.unicef.org/blog/child-hunger-and-its-long-term-effects/> (visited 20 March 2019).

V. Zarulli et al., 'Women Live Longer than Men Even During Severe Famines and Epidemics', 115(4) *Proceedings of the National Academy of Sciences* (2018) 832–840.

S. Zeć et al., 'Nutrition in Pre-war Sarajevo', 49 *European Journal of Clinical Nutrition* (1995) 6–10.

T. Zhurzhenko, 'Commemorating the Famine as Genocide: The Contested Meanings of Holodomor Meanings in Ukraine', in S. Buckley-Zistel and S. Schäfer (eds), *Memorials in Times of Transition* (Cambridge: Intersentia, 2014) 221–242.

T. Zintl, 'The Co-option of Foreign-Educated Syrians: Between Legitimizing Strategy and Domestic Reforms', in R. Hinnebusch and R. Zintl (eds), *Syria from Reform to Revolt, Vol. 1: Political Economy and International Relations* (Syracuse: Syracuse University Press, 2015) 113–132.

United Nations Documents

United Nations, *Charter of the United Nations*, 24 October 1945, UN Doc. 1 UNTS XVI.

Convention against Torture and Other Cruel, Inhuman or Degrading Treatment or Punishment, General Comment No. 2, UN Doc. CAT/C/GC/2, 24 January 2008.

General Assembly

United Nations, *Universal Declaration of Human Rights*, UN Doc. A/RES/217 (III), 10 December 1948.

International Covenant on Civil and Political Rights, UN Doc. A/RES/2200A(XXI) 16 December 1966.
GA Res. 2444 (XXII), 9 December 1968.
GA Res. 3068, A/9030, 18 July 1976.
Convention Against Torture, UN Doc. A/RES/39/46 10 December 1984.
Report of the Preparatory Committee on the Establishment of an International Criminal Court, GA Supplement No. 22, UN Doc. A/51/22, 1996.
International Covenant on Economic, Social and Cultural Rights, UN Doc. A/Res/21/2200, 16 December 1966.
Proposal submitted by the United States of America regarding an Annex on Definitional Element for Part 2 Crimes, UN Doc. A/CONF.183/C.1/L.10, 19 June 1998.
Report of the International Law Commission, Fifty-Third Session, UN Doc. A/56/10, 9 August 2001.
Report of the International Law Commission, Fifty-Eighth Session, UN Doc. A/61/10, 2006.
GA Res. 63, 10 December 2008.
Report of the International Law Commission, Sixty-Fourth Session, UN Doc. A/67/10, 2012.
Sixty-eighth Plenary Meeting of the GA, 'World Leaders Highlight Link between Peace, Development as General Assembly's Sixty-eighth Session Holds Second Day of Annual Debate', UN Doc. GA/114, 25 September 2013.
Report of the International Law Commission, Sixty-Eighth Session, UN Doc. A/71/10, 2016.
Interim report of the Special Rapporteur on the Right to food, UN Doc. A/72/188, 21 July 2017.
2030 Agenda for Sustainable Development, UN Doc. A/HRC/40/34, 5 March 2019.
Interim Report of the Special Rapporteur on the right to food, UN Doc. A/74/164, 15 July 2019.
Report of the Detailed Findings of the Group of Eminent International and Regional Experts on Yemen, UN Doc. A/HRC/42/CRP.1, 3 September 2019.

Secretary General

Report to the Secretary-General on Humanitarian Needs in Kuwait and Iraq in the Immediate Post-crisis Environment by a Mission to the Area Led by Mr. Martii Ahtisaari, Under-Secretary-General for Administration and Management, UN Doc S/22366, 20 March 1991.
Final Report of the Panel of Experts on Somalia, UN Doc S/2020/949, 28 September 2020.
Report of the UN Secretary-General on the Protection of Civilians in Armed Conflict, S/1999/957, 8 September 1999.
Prevention of Armed Conflict: Report of the Secretary General, UN Doc. A/55/985-S/2001/574, 1 June 2001.
The rule of law and transitional justice in conflict and post-conflict societies, UN Doc. S/2004/616, 23 August 2004.
Report of the Secretary-General on the implementation of Security Council resolution 2139, UN Doc. S/2014/208, 24 March 2014.
Letter dated 21 August 2015 from the Panel of Experts on South Sudan established pursuant to Security Council resolution 2206 (2015) addressed to the President of the Security Council, UN Doc. S/2015/656, 21 August 2015.
Final report of the Panel of Experts on Yemen, UN Doc. S/2018/68, 26 January 2018.
Letter dated 26 January 2018 from the Panel of Experts on Yemen mandated by Security Council resolution 2342 (2017) addressed to the President of the Security Council, UN Doc. S/2019/594, 26 January 2018, Annex 58 ('Case Studies of Air Strikes in Yemen (2017)').

Report of Secretary General to the United Nations Security Council, Implementation of Security Council resolutions 2139 (2014), 2165 (2014), 2258 (2015), 2332 (2016), and 2393 (2017), UN Doc. S/2018/243, 20 March 2018.

Letter dated 25 January 2019 from the Panel of Experts on Yemen addressed to the President of the Security Council, UN Doc. S/2019/83, 25 January 2019.

Children and Armed Conflict in Yemen: Report of the Secretary General, UN Doc. S/2019/453, 3 June 2019.

Letter dated 27 January 2020 from the Panel of Experts on Yemen addressed to the President of the Security Council, UN Doc. S/2020/70, 27 January 2020.

Letter dated 29 May 2020 from the President of the Security Council addressed to the Secretary-General and the Permanent Representatives of the members of the Security Council, UN Doc. S/2020/459, 29 May 2020.

Letter dated 29 May 2020 from the President of the Security Council addressed to the Secretary-General and the Permanent Representatives of the members of the Security Council, UN Doc. S/2020/466, 1 June 2020.

The situation in the middle east: Briefing by Mr. Martin Griffiths, Special Envoy of the Secretary-General for Yemen; and Mr. Mark Lowcock, Under-Secretary-General for Humanitarian Affairs and Emergency Relief Coordinator, UN Doc. S/PV.8757, 15 September 2020.

Interim Report of the Panel of Experts on South Sudan Submitted Pursuant to Resolution 2521 (2020), UN Doc S/2020/1141, 25 November 2020.

Letter dated 12 March 2021 from the President of the Security Council addressed to the Secretary-General and the Permanent Representatives of the members of the Security Council, UN Doc. S/2021/255, 12 March 2021.

Security Council

SC Res. 1844, 20 November 2008.

Report of the Monitoring Group on Somalia pursuant to Security Council resolution 1853 (2008), UN Doc. S/2010/91, 10 March 2010.

SC Res. 2002, 29 July 2011.

SC Res. 2093, 6 March 2013.

SC Res. 2140, 26 February 2014.

SC Res. 2216, 15 April 2015.

Final Report of the Panel of Experts on Yemen Established Pursuant to Security Council Resolution 2140 (2014), UN Doc S/210/192, 26 January 2016.

Letter dated 27 January 2017 from the Panel of Experts on Yemen addressed to the President of the Security Council, UN Doc. S/2018/193, 31 January 2017.

Final Report of the Panel of Experts on South Sudan, UN Doc. S/2017/326, 13 April 2017.

Security Council 8213th meeting, UN Doc. S/PV.8213, 23 March 2018.

SC Res. 2417, 24 May 2018.

SC Res. 2417 24 May 2018.

SC Res 2428, 13 July 2018.

SC Res 2428, 13 July 2018.

SC Res. 2451, 21 December 2018.

SC Res. 2451, 28 December 2018.

Final Report of the Panel of Experts on Yemen, UN Doc S/2019/83, 25 January 2019.

SC Res. 2472, 31 May 2019.

SC Res. 2474, 11 June 2019.

Final Report of the Panel of Experts on Yemen, UN Doc S/2020/70, 28 April 2020.
SC Res. 2520, 29 May 2020.
SC Res. 2568, 12 March 2021.
SC Res. 2567, 12 March 2021.

Economic and Social Council

Report on the Third Session, UN Doc. E/1989/22/, 27 July 1981.
Review of the composition, organization and administrative arrangements of the Sessional Working Group of Governmental Experts on the Implementation of the International Covenant on Economic, Social and Cultural Rights, ECOSOC Res. 1985/17, 28 May 1985.
The Limburg Principles on the Implementation of the ICESCR, UN Doc. E/CN.4/1987/17, 8 January 1987.
A. Eide, the former UN Special Rapporteur on the Right to Food, UN Doc. E/CN.4/Sub.2/1987/23, 7 July 1987.
General Comment No. 3: The Nature of States Parties' Obligations, UN Doc. E/1991/23, 14 December 1990.
Report on the Situation of Human Rights in Kuwait under Iraqi Occupation, prepared by W. Kälin, Special Rapporteur of the Commission on Human Rights, UN Doc. E/CN.4/1992/26, 16 January 1992.
Concluding Observations: Guatemala, UN Doc. E/C.12/1/Add.3, 28 May 1996.
Maastricht Guidelines on Violations of ESCR, UN Doc. E/C.12/2000/13, 22-26 January 1997.
Concluding Observations: Sri Lanka, UN Doc. E/C.12/1/Add.24, 16 June 1998.
General Comment No. 9: The Domestic Application of the Covenant, UN Doc. E/C.12/1998/243 December 1998.
General Comment No. 12: The right to adequate food, UN Doc. E/C.12/1999/5, 12 May 1999.
Concluding Observations: Sri Lanka, UN Doc. E/C.12/LKA/CO/2-4, 9 December 2010.
Protection of Economic, Social and Cultural Rights in Conflict, UN Doc. E/2015/59, 19 May 2015.
IDG v. Spain, Communication No. 2/2014, UN Doc. E/C.12/55/D/2/2014, 13 October 2015.
Concluding observations on the fifth periodic report of Sri Lanka, UN Doc. E/C.12/LKA/CO/5, 4 August 2017.
General Comment No. 14: The Right to the Highest Attainable Standard of Health, UN Doc. E/C.12/2000/4, 11 August 2000.
Concluding Observations: Sudan, UN Doc. E/C.12/1/Add.48, 1 September 2000.
Concluding Observations of the CESCR on Israel, UN Doc. E/C.12/1/Add.69, 31 August 2001.
Concluding Observations: Colombia, UN Doc. E/C.12/1/Add.74, 6 December 2001.
Statement on 'An evaluation of the obligation to take steps to the maximum of available resources under an optional Protocol to the Covenant', UN Doc. E/C.12/2007/1, 21 September 2007.
Concluding Observations: Nepal, UN Doc. E/C.12/NPL/CO/2, 16 January 2008.
Guidelines on Treaty-Specific Documents to be submitted by states parties under articles 16 and 17 of the International Covenant on Economic, Social and Cultural Rights, UN Doc. E/C.12/2008/2, 24 March 2009.
Concluding Observations: Democratic Republic of the Congo, UN Doc. E/C.12/COD/CO/4, 16 December 2009.

Human Rights Committee

Luciano Weinberger Weisz and Ismael Weinberger v. Uruguay, HRC Communication No. 28/1978, UN Doc. CCPR/C/11/D/28/1978, 29 October 1978.

Select Decisions under the Optional Protocol, UN Doc. CCPR/C/OP/1, 1985.

General Comment No. 24: Issues Relating to Reservations Made upon Ratification or Accession to the Covenant or the Optional Protocols thereto, or in Relation to Declarations under Article 41 of the Covenant, UN Doc. CCPR/C/21/Rev.1/Add.6, 4 November 1994.

General Comment No. 29: Derogations during a State of Emergency, UN Doc. CCPR/C/21/Rev.1/Add.11, 31 August 2001.

General Comment No. 31: The nature of the general legal obligation imposed on States Parties to the Covenant, UN Doc. CCPR/C/21/Rev.1/Add. 13, 26 May 2004.

Human Rights Council

Report of the Commission of Inquiry on Human Rights in the Democratic People's Republic of Korea, UN Doc. A/HRC/25/63, 7 February 2014.

Report of the detailed findings of the Commission of Inquiry on human rights in the DRK, UN Doc A/HRC/25/CRP.1, 7 February 2014.

Situation of human rights in Yemen, including violations and abuses since September 2014: Report of the detailed findings of the Group of Eminent International and Regional Experts on Yemen, UN Doc. A/HRC/39/43, 17 August 2018.

Report of the Commission on Human Rights in South Sudan, UN Doc. A/HRC/40/CRP.1, 21 February 2019.

Report of the Commission on Human Rights in South Sudan', UN Doc. A/HRC/40/69, 12 March 2019.

Report of the Group of Eminent International and Regional Experts as submitted to the UN High Commissioner for Human Rights, UN Doc. A/HRC/42/17, 9 August 2019.

Situation of human rights in Yemen, including violations and abuses since September 2014: Report of the detailed findings of the Group of Eminent International and Regional Experts on Yemen, UN Doc. A/HRC/42/CRP.1, 3 September 2019.

Report of the Commission on Human Rights in South Sudan, UN Doc. A/HRC/43/56, 31 January 2020.

Report of the detailed findings of the Group of Eminent International and Regional Experts on Yemen, UN Doc. A/HRC/45/6, 14 September 2020.

Situation of human rights in Yemen, including violations and abuses since September 2014: Detailed findings of the Group of Eminent International and Regional Experts on Yemen, UN Doc. A/HRC/45/CRP.7, 29 September 2020.

Conference Room Paper of the Commission on Human Rights in South Sudan, UN Doc. A/HRC/45/CRP.4, 5 October 2020.

Commission on Human Rights in South Sudan, *'There is nothing left for us': starvation as a method of warfare in South Sudan*, UN Doc. A/HRC/45/CRP.3, 5 October 2020.

HRC Res. 45/15, 12 October 2020.

Right to Food, Report of the Special Rapporteur on the right to food, Michael Fakhri, UN Doc. A/HRC/46/33, 24 December 2020.

Report of the Independent International Commission of Inquiry on the Syrian Arab Republic, UN Doc. A/HRC/46/54, 21 January 2021.

Report of the Commission on Human Rights in South Sudan, UN Doc. A/HRC/46/53, 4 February 2021.
Detailed Findings of the Commission on Human Rights in South Sudan, UN Doc. A/HRC/46/CRP.2, 18 February 2021.
Detailed findings of the Commission on Human Rights in South Sudan, UN Doc. A/HRC/46/CRP.2, 18 February 2021.
HRC Res. 46/23, 30 March 2021.

UN Committee on the Rights of the Child

Consideration of Reports Submitted by States parties under article 44of the Convention, Concluding observations: Sudan, UN Doc. CRC/C/SDN/CO/3-4, 22 October 2010.

Preparatory Commission for the International Criminal Court

Proposal Submitted by the United States of America: Draft Elements of Crime, UN Doc. PCNICC/1999/DP.4/Add.2, 4 February 1999.

Author Interviews

M. Kanfash and A. Aljasem, Interview with An officer manning the Maliha checkpoint, 2013.
M. Kanfash and A. Aljasem, Interview with H. Bashar; Head of Erbeen Local Council Humanitarian Committee, 29 November 2017.
M. Kanfash and A. Aljasem, Interview with E. Amer; humanitarian worker in Touba, a local NGO active in Ghouta, 20 February 2018.
M. Kanfash and A. Aljasem, Interview with S. Moutasem; head of negotiation committee in eastern Ghouta: southern sector, 1 March 2018.
M. Kanfash and A. Aljasem, Interview with Q. Abdullah; Head of Local Council Irrigation Office in Deir-Hafer, 15 January 2019.
M. Kanfash and A. Aljasem, Interview with Y. Safwan; Interview with a paramedic from Al-Bab city, 12 February 2019.
D. Mazurana, Phone interview with medical care provider from Tigray, 18 June 2021.

National Laws and Legal Codes

Argentina Law of War Manual (1989) Leyes de Guerra, PC-08-01, Público, Edición 1989, Estado Mayor Conjunto de las Fuerzas Armadas, aprobado por Resolución No. 489/89 del Ministerio de Defensa, 23 April 1990.
Australia LOAC Manual (2006) The Manual of the Law of Armed Conflict, Australian Defence Doctrine Publication 06.4, Australian Defence Headquarters, 11 May 2006, 10-11.
Benin, Le Droit de la Guerre, III fascicules, Forces Armées du Bénin, Ministère de la Défense nationale (Military Manual, 1995).
Canada, The Law of Armed Conflict at the Operational and Tactical Levels, Office of the Judge Advocate General, 13 August 2001.

Colombia (Directive on IHL) Normas de Derecho Internacional Humanitario, Directiva Permanente No. 017, Ministerio de Defensa Nacional, 17 August 1993.

Croatia, 'Basic Rules of International Humanitarian Law Applicable in Armed Conflicts', Republic of Croatia, Ministry of Defence, 1993.

France (OAC Manual) Manuel de droit des conflits armés, Ministère de la Défense, Direction des Affaires Juridiques, Sous-Direction du droit international humanitaire et du droit européen, Bureau du droit des conflits armés (2001).

Germany (IHL Manual), ZDv 15/1, Humanitäres Völkerrecht in bewaffneten Konflikten—Grundsätze, DSK VV230120023, Bundesministerium der Verteidigung, June 1996.

Hungary (Military Manual) A Hadijog, Jegyzet a Katonai, Föiskolák Hallgatói Részére, Magyar Honvédség Szolnoki Repülötiszti Föiskola (1992).

Kenya (LOAC Manual) Law of Armed Conflict, Military Basic Course (ORS), 4 Précis, The School of Military Police.

Republic of Korea, Military Law Manual (1996).

Madagascar (Military Manual) Le Droit des Conflits Armés, Ministère des Forces Armées, August 1994.

New Zealand (Military Manual, 2005); Humanitair Oorlogsrecht: Handleiding, Voorschrift No. 27-412, Koninklijke Landmacht, Militair Juridische Dienst (2005).

Nigeria (Military Manual) International Humanitarian Law (IHL), Directorate of Legal Services, Nigerian Army (1994).

Russian Federation (Military Manual), Instructions on the Application of the Rules of International Humanitarian Law by the Armed Forces of the USSR, Appendix to Order of the USSR Defence Minister No. 75 (1990).

Spain (LOAC Manual) Orientaciones, El Derecho de los Conflictos Armados, Tomo 1, Publicación OR7–004 (Edición Segunda), Mando de Adiestramiento y Doctrina, Dirección de Doctrina, Orgánica y Materiales, 2 November 2007.

Togo (Military Manual) Le Droit de la Guerre, III fascicules, Etat-major Général des Forces Armées Togolaises, Ministère de la Défense nationale (1996).

The former Yugoslavia (Military Manual) Propisi o Primeri Pravila Medjunarodnog Ratnog Prava u Oruzanim Snagama SFRJ, PrU-2, Savezni Sekretarijat za Narodnu Odbranu (Pravna Uprava) (1988).

Index

For the benefit of digital users, indexed terms that span two pages (e.g., 52–53) may, on occasion, appear on only one of those pages.

Tables and figures are indicated by *t* and *f* following the page number